MANAGERIAL ECONOMICS

IRWIN PUBLICATIONS IN ECONOMICS
Advisory Editor: Martin S. Feldstein, *Harvard University*

MANAGERIAL ECONOMICS
Applied Microeconomics for Decision Making

S. Charles Maurice
Professor of Economics   Texas A&M University

Charles W. Smithson
Managing Director   The Continental Bank

Third Edition 1988

Homewood, Illinois 60430

© RICHARD D. IRWIN, INC., 1981, 1985, and 1988

This book was set in Times Roman by Carlisle Communications Limited.
The editors were Gary L. Nelson, Ethel Shiell, and Merrily D. Mazza.
The production manager was Irene H. Sotiroff.
The designer was Michael Warrell.
The drawings were done by Jay Bensen, The Artforce.
R. R. Donnelley & Sons Company was the printer and binder.

ISBN 0-256-05914-4

Library of Congress Catalog Card No. 87–81579

Printed in the United States of America

4 5 6 7 8 9 0 DO 5 4 3 2 1 0

PREFACE

In the preface to our second edition, we admitted, "When we began this revision, we fully expected that our changes would be rather minor. But, as we read the comments of users, we eventually came to the opinion that a major revision was needed."

When we began this, our third edition, we again expected that our changes would be rather minor. And yet again we came to the opinion that a major revision was necessary.

In the case of this revision, two factors led us to revise our expectations and opt for a major revision. First, as with the previous revision, we listened to the people who used the text. Our users had asked for some reorganization, for still more business-oriented applications, and for the discussion of linear programming that had been dropped in the second edition to be included once again. Second, in the interim since the second edition was written, Charles Smithson spent two years teaching managerial economics and corporate finance to officers of Chase Manhattan Bank throughout the world. As is always the case, the person in the class who learns the most is the teacher; and this was definitely the case with Charles' experience with Chase. Most significantly, he got a much fuller appreciation of the way managerial economics and managerial finance fit together, and he wanted to try to incorporate that appreciation in this text.

Hence, to the two fundamental objectives described in the preface to our second edition:

1. To present the core of microeconomic theory.
2. To show how the theoretical concepts can actually be implemented.

we add a third objective in this edition:

3. To demonstrate the relation of managerial economics to finance and to the other courses in a business school curriculum.

Indeed, these three objectives illuminate the primary distinguishing characteristics of our approach to managerial economics.

First, this text can "stand alone" in the sense that it contains all of the principles of microeconomic theory needed to understand specific managerial economics concepts; no supplemental text is necessary. By presenting the basic theory and the specific managerial economics constructs together, we demonstrate that managerial economics is simply an application of microeconomics.

Second, we stress that the theoretical principles of microeconomics are *useful* in the real world. We use a "three-pronged attack" to make this crucial point. (1) We show that the principles of microeconomic theory will invariably lead the manager to decisions that will increase the value of the firm. (2) Using some simple numerical examples, we show that the implementation of the principles using real-world data and some basic empirical models and techniques is not all that hard. (3) Drawing on recent articles in publications like *The Wall Street Journal*, we show that real-world managers are actually using the theoretical principles to make decisions on a day-to-day basis.

Third, we demonstrate how managerial economics—applied microeconomic theory—is related to the other disciplines the student will encounter in a business school curriculum. We point out how managerial economics relies on material from other disciplines (e.g., the importance of the theory of efficient markets to the issue of forecasting future sales) and how economics provides a theoretical framework for questions asked in other disciplines (e.g., the use of the indifference curves to evaluate the effect of advertising programs).

The reorganization of material reflected in this edition resulted solely from requests from our users. There are three major areas in which the reorganization appears.

As has been the case since its inception, the body of the text contains no calculus; only algebra and basic geometry are required for complete understanding of the material presented. In the past, the calculus was presented in footnotes. In this edition, we have moved those mathematical discussions, as well as any difficult material that could be bypassed without a loss of continuity, to appendices to the relevant chapters.

For the reasons given in the preface to our second edition, we still believe that it is easier to teach production and cost first and then teach demand. This belief notwithstanding, our current role as textbook writers requires us to listen to our users about the topic order they think is easier to teach. We have listened. Consequently, we have in this edition returned to the traditional topic organization of demand first (Part 2, following the methodological preliminaries in Part 1) and then production and cost (Part 3).

As noted earlier, a number of users asked that we reinstate the topic of linear programming. While we do not use linear programming directly in any of our applications, we have added this topic in an appendix to this text.

The response of instructors and students to the applications in our previous editions has been gratifying. And, if you liked those, you should love the new ones. In this revision, we gave particular attention to the applications.

We searched *The Wall Street Journal* and other publications to find stories that illustrate the theoretical principles. In particular, our goal was to find timely and amusing stories. We think that, with applications like " 'People Watching' to Estimate Demand" (Chapter 7), "Insurance and Litigation Expenses: A Different Type of Production Cost" (Chapter 12), "An Advertiser's Dilemma: Baby Food and Burger Wars" (Chapter 15), and "Selling off the Crown Jewels" (Chapter 18), we succeeded.

For more complicated topics and/or those that required numerical solutions, we were sometimes forced to make up stylized applications. We developed these stylized applications to correspond to real-world events as much as possible. For example, our applications for hostile takeovers— "What Happened to the Golden Boys at EasTex Oil?" and "Goodbye to the Golden Boys at EasTex Oil" (Chapter 18)—are simply stylized versions of stories that were repeated many times in the 1980s.

In addition to the revised applications, we have made extensive revisions and, we believe, improvements to the text. For example, the chapters on production and cost have been expanded to make the material more accessible. Moreover, much of the material on market structures, particularly oligopoly, has been reordered and expanded. Indeed, we have added new text material to every chapter—as we continue to learn new material, we pass it on to the users of this text.

The effect on our thinking of Charles' experiences at Chase appear throughout the text. Examples include estimation of the market model (Chapter 4), the discussion of efficient markets as they relate to demand forecasting (Chapter 8), and price forecasts obtained from the futures markets and random walk price forecasts (Chapter 13).

However, the most significant changes are reflected in Part 6 of the text, all of which is new material. In Parts 1 through 5 of the text, we implicitly consider a firm that is owned and managed by a single entre-preneur, has only a single-period time horizon, and faces no uncertainty. In Part 6, we explicitly consider the shareholder-owned firm. Chapter 18 examines the effects of a multiperiod time horizon, considering the con-cept of present value, the net present value rule for maximizing the value of a firm, the relation between single-period profit maximization and max-imizing the value of the firm, the way maximizing the value of the firm eliminates potential conflicts among shareholders, and how the net present value rule can explain much of the recent merger and acquisition activity in the United States. Chapter 19 examines the effects of uncertainty. After looking at some basic features of probability distributions and showing how the variance of a distribution can be used as a measure of risk, we concentrate on the valuation of a stream of risky cash flows, with partic-ular emphasis on the appropriate discount rate for a risky project. In the process, we consider risk-adjusted discount rates, the weighted average cost of capital, and the capital asset pricing model. Chapter 20 brings together Chapters 18 and 19 by considering the investment decision. We compare the net present value rule with other competing investment cri-teria—payback, return to investment, and internal rate of return—and then briefly examine the capital rationing problem.

The material in Part 6 is an integral part of managerial economics. In Parts 1 through 5, we look at three questions a manager must answer when maximizing single-period profit:

How much output do I produce?

What price do I charge?

What levels of input usage is optimal?

In Part 6, we look at the fourth question a manager must answer:

What investment projects will I undertake?

Moreover, as is apparent from the topics covered and the order of pre-sentation, the material in Part 6 will lead into or reinforce the material learned in the student's finance courses. Hence, it provides an integration of managerial economics with finance, which is part of our third objective for this text.

Chuck Maurice
Charles Smithson

ACKNOWLEDGMENTS

We are indebted to a number of people for their help and support in this revision. In particular, we want to acknowledge the significant contribution made by Niccie McKay at Texas A&M University. She has been involved with every part of this revision, suggesting changes, commenting on the entire draft manuscript, and providing new end-of-chapter questions.

We are also indebted to the persons we met through Richard D. Irwin, Inc., who helped us with this text. Daryl Winn (University of Colorado) has been particularly helpful, making suggestions about the design of the revision and commenting on the draft manuscript for the third edition. We also were helped by the comments and suggestions of Daniel Blakey (University of San Francisco), Charles Brumfield (California State University, Hayward), James Overdahl (University of Texas, Dallas), and Pat Sanderson (Mississippi State University).

We want to thank the people Charles Smithson met and learned from through his affiliation with Chase. Clifford W. Smith, Jr. (University of Rochester) deserves particular thanks for teaching Charles the principles of modern corporate finance that could subsequently be added to this text. Roberto Wessels (Erasmus University) convinced us that Part 6 had to be revised and helped us to revise it. J. Nicholas Robinson (Chase), Dylan Thomas (London Polytechnic), and D. Sykes Wilford (then of Chase, now of Drexel, Burnham, Lambert) read and provided useful comments on much of the manuscript. But most of all, we want to thank officers of Chase Manhattan Bank who came as students but ended up teaching us that managerial economics is a real-world discipline with real-world answers to real-world problems.

S. C. M.
C. W. S.

CONTENTS

1

SCOPE OF MANAGERIAL ECONOMICS

H ow does managerial economics differ from "regular" economics? There is no difference in the theory; standard economic theory provides the basis for managerial economics. The difference is in the way the economic theory is applied.

The primary emphasis of a course in microeconomic theory (also called price theory) is on how individual decisions of buyers and sellers lead (or possibly fail to lead) to efficient outcomes for society as a whole. In most price theory courses, the applications generally concern the effects of the actions of private or governmental decision makers on the economy. There is little concern with the way decisions *should be made;* the focus is on the costs and benefits of the decisions to society as a whole.

Managerial economics (also called applied microeconomics), on the other hand, deals with *how decisions should be made by managers to achieve the firm's goals*—in particular, how to maximize profit. These decisions, or their results, may or may not be beneficial from society's viewpoint. Although important, such welfare consequences are of secondary consideration in managerial economics.

Despite the difference in emphasis, a primary concern in a managerial economics course is the fundamentals of microeconomic theory—the basic tools used by economists. Let us emphasize at the beginning that while these theories are relatively simple, they are the same theoretical methods used by "real-world" decision makers. In other words, although the economic theory used in this text is relatively simple, it is sophisticated enough to be used in real-world managerial decision making.

In this text, you will use economic theory to analyze economic problems that are relevant to firms. You will learn to analyze decision-making problems similar to those currently being considered by analysts in the nation's largest firms. It is not our intention to make you into a professional economist. This text is designed to help you learn basic economic theory and to allow you to practice using economics in order to become a competent professional decision maker and manager: The basic theoretical tools, the fundamental methods of analysis, and the basic approaches to problem solving used by professional economists and business analysts are those you will learn to use.

The major reason for studying managerial economics is that it is useful. Every manager—in fact, every person—makes economic decisions every day. We will always face problems of scarcities and consequently must make choices. A knowledge of economics helps us make wise choices. Therefore, all students will find managerial economics useful in both their professional and their private lives.

Students who choose business as a career will find economics particularly useful. (Note that people who become doctors, lawyers, or other professionals are in business also.) Economics is extremely useful in making decisions designed to increase the firm's profit and enable the firm to operate more efficiently. Economics is useful in helping decision makers decide how to adapt to external changes in economic variables. The appropriate level of advertising and the investment decision are also economic decisions, and an understanding of economic theory helps managers make the most profitable decisions.

A knowledge of economics is useful also to people who work for government agencies or nonprofit institutions. Although the goals of these agencies and institutions do not include profit maximization, they do involve economic efficiency. For example, a government agency may be required to allocate a given budget to attain the maximum benefit—in education, health care, and so forth—permitted by the size of the budget. Or it may be charged with attaining a certain goal at the lowest possible cost. These are economic problems, and managerial economics provides the tools needed to solve these problems. Just as it helps business managers, economics helps these managers of nonprofit organizations adapt to changes in the economic environment in the most efficient manner.

We have barely skimmed the surface, mentioning only a few types of decisions for which economic reasoning is useful. We will consider many such examples throughout the text. You will be able to increase your ability to analyze and solve decision-making problems through practice. The better your understanding of economic theory and the more you practice applying the theory, the better prepared you will be for carrying out the tasks of managers.

1.1 WHY FIRMS EXIST

Since most of this text will be concerned with the behavior of firms, it would be useful at the outset to discuss why firms exist. For analytical purposes, economists divide the economy into two sectors—households, which purchase goods and services and sell their inputs, and business firms, which purchase inputs and sell goods and services.

An economy could, of course, function without firms. Some have in the past; some do so today. In the "pioneer era," households were virtually self-sufficient. However, this method of production is inefficient. Society loses the advantage of specialization, and households do not gain from trade.

Over time, households began to specialize in one type of production and to trade their products in the marketplace. This method was more efficient than producing all of the household's goods under a single roof. But large transportation and transaction costs were involved in such exchanges. People discovered that it was more efficient to bring together resources in one place and cooperate in the production of goods and services. This system of production permitted the advantages of specialization and division of labor. And, if there were cost savings associated with producing larger outputs, this cooperative form of organization would produce at a lower cost and drive out other organizational forms of production. Historically, this method of production did develop very rapidly during the 19th century. It is often referred to as the factory system.

But mere cooperation of resources does not necessarily make a firm efficient. To see why, let's look at a very simplified example. Suppose four of us bought a boat and entered the fishing business. We agree to split the profits equally. But, we soon find out that fishing is hard work. We each know that if one of us goofs off a little, we catch fewer fish than if we all fished hard all of the time. But every fish "the loafer" does not catch costs the person doing the loafing only one fourth of the value of that fish, because its value is divided into four parts. Thus, since the cost of goofing off is lower than if each of us received only the value of our own product, we are all induced to goof off more. So, production falls off. The same situation would clearly hold in a factory setting.

Hence, separating the ownership from the productive activity itself has certain advantages. The owners can contract with workers for a fixed amount of their labor per period in return for a fixed payment per period. The owners can then claim any residual after the output is sold and the workers paid. (They would also suffer the loss if that should result.) The residual claimants (owners) could either personally assume the task of monitoring the workers to make sure they fulfilled their contracts or they could hire monitors, sometimes called *managers,* to do the job.

Firms of various types arise in an economy because they have been able to organize production more efficiently than other types of institutions could. Generally, we think of the owners of capital as doing the task of contracting with other resources and either hiring managers (monitors) or carrying out this task themselves. While this may be the most prominent form of organization, it is not the only one. In some countries, the labor-managed firm is a frequently used form of organization. Less frequently, we find the consumer-managed firm. But the point is that most production takes place in business firms. These firms are not merely forced onto a helpless society. The institution of business firms exists because this is an efficient form for organizing production. If some more efficient way of organizing production is discovered, that organization will replace the business firm. Until then, economics texts will treat production of goods and services as generally being organized in firms.

1.2 ROLES OF MANAGERS

Making decisions and processing information are the two primary tasks of managers. We separate these two tasks for analytical purposes; in reality, they are inseparable. In order to make intelligent decisions, managers must be able to obtain, process, and use information. Economic theory helps managers know what information should be obtained, how to process the information, and how to use it.

The task of organizing and processing information in conjunction with basic economic theory can take two general forms. The first involves a specific decision that must be made by the manager. The second general form involves using readily available information to carry out a course of action that furthers the goals of the organization.

Examples of the first form of decisions that managers might have to make are (1) whether or not to close down a branch of the firm, (2) whether or not a store or restaurant should stay open more hours a day, (3) how a government agency can be reorganized to be more efficient, (4) how a hospital can treat more patients without a decrease in patient care, and (5) whether to install an in-house computer rather than pay for outside computing services. These and a myriad of other managerial decisions require the use of basic economics. Economic theory helps decision makers know what information is necessary to make the decision and how to process and use that information. In other words, an important purpose of economic theory is to indicate what information will be useful in solving problems and enabling firms to operate more efficiently. After obtaining the desired information managers must then analyze this information and use it in connection with the theoretical and statistical tools available to make the best decision possible under the circumstances.

The second general form of managerial decision making involves using readily available information to carry out a course of action that furthers the goals of the organization. Basic economic theory is extremely useful to managers in this task also. Managers receive useful information every day from many sources. Some of these sources are *The Wall Street Jour-*

nal, business magazines such as *Business Week,* local newspapers, television, private newsletters, and conversations with others. Successful managers know how to pick out the useful information from the vast amount of information they receive. They know how to evaluate this information and act on it in order to further the goals of their organizations.

Of course, a manager must know the goals of the organization. As we mentioned above, managerial economics is useful not only to managers in profit-maximizing firms but also to managers in government and in nonprofit organizations. The primary goal of a manufacturing firm would be to maximize profits. The primary goal of a foundation could be to further some cause. A public hospital could have the goal of treating as many patients as possible—subject, of course, to certain standards. A state university could have the goal of educating, above a certain standard, as many students as possible.

We should emphasize, however, that the tasks of managers in practically all of these situations are the same. Each goal involves an optimization problem. The manager attempts either to maximize or minimize some objective function (frequently subject to some constraint). And, for all goals that involve an optimization problem, the same general economic principles apply, a point we will stress in a forthcoming chapter.

1.3 MANAGERIAL ECONOMICS AS PART OF A BUSINESS CURRICULUM

Managerial economics deals with the decisions a manager must make in the course of maximizing profit or maximizing the value of the firm. Hence, managerial economics must make use of principles and techniques from the other disciplines in a business curriculum. And, not surprisingly, the other business disciplines also make use of principles and techniques from economics.

When, in Chapter 5, we consider the impact of advertising on the demand function for a firm's output we turn to the marketing literature for guidance. Clearly, no other discipline has spent as much time considering the impacts of advertising. We again rely considerably on the marketing literature when we look at some of the pricing models—for example, cost-plus pricing in Chapter 16.

Our discussion of the optimal combinations of inputs is clearly of interest to professionals in both management and economics. However, the material we present that is closest to topics found in a management course is our discussion of the potential conflicts between shareholders and managers and the subsequent discussion of mergers and acquisitions in Chapter 18.

The material on optimization in Chapter 3, regression analysis in Chapter 4, and linear programming in the appendix cover topics you might have seen in an operations research or business analysis course. All of the business disciplines share a common core of quantitative methods.

Throughout this text we make a significant use of principles and examples drawn from finance. The market model described in Chapter 4 is taken directly from the finance literature, as is the discussion of efficient markets in Chapters 8 and 13. However, the largest contribution of finance is found in Part Six of this text where we discuss the behavior of a firm attempting to maximize profit over time in an uncertain environment.

Finally, it is obvious that few of the quantitative analyses in this text would be possible without accounting data. Without reliable data, reasoned decision making would be impossible. Accounting data is increasingly coming to reflect the concept of opportunity cost emphasized in economics. Indeed, in a conversation with one of the principals of Price Waterhouse on a flight back from Europe, we were struck by the degree to which accounting and economics are converging.

Managerial economics fits closely with the other courses you are taking or have taken or will take during your course of study. Those other courses will help you in this managerial economics course. In turn, managerial economics will aid you in other business courses.

1.4 PURPOSE OF ECONOMIC THEORY

Economics might be best described as "a way of thinking about problems"—a logical system for processing and using information. Since this text is in large part concerned with economic theory and its application, we might take time to explain how and why theory is used. No doubt you have heard statements such as "That's OK in theory, but how about the real world?" The fact is that theory is designed to apply to the real world; it allows us to gain insights into problems that would be impossible to solve without a theoretical structure. We can make predictions from theory that will hold in the real world even though the theoretical structure abstracts from many actual characteristics of the world.

The purpose of theory is to make sense out of confusion. The real world is a very complicated place. There are an infinite number of variables that continually change. Theory is concerned with determining which variables are important to the issue at hand and which are not. The theoretical structure allows us to concentrate on a few important forces and ignore the many, many variables that are unimportant. In other words, when using theory we abstract away from the irrelevant.

It is this ability to abstract—to cast aside all factors insignificant to the problem—that allows managers to come to grips with the issue at hand without becoming bogged down in unimportant issues. The ability to abstract and ignore unimportant factors helps managers know what information is useful in making decisions and what is not. As we emphasized above, a major role of managers is obtaining and processing information. Economic theory indicates what information is relevant to the decision at hand and how to use that information.

1.5 PURPOSE OF EMPIRICAL ANALYSES

In this text we will describe several types of empirical (or quantitative) analysis—in particular, regression analysis. Why should we be talking about statistical techniques in an *economics* text?

The purpose of these discussions of empirical techniques is the same as the purpose of learning economic theory: We need some method of making sense out of the confusion that is inherent in real-world data. But simply collecting data is not enough. The data must somehow be organized in such a fashion that economic theory can be used in making decisions. It is the empirical analyses that provide this necessary organization. Economic theory determines what information should be collected; the empirical analyses provide a structure for organizing this information.

While we will concentrate on regression analysis as a means of organizing real-world data, we do not mean to imply that this is the only method that can be used. We concentrate on regression analysis simply because it is a widely used technique and because space limitations preclude a comprehensive discussion of all of the available empirical techniques. At this point, let us mention something we will stress throughout this text: Our purpose is *not* to teach you how to do statistics. That is a task appropriately left to courses in statistics, business analysis, or econometrics. Rather, our objective is to show how these empirical analyses can be, and are, used in managerial decision making.

1.6 A PREVIEW

Since this text is concerned with using economic theory in conjunction with real-world data to make optimizing (e.g., profit-maximizing) decisions, it might be helpful to look at the kind of decisions a manager is faced with. At this point, we limit ourselves to some simple applications. Subsequent chapters will deal with these topics in more detail.

A decision of primary importance to the manager is the output decision: How much should the firm produce? In a service industry this question might involve the hours of operation.

APPLICATION

Hours of Operation for a Store

A retailer is considering keeping the store open an additional four hours a day. What information does the retailer need in order to make the decision? The first piece of information necessary is the additional (or incremental) cost of remaining open the additional four hours.

These additional costs could be estimated by calculating the added labor required, the additional cost of electricity and gas, perhaps added maintenance and management costs, and any other costs that would not be incurred unless the store stays open the additional hours. Note, as will be obvious later in the text, that the overhead or fixed cost is irrelevant in the decision-making process. The fixed costs must be paid by the store regardless of how many hours the store remains open and therefore can be ignored.

Next, the additional sales revenue that can be expected from remaining open must be estimated. The retailer must consider in making this estimation any sales lost during the regular operating hours because of remaining open the additional hours.

If the additional sales expected from staying open longer exceed the expected additional costs, the store should stay open the additional hours. If the added costs exceed the expected additional sales revenue, the store should not extend its hours of operation. The decision is based only on additional (marginal) revenues and additional (marginal) costs.

The preceding application is an example of a maximization problem—maximizing profit. However, the manager is also faced with minimization problems, most frequently the problem of how to minimize cost.

APPLICATION

Breakage in the Factory—Should It Be Eliminated?

The manager of a firm is aware that in the course of day-to-day operation, there is a considerable amount of breakage occurring, particularly containers getting crushed on the loading dock of the factory. The breakage is occurring on the conveyor and to some extent because of the way the forklifts are used. The engineering department notes that the conveyor can be modified and the stacking process changed to eliminate the breakage.

Should the manager authorize the modifications and changes to eliminate breakage? The manager must first determine the benefit from making the modifications: the engineering and accounting departments would need to determine the savings—the reduction in costs—that could be expected. Next, the manager must assess the additional cost of the modifications: the costs associated with modifying the conveyor, altering the work rules for the forklift drivers, and hiring additional forklift drivers or inspectors. Then the manager can compare the additional benefits—the savings—with the additional cost. If the additional benefits exceed the additional cost, the modifications should be made.

It may well be the case that the cost of eliminating (or even reducing) the breakage exceeds the savings that could be obtained. In this case no modification should be made.

It is even possible that more, not less, breakage is optimal. This would be the case if the cost of additional breakage is less than the expected cost of the labor and other resources that control breakage. In any case, there is an optimal amount of breakage—and this amount is probably not zero.

To illustrate this important point, suppose the manager obtains the following data for breakage costs and the costs of breakage control for the firm:

(1) Daily Cost of Breakage Control (dollars)	(2) Average Number of Containers Damaged per Day	(3) Average Daily Breakage Cost (dollars)
$ 0	100	$1,000
100	70	700
200	45	450
300	25	250
400	10	100
500	4	40
600	0	0

Column 1 shows the costs of the modifications: the amounts the firm might spend daily on breakage control. As more is spent on breakage control, the average number of containers damaged per day (Column 2) declines. Column 3 summarizes the benefits which could be realized from less breakage. The average expense associated with each damaged container is $10, so column 3 is simply $10 times the corresponding number in column 2 and, therefore, shows the average daily breakage cost associated with each level of expenditure in column 1.

From the table we can see that if the firm spends nothing on damage control, the average daily damage from breakage is 100 units at a cost of $1,000. If the firm increases its expenditure to $100, breakage cost falls to $700, a reduction of $300. Clearly the firm should increase its expense on damage control. Moreover, an additional increase in expenditure to $200 reduces breakage cost by $250. Likewise, you can verify that increases in expenditure from $200 to $300 and from $300 to $400 reduce breakage costs by more than each additional $100 expenditure. But an increase in expenditure from $400 to $500 reduces breakage costs by only $60. Obviously the firm would not make this increase. Thus, the firm would spend $400 daily on reducing damage, with an associated $100 breakage cost. The total cost of this operation is $500. You may, by summing the amounts in columns 1 and 3, verify that the $500 total cost is the lowest total cost possible. Note that the firm could reduce breakage to zero by spending $600, but this method would not give the lowest total cost of the operation.

To summarize, the factory should increase or reduce breakage as long as the added saving is more than the added cost. An engineer might say any amount of breakage is inefficient. An economist would say a positive amount is optimal if the additional cost of a change from that amount exceeds the expected additional saving.

As we will see in Chapter 3 and subsequent chapters, in a large number of managerial decisions the manager's ability to maximize profit or minimize cost is constrained. It may be that the manager must minimize the cost of a given level of output, or, as is the case in the following example, the manager may be required to maximize some measure of output for a given level of expenditures.

APPLICATION

The Optimal Mix of Advertising Media

In many firms, the marketing department is given a fixed advertising budget. The problem facing the vice president for marketing is to select the mix of advertising media—television, radio, print ads, cents-off coupons, rebates, sweepstakes, and so on—that will maximize the firm's sales while satisfying the constraint imposed by the fixed advertising budget.

In the previous examples, the manager selected the optimal level of operating hours or expenditures on breakage control by equating the incremental benefits from the activity with the incremental cost of the activity. In the case of this constrained decision, that rule is not sufficient: it is not sufficient to advertise on television as long as the addition to sales (revenues) exceeds the addition to costs. While such a strategy could add to total profit, it may not satisfy the expenditure constraint faced by the vice president for marketing.

Instead, the marketing department must consider the additional revenues generated by an additional dollar's worth of advertising in each media. The advertising budget can then be allocated by spending the budget where "we get the biggest bang for a buck."

So far, the applications presented have considered situations in which the manager is maximizing profit in a single period and faces no uncertainty. Decisions like the investment decision—whether or not to undertake a project or acquire an asset—require us to take into account that the manager's objective is to maximize the value of the firm when future cash flows are uncertain.

APPLICATION

Do I Acquire a New Machine?

Almost all managers are confronted with the decision about acquiring a new piece of equipment. Managers know with certainty the current purchase price of the equipment. However, they can only estimate future revenues and costs associated with the equipment. Thus, actual net cash flows in the future are uncertain and the best the manager can do is to get a measure of *expected* net cash flows in the future periods.

Moreover, the problem is further complicated because the net cash flows occur in the future, not in the current period. And, a dollar inflow in the future is worth less to the firm than a dollar inflow today. Thus, the future net cash flows will have to be *discounted;* that is, the net cash flows will have to be converted from their values in the future to their equivalent values today. And, the selection of the appropriate discount rate for a risky investment project is not always that simple.

The specifics of this issue will be taken up in Chapters 18, 19, and 20. However, at this point, we can see the basics of how this investment decision must be made: The value in today's dollars—the *present value*—of the prospective equipment purchase must be compared with the cost of acquiring the equipment. If the present value of the project (the addition to revenues) exceeds the cost of the project (the addition to costs), the equipment should be acquired. If the present value of the project is less than the cost of acquiring the equipment, the investment should not be undertaken.

From the preceding applications, two points should be emphasized. First, economic theory allows managers to ignore variables that are unimportant or irrelevant in the decision-making process. One can deduce conclusions, using simple assumptions, while ignoring forces that could have an effect on the outcome but in all likelihood will not. Economic theory gives a formalized structure (or method of analysis) for handling business decisions. When carrying out analysis we should remember that, while everything depends on everything else, most things depend in an essential way upon only a few other things. We usually ignore the general interdependence of everything and concentrate only upon the close interdependence of a few variables. If pressed far enough, the price of beef depends not only on the prices of pork and other meats, but also on the prices of butane, color television, and airline tickets. But as a first approximation we ignore the prices of butane, TVs, and so on, because a change in the price of one of these items would have little or no effect on the price of beef. We temporarily hold other things constant and concentrate our attention on a few closely related variables where a change may have a significant impact on the subject variable.

The second major point that should be stressed is that managerial decision making involves marginal analysis in comparing the costs and benefits of a particular activity. Marginal analysis simply means that the decision maker compares incremental or additional changes in the variables. For example, a firm would attempt to increase output if the manager expected the additional revenue from expansion to exceed the additional cost. If the additional or marginal cost is expected to exceed the additional or marginal revenue, output would not be expanded. Managers use this type of analysis to solve many, many similar types of problems. You will receive a considerable amount of practice using this type of analysis throughout this text.

1.7 STRUCTURE OF THE TEXT

This text is divided into six parts. In Part One we provide what we refer to as the preliminary material. In addition to an overview of demand and supply, we provide a general discussion of optimization (i.e., maximization or minimization) and a brief review of how to interpret regression results. While all of this material is simple (and may well be a review for many students), an understanding of this material is essential for the subsequent discussions.

Part Two deals with demand. Although it provides the theoretical basis for demand, the emphasis is on the way the theory of demand is used in decision making. In this vein, we will describe the techniques of demand estimation. The purpose of the material that deals with estimation is not to teach sophisticated statistical methods of estimation; rather, the concern is to teach you how to have demand estimated and how to interpret these estimations. This part of the book also considers the techniques used in forecasting demand in the future. Again, the emphasis is placed on use and interpretation rather than on statistical methodology.

Part Three is concerned with the underpinnings of supply—production and cost. It begins with a consideration of the production process, the method of organizing inputs to produce an output, a subject more general than the title suggests. It is clear that managers of manufacturing firms are concerned with organizing inputs to produce an output. But managers in service industries or government are also concerned with production processes. Marketing personnel organize inputs—their time, selling aids, travel, and so on—to produce sales. Hospital administrators and educators also use inputs to produce outputs—in these cases, health and education. Doctors, lawyers, and governmental employees also produce an output, even though it may be more difficult to measure than the number of cars or tons of steel produced by a firm. Since much of the theory and methods of processing information apply to these types of managers as well as to manufacturers, the theoretical and empirical discussions will be quite general. The applications will be concerned with all aspects of production processes, not simply manufacturing. Then, the theory of production is used to derive the cost function facing the organization. Part Three also provides an empirical approach to production and cost.

In essence, Parts Four and Five combine the material developed in Parts Two and Three in order to show how a manager can make profit-maximizing decisions. Specifically, the objective is to show how the manager of a firm will answer three questions: (1) How much should the firm produce? (2) What price should be charged? (3) What amounts of the inputs should be employed? In Part Four these questions are answered for a firm in a perfectly competitive industry. In Part Five the same questions are considered for firms that possess some market power. We present implementation methodologies for both structures.

Part Six provides a discussion of how the time dimension and uncertainty affect the firm's decision process. We then demonstrate how the basic optimization rules can be applied to the firm's decisions about which investment projects to undertake.

A large part of the text is devoted to the development of the theoretical and empirical techniques and analyses. But much of the book is concerned with applications. New theoretical material is generally not introduced in the "Applications" sections. Spaced throughout each chapter, they are designed to show how the text material is used and to give you practice in using the techniques set forth.

Finally, we should stress that this text does not assume that the student has a mathematical background. All of the analysis uses simple algebraic manipulations. However, for the student with a mathematical background, we provide mathematical expositions in the appendix to the relevant chapter.

PART ONE

THE PRELIMINARIES

2

DEMAND AND SUPPLY

Q uite possibly the most important tools of economic analysis are the concepts of demand and supply. A thorough knowledge of demand and supply is absolutely essential for sound economic decision making.

In later chapters we will develop these concepts more completely; the purpose of this chapter is to set forth a short overview of demand, supply, and market equilibrium. This overview is meant to be an introduction to, or to most students a review of, these important tools of economic analysis and how they are used.

The primary importance of demand and supply is the way they determine prices and quantities sold in the market. As we stressed in Chapter 1, managers are extremely interested in forecasting future prices and output, both for the goods and services they sell and for the inputs they use.

A familiarity with the concept of comparative statics, the comparison of market equilibrium conditions before and after certain conditions change, is essential if you want to be able to forecast future market conditions. This technique enables managers to make qualitative forecasts—forecasting the direction of change in price and output—and to know what techniques should be used to forecast the magnitude of the changes. For instance, if you read in *The Wall Street Journal* that Congress is considering a tax cut, comparative statics enables you to forecast whether the price and output of a product will increase or decrease.

We begin with an analysis of demand (2.1), then develop the foundations of supply (2.2). Section 2.3 puts these two concepts together to show how they determine the equilibrium price and quantity sold in the market. Then section 2.4 describes comparative statics—how changes in demand and supply affect equilibrium price and quantity sold.

2.1 DEMAND

Economists are frequently accused of implying that the only factor that affects the amount of a good or service purchased is its price. This allegation is simply not correct. While economists do stress the importance of price, they recognize that many factors determine the amount of a good or service consumers will purchase during a given period. But, in order to make analysis manageable, economists concentrate on the more important influencing forces and ignore those that have little or no effect.

In general, economists assume that the quantity of a good or service that individuals are willing and able to purchase during a particular period depends upon six major variables: (1) the price of the good itself, (2) the incomes of the consumers, (3) the prices of related goods and services, (4) the expected price of the good in future periods, (5) the tastes of the consumers, and (6) the number of potential consumers.

As you would expect, consumers are willing and able to buy more of a good the lower the *price* of the good, when the other variables are held constant. This relation is so important that it is called the "law of demand." (If you have doubts about the validity of the law of demand, try to think of specific items you would buy in larger quantities if the price were higher, again holding the other variables constant.) The law of demand holds because, when the price of a good rises, consumers tend to shift from that good to now relatively cheaper goods. Conversely, when the price of a good falls, they tend to purchase more of that good and less of other goods that are now relatively more expensive.

Next let's look at changes in *income*. Holding the other variables constant, an increase in income can cause the amount of a commodity consumers purchase either to increase or to decrease. If an increase (a decrease) in income causes quantity purchased to increase (decrease), we refer to such a commodity as a "normal" good. That is, in the case of a normal good, income and sales vary directly. There can, however, exist goods for which an increase in income would reduce the quantity purchased—other variables held constant. These types of commodities are referred to as "inferior" goods.

Commodities may be *related in consumption* in either of two ways: as substitutes or complements. In general, goods are substitutes if one good can be used in the place of the other; an example might be Fords and Chevrolets. If two goods are substitutes, an increase in the price of one good will increase the quantity purchased of the other (holding the price of the good under consideration constant). If the price of Fords rises while the price of Chevrolets remains constant, we would expect consumers to purchase more Chevrolets. A decrease in the price of a substitute good will decrease the quantity purchased of the other good. For example, if the price of beef falls, we would expect the quantity of pork purchased to fall, given a constant price of pork.

Goods are said to be complements if they are used in conjunction with each other. Examples might be lettuce and salad dressing or cameras and film. An increase in the price of either complementary good will decrease the quantity purchased of the other good, the price of the other good held constant.

The preceding discussion does not mean that all commodities are either substitutes or complements in consumption. Many commodities are *essentially* independent. For example, we would not expect the price of lettuce to significantly influence the sales of automobiles. Thus, we can treat these commodities as independent and ignore the price of lettuce when evaluating the demand for automobiles.

Expectations of consumers also influence the quantity purchased of a commodity. More specifically, consumers' expectations about the future price of the commodity can change their current purchases. If consumers expect the price to be higher in a future period, sales would probably tend to rise in the current period. On the other hand, expectations of a price decline in the future would cause some purchases to be postponed; thus sales in the current period would fall.

A change in *tastes* or *preferences* can change the quantity purchased of a commodity, the other variables held constant. Clearly, taste changes could either increase or decrease sales. Given the difficulty of measuring tastes, economists frequently assume that this variable is constant. However, this factor is very important in understanding the effects of advertising, a topic to which we will turn later. Finally, an increase in the number of potential consumers will increase the quantity purchased, and a decrease in the number will decrease quantity purchased of a commodity, the other variables held constant.

We can write the function describing the quantity that consumers are willing and able to purchase during a particular time period as:

$$Q_{X,t} = f(P_{X,t}, Y_t, P_{R,t}, P^e_{X,t+i}, \mathcal{T}, N),$$

where "f" means "is a function of" (depends upon)

$Q_{X,t}$ = The quantity purchased of good X in period t,
$P_{X,t}$ = The price of good X in period t,
Y_t = The consumers' incomes in period t,
$P_{R,t}$ = The price of related goods in period t,
$P^e_{X,t+i}$ = The expected price of good X in some future period, $t + i$,
$\mathcal{T}$ = The taste patterns of consumers,
N = The number of potential consumers.

The effects of changes in the variables that determine the quantity purchased in a market during a particular time period may be summarized as follows, where the symbol Δ means "the change in":[1]

$$\frac{\Delta Q_{X,t}}{\Delta P_{X,t}} < 0$$

$$\frac{\Delta Q_{X,t}}{\Delta Y_t} \quad \begin{array}{l} > 0 \text{ if the good is normal} \\ < 0 \text{ if the good is inferior} \end{array}$$

$$\frac{\Delta Q_{X,t}}{\Delta P_{R,t}} \quad \begin{array}{l} > 0 \text{ if the goods are substitutes} \\ < 0 \text{ if the goods are complements} \end{array}$$

$$\frac{\Delta Q_{X,t}}{\Delta \mathcal{T}} \quad ? \text{ (The sign is indeterminant)}$$

$$\frac{\Delta Q_{X,t}}{\Delta P^e_{X,t+i}} > 0$$

$$\frac{\Delta Q_{X,t}}{\Delta N} > 0.$$

Again let us stress that these relations are in the context of all other things equal. An increase in the price of the commodity will lead to a decrease in quantity purchased as long as the other variables—income, the price of related commodities, tastes, price expectations, and the number of potential consumers—remain constant.

THE WALL STREET JOURNAL

APPLICATION

Gasoline Prices and the Demand for Burgers

Recall that we said two goods are complements if a decrease in the price of one leads to an increase in the sales of the other. When we think of complements, we typically think of goods that are consumed together, such as bread and butter, hamburgers and catsup, or automobiles and gasoline. But a change in the price of one good may well lead to an increase in the sales of other goods without there being any complementary relation at all. Let's look at why this relation occurs.

From the summer of 1985 to May 1986, average gasoline prices in the United States fell from $1.20 to 90 cents. In some places the price of regular

Continued on page 21

----

[1]Students with a mathematical background will note that we are dealing with partial derivatives of the demand relation. The derivatives evaluate the effect of a change in one variable, holding the other variables constant.

THE WALL STREET JOURNAL

APPLICATION

Continued from page 20 plunged to 65 cents. Betsy Morris, in an article in *The Wall Street Journal,* May 19, 1986,* presented a few predictions about the effect of lower gasoline prices that, at first glance, seemed a bit unusual. The *WSJ* did predict that people would buy more gasoline in the summer of 1986, as we would expect. And this did occur. Morris also predicted, on the basis of consumer interviews, that more vacations would be taken in automobiles. This would also be expected. Gasoline and automobile trips are probably complements.

Morris did not predict an increase in automobile sales because of the reduced price of gasoline. She did, however, make some unexpected predictions about increases in sales of some other goods and services. For example, she predicted an increase in entertainment purchases, eating out, fast foods such as pizzas and burgers, video rentals, upscale frozen dinners, specialty foods, and, of all things, lottery tickets. How would these things be considered complements to gasoline? In the sense of being consumed jointly, they aren't. Then why would a decrease in the price of gasoline be expected to increase their sales?

These predictions were based upon the following information. Americans were expected to purchase about 109 billion gallons of gasoline in 1986. Other things equal, every one-cent fall in the price of gasoline means a saving to consumers of $1 billion. Even though the lower gasoline price might have caused people to buy more gasoline, the saving was expected to be huge with a 30-cent reduction in price. So Morris's predictions were based upon this large expected increase in consumer purchasing power.

The saving, spread over all gasoline consumers, would not be large enough to spur spending on expensive items such as automobiles. Any one family's saving on gasoline would not stretch that far. But, these savings would stretch far enough to induce increased spending on low-priced, impulse purchases such as those mentioned above.

The lower gasoline prices, in effect, increased the disposable income of gasoline consumers. Then the increase in income would induce these consumers to purchase more of these relatively low-priced goods and services. So the predictions were made on the basis of increased purchasing power rather than any

Continued to page 22

*"Low Gasoline Prices May Inspire Splurging on Small-Ticket Items." Adapted by permission of *The Wall Street Journal.*

The Demand Function

Demand functions show the relation between the quantity demanded by
consumers and the price of the product. These functions are among the
most important tools used by economists. While we emphasized above
that many variables determine the quantity consumers wish to purchase
in a market, the price of the commodity is an extremely important, probably the most important, determinant for economic analysis. We begin
with the definition of a demand function:

*Definition.   A demand function is a list of prices and the corresponding
quantities that consumers are willing and able to purchase in some
time period, all other things held constant. Consumers are willing and
able to purchase more of an item the lower its price; that is, quantity
demanded per time period varies inversely with price.*

Note that *demand* is a function (or schedule), not a specific quantity.
Hence, when we refer to the demand for beef or the demand for automobiles in the United States, we are considering the amounts that consumers are willing and able to purchase at *various* prices. When we talk
about demand, we are talking about the entire schedule of quantities and
prices. Only when we specify a single price do we consider a single point
on the demand schedule, and we refer to this point on the schedule as
the *quantity demanded* at that given price.

We generally specify consumer demand in any of three ways: as a
schedule, a graph, or a function. A typical market demand schedule is
shown in Table 2.1. This table shows the list of prices and the corresponding quantities that consumers demand (i.e., are willing and able to
purchase) per period of time. Note again that quantity demanded and
price vary inversely in the market.

Quite often it is more convenient to work with the graph of a demand
schedule, called a demand curve, rather than with the schedule itself.

Table 2.1 **Market Demand Schedule**

Quantity Demanded (units)	Price per Unit (dollars)
2,000	$6
3,000	5
4,000	4
5,000	3
5,500	2
6,000	1

Figure 2.1 **Market Demand Curve**

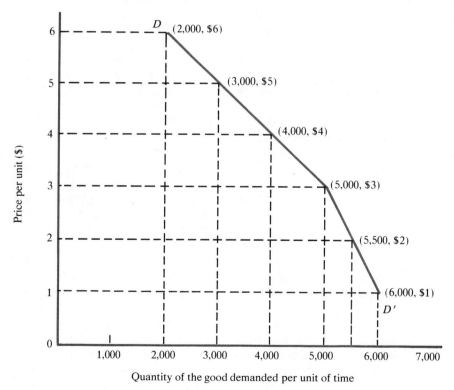

Quantity of the good demanded per unit of time

Figure 2.1 provides the demand curve corresponding to the schedule in Table 2.1. Each quantity-price combination—(2,000, $6), (3,000, $5), and so on—is plotted, then the six points are connected by the curve labeled *DD'*. This curve indicates the quantity of the good consumers are willing and able to buy per unit of time at every price from $6 to $1. Since price and quantity demanded are inversely related, the curve slopes downward.

Indeed, all market demand curves must be drawn downward sloping to conform with the law of demand. Individuals purchase less as price increases. Furthermore, as price increases, some individuals may purchase nothing at all, again causing the quantity demanded at each price to decrease.

Alternatively, we can express demand as a function[2]

$$Q_X = f(P_X),$$

meaning the quantity of X demanded is a function of (depends on) the price of X. In this function the other variables (income, and so on) are held constant. Quantity demanded is a function of the price of the good, holding constant the other determining variables.

Shifts in Demand

From our earlier discussion you know that price is not the sole determinant of the amount of the commodity consumers wish to purchase. Obviously the amount of beef or number of automobiles consumers wish to purchase during a given period depends on other variables, including income, the price of related goods, and so on. In other words, changes in these other variables change the quantity demanded at each price—they change (shift) the demand function. We refer to these other variables as the *determinants of demand* since they determine where the demand function will be located.

As we emphasized above, when we draw a demand curve like the one in Figure 2.1, we do so under the assumption that other things remain the same. The other things are: (1) consumers' incomes, (2) the prices of related goods, (3) price expectations, (4) tastes, and (5) the number of potential consumers. When price falls (rises) and consumers purchase more (less) of a good, other things remaining the same, we say that *quantity demanded* increases (decreases). *Demand* does not increase or decrease when price changes.

Demand is said to increase or decrease only if one or more of the determinants of demand change. For example, if incomes of consumers increase and they wish to purchase more of a good at each price than they did previously, we say that the demand for the good has increased. That is, consumers demand a larger quantity at each price. If the increase in income causes consumers to demand less of the good than before at each price (i.e., if the good is inferior), then demand decreases.

In this discussion we have been differentiating between (1) changes in quantity demanded, due to a change in the price of the product, and (2) changes (shifts) in demand due to changes in one or more of the determinants of demand (e.g., income). Figure 2.2 might help to make this difference clearer.

---

[2]In this functional notation, the inverse relation between price and quantity demanded is expressed by the derivative $dQ_X/dP_X < 0$ or $f'(P_X) < 0$.

Figure 2.2   Changes in Demand versus Changes in Quantity Demanded

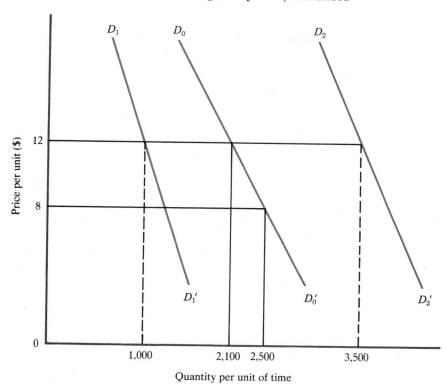

Quantity per unit of time

In Figure 2.2 the original demand curve is given by D_0D_0'. Given this demand curve, at a price of $12, the quantity demanded by the consumers is 2,100 units. If price falls from $12 to $8, quantity demanded will increase to 2,500 units. Changes in quantity demanded are caused only by changes in the price of the product itself and are reflected in movements along the existing demand curve.

Now, beginning again with demand curve D_0D_0', let's look at a change in demand. Suppose that income decreases and the good in question is a normal commodity. Consumers will now demand less of the commodity at every price. The demand for the product will decrease as is illustrated by the leftward shift from D_0D_0' to D_1D_1' in Figure 2.2. At every price, quantity demanded is less than before; for example, at a price of $12 per unit the quantity demanded is now 1,000 units. In this case, the decrease in the amount consumers are willing and able to purchase (from 2,100 to 1,000 at a price of $12 per unit) is the result of a change in demand. Alternatively, an increase in demand would be as illustrated by the rightward shift from D_0D_0' to D_2D_2' in Figure 2.2. Now, consumers demand 3,500 units at a price of $12. In either case, changes in demand are caused by changes in one or more of the determinants of demand (income, prices of related goods, price expectations, tastes, and the number of consumers). Changes in demand are reflected in shifts of the demand curve, either to the right for an increase in demand or the left for a decrease in demand.

Let's look more specifically at the effects of changes in the various determinants of demand, beginning with income. As we noted earlier, an increase in income causes consumers to demand more of the good at every price, if the good is a normal good. If the good is inferior, consumers will demand less of the good at every price after an increase in income. Thus, an increase in income increases the demand (shifts the curve rightward) for a normal good, but decreases the demand (shifts the curve leftward) for an inferior good. Conversely, a decrease in income will decrease (increase) the demand for a normal (an inferior) good.

If goods A and B are *substitutes,* an increase in the price of good B will cause an increase in the demand for A. For example, if the price of Fords increases by $500, we would expect consumers to demand more Chevrolets at each relevant price. If two goods are substitutes, an increase (decrease) in the price of one will cause the demand for the other to increase (decrease).

On the other hand, if two goods are *complements,* an increase in the price of one good will decrease the demand for the other. For example, since cameras and film are consumed together, they are complements. If the price of cameras rises, we would expect consumers to demand less film at each price, because the good used with film is now more expensive. If the price of one good rises (falls), we would expect the demand for the other to decrease (increase), if the two goods are complements.

When the price of a good is expected to increase (decrease) in the future, the demand for the good in the current period will increase (decrease). For example, widespread consumer expectations that automobile prices will decline in the future will cause some consumers to postpone purchasing a car and therefore cause a decrease in the current demand for automobiles.

Tastes are extremely difficult to quantify. We can only say that if something causes consumers' tastes to change toward (away from) a particular good, the demand for that good will increase (decrease). Finally, if the number of consumers increases (decreases), demand will increase (decrease).

In this section we have developed the following principles:

Principle.   The amount of a product that consumers will purchase depends upon many things, the most important of which are the price of the product, the price of related products, income, tastes, the price expected in the future, and the number of potential consumers.

Principle.   Market demand is a list of prices and the corresponding quantities that consumers are willing and able to purchase per unit of time. Demand can be a schedule, a graph, or a function. Quantity demanded is determined by and varies inversely with price.

Principle. An increase in demand means that, at each price, more is demanded; a decrease in demand means that, at each price, less is demanded. Demand changes when one of the determinants of demand changes. These determinants are income, prices of related goods, expected future price, tastes, and the number of consumers.

Principle. When income increases (decreases), the demand for a normal good increases (decreases) and the demand for an inferior good decreases (increases). An increase (decrease) in the price of a substitute good increases (decreases) the demand for the good it is a substitute for. An increase (decrease) in the price of a complement good decreases (increases) the demand for the good it is a complement for. If the price of a good is expected to rise (fall), current demand for the good increases (decreases). An increase (decrease) in the number of consumers increases (decreases) the demand for the good.

As you will see, demand theory along with demand estimation and forecasting is one of the most important concepts used by business decision makers as well as economists. We shall therefore return to demand later in the text and devote two full chapters to demand theory and two chapters to demand estimation and forecasting.

THE WALL STREET JOURNAL
APPLICATION

Demand for Remodeling: Why Does Demand Increase?

On August 13, 1986, *The Wall Street Journal* reported that U.S. homeowners were installing new kitchens, renovating bathrooms, and adding new rooms at a record pace.* Department of Commerce figures showed that homeowners spent 78 percent more on remodeling and repairs in 1985 than they did in 1982. The *WSJ* set forth several reasons for the boom. Let's put these into our framework of demand theory.

The first reason given was lower interest rates. Since most homeowners borrow to finance remodeling, the loan can be thought of as a complement good to remodeling. When the interest rate fell, it had the same effect as a decline in the price of any complement. It increased the demand for remodeling.

The second reason given was the increase in the price of newly built homes. Remodeling is a substitute for the purchase of a newly built home, and such homes were becoming more

Continued on page 28

---

*Robert Guenther, "Remodelers Post Record Year as Rates Sink and Sales Rise." Adapted by permission of *The Wall Street Journal*. © Dow Jones & Company, Inc., 1986. All rights reserved.

THE WALL STREET JOURNAL

APPLICATION

Continued from page 27
expensive at the time. The price
of a substitute rose, and the
demand for remodeling increased.

Finally, the *WSJ* noted that the
average American home was
getting older. At least 30 percent
of the 92 million permanent
residences were over 45 years
old. The substantial increase in
remodeling began in 1982. Since
this was a year of severe
recession, incomes were lower
than they were three years later.
As the economy recovered from
the recession, incomes rose.

Owners of older homes had
postponed remodeling when
times were bad. The increase in
income increased the demand for
remodeling these older homes,
since remodeling is probably a
normal good.

So basically three things
increased the demand for
remodeling during this period.
The price of a complement (the
interest rate on a loan) declined.
The price of a substitute, newly
built homes, increased. And, an
increase in income increased the
demand for a normal good.

2.2 SUPPLY

The amount of a good or service offered for sale in a market depends
upon an extremely large number of variables. But, as we did for demand,
we ignore all of the relatively unimportant variables in order to concentrate upon those that have the greatest effect upon quantity supplied.

Certainly, the *price* of the product would affect the quantity offered
for sale. The greater the price of the product, the more that would be
offered. This relation is attributable to two reactions: (1) A higher price
would lead to greater profits for firms already producing and selling the
good or service, and thus they would be induced to produce and sell more;
and (2) The higher price and consequent higher profits would tend to lure
new firms into the market and therefore cause more goods to be supplied.
(We shall analyze the determinants of a particular firm's output decisions
more completely in later chapters.)

While the price of the good itself is the most important variable affecting
the amount of the good offered for sale (we will return to this relation
below), several other variables can also have an effect. The first of these
is the level of available *technology*. An improvement in the state of technology would lower the costs of producing the good and therefore would,
other things remaining the same, increase the quantity offered for sale.
(Note, however, that the level or state of technology is difficult if not
impossible to quantify.)

Changes in the *prices of inputs* used to produce the good will also change the quantity supplied *at any given price of the good.* An increase in the prices that must be paid for the inputs would raise costs and hence decrease the quantity supplied at a given price. Alternatively, a decrease in the prices of inputs would lower costs and increase the quantity offered for sale.

The price of *substitute goods* in production can affect the quantity of a good offered for sale. For example, if the price of corn increases while the price of wheat remains the same, some farmers may well change from growing wheat to growing corn, and less wheat will be supplied. Or, in the case of manufactured goods, firms can switch resources from the production of one good to the production of a substitute commodity, the price of which has risen. Alternatively, it could be the case that commodities are complementary in production. If the price of a complementary commodity increases, the firm should be willing to supply more of the commodity in question.[3] If firms expect the price of a good they produce and sell to rise in the future relative to the prices of other goods, they may withhold the sales of some amount of the good. Finally, if the number of firms producing the product increases, more will be supplied.

From our discussion so far, it should be clear that the quantity of a good that will be offered for sale in a particular time period depends upon many variables. To summarize the preceding, let us specify a relation describing the amount of a commodity that is offered for sale in a particular time period as

$$Q_{X,t} = g(P_{X,t}, T_t, P_{F,t}, P_{R,t}, P^e_{X,t+i}, F_t).$$

That is, the quantity of a particular commodity X offered for sale in period t ($Q_{X,t}$) is determined not only by the price of that commodity ($P_{X,t}$) but also by the level of available technology (T_t), the price of the factors of production (inputs) used ($P_{F,t}$), the prices of any commodities related in production ($P_{R,t}$), the expectations of the producers concerning the future price of the commodity ($P^e_{X,t+i}$), and the number of firms (F_t). We can summarize the relations between the quantity offered for sale and the various variables as follows. Holding other things constant,[4]

$$\frac{\Delta Q_{X,t}}{\Delta P_{X,t}} > 0$$

$$\frac{\Delta Q_{X,t}}{\Delta T_t} > 0$$

$$\frac{\Delta Q_{X,t}}{\Delta P_{F,t}} < 0$$

---

[3] An example of such complementary commodities is found in mineral extracting industries. Often nickel and copper occur in the same deposit. Therefore, copper ore is a by-product of mining nickel, or vice versa. If the price of nickel rises, the firm would be expected to extract more ore, and so the output of copper would increase.

[4] The student with a background in mathematics will again note that these relations are more properly expressed as partial derivatives.

$\dfrac{\Delta Q_{X,t}}{\Delta P_{R,t}}$ > 0 if the related commodity is a complement in production

$\phantom{\dfrac{\Delta Q_{X,t}}{\Delta P_{R,t}}}$ < 0 if the related commodity is a substitute in production

$$\frac{\Delta Q_{X,t}}{\Delta P^e_{X,t+i}} < 0$$

$$\frac{\Delta Q_{X,t}}{\Delta F_t} > 0.$$

The Supply Function

While we can analyze the relation between the quantity offered for sale and any of the determinants, economists focus upon the relation between quantity supplied and the product price: As the price of a product increases (decreases), more (less) is supplied by sellers, holding everything else constant. We use the following definition:

Definition. Supply is a list of prices and the corresponding quantities that a group of suppliers (firms) would be willing and able to offer for sale at each price per period of time, other things held constant.

We can write the supply function as

$$Q_X = g(P_X),$$

or supply can be specified by a schedule or a graph. Consider the market supply schedule shown in Table 2.2. This table shows the minimum price necessary to induce firms to supply, per unit of time, each of the six quantities listed. In order to induce the firms to supply greater quantities, price must rise. For example, if price increases from $4 to $5, firms will increase quantity supplied from 6,000 units to 6,500 units.

This schedule shows the minimum price that induces firms to supply each amount in the list. Note that price and quantity supplied are directly related; as price falls, firms supply less. While this relation is intuitively appealing, we shall postpone the explanation of why price and quantity vary directly until a later chapter, after analyzing cost and production.

Table 2.2 **Market Supply Schedule**

Quantity Supplied (units)	Price per Unit (dollars)
7,000	$6
6,500	5
6,000	4
5,000	3
4,000	2
3,000	1

For the present we assume that the supply schedule shows the minimum price necessary to induce producers voluntarily to offer each possible quantity for sale and that an increase in price is required to induce an increase in quantity supplied, other things remaining constant.

Figure 2.3 shows a graph drawn using the schedule in Table 2.2. The price per unit of the product is measured along the vertical axis; quantity supplied per period of time, along the horizontal. All price-quantity combinations in Table 2.2 are plotted; then these points are joined by a curve labeled *SS'*. This curve is called a supply curve or simply supply. Since quantity supplied and price are directly related, the resulting supply curve is upward sloping.

Shifts in Supply

We should emphasize that a supply schedule is derived or a supply curve drawn under the assumption that the other variables that affect the quantity offered for sale (technology, the prices of inputs, the prices of goods related in production, price expectations, and the number of firms) are

Figure 2.3 **Market Supply Curve**

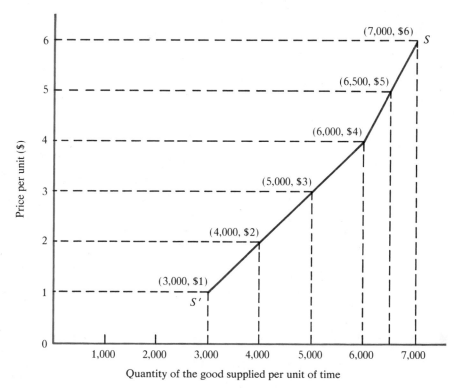

held constant. Just as we differentiated between a change in quantity demanded due to a change in price and a shift in demand because of a change in one of the variables held constant when drawing a demand curve, we must make the same distinction with supply. When the price of the commodity in question rises and firms are induced to offer a greater amount for sale, we say that *quantity supplied* increases. If the price of the product falls, quantity supplied decreases. Such an effect is illustrated in Figure 2.4. Considering the supply curve S_0S_0', if the price falls from $5 to $4, the quantity supplied of X decreases along that supply curve from 6,500 to 6,000.

If, however, one or more of the other variables (the determinants of supply) change, firms are induced to offer more or less of the commodity at each price. In this case, we say that supply has shifted. A decrease and increase in supply are illustrated in Figure 2.4 as a shift from S_0S_0' to S_1S_1' and S_2S_2', respectively. (At the original price, $5, 5,000 units are supplied when supply decreases to S_1S_1' and 8,500 units are supplied when supply increases to S_2S_2'.)

Considering the individual determinants, we would expect the following: An increase in the level of available technology should increase supply. Since an increase in the price of the inputs increases the costs of production, an increase in the price of inputs should cause supply to

Figure 2.4 Changes in Supply versus Changes in Quantity Supplied

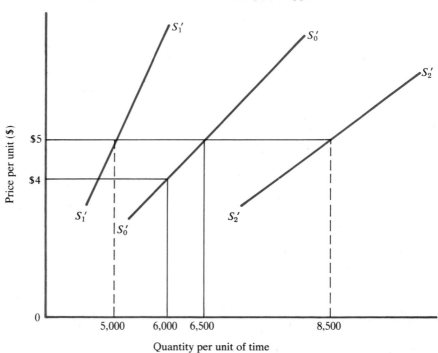

decrease. If the price of a good that is a substitute in production increases, the supply of the commodity in question decreases. If the price of a good that is a complement in production increases, the supply of the commodity in question increases. If producers expect the price of a good to increase in the future, they will withhold some current production (i.e., increase inventories); thus, supply in the current period will decrease. And, if the number of firms producing the good increases, supply will increase.

The preceding discussion can be summarized as follows:

Principle.   The quantity of a good or service offered for sale in a particular market depends upon the price of the good or service, the state of technology, the prices of inputs, the prices of related goods or services (in production), the expected future price of the good or service, and the number of firms.

Principle.   The supply function or schedule is a list of prices and the corresponding quantities that sellers are willing and able to sell at each price in the list per period of time. A particular supply function is specified holding constant the values of the other variables that affect the quantity offered for sale. Other things held constant, an increase (decrease) in price causes quantity supplied to increase (decrease).

Principle.   If one of the other variables (e.g., the prices of inputs) changes, the entire supply function shifts. As supply increases (decreases), suppliers will supply more (less) to the market, at each price.

THE WALL STREET JOURNAL

APPLICATION

Supply in the Oil Industry

The August 26, 1986, edition of *The Wall Street Journal* reported that the oil drilling slump appeared to have bottomed out.* The oil rig count had plunged to 663 in mid-July, the lowest since Hughes Tool of Houston began counting in 1940. This compared with 4,500 in 1981. But after mid-July the count had risen during five of the next six weeks. Many experts expected the oil recovery to continue. Let's see why.

First, the average price paid for oil by U.S. refiners had risen $2 a barrel during August. OPEC had instituted a policy restricting output. Since imported oil is a

Continued on page 34

*James Tanner, "Drilling Industry Slump Is Seen Easing; Oil and Gas Prices, Tax Bill Are Cited." Adapted by permission of *The Wall Street Journal.* © Dow Jones & Company, Inc., 1986. All rights reserved.

THE WALL STREET JOURNAL

APPLICATION

Continued from page 33
substitute for U.S. oil, this policy helped drive up the price of U.S. oil. And, most observers expected OPEC to continue this policy. A vice president of Hughes Tool projected an average rig count of 900 if oil prices stayed around $15 a barrel and higher drilling activity if prices rose further. Another analyst felt that OPEC's production curbs would work and believed that a price of $20 was "probable." Hence, the projected increase in the price of oil would increase the *quantity supplied* of oil—and therefore the number of oil rigs in service. In addition, the *WSJ* pointed out that two other forces would increase U.S. production by increasing supply.

First, the *WSJ* pointed to the recent sharp drop in drilling costs, which in many cases had plunged more steeply than oil prices. One producer pointed out that drilling costs were down to their 1976 level, while oil prices, although down from their peak, were higher than in 1976. Thus lower costs, because of lower capital cost and some improvement in technology, were, as our theory says, predicted to increase supply and, therefore, production.

Finally, there had been a change in the suppliers' expectations about the future *after-tax* price of oil. The tax revision of 1986, although viewed negatively by most industry officials, was by August 1986 not expected to be as adverse to the oil industry as had been expected earlier in the year. The new bill preserved the percentage depletion allowance and relatively fast write-offs of drilling costs. Expectations concerning after-tax price (and profits) had improved. This would, in effect, lead to an increase in supply, relative to what the supply would have been with harsher tax laws. Also, many predicted stepped-up drilling activity during the remainder of 1986 as the industry rushed to use tax incentives that appeared likely to expire at the end of the year.

So in 1986 experts were predicting increased drilling in the future for several reasons. Price was expected to continue rising, causing an increase in quantity supplied. Also, supply was expected to increase because of lower costs and a change in the suppliers' expectations. All of this would lead to more drilling.

2.3 MARKET EQUILIBRIUM

The purpose of studying demand and supply is to prepare us to analyze their interaction, the market equilibrium, which determines market price and quantity sold. Let us begin our analysis of the market equilibrium with a hypothetical example. Suppose that in a market for some commodity, the demanders and suppliers have the particular schedules we previously set forth in Tables 2.1 and 2.2. These schedules are combined in Table 2.3. Note that only one price, $3, clears the market (quantity demanded equals quantity supplied).

Suppose that the price is $5. With this price, 3,000 units are demanded but 6,500 are offered for sale, leading to an excess supply (sometimes called a surplus) of 3,500 units. When there is excess supply, firms cannot sell all they wish at that price and they must reduce price to keep from accumulating surpluses. Indeed, at any price above $3, you can see that there will be an excess supply and price will fall.

Alternatively, let price be $1. Consumers demand 6,000 units, but producers are willing to supply only 3,000, creating an excess demand (a shortage) of 3,000 units. Since their demands are not satisfied, consumers bid the price up. As they continue to bid up the price, quantity demanded decreases and quantity supplied increases until a price of $3 is reached and 5,000 units are sold per period of time.

We can also express the equilibrium solution graphically. Figure 2.5 shows the demand and supply curves associated with the schedules in Table 2.3. These are the demand and supply curves previously shown in Figures 2.1 and 2.3. Clearly, $3 and 5,000 units are the market-clearing (equilibrium) price and output. Only at a price of $3 does quantity demanded equal quantity supplied, and market forces will drive the price toward that equilibrium price.

As in the table, if price is $5, producers supply 6,500 units, but only 3,000 units are demanded. An excess supply of 3,500 units develops. Producers must lower price in order to keep from accumulating unwanted inventories. At any price above $3 excess supply results, and producers will lower price.

If price is $2, consumers are willing and able to purchase 5,500 units, while suppliers offer only 4,000 units for sale. An excess demand of 1,500

Table 2.3 Market Demand and Supply

Price	Quantity Supplied	Quantity Demanded	Excess Supply (+) or Excess Demand (−)
$6	7,000	2,000	+5,000
5	6,500	3,000	+3,500
4	6,000	4,000	+2,000
3	5,000	5,000	0
2	4,000	5,500	−1,500
1	3,000	6,000	−3,000

Figure 2.5 **Market Equilibrium**

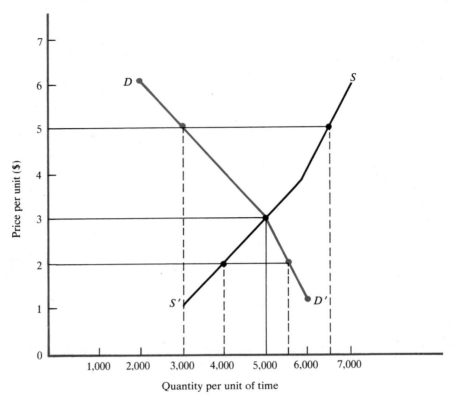

units results. Since their demands are not satisfied, consumers bid the price up. Any price below $3 leads to an excess demand, and the shortage induces consumers to bid up the price.

Given no outside influences that prevent price from being bid up or down, an equilibrium price and quantity is attained. This equilibrium price is the price that clears the market; both excess demand and excess supply are zero in equilibrium. Equilibrium is attained in the market because of the following:

Principle. The equilibrium price is that at which quantity demanded is equal to quantity supplied. When the current price is above the equilibrium price, quantity supplied exceeds quantity demanded. The resulting excess supply induces sellers to reduce price in order to sell the surplus. If the current price is below equilibrium, quantity demanded exceeds quantity supplied. The resulting excess demand causes the unsatisfied consumers to bid up price. Since prices below equilibrium are bid up by consumers and prices above equilibrium are lowered by producers, the market will converge to the equilibrium price-quantity combination.

THE WALL STREET JOURNAL

APPLICATION

Do Buyers Really Bid up Prices?

We have emphasized that when a surplus exists unwanted inventories accumulate and sellers lower prices. And, when there is a shortage, consumers, unable to buy all they want at the going price, bid up the price. It's easy to see that a surplus would induce sellers to lower the price. But do consumers actually bid up the price during a shortage?

An article in *The Wall Street Journal* describes how the bidding process took place in housing markets in many areas of the country.* During the spring of 1986 a huge influx of home buyers, lured by lower mortgage rates, began offering sellers $100 to $45,000 extra for scarce houses in desirable suburbs or prestigious urban neighborhoods. The *WSJ* reported that bidding contests were breaking out in a growing number of hot housing markets for the first time since the late 1970s. The trend began in Boston and upstate New York, then appeared in most of the Northeast, suburbs of Chicago, Detroit, Minneapolis, parts of Ohio, and major California cities. The connection is that all of these areas were experiencing substantial economic growth at the time.

While overbidding wasn't the norm, it occurred in 25 percent of home sales in some booming areas. As the *Journal* noted, "Its pervasiveness is helping to drive house prices sky high."

The median price of existing homes in April 1986, was 8.4 percent higher than the year before, the biggest year-to-year gain in five years. (The increase in price was only 4.3 percent in 1985.) One economist predicted an additional gain of 8 to 10 percent during the rest of the year. He said, "There is too much overbidding to hold down prices."

The article reports several specific examples. A New York couple offered $2,000 above the $181,000 asking price for a New Jersey home that needed a new furnace, a repainted garage, and extensive bathroom repairs. They made the offer to win a bidding war with two other buyers. And they said they were happy because they knew people who had paid as much as $10,000 above the asking price.

A Washington, D.C., couple paid $4,500 above the asking price for a home in a fashionable neighborhood, after simply driving by. Many people were

Continued on page 38

THE WALL STREET JOURNAL

APPLICATION

Continued from page 37
even giving up some purchase conditions, such as demanding structural inspection for hidden flaws, in order to win bidding contests. A California couple reported paying $135,000 for a two-bedroom house priced at $120,000. An Alexandria, Va., lawyer, after she was outbid for another home, paid $170,000 for a $167,000 house that needed $25,000 in repairs. A Realtor® in Albany, N.Y., said that one fourth of the homes in the area priced between $65,000 and $170,000 sold for more than the asking price.

A statement by a senior vice president of a securities firm sums up the process: "The baby-boom generation wants suburban housing. The drop in interest rates sort of really got the process going. Given the current scarcity of suburban homes, this [overbidding] could last longer than the rates dropping."

Translated into demand and supply, when interest rates fell and as more people wanted to live in the suburbs, the demand for homes in many suburban areas increased substantially. Quantity demanded exceeded quantity supplied at the old equilibrium price. Consumers, not able to get all the houses they wanted at that price, bid the price up. Not until the new price reaches the new, higher equilibrium will overbidding cease.

2.4 CHANGES IN MARKET EQUILIBRIUM

So far, we have examined demand, supply, and the market equilibrium. On a practical basis, managerial decision makers are frequently interested in the effect of changes in the determinants of demand and supply on price and quantity purchased. In the preceding application, we saw the effects of lower mortgage interest rates on the price of housing. Other questions that might be asked include: What will happen to the price of automobiles as the price of energy falls (or rises) or as income rises? What will happen to the quantity of furniture sold as the price of houses rises? What will happen to teachers' salaries as the population becomes older? All of these types of questions are important and interesting for economic decision makers.

And these are precisely the types of questions we are now ready to address. In a general sense all of these questions become: What will be the impact on market price and output (sales) of changes in those determinants that cause a shift in the demand or supply curves? By comparing the market equilibrium positions before and after the changes, we will be able to determine the direction, if not the magnitude, of such effects.

It should be clear from the discussion so far that changes in the price of the commodity in question will not cause shifts in demand and supply. As we have shown, price adjusts along the prevailing demand and supply curves to eliminate excess demand or excess supply. Thus, price and output are endogenous variables—variables determined by the market equilibrium.

The variables that may be altered to generate forecasts about price and quantity are the exogenous variables—those determined outside the market under consideration. Briefly, let us review these determinants. In the case of demand, we include as exogenous variables the incomes of consumers, the prices of those commodities related in consumption to the good in question (i.e., substitutes and complements), tastes, consumers' expectations about the future price of the commodity, and the number of consumers. In the case of supply, the exogenous variables include the level of available technology, the prices of inputs used in producing the commodity, the prices of those commodities that are related (in production) to the one in question, the producers' expectations about the future price of the commodity, and the number of firms selling the product. In earlier sections we determined how each of these variables will shift the demand curve or the supply curve.

Given that we can identify the effects of the specific determinants of demand and supply, let's examine the effects of shifts in the demand and/or supply curves. In Figure 2.6, p_0 and q_0 are the equilibrium price and quantity when demand and supply are D_0D_0' and SS'. Suppose demand decreases to D_1D_1'. At price p_0, quantity supplied exceeds by AB the new quantity demanded; that is, excess supply at p_0 is AB. Faced with this surplus, sellers reduce price and quantity until the new equilibrium is reached at p_1 and q_1. Alternatively, suppose that demand increases from D_0D_0' to D_2D_2'. At price p_0, quantity demanded exceeds quantity supplied, and a shortage of BC occurs. The excess demand causes consumers to bid the price up until the new equilibrium at p_2 and q_2 is reached. From this figure, we can see that if supply remains fixed and demand decreases, quantity and price both fall; if demand increases, price and quantity both rise. This direct relation between price and quantity would be expected because the movements take place along the supply curve, which is positively sloped.

Figure 2.7 shows what happens to price and quantity when demand remains constant and supply shifts. Let demand be DD' and supply be

Figure 2.6   Effect of Shifts in Demand

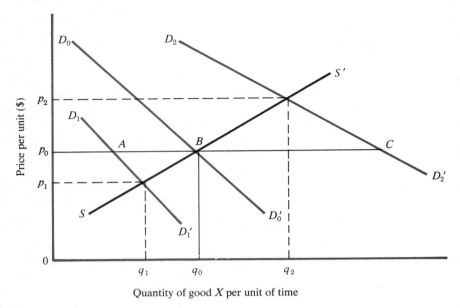

Quantity of good X per unit of time

S_0S_0'. The original equilibrium thus occurs at price p_0 and quantity q_0. Now let supply decrease to S_1S_1'. The shortage of EF at p_0 causes consumers to bid up price until equilibrium is reached at the price p_1 and quantity q_1. Alternatively, let supply increase from S_0S_0' to S_2S_2'. The surplus of FG at p_0 causes producers to lower price. Equilibrium occurs at p_2 and q_2. Thus, we see that if demand remains constant and supply decreases, equilibrium price rises and quantity falls; if supply increases, equilibrium price falls and quantity increases. This inverse relation is expected since the movement is along a negatively sloped demand curve.

Of course, both demand and supply can change simultaneously. In these cases the resulting changes in equilibrium price and quantity are not so predictable. The total effects frequently depend upon the relative strengths of the shifts in the two curves. In any case, we have established the following principle.

Principle.   When demand increases (decreases), supply remaining constant, both price and equilibrium quantity increase (decrease). When supply increases (decreases), demand remaining constant, price falls (rises) and equilibrium quantity rises (falls).

Figure 2.7 **Effect of Shifts in Supply**

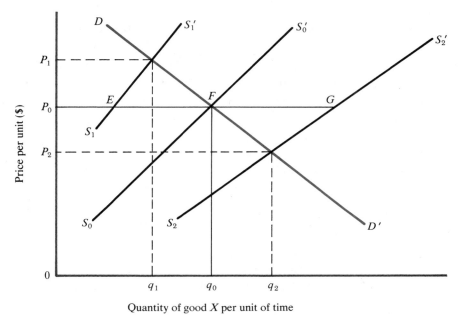

Quantity of good X per unit of time

We should note in closing that prices serve two functions: they are a rationing device and a signaling device. The price of a product determines who gets what is produced. Those who are willing and able to pay the price can consume the good. Those who are not willing and able to pay the price for an additional unit of the good do not consume that unit. Thus the rationing function of prices ensures that society allocates products to their highest-valued uses—to those who will pay the price.

The second function of prices is to signal producers of a good to supply more when consumers want more, and less when consumers want less. When consumers want more, demand increases. The increase in demand drives up price, thereby inducing producers to supply more. When consumers want less, demand decreases, driving price down, and inducing sellers to produce less.

For managers to make successful decisions by watching for changes in economic conditions, they must be able to predict how these changes will affect the market. As we hope you have seen, this is precisely what economic analysis is designed to do. This ability to use economics to make predictions is one of the topics we will emphasize throughout the text. Let's look at a hypothetical example in the next application to see how the process works.

APPLICATION

World Economic Conditions and the Price of Platinum

Suppose you manage a small manufacturing firm that uses platinum as one of the inputs. Clearly, in order to make plans for the future, you want to predict what the price of platinum will be. You have recently read that the following events, all of which affect the price of platinum, have occurred:

1. South Africa, which produces 85 percent of the world's platinum, is experiencing considerable civil unrest and riots, which could turn into civil war.
2. The U.S. Department of Defense has received a large appropriation for a new weapons system; although the system is classified, it is known that platinum is a key input in its manufacture.
3. The world economy is recovering from a recession. Automobile sales are increasing.
4. The price of gold is rising and is expected to continue to rise.
5. The platinum miners union has negotiated a large wage increase.

Let's use the figure below to analyze how these events would affect the platinum market. The current demand and supply in the world market are, respectively, D_0D_0' and S_0S_0'. Price is therefore P_0. Each of the five events would be expected to affect demand or supply.

The political turmoil in South Africa, where a huge portion of the world's platinum is produced, will in all likelihood disrupt platinum production. Certainly, a civil war would have a much more disruptive effect. So these events will probably decrease supply to, say, S_1S_1'. The other supply-decreasing event is a large wage increase for the platinum miners. When input prices increase, supply decreases, in this case to S_2S_2', which will be the new supply curve.

The other three events will affect demand. The new U.S. weapons system, which will require considerable platinum, will increase the demand for platinum. So let future demand shift to D_1D_1'. The recovery from recession is increasing automobile sales. Each new automobile sold in the United States, Japan, and parts of the Common Market is required to have an emission controlling catalytic converter. About one third of the annual production of platinum is used in the manufacture of catalytic converters for U.S. and Japanese cars. Thus higher automobile sales will increase the demand for platinum even more to D_2D_2'. Finally, gold is a good substitute for platinum in the manufacture

Demand and Supply in the Platinum Market

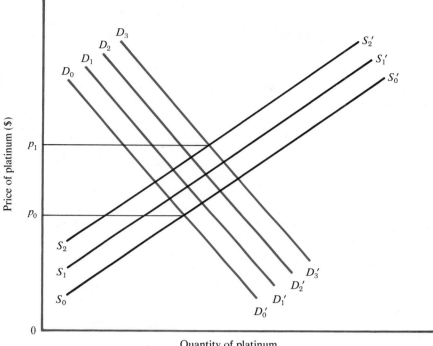

of much jewelry. The increase in the price of this substitute should increase the demand for platinum to D_3D_3'.

So the expected demand and supply of platinum should be D_3D_3' and S_2S_2'. Thus, the price of platinum would be expected to rise—in terms of the figure to p_1. If you are a manufacturer who uses a great deal of platinum in the manufacturing process, you need to adjust your production plans accordingly.

We should note before ending this application that we were interested only in the *direction* of the price change, not in the magnitude of the change. Managers are certainly interested in whether a price will increase or decrease. They are also interested in *how much* price will increase or decrease. We will introduce how the magnitude of price changes can be estimated in Chapters 7 and 8 on demand estimation and forecasting.

Source: Much of the information in this application is taken from "The Emperor's New Gold Rush," *Newsweek,* September 15, 1986, pp. 58–59.

2.5 SUMMARY

This chapter has established the basic framework for a great deal of economic analysis. We have developed the important tools of demand and supply and the concept of market equilibrium. We have not, however, fully developed these points. Later chapters will be devoted to the theory of consumer behavior (the underpinning of demand) and the theory of competitive firms and industries (the underpinning of supply). We will also discuss at some length the techniques that can be used for the estimation and forecasting of demand and supply. For now we have the following important definitions and principles.

Definition. Demand is a list of prices and the quantities that consumers are willing and able to purchase at each price in the list during a particular period of time. The law of demand requires that when price rises (falls), quantity demanded falls (rises). A given demand schedule (graph) holds constant other variables, such as income, prices of other goods, expectations, tastes, and the number of consumers. When these variables change, demand shifts. If demand increases (decreases), consumers demand more (less) at each price in the list. When the price of the good itself changes, demand does not change, quantity demanded changes.

Definition. Supply is a list of prices and the quantities of a good or service that producers are willing and able to sell at each price in the list per period of time. In general, when price rises (falls), quantity supplied increases (decreases). A given supply schedule (graph) holds constant other variables, such as technology, the prices of inputs, the prices of other goods related in production, price expectations, and the number of firms. When one or more of these variables change, supply shifts, indicating that firms will supply more or less of the product at each price in the list. When the price of the good itself changes, supply does not change, quantity supplied changes.

Principle. Equilibrium occurs at the price at which quantity demanded equals quantity supplied. When price is above the equilibrium price, quantity supplied exceeds quantity demanded, and a surplus results. Faced with this surplus, producers will decrease price until equilibrium is reached. If price is below equilibrium, quantity demanded exceeds quantity supplied and a shortage occurs. Unable to purchase all they wish at this low price, consumers will bid up the price until the shortage is eliminated and equilibrium is attained.

Principle. When supply increases (decreases) and demand remains constant, price falls (rises) and quantity sold rises (falls). When demand increases (decreases) and supply remains constant, price and quantity sold both rise (fall). When both supply and demand shift, the resulting price and quantity sold depend on the relative strengths of the shifts.

In this chapter we had two purposes. The first was to show you how managers can use economic theory to make qualitative predictions about the effect of exogenous events upon prices and other aspects of their businesses. We have attempted to show what to expect about price and quantity in specific markets when certain variables changed or were expected to change. As we will show in later chapters, the ability to make correct forecasts under difficult conditions separates good (successful) managers from those who are not so good (unsuccessful).

The second purpose was to prepare you for the material we will present in the following chapters. These chapters will show how demand and supply functions are derived from the behavior of consumers and firms and how these functions can be estimated. A thorough understanding of the material set forth in this chapter is essential to developing the ability to use and interpret demand and supply estimations and make accurate forecasts about the future.

TECHNICAL PROBLEMS

1. What happens to *demand* when the following changes occur?
    a. The price of the commodity falls.
    b. Income increases and the commodity is normal.
    c. Income increases and the commodity is inferior.
    d. The price of a substitute good increases.
    e. The price of a substitute good decreases.
    f. The price of a complement increases.
    g. The price of a complement decreases.
    h. The price of the good is expected to increase.
    i. The price of the good is expected to decrease.

2. How would the following changes affect the *demand* for french fries?
    a. Fast-food stores offer a half-price special on french fries.
    b. Fast-food stores offer a half-price special on hamburgers.
    c. Fast-food stores offer a half-price special on onion rings.
    d. A flood destroys half of this year's potato crop.
    e. Researchers discover a new method of preparing french fries that reduces production costs by 25 percent.
    f. The unemployment rate increases.
    g. Congress passes a law that all high school and college students will receive a weekly allowance of $100.
    h. A scientific study concludes that people who eat more french fries are more attractive to the opposite sex.

3. Other things remaining the same, what would happen to the *supply* of a particular commodity if the following changes occur?
   a. The price of the commodity decreases.
   b. A technological breakthrough enables the good to be produced at a significantly lower cost.
   c. The prices of inputs used to produce the commodity increase.
   d. The price of a commodity that is a substitute in production decreases.
   e. The managers of firms that produce the good expect the price of the good to rise in the near future.

4. Although we have concentrated on the demand and supply of goods and services in this chapter, we can also look at the demand and supply for workers in particular industries or occupations. How would the following changes affect the *demand* for automobile workers in the United States?
   a. The price of U.S. automobiles rises.
   b. Quotas are placed on Japanese cars.
   c. Interest rates on consumer loans rise.
   d. The U.S. experiences a serious recession.
   e. The United Automobile Workers (UAW) union negotiates a large wage increase for auto workers.
   f. The government imposes much stricter pollution standards on new cars.

5. How would the following changes affect the *supply* of high school math teachers?
   a. The annual salary of a high school math teacher increases.
   b. The annual salary of a junior high school math teacher decreases.
   c. The price of a college education increases.
   d. The number of high school students decreases.
   e. A new curriculum for potential high school math teachers allows them to graduate from college in three years.
   f. The annual salary of math graduates in private industry increases.
   g. Average household income increases.
   h. The state school system abolishes continuing education requirements for high school math teachers.

6. Suppose that the demand and supply functions for good X are:

   $$Q_d = 50 - 8P$$
   $$Q_s = 22 + 6P.$$

   a. What are equilibrium price and quantity?
   b. What is the market outcome if price is $0.50? What do you expect to happen? Why?
   c. What is the market outcome if price is $3? What do you expect to happen? Why?

    d. What happens to equilibrium price and quantity if supply remains constant and the demand function becomes 64 − 8*P*?

    e. What happens to equilibrium price and quantity if demand remains constant and the supply function becomes 43 + 6*P*?

7. This question anticipates material in later chapters. Suppose that the demand function for good X is:

$$Q_d = 60 - 2P_X + 10M + 7P_Y,$$

where

    Q_d = Quantity of X demanded,
    P_X = Price of *X*,
    M = Income,
    P_Y = Price of related good Y.

    a. Is good X normal or inferior? Explain.

    b. Are goods X and Y substitutes or complements? Explain.

    Suppose that M = \$40, P_Y = \$20, and the supply function is $Q_s = 120 + 10P_X$.

    c. What is the demand function for good X?

    d. What are equilibrium price and quantity?

    e. What happens to equilibrium price and quantity if other things remain the same and income increases to \$52?

    f. What happens to equilibrium price and quantity if other things remain the same and the price of good Y decreases to \$14?

    g. What happens to equilibrium price and quantity if other things remain the same and supply shifts to $Q_s = 240 + 10P_X$?

8. Determine the effect upon equilibrium price and quantity sold if the following changes occur in a particular market:

    a. Consumers' income increases and the good is normal.

    b. The price of a substitute good (in consumption) increases.

    c. The price of a substitute good (in production) increases.

    d. The price of a complement good (in consumption) increases.

    e. The prices of inputs used to produce the good increase.

    f. Consumers expect the price of the good will increase in the near future.

    g. It is widely publicized that consumption of the good is hazardous to one's health.

    h. Cost-reducing technological change takes place in the industry.

9. What would you expect to happen to the price and quantity sold of orange juice if the following changes occurred?

    a. The price of grapefruit juice falls.

    b. A major freeze destroys a large number of the orange trees in Florida.

     c. Scientists in the agricultural extension service of the University of Florida discover a way to double the number of oranges produced by each orange tree.

     d. The American Medical Association announces that orange juice prevents heart attacks.

10. Suppose that you own a winery in California. How would you expect the following events to affect the price you receive for a bottle of wine?

     a. The price of comparable French wines decreases.

     b. One hundred new wineries open in California.

     c. The unemployment rate decreases.

     d. The price of cheese increases.

     e. The price of a glass bottle increases significantly due to new government antishatter regulations.

     f. Researchers discover a new winemaking technology that reduces production costs.

     g. The price of wine vinegar, which is made from the leftover grape mash, increases.

     h. The average age of consumers increases and older people drink less wine.

ANALYTICAL PROBLEMS

1. Several economics faculty members were standing in line in the student union cafeteria for lunch. One was heard to say, "I sure wish the union would raise their food prices." The others agreed. What in the world would motivate such a wish?

2. Suppose that you are considering investing in an apartment complex in a medium-sized city. There exists a certain demand for apartments in this city. Several conditions are occurring, and you expect these conditions to continue. The city is growing rapidly. Inflation is running at about 5 to 7 percent, but wages in the city are not quite keeping up. The rate of interest has risen to about 12 percent, but, because of the tight money policy undertaken by the Federal Reserve, most authorities expect the interest rate to fall. Some new industries, which will employ a large proportion of white-collar workers, are moving to the city. Finally, the university is undertaking a massive dormitory construction project which is expected to increase the number of dormitory rooms by 50 percent in the next two years. Analyze the effect of each of these influences on the demand for apartments. Show the effects graphically.

3. Some firms experience extreme seasonal fluctuation in the demand for the goods or services produced by their firms. Some examples

are air-conditioning repair services, toy retailers, and tax accounting firms.

    a. What problems can you think of that would evolve from such seasonal fluctuations in demand?

    b. What can managers of such types of firms do to help solve these problems?

    c. Would the problems and/or the solutions be different if the extreme fluctuations in demand were not seasonal or regular? An example might be a firm that manufactures a product the demand for which is extremely sensitive to general economic conditions.

4. Suppose that you manage a retail store. How would you know if the prices of some of the goods you sell were "too low"? How would you know if they were "too high"?

5. In the application on "overbidding" in the housing market, some sellers were clearly selling their houses at "too low" a price. Why didn't they set a higher price?

6. In that application, we noted that the price of housing rose about 8 percent in 1986 and was expected to rise even more. What would you expect would happen to:

    a. The demand for owner-occupied housing?

    b. The demand for rental housing?

    c. The supply of newly built houses?

    d. The demand for household appliances?

7. Why would the supply of people to a particular occupation, say the law profession, be upward sloping? Why would the demand for lawyers be downward sloping?

8. Suppose that you sell a product, but the price you can charge is regulated by law; that is, you are not permitted to raise the price. But you cannot obtain enough of the product so that all who want to buy it at that price can buy as much as they want. How would you decide who gets what?

9. Consider again the housing application. Suppose that the home sellers were forbidden by law from accepting the higher bids of the prospective buyers. Who would get the houses?

10. Consider the market for microcomputers from 1984 through 1986. Some facts that we consider relevant to this market are as follows:

    a. Business schools were offering more and more courses in computer programming and use.

    b. Techniques were developed by which silicon chips, which are the basis of these machines, could be mass produced at a much lower cost.

    c. In 1985 corporate profits were rising substantially.

   d. Many new firms began to produce microcomputers.
   e. The rate of inflation fell and the economy continued to recover
       from a severe recession.
   Using the analysis developed in this chapter, evaluate the
impact of these forces on price and quantity sold in the
microcomputer market.
   As you may be aware, sales rose dramatically during this
period, while prices fell. What does this imply in the context of
your evaluation? Assume that prevailing conditions continued.
What would your forecast be for prices and sales in this market?

3

THEORY OF OPTIMIZING BEHAVIOR

M anagerial decision-making problems are optimization problems. The manager must base decisions on solutions to maximization or minimization problems. In general, people seek to maximize the benefits they receive or to minimize the costs from the activities they undertake. In the case of a firm, the manager makes decisions to maximize profits (or the present value of a stream of profits over time). At the same time, the manager also makes decisions to minimize the cost of producing a specific level of output.

The optimization process can be divided into two fundamental types of problems: unconstrained optimization and constrained optimization. An example of unconstrained optimization is the manager's decision about how to attain maximum profit. The manager must decide how much output to produce, how many inputs to hire, how much advertising to buy, what quality to produce, and much more—all with an eye to making profit.

An example of constrained optimization is the problem of producing a given level of output at the lowest possible cost—that is, deciding how to minimize cost subject to the constraint that a specified level of output is produced. The firm must choose among many possible input combinations to find the combination that yields the lowest cost, subject to the constraint.

There are countless maximizing or minimizing decisions, both unconstrained and constrained. But, as you will see, all optimizing decisions follow either one or the other of two simple rules; one for unconstrained decisions and one for constrained decisions. We turn first to the unconstrained decision.

3.1 UNCONSTRAINED OPTIMIZATION

Unconstrained optimization involves choosing a level of some activity (or set of activities) that will maximize the returns (benefits) from or minimize the costs of the activity. The simplest case of unconstrained optimization occurs when there is only one choice variable.

A frequently encountered example of such a decision is the firm's profit-maximization decision. The owners of a firm try to maximize profits; other things remaining the same, they prefer more profit to less.

Only Profit Maximization?

A manager may seek other goals, but one who ignores profits or prefers less profit to more would be rather unusual. In any case, a firm cannot remain in business very long unless some profits are earned. To be sure, there have been several criticisms of the profit-maximizing assumption, but this assumption is the only one providing a general theory of firms, markets, and resource allocation that is successful both in explaining and predicting firm behavior. In short, the profit-maximization assumption is used, first, because it works well and, second, because it describes to a large extent the way that firms behave.*

---

*We concentrate our attention on profit maximization. For a discussion of other potential objectives, for example, revenue (sales) maximization—see the text by W. J. Baumol referenced at the end of this chapter.

The principles of profit maximization are really quite simple. A firm will increase any activity so long as the *additional revenue* from the increased activity *exceeds* the *additional cost* of the increase in the activity. The firm will reduce the activity if the additional revenue is less than the additional cost.

Suppose, for a more concrete example, that the activity (or choice variable) is the firm's level of output. As the firm increases its output, each additional unit produced and sold adds to the total revenue of the firm. This change in revenue per unit change in output is called *marginal revenue*. As the firm increases its level of output, each unit increase in output also increases the firm's total cost. The additional cost per unit increase in output is called *marginal cost*.

Thus, the firm will expand output so long as the added revenue from the expansion (marginal revenue) is greater than the added cost of the expansion (marginal cost). The firm would decrease output if marginal cost is greater than marginal revenue. Therefore, in order to maximize profit, the firm would select that level of output at which marginal revenue is equal to marginal cost.

We can easily extend the analysis to consider other choice variables. Suppose, for example, that a manager wishes to determine how much to advertise. Each additional (marginal) unit of advertising leads to both increased revenues and increased costs. The marginal benefit to the firm is the higher revenues; the marginal cost is the amount that the firm must pay for an additional unit of advertising.

As long as the marginal revenue derived from an increase in advertising exceeds the marginal cost of the increase, the firm would expand its advertising budget. If, beyond some level, the additional cost is expected to be greater than the increased revenue, the firm would no longer increase its advertising. The optimizing decision is the same as the one for output: The firm would choose the level of advertising at which the marginal revenue derived from the last unit of advertising equals the marginal cost of that unit. The same type of reasoning would apply to a firm's choice of the optimal level of quality or any of its other choice variables. In order to maximize profits, the marginal revenue of the last unit must equal the marginal cost of that unit.

We can generalize the theory of unconstrained maximization quite easily. Suppose any activity (e.g., output in one of the previous examples) adds to benefits but also adds to cost. The positive difference between total benefits and total costs (profit in that preceding example) increases as long as the marginal (incremental) benefit exceeds the marginal (incremental) cost of increasing the activity. The difference between total benefits and total cost decreases if the marginal benefit from increasing the activity is less than marginal cost. Thus, the difference between total benefits and costs is maximized at the point at which marginal benefits are equal to marginal costs.

We illustrate the situation graphically in Figure 3.1. The level of some activity is plotted along the horizontal axis. Marginal costs and benefits are plotted along the vertical axis. The positively sloped curve shows the marginal cost of increasing the level of the particular activity by one unit. The negatively sloped curve shows the marginal benefit from increasing the activity by one unit. Until the level of the activity is increased to A_2 the marginal benefit from increasing the activity exceeds the marginal cost of the increase. Thus, the decision maker would never choose a level such as A_1, because increasing the activity by one more unit adds more to benefit (M_2) than to cost (M_1). The level of total benefits minus total costs would be increased, and it would be increased until A_2 is reached. Certainly the decision maker would never increase the level of the activity beyond A_2, because beyond this level the marginal cost of an increase always exceeds the marginal benefit.

Figure 3.1 Principle of Optimization

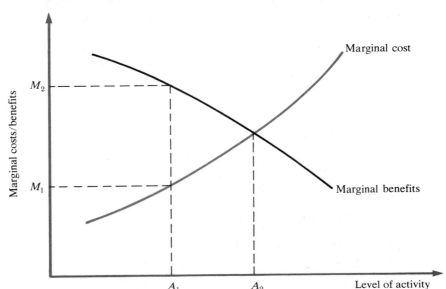

Principle. **An optimizing decision maker will always choose that level
of an activity where the marginal benefit from the activity equals the
marginal cost.**

As you can see, a firm's profit-maximizing choice of output, advertising, or quality is simply a specific application of this general principle.
So is the decision concerning how much of any input to hire. A firm should
hire additional workers as long as each additional worker hired adds more
to the firm's revenue than to cost. It would not hire any additional workers
if these workers would add more to the firm's cost than to the firm's
revenue. For example, if an additional worker will add $100 a day to the
firm's total revenue and the wage rate is $80 a day, the worker should be
hired. Conversely, if the wage rate is $120 a day, the additional worker
should not be hired. Thus the firm hires workers, or any other factor of
production, until the amount an additional worker adds to revenue equals
the addition to cost.

APPLICATION

Upscale Migrant Workers

We don't want to give you the impression that the optimization rule for
input usage applies only to factory labor or production workers. That's

not the case at all. The rule works equally well for all employee decisions. The rule can be used to determine the maximum amount a firm would pay to hire an additional employee of any type—from unskilled laborers to highly paid executives.

As an example of the latter, consider the salaries of investment bankers in New York City. These are the people on Wall Street who put together the multimillion-dollar mergers, acquisitions, and other "deals" we hear about so much in the news. Compensation packages of $350,000 to $750,000 a year for 35-year old investment bankers are not uncommon. Neither is it uncommon to observe young investment bankers migrating from one firm to another early in the calendar year—after bonuses have been paid.

Why would a firm be willing to pay so much for an employee? The answer is simple. The owners of the brokerage firms and investment banks think the new investment bankers they hire will add more to the firm's revenues, or at least as much, than the salaries they are paid. After all, a huge merger or acquisition brings millions of dollars to the firm.

So the maximum amount a firm would pay investment bankers is what it expects them to add to revenue. Clearly they are expected to add a lot.

And the reason for the migration problem is also simple: to realize the largest compensation possible, an investment banker should induce prospective employers to compete among themselves for his or her services. If several firms are competing for the services of each investment banker, some migration is inevitable. So, when you hear about people being paid what some call outrageous salaries, remember that employers must think they will be worth it.

Not surprisingly, the optimization rule works equally well for profit maximization over time. As we will show in Chapter 18, the value of the firm is maximized by accepting all investment projects that add more to value than they add to cost. Put another way, our basic optimization rule requires that we accept only projects for which the [present] value of the project exceeds its cost; by defining the net present value of a project as its present value minus its cost, the basic optimization rule requires that the manager accept only positive net present value projects.

To this point, we have considered only one choice variable. However, when decision makers wish to maximize the net benefits from several activities, precisely the same principle applies: the firm maximizes net benefits when the marginal benefit from any activity equals the marginal cost of that activity. The problem is more complicated because the marginal benefit or return from increasing one activity may depend on the levels of the other activities. The same can be said for the marginal cost.

However, this complication does not change the fundamental principle: At the optimal choice, the marginal return from each activity equals its marginal cost.

To illustrate this, let us extend our profit maximization problem to include output and advertising as simultaneous decision variables, rather than considering them separately as we did above. Increased advertising, over some range, increases the quantity demanded, and hence the revenue obtained, at each price. Suppose that, at a given level of output and advertising, the marginal revenue from an increase in output equals its marginal cost ($MR_Q = MC_Q$). But suppose that, at these levels of output and advertising, the marginal revenue from an increase in advertising exceeds its marginal cost ($MR_A > MC_A$). The firm should clearly increase its level of advertising in order to increase its profits. (Since additional expenditures on advertising add more to revenue than to cost, additional advertising will lead to higher profits.) But the increase in advertising will change the firm's level of output because increased advertising leads to an increase in demand. When output changes, the marginal revenue and marginal costs associated with output are no longer equal. For instance, with the increase in output, it may be that $MR_Q < MC_Q$, and so the firm would want to decrease output. Then, if output is decreased, the marginal revenue and marginal costs associated with advertising may again change. The point is that the firm will have to adjust both output and advertising until the marginal returns equal the marginal costs in both activities; the firm will have to equate marginal revenue and marginal cost for output and advertising simultaneously.

Another example of unconstrained optimization with several choice variables occurs when a profit-maximizing firm uses several inputs in the production process (when the level of output depends upon the levels of usage of several inputs). The firm would hire the amount of each input at which the marginal benefit (increased revenue) from each input equals its marginal cost (e.g., the wage rate in the case of labor). The complication is that the marginal revenue generated by any one input depends on the level of usage of the other inputs. Therefore, if for any one input marginal revenue is not equal to marginal cost, the firm will have to adjust (increase or decrease) its usage of that input; and, since this change in the usage of that input will change the marginal revenues from the other inputs, their levels of usage must also be adjusted until equilibrium is reached. Again, the complication of multiple choice variables does not change the principle of unconstrained optimization. Each choice variable is set such that $MR = MC$. The only difference is that the several optimization conditions must be satisfied simultaneously.

Thus far we have been looking at unconstrained *maximization*. While there are fewer examples of unconstrained *minimization* in business decision making, the main thing we want you to remember is that the basic principle is the same: Optimization occurs when the level of the activity is such that marginal benefit is equal to marginal cost.

For instance, consider the case of a retail merchant confronted with shoplifting. The objective is to minimize the total cost associated with shoplifting. Note that there are two costs involved in the *total cost* associated with shoplifting: (1) the cost of the merchandise lost through theft and (2) the cost of reducing theft by policing or other security measures.

For any given amount of security measures, there exists an expected amount of shoplifting. The store could decrease shoplifting by increasing its policing activities and taking additional security measures. However, the added security also imposes a cost. Therefore, the manager would increase store policing and security as long as the marginal cost of the additional security is less than the marginal reduction in the loss from shoplifting resulting from the additional security. This marginal reduction in the loss from theft is the marginal benefit from the added security. If the added security costs more than the resulting reduction in losses from theft, security should not be increased. Thus, the store manager will minimize total cost by employing the amount of security at which the marginal cost of security equals the marginal reduction in the losses through theft.

For any type of unconstrained optimization the rule is always the same: Adjust the level of the activity until marginal benefit is equal to marginal cost. To see how a firm actually accomplished this, let's look at an application.

THE WALL STREET JOURNAL

APPLICATION

Optimal Product Quality

A crucial managerial decision is how much should be spent on improvements in product quality. Certainly the firm's customers value quality, so quality improvements would probably increase sales and revenue. But, quality improvements and quality control also cost money. So what should a firm do about quality?

The Wall Street Journal in 1983 reported what one large electronics firm, Hewlett-Packard, did.* John A. Young, the chief executive officer of Hewlett-Packard, related his firm's experience when, in the early 1980s, they undertook an analysis of product quality. To their surprise, they found that 25 percent of all manufacturing assets were being tied up in reacting to quality problems. They also found that production

Continued on page 58

*"One Company's Quest for Improved Quality," The Wall Street Journal, July 25, 1983. Adapted by permission of The Wall Street Journal. © Dow Jones & Company, Inc., 1983. All rights reserved.

THE WALL STREET JOURNAL

APPLICATION

Continued from page 57
costs and prices were being driven up because of these quality problems. Therefore, Hewlett-Packard was less competitive than would otherwise have been the case.

Consequently, a series of improvements and controls were undertaken including an extensive training program, competition and rewards for improved quality, and improved methods for spreading information. The firm set up a computer system to monitor quality and emphasized increased inspection. The company substantially increased the resources devoted to quality improvement and control.

The results were impressive. Within a short time, tangible improvements were becoming evident. For example, the cost of service and repair of desk top computers was reduced 35 percent. For other products, production time fell as much as 30 percent, with product defects declining substantially. These improvements allowed Hewlett-Packard to cut prices on many products. The quality program also permitted the company to cut inventories from 20.2 percent of sales to 15.5 percent within two years. This decrease meant a saving of $200 million that did not have to be tied up in inventories.

The improved product quality had benefits: reduced repair and services, lower inventory costs, and decreased manufacturing costs. Also, when production costs fell, prices were reduced and sales increased. Moreover, the reputation for high quality can stimulate business. In an industry like the microcomputer industry, all of these forces increase revenues. But improved quality also costs something. The measures set up by Hewlett-Packard certainly cost the firm money. The new computers, the added inspectors, and the added expenses for training added to costs.

Hewlett-Packard's decisions certainly enhanced the profitability of the firm. The management decision *to invest* resources in quality control was *correct*. However, whether or not the firm invested the optimal *amount* remains uncertain. Did the last $1 spent on product quality return more than $1 in increased revenues and reduced costs? If so, Hewlett-Packard should spend still more on quality assurance. Or, did the last $1 spent on product quality return less than $1? If this were the case, Hewlett-Packard would have spent too much on quality.

Figure 3.2 **A Marginal Revenue (Benefit) Curve for Advertising**

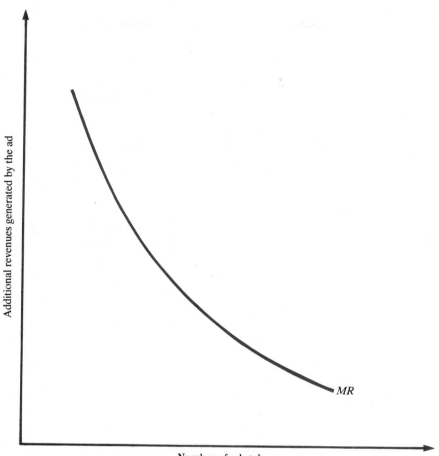

3.2 CONSTRAINED OPTIMIZATION

Since the concept of constrained optimization is more difficult than the concept of unconstrained optimization, let's begin with an example. Suppose that the manager faces the decision of allocating a fixed advertising budget between two media—newspaper and radio ads. Hence, the manager is confronted by a problem of constrained maximization: The manager must determine the levels of use of the two media that will maximize total revenue subject to the constraint of a limited advertising budget.

The marginal benefit of an additional ad is the additional revenues that the ad will generate. Let's denote this marginal revenue for newspaper ads as MR_N and illustrate it as in Figure 3.2. (Note that this marginal benefit curve has the same shape as that in Figure 3.1.) Figure 3.2 implies that additional newspaper ads result in additional sales; but, as more and more ads are taken out, the additions to sales get progressively smaller. The marginal cost of an additional newspaper ad is simply the price of the ad, which we denote as P_N. Similarly, let's denote the (downsloping) marginal revenue for radio ads as MR_R and the marginal cost (price) for radio ads as P_R.

If it were not for the fixed advertising budget, the firm would advertise in the two media until $MR_N = P_N$ and $MR_R = P_R$. But the budget constraint prevents this. It must, therefore, allocate advertising in the two media so that the constraint is met.

Suppose that the original allocation of the advertising budget between newspaper and radio ads is such that

$$\frac{MR_N}{P_N} > \frac{MR_R}{P_R}.$$

Is this allocation optimal? Certainly not. The additional revenue per dollar spent on newspaper advertising (MR_N/P_N) is greater than that for radio ads (MR_R/P_R). In this case, the firm could increase revenues—without changing its total advertising expenditures—by shifting expenditures from radio ads to newspaper ads. For every dollar increase in newspaper advertising, total revenue increases by MR_N/P_N. For every dollar taken away from radio advertising, total revenue falls by MR_R/P_R, clearly a lesser amount. Thus the total effect is an increase in revenue.

As this reallocation continues, more newspaper ads will be purchased; as is shown in Figure 3.2 the marginal revenue from the last ad will become smaller. Conversely, since fewer radio ads are used, the marginal revenue from the last radio ad will get larger. Hence, as the manager reallocates the advertising budget by shifting expenditures from radio to newspaper ads, MR_N/P_N decreases and MR_R/P_R increases. The manager will continue to reallocate the advertising budget from radio ads to newspaper ads as long as the additional revenue per dollar's worth of newspaper advertising exceeds that of radio advertising. Only when

$$\frac{MR_N}{P_N} = \frac{MR_R}{P_R}$$

will this reallocation cease.

Alternatively, if the original allocation of the advertising budget had been such that

$$\frac{MR_N}{P_N} < \frac{MR_R}{P_R},$$

the manager would recognize that revenues, and therefore profits, could be increased by shifting expenditures from newspaper ads to radio ads. Again, with decreasing marginal revenue from increased advertising, as shown in Figure 3.2, you can see that as this reallocation occurs, MR_N/P_N will increase and MR_R/P_R will decrease, since MR_N increases with less newspaper advertising while MR_R decreases with more radio advertising. The manager would continue to reallocate expenditures from newspapers to radio until

$$\frac{MR_N}{P_N} = \frac{MR_R}{P_R}.$$

Therefore, in order to maximize revenue subject to an expenditure constraint, the manager should select those levels of usage of the two media at which the marginal revenues per dollar of expenditure are equal. If $MR_N/P_N > MR_R/P_R$, revenues could be increased by shifting expenditures from radio ads to newspaper ads. If $MR_N/P_N < MR_R/P_R$, revenues could be increased by shifting expenditures from newspaper ads to radio ads.

To make this advertising example more concrete, let's use some numerical values:

APPLICATION

The Optimal Allocation of Advertising Expenditures— A Hypothetical Example

To see how a typical firm should allocate its advertising budget, let's look at a hypothetical example. The manager of a small retail firm wants to maximize the effectiveness of the firm's weekly advertising budget of $1,100. The manager has the option of advertising on the local television station, on the local AM radio station, or in the local newspaper. As a class project, a managerial economics class at a nearby college estimated the impact on the retailer's sales of varying levels of advertising in the three media. The estimates of the *increases* in weekly sales are as follows:

Number of Ads	Increase in Units Sold		
	TV	Radio	Newspaper
1	40	15	20
2	30	13	15
3	22	10	12
4	18	9	10
5	14	6	8
6	10	4	6
7	7	3	5
8	4	2	3
9	2	1	2
10	1	0	1

As is obvious, TV ads are more "powerful" than radio or newspaper ads, in the sense that the marginal benefits from TV ads tend to be larger than those for the other media. However, since the manager is constrained by the limited advertising budget, the relevant measure is not simply marginal benefit but rather marginal benefit per dollar expenditure. The prices of ads in the three media are $300 for each TV ad, $100 for each radio ad, and $200 for each newspaper ad. Although the first TV ad dominates the other two in terms of its marginal benefit, the marginal benefit per dollar's worth of expenditure for the first radio ad is greater than for either of the other two media:

	Marginal Benefit/Price		
	TV	**Radio**	**Newspaper**
Ad 1	$\dfrac{40}{300} = 0.133$	$\dfrac{15}{100} = 0.15$	$\dfrac{20}{200} = 0.10$

Therefore, when allocating the budget, the first ad selected by the manager will be a radio ad—the activity with the largest marginal benefit per dollar expenditure. Following the same rule, the $1,100 advertising budget was allocated as follows:

Ad Selected	**MB/P**	**Ranking of MB/P**	**Cumulative Expenditures**
Radio Ad 1	$\dfrac{15}{100} = 0.150$	1	$ 100
TV Ad 1	$\dfrac{40}{300} = 0.133$	2	400
Radio Ad 2	$\dfrac{13}{100} = 0.130$	3	500
TV Ad 2	$\dfrac{30}{300} = 0.100$		800
Radio Ad 3	$\dfrac{10}{100} = 0.100$	4	900
Newspaper Ad 1	$\dfrac{20}{200} = 0.100$		1,100

By selecting three radio ads, two television ads, and one newspaper ad, the manager of the firm has maximized sales subject to the expenditure constraint. Note that for this combination

$$\frac{MB_{TV}}{P_{TV}} = \frac{MB_{Radio}}{P_{Radio}} = \frac{MB_{Newspaper}}{P_{Newspaper}} = 0.10.$$

The fact that the preceding application used artificially simplistic numbers shouldn't make you think that the problem is artificial. If we add a few zeros and make the price of the 30-second TV ad $300,000 rather than $300, we have the current situation faced by advertisers, a constrained optimization problem described in *The Wall Street Journal:*

THE WALL STREET JOURNAL

APPLICATION

The Optimal Allocation of Advertising Expenditures—An Actual Example*

The advertising decision is not as straightforward as it was not too long ago. As Joel Weiner, the executive vice president of marketing for Kraft, remembered, "In the olden days . . . you ran your commercials on the Big Three network stations and one or two locals [and] you basically reached everybody." In the context of our discussion to this point we could restate Mr. Weiner's position as:

> In the past, the marginal benefit per dollar's worth of expenditures in television advertising was so large that TV advertising was essentially the only game in town.

However, cable television, video recorders, and independent stations have reduced the power of network commercials. A. C. Nielsen Co. reports that the networks' share of the TV viewing audience has declined from 90 percent in 1979–80 to 76 percent in 1985–86. At the same

time, factors like the increased number of working women has made it more difficult to reach that critical female audience responsible for so many consumption decisions.

The result has been that firms are using a much wider range of media to get their messages to consumers. Firms are using public relations (Cabbage Patch dolls were introduced with PR blitz) and event sponsorships (AT&T is sponsoring golf and tennis tournaments and Pepto-Bismol sponsors a chili cook-off). However, the primary alternative means of reaching consumers is through sales promotions: cents-off coupons, sweepstakes, and direct mail.

Why did the advertisers turn to these alternative methods? Why turn away from television advertising when the price of network TV ads is declining? The answer is that the marginal benefit—the increased sales—per dollar spent on TV advertising

Continued on page 64

THE WALL STREET JOURNAL

APPLICATION

Continued from page 63
was decreasing. As the TV ad dollar brought in fewer additional sales, these other media became more attractive.

And, if a firm is going to spend money on all of these different kinds of promotions, how does it determine how to allocate its spending? The answer is simple. It will maximize the effectiveness of its promotion budget by allocating its spending so that the marginal benefits from the last dollar spent in each of the media are equal:

$$\frac{MB_{\text{Network TV}}}{P_{\text{Network TV}}} = \frac{MB_{\text{cents-off coupons}}}{P_{\text{cents-off coupons}}}$$
$$= \frac{MB_{\text{sweepstakes}}}{P_{\text{sweepstakes}}} = \dots$$

Generalizing the results obtained from the preceding example, let's consider two activities, A and B. The objective of the manager is to maximize (or minimize) an objective function determined by these activities, subject to a constraint. If we denote the marginal benefits from activities A and B as MB_A and MB_B and the marginal costs as MC_A and MC_B, the optimal levels for activities A and B are those at which

$$\frac{MB_A}{MC_A} = \frac{MB_B}{MC_B}.$$

This condition can be expanded to include more than two activities. If we were to consider activities A,B,C, . . . ,Z, the condition for constrained optimization is

$$\frac{MB_A}{MC_A} = \frac{MB_B}{MC_B} = \frac{MB_C}{MC_C} = \dots = \frac{MB_Z}{MC_Z}.$$

Hence, we can express the principle of constrained optimization as follows:

Principle. An objective function is maximized or minimized subject to a constraint if, for all of the variables in the objective function, the ratios of marginal benefit to marginal cost are equal.

To further illustrate this principle let's look at a constrained minimization problem that we will consider in much more detail in Chapter 9. Suppose that a firm produces its output using two inputs, capital (K) and labor (L). The manager of the firm desires to produce some given level of output, say, 1,000 units. The problem confronting the manager is how to select the combination of the inputs, K and L, to result in the lowest possible cost to the firm: the manager wants to minimize cost, subject to the constraint that the combination selected must yield an output of 1,000 units.

Using the principle set out above, let's see how the manager can solve this problem. In this case, the objective function that is to be minimized is a cost function, which is determined by the levels of usage of the two inputs. That is,

$$C = f(K,L).$$

The question facing the manager is how much of the two inputs to use. Let's look first at capital. The marginal benefit to the firm from using an additional unit of capital is the additional output that would be produced—the marginal product of capital,

$$MB_K = \frac{\Delta Q}{\Delta K} = MP_K,$$

where Δ means "the change in." The marginal cost to the firm of using this additional unit of capital is the price the firm must pay to use this unit of capital. We denote this price as the rental rate on capital (r), so $MC_K = r$. Likewise, the marginal benefit from using an additional unit of labor is its marginal product,

$$MB_L = \frac{\Delta Q}{\Delta L} = MP_L,$$

and the marginal cost of using the additional unit of labor is the wage rate (w) that must be paid; $MC_L = w$. Using the preceding principle, cost will be minimized subject to the output constraint if the manager selects the levels of usage of capital and labor at which

$$\frac{MP_K}{r} = \frac{MP_L}{w}.$$

To see that this is a constrained optimum, suppose that the firm is using labor and capital such that

$$\frac{MP_K}{r} < \frac{MP_L}{w}.$$

In this case, the additional output per dollar expenditure for labor exceeds that for capital, and so the firm could reduce cost by releasing some capital and hiring more labor. To see this more clearly, let's look at an example.

APPLICATION

The Optimal Combination of Inputs

Cyber, Inc., is currently producing 10,000 units of output using two inputs, capital and labor. At the existing input usage level, the marginal product of capital is 300—the last unit of capital increased annual output by 300 units—and the marginal product of labor is 150—the last worker hired increased output by 150 units per year.

The current wage rate is $30,000 per year (including fringe benefits). Each unit of capital has a market value of $1 million and Cyber's cost of capital is 8 percent per year, so the annual cost of using a unit of capital is ($1,000,000) (0.08) = $80,000.

Combining the data,

$$\frac{MP_K}{r} = \frac{300}{\$80,000} < \frac{150}{\$30,000} = \frac{MP_L}{w}.$$

Cyber is currently using too much capital relative to labor. Were Cyber to reduce capital usage by 1 unit, output would fall by 300 units per year and annual cost would decline by $80,000. Then—to hold output at 10,000 units per year—approximately 300 units per year could be produced by employing two more workers, at a cost of only $60,000 (each of the two workers would add 150 units of output, ignoring slightly diminishing marginal product):

Action	Cost	Output
Reduce capital by one unit	− $80,000	− 300
Employ two additional workers	+ $60,000	+ 300
Net change	− $20,000	0

As the preceding indicates, the firm can save $20,000 while continuing to produce 10,000 units per year by replacing some of its capital with labor. And Cyber would continue reducing its capital and adding labor, holding output constant, as long as the above inequality held.

In contrast to the preceding example, if the firm had originally been using levels of capital and labor at which $MP_K/r > MP_L/w$, the firm could reduce total cost by substituting some capital for labor. Only in the case in which $MP_K/r = MP_L/w$, is there no reallocation between capital and labor that would reduce cost.

Until now we have concentrated upon problems involving activities that cost money. Economic decision makers do, however, operate under nonmonetary constraints. An excellent example is a time constraint. Each of us has a fixed amount of time available and must decide how to allocate this time among several types of activities, each of which takes time and yields benefits. From the principle of constrained optimization, time should be allocated so that the marginal benefit per unit of time spent is equal for all activities. To illustrate this point, consider the constrained optimization problem faced by all college students.

APPLICATION

The Optimal Allocation of Study Time

A student decides to study nine hours for examinations in statistics, economics, and mathematics coming up the next day. The student's objective is to allocate the study time so as to maximize the total of the scores on the three exams (and therefore maximize the average score). The student's assessment of the grade in each exam for each given amount of study time is shown in the following table.

From the table we can see that were the student to spend no time studying, the grades will be 50 in statistics, 53 in economics, and 65 in mathematics. If one hour is added to study time, it would add 13 points to the statistics grade, 12 points to the economics grade, or 10 points to the mathematics grade. So, the first hour of study would be allocated to statistics, where the return is highest. The second hour would be allocated to economics, since it would add 12 points in this subject but only 10 in each of the others. The third and fourth hours should go to statistics and math, since the grade increases are 10 points in each of these subjects, but only 8 in economics. Following the same line of reasoning, the fifth hour would go to economics and the sixth to statistics. The student's nine-hour study time constraint leaves three more hours of study time. The added points from an additional hour of study in each subject at this point are the same—five. Thus the student would allocate one more hour to each course.

Study Time (hours)	Grade in		
	Statistics	**Economics**	**Mathematics**
0	50	53	65
1	63	65	75
2	73	73	80
3	80	78	84
4	85	81	87
5	89	83	89
6	92	84	90

Therefore, the optimal allocation of the nine hours would be for the student to spend four hours studying statistics, three hours studying economics, and two studying math. The total expected points would be 243, with an average grade of 81. This is the highest average possible with the nine-hour study constraint. (You can verify this by trying to reallocate the nine hours in different ways.)

Note that this allocation decision is simply a specific application of the principle set forth above for constrained optimization. The marginal cost (in hours) of allocating an additional hour to a particular course is one. The marginal benefit of allocating an additional hour to a particular course is the grade increase that would result. As we know, the optimization rule is to allocate so that

$$\frac{MB_S}{P_S} = \frac{MB_E}{P_E} = \frac{MB_M}{P_M}.$$

Using the above table with the allocation we have proposed, the ratios of marginal benefit to marginal cost for the last hour spent in each course are

$$\frac{5}{1} = \frac{5}{1} = \frac{5}{1}.$$

The marginal benefit for the last unit of expenditure in time is the same for all three subjects, and the nine-hour constraint is met. Thus the student maximizes the total, and hence the average, grade possible, given the constraint.

3.3 SUMMARY

This chapter has set forth the fundamental tools of analysis that will be used throughout this text. Problems in managerial economics involve a decision maker who is attempting either to maximize the total benefits from various activities or to minimize the costs. These decisions always involve marginal analysis and follow either of two fundamental principles.

Principle.   Unconstrained Optimization: To maximize or minimize an objective function, the value of which depends on certain activities or variables, each activity is carried out until the marginal return (marginal benefit) from an increase in the activity equals the marginal cost of the increase,

$$MB_A = MC_A, \; MB_B = MC_B, \cdots, MB_Z = MC_Z.$$

Principle. Constrained Optimization: To maximize or minimize an objective function subject to a constraint, the ratios of the marginal benefit to marginal cost must be equal for all activities,

$$\frac{MB_A}{MC_A} = \frac{MB_B}{MC_B} = \cdots = \frac{MB_Z}{MC_Z}.$$

If you follow these simple rules, economic analysis will be clear and straightforward. These two rules, although simple, are the essential tools for making economic decisions. And, as the rules emphasize, *marginal changes* are the key to optimization decisions.

TECHNICAL PROBLEMS

1. A toy manufacturer is experiencing quality problems on its assembly line. The marketing division estimates that each defective toy that leaves the plant costs the firm $10, on average, for replacement or repair. The engineering department recommends hiring quality inspectors to sample for defective toys. In this way many quality problems can be caught and prevented before shipping. After visiting other companies, a management team derives the following schedule showing the approximate number of defective toys that would be produced for several levels of inspection.

Number of Inspectors	Average Number of Defective Toys (per day)
0	92
1	62
2	42
3	27
4	17
5	10
6	5

The daily wage of inspectors is $70.
   a. How many inspectors should the firm hire?
   b. What would your answer be if the wage rate is $90?
   c. What if the average cost of a defective toy is $5 and the wage rate of inspectors is $70?

2. A radio manufacturer is experiencing theft problems at its warehouse and has decided to hire security guards. The firm wants

to minimize the total cost of warehouse thefts. The following table shows how the number of security guards affects the number of radios stolen per week.

Number of Security Guards	Number of Radios Stolen per Week
0	50
1	30
2	20
3	14
4	8
5	6

a. If each security guard is paid $200 a week and the cost of a stolen radio is $25, how many security guards should the firm hire?

b. If the cost of a stolen radio is $25, what is the most the firm would be willing to pay to hire the first security guard?

c. If each security guard is paid $200 a week and the cost of a stolen radio is $50, how many security guards should the firm hire?

3. A mining firm believes that it can increase labor productivity and, therefore, net revenue by reducing air pollution in the mine. It estimates that the marginal cost function for reducing pollution by installing additional capital equipment is

$$MC = 40P,$$

where P represents a reduction of one unit of pollution. It also feels that for every unit of pollution reduction the marginal increase in net revenue (MR) is

$$MR = \$1,000 - 10P.$$

How much pollution reduction should the firm undertake?

4. Consider again the application titled "The Optimal Allocation of Advertising Expenditures—A Hypothetical Example." What would be the optimal ad selection if the weekly advertising budget is $2,300? Show that the allocation you suggest satisfies the condition for constrained optimization.

5. Ms. Waller, the manager of the customer service department at a bank, can hire employees with a high school diploma for $20,000 annually and employees with a bachelor's degree for $30,000. She wants to maximize the number of customers served given a fixed payroll. The table below shows how the total number of customers served varies with the number of employees.

Number of Employees	Total Number of Customers Served	
	High School Diploma	Bachelor's Degree
1	120	100
2	220	190
3	300	270
4	370	330
5	430	380
6	470	410

a. If Ms. Waller has a payroll of $160,000, how should she allocate this budget in order to maximize the number of customers served?

b. If she has a budget of $150,000 and currently hires three people with high school diplomas and three with bachelor's degrees, is she making the correct decision? Why or why not? If not, what should she do? (Assume she can hire part-time workers.)

c. If her budget is increased to $240,000, how should she allocate this budget?

6. A large shipping firm has established a minimum standard of truck maintenance and repair. It uses a combination of skilled mechanics and unskilled labor to perform the maintenance. The director of the maintenance division believes that any of the following combinations of unskilled and skilled labor would achieve this minimum requirement.

Combination	Skilled Mechanics	Unskilled Labor
A	2	30
B	5	22
C	8	15
D	12	8

The table demonstrates that, if less unskilled labor is used, more skilled mechanics must be added, and vice versa. Clearly the two are substitutable.

The wage of skilled mechanics is $180 a day and the wage of unskilled labor is $40 a day.

a. Which combination results in the minimum cost for performing the required maintenance?

b. If the combination you found is indeed optimal and the marginal product of a skilled mechanic is 90, what would the marginal product of unskilled labor be?

    c. If the price of unskilled labor rises to $80 per day, what combination will the firm choose?

7. Suppose that, in this "new tech" world in which we live, someone came up with a machine that could measure the increase in an individual's happiness as he or she consumed more of a product. Using this machine on one of our friends who consumes only beer and sandwiches, we found that her additional happiness function—let's call it a marginal happiness function—for beer was

$$MH_B = 25 - 2B.$$

That is, the first beer gave her 23 extra units of happiness, the second gave her 21 extra units, the third 19, and so on. Likewise, her additional happiness function for sandwiches was

$$MH_S = 36 - 4S.$$

    If the price of beer is $1.50 per bottle, the price of sandwiches is $2.00 each, and if our friend has a daily budget of $15.50, how much of each of these commodities would we expect her to consume each day?

ANALYTICAL PROBLEMS

1. In an article in *The Wall Street Journal,* January 5, 1984— "Fast-Food Firms' New Items Undergo Exhaustive Testing"—John Koten reported that before switching to Pepsi from Coke in 1983, Burger King Corporation spent more than two years examining data from the soft-drink industry and doing its own market research. Burger King went so far as to send employees on "undercover missions" to Jack-in-the-Box franchises to clock how much time was wasted informing customers who asked for Coke that the chain serves Pepsi instead.

    What information was Burger King looking for? Why was it collecting this information? What other information would be relevant other than time wasted?

2. We know that consumers engage in price search—shopping for lower prices for the products they wish to purchase.
   a. How, in general, would a consumer determine how much time to spend in price search?
   b. For what kinds of goods would we expect to see consumers engaging in more price search?
   c. How might the manager of a firm be able to use the existence of this price searching to increase the firm's profit?

3. An article in *The Wall Street Journal,* November 3, 1983, presented some results from a survey by the Association of National

Advertisers. Of the 138 national marketers surveyed, 92 claimed that at least half of their new products were profitable. This clearly represented a lot of successes but there were also a lot of failures. From the results of the survey the *WSJ* concluded that to improve the odds of finding a successful new product, a firm should spend more time studying markets and less time designing new products. Many of the companies surveyed recommended that more resources be devoted to searching for promising markets rather than on developing and testing new products.

Suppose the "new product" division of a firm is allocated a specific budget for its activities. Within this budget, the firm can spend on product development and/or market research. Discuss how the manager of the new-products division could obtain the necessary data and make the decision regarding the allocation of this limited budget between product development and market research.

4. The business section of the December 12, 1986, *International Herald Tribune* carried a story with the headline "Hark! The Herald Angels Sing of Teleconferencing" (Peter H. Lewis, New York Times Service). The story described how video teleconferencing—two-way telecasts—has been gaining popularity with businesses. Indeed, it was reported that some firms are regarding teleconferencing as an effective substitute for in-person conferences. And the cost has been declining to the point where it is comparable to "having four or five executives jump on a plane to go to a common point."

Your boss asked you to evaluate teleconferencing as an alternative to the six global conferences the firm is currently holding each year. In his instructions to you, he said that "it looks like we might be able to realize substantial savings without reducing the impact of the conferences."

Set up a plan for solving this optimization problem. What are the benefits? What are the costs? Should this problem be treated as a constrained or unconstrained optimization problem? Why?

SUGGESTED ADDITIONAL REFERENCES

Allen, R. D. G. *Mathematical Analysis for Economists.* New York: St. Martin's Press, 1938.

Baumol, W. J. *Business Behavior, Value, and Growth.* New York: Harcourt Brace Jovanovich, 1967.

Chiang, A. C. *Fundamental Methods of Mathematical Economics,* 3rd ed. New York: McGraw-Hill, 1984.

APPENDIX: THE MATHEMATICS OF OPTIMIZATION

Unconstrained Optimization

The General Case   Consider some arbitrary activity, the level of which is denoted by A. The activity generates benefits,

$$B = B(A),$$

and costs,

$$C = C(A).$$

The objective is to maximize net benefits,

$$\text{Net benefits} = B(A) - C(A).$$

From differential calculus, we know that the necessary condition for maximization of the objective function is that the derivative of the objective function with respect to the choice variable be equal to zero:

$$\frac{d(\text{Net benefits})}{dA} = \frac{dB(A)}{dA} - \frac{dC(A)}{dA} = 0.$$

Hence, the objective function is maximized when

$$\frac{dB(A)}{dA} = \frac{dC(A)}{dA}.$$

That is, the objective function is maximized when the marginal benefit from the activity (dB/dA) is equal to its marginal cost (dC/dA).

An Example   Suppose that the firm attempts to maximize profit (total revenue minus total cost),

$$\pi = R(Q) - C(Q),$$

with respect to its level of output, Q. The necessary condition for profit maximization requires that the derivative of the objective function with respect to output be equal to zero,

$$\frac{d\pi}{dQ} = \frac{dR}{dQ} - \frac{dC}{dQ} = 0.$$

Thus, profit will be maximized when marginal revenue $\left(\dfrac{dR}{dQ}\right)$ is equal to

marginal cost $\left(\dfrac{dC}{dQ}\right)$.

Constrained Optimization

The General Case   Consider an objective function with n choice variables,

$$\theta = \theta(X_1, X_2, X_3, \cdots, X_n).$$

The partial derivatives of this objective function, $\partial\theta/\partial X_i$, represent the marginal benefit associated with X_i. Now, consider a constraint function,

$$\phi = \phi(X_1, X_2, X_3, \cdots, X_n) = 0.$$

In this case, the partial derivatives, $\partial\phi/\partial X_i$, represent the marginal cost of X_i.

To obtain an optimum, we specify the Lagrangian function:

$$L = \theta(X_1, X_2, X_3, \cdots, X_n) - \lambda[\phi(X_1, X_2, X_3, \cdots, X_n)].$$

The necessary condition for an optimum requires that the partial derivatives of this function all equal zero

$$\frac{\partial L}{\partial X_1} = \frac{\partial\theta}{\partial X_1} - \lambda\frac{\partial\phi}{\partial X_1} = 0$$

$$\frac{\partial L}{\partial X_2} = \frac{\partial\theta}{\partial X_2} - \lambda\frac{\partial\phi}{\partial X_2} = 0$$

$$\vdots$$

$$\frac{\partial L}{\partial X_n} = \frac{\partial\theta}{\partial X_n} - \lambda\frac{\partial\phi}{\partial X_n} = 0.$$

Combining these, the condition for an optimum is

$$\frac{\partial\theta/\partial X_1}{\partial\phi/\partial X_1} = \frac{\partial\theta/\partial X_2}{\partial\phi/\partial X_2} = \frac{\partial\theta/\partial X_3}{\partial\phi/\partial X_3} = \cdots = \frac{\partial\theta/\partial X_n}{\partial\phi/\partial X_n}.$$

That is, a constrained optimum requires that the ratios of marginal benefit to marginal cost are equal for all of the choice variables.

An Example   Suppose that the firm wants to maximize the output attainable for a given cost. In this case, the objective function is the production function,

$$\theta = Q = Q(X_1, X_2, X_3, \cdots, X_n),$$

where X_i represents the levels of input usage. The partial derivatives $\partial Q/\partial X_i$ represent the additional output generated by an additional unit of

X_i (i.e., the marginal benefit from an increase in X_i). In general, cost can be specified to be a function of the levels of input usage,

$$C = C(X_1, X_2, X_3, \cdots, X_n).$$

In this example, the constraint is that cost be equal to some fixed amount. That is, $C = \bar{C}$, or

$$\phi = C(X_1, X_2, X_3, \cdots, X_n) - \bar{C}.$$

Note that $\partial\phi/\partial X_i = \partial C/\partial X_i$ (i.e., the marginal cost of the input). Using the Lagrangian function, it follows that a constrained maximum occurs when

$$\frac{\partial Q/\partial X_1}{\partial C/\partial X_1} = \frac{\partial Q/\partial X_2}{\partial C/\partial X_2} = \frac{\partial Q/\partial X_3}{\partial C/\partial X_3} = \cdots = \frac{\partial Q/\partial X_n}{\partial C/\partial X_n}.$$

That is, constrained output maximization occurs when the ratio of marginal product (benefit) to marginal cost is equal for all inputs. (Note that, if the input prices are fixed, marginal cost is equal simply to input price.)

4

BASIC ESTIMATION TECHNIQUES

I n order for managers of firms to be able to use the various techniques that will be described in this text, it is necessary that they be able to obtain estimates of the functions we will describe—production functions, cost functions, and demand functions. While there do exist alternative estimating techniques—some of which we will describe—these estimates are often obtained from *regression analysis*.

In this chapter, we will review the *basics* of regression analysis: how a regression line is fitted, how tests of hypotheses are conducted, and how the estimates can be used in managerial decision making. Throughout this discussion and the applications of regression analysis that will appear later in this text, please keep in mind that we are not so interested in your knowing the way the various statistics are calculated as we are in your knowing the way these estimates can be employed. We are primarily concerned with familiarizing you with the interpretation of statistical results rather than with the estimating techniques themselves. We want you to be able to *use* the results of estimations in making managerial decisions.

4.1 FITTING A REGRESSION LINE

Regression analysis is simply a statistical technique used to ascertain the relation between one variable (called the dependent or endogenous variable) and one or more other variables (called the independent or exogenous variables). Let's consider a simple, two-variable case. Suppose you believe that there exists a linear relation between Y and X. That is, you hypothesize the linear relation

$$Y = a + bX.$$

Put most simply, the objective of regression analysis is to provide estimates of the parameters a and b.

To obtain such estimates, an analyst would first collect data on the values of Y and X. The data could be collected over time for a given firm (or a given industry, etc.), or the data could be collected from many different firms, industries, and so forth, at a given point in time. (The former is called time-series data, while the latter is called cross-section data.) No matter how the data were collected, the result would be a scatter of data points through which a regression line would be fit.

To see how this would be done, let's consider a simplified example. Suppose that you wanted to examine the relation between advertising expenditures and sales. Suppose further that you had the cross-section data set on the sales and corresponding advertising expenditures for six firms as provided in Table 4.1.

A regression line is nothing more than a method of organizing the data into a simplified form in order to obtain an estimate of the relation between the dependent variable (sales) and the independent variable (advertising). To illustrate, the six observations on quantity sold and advertising expenditures presented in Table 4.1 are plotted in Figure 4.1. Note that there seems to be a positive relation between advertising expenditures (the independent variable) and sales (the dependent variable). The higher the level of advertising, the greater are sales. We have drawn a regression line through the scatter of data points that seems to ''fit'' the data rather well.

But this line is only one of the many possible lines that fit the data. The objective of regression analysis is to determine the straight line that ''best fits'' this scatter of data points. Regression analysis is designed to determine this best-fitting line statistically.

In our hypothetical example we want to obtain an *estimate* of the relation between advertising expenditures (A) and sales (S). For simplicity, we assume that this relation is linear; so, we want to obtain an estimate of the relation

$$S = a + bA,$$

where the parameter a measures expected sales with no advertising and the parameter b represents the additional sales that would be generated by an additional \$1 expenditure on advertising. In terms of the discussion in Chapter 3, b provides a measure of the marginal addition to sales generated by an additional unit (dollar's worth) of advertising; that is, $b = \Delta S/\Delta A$. Hence, our objective is to obtain estimates of a and b. We will denote these estimates as $\hat{a}$ and $\hat{b}$ respectively.

Once we have these estimates, we can use them in making managerial decisions. For example, given the estimate of b and the optimization

Table 4.1

Firm	Sales ($000)	Advertising Expenditures
1	$40	$ 6,000
2	40	10,000
3	60	15,000
4	50	14,000
5	20	4,000
6	30	8,000

Figure 4.1 **A Regression Line**

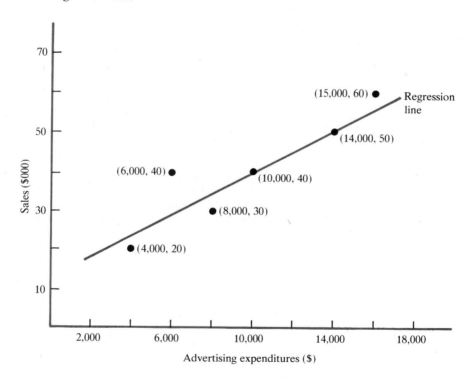

techniques described in Chapter 3, we can determine the optimal level of advertising. Or, we might use the estimated regression line (regression equation) to provide forecasts of future sales.

In Figure 4.2 we have reproduced our data scatter on the more general X and Y axes. Through the data scatter we have put a representative regression line, $\hat{Y} = \hat{a} + \hat{b}X$. The vertical distance of a data point from the regression line is called the error. A representative error is shown in

Figure 4.2   **Fitting a Regression Line**

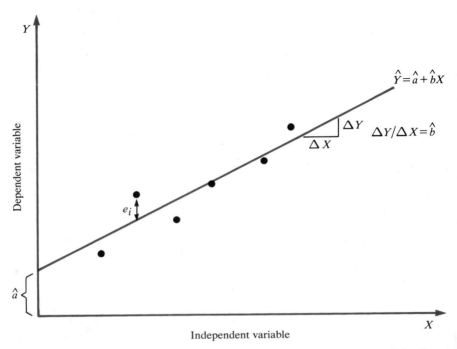

Independent variable

Figure 4.2 as the distance e_i. Regression analysis selects the straight line, $\hat{Y} = \hat{a} + \hat{b}X$, that minimizes the sum of the squared errors (Σe_i^2).[1]

Regression analysis is simply a technique that employs available data to provide an estimate of the relation between the independent and dependent variables. Given the existing data on Y and X, regression analysis is a way of calculating values for $\hat{a}$ and $\hat{b}$ so that regression equation

$$\hat{Y} = \hat{a} + \hat{b}X$$

best fits the data. The criterion for selecting the line that best fits is the minimization of the sum of the squared errors. (Since regression analysis uses this criterion, it is often referred to as least squares analysis.)

4.2 TESTS FOR SIGNIFICANCE

The output of any regression computer program will provide the analyst with estimates of the parameters (i.e., $\hat{a}$ and $\hat{b}$). However, the question remains whether or not these estimates are "statistically significant." For

---

[1]Alternatively, we can denote the error as the difference between the actual value of the dependent variable, Y_i, and the value that would be predicted from the regression line, $\hat{Y}_i = \hat{a} + \hat{b}X_i$. Thus, regression analysis means that the values $\hat{a}$ and $\hat{b}$ are selected in order to minimize

$$\Sigma(Y_i - \hat{Y}_i)^2 = \Sigma(Y_i - \hat{a} - \hat{b}X_i)^2.$$

example, suppose we used a regression program to estimate $Y = a + bX$ and that we obtained a positive estimate of b (i.e., $\hat{b} > 0$). But, the *estimate* $\hat{b}$ is a random variable. Since $\hat{b}$ is calculated on the basis of the available data, $\hat{b}$ has a variance which is itself dependent on the variance of the data in the sample. Although the estimate of b is positive ($\hat{b} > 0$), the *true* value of b may be zero; and, if $b = 0$, there is no relation between X and Y. (For our example in the preceding section, this would mean that advertising does not alter sales.)

Thus, we normally test for *statistical significance* of the estimated parameters. If the estimated value of b is close to zero, it could be that the positive estimate occurred purely by chance. On the other hand, if $\hat{b}$ is sufficiently large, we would say that there is a positive relation between X and Y because there is a very small probability of obtaining that large an estimate of b when in reality there is no relation between the variables. The problem is determining the value below which the estimate is "close" to zero and that above which it is "sufficiently large."

We normally test for statistical significance of the estimated parameters using what is referred to as a *t*-test. To see what a *t*-test means, let's continue to consider a case in which the estimate of b is positive ($\hat{b} > 0$). As noted above, the estimate $\hat{b}$ is a random variable. Thus, $\hat{b}$ has a variance associated with it and this variance measures the dispersion of the possible values of $\hat{b}$ about its mean. In Figure 4.3 we have illustrated two possible distributions for our estimate of $\hat{b}$. Both of these distributions have the same mean value (2.0), so the estimated value of b is 2.0 in both cases. But, the variance of $\hat{b}$ in distribution A is much larger than the variance illustrated as distribution B. (The dispersion about the mean is larger in distribution A.)

In which case is it more likely that b is *really* positive—really greater than zero? Another way of asking this question is to say: In which case is it less likely that the true value of b is zero? As you can see from Figure 4.3, the probability that $\hat{b}$ is equal to zero is much less for distribution B than for distribution A. In both of the two cases illustrated, the estimated value for b is

Figure 4.3 Possible Distributions for $\hat{b}$

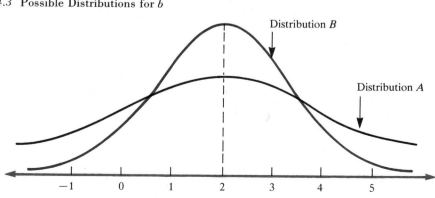

2.0: In both cases, the estimated values indicate that the true value of b is positive. But, if the distribution of $\hat{b}$ is that illustrated as distribution B, we are more sure that b is *really* positive than we would be if the distribution of $\hat{b}$ is that illustrated as distribution A. Clearly then, the variance of our estimate of b will play a large part in the determination of statistical significance.

To generalize this somewhat, let's try the following: Let's define a measure of the variance of $\hat{b}$ as its "standard error,"[2] and denote this standard error as $S_{\hat{b}}$. As the variance of $\hat{b}$ gets larger, $S_{\hat{b}}$ gets larger. (For example, in Figure 4.3, the value for $S_{\hat{b}}$ for distribution A would be much larger than that for distribution B.) Now, let's form the ratio:

$$\frac{\hat{b}}{S_{\hat{b}}}.$$

In terms of this ratio, when would we be more sure that the true value of b actually is larger than (significantly different from) zero? Clearly, the larger is this ratio, the more sure we are that the true value of b is greater than zero. Note that if we had estimated $\hat{b}$ to be negative (for example if we were estimating the relation between profits and shoplifting), we would be more sure that b was really negative if the preceding ratio had a larger (negative) magnitude. Hence, in general terms, we could say that we are more sure that the true value of b is significantly different from zero if *the absolute value* of $\hat{b}/S_{\hat{b}}$ is sufficiently large.

But, how large is large enough? For this purpose, we use the t-test alluded to earlier. The ratio we defined above is called a t-statistic,

$$t = \frac{\hat{b}}{S_{\hat{b}}}.$$

Using the calculated value of t, we can test the hypothesis that the true value of b equals zero in order to find out if b is significantly different from zero. If the calculated value of t is larger than some "critical value," we can say that the true value of b is significantly different from (greater than or less than) zero.

In regression analysis, it is often said that something is significant at a 90 percent, 95 percent, or 99 percent confidence level. Thus, if we say that sales and advertising expenditures are significantly related at the 95 percent confidence level, we mean that the calculated value of $\hat{b}$ is far enough from zero that there is only a 5 percent probability that the true value of b is zero.

We obtain the critical value of t from the t-table provided at the end of this book along with explanatory text. The critical value of t is defined by the risk level (the level of confidence) and the appropriate degrees of freedom. The t-statistic will have $n - k$ degrees of freedom, where n is the number of observations in the sample and k is the number of param-

---

[2]More correctly, the standard error is the square root of estimated variance.

eters estimated. (In our advertising example, we have $6 - 2 = 4$ degrees of freedom since we had six observations and estimated two parameters, *a* and *b*.) As noted above, the risk level may be described simply as the probability of finding the parameter to be statistically significant, when in fact it is not. The appropriate risk level is determined by the analyst on the basis of the "cost" of making an error. For example, if you will lose your job if you make a mistake, you will probably want to use a low risk level (a high confidence level).

If the absolute value of the calculated *t*-coefficient is greater than the critical value of *t* (obtained from the table), we can say that the estimated parameter is statistically significant. If the calculated *t*-coefficient is smaller than the critical value of *t*, no statistically significant relation exists.

4.3 EVALUATION OF THE REGRESSION EQUATION

Two other statistics are frequently employed to evaluate the overall acceptability of a regression equation. The first of these statistics is called the coefficient of determination, normally denoted as R^2. This statistic reflects the percentage of the total variation in (dispersion of) the dependent variable (about its mean) that is explained by the regression equation. In terms of the example we used earlier, it is the percent of the variation in sales that is explained by variation in advertising expenditures. Therefore, the value of R^2 can range from 0 (the regression equation explains none of the variation) to 1 (the regression equation explains all of the variation).

If the value of R^2 is high, we say there is high correlation between the dependent and independent variables; if it is low, there is low correlation. For example, in Figure 4.4, Panel A, the observations in our data scatter all lie very close to the regression line. Since the deviations from the line are small, the correlation between *X* and *Y* is high and the value of R^2 will approach 1. (At the extreme, if all of the observations were on the line, R^2 would be equal to 1.) In Panel B the observations are scattered widely about the regression line. The correlation between *X* and *Y* in this case is much less; so the value of R^2 is closer to zero. (We might note that high correlation between two variables or a statistically significant regression coefficient does not necessarily mean the variation in the dependent variable is caused by variation in the independent. Variations in the two may be caused by something else.)

Although the R^2 is a widely used statistic, it is subjective in the sense of how much explained variation—explained by the regression equation—is enough. An alternative is the *F*-statistic. In very general terms, this statistic provides a measure of the ratio of explained variation (in the dependent variable) to unexplained variation. To test whether the overall equation is significant, this statistic is compared to a critical *F*-value obtained from an *F*-table (at the end of this book). The critical *F*-value is identified by two degrees of freedom and the confidence level. The first

Figure 4.4 High and Low Correlation

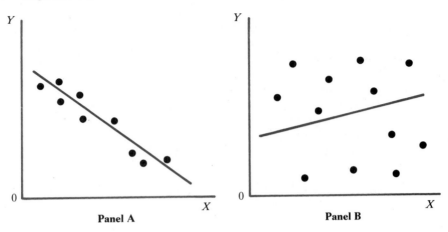

Panel A   Panel B

of the degrees of freedom is $k - 1$ (i.e., the number of independent variables) and the second is $n - k$. If the value for the calculated F-statistic exceeds the critical F-value, we can say that the regression equation is statistically significant at the specified confidence level.

All of the statistics you will need in order to analyze a regression—the coefficient estimates, the standard errors, R^2, and F—are automatically calculated and printed by many available regression programs. For example, a computer program for the regression equation $Y = a + bX$ might present results in the following format:

```
DEPENDENT VARIABLE: Y        F-RATIO: ...

OBSERVATIONS: ...            R-SQUARE: ...

                PARAMETER    STANDARD
    VARIABLE    ESTIMATE     ERROR

INTERCEPT         ...           ...
X                 ...           ...
```

Indeed we will use this format to provide you with regression output in the remainder of this text.

As we have mentioned before, our objective is not that you understand how these statistics are calculated. Rather, we want you to know how to set up a regression and interpret the results. In this vein, let us provide you with an example to illustrate the topics we have discussed.

APPLICATION

The Market Model

A widely used application of regression analysis in finance and financial economics (and one we will return to in Chapter 19) is the *market model*. The purpose of the market model is to relate the returns from a single asset/project/security to the returns from holding a well-diversified portfolio—a market portfolio. In terms of a regression equation, we would write the return from holding security j as a linear function of the return from the market portfolio,

$$R_j = \alpha + \beta R_m.$$

Let's look at Chase Manhattan Bank to see how the returns from holding a share of Chase stock moved relative to the market. To this end, we estimated

$$R_{\text{Chase}} = \alpha + \beta R_{\text{Market}}$$

using weekly returns* for the period January 14, 1983, to August 29, 1986. Presented below are the regression output and a plot of the relation between the 190 data points and the estimated regression line.

```
DEPENDENT VARIABLE: RCHASE        F-RATIO: 111.906

OBSERVATIONS: 190                 R-SQUARE: 0.3731

                    PARAMETER         STANDARD
    VARIABLE        ESTIMATE          ERROR

    INTERCEPT       0.00183           0.00238
    RMARKET         1.36926           0.12944
```

Look first at the estimate of α, the intercept. Although the parameter estimate is positive—0.00183—is it *really* greater than zero? To find out, we need to calculate the t-value for $\hat{\alpha}$ as the ratio of the parameter estimate to its standard error,

$$t\hat{\alpha} = \frac{\hat{\alpha}}{S_{\hat{\alpha}}} = \frac{0.00183}{0.00238} = 0.76891,$$

*The return to holding Chase stock included dividends. The return on the market portfolio was calculated using returns on the S&P 500 Index.

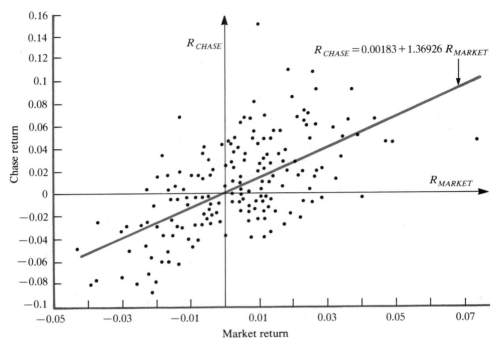

and compare this value to the critical value of t. Let's use a 95 percent confidence level (a 5 percent risk level). Since we used 190 observations and estimated 2 parameters, we have $190 - 2 = 188$ degrees of freedom. The table (Critical T-values) at the end of the text does not have a value for 188 degrees of freedom; instead, it has a value for 120 degrees of freedom (1.980) and a value for an infinitely large sample (1.960). Our calculated t-value for $\hat{\alpha}$ is smaller than either; so, we cannot be sure that our estimate is *really* positive. It is quite possible that the true value of α is zero. In terms of the equation we estimated, this means that if the market as a whole earned nothing, Chase shareholders would also earn nothing.

The estimate of β—1.36926—is also positive. And, we can be confident that our estimate of β is *really* positive—it is significantly greater than zero. The calculated t-value is

$$t_{\hat{\beta}} = \frac{\hat{\beta}}{S_{\hat{\beta}}} = \frac{1.36926}{0.12944} = 10.57834,$$

which is substantially greater than the critical value of t.[†] The interpretation of $\hat{\beta}$ is that, if the return on the market portfolio changes by $+10$ percent (-10 percent), the return on Chase stock is expected to change by $+13.7$ percent (-13.7 percent).

[†] An even more important question is whether $\hat{\beta}$ is significantly greater than 1.0; that is, whether Chase returns do in fact move more than proportionately to market returns. Such a test will be described later in this text.

The R^2 for the regression equation indicates that 37.31 percent of the total variation in the returns to Chase stock is explained by the regression equation. That is, 37.31 percent of the variation in Chase's returns are explained by variation in returns on the market portfolio.

The F-ratio is used to test for significance of the entire equation. To determine the critical value of F (with a 95 percent confidence level), it is necessary to determine the degrees of freedom. In this case, we have $k - 1 = 2 - 1 = 1$ and $n - k = 190 - 2 = 188$ degrees of freedom. In the table of values of the F-statistic at the end of the book, we look down the $k - 1 = 1$ column until we get to $n - k = 188$ row. However, there is no 188 entry; instead there are 95 percent confidence level F-values for $F_{1,150}$ (3.91) and for $F_{1,200}$ (3.89). Since our calculated F-value (111.906) exceeds either of these, we can be sure that our regression equation is significant at the 95 percent confidence level.

4.4 MULTIPLE REGRESSION

Thus far we have dealt with simple regressions involving a linear relation between only two variables—one dependent variable and one independent variable. Frequently we use two or more independent variables. Again we are interested in obtaining the equation for the line that gives us the best fit.

Linear Equations

Continuing to use a linear specification, a typical multiple regression equation would be

$$Y = a + b_1X_1 + b_2X_2 + b_3X_3.$$

In this equation, Y is the dependent variable, a is the intercept term, X_1, X_2, and X_3 are the independent variables, and b_1, b_2, and b_3 the coefficients for the independent variables.

As in simple regression, the coefficients b_1, b_2, and b_3 measure the degree of variation in the dependent variable associated with variation in each independent variable. That is, $b_i = \Delta Y/\Delta X_i$. These coefficients are estimated in the computer program, as is the coefficient of determination, R^2 (which, as above, measures the proportion of variation in the dependent variable associated with variation in the independent variables), and the value of the F-statistic (the F-ratio). The significance of the coefficients and of the regression equation can be determined by t-tests and an F-test. Indeed, the only real complication introduced by multiple regression is that we will have more t-tests to perform. Although (as many of you know from courses in statistics) the *calculation* of the parameter estimates gets much more difficult as additional independent variables are added, the manner in which they are *interpreted* does not change.

APPLICATION

A Simple Consumption Function

Suppose we wish to examine the relation between a household's consumption expenditures and two independent variables—family income and the number of children in the household. We could specify a linear relation

$$C = a + bY + cN,$$

where C is monthly consumption expenditures, Y is monthly income, and N is the number of children. Since we expect income and consumption to be positively related, we expect b to be positive. Likewise, we should expect c to be positive. Furthermore, we would also expect a to be positive since it reflects something like minimum subsistence expenditures for a family with no children.

In order to estimate a, b, and c we could obtain data from a sample of families. Suppose that such data were obtained from 30 families and used in an available regression program. We provide below the output from the estimation of our simple consumption function:

```
DEPENDENT VARIABLE: C        F-RATIO: 141.391

OBSERVATIONS: 30             R-SQUARE: 0.8347

                 PARAMETER            STANDARD
VARIABLE         ESTIMATE             ERROR

INTERCEPT        443.7286             124.8189
Y                  0.80572              0.06776
N                132.5073              66.9560
```

As we expected, our estimates of a, b, and c are all positive. Looking at the estimates, this regression equation suggests that the "minimum monthly subsistence" expenditures for a family with no children is \$443.73. Each child is estimated to add \$132.51 to monthly subsistence expenditures. (Minimum monthly subsistence expenditures for a family with one child is estimated to be \$443.73 + 132.51 = \$576.24. For a family with two children this figure is \$443.73 + (2 × 132.51) = \$708.75.) The estimate of b indicates that households will spend 81 cents of each additional dollar received on consumption expenditures (and, presumably, save the remaining 19 cents).

However, we need to determine if these estimates are statistically significant. That is, are *a*, *b*, and *c* "really" positive? As we have explained, this entails a *t*-test.

First, let's obtain the critical value of *t*. Since we have 30 observations and have estimated 3 parameters, the degrees of freedom are $n - k = 30 - 3 = 27$. Let's use a 5 percent risk level (a 95 percent confidence level). From the table at the end of the book, the critical value of *t* is 2.052.

Next, we calculate the *t*-values for $\hat{a}$, $\hat{b}$, and $\hat{c}$ as the ratio of the estimated parameter to its standard error,

$$t_{\hat{a}} = \frac{\hat{a}}{S_{\hat{a}}} = \frac{443.7286}{124.8189} = 3.555$$

$$t_{\hat{b}} = \frac{\hat{b}}{S_{\hat{b}}} = \frac{0.80572}{0.06776} = 11.891$$

$$t_{\hat{c}} = \frac{\hat{c}}{S_{\hat{c}}} = \frac{132.5073}{66.9560} = 1.979.$$

Comparing the calculated *t*-values with the critical *t*, we see that the absolute values of $t_{\hat{a}}$ and $t_{\hat{b}}$ exceed the critical value; so, we can say that the estimates of *a* and *b* are statistically significant—in this case both are significantly positive. However, the calculated value of $t_{\hat{c}}$ is less than the critical value ($1.979 < 2.052$). In this estimation, the parameter *c* is not indicated to be significantly positive at a 95 percent confidence level. (Although, as you can confirm, it is significant at a 90 percent confidence level.) The upshot is that we are less sure about the impact of the number of children on monthly consumption expenditures.

We can also consider the overall equation. From the value of R^2, we can see that 83.47 percent of the total variation in consumption is explained by the regression equation; that is, by variation in *Y* and *N*. To test for significance of the entire equation, it is necessary to use the *F*-statistic. To obtain the critical *F*-value, note that we have $k - 1 = 3 - 1 = 2$ and $n - k = 30 - 3 = 27$ degrees of freedom. From the table of *F*-statistics at the end of the book, the critical *F*-value for $F_{2,27}$ at a 5 percent risk level is 3.35. Since our *F*-statistic exceeds this value, we can say that our regression equation is statistically significant.

Nonlinear Equations

So far, we have considered only linear equations such as

$$Y = a + bX + cZ.$$

However, as will be evident in subsequent chapters, there will be times when economic theory requires that we use a nonlinear specification. In this text, we will use two types of nonlinear equations.

The first of these nonlinear equations involves nonlinearity in the variables. More specifically, we will want to estimate an equation of the form

$$Y = a + bX + cX^2.$$

This equation is clearly not linear; but it presents no real problem in estimation. Indeed, the simplest way to look at this kind of estimation is to define $Z = X^2$. This nonlinear equation then becomes a linear, multiple regression equation

$$Y = a + bX + cX^2 = a + bX + cZ.$$

The other kind of nonlinear equation we will use is a little more difficult to work with. This second kind of nonlinearity is referred to as nonlinearity in the parameters. The form we will employ in this text is

$$Y = aX^bZ^c.$$

This functional form is particularly useful because of the interpretation of the parameters b and c:

$$b = \frac{\text{Percentage change in } Y}{\text{Percentage change in } X} = \frac{\Delta Y/Y}{\Delta X/X} = \left(\frac{\Delta Y}{\Delta X}\right) \cdot \left(\frac{X}{Y}\right)$$

$$c = \frac{\text{Percentage change in } Y}{\text{Percentage change in } Z} = \left(\frac{\Delta Y}{\Delta Z}\right) \cdot \left(\frac{Z}{Y}\right) \cdot$$

As you should remember from your course in the principles of economics, these parameters measure elasticities—a concept to which we will return in later chapters. Hence, using this form for our equation permits us to estimate elasticities directly—the parameter estimates are elasticity estimates.

But, the problem we face is how to estimate such a function. While it is clearly not linear, it is linear in its logarithms. That is, taking the logarithm of the function $Y = aX^bZ^c$, we obtain

$$\log Y = (\log a) + b(\log X) + c(\log Z).$$

So, if we define

$$Y' = \log Y$$
$$X' = \log X$$
$$Z' = \log Z$$
$$a' = \log a,$$

we once again have a linear, multiple regression equation

$$Y' = a' + bX' + cZ'.$$

Once estimates have been obtained, significance tests and evaluation of the equation are done precisely as we have described earlier. The only difference is that the intercept estimate provided by the computer output is not $\hat{a}$; rather it is log $\hat{a}$.

APPLICATION

A Log-Linear Regression

To illustrate a log-linear regression, let's look ahead to an equation we will describe in detail in Chapter 11. Suppose an analyst specified output to be a function of the firm's levels of usage of capital and labor,

$$Q = f(K,L),$$

and wanted to use a log-linear specification,

$$Q = aK^bL^c.$$

The analyst collected a cross-section data set made up of data from 32 firms. Using these data, the analyst estimated the equation

$$\log Q = (\log a) + b(\log K) + c(\log L).$$

The resulting computer output was as follows:

	DEPENDENT VARIABLE: LOG Q	F-RATIO: 160.621
	OBSERVATIONS: 32	R-SQUARE: 0.9172

VARIABLE	PARAMETER ESTIMATE	STANDARD ERROR
INTERCEPT	-0.693	0.106
LOG K	0.578	0.216
LOG L	0.423	0.186

From these results, the analyst knows that

$$\hat{a}' = \log \hat{a} = -0.693$$
$$\hat{b} = 0.578$$
$$\hat{c} = 0.423.$$

As noted earlier, and will be stressed in Chapter 11, $\hat{b}$ and $\hat{c}$ are estimates of elasticities. (Specifically, $\hat{b}$ is the estimate of the elasticity of output with respect to capital usage—the output elasticity of capital. Likewise, $\hat{c}$ is an estimate of the output elasticity of labor.)

Tests for significance are performed in precisely the same way as for a "normal" equation: Since there are $32 - 3 = 29$ degrees of freedom, the critical value of t at a 95 percent confidence level is 2.045. The calculated t-values are

$$t_{\hat{a}} = \frac{-0.693}{0.106} = -6.538$$

$$t_{\hat{b}} = \frac{0.578}{0.216} = 2.676$$

$$t_{\hat{c}} = \frac{0.423}{0.186} = 2.274.$$

And, since the absolute values for all of these exceed the critical value, all of the estimates are statistically significant.

The R^2 value indicates that 91.72 percent of the variation in output is explained by the regression equation. And, given that the critical value for F at a 95 percent confidence level is 3.33 (2 and 29 degrees of freedom), the analyst knows that the equation is statistically significant.

In order to find the value of $\hat{a}$, it is necessary to take the antilog of $\hat{a}'$,*

Antilog$(-0.693) = 0.5.$

Using this value, the estimated function could be written as

$$Q = 0.5K^{0.578}L^{\,0.423}.$$

---

*In this text we will use natural logarithms; that is, $\log_e$. Hence

Antilog$(-0.693) = e^{-0.693}.$

4.5 REGRESSION IN MANAGERIAL DECISION MAKING

From this brief overview of regression analysis, we hope that you have been able to see that this technique will be very useful in obtaining measures of those marginal benefits and marginal costs that we discussed in Chapter 3. While we will have more to say about the specific applications of regression in later chapters, at this point we want you simply to understand that it is actually used in managerial decision making.

As Robert F. Soergel (general marketing manager, E. L. Weingard Division, Emerson Electric Company) put it, "regression analysis can be extremely helpful, and it's not as difficult as its name suggests."[3] Regression analysis is simply a tool to provide the information necessary for a manager to make decisions which will maximize profits, or as Mr. Soergel observed, "the computer is a tool, not a master." We will use this tool

---

[3]"Probing the Past for the Future," *Sales & Marketing Management,* March 14, 1983.

to find estimates of the various functions we will describe later in the text. It's not that hard, and we would agree with Mr. Soergel's conclusion of "the best part: it's not expensive."

The statistical analyses (or, if you wish, econometrics) that we are going to use in this book are really very simple. Our two major objectives are also simple:

1. We want you to be able to set up a regression equation that could subsequently be estimated using one of the readily available regression packages.
2. We want you to be able to use the output of a regression to examine those economic issues that are of interest to the manager of an enterprise.

Hence, in terms of the field of study known as econometrics, we will concentrate our attention on helping you to avoid what are called *specification errors*. In simple terms, this means that we will show you how to set up an estimation equation that is appropriate for the use to which it is to be put. Specification errors—such as excluding important explanatory variables or using an inappropriate form for the equation—are very serious; they can result in the estimates being *biased*.

Unbiased Estimates

An estimate is unbiased if the expected value of the estimate is equal to the actual value of the parameter being estimated. Defining $\hat{b}$ to be an estimate of b, this means

$$E(\hat{b}) = b.$$

The estimate $\hat{b}$ is a random variable with some distribution. Graphically, this definition requires that the mean of the distribution of $\hat{b}$ is at the true value of b.

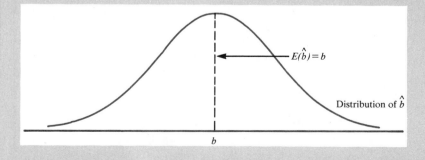

Later in this text, we will introduce you to another problem in econometrics that we feel is particularly relevant for managerial economics—the so-called *identification problem*. This problem, like specification errors, is very serious, since it could also lead to biased estimates of the coefficients of a regression equation.

In addition to specification errors and the identification problem, there are other problems that can be encountered in regression analysis. These problems, which are more difficult than the material we want to cover in this text, are reviewed briefly in the appendix to this chapter (and covered more completely in the references listed at the end of this chapter).

TECHNICAL PROBLEMS

1. Define endogenous and exogenous variables.
2. Contrast time-series and cross-section data sets.
3. Regression analysis is often referred to as "least squares" regression. Why is this name appropriate?
4. Following is the computer output obtained from a regression used to estimate the equation $Y = a + bX$.

DEPENDENT VARIABLE: Y		F-RATIO: 141.391
OBSERVATIONS: 25		R-SQUARE: 0.8347
VARIABLE	PARAMETER ESTIMATE	STANDARD ERROR
INTERCEPT	443.72	124.82
X	0.80572	0.06776

   a. How many degrees of freedom remain?
   b. What is the critical value for *t* at a 95 percent confidence level?
   c. Test to see if the estimates of *a* and *b* are statistically significant.
   d. What does the R^2 statistic tell us?
   e. What are the appropriate degrees of freedom for the *F*-statistic?
   f. What is the critical value for the *F*-statistic at a 95 percent confidence level? Is the regression equation statistically significant?

5. What does an analyst mean by saying that a regression coefficient is statistically significant at a 95 percent confidence level?
6. Look again at the application titled "The Market Model." In this application we graphed the relation between the regression line and

the data points. *Sketch* alternative graphs supposing that R^2
a. Rose to 0.9052.
b. Fell to 0.1072.

7. An analyst wanted to determine the relation between a firm's sales and its advertising levels in newspapers and on radio. That is, the function presupposed was

$$S = f(N,R).$$

Suppose the relation was specified as

$$S = a + bN + cR.$$

  a. Interpret the parameters a, b, and c (e.g., what does the parameter b measure?).
Alternatively, suppose the relation was specified as

$$S = aN^bR^c.$$

  b. Interpret the parameters a, b, and c.
  c. How could this nonlinear function be estimated?

8. Suppose the "true" relation was

$$Y = a + bX + cZ,$$

but the analyst estimated

$$Y = a + bX.$$

What might be the result on the parameter estimates?

SUGGESTED ADDITIONAL REFERENCES

Kelejian, Harry H., and Wallace E. Oates.   *Introduction to Econometrics.* New York: Harper & Row, 1974.

Kmenta, Jan.   *Elements of Econometrics.* New York: Macmillan, 1971.

Rao, Potluri, and Roger LeRoy Miller.   *Applied Econometrics.* Belmont, Calif.: Wadsworth, 1971.

Wonnacott, Ronald J., and Thomas H. Wonnacott.   *Econometrics.* New York: John Wiley & Sons, 1979.

APPENDIX: SOME ADDITIONAL PROBLEMS

Multicollinearity

When using regression analysis, we assume that the explanatory (right-hand side) variables are linearly independent of one another. If this assumption is violated, we have the problem of multicollinearity. Under normal circumstances, multicollinearity will result in the estimated standard errors being larger than their true values. This means, then, that if multicollinearity exists, finding statistical significance will be more difficult. More specifically, if moderate multicollinearity is present, the estimate of the coefficient, $\hat{b}$, will be unbiased; but the estimated standard error, $S_{\hat{b}}$, will be increased. Thus, the *t*-coefficient, $t = \hat{b}/S_{\hat{b}}$, will be reduced and it will be more difficult to find statistical significance.

Multicollinearity is not unusual. The question is what to do about it. As a general rule, the answer is *nothing*. To illustrate, consider the following function that denotes some "true" relation,

$$Y = a + bX + cZ.$$

If X and Z are not linearly independent—if X and Z are collinear—the standard errors of the estimates for $\hat{b}$ and $\hat{c}$ will be increased. Shouldn't we just drop one? Not in the normal instance. If Z is an important explanatory variable, the exclusion of Z would be a *specification error* and would result in biased estimates of the coefficients—a much more severe problem.

Heteroscedasticity

The problem of heteroscedasticity is encountered when the variance of the error term is not constant. It can be encountered when there exists some relation between the error term and one or more of the explanatory variables—for example, when there exists a positive relation between X and the errors (i.e., large errors are associated with large values of X).

In such a case, the estimated parameters are still unbiased, but the standard errors of the coefficients are biased; so the calculated *t*-coefficients are unreliable. This problem, most normally encountered in cross-section studies, can sometimes be corrected by performing a transformation on the data or equation. Otherwise, it becomes necessary to employ a technique called weighted least squares estimation.

Autocorrelation

The problem of autocorrelation, associated with time series data, occurs when the errors are not independent over time. For example, it could be the case that a high error in one period tends to promote a high error in the following period. Such a phenomenon is sometimes called *tracking*.

With autocorrelation (sometimes referred to as serial correlation) the estimated parameters are unbiased, but the standard errors are again biased, resulting in unreliability of the calculated *t*-coefficients. Tests for determining if autocorrelation is present (most notably the Durbin-Watson test) are included in most of the available regression packages. Furthermore, most packages also include techniques for estimating an equation in the presence of autocorrelation.

PART TWO

DEMAND

5

THEORY OF CONSUMER BEHAVIOR: INDIVIDUAL DEMAND CURVES

I n Chapter 2 we described some of the characteristics of market demand curves. But, in that analysis we simply asserted the characteristics, we did not use the theory of consumer behavior to derive the demand curves or to develop their characteristics. Since market demand is directly related to the way consumers are willing and able to act, it is necessary to understand consumer behavior in order to understand the fundamentals of demand. It is useful for managers to be aware of what underlies demand in order to understand, estimate, and forecast the demand for the products they sell. Hence, in this chapter, we will derive the demand curve of an individual consumer and examine the determinants of this demand function. In Chapter 6 we will aggregate these individual demand curves to obtain a market demand curve.

The basic theory of consumer behavior is really quite simple. As a matter of fact, it follows directly from the theory of constrained optimization we described in Chapter 3. (Indeed, as you go through this chapter, you may want to look back at Chapter 3 to see how closely the analysis here follows that general framework.) Few, if any, people have incomes sufficient to purchase as much as they desire of every good or service. So the consumer attempts to maximize his or her satisfaction given the constraint of a limited income. To see how this works, let's begin by looking at a "satisfaction function."

5.1 THE UTILITY FUNCTION

The individual consumer attempts to maximize his or her level of satis-faction—or, as economists call it, *utility*. More precisely, the consumer chooses the goods and services that maximize utility (subject to an income constraint). We define utility as follows:

Definition.   Utility is an individual's perception of his or her own satisfaction from consuming any specific bundle of goods and services.

We can write a consumer's utility function in the form

$$U = f(X_1, X_2, X_3, \ldots, X_n),$$

where X_i is the amount of the i-th good or service to be consumed. If U is some index of utility, the value of this index depends upon the quantities of goods one through n consumed.

For analytical convenience, we will consider the case of a consumer choosing among bundles consisting of only two goods (or services)—X and Y. The utility function can then be written as

$$U = f(X, Y),$$

where X and Y are, respectively, the levels of consumption of the two commodities. We should emphasize, however, that the principles we de-velop will apply to situations in which individuals make consumption decisions about any number of goods and services.

As with all economic models, the theory of consumer behavior employs some simplifying assumptions. These assumptions permit us to go directly to the fundamental determinants of consumer behavior and to abstract away from the less important aspects of the consumer's decision process. Let us briefly describe these assumptions.

Complete Information

We assume for now that consumers have complete information pertaining to their consumption decisions. They know the full range of goods and services available and the capacity of each to provide satisfaction (or utility). Further, the price of each good is known exactly, as is each consumer's income during the time period in question.

Admittedly, to assume perfect knowledge is an abstraction from reality. But the assumption of complete information does not distort the relevant aspects of the real world. It allows us to concentrate upon how real consumption choices are made.

Preference Ordering

Our second assumption is that consumers are able to rank all conceivable bundles of commodities on the basis of the ability of each bundle to provide satisfaction. When confronted with two or more bundles of goods, consumers can determine their order of preference among them. Let's look at an example.

Suppose a consumer is confronted with two bundles consisting of different combinations of two goods. Bundle 1 consists of five candy bars and one soft drink. Bundle 2 consists of three candy bars and three soft drinks. Ranking the two bundles, the person can make one of three possible responses: (1) I prefer bundle 1 to bundle 2, (2) I prefer bundle 2 to bundle 1, or (3) I would be equally satisfied with—indifferent between—either.

The same is true when ranking any two bundles of goods and services. The consumer either prefers one bundle to the other or is indifferent between the two. A consumer who is indifferent between two bundles clearly feels that either bundle would yield the same level of utility. A preferred bundle would yield more utility than the other, less-preferred bundle.

Relations. Consumers have a preference pattern that (1) establishes a rank ordering of all bundles of goods and (2) compares all pairs of bundles, indicating that bundle 1 is preferred to bundle 2, 2 is preferred to 1, or the consumer is indifferent between 1 and 2. In a three- (or more) way comparison, if 1 is preferred (indifferent) to 2, and 2 is preferred (indifferent) to 3, 1 must be preferred (indifferent) to 3. A larger bundle, in the sense of having at least as much of every good and more of at least one good, is always preferred to a smaller one.

5.2 INDIFFERENCE CURVES AND MAPS

A fundamental tool for the analysis of consumer behavior is an indifference curve, defined as follows:

Definition. An indifference curve is a locus of points—bundles of goods and services—each of which yields an individual the same level of total utility or satisfaction.

For simplicity we continue to assume that the consumer chooses among bundles consisting of only two goods. This assumption enables us to analyze consumer behavior using two-dimensional graphs.

Figure 5.1 shows a representative indifference curve with the typically assumed slope. The quantity of some good X is plotted along the horizontal axis; the quantity of good Y (possibly some composite of all other goods) is plotted along the vertical axis.

All combinations of goods X and Y along indifference curve I yield the consumer the same level of utility. In other words, the consumer is indifferent among all points such as *A*, with 10 units of X and 50 units of Y; point *B*, with 20X and 35Y; point *C*, with 40X and 18Y; and so on. At any point on I, it is possible to take away some amount of X and add some amount of Y (though not necessarily the same amount) and leave

Figure 5.1   **A Typical Indifference Curve**

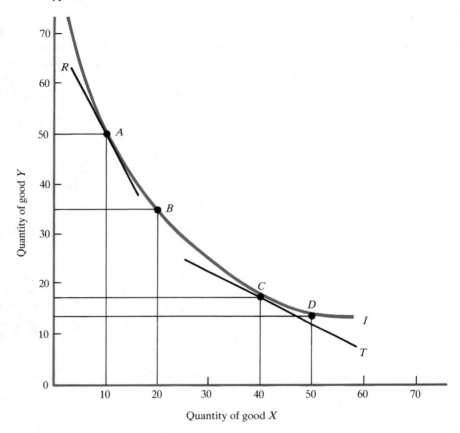

the consumer with the same level of utility. Conversely, we can add X and take away just enough Y to make the consumer indifferent between the two combinations.

The indifference curve is downward sloping. This reflects the fact that the consumer obtains utility from both goods. Thus, if we add X, we must take away Y in order to keep the same level of utility. If the curve in Figure 5.1 would begin to slope upward at, say, 70 units of X, it would mean that the consumer has so much X that any additional X would reduce utility if the quantity of Y remains constant. In such a case, to keep the consumer at the same level of utility when X is added, more Y would have to be added to compensate for lost utility from having more X. Likewise, if the curve begins to bend backward at, say, 70 units of Y, it would mean that the consumer experiences reduced levels of utility with increases in Y.

Indifference curves are convex. This shape requires that as the consumption of X is increased relative to Y, the consumer is willing to accept a smaller reduction in Y for an equal increase in X, in order to stay at the same level of utility. This property is apparent in Figure 5.1. Suppose we begin at point *A* with 10 units of X and 50 units of Y. In order to increase consumption of X by 10 units, to 20, the consumer is willing to reduce consumption of Y by 15 units, to 35. Given indifference curve I, the consumer will be indifferent between the two combinations represented by *A* and *B*. Next begin at *C*, with 40X and 18Y. From this point, to gain an additional 10 units of X (move to point *D*), the consumer is willing to give up only 6 units of Y, much less than the 15 units willingly given up at *A*. The convexity of indifference curves implies a diminishing marginal rate of substitution, to which we now turn.

Marginal Rate of Substitution

An important concept in indifference curve analysis is the marginal rate of substitution, defined as follows:

Definition. The marginal rate of substitution of X for Y measures the number of units of Y that must be given up per unit of X added so as to maintain a constant level of utility. The marginal rate of substitution is given by the negative of the slope of an indifference curve at a point. It is defined only for movements along a given curve.

Returning to Figure 5.1, we can see that the consumer is indifferent between combinations *A* (10X and 50Y) and *B* (20X and 35Y). Thus the rate at which the consumer is willing to substitute is

$$\frac{\Delta Y}{\Delta X} = \frac{50 - 35}{10 - 20} = -\frac{15}{10} = -1.5.$$

The marginal rate of substitution is 1.5, meaning that the consumer is willing to give up 1.5 units of Y for each unit of X added. Since we would find it cumbersome to have the minus sign on the right side of the equation, we define the marginal rate of substitution as

$$MRS = -\frac{\Delta Y}{\Delta X} = 1.5.$$

For the movement from *C* to *D* along I, the marginal rate of substitution is

$$MRS = -\frac{\Delta Y}{\Delta X} = -\frac{(18 - 12)}{(40 - 50)} = \frac{6}{10} = .6.$$

In this case the consumer is willing to give up only .6 units of Y per additional unit of X added.

Thus we say that the marginal rate of substitution diminishes along an indifference curve. When consumers have a small amount of X relative to Y, they are willing to give up a lot of Y to gain another unit of X. When they have less Y relative to X, they are willing to give up less Y in order to gain another unit of X.

The marginal rate of substitution is, as noted, the negative of the slope of an indifference curve for very small changes in X and Y. For example, the negative of the slope of the tangent *R* at point *A* is the marginal rate of substitution at that point. The same is the case for tangent *T* at point *C*. Looking at these tangents, it is easily seen that the slope of the indifference curve, and hence the marginal rate of substitution, declines as X is increased relative to Y.

We can summarize the discussion in the following:

Principles.   Indifference curves are negatively sloped and convex. Therefore, if the consumption of one good is increased, consumption of the other must be reduced to maintain a constant level of utility, and the marginal rate of substitution—the negative of the slope of the indifference curve—diminishes as we move downward along an indifference curve, increasing X relative to Y.

Indifference Maps

An indifference map is simply a graph showing a set of two or more indifference curves. Figure 5.2 shows a typical indifference map, made up of four indifference curves, I, II, III, and IV. Any indifference curve

---

Figure 5.2   Indifference Map

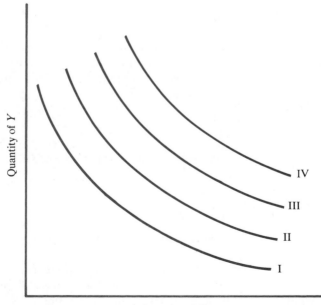

Quantity of *X*

lying above and to the right of another represents a higher level of utility. Thus any combination of X and Y on IV is preferred to any combination on III, any combination on III is preferred to any on II, and so on. All bundles of goods on the same indifference curve are equivalent; all combinations lying on a higher curve are preferred.

The indifference map in Figure 5.2 consists of only four indifference curves. We could have drawn many, many more. In fact, the X-Y space actually contains an infinite number of indifference curves. Each point in the space lies on one and only one indifference curve; that is, indifference curves cannot intersect.

We can summarize with the following:

Principles.   An indifference map consists of several indifference curves. The higher (or further to the right) an indifference curve, the greater the level of utility associated with the curve. Combinations of goods on higher indifference curves are preferred to combinations on lower curves.

APPLICATION

Indifference Curves in Investments

How do you structure your investment portfolio? This question receives a great deal of attention in finance courses. Indeed, a major field of study in finance is referred to as portfolio theory.

In portfolio theory any investment can be characterized by two parameters: the expected return on the investment and its risk.* Consider the figure below in which three investments are illustrated.

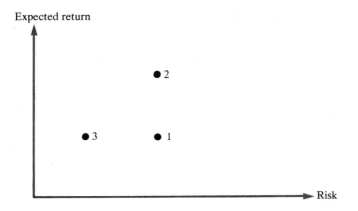

*Risk is measured as the variance of returns; that is, Risk = Var (Returns) = σ^2. We will return to this concept of risk in Chapter 19.

Clearly investment 2 is preferred to investment 1, since investment 2 has the same level of risk as investment 1, but a higher expected return. Likewise, investment 3 is preferred to investment 1, because investment 3 has a smaller level of risk for the same expected return. But, how do investments 2 and 3 compare? Investment 3 has a lower expected return than investment 2, but it also has a lower level of risk. And since investors are normally willing to give up some return for less risk, it might be that you are indifferent between investments 2 and 3. Illustrated below is an indifference map consistent with these rankings:

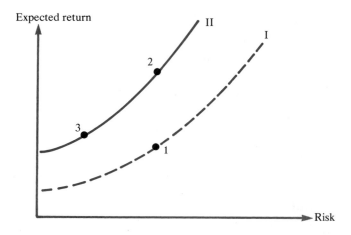

The investor is indifferent between investments on curve II (or curve I), but investments on curve II are strictly preferred to those on curve I.

We could thus draw an indifference map portraying the investor's trade-off between expected return and risk. However, this indifference map looks very different from that in Figure 5.2. The reason is that Figure 5.2 illustrates the trade-off between two "goods," while our investment curves illustrate the trade-off between one "good"— expected return—and one "bad"—risk. If, as is illustrated below, we

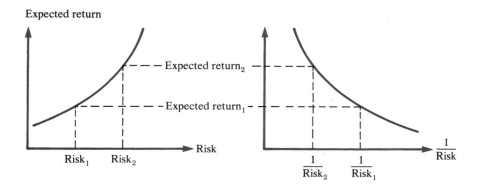

redraw our investment curves in terms of 1/Risk—a "good"—the indifference curves resume their "normal" shape.

Marginal Utility Approach

The concept of marginal utility can give additional insight into the properties of indifference curves. We define marginal utility as follows:

Definition. Marginal utility is the addition to total utility that is attributable to the addition of one unit of a good to the current rate of consumption, holding constant the amounts of all other goods consumed. We typically assume that, as the consumption of a good increases, the marginal utility from an additional unit of the good decreases.

While many economists object to the concept of marginal utility on the grounds that utility is not measurable, we find it useful to relate marginal utility to the marginal rate of substitution along an indifference curve. Assume for now that utility (U) depends upon the rate of consumption of only two goods, X and Y. The total change in utility resulting from a small change in both X and Y can be represented as[1]

$$\Delta U = [(MU \text{ of } X) \times \Delta X] + [(MU \text{ of } Y) \times \Delta Y].$$

For points on a given indifference curve, all combinations of goods yield the same level of utility, so ΔU is zero for all changes in X and Y that would keep the consumer on the same indifference curve. From the above equation, if $\Delta U = 0$, it follows that

$$\frac{MU_X}{MU_Y} = -\frac{\Delta Y}{\Delta X},$$

where $(-\Delta Y/\Delta X)$ is the negative of the slope of the indifference curve; that is, the marginal rate of substitution.

5.3 THE CONSUMER'S BUDGET CONSTRAINT

Indifference curves are derived from the preference patterns of consumers. As such, they give us a method of analyzing what consumers are willing to do. But recall from Chapter 2 that demand functions indicate what consumers are both *willing and able* to do. Consumers are con-

---

[1] Note that we have stretched one of the assumptions in this analysis. Recall that marginal utility is the increase in utility from a one-unit increase in the rate of consumption in a good, holding the consumption of all other goods constant. In this example, we speak of marginal utility while letting the consumption of both goods change at the same time. However, if the change in each is small, this presents little or no problem.

strained in what they are able to do by market-determined prices and their income. We now turn to an analysis of the constraint that consumers face—the determinants of what consumers are able to do.

Budget Lines

If consumers had unlimited money incomes there would be no problem of economizing and no jobs for economists. People could buy whatever they wanted when they wanted it and would have no problem of choice. But this is not generally the case.

Consumers normally have limited incomes. Thus their problem is to spend this limited income in a way that gives the maximum possible satisfaction. Let's look at this constraint faced by consumers.

We continue to consider only two goods, bought in quantities X and Y. (We can assume, as before, that there are only two goods in the consumption bundle or that good Y is a composite of all goods other than X.) The consumer has a fixed money income, M, which is the maximum amount that can be spent on the two goods. For simplicity, we assume that the entire income is spent on X and Y.[2] Thus the amount that is spent on X ($p_x X$) plus the amount that is spent on Y ($p_y Y$) must equal income (M):

$$M = p_x X + p_y Y.$$

This equation can be rewritten in the intercept-slope form as:

$$Y = \frac{M}{p_y} - \frac{p_x}{p_y} X.$$

Such equations are called budget lines, defined as follows:

Definition.   A budget line is the locus of all combinations or bundles of goods that can be purchased if the entire money income is spent.

The first term, M/p_y, gives the amount of Y the consumer can buy if no X is purchased. Suppose that income is $1,000 and the price of Y is $5 per unit. If the consumer spends the entire income on Y, 200 units of Y can be purchased.

The slope of the line ($-p_x/p_y$) indicates the amount of Y that must be given up if one more unit of X is purchased. Suppose the price of Y is $5, and the price of X is $10. For every additional unit of X, the consumer must give up $10 worth of Y, or two units of Y. Thus the rate at which a consumer can trade Y for more X is 10/5 = 2—two units of Y for one of X. If, instead, the price of X is $2.50, the rate that Y can be traded for

---

[2]More advanced theories permit consumers to save and borrow between periods. We shall address these more complicated topics later when we analyze the effect of time and the interest rate.

Figure 5.3 **A Typical Budget Line**

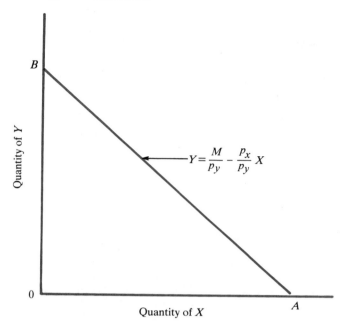

X is 2.50/5.00 = 1/2. For every additional unit of X, the consumer must give up ½ unit of Y.

A typical budget line is shown in Figure 5.3. The line *BA* shows all combinations of Y and X that can be purchased with the given money income and given prices of the goods. The intercept on the *Y* axis, *B*, is M/p_y; the horizontal intercept, *A*, is M/p_x. The slope of the budget line is $-p_x/p_y$.

Shifting the Budget Line

If money income (*M*) or the price ratio (p_x/p_y) changes, the budget line changes. Panel A of Figure 5.4 shows the effect of changes in income. Begin with the original budget line *BA*. Next let money income increase, holding the prices of X and Y constant. Since the prices do not change, the slope of the budget line remains the same. But since money income increases, M/p_y, the vertical intercept must increase (shift upward). That is, if the consumer spends the entire income on good Y, more Y can be purchased than before. The horizontal intercept (M/p_x) also increases, and the result of an increase in income is a parallel shift in the budget line from *BA* to *RN*. The increase in income increases the set of combinations of the goods that can be purchased.

Figure 5.4 Shifting Budget Lines

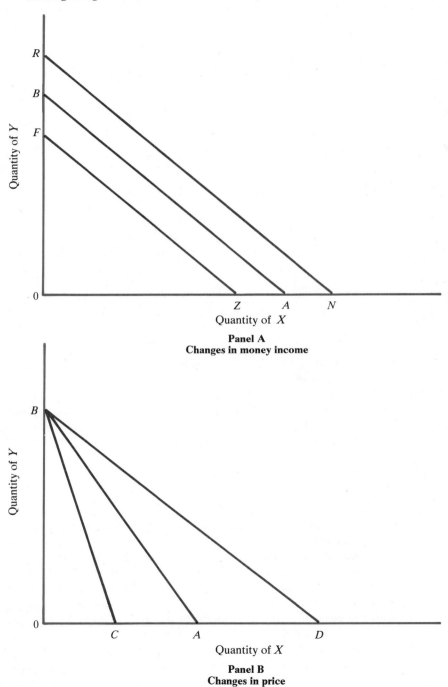

Panel A
Changes in money income

Panel B
Changes in price

Alternatively, begin with budget line *BA* and let money income decrease. In this case the set of possible combinations of goods decreases. The vertical and horizontal intercepts decrease, causing a parallel shift in the budget line to *FZ*.

Panel B shows the effect of changes in the price of good X. Begin once more with the budget line *BA*, then let the price of X fall. Since M/p_y does not change, the vertical intercept remains at *B*. But when p_x decreases, the absolute value of the slope, p_x/p_y, must also fall. In this case, the budget line becomes less steep. In Panel B the budget line pivots from *BA* to *BD*. In other words, if the price of X falls, more X can be purchased if the entire money income is spent on X. Thus the horizontal intercept increases from *A* to *D*.

An increase in the price of good X causes the budget line to pivot backward, from *BA* to *BC*. That is, if p_x increases, the absolute value of the slope of the line, p_x/p_y, must increase. The budget line becomes steeper, while the vertical intercept remains constant.

These results can be summarized in the following:

Relations. An increase (decrease) in money income causes a parallel outward (backward) shift in the budget line. An increase (decrease) in the price of X causes the budget line to pivot backward (outward) around the original vertical intercept.

5.4 UTILITY MAXIMIZATION

We now have the tools to analyze the utility maximization problem. The budget line shows all bundles of commodities that are available to the consumer, given the limited income and market-determined prices. The indifference map shows the preference ordering of all conceivable bundles of goods. The consumer's task is to choose, from all available bundles of goods, the bundle that leads to the highest attainable level of utility.

Maximizing Utility Subject to a Limited Money Income[3]

The maximization process is shown in Figure 5.5. Indifference curves I–IV represent the indifference map. Budget line *BA* shows all bundles of X and Y available to the consumer. Clearly the highest possible level of satisfaction possible given the consumer's budget is attained at *P* on indifference curve III, where the individual consumes x^* units of X and y^* units of Y. Many bundles of goods, such as combinations on IV, are preferred to the bundle given by *P*, but they are not available because of the consumer's limited money income. All combinations on indifference curves higher than III are unattainable.

---

[3]A mathematical approach to constrained utility maximization is provided in the appendix to this chapter.

Figure 5.5   **Constrained Utility Maximization**

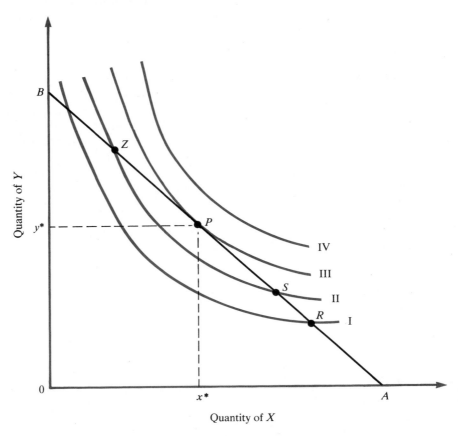

Quantity of X

Other bundles are attainable but lie on lower indifference curves and are therefore less preferred. Consider the bundle given by point *R*. The consumer could move upward along the budget line, giving up X and adding Y, through combinations such as that at *S*. And the consumer would not stop substituting Y for X until *P* is reached, because such substitution leads to a higher level of utility.

The consumer would not move beyond *P* to points such as *Z*, because that would lead to consumption on a lower indifference curve. If the consumer began at combination *Z*, for example, he or she could substitute X for Y—take more X and give up some Y—along the budget line and attain higher levels of utility until *P* is reached.

Thus the highest attainable level of utility is reached by consuming the combination at which the marginal rate of substitution (the slope of the indifference curve) equals the price ratio (the slope of the budget line). The marginal rate of substitution is the rate at which the consumer is *willing* to substitute X for Y. The price ratio is the rate at which the consumer is *able* to substitute X for Y in the market. Thus, equilibrium occurs where the rate at which the consumer is willing to substitute equals the rate at which he or she is able to substitute.

To develop the concept further, consider a combination such as *S* in Figure 5.5. At this point, the marginal rate of substitution is less than the price ratio. Suppose at this point $MRS = 2$ and $P_x/P_y = 4$. The consumer is willing to give up one unit of X to get two units of Y. The price ratio allows the consumer to obtain four units of Y for each unit of X given up. Thus the consumer can be made better off by substituting Y for X.

Conversely, suppose the consumer is at a point such as *Z*, where the *MRS* is greater than the price ratio. Suppose at this point the *MRS* is six and the price ratio remains four. The consumer is willing to give up six units of Y to obtain one X. The price ratio allows the consumer to give up only four units of Y to obtain each additional unit of X. Thus the consumer is made better off by substituting X for Y.

We can summarize consumer optimization in the following:

Principle. The maximization of satisfaction subject to a limited money income occurs at the combination of goods for which the MRS *of X for Y equals the ratio of the price of X to the price of Y.*

APPLICATION

The Optimal Portfolio of Investments

In an earlier application, we discussed an investor's indifference curve between an investment's expected return and its risk. As with our consumer goods examples, this indifference curve reflects *willingness*—in this case an investor's willingness to trade off expected return for a reduction in risk. Recall that an investor's indifference curves between rate of return and risk are upward sloping, reflecting that risk is a "bad"; that is, investors must be compensated by a higher rate of return if the risk is increased. These curves became steeper as risk increases. An indifference curve above and to the left of another signifies a higher level of utility.

Comparable to the consumer's budget line, an investor faces a budget constraint indicating how the market will permit the investor to trade off between expected return and risk. Such a constraint is illustrated in the figure on the following page. The investor, with a fixed amount to invest, has essentially three choices:

1. Invest 100 percent in risk-free securities (e.g., government securities), earning R_f with risk equal to zero;
2. Invest 100 percent in risky assets (e.g., stocks) by holding the market portfolio, *p*, thereby earning the market return R_M with risk as denoted $Risk_M$;

3. Invest some percent between zero and 100 in risk-free
    securities and the remainder in the market portfolio
    (illustrated by point A), thereby earning a rate between R_f and
    R_M but subject to risk between 0 and Risk$_M$.

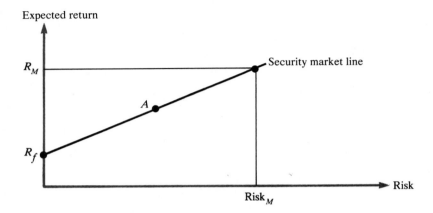

As should be evident from the figure, the risk/return budget line
indicates the highest expected return available for any level of risk. Put
another way, the risk/return budget line illustrates the maximum
increase in return available for an increase in the riskiness of the
portfolio.

Marginal Utility Interpretation

Recall that the *MRS* can be defined as the ratio of the marginal utilities
of the two goods. Therefore, equilibrium occurs when

$$MRS = \frac{MU_X}{MU_Y} = \frac{P_x}{P_y},$$

or

$$\frac{MU_X}{P_x} = \frac{MU_Y}{P_y}.$$

This condition means that the marginal utility per dollar spent on good X
equals the marginal utility per dollar spent on Y. For example, if $MU_X =$
10 and $P_x =$ \$2, $MU_X/P_x = 5$, meaning that one additional dollar spent
on X increases utility by five units. The principle set forth above is plausible. To see this, suppose that the condition did not hold and that

$$\frac{MU_X}{P_x} < \frac{MU_Y}{P_y}.$$

Combining the investor's indifference map for risk and expected
return with the budget line imposed by the market, we have the utility
maximization problem described above. The investor will maximize
utility by selecting the portfolio of risk-free securities and risky assets
for which the indifference curve is just tangent to the budget line.

Risk/Return Indifference Map

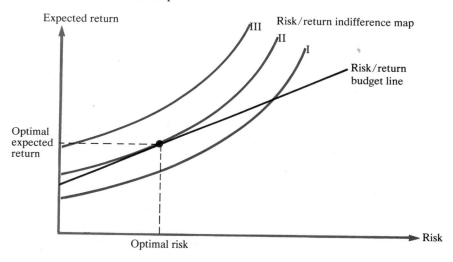

The marginal utility per dollar spent on good X is less than the marginal
utility per dollar spent on Y. The consumer can take dollars away from
X and spend them on Y. As long as the inequality holds, the lost utility
from each dollar taken away from X is less than the added utility from
each additional dollar spent on Y, and the consumer continues to substitute
Y for X. As the consumption of X decreases, we would expect the marginal utility of X to rise. As Y increases, its marginal utility would decline.
The consumer continues substituting until MU_X/p_x equals MU_Y/p_y.
   Alternatively, if

$$\frac{MU_X}{P_x} > \frac{MU_Y}{P_y},$$

the marginal utility per dollar spent on X is greater than the marginal
utility per dollar spent on Y. The consumer takes dollars away from Y
and buys additional X, continuing to substitute until the equality holds.

Principle. *To obtain maximum satisfaction from a limited money
income, a consumer allocates money income so that the marginal
utility per dollar spent on each good is the same for all commodities
purchased.*

APPLICATION

The Allocation of Retail Display Space

Suppose a store sells both a national brand and a generic (store) brand of a particular product; for example, Kroger food stores sell both Campbell soup and Kroger brand soup (or Tide soap and Kroger soap). Likewise, Sears sells both national brand sporting goods and sporting goods carrying their own brand name. Undoubtedly you can think of many other examples. How should the manager of the store allocate display space between these two types of goods in order to maximize profits?

For generality, let's simply speak of a brand good (B) and a generic good (G) sold by a specific retail store. We would expect that the store is limited by its competitors as to the price it can charge for the brand good B. If Kroger charges more than its competitors for Campbell soup and other national brands, it gets a reputation as being a "high-priced store." Shoppers can compare prices of brand goods among stores and, if a store prices its brand name items high relative to competitors, it loses customers. But Kroger can determine the price of Kroger soup. So the store has flexibility in setting the price of the generic good G (as long as the generic good is priced below the brand good).

How high a price can the retailer charge for the generic good without losing substantial sales to the brand good? Brand goods generally cost the store more than generic goods and, because of competition, have a lower markup (profit margin). Obviously, the manager wants to obtain as high a markup on G as possible. How does the store induce customers to choose G over B, given that we would expect consumers to prefer the brand good to the generic good, other things being the same?

We know from economic theory that, for any consumer, the equilibrium condition for the generic and brand name products is

$$\frac{MU_G}{MU_B} = \frac{P_G}{P_B}.$$

The retailer has little control over consumers' willingness to substitute between G and B (MRS). Also, as noted above, the nominal price of B—the price charged at the checkout—is given by competition. But, the retailer *does* have a choice about the allocation of shelf space. The retailer can raise the "full price" of the brand name good by giving the generic good a more accessible location—possibly by displaying the generic good at eye level and the brand good on one of the bottom shelves. The relative inaccessibility of the brand good increases its full price to consumers by making it relatively more difficult to locate and purchase.

Thus displaying the brand good in a less accessible location in effect raises its price and allows the store to increase the nominal price charged for the generic good. Considering the full price (price plus transaction cost) the consumer equilibrium is attained at a higher generic price, and the store increases its profits above those that could be made if the goods were located side by side on the shelf.

If you doubt the analysis, notice the location of brand goods and generic goods when you go shopping. We doubt if you will find many instances where the brand good has a more accessible location than the generic good. There has to be some economic reason for this, and the reason must be to make the full price of the brand good relatively higher so the store can increase the price of the generic good, therefore making more profit.

5.5 AN INDIVIDUAL CONSUMER'S DEMAND CURVE

Recall from Chapter 2 that demand was defined as the quantities of a good the consumer is willing and able to purchase at each price, holding other things constant. We have just seen that consumers maximize utility when the rate at which they are *willing* to substitute one good for another just equals the rate at which they are *able* to substitute. So it would seem that the two theories are closely related, and they are. The theory of demand can be easily derived from the theory of consumer behavior.

We use Figure 5.6 to see this relation and show how an individual consumer's demand curve is obtained. We begin with a given money income and prices of good X and good Y. The corresponding budget line is given by budget line 1 in the upper panel of the figure. Let the original price of X be $8. The consumer maximizes utility where budget line 1 is tangent to indifference curve I, consuming 200 units of X. Clearly one point on this consumer's demand for X is $8 and 200 units of X. This point is illustrated on the price-quantity graph in the lower panel of Figure 5.6.

Now, following our definition of demand, we hold money income and the price of the other good constant, while letting the price of X fall from $8 to $6. The new budget line is budget line 2. Since money income and the price of Y remain constant, the vertical intercept does not change, but, because the price of X has fallen, the budget line must pivot outward along the X-axis. With this new budget line, the consumer now maximizes utility where budget line 2 is tangent to indifference curve II, consuming 300 units of X. Thus another point on the demand schedule in the lower panel must be $6 and 300 units of X.

Next, letting the price of X fall again, this time to $4, the new budget line is budget line 3. Again the price of Y and money income were held

Figure 5.6 Deriving a Demand Curve

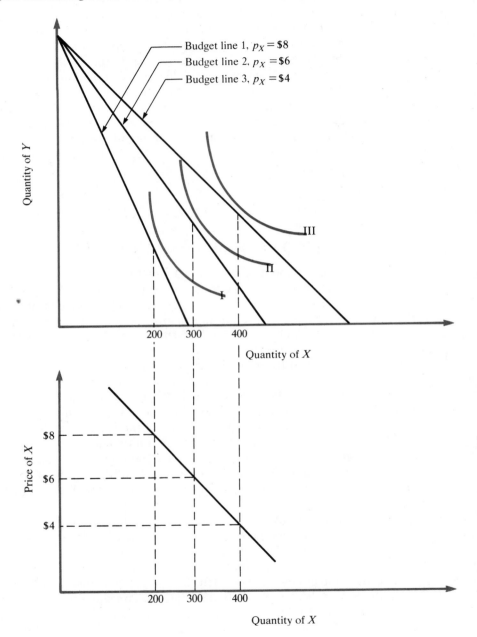

constant. The new equilibrium is on indifference curve III. At the price $4, the consumer chooses 400 units of X, another point on this consumer's demand curve.

Thus we have the following demand schedule for good X.

Price	Quantity Demanded
$8	200
$6	300
$4	400

This schedule is graphed as a demand curve in price-quantity space in the lower part of Figure 5.6. This demand curve is downward sloping. As we let the price of X fall, the quantity of X the consumer is willing and able to purchase increases, following our rule of demand. Furthermore, we followed our definition of demand, holding money income and the price of the other good (goods) constant. Thus we see that an individual's demand for a good is derived from a series of utility-maximizing equilibrium points. We only used three such points, but we could easily have used more in order to obtain more points on the demand curve.

Definition.   The demand curve of an individual for a specific commodity relates utility-maximizing equilibrium quantities purchased to market prices, holding constant money income and the prices of all other goods. The slope of the demand curve illustrates the law of demand: quantity demanded varies inversely with price.

5.6 SUBSTITUTION AND INCOME EFFECTS

Recall from Chapter 2 that when the price of a good decreases, consumers tend to substitute that good for other goods, since the good in question has become cheaper relative to other goods. Conversely, when the price of a good rises, it becomes more expensive relative to other goods, and consumers tend to substitute some of the other goods for some of the good with the now higher price. This is called the substitution effect.

But, there is also another effect, called the income effect. If a good becomes cheaper, people who are consuming that good are made better off. Since the price of that good has fallen, people can consume the same amount as before, but, because of the reduced price, they have some income left over which can be spent on the good with the now lower price and on other goods. The opposite happens when the price of a good increases. Consumers are worse off in the sense that they cannot now

Figure 5.7 **Substitution Effect**

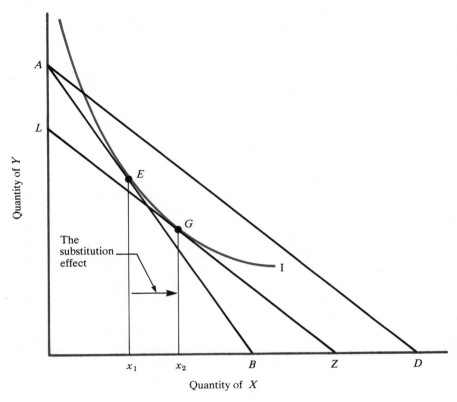

afford the bundle they originally chose. They must consume less of the now more expensive good, less of other goods, or less of both. This is called the income effect. Let us analyze each effect in turn.

Substitution Effect

We begin our analysis of the substitution effect with a definition:

*Definition. **The substitution effect of a change in the price of a good is the change in the consumption of the good that would result if the consumer remained on the same indifference curve.***

To develop the substitution effect formally, consider Figure 5.7 in which we analyze a reduction in price. Begin with a consumer in equilibrium where the original budget line AB is tangent to indifference curve I at point E. The consumer chooses x_1 units of good X. Now let the price of X decline so that the budget line pivots outward to AD.

The consumer, being better off, can now move to an indifference curve higher than I. But, the substitution effect deals with changes on the same indifference curve; so let's theoretically "take away" just enough of the consumer's income to force the new budget line, *AD,* to become tangent to the original indifference curve I. This is shown as the parallel shift of *AD* to the adjusted budget line *LZ.* It is important to note that the slope of *LZ* reflects the new, lower price of X, but is associated with a lower money income than is the original budget line, *AB.* Since budget line *LZ* is tangent to indifference curve I at point *G,* the consumer now chooses x_2 units of X.

The substitution effect is shown as the distance x_1 to x_2, or the movement along I from *E* to *G.* It is clear that this effect is negative—a decrease in price must result in an increase in consumption of the good when utility is held constant. And this must always be the case, given the shape of our indifference curves. That is, a decrease in the price of X causes the budget line to become less steep, so the budget line, after taking away some income, must be tangent to the original indifference curve at a point with a lower slope (*MRS*) than was the case at the original equilibrium. This can only occur with increased consumption of X.

We have established the following principle:

Principle. The substitution effect is the change in the consumption of a good after a change in its price, when the consumer is forced by a change in money income to consume at some point on the original indifference curve. Considering the substitution effect only, the amount of the good consumed must vary inversely with its price. That is, utility held constant, $\Delta X / \Delta P_x < 0$.

Income Effect

We cannot be as certain about the direction of the income effect as was the case for the substitution effect. Before we analyze the income effect, let us define it:

Definition. The income effect from a price change is the change in the consumption of a good resulting strictly from the change in purchasing power.

Earlier we noted that a decrease in the price of a good makes a consumer of that good better off in the sense of being able to purchase the same bundle and have income left over; that is, the consumer can move to a higher indifference curve. An increase in the price of a good makes a consumer worse off because he or she is unable to purchase the original bundle; that is, the consumer must move to a lower indifference curve. Since the consumer moves to a higher or lower indifference curve, depending upon the direction of the price change, and the substitution effect takes place along the original indifference curve, the income effect is simply the difference between the total effect of the price change—the movement from one indifference curve to another—and the substitution effect.

We can isolate these effects for a price decrease in Figure 5.8. First consider Panel A. Begin with budget line AB and equilibrium at E (x_1 units of X) on indifference curve I. Suppose the price of X falls and the budget line pivots to AC. The new equilibrium is at point F on indifference curve II. The total effect of the price decrease is to increase the consumption of X from x_1 to x_3. As we have already demonstrated, the substitution effect is the movement from x_1 to x_2 (or from E to R).

Since the total effect is x_1x_3 and the substitution effect is x_1x_2, the remainder of the change—x_2x_3, or the movement from R to F between indifference curves—must be the income effect. That is, as we return the income that was "taken away" to isolate the substitution effect, the consumer increases the consumption of X from x_2 to x_3.

Note that in Panel A the good is a normal good. Recall from Chapter 2 that consumption of a normal good increases when income increases, prices held constant. This is precisely what we did when we shifted the budget line from LZ back to AC.

As can be seen from the graph, in the case of a normal good, the income effect reinforces the substitution effect. Thus, for a normal good both effects are negative. When price falls both the substitution effect and the income effect cause the consumer to purchase more of the good. Likewise, when the price of the good rises, both effects will cause the consumer to purchase less of the good.

The situation is different for an inferior good. Recall from Chapter 2 that if a good is inferior, an increase in income, holding prices constant, causes less of the good to be consumed.

The case of an inferior good is illustrated in Panel B of Figure 5.8. Begin, as before, with budget line AB. Equilibrium is at E on indifference curve I with x_1 being consumed. Let the price of X fall, so that the budget line pivots out to AC. The new equilibrium is at F on indifference curve II, with x_3 being consumed. The total effect is therefore shown as x_1x_3.

Shifting the new budget line back to LZ, we see that the substitution effect is x_1x_2. Note that the substitution effect is greater than the total effect; x_2 is greater than x_3 (or x_1x_2 exceeds x_1x_3). It is apparent that the income effect must have partially offset the substitution effect. Such will always be the case for an inferior good.

To see why this must be so, return the income taken away when isolating the substitution effect. The budget line moves from LZ back to AC. Since the good is inferior, this increase in income causes less X to be consumed than was the case when the budget line was LZ. The income effect is therefore the movement from x_2 back to x_3 (or the movement from R to F between indifference curves I and II). We can see that in this case the income effect is positive—the decrease in the price of X causes a decrease in the consumption of X (income effect only). As you should be able to

Figure 5.8 **Income and Substitution Effects**

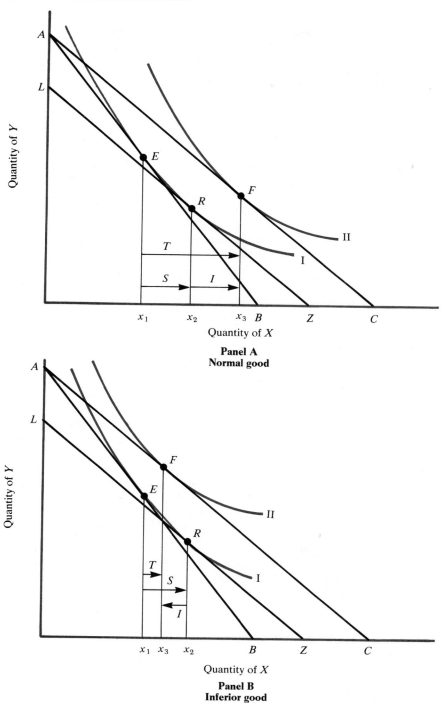

Quantity of Y

Quantity of X

Panel A
Normal good

Panel B
Inferior good

demonstrate, if the price of an inferior good rises, the income effect alone leads to an increase in consumption.

Thus we have established the following principle:

Principle.   Considering the substitution effect alone, an increase (decrease) in the price of a good causes less (more) of the good to be demanded. For a normal good, the income effect—from the consumer's being made better or worse off by the price change—adds to or reinforces the substitution effect. The income effect in the case of an inferior good offsets or takes away from the substitution effect.

Why Demand Slopes Downward

In the case of a normal good, it is clear why price and quantity demanded are negatively related. From the substitution effect alone, a decrease in price is accompanied by an increase in quantity demanded. (An increase in price decreases quantity demanded.) For a normal good, the income effect must add to the substitution effect. Since both effects move quantity demanded in the same direction, demand must be negatively sloped.

In the case of an inferior good, the income effect does not move in the same direction, and to some extent offsets the substitution effect. However, looking at Panel B of Figure 5.8 again, we see that the income effect only *partially* offsets the substitution effect, so that quantity demanded still varies inversely with price. And this is generally the case: Even if the commodity is inferior, the substitution effect dominates the income effect and the demand curve still slopes downward.

It is *theoretically* possible that the income effect for an inferior good could dominate the substitution effect. In this case—the so-called Giffen good—quantity demanded would vary directly with price and the demand curve would be upward sloping. However, in this text, we will ignore Giffen goods. While experimental economists have suggested that a Giffen good may exist for an individual, we have as yet seen no convincing evidence of the existence of a Giffen good for a group of consumers.

5.7 ADVERTISING AND INDIFFERENCE CURVES

It is surely an understatement to say that advertising is big business: U.S. advertising expenditures are approaching $100 billion annually. Indeed, firms like Procter & Gamble, General Foods, Philip Morris, and R. J. Reynolds/Nabisco Brands each spend more than $1 billion each year on advertising.

As you already know, the purpose of these expenditures is to increase sales. And, as you may know from your marketing courses, sources like the *Journal of Marketing Research* have provided substantial evidence that increased advertising does, to a point, increase sales.

But the question remains, WHY? Why are advertising campaigns expected to increase sales? What is it that an advertising campaign is trying to do?

What you have seen in this chapter should provide you with the answer: Advertising campaigns are intended to modify consumers' indifference curves. Successful advertising shifts and/or twists the indifference map.

To illustrate how advertising affects indifference curves, we use two classifications for advertising. We call ads that are primarily designed to convey price, quality, or availability information about the product informative advertising. Ads that are intended to convey an image about the product we refer to as image advertising. (Our informative advertising is much like the comparative advertising described in marketing courses, and image advertising is similar to the selective/competitive advertising classification.)

Informative Advertising

Purely informative advertising conveys price and quality information. Examples of this type of advertising are newspaper ads for food and drug stores, catalog ads, and ads in technical publications.

Until now we have assumed that consumers have complete information about both product price and the ability of goods to satisfy their wants. But we know that this is not the case in the real world. People do not always have full information about prices or the quality of all products.

We might depict the budget line of a consumer who is only partially informed about the price of a product as in Panel A of Figure 5.9. Consider a consumer who is choosing between a particular good, commodity X, and a composite good, that is, all other goods. This consumer does not know with certainty the price of product X; instead he or she knows that the price of commodity X lies within a certain range. The upper bound of this range would give the budget line LZ. This is the budget line if the price of commodity X is the highest that the customer thinks possible. Budget line LR is the budget line for the lowest price of X in the potential range. The true budget line would probably lie somewhere in the shaded area between the two.

We have illustrated a similar situation for the indifference curves of a consumer who is only partially informed about the quality of a product in Panel B of Figure 5.9. In this figure, indifference curve I is the indifference curve that would be relevant if the consumer were completely informed about the quality of commodity X. But, with lack of full information, the consumer can't determine exactly where the indifference curve will be located. The perception of this consumer is that the indifference curve could be anywhere between indifference curves I_A and I_B. So, the indifference curve under incomplete information is a band rather than a line.

Figure 5.9   Budget Lines and Indifference Curves without Complete Information

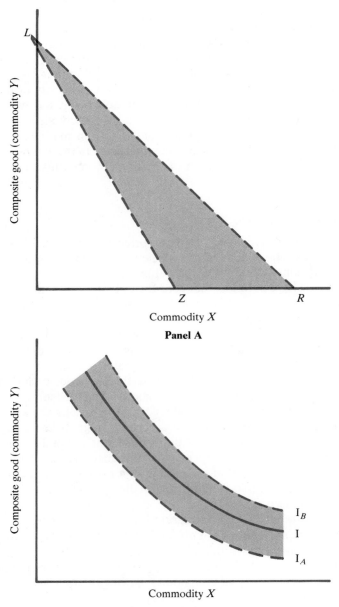

Panel A

Panel B

What would a consumer do when faced with this uncertainty? One possibility is to purchase (or not purchase) given the limited information available. However, this could result in a lower level of utility for the consumer than would exist if he or she has complete information. Alternatively, the consumer might elect to search for price and quality information about the product in order to isolate the true budget line and indifference curve. But, searching takes time, and since "time is money," search is costly.

How can the manager of a firm benefit from the fact that acquiring information is costly? If the manager can make it less costly for consumers to acquire information about the firm's product, the manager can increase the probability that the consumer will purchase from the manager's firm rather than continue to search.

This is the reason for pure information advertising. If information about a firm's product is easily available, consumers would be more likely to conserve their valuable search time and purchase the product about which they have information. Thus, the purpose of informative advertising is to lower the search cost of the product, in the expectation that consumers will purchase the advertised product.

APPLICATION

Informative Advertising

As we have already mentioned, the grocery and drugstore ads that appear weekly or biweekly in newspapers are classic illustrations of price/availability informative advertising. Indeed ads like the one reproduced in the figure on the next page generally provide nothing more than a listing of the products available and their prices. The message provided by the advertiser is that A&P is offering the lowest price for brand name products and that the consumer can minimize the cost of the products by shopping at A&P. The implication is that A&P has the lowest costs overall and that consumers can minimize total shopping costs by purchasing all their groceries at A&P.

Interestingly, as more competitors have entered the market for personal computers, newspaper ads for computers have become increasingly informative ads. The ad reproduced in the figure on page 129, similar to one you might see in your local newspaper, provides an excellent example. This ad provides information about the availability of the machine, its price, and what it will do.

J

The supermarket with warehouse prices.

GROCERY

HAWAIIAN GUAVA FRUIT DRINK

Ocean Spray Mauna Lai

48-oz. btl.   **1³⁹**

CHOCOLATE CANDIES
M&M's Plain or Peanut   16-oz. pkg.   **2¹⁹**

SUGAR FREE 10 CT. OR REGULAR
Swiss Miss Hot Coca Mix   12-ct. pkg.   1.39

MILK CHOC. 11.5-OZ. OR 12-OZ. PKG.
Nestle Semi-Sweet Morsels   1.89

COCOA OR
Post Fruity Pebbles   11-oz. pkg.   1.79

REGULAR OR NATURAL
Mott's Apple Juice   64-oz. btl.   1.49

19-OZ. CLAM CHOWDER, SPLIT PEA W/HAM OR
Progresso Chickarina Soup   99¢

PUREE 29-OZ. CAN OR CRUSHED
Contadina Tomatoes   28-oz. can   79¢

REGULAR TOMATO
Contadina Sauce   5   8-oz. cans   1.00

STEWED
Contadina Tomatoes   14½-oz. can   59¢

REGULAR OR ITALIAN
Contadina Tomato Paste   2   6-oz. cans   69¢

NEW YORK
Wise Deli Potato Chips   7-oz. bag   1.29

REGULAR OR LOW SALT
Nabisco Ritz Crackers   16-oz. box   **1⁷⁹**

GROCERY

TRADITIONAL OR GARDEN STYLE

Ragu Spaghetti Sauce

32-oz. jar   **1³⁹**   Any Variety

TOMATO PLUS OR
Sacramento Tomato Juice   46-oz. can   **79¢**

NATURAL
Poland Spring Water   gallon jug   89¢

WHITE OR ASSORTED
Scotties Facial Tissues   300 in pkg.   79¢

ECONOMY PACK...300 IN PKG.
Scott Family Napkins   1.09

REGULAR OR LIGHT
Kraft Mayonnaise   32-oz. jar   1.79

PLUS DEPOSIT IN N.Y...REGULAR OR
A&P 2-Liter Diet Soda   67.6-oz. bottle   79¢

ASSORTED IMPORTED VARIETIES
Spigadoro Pasta   2   1-lb. pkgs.   **1⁰⁰**

ARTS 'N FLOWERS, DECORATED OR ASS'T
Scott Paper Towels   124 ct. roll   79¢

FOR AUTOMATIC DISHWASHERS
Sunlight Detergent   50-oz. box   1.99

FOR THE LAUNDRY...LIQUID
Wisk Detergent   64-oz. jug   2.99

PLUS DEPOSIT IN N.Y...ASS'T FLAVORS
Faygo Diet Soda   5   12-oz. cans   **1⁰⁰**

Courtesy The Great Atlantic and Pacific Tea Company

Image Advertising

The principal aim of image advertising is to make consumers associate the advertised image with consumption of the product. The image is intended to literally become a characteristic of the product. Image advertising is designed to change the consumer's preference patterns, that is, the consumer's indifference curves. For analytical simplicity, we decompose the total effect on the indifference map into two effects: (1) the change in the marginal rate of substitution and (2) the shift in the indifference map. Let's analyze each of these effects separately and look at the resulting effect upon the demand for the advertised product.

In Figure 5.10 we illustrate the desired effect of image advertising on a consumer's marginal rate of substitution. In this figure we consider commodity A. Let the solid indifference curve I be the relevant curve if commodity A is not advertised, and let LZ be the consumer's original budget line. Equilibrium is attained at E, with the consumer purchasing A_1 units of commodity A. If the price of commodity A increases relative to the price of the composite commodity,[4] the new budget line, MN, is steeper and is tangent to indifference curve I at B. The substitution effect is the movement from E to B, and will result in a decrease in the consumption of good A from A_1 to A_2.

The desired effect of image advertising is illustrated as the change in the indifference curve from I to the dashed line I'. Note that the only thing that has changed is the shape of the indifference curve. With budget line LZ, equilibrium still occurs at E.

With this new indifference curve, let's again let the price of A rise relative to the price of the composite commodity. Since the relative price

---

[4]We should note that in this analysis we are considering only the substitution effect from a change in price.

Figure 5.10   Effect of Advertising on *MRS*

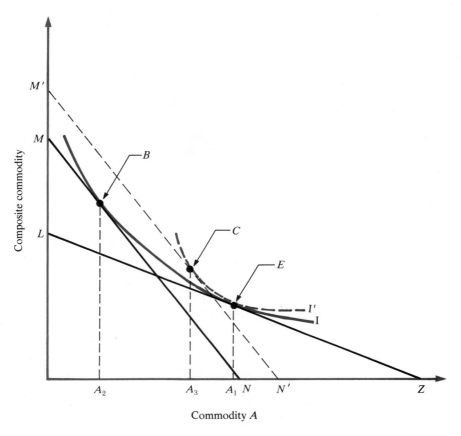

Commodity *A*

change is the same as in the preceding case, the slope of the new budget line *M'N'* is the same as *MN*. Again isolating the substitution effect, the new budget line *M'N'* is now tangent to indifference curve I' at *C*. Now the substitution effect is the movement from *E* to *C* along indifference curve I', or the decrease in the consumption of good A from A_1 to A_3. The substitution effect is still negative—an increase in the relative price of A causes a decrease in its consumption—but the decrease in the consumption of commodity A is much less with advertising than was the case without advertising.

The reason for the difference is that image advertising reduces the substitutability between good A and the composite good. This means that, with advertising, the consumer is willing to give up much less A to obtain an equal amount of the composite good. Thus, if image advertising is successful, the firm can increase price with a much lower decrease in sales than would be the case without advertising. Or, the loss in sales would be reduced if the firm's competitors decrease the price of their product.

APPLICATION

Ads to Reduce Substitutability

Examples of image advertisements designed to reduce substitutability are not hard to find. When John Houseman told us that they made "money the old fashioned way . . . they earned it," Smith Barney was

It's no coincidence that the Bentley logo sports wings. It's been an appropriate symbol of Bentley performance throughout 65 years of automotive history.

In the 20's and 30's, Bentley was a frequent visitor to the winner's circle at Le Mans and Brooklands. Today's version, the Bentley 8, is every bit as triumphant.

The Bentley 8 engine is a substantial 6.75 litres with an 8-to-1 compression ratio and electronically controlled continuous fuel injection. It will certainly get you out and about.

What's most astonishing about the 8, however, is that a car this grand and glorious can be so nimble and quick. You don't quite expect its hard, firm cornering stance. The feel of the ride defies description, particularly at high speeds. Which the Bentley 8 is very wont to do.

Of course, underlying all its engineering attributes is Bentley's historic sense of elegance and restraint. Bentley is manufactured by Rolls-Royce. Assurance enough that the particulars are particularly exemplary.

The Bentley 8, at $89,900,* is for people who want something on a higher plane than the top European imports. If you're interested in that pleasantly lofty position, stop into a Bentley dealer for a test flight.

*MANUFACTURER'S SUGGESTED RETAIL PRICE. TITLE, TAXES, TRANSPORTATION, REGISTRATION, ETC. ADDITIONAL.

Bentley

Courtesy Rolls-Royce Motor Cars, Inc.

forever marked as the brokerage house for those of us who had worked hard for our money. The classic image advertisement is, of course, the Marlboro man. Even those of us who no longer smoke always get a steely glint in our eyes when we come across one of those ads.

Automobile ads have traditionally been designed to point out how unique the Ford or the Chrysler or the Buick is. We decided to use a car ad as our example. Interestingly enough, the one we selected contains price information. However, we propose the following ad as an example of an image ad designed to differentiate the product from other automobiles. In our opinion, it succeeded.

So, image advertising can reduce the substitution effect of a price change. But, image advertising can also have another effect on demand. This effect is shown in Figure 5.11. Let's begin with a consumer facing the income constraint given by budget line *LZ*. Again, the solid indifference curves I and II make up a portion of the consumer's original (pre-advertising) indifference map. As we know, the consumer attains utility-maximizing equilibrium at *E* on indifference curve I, consuming A_1 units of good A.

Now suppose that commodity A is advertised and the image advertising is successful in increasing the perceived value of commodity A. In effect, the advertising shifts the indifference map downward. We have illustrated this new indifference map with the dashed indifference curves I' and II'. Combinations of goods on the new (post-advertising) indifference curve I' denote the same level of utility as combinations on the original (pre-advertising) indifference curve I. Likewise, combinations on indifference curve II' give the same utility level as those on indifference curve II. At any given level of consumption of good A, the consumer attains the same level of utility with less of the composite good when A is advertised. Advertising has increased the perceived value of the advertised good, in the sense that the satisfaction is not reduced from having less of good G and the same amount of A. With no change in the budget line, the new equilibrium is reached at *B* on curve II', with the consumer purchasing A_2 units of commodity A. The effect of the advertising is to increase the demand for the advertised commodity. The *MRS* still equals the price ratio, but more A and less G are consumed at the new equilibrium.

Figure 5.11 Demand-Increasing Advertising

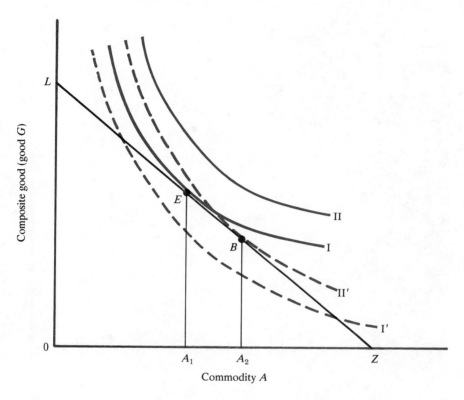

APPLICATION

Ads to Increase Demand

In order to increase the demand for a product, the advertisement must increase the perceived value of the product. Such ads tend to be placed by trade associations rather than individual firms. Most of the examples are from such organizations as Florida orange juice producers or beef producers or coffee growers. In that vein, the following ad was particularly interesting as it obliquely referred to the concern of women about osteoporosis to suggest that dairy products are more valuable than other products.

Courtesy National Dairy Board

5.8 SUMMARY

This chapter has provided the theoretical underpinnings for demand analysis. We began with a utility function,

$$U = U(X, Y),$$

and the fact that the consumer can rank various bundles of consumption goods as to whether he or she prefers one bundle to another or is indifferent between the two. We then constructed an indifference curve showing all combinations of two commodities among which the consumer is indifferent. The collection of all indifference curves—the consumer's indifference map—tells us what the consumer is willing to purchase: consumers gain utility by consuming more of the commodities. On a more technical level, we showed that the marginal rate of substitution diminishes as more of good X is consumed and the slope of the indifference curve—the marginal rate of substitution—is equal to the ratio of the marginal utilities of the two commodities:

$$MRS = MU_X/MU_Y.$$

The consumer's budget line determines what the consumer is able to consume. The budget line is a straight line with a slope equal to the ratio of the prices of the two commodities:

$$Y = (M/P_Y) - (P_X/P_Y)X.$$

As income changes, the budget line shifts. As prices change, the budget line rotates.

The consumer will maximize utility subject to the constraint of a limited income by consuming that combination of the two commodities at which the budget line is tangent to an indifference curve. At that point, the slope of the budget line is equal to the slope of the indifference curve, so the equilibrium condition can be expressed as:

$$MU_X/MU_Y = P_X/P_Y.$$

An individual consumer's demand curve can be derived by holding income and the prices of all other commodities constant, then altering the price of one commodity and observing how the constrained utility-maximizing consumption of that commodity changes. Price changes have two effects: a substitution effect and an income effect. The substitution effect of a price change upon the consumption of that good is always negative; that is, quantity demanded varies inversely with price, holding utility constant and considering the substitution effect only. If the good is normal, the income effect reinforces the substitution effect. If the good is inferior, the income effect offsets to some extent the substitution effect.

Using indifference curves, we were able to gain some insight into the rationale for advertising. Some advertisements are designed to provide price, availability, and quality information that will lower search costs and thereby attract consumers. Other advertisements are designed to reduce the substitutability between the advertised product and other commodities. Or an advertisement may be designed to increase the consumer's perception of the value of the product and thus increase the consumer's demand for the product.

TECHNICAL PROBLEMS

1. Suppose that two units of X and eight units of Y give a consumer the same satisfaction as four units of X and two units of Y. Over this range:
   a. If the consumer obtains one more unit of X, how many units of Y must be given up in order to keep utility constant?
   b. If the consumer obtains one more unit of Y, how many units of X must be given up in order to keep utility constant?
   c. What is the marginal rate of substitution?
   d. What is the ratio of the marginal utility of X to the marginal utility of Y?

2. In the figure on the next page, suppose a consumer has the specified indifference map. The relevant budget line is *LZ*. The price of good Y is $10.
   a. What is the consumer's income?
   b. What is the price of X?
   c. Write the equation for the budget line *LZ*.
   d. What combination of X and Y will the consumer choose? Why?
   e. What is the marginal rate of substitution at this combination?
   f. Explain in terms of the *MRS* why the consumer would not choose combinations designated by A or B.
   g. Suppose the budget line pivots to *LM*, money income remaining constant. What is the new price of X? What combination of X and Y is now chosen?
   h. What is the new *MRS*?
   i. What are two points on the individual's demand curve for X?

3. Suppose that the marginal rate of substitution of X for Y is 2, the price of X is $3, and the price of Y is $1.
   a. If the consumer obtains one more unit of X, how many units of Y must be given up in order to keep utility constant?
   b. If the consumer obtains one more unit of Y, how many units of X must be given up in order to keep utility constant?
   c. What is the rate at which the consumer is willing to substitute X for Y?
   d. What is the rate at which the consumer is able to substitute X for Y?
   e. Is the consumer making the utility-maximizing choice? Why or why not? If not, what should the consumer do? Explain.

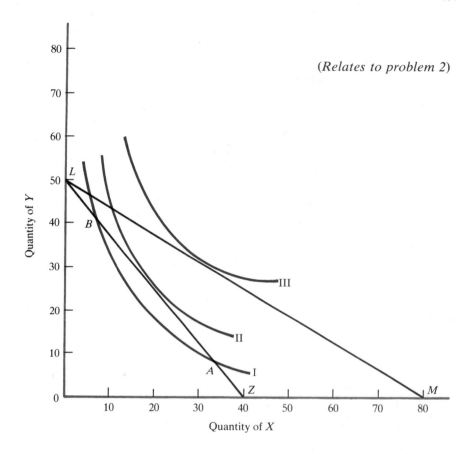

(Relates to problem 2)

4. Gigi has a limited income and consumes only wine and cheese; her current consumption choice is 4 bottles of wine and 10 pounds of cheese. The price of wine is $10 per bottle and the price of cheese is $4 per pound. The last bottle of wine added 50 units to Gigi's utility, while the last pound of cheese added 40 units.
   a. Is Gigi making the utility-maximizing choice? Why or why not?
   b. If not, what should she do instead? Why?

5. In the first figure on the following page, indifference curves I, II, and III make up a portion of an individual's indifference map. The consumer's income is $1,000; the price of Y is $20. Derive three points on the individual's demand curve for good X.

6. A person's marginal rate of substitution between X and Y is 4. The price of X is $12 and the price of Y is $3. The consumer is in equilibrium. The price of X rises to $15 and the price of Y rises to $5. Income is varied to restrict the consumer to the original level of utility. Does the person choose more X and less Y or less X and more Y? Explain.

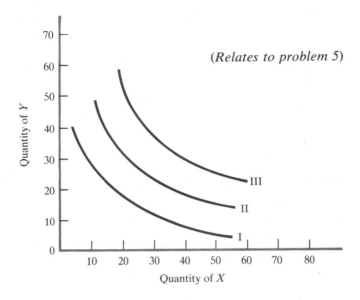

(*Relates to problem 5*)

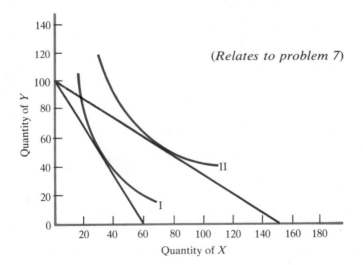

(*Relates to problem 7*)

7. The above figure contains a portion of a consumer's indifference map. Income is $600 and the price of Y is $6. The price of X rises from $4 to $10. Derive the total, the substitution, and the income effects on the consumption of good X from the price increase.

8. What would budget lines look like if consumers received a lower price for a good the more they purchased during a period? Assume that the reduction varies continuously over the range of quantities

of the good. Would the utility-maximizing equilibrium condition be substantially changed from that prevailing under fixed prices?

9. Suppose a consumer spends his or her entire income on some composite commodity (G) and purchases none of good X. What can you say about the marginal utility per dollar spent of the first unit of good X that could be purchased, relative to the marginal utility per dollar of the last unit of G purchased?

10. In our discussion of informative advertising, we noted that, if the consumer does not have complete information, he or she could spend time searching for information, but search is costly.

    Describe how a consumer could determine how much time to spend searching for price and quality information.

11. In our application on informative advertising, we noted that grocery store ads generally contain nothing more than price and availability information. Why is no quality information presented?

    For what kind of products would we be likely to find no quality information in the ad? What kind of products will require that quality information be presented?

ANALYTICAL PROBLEMS

1. Explain what types of effects firms would like their advertising to have upon the indifference curves of purchasers of the products they sell. Why would this be desired by the advertiser?

2. A retailer of video recorders advertises a large price reduction on one of the recorders it sells. How would the retailer allocate display space for the advertised recorders and the merchandise that is not marked down?

3. The wife of one of our colleagues took exception to our application about the allocation of retail shelf space. As she said, "I spend a lot of time shopping, and it's not uncommon to see brand-name products side by side with the generic goods. For example, Campbell soup is often next to the supermarket's own brand. If you guys are so smart, explain that one." We pass her question on to you: How can you explain the fact that brand-name products sometimes are shelved side by side with the generic products?

4. What methods, other than advertising, can firms use to shift consumers' indifference curves or change the marginal rates of substitution between the product they sell and substitute products?

5. Can you think of hypothetical cases in which someone would not give up a single unit of a good no matter what is offered in exchange? What type of goods would these extreme examples be?

6. Suppose a firm's manager/owner obtains utility from income (profit) and from having the firm be "socially conscious"—possibly making charitable contributions or civic expenditures. Can you set up the

problem and derive equilibrium conditions if the manager/owner wishes to obtain a specific level of utility at the lowest possible cost? Do these conditions differ from the utility-maximizing conditions?

7. Why do ads designed to increase the demand for a product tend to be placed by trade associations rather than individual firms?

APPENDIX: UTILITY MAXIMIZATION SUBJECT TO AN INCOME CONSTRAINT

In the text of this chapter, we considered the problem of maximizing utility subject to an income (budget) constraint. We provided both a graphical and a verbal description of this constrained optimization problem. For the student with a mathematical background, this problem can be solved easily using the tools of differential calculus.

The consumer maximizes utility,

$$U = U(X, Y),$$

subject to the income (budget) constraint,

$$M = P_X X + P_Y Y.$$

Thus, the Lagrangian function to be maximized is

$$\mathcal{L} = U(X, Y) + \lambda(M - P_X X - P_Y Y).$$

Maximization of this function with respect to the levels of consumption of X and Y requires that the partial derivatives be equal to zero:

$$\frac{\partial \mathcal{L}}{\partial X} = \frac{\partial U}{\partial X} - P_X = 0$$

and

$$\frac{\partial \mathcal{L}}{\partial Y} = \frac{\partial U}{\partial Y} - P_Y = 0.$$

Combining the two equations, the necessary condition for maximizing utility subject to the income constraint is

$$\frac{\partial U/\partial X}{\partial U/\partial Y} = \frac{P_X}{P_Y}.$$

Note that $\partial U/\partial X$ and $\partial U/\partial Y$ are the marginal utilities of the two goods; their ratio is the marginal rate of substitution. The ratio P_X/P_Y is the absolute value of the slope of the budget line. Hence, the necessary condition for income-constrained utility maximization is that the marginal rate of substitution between the two commodities be equal to the ratio of their prices.

6

MARKET DEMAND AND ELASTICITY

F or managerial decision making, we are normally more interested in the market demand for a product than in the demand of an individual consumer. Nonetheless, the behavior of individual consumers in the market determines market demand. Recall that in Chapter 2 we defined market demand as a list of prices and the corresponding quantities consumers are willing and able to purchase at each price in the list, holding constant money income, the prices of other goods, tastes, price expectations, and the number of consumers. When deriving individual demand in Chapter 5, we pivoted the budget line around the vertical intercept, therefore holding income and the prices of other goods constant. Since the indifference curves remained constant, tastes and price expectations were unchanged.

Thus the discussion in Chapter 5 meets all of the conditions of market demand. To obtain the market demand function we need only to aggregate the individual demand functions of all potential consumers in the market. In this chapter we will demonstrate this aggregation and analyze some of the more important characteristics of market demand curves.

6.1 AGGREGATING INDIVIDUAL DEMANDS

Suppose there are only three individuals in the market for a particular commodity. The quantities demanded by each consumer at each price in column 1 are shown in columns 2, 3, and 4 of Table 6.1. Column 5 shows the sum of these quantities demanded at each price and is therefore the

Table 6.1 Aggregating Individual Demands

| | Quantity Demanded | | | Market |
Price	Consumer 1	Consumer 2	Consumer 3	Demand
$6	3	0	0	3
5	5	1	0	6
4	8	3	1	12
3	10	5	4	19
2	12	7	6	25
1	13	10	8	31

Figure 6.1 Derivation of Market Demand

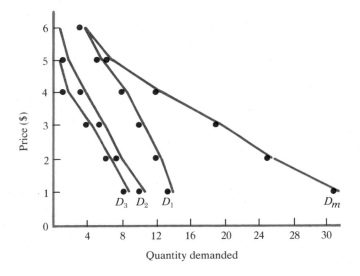

market demand. Since the demands for each consumer are negatively sloped, market demand is negatively sloped also. Quantity demanded is inversely related to price.

Figure 6.1 shows graphically how a market demand curve can be derived from the individual demand curves. The individual demands of consumers 1, 2, and 3 from Table 6.1 are shown graphically as D_1, D_2, and D_3, respectively. The market demand curve, D_m, is simply the sum of the quantities demanded at each price. At $6 consumer 1 demands 3 units. Since the others demand nothing, 3 is the quantity demanded by the market. At every other price D_m is the horizontal summation of the quantities demanded by the three consumers. And if other consumers came into the market, their demand curves would be added to D_m to obtain the new market demand. Thus we have shown the following general principle.

Principle.   The market demand curve is the horizontal summation of the demand curves of all consumers in the market. It therefore shows how much all consumers demand at each price in the relevant range of prices.

6.2 DEMAND ELASTICITY—OWN-PRICE ELASTICITY

We have emphasized that quantity demanded rises when price falls, and vice versa—the law of demand. Those who use economics in decision making are frequently interested in how total expenditure on a commodity changes when there is a movement along the demand curve. Total expenditure by the consumers (or total revenue, R, to the firm) is simply price times quantity demanded, or

$$R = P \cdot Q.$$

Remember that, along a demand curve, P and Q move in opposite directions and, consequently, have offsetting effects on R. For example, an increase in price alone would tend to increase consumer expenditure, whereas the resulting decrease in quantity would tend to decrease expenditure. Thus, the net effect of a price change on total expenditure depends upon which force dominates, the increase in price or the decrease in quantity demanded.

The price effect dominates the quantity effect if the percentage increase in price exceeds the percentage decrease in quantity demanded; in this case, total expenditure rises when price rises. Total expenditure falls, however, if the percentage increase in price is less than the percentage decrease in quantity demanded. Looking at a decrease in the price of the commodity, if the percentage decrease in price exceeds (is less than) the percentage increase in quantity demanded, total expenditure falls (rises). We see then that the overall effect of a price change on total expenditure (revenue) depends upon the relative sensitivity of quantity demanded to price along a demand curve. The measure of this relative sensitivity is called the (own-price) elasticity of demand.

This concept is of great interest to managerial decision makers. Obviously, a manager would like to know the effect of a change in price on sales revenue and what determines such an effect. For some products, a small change in price over a certain range of the demand curve results in a significant change in quantity demanded. In this case, quantity demanded is very responsive to changes in price, and the total revenue collected by the seller falls when price increases. For other products (or perhaps for the same product over a different range of the demand curve), a relatively large change in price leads to a correspondingly smaller change in quantity demanded. That is, quantity demanded is not particularly responsive to price changes.

A graph can help us see how price and quantity interact to determine the effect on total revenue of a movement along the demand curve. In Figure 6.2, suppose a firm sets a price of p_0 and therefore sells quantity

Figure 6.2   Change in Revenue from a Price Increase

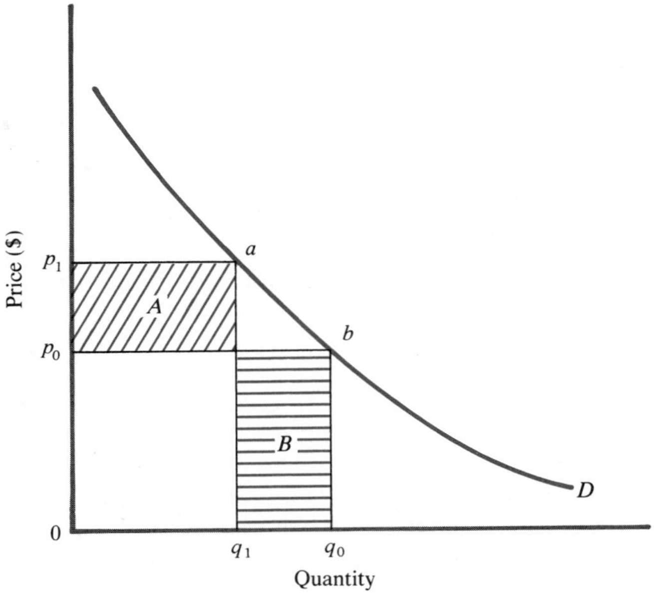

q_0. Suppose that the firm then raises price to p_1. As shown in Figure 6.2, the quantity sold falls to q_1. Before the price change, total revenue to the firm or total consumer expenditure was

$$R_0 = p_0 q_0.$$

In terms of Figure 6.2, total revenue prior to the price change is the area of the rectangle $0p_0bq_0$. After the price change, total revenue is

$$R_1 = p_1 q_1.$$

In Figure 6.2 this new total revenue is the area of the rectangle $0p_1aq_1$. The independent effect of the price increase was to increase revenue by an amount shown as rectangle A. However, the consequent reduction in sales reduced total revenue by the amount shown as rectangle B. Total revenue rises if area A is greater than area B; it falls if area A is less than area B; and it stays the same if area A equals area B.

Economists have a precise way of classifying demand according to the responsiveness of quantity demanded to a change in price and the resulting effect of the price change on total revenue (total expenditure). Demand is classified as elastic or inelastic according to the degree of responsiveness. Specifically, demand is said to be *elastic* if the percentage change in quantity demanded is greater than the percentage change in price. Since the quantity effect outweighs the price effect, total expenditure falls when

Table 6.2 Relations between Demand Elasticity and Total Revenue (*TR*)

	Elastic Demand $\|\%\Delta Q\| > \|\%\Delta P\|$	Unitary Elasticity $\|\%\Delta Q\| = \|\%\Delta P\|$	Inelastic Demand $\|\%\Delta Q\| < \|\%\Delta P\|$
Price rises	*TR* falls	No change in *TR*	*TR* rises
Price falls	*TR* rises	No change in *TR*	*TR* falls

price increases and quantity demanded decreases, and rises with a price decrease and quantity increase. Demand is *inelastic* if the percentage change in quantity demanded is less than the percentage change in price. For an inelastic demand, total expenditure rises when price rises and falls when price falls. Finally, demand is *unitary elastic* if the percentage changes in quantity demanded and price are equal. If demand is unitary elastic, total expenditure is unaffected by a change in price.

Thus the effect of a price change on total revenue depends solely upon how responsive quantity demanded is to price changes. The relations we have developed are summarized in Table 6.2, where the terms $\|\%\Delta P\|$ and $\|\%\Delta Q\|$ denote the absolute values of the percentage changes in price and quantity demanded.

Computation of Elasticity

We have thus far talked of elasticity in very general terms. It is useful, at times, to have a specific measure of relative responsiveness rather than merely speaking of demand as being elastic or inelastic. We should emphasize, however, that it is not accurate to say that a given demand curve is elastic or inelastic. In many cases, demand curves have both an inelastic and an elastic range, as well as a point or range of unitary elasticity. Thus, it is more accurate to speak of demand as being elastic or inelastic over a particular range of prices and quantities. We might wish to determine, over a certain range of prices, which of two demand curves is more elastic. For this we need a measuring device. That device is the coefficient of elasticity (*E*):

$$E = -\frac{\text{Percentage change in quantity demanded}}{\text{Percentage change in price}} = -\frac{\%\Delta Q}{\%\Delta P}.$$

Note that, since price and quantity demanded are inversely related, the negative sign makes *E* a positive number. The percentage change in any variable can be expressed as the change in the variable divided by the value of the variable, so we can rewrite the coefficient of elasticity as[1]

---

[1]We can also express the coefficient of elasticity at a point on the demand curve as $E = -(dQ/Q)/(dP/P)$.

$$E = -\frac{\Delta Q/Q}{\Delta P/P}$$

or

$$E = -\frac{\Delta Q}{\Delta P} \cdot \frac{P}{Q}.$$

From the formula, we see that the relative responsiveness of quantity demanded to changes in price (which we summarized in Table 6.2) is reflected precisely in the ratio of the proportional change in quantity demanded to the proportional change in price. That is, if E is less than one, demand is inelastic, since $|\%\Delta Q| < |\%\Delta P|$. Likewise, if E is greater than one, demand is elastic, since $|\%\Delta Q| > |\%\Delta P|$. If E is equal to one, demand has unitary elasticity, since $|\%\Delta Q| = |\%\Delta P|$.

Returning to Figure 6.2 you can see that, for a price increase, if total revenue goes up, demand is inelastic. If total revenue rises, then in Figure 6.2 area $A >$ area B. We can rewrite this inequality as

$$q_1 \cdot (p_1 - p_0) > p_0 \cdot (q_0 - q_1),$$

or, using the Δ sign again, as

$$|q_1\Delta p| > |p_0\Delta q|.$$

Dividing both sides by $|q_1\Delta p|$ gives

$$1 > \left|\frac{\Delta q}{\Delta p} \cdot \frac{p_0}{q_1}\right|.$$

As you can verify, the absolute value of $(\Delta q/\Delta p) \cdot (p_0/q_1)$ is the elasticity coefficient for a price change from p_0 to p_1. This means that

$$E < 1.$$

Hence, if total revenue rises when price increases, the measured elasticity of demand must be less than one.

If total revenue goes down when price is increased, we reverse the inequality: area $A <$ area B. Again rewriting

$$|q_1\Delta p| < |p_0 \Delta q|$$

and, dividing by $|q_1\Delta p|$,

$$1 < \left|\frac{\Delta q}{\Delta p} \cdot \frac{p_0}{q_1}\right|.$$

Using our definition of the elasticity coefficient,

$$E > 1.$$

So, if total revenue decreases when price increases, the measured elasticity of demand must be greater than one. Using the same type of analysis, it is easy to show that if a price increase has no effect on total revenue

Table 6.3 Calculating Elasticity

Price	Quantity Demanded	Total Revenue	Elasticity
$1.00	100,000	$100,000	
			>——ELASTIC
0.50	300,000	150,000	
			>——UNITARY
0.25	600,000	150,000	
			>——INELASTIC
0.10	1,000,000	100,000	

(i.e., area A = area B), the measured elasticity of demand must be equal to one.

The process of deriving the coefficient of elasticity between two price-quantity combinations involves a simple computation. The only problem encountered is how to select the proper base. Consider the hypothetical demand schedule given in Table 6.3. From the change in total revenue, we know that demand is elastic for a price change between $1.00 and $0.50. Indeed, if in our elasticity formula, we used $1.00 for the base price (P) and 100,000 for our base quantity (Q), the calculated elasticity is 4. But, if we use $0.50 as P and 300,000 as Q, we get $E = \frac{2}{3}$—demand appears to be inelastic.

The difficulty lies in the fact that elasticity has been computed over a wide range of the demand curve but evaluated at a specific point. Therefore, we get a much better approximation of elasticity between two points on a demand curve by using the average values of price and quantity demanded between the two points. That is, for large changes such as this, we should compute elasticity using the "arc formula." Arc elasticity, $\bar{E}$, is

$$\bar{E} = -\frac{\%\Delta Q}{\%\Delta P} = -\frac{(Q_1 - Q_0)}{(Q_1 + Q_0)/2} \Big/ \frac{(P_1 - P_0)}{(P_1 + P_0)/2}$$

$$= -\frac{(Q_1 - Q_0)}{(Q_1 + Q_0)} \Big/ \frac{(P_1 - P_0)}{(P_1 + P_0)},$$

where subscripts 0 and 1 refer, respectively, to the initial and the new prices and quantities demanded.

Using this formula for the first two points on the demand schedule in Table 6.3, we obtain

$$\bar{E} = -\frac{(100,000 - 300,000) \ / \ (100,000 + 300,000)}{(\$1 - \$0.50) \ / \ (\$1 + \$0.50)} = \frac{3}{2},$$

for either a price increase from $0.50 to $1.00 or a price decrease from $1.00 to $0.50. Using the same formula we can calculate that between $0.50 and $0.25, $\bar{E} = 1$, and between $0.25 and $0.10, $\bar{E} = \frac{7}{12}$.

Principle.   Demand is said to be elastic, unitary elastic, or inelastic according to the value of E. If E > 1, demand is elastic; a given percentage change in price results in a greater percentage change in quantity demanded. When E = 1, demand has unitary elasticity, meaning that the percentage changes in price and quantity demanded are precisely the same. Finally, if E < 1, demand is inelastic; a given percentage change in price results in a smaller percentage change in quantity demanded.

APPLICATION

Texas Calculates Elasticity

In addition to its regular license plates, the state of Texas, as do other states, sells personalized or "vanity" license plates. To raise additional revenue, the state will sell a vehicle owner a license plate saying whatever the owner wants as long as it uses six letters (or numbers), no one else has the same license as the one requested, and it isn't obscene. For this service, the state charges a higher price than the price for standard licenses. Many people are willing to pay this higher price rather than display a license of the standard form such as 387 BRC.

For example, an ophthalmologist announces his practice with the license MYOPIA. Others tell their personalities with COZY-1 and ALL MAN. A rabid Star Trek fan has BM ME UP.

In 1986, Texas increased the price for such plates from $25 to $75. The *Houston Post,* October 19, 1986, reported that before the price increase, about 150,000 cars in Texas had personalized licenses. After the increase in price, only 60,000 people ordered the vanity plates. As it turned out, demand was rather inelastic over this range. As you can calculate, the own-price elasticity is .86. Thus revenue rose after the price increase, from $3,750,000 to $4,500,000.

But the *Post* article quoted the assistant director of the Texas Division of Motor Vehicles as saying, "Since the demand dropped,* the state didn't make money from the higher fees, so the price for next year's personalized plates will be $40." If the objective of the state is to make money from these licenses and if the numbers in the article are correct, this is the wrong thing to do. It's hard to see how the state lost money by increasing the price from $25 to $75—the revenue increased and the cost of producing plates must have decreased since fewer were produced. So the move from $25 to $75 was the right move.

---

*It was, of course, quantity demanded that decreased, not demand.

Moreover, let's suppose that the elasticity between $75 and $40 is essentially the same as that calculated for the movement from $25 to $75—.86. We can use this estimate to calculate what will happen to revenue if the state drops the price to $40. We must first find what the new quantity demanded will be at $40. Using the arc elasticity formula and our elasticity of .86,

$$\bar{E} = -\frac{\%\Delta Q}{\%\Delta P} = \frac{-(60,000 - Q) / (60,000 + Q)}{(75 - 40) / (75 + 40)} = .86,$$

where Q is the new quantity demanded. Solving this equation for Q, we find that the estimated sales are 102,000 (rounded) at a price of $40. With this quantity demanded and price, total revenue would be $4,080,000 representing a decrease of $420,000 from the revenue at $75 a plate. If the state's objective is to raise revenue by selling vanity plates, it should increase rather than decrease price.

This application actually makes two points. First, even decision makers in organizations that are not run for profit, like government agencies, should be able to use economic analysis. Second, managers whose firms are in business to make a profit should make an effort to know (or at least have a good approximation for) the elasticity of demand for the products they sell. Only with this information will they know what price to charge.

Source: This application is based upon "A License for Vanity," Barbara Boughton, *Houston Post*, October 19, 1986, pp. 1G, 10G.

Factors Affecting Elasticity

To this point in our discussion we have described the importance of price elasticity and have demonstrated a methodology for measuring price elasticity for a specific demand function. We now turn to an examination of the factors that affect the price elasticity of demand. We will indicate those characteristics of a commodity that make it more or less elastic, and demonstrate how, even in the absence of direct measures of price elasticity, a manager would be able to obtain a subjective estimate of the price elasticity of a particular commodity based upon the characteristics of that commodity. As was the case with the determinants of demand, there may well be a large number of characteristics that affect the price elasticity of demand for a commodity. In this discussion we limit our attention to those factors that appear to be most significant: (1) the number and availability of substitute commodities, (2) the expenditure on the commodity in relation to the consumer's budget, (3) the durability of the product, and (4) the length of the time period under consideration.

Of these factors, the number and availability of substitute commodities is the most significant determinant of the price elasticity of demand. The more and better the substitutes for a specific good, the greater its price elasticity will be at a given set of prices. Goods with few and poor substitutes—wheat and salt, for example—will tend to have low price elasticities. Goods with many substitutes—wool, for which cotton and synthetic fibers may be substituted, for instance—will have higher elasticities.

Of course, the definition of a good greatly affects the number of substitutes and thus its elasticity of demand. For example, if all of the gasoline stations in a city raised the price of gasoline by 10 cents per gallon, total sales of gasoline would undoubtedly fall—but probably not by much. If, on the other hand, only the Gulf stations raised price by 10 cents, the sale of Gulf gasoline would probably fall substantially. There are many good substitutes for Gulf gasoline at the lower price, but there are not as many substitutes for gasoline in general. Moreover, if only one service station raised its price, that station's sales would be expected to fall almost to zero in the long run. The availability of so many easily accessible substitutes would encourage most customers to trade elsewhere, since the cost of finding a substitute service station is so small.

The percentage of the consumer's budget that is spent on the commodity is also important in the determination of price elasticity. All other things equal, we would expect the price elasticity to be directly related to the percentage of consumers' budgets spent on the good. For example, we expect the demand for refrigerators to be more price elastic than the demand for toasters, since the expenditure required to purchase a refrigerator would make up a larger percentage of the budget of a "typical" consumer. Note that we are not saying that price elasticity is determined by the price of the good. Rather, price elasticity is influenced by the relation between total expenditure on the good and the budget of potential consumers of the commodity.

Next, all other things equal, durable goods tend to be more price elastic than nondurable commodities. This relation results simply from the fact that the purchase of a durable good may be postponed. If the price of a durable commodity rises, quantity demanded would be expected to fall by a larger percentage than would be the case for nondurables because potential buyers have the option of "making do" with their existing durables. Returning to our earlier example, the demand for refrigerators would be more elastic than that for toasters since the refrigerator is more durable. The consumer can make do with the old refrigerator longer while searching for the lowest price.

Finally, the length of the time period under consideration affects the price elasticity of demand. In general, the longer the time period, the more elastic is demand. This relation is the result of consumers having more time to adapt to the price change. Excellent examples of the effect of time on demand elasticity are found in the demands for commodities such as gasoline or natural gas. The demand for such commodities is referred to as a "derived demand." That is, consumers do not desire gasoline per se, rather, they desire the services of automobiles or other machines that use gasoline. Hence, for consumers to adjust to changes in the price of gasoline, it is necessary for them to adjust their usage and stock of those machines that use gasoline. In the short run, an increase in the price of gasoline reduces quantity demanded, but this reduction is limited by the fact that consumers still own their original stock of gasoline-using machinery. Given a longer period of adjustment, consumers can alter their stock of gasoline-using equipment (for example, by switching to smaller automobiles). The response to the increased price of gasoline would then be more pronounced. Given a still longer period, it is possible that manufacturers will develop machinery that requires less gasoline and the reduction in quantity demanded would become even more significant. The point is that, given a longer time period to adjust, the demand for the commodity exhibits more responsiveness to changes in price—the demand curve is more elastic. Of course, we can treat the effect of time within the framework of the effect of available substitutes on elasticity. The greater the time period available for consumer adjustment, the more substitutes become available and economically feasible. As we stressed above, the more available are substitutes, the more elastic is demand.

APPLICATION

Time and the Demand for Petroleum

As you are aware, the United States and most of the world experienced tremendous fluctuations in oil prices from 1973 through 1986. The price of petroleum at the wellhead rose from about $5 a barrel in the early 1970s to almost $40 in 1981. Price then fell to between $12 and $15 in 1986. Consequently, the prices of gasoline and heating oil first increased dramatically then fell even more rapidly over this period. The adaptation to changing energy prices over this period provides an excellent example of the effect of time on elasticity of demand.

After the Arabian oil embargo in 1973–74, most people were predicting disastrous consequences because of the supposed inability, or unwillingness, of consumers to cut back on the amount of oil they were consuming. In other words, the experts thought the demand for gasoline and heating oil was extremely inelastic. As it turned out, they were right in the short run but wrong in the long run.

Shortly after 1973, the price of oil tripled. The fact that people did not immediately cut back on consumption led to dismal predictions based upon an inelastic demand for oil. Experts were saying that Americans were just naturally wasteful. But this prediction turned out to be wrong. Americans did decrease their consumption of oil—

substantially. We adapted to the higher prices, but the adaptation took time.

Consider the time that was required to adjust to the higher price of heating oil. When the price went up, people added some insulation to their attics, but they did not immediately hire someone to rip out and reinsulate the walls. This costs a considerable amount of money, so many people simply paid the higher heating bills in order to save the expense of reinsulation. Of course, they did keep their homes a little cooler in winter and a little warmer in the summer, both of which helped conserve some energy. But the new homes that were built were becoming much more energy efficient. And, as people realized that the higher energy prices were likely to be around for a long time, many did reinsulate their homes. Likewise, when the price of energy first increased, most people did not immediately replace their home appliances with more energy efficient appliances. But the appliances that were installed in new homes were more energy saving. And when people had to replace their old appliances, the ones they purchased were usually more energy efficient. This substitution helped decrease the consumption of energy over time.

The same thing was happening in the market for gasoline. Again, when the price of gasoline tripled, people didn't immediately replace their "gas-guzzlers" with economy cars. But when it became time to trade, they frequently opted for smaller, more fuel efficient automobiles. The owners of the largest cars generally didn't trade for the smallest compacts. But there was a general movement downward in size. The overall effect was a gradual decrease in automobile size, and a resulting increase in gasoline mileage. From 1973 to 1983 the average fuel efficiency of automobiles increased 18 percent. In addition, driving habits changed. Encouraged in part by lower speed limits and in part by the higher price of gasoline, people began driving more slowly, and consequently decreased their gasoline consumption.

So, the overall result was a decline in the amount of oil consumed. The United States reduced its dependence on imported oil from 50 percent of the total consumed to 30 percent. And together with the increased production of domestic oil, the decrease in oil consumption significantly reduced the power of the OPEC nations.

With the decline of OPEC's power in the 1980s, the price of oil decreased substantially. The price fell from a high of $40 in 1981 to between $12 and $15 in 1986. Just as demand was relatively inelastic in the short run as the price rose, it has been quite inelastic during the short period of rapidly declining prices. Gasoline consumption remained relatively constant over this period. People didn't immediately replace their fuel efficient cars with gas-guzzlers. Nor did they begin shifting their purchases to fuel wasting appliances. Many were not convinced the prices would remain low. But, just as demand became much more elastic in the long run as people adapted to much higher energy prices, so will it become more elastic as people change their energy-using habits and adapt to low oil prices.

The point is that the price-induced decrease in consumption took time. The adaptation did not come overnight. It was practically impossible and certainly not economically feasible to adapt immediately to the change in relative prices. While the demand for energy was relatively inelastic at first, given a sufficient period of time, demand became much more elastic.

6.3 OTHER ELASTICITIES

In addition to own-price elasticity, we should note two other elasticities that are used in economic analysis: income elasticity and cross-price elasticity. Recall that when we derived the demand schedule we held constant the consumer's money income and the prices of other goods. Consequently, these are held constant when deriving market demand curves and evaluating the own-price elasticity of demand. But sometimes economists and business decision makers are interested in the effect of changes in one of these variables on quantity (sales) when the price of the good itself remains constant.

Let's first consider income elasticity, defined as follows:

Definition. Income elasticity measures the relative responsiveness of quantity purchased when income changes, holding the price of the good and the prices of other goods constant. It is, therefore, the percentage change in quantity purchased in response to a given percentage change in income.

We can express the preceding definition as

$$E_M = \frac{\%\Delta Q}{\%\Delta M} = \frac{\Delta Q/Q}{\Delta M/M} = \frac{\Delta Q}{\Delta M} \cdot \frac{M}{Q},$$

where E_M is income elasticity and M is income. (For market demand, per capita income is normally used.) Note that the sign of E_M depends upon the sign of $\Delta Q/\Delta M$, which may be positive (if the good is normal), negative (if the good is inferior), or zero. Thus, if the good is normal (inferior), the income elasticity is positive (negative).

The cross-price elasticity of a good is defined as follows:

Definition. Cross-price elasticity measures the relative responsiveness of the quantity purchased of one good when the price of another good changes, holding the price of the good and money income constant. It is, therefore, the percentage change in quantity purchased in response to a given percentage change in the price of another good.

We can express the cross-price elasticity between the good in question, X, and another good, Y, as

$$E_{XY} = \frac{\%\Delta Q_X}{\%\Delta P_Y} = \frac{\Delta Q_X/Q_X}{\Delta P_Y/P_Y} = \frac{\Delta Q_X}{\Delta P_Y} \cdot \frac{P_Y}{Q_X},$$

where Q_X is the amount of commodity X consumed and P_Y is the price of good Y. The sign of E_{XY} depends upon the sign of $\Delta Q_X/\Delta P_Y$, which can be positive or negative. Recall from Chapter 2 that if an increase in the price of one good causes the quantity purchased of another good to increase, we say the goods are substitutes (i.e., $\Delta Q_X/\Delta P_Y > 0$). If the rise in the price of one good causes the quantity purchased of another good to fall, the goods are complements (i.e., $\Delta Q_X/\Delta P_Y < 0$). If there is no change in the quantity purchased of the other good, the two goods are independent (i.e., $\Delta Q_X/\Delta P_Y = 0$). Thus, E_{XY} is positive (negative) when X and Y are substitutes (complements).[2]

We should note that when calculating income and cross-price elasticities for discrete changes, we would use the averaging or arc elasticity formula similar to the one set forth for own-price elasticity. Thus in the above formulas,

$$\%\Delta Q = \frac{Q_1 - Q_0}{(Q_1 + Q_0)/2}, \quad \%\Delta M = \frac{M_1 - M_0}{(M_1 + M_0)/2},$$

$$\%\Delta Q_X = \frac{Q_{X_1} - Q_{X_0}}{(Q_{X_1} + Q_{X_0})/2}, \quad \%\Delta P_Y = \frac{P_{Y_1} - P_{Y_0}}{(P_{Y_1} + P_{Y_0})/2},$$

where subscripts 0 and 1 refer, respectively, to the initial and new values of the variables. This solves the problem of which value to use as a base.

And finally, we should point out that when calculating an elasticity (own-price, income, or cross-price), the values of all other variables that affect quantity demanded must be held constant. Otherwise, the effect of changes in not just one, but two or more variables would be captured in the elasticity coefficient.

6.4. MARGINAL REVENUE AND ELASTICITY

Closely related to the own-price elasticity is the concept of marginal revenue, a concept which becomes quite important when we begin to analyze the production and pricing decisions of firms under various market structures. We begin with a definition:

---

[2]Note that, because of the possibility of different income effects, the cross-price elasticity of X for Y need not equal the cross-price elasticity of Y for X.

Table 6.4 Demand and Marginal Revenue

(1) Unit Sales	(2) Price	(3) Total Revenue	(4) Marginal Revenue
1	$4.00	$ 4.00	$ 4.00
2	3.50	7.00	3.00
3	3.10	9.30	2.30
4	2.80	11.20	1.90
5	2.40	12.00	0.80
6	2.00	12.00	0.00
7	1.50	10.50	-1.50

Definition. Marginal revenue is the addition to total revenue attributable to one additional unit of output (per period of time),

$$MR = \Delta TR / \Delta Q.$$

Thus marginal revenue must be related to the way price and output change along a demand curve. To show the relation between marginal revenue and price, let's first use a numerical example. The demand schedule for a product is presented in columns 1 and 2 of Table 6.4. Price times quantity gives the total revenue obtainable from each level of sales, shown in column 3.

Marginal revenue, shown in column 4, indicates the change in total revenue from an additional unit of sales. Note that marginal revenue equals price only for the first unit sold. At zero sales, total revenue is zero; for the first unit sold total revenue is the demand price for one unit. Thus the change in total revenue is the same as price. However, since price must fall in order to sell additional units, marginal revenue must be less than price at every other level of sales (output).

As shown in column 4, marginal revenue declines for each additional unit sold. Notice that it is positive for each unit 1 through 5. However, marginal revenue is zero for the sixth unit sold, and marginal revenue becomes negative thereafter. That is, the seventh unit sold actually causes total revenue to decline.

Relation. Marginal revenue must be less than price for all units sold after the first, because the price must be lowered in order to sell more units. When marginal revenue is positive, total revenue increases when quantity increases. When marginal revenue is negative, total revenue decreases when quantity increases.

Figure 6.3 **Demand, Marginal Revenue, and Total Revenue**

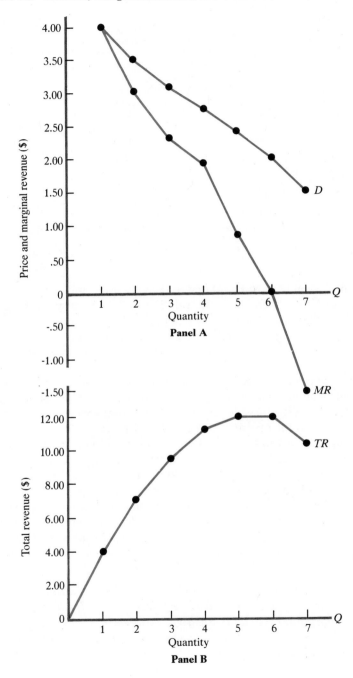

Figure 6.4 **Demand, Marginal Revenue, and Elasticity**

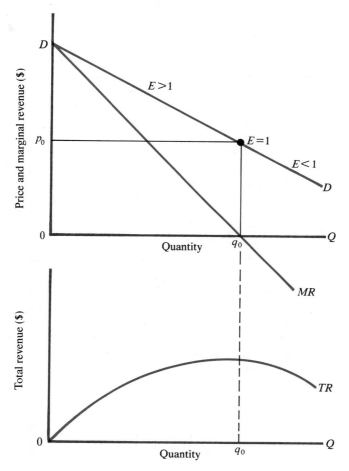

Figure 6.3 shows graphically the relations among demand, marginal revenue, and total revenue for the demand schedule in Table 6.4. As noted above, *MR* is below price (in Panel A) at every level of output except the first. When total revenue (in Panel B) begins to decrease, marginal revenue becomes negative. Since demand is negatively sloped, marginal revenue is negatively sloped also.

Figure 6.4 shows these relations for a general linear demand curve when output, and hence price and revenue, are continuous. In this figure, as is the case for all continuous linear demand curves, marginal revenue lies exactly halfway between demand and the vertical axis. Thus the *MR* curve must be twice as steep as the demand curve.[3]

---

[3]We show this relation mathematically in the appendix to this chapter.

Using Figure 6.4, we can examine the relation of own-price elasticity to demand and marginal revenue. Recall that if total revenue increases when price falls and quantity rises, demand is elastic; if total revenue decreases when price falls and quantity rises, demand is inelastic. When marginal revenue is positive, from a quantity of zero until q_0, total revenue increases as price declines; thus demand is elastic over this range. Conversely, when marginal revenue is negative, at quantities greater than q_0, total revenue declines when price falls; thus demand must be inelastic over this range. Finally, if marginal revenue is zero, at q_0, total revenue does not change when quantity changes, so the elasticity of demand is unitary at q_0.

Except for marginal revenue lying exactly halfway between demand and the vertical axis, all of the above relations hold for nonlinear demands. Thus for all demand curves the following relation must hold.

Relation. Marginal revenue is less than price at every level of output after the first unit. When MR *is positive (negative), total revenue increases (decreases) as quantity increases, and demand is elastic (inelastic). When* MR *is zero, the elasticity of demand is unitary.*

The relation between marginal revenue and price at any quantity can be expressed still more precisely. Suppose that at price p_0, quantity demanded is q_0. In order to sell an additional unit, price must fall from p_0 to p_1. That is, as price falls from p_0 to p_1, quantity increases from q_0 to $q_0 + 1$. Since the price has been decreased, the revenue generated by the original level of sales must fall. The decline in total revenue due to the decrease in price is

$$(p_1 - p_0)q_0 = (\Delta p)q_0.$$

But this decline is to a greater or lesser extent offset by the revenue generated by the additional unit sold at price p_1. This increase is $p_1 \times 1$, or p_1. Combining the two changes in revenue resulting from the price change, marginal revenue—the change in total revenue—is therefore

$$MR = p_1 + \Delta p \cdot q_0,$$

where Δp is negative.

Since $\Delta q = 1$, we can divide Δp by Δq with no change in the value of the expression,

$$MR = p_1 + \frac{\Delta p}{\Delta q}q_0.$$

Now, let's factor p_1 out of the right-hand side of this equation,

$$MR = p_1\left(1 + \frac{\Delta p}{\Delta q} \cdot \frac{q_0}{p_1}\right),$$

and rewrite this equation as

$$MR = p_1 \left[1 - \frac{1}{\left(-\dfrac{\Delta q}{\Delta p} \cdot \dfrac{p_1}{q_0} \right)} \right]$$

At this point you should see what we have been moving toward. The expression

$$-\frac{\Delta q}{\Delta p} \cdot \frac{p_1}{q_0}$$

is a very close approximation to the own-price elasticity of demand. Hence, we can rewrite our equation as

$$MR = p_1 \left(1 - \frac{1}{E} \right),$$

or, as long as $p_0 - p_1$ is small,

$$MR = p \left(1 - \frac{1}{E} \right),$$

where E is the own-price elasticity of demand.[4] From this equation it is apparent that when marginal revenue is negative, demand is inelastic ($E < 1$). When marginal revenue is positive, demand is elastic ($E > 1$). Finally, when marginal revenue is zero, demand has unitary elasticity.

6.5 SUMMARY

Market demand is simply the aggregation of the demands of all individual consumers in the market. Specifically, the market demand function is the horizontal summation of all the individual demand functions. Since the demands of individual consumers are downward sloping, the market demand function must be downward sloping.

Demand elasticity—the own-price elasticity of demand—is the percentage change in quantity demanded in response to a given percentage change in price. Demand elasticity is said to be unitary ($E = 1$) when the two percentage changes are equal. Demand is elastic (inelastic) when the percentage change in quantity demanded is greater (less) than the percentage change in price. If demand is elastic (inelastic) over a range of output, an increase in price and the resulting decrease in quantity demanded cause total revenue (total expenditure on the good by consumers) to fall (rise). A decrease in price causes total revenue to rise (fall) if demand is elastic (inelastic). Several factors affect the own-price elasticity of demand. The most important of these factors is the availability of good

---

[4]This relation is derived mathematically in the appendix to this chapter.

substitutes. The better and more numerous are its substitutes, the more elastic is the demand for a good.

Two other elasticities are income elasticity, measuring the relative responsiveness of quantity purchased to changes in income, and cross-price elasticity, measuring the relative responsiveness of the quantity purchased of one good to changes in the price of another good. These elasticities can be positive or negative. In the case of income elasticity, the elasticity measure is positive (negative) if the good is normal (inferior). In the case of cross-price elasticity, the elasticity measure is positive (negative) if the two goods are substitutes (complements).

Marginal revenue is the change in total revenue resulting from an additional unit of output. Marginal revenue declines as output increases and is less than price for every quantity except the first unit, in which case *MR* equals price. Marginal revenue can be expressed as

$$MR = p\left(1 - \frac{1}{E}\right),$$

where *E* is the own-price elasticity of demand. Hence, if demand is elastic (inelastic), marginal revenue is positive (negative). If demand is unitary elastic, marginal revenue is equal to zero.

TECHNICAL PROBLEMS

1. Your firm supplies output to a market in which there are only five buyers. The demand for each buyer is shown in the following table. Derive and graph the market demand.

Price	Quantity Demanded by				
	Buyer 1	**Buyer 2**	**Buyer 3**	**Buyer 4**	**Buyer 5**
$500	20	0	0	4	6
400	25	5	0	6	24
300	32	8	8	10	32
200	40	14	16	20	40
100	50	22	38	32	48

2. If the quantity of video cassette recorders (VCRs) demanded decreases 8 percent when price increases 10 percent, what is the own-price elasticity of demand?

   a. Given the own-price elasticity of demand calculated above, what would happen to quantity demanded if price now decreases 4 percent?

   b. Based on the above own-price elasticity of demand, what must have happened to price if quantity demanded increases 6 percent?

3. Assume that the demand for plastic surgery is price inelastic. Are the following statements true or false?
   a. When the price of plastic surgery increases, the number of operations decreases.
   b. The percentage change in the price of plastic surgery is less than the percentage change in quantity demanded.
   c. Changes in the price of plastic surgery do not affect the number of operations.
   d. Quantity demanded is quite responsive to changes in price.
   e. If more plastic surgery is performed, expenditures on plastic surgery will decrease.
   f. The marginal revenue of another operation is negative.

4. How would the following events affect the own-price elasticity of demand for good X?
   a. A new good, Y, is introduced. Good Y can often be used in place of X.
   b. Higher unemployment reduces consumer incomes and increases the share of expenditures on X.
   c. The cost of producing X decreases.
   d. Laboratory studies show that the expected life span of X has decreased.
   e. A new, improved version of X is introduced.

5. Suppose that government sales of wheat to foreign buyers reduce the amount of wheat available for U.S. consumers.
   a. What will happen to the domestic price of wheat?
   b. What will happen to the amount spent on wheat by U.S. consumers? What additional information must you have?

6. Use the information in the following table and the arc formula to calculate the own-price, income, and cross-price elasticities of demand. (Recall that each elasticity is calculated holding all other variables constant.)

Price of X	Quantity Demanded of X	Income ($1,000)	Price of Related Good Y
$20	200	$25	$4
20	300	25	8
20	280	23	4
10	400	25	4

   a. Is demand elastic or inelastic?
   b. Is X a normal or an inferior good?
   c. Are X and Y substitutes or complements?

d. If the price of X increases 5 percent, what will happen to the quantity of X demanded? What will happen to total expenditure on X?

e. If income increases 10 percent, what will happen to the quantity of X demanded?

f. If the price of Y decreases 20 percent, what will happen to the quantity of X demanded?

7. Using the following demand schedule, calculate total revenue, marginal revenue, and own-price elasticity of demand. Then show the relation among marginal revenue, price, and elasticity of demand.

Price	Quantity Demanded	Total Revenue	Marginal Revenue	Elasticity of Demand
$60	8			
50	16			
40	24			
30	32			
20	40			
10	48			

8. "I earn $20 a day and spend it all on beer, no matter what the price of beer is." What is this person's elasticity of demand for beer?

9. Seltzer Company sells spring water at a desert oasis; its costs are virtually zero. Seltzer knows that its demand function is $Q = 25 - (\frac{3}{2})P$. Presently it charges a price of $2. Seltzer wishes to increase its profits. Do you recommend a price change? If so what price would you suggest?

ANALYTICAL PROBLEMS

1. Suppose that a quota on imported steel substantially increases the price of steel in the United States. The higher price is expected to last a long time. Discuss the effect of time on the elasticity of demand for steel.

2. It has often been argued that the demand for agricultural products is (own) price inelastic. Given that farmers want to increase their incomes, what policies should they try to implement? How could they enforce these policies? What problems might be involved?

3. Consider the demand for automobiles. Would you expect it to be relatively elastic or inelastic? What characteristics of this commodity lead to your assertions?

4. Analyze the effect of time on the elasticity of demand for the following goods:
   a. Milk.
   b. Refrigerators.
   c. Textbooks.
   d. Personal computers.
   e. Electricity.
   f. Football tickets.

5. The city of Metro recently attracted several new manufacturing plants. As a result Metro is beginning to experience an economic boom. Which businesses would you expect to benefit from the boom? Which would you expect to be hurt?

6. You are assistant to the president of a large state university. The university, faced with declining enrollment, is considering a large decrease in tuition. You are asked to forecast the effect. What factors would you have to consider? Explain.

7. Assume that the owner of an appliance store decides to undertake a large advertising campaign. Should the owner cut prices during the campaign or advertise at the "regular" prices? What factors would you need to consider?

8. In the application on personalized license plates in Texas, we assumed that the elasticity of demand is constant at .86 between any two prices along the demand curve. Using the numbers in the application, suppose that demand is actually a straight line when price is between $25 and $75. What would quantity demanded be at a price of $40? What would be the elasticity if price is reduced from $75 to $40? What would happen to revenues?

APPENDIX

1. For a straight line demand, marginal revenue is twice as steep and has the same vertical intercept as demand. A general straight line demand has the form

   $$P = a + bQ, \text{ where } a > 0, b < 0.$$

   Total revenue is therefore

   $$TR = P \cdot Q = (a + bQ) Q = aQ + bQ^2.$$

   Marginal revenue is

   $$\frac{dTR}{dQ} = a + 2bQ.$$

   In absolute value, the slope of *MR*, $2b$, is twice as great as the slope of demand, b. Both curves have the same vertical intercept, a.

2. Relations among own-price elasticity, price, and marginal revenue.

$$TR = P \cdot Q.$$

Thus,

$$MR = \frac{dTR}{dQ} = P + \frac{dP}{dQ} Q.$$

Factoring out P,

$$MR = P\left(1 + \frac{dP}{dQ} \frac{Q}{P}\right).$$

Since

$$E = -\frac{dQ}{dP} \frac{P}{Q},$$

$$MR = P\left(1 - \frac{1}{E}\right).$$

7

EMPIRICAL DEMAND FUNCTIONS

W̄ e have looked at demand from a theoretical perspective in previous chapters. In Chapter 2 we presented an overview of demand theory. Chapter 5 examined an individual consumer's demand function, using the theory of consumer behavior. Then, in Chapter 6, we described the market demand function and the important concept of demand elasticities.

However, we have not yet discussed how demand functions can be estimated or how managers can interpret and use the resulting estimations. From the discussion in the earlier chapters, it should be clear how important knowledge about the demand function is to a manager. In planning and in making policy decisions, managers must have some idea about the characteristics of the demand for their product in order to attain the objectives of the firm or even to enable the firm to survive. In this chapter, we will show you some of the methods used in the estimation and interpretation of demand functions.

We begin with a description of some of the more direct methods of demand estimation—consumer interviews and market studies. We deal rather briefly with these methods, attempting only to point out the strengths and weaknesses in each. The primary topic of the chapter is the use of regression analysis to estimate demand functions. As always, our fundamental concern is with how an analyst can use regression analysis and interpret the results, rather than with the precise statistical concepts underlying the estimation. To this end, we will provide some examples to show how actual demand functions have been estimated and interpreted.

7.1 DIRECT METHODS OF DEMAND ESTIMATION

Consumer Interviews

Since consumers themselves should be most knowledgeable about their individual demand functions for particular commodities, the most straight-forward method of demand estimation would be simply to ask potential buyers how much of the commodity they would buy at different prices with alternative values for the determinants of demand (i.e., the price of substitute commodities, the price of complement commodities, and so on). At the simplest level, this might be accomplished by stopping shop-pers and asking them how much of the product they would buy at various prices. At a more sophisticated level, this procedure would entail admin-istering detailed questionnaires to a selected sample of the population by professional interviewers. While this procedure appears very simple, there exist several substantial problems. Among these problems are (1) the selection of a representative sample, (2) response bias, and (3) the inability of the respondent to answer accurately. Let's look at each of these prob-lems briefly.

If the results of a survey accomplished by using a sample of the pop-ulation are to be reliable, *the sample must be representative* of the total population. More specifically, the sample should be random. In actuality, it is very difficult to obtain a truly random sample. A classic illustration of what can happen if the sample is not random occurred during the presidential campaign of 1948. A survey was performed that predicted an overwhelming victory for Dewey. In fact Truman won the election. The problem with this survey was that the sample was drawn from the sub-scription list of a particular magazine. The subscribers were not repre-sentative of the entire population of the United States; they were instead a subgroup of the voting population having several important character-istics in common. Thus, the biased sample led to biased results.

A *bias in response* can result simply from the fact that those interviewed are giving hypothetical answers to hypothetical questions. The answers do not necessarily reflect what the individual will do, rather, they may reflect intentions or desires. More importantly, however, the responses may be biased by the manner in which the question is asked. In many cases, the questions may be such that the respondents give what they view as a more socially acceptable response rather than reveal their true preferences.

One example of response bias is found in a survey by an automobile manufacturer taken many years ago—during the time of cheap gasoline. The potential consumers were asked if they would be interested in buying small economical cars (i.e., fuel-efficient) which were not flashy, fast, or showy. A large number of people said they would indeed buy such a car. On the basis of this survey, the manufacturer introduced a small, fuel-efficient car—with disastrous results. Perhaps had the respondents—who indicated that they wanted economy cars—been asked whether their *neighbors* would buy such cars they might have provided more valid responses. It's easier to say that your neighbor wants a flashy car than to admit that you do. The point is that the wrong question was asked. The way the question was asked induced a response bias. As you might expect, it takes an expert to design a questionnaire that avoids such bias.

Finally, it is quite possible that the respondent is simply *unable to answer accurately the question posed.* Conceptually, the firm performing the survey may want to know about the elasticity of demand for its products. Thus, the firm is interested in the response of consumers to incremental changes. For example, the firm needs to know how the consumers would react to such things as a 1, 2, or 3 percent increase (or decrease) in price or a 5 percent increase (decrease) in advertising expenditures. Obviously, most persons interviewed are not able to answer such questions precisely.

THE WALL STREET JOURNAL

APPLICATION

Problems with Consumer Interviews

As *The Wall Street Journal* noted, the food industry has a lot riding on the claims people make about what they eat.* Food companies have, in the past, conducted their market research by asking people what they eat. Based on the results of these surveys, the food manufacturers would develop their new products. But, as the *Journal* noted, there is one big problem: "People don't always tell the truth."

As Harry Balzer (the vice president of a market research firm) put it: "Nobody likes to admit he likes junk food." In this instance, the problem is that there exists a response bias in such surveys. Instead of answering truthfully, the consumer is very likely to give a socially acceptable answer. As Mr. Balzer said, asking a sweet-eater how many Twinkies he eats "is like asking an alcoholic if he drinks much."

A different problem was encountered by Owens-Corning Fiberglass Corporation.† During a home-building convention, the firm commissioned a survey to determine the industry's outlook

Continued to page 168

---

*"Study to Detect True Eating Habits Finds Junk-Food Fans in the Health-Food Ranks," by Betsy Morris, *The Wall Street Journal,* February 3, 1984. Reprinted by permission of *The Wall Street Journal.* © Dow Jones & Company, Inc., 1984. All rights reserved.

†"Stupid Questions," *The Wall Street Journal,* February 7, 1984. Reprinted by permission of *The Wall Street Journal.* ©Dow Jones & Company, Inc., 1984. All rights reserved.

THE WALL STREET JOURNAL

APPLICATION

Continued from page 167
for 1984. The results were startling: The survey indicated that builders were planning to increase housing starts by an amazing 30 percent!

Owens-Corning convened a news conference to announce their findings, but the star of the news conference turned out to be Michael Sumichrast (chief economist for the National Association of Home Builders).

When asked to interpret the bullish forecast he replied that "it shows when you ask stupid questions, you get stupid answers." Mr. Sumichrast's point was that the survey did not use a representative sample. According to the *Journal,* the survey was taken only among the builders who attended the convention and these builders tend to be the larger and more aggressive companies.

Although the survey technique is plagued with these inherent difficulties, it can still be an extremely valuable tool for a manager to use in quantifying demand. The trick in doing a survey is to avoid the pitfalls, and, as the following application indicates, it can be done.

Market Studies and Experiments

A somewhat more expensive and difficult technique for estimating demand and demand elasticity is the controlled market study or experiment. The analyst attempts to hold everything constant during the study except for the price of the good.

Those carrying out these market studies normally display the products in several different stores, generally in areas with different characteristics, over a period of time. They make certain that there are always sufficient amounts available in every store at each price to satisfy demand. In this way the effect of changes in supply is removed. There is generally no advertising. During the period of the experiment, price is changed in relatively small increments over a range, and sales are recorded at each price. In this way, many of the effects of changes in other things can be removed, and a reasonable approximation of the actual demand curve can be estimated.

A relatively new technique for estimating demand is the use of experiments performed in a laboratory or in the field. Such experiments are a compromise between market studies and surveys. In some types of lab-

THE WALL STREET JOURNAL

APPLICATION

"People Watching" to Estimate Demand

We certainly aren't the first to note that, in interviews, people tend to portray themselves as they would like to be rather than as they are. There are a lot of advertising agencies that are only too familiar with this problem, and, since they have a lot riding on accurate estimates, they have found a number of ways around the problem.

As reported in *The Wall Street Journal*, advertising agencies have gone far beyond simply asking consumers questions. They now eavesdrop on consumers by looking in their garbage, hanging out with teenagers on the corner, snooping through the kitchen cabinets, and putting cameras in the home to record what their sample consumers *actually do*.* While a consumer might embellish the truth about how much ice cream (or how many Twinkies) he eats, his garbage doesn't lie.

And, if it is hard for consumers to accurately answer the question posed, the problem may be that the wrong question was asked. Kimberly-Clark Corporation is quite interested in knowing how consumers would react to more or fewer Kleenex tissues in a box. But there are very few of us who could answer accurately about the responsiveness of our demand functions to five more or five less tissues. Indeed, that would have been the wrong question to ask. Instead, Kimberly-Clark asked sample consumers to keep a record of how many times they blew their nose when they were suffering from a cold. In this way, the company had much less doubt that 60 tissues per pack was the optimal package size.†

*"People Watchers Seek Clues to Consumers' True Behavior," by Ronald Alsop, *The Wall Street Journal*, September 4, 1986. Reprinted by permission of *The Wall Street Journal*. © Dow Jones & Company, Inc., 1986. All rights reserved.

†"Why Do Hot Dogs Come in Packs of 10 and Buns in 8s or 12s," by John Koten, *The Wall Street Journal*, September 21, 1984. Reprinted by permission of *The Wall Street Journal*. © Dow Jones & Company, Inc., 1984. All rights reserved.

oratory experiments, volunteers are paid to simulate actual buying conditions without going through real markets. Volunteer "consumers" are given money to go on simulated market trips. The experimenter changes relative prices between trips. After many "shopping trips" by many "consumers" an approximation of demand is obtained. The volunteers have the incentive to act as though they are really shopping, because there is a probability that they may keep their purchases.

THE WALL STREET JOURNAL

APPLICATION

Why 42 Oreo Cookies to a Package?

As reported by John Koten, the question of the profit-maximizing quantity of cookies or candy, or tissues, or whatever is fraught with complexities.* Indeed, a former Procter & Gamble manager indicated that, during his tenure, "the company was in an almost constant state of agony over how many paper towels it should put on a roll of Bounty."

Such a question is often answered by a market study. For example, M&M/Mars wanted to determine the optimal weights for its candy bars. To do so, it conducted a 12-month test in 150 stores. Instead of altering the price from store to store, the company kept price constant and altered the size of the product. As the director of sales development reported, in stores where the size was increased "sales went up 20 percent to 30 percent almost overnight." As a result, M&M decided to change much of its product line.

But market studies are not without problems that must be considered and accounted for. One is regional differences. A case in point is the toilet-paper business, where the issue is the trade-off between the number and thickness of tissues. As a marketing director for the manufacturer of Northern tissue reported, Californians like more sheets to the roll, while Southerners prefer thicker sheets. A market study that was done without accounting for these regional differences would probably yield very unreliable results.

With respect to the question we began with, we can't tell you why Oreos come in a package of 42. Market studies are expensive and firms often guard the results jealously. Indeed it wasn't too surprising that the executive of Nabisco Brands reacted to the question with "We can't tell you something like that. We'd have to go into our whole marketing strategy, how we target consumers, and so on. That's all highly confidential information."

*"Why Do Hot Dogs Come in Packs of 10 and Buns in 8s or 12s," by John Koten, *The Wall Street Journal,* September 21, 1984. Reprinted by permission of *The Wall Street Journal.* © Dow Jones & Company, Inc., 1984. All rights reserved.

Going a step further, some economists have conducted experiments about consumer behavior—with the help of psychologists—in mental institutions and in drug centers, by setting up token economies (which incidentally are supposed to have therapeutic value). Patients receive tokens for jobs performed. They can exchange these tokens for goods and services. The experimenters can change prices and incomes and thus generate demand curves, the properties of which are compared with the theoretical properties of such curves.

In field experiments, the researchers want to be able to change the price of goods and actually observe the behavior of the consumers. To illustrate this type of experiment, let us give you an example.

APPLICATION

The Residential Demand for Electricity*

Some of our colleagues at Texas A&M were interested in estimating the own-price elasticity of the demand for energy— electric energy. They recruited a sample of 100 households to participate in their experiment. The objective of the study was to observe these households' weekly consumption of electric power. After first establishing the households' baseline levels of usage, the researchers experimentally changed the price of electric power for part of their sample by paying rebates for reduction in weekly electricity usage.

For example, in one of their subgroups, the researchers paid the household 1.3 cents for every kilowatt-hour (kwh) reduction in weekly usage. At the time this study was conducted, the cost of electrical power to the residential consumers was 2.6 cents per kwh. Therefore, for this subgroup, the price of consuming an additional kwh was increased: To consume an additional kwh, the household not only had to *pay* 2.6 cents but also had to *forego* the rebate of 1.3 cents they could have received had they conserved rather than consumed electricity. Hence, for this subgroup, the price of electricity increased by 50 percent, from 2.6 to 3.9 cents per kwh.

Other subgroups were given other rebate schedules. And one subgroup—the control group—was given no rebate. The researchers could then actually measure the reduction in electricity consumption due to the experimentally imposed price increase by comparing the change in the consumption of the subgroup receiving the rebate with the change in the consumption of the control group.

The results of this experimental study indicated that the maximum own-price elasticity of the residential demand for electricity was 0.32. That is, the experiment indicated that the residential demand for electricity was very price inelastic. However, as the researchers

---

*This application is taken from Raymond C. Battalio, John H. Kagel, Robin C. Winkler, and Richard A. Wineh, "Residential Electricity Demand: An Experimental Study." *The Review of Economics and Statistics,* May 1979, pp. 180–89.

indicated, this study measured a very short-run elasticity. (As we noted in Chapter 6, we would expect the price elasticity to increase as the time period for adjustment gets longer.)

The experimental approach to estimating the demand for products has rapidly moved out of the laboratories and off the college campuses to the real-world applications more of interest to Wall Street and Main Street. The rapid growth of microcomputers and cable television systems has made possible market experiments that could only have been dreamed of a few years ago.

APPLICATION

High-Tech Market Experiments*

The newest buzzword in market research is single-source data—data on both the advertisements received and the purchases made by an individual household. The idea is very simple. If a firm wants to know how a consumer will react to a 10 percent increase in exposure to its ads or a 25-cents off coupon, it can actually do the experiment and see what happens. The technology for this analysis was pioneered in 1980 by Information Resources Inc. (Behaviorscan). Recently, two new competitors have entered the scanning service business: a joint venture between Arbitron Ratings Company and Selling Areas Marketing Inc. (ScanAmerica) and the A. C. Nielsen Company.

For example, Nielsen uses Sioux Falls, South Dakota, as its test site, in part because the demographics of this city of 81,000 population closely match those of the entire country. From this population, Nielsen selected a random sample of 3,500 households who agreed to let Nielsen record their viewing habits and purchases. (The households receive discount coupons and a chance to win small prizes in a sweepstakes.)

Via special devices attached to the television sets of the test households, Nielsen can replace broadcast commercials with test commercials from the same firm. (For example, Nielsen can replace the nationally broadcast Campbell Soup commercial with one that Campbell Soup wants to test.) And, given an arrangement with the

---

*This application is based on "Test-Market Programs Stir Surprises" by Richard W. Stevenson, *The New York Times*, July 24, 1986 and "High-Tech Shocks in Ad Research" by Felix Kessler, *Fortune*, July 7, 1986.

local newspaper, the test households get special editions of the paper containing test print ads.

When the test households get to the grocery stores, optical scanners at the checkout provide Nielsen with a record of purchases actually made. Thus, by combining data on what commercials and ads the households received with data on what they actually bought, a client firm can determine what happens if it increases or decreases its ad frequency. Or if it substitutes one kind of ad for another. Or if it uses a 25-cents off coupon instead of a 10-cents off coupon. Or if it combines several of these strategies.

As a case in point, the *New York Times* reported that Campbell Soup used this approach for its Swanson frozen dinners to determine which of two types of ads to run and how large an advertising budget to employ. Using several groups of test households, Campbell Soup was able to evaluate combinations of these strategies for much less than if it had used a test market approach for each of the strategies. (*Fortune* reported that these scanning service tests cost a tenth of the $2 million for a regional market study.) And the group manager for market research has credited this scanning service test with making a large contribution to improved sales for Swanson.

7.2 ESTIMATION OF DEMAND USING REGRESSION ANALYSIS

The techniques of regression analysis can also be used to obtain estimates of the market demand function. In general, this procedure follows the lines outlined in Chapter 4. However, a special problem is encountered when we estimate a demand function—the simultaneous equations problem. While the statistics involved in this problem is beyond the scope of this text, we do want to indicate the nature of the problem and note that there are readily available "canned" computer programs that can handle this problem. Again, as we have stressed before, we don't intend to teach you statistics (or econometrics). Instead, we want to give you an idea as to how these techniques can provide the information needed for managerial decision making.

In order to estimate a demand function, it will first be necessary to use a specific functional form. We will consider both linear and nonlinear demand functions. Before proceeding, however, let us simplify the demand function. We have already noted the difficulties inherent in quantifying taste and price expectations; therefore, let us eliminate those variables for now and rewrite the demand function as

$$Q_X = f(P_X,\ Y,\ P_R)\ ,$$

where

Q_X = Quantity purchased of commodity X.
P_X = Price of X.
Y = Consumers' income.
P_R = The price of related commodities.

A Linear Demand Function

The simplest demand function would be one that specifies a linear relation. That is, using the general demand function above, we could write our empirical demand function as

$$Q_X = a + bP_X + cY + dP_R .$$

In this equation, the parameter b measures the change in quantity demanded that would result from a one unit change in the price of X. That is, $b = \Delta Q_X / \Delta P_X$, which is assumed to be negative. Likewise,

$$c = \Delta Q_X / \Delta Y > 0 \text{ if } X \text{ is a normal good}$$

$$d = \Delta Q_X / \Delta P_R \overset{>}{\underset{<}{}} 0 \text{ if commodity } R \text{ is a } \begin{cases} \text{substitute.} \\ \text{complement.} \end{cases}$$

Using the techniques of regression analysis, this linear demand function could be estimated to provide estimates of the parameters a, b, c, and d. Then t-tests would be performed to determine if these parameters are statistically significant.

As we stressed in Chapter 6, the elasticity of demand is a crucial feature. The elasticities of demand—with respect to own price, income, and the prices of related commodities—can be calculated from a linear demand function without much difficulty. Consider first the own-price elasticity, defined as

$$E = -\frac{\Delta Q_X}{\Delta P_X} \cdot \frac{P_X}{Q_X} .$$

With the linear specification, $b = \Delta Q_X / \Delta P_X$, so the estimated own-price elasticity is

$$\hat{E} = -\hat{b} \cdot \frac{P_X}{Q_X} .$$

The problem is the choice of the price and quantity values to be used. Obviously, this elasticity could be evaluated at any price and output combination. Given the properties of regression analysis, it might be most meaningful to evaluate the elasticity at the mean values for price and output (i.e., at $\overline{P_X}$ and $\overline{Q_X}$). Note that if $\hat{b}$ is statistically significant, the estimated elasticity, $\hat{E}$, will also be statistically significant.

In a similar manner, the income elasticity may be estimated as

$$\hat{E}_Y = \hat{c} \cdot \frac{Y}{Q_X}.$$

Likewise, the estimated cross-price elasticity is

$$\hat{E}_{XR} = \hat{d} \cdot \frac{P_R}{Q_X}.$$

A Nonlinear Demand Function

The most commonly employed nonlinear demand specification is the log-linear (or constant elasticity) form. Using the general specification above, a log-linear demand function would be written as

$$Q_X = aP_X^b Y^c P_R^d.$$

The obvious potential advantage of this form is that it would provide a better estimate if the true demand function is indeed nonlinear. Furthermore, as we know from Chapter 4, this specification allows for the direct estimation of the elasticities. Specifically, the absolute value of parameter b measures the own-price elasticity of demand.[1] Likewise, c and d, respectively, measure the income elasticity and cross-price elasticity of demand.

As we learned in Chapter 4, in order to obtain estimates from the log-linear demand function, we must convert it to logarithms. Thus, the function to be estimated is

$$\log Q_X = \log a + b \log P_X + c \log Y + d \log P_R.$$

The Identification Problem

To this point we have approached the problem of estimating a demand function as a simple application of regression analysis—that is, a regression of observed quantity sold on observed price and the other variables. However, a problem arises here from the fact that the observed quantities sold and observed prices are not simply points on a specific demand curve but rather represent points of market equilibrium. The observed points are the result of the *simultaneous* interaction of supply and demand.

To illustrate the difficulties that can be encountered, let's consider the following simplified forms of the demand and supply functions:

Demand: $Q = \alpha + \beta P$
Supply: $Q = a + bP.$

---

[1]See the appendix to this chapter for the derivation of this relation.

From an empirical standpoint, four situations might exist:

1. Both the demand and supply functions are stable.
2. The supply function is stable, but the demand function is shifting (due perhaps to changes in income).
3. The demand function is stable, but the supply function is shifting (due perhaps to changes in the price of inputs).
4. Both the demand and supply functions are shifting.

Let us examine each of these situations in turn to see what happens if we attempt to estimate the demand function by simply regressing observed quantity sold on observed price.

Case 1 is illustrated in Panel A of Figure 7.1. If both demand and supply are stable, the equilibrium price and quantity will be subject only to random variation; thus, the observed price and quantity points would be as shown by the scatter of points in this figure. Then, if price were regressed on output, one would obtain a horizontal line (the dashed line in this figure). That is, in this situation, regressing observed output on observed price would result in a conclusion that no relation exists between price and output. Clearly, interpreting this line as a demand function would be a serious error.

Case 2 is illustrated in Panel B. In this case we have shifted demand from D_1 to D_2 and then to D_3 (as would be the case if the good is normal and income increases). Thus, there are three points of equilibrium. As before, since the actual price-quantity points are subject to random variation about the equilibrium, the observed points would be similar to the scatter presented in this figure. In this instance, attempting to obtain an estimate of the demand function by simply regressing output on price would result in a positive relation between price and output. More specifically, in this case, such a simple estimation would result in an estimate of the supply function rather than the demand function.

In case 3, shown in Panel C of Figure 7.1, supply has shifted from S_1 to S_2 and then to S_3 (as a result, for instance, of increasing input prices), while demand has remained stable. Again, the actual observed price and quantity points are distributed around the equilibrium points. Regressing output on price will indeed result in a good estimation of the demand function. That is, in this case, fitting a regression line through the illustrated scatter of points will provide an estimate of the true demand function, D.

Finally, Panel D illustrates a possible result if both the demand and supply functions are shifting. In this case, we again have three equilibrium points (the intersections of D_1S_1, D_2S_2, D_3S_3) with the observed price-quantity points scattered randomly around these equilibria. It is easily seen that a regression of quantity on price will, in this case, provide an estimate of neither the demand nor the supply function. Such a regression would be analogous to simply connecting the equilibrium points for different demand and supply functions.

Figure 7.1 Problems in Estimating Demand Functions

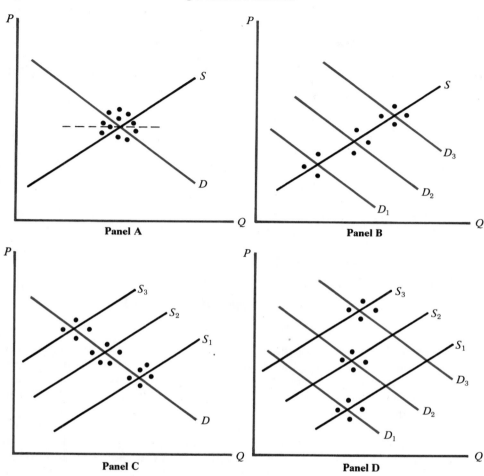

From the preceding discussion it would appear that simple regression analysis is useful only in the case in which the demand curve is stable and the supply curve is shifting—a circumstance that is generally not guaranteed. Statistical techniques designed to handle this problem do exist. But, in order to estimate a demand function, it must first be *identified*.

To illustrate what we mean by a demand function being identified, look again at Figure 7.1. Only in case 3 (Panel C) would regression analysis provide a meaningful estimate of the true demand function. More specifically, only in case 3 was the demand function identified. Mathematically, this is a case in which the demand curve is stable,

$$D: Q = \alpha + \beta P,$$

and the supply curve is shifting in response to changes in, say, the price of inputs (P_F),

$$S: Q = a + bP + cP_F .$$

In this case, because both output, Q, and price, P, are determined in the marketplace, they are both *endogenous* variables. The price of inputs, P_F, is determined outside of this market and is, therefore, *exogenous*. The demand function contains one endogenous variable on the right-hand side; the supply function contains one exogenous variable not included in the demand function. These circumstances cause the demand function to be identified. In more general terms, the necessary conditions for the identification of a demand function can be stated as follows:[2]

Definition. The demand function is identified if the supply function contains at least one exogenous variable that is not in the demand function.

Conversely, the supply function will be identified if the demand function contains at least one exogenous variable not in the supply function.

Using this rule, let us return to a more general formulation. In linear form, our demand function is

$$Q_X = a + bP_X + cY + dP_R .$$

We could specify a simplified, linear supply function as

$$Q_X = e + fP_X + gT + hP_F ,$$

where T is the level of technology. Since the output and the price of X are determined within the market, Q_X and P_X are endogenous. The remainder of the variables (Y, P_R, T, P_F) are exogenous because they are determined outside the market. Is the demand function identified? The demand function contains one endogenous variable on the right-hand side, P_X. There exist, however, two exogenous variables in the supply equations that are excluded from the demand equation, T and P_F. Thus, the demand function is identified and can be estimated. (You should be able to see that, in this system of equations, the supply function is also identified.)

If the demand function is log-linear,

$$\log Q_X = \log a + b \log P_X + c \log Y + d \log P_R ,$$

the same technique applies. We need to specify the supply function and, for reasons that become more clear in the following discussion, we probably will want to use a log-linear form,

$$\log Q_X = \log e + f \log P_X + g \log T + h \log P_F .$$

---

[2]In a more general case, if we want to be able to identify one equation in a system of simultaneous equations, the necessary condition for identification is:

The number of exogenous variables in the system excluded from the equation must be greater than or equal to the number of endogenous variables included on the right-hand side of the equation.

In this instance, the endogenous variable on the right-hand side of the demand equation is log P_X. Since, however, the supply function contains two exogenous variables (log T and log P_F) the demand function is again identified.

Estimation of the Demand Function

Once the demand function has been identified, it can be estimated using any of a number of available techniques. Perhaps the most widely used of these techniques—and the one that is most likely to be preprogrammed into the available regression packages—is two-stage least squares (2SLS).

In the discussion to follow, we will provide only a brief sketch of the basic technique of 2SLS. Keep in mind what our problem is: Regression techniques normally assume that the right-hand side variables are exogenous. However, in the case of simultaneous equations—like the demand and supply functions considered here—one of the right-hand side variables is endogenous.

Conceptually, what we want to do is to make this endogenous right-hand side variable (in our case, price) behave as if it is exogenous, then use traditional regression techniques to obtain estimates of the parameters. In the example we have been using we have a system of two simultaneous equations:

$$\text{Demand: } Q_X = a + bP_X + cY + dP_R$$
$$\text{Supply: } Q_X = e + fP_X + gT + hP_F .$$

In these, P_X is an endogenous variable. To obtain unbiased estimates of a, b, c, and d, the estimation of the demand function proceeds in two steps or stages.

Stage 1   The endogenous right-hand side variable is regressed on all of the exogenous variables in the system:

$$P_X = \alpha + \beta Y + \gamma P_R + \delta T + \theta P_F .$$

From this estimation, we obtain estimates of the parameters, i.e., $\hat{\alpha}$, $\hat{\beta}$, $\hat{\gamma}$, $\hat{\delta}$, and $\hat{\theta}$. Using these estimates and the actual values of the exogenous variables, we generate a "new" price series—predicted price—as follows

$$\hat{P}_X = \hat{\alpha} + \hat{\beta} Y + \hat{\gamma} P_R + \hat{\delta} T + \hat{\theta} P_F .$$

Note how the predicted price $\hat{P}_X$ is obtained. $\hat{P}_X$ is simply a linear combination of the exogenous variables, so it follows that $\hat{P}_X$ is also exogenous. However, given the way that we obtained our predicted price series, the values of $\hat{P}_X$ will correspond closely to the original values of P_X. In essence, in this first stage, we have made price behave as if it is exogenous.

Stage 2 We then use the predicted price variable ($\hat{P}_X$) in the demand function we wish to estimate. That is, in the second stage, we estimate the regression equation:

$$Q_X = a + b\hat{P}_X + cY + dP_R .$$

Note that, in this estimation, we use the exogenous variable we constructed in the first stage. We use predicted price, $\hat{P}_X$, rather than the actual price variable, P_X, in the final regression.

At this point, we probably should remove some of your fears by noting that in the regression programs with which we are familiar, these two stages are done automatically. It is normally necessary for the user only to specify which variables are endogenous and which are exogenous.

Once the estimates for a, b, c, and d have been obtained from the second stage of the regression, they can be tested for significance (using a t-test) in precisely the same manner as for any other regression equation. However, due to the manner in which 2SLS estimates are calculated, the R^2 and F-statistics are not meaningful. Indeed, these statistics are usually not even reported in the output of standard regression packages.

APPLICATION

The World Demand for Copper

In its simplest form, we can define the world demand for copper to be a function of the price of copper, income, and the price of any related commodities. Let's use aluminum as the related commodity, because it is the primary substitute for copper in manufacturing, and write our demand function as

$$Q_{copper} = f(P_{copper}, Y, P_{aluminum})$$

As we have noted, we could specify either a linear or a nonlinear demand function. Let's use a linear form in this application,

$$Q_{copper} = a + bP_{copper} + cY + dP_{aluminum}.$$

It is tempting to simply regress consumption on the price of copper, income, and the price of aluminum. However, as we have pointed out, such a procedure is normally not appropriate. Instead, it is first necessary to identify the demand function. As we have shown, this requires that we specify the supply function.

The quantity supplied of copper depends, as usual, on the price of copper and the level of available technology. In this market, inventories are also of particular importance. If inventories are rising, we would expect current production to be reduced. Therefore, we need an additional variable to reflect inventory changes. We define the ratio of consumption to production in the preceding period (denoted simply as X) to be this variable. As consumption declines relative to production, X will fall, and we would expect a decline in current production. Thus, our supply function becomes

$$Q_{copper} = g(P_{copper}, T, X),$$

or, using a linear specification,

$$Q_{copper} = e + fP_{copper} + gT + hX .$$

We can now turn to the question of whether or not the demand function is identified. Since the supply function includes two exogenous variables that are excluded from the demand equation (T and X), the demand function is identified and may be estimated.

Once we knew that the demand function was identified, we collected the necessary data: (1) The world consumption (sales) of copper in 1,000 metric tons, (2) the price of copper and aluminum in cents per pound, deflated by a price index to obtain the real (i.e., constant dollar) prices, (3) an index of real per capita income, and (4) the world production of copper (in order to calculate our "inventory" variable, X). We used time as our proxy for available technology (i.e., assuming that the level of technology has increased steadily over time). The resulting data set is presented in Table 7.1.

Using these data, we estimated the demand function using 2SLS. In this estimation, the endogenous variable P_{copper} is first regressed on all of the exogenous variables: Y, $P_{aluminum}$, X, and T. Then, as we described earlier, this estimation is used to generate the predicted value of P_{copper}. Finally, consumption, Q_{copper}, is regressed on this predicted price of copper as well as on income and the price of aluminum. The results of these estimations are:

```
SECOND STAGE STATISTICS

DEPENDENT VARIABLE: QC

OBSERVATIONS: 25


                        PARAMETER              STANDARD
        VARIABLE        ESTIMATE               ERROR

        INTERCEPT       -6837.8                1264.5
        PC.HAT            -66.495                31.534
        Y               13997.                 1306.3
        PA                107.66                 44.510
```

Table 7.1 The World Copper Market*

Year	(QC) World Consumption	(PC) Real Price Copper	(Y) Index of Real Income	(PA) Real Price Aluminum	X	T
1	3,173.0	26.56	0.70	19.76	0.97679	1
2	3,281.1	27.31	0.71	20.78	1.03937	2
3	3,135.7	32.95	0.72	22.55	1.05153	3
4	3,359.1	33.90	0.70	23.06	0.97312	4
5	3,755.1	42.70	0.74	24.93	1.02349	5
6	3,875.9	46.11	0.74	26.50	1.04135	6
7	3,905.7	31.70	0.74	27.24	0.97686	7
8	3,957.6	27.23	0.72	26.21	0.98069	8
9	4,279.1	32.89	0.75	26.09	1.02888	9
10	4,627.9	33.78	0.77	27.40	1.03392	10
11	4,910.2	31.66	0.76	26.94	0.97922	11
12	4,908.4	32.28	0.79	25.18	0.99679	12
13	5,327.9	32.38	0.83	23.94	0.96630	13
14	5,878.4	33.75	0.85	25.07	1.02915	14
15	6,075.2	36.25	0.89	25.37	1.07950	15
16	6,312.7	36.24	0.93	24.55	1.05073	16
17	6,056.8	38.23	0.95	24.98	1.02788	17
18	6,375.9	40.83	0.99	24.96	1.02799	18
19	6,974.3	44.62	1.00	25.52	0.99151	19
20	7,101.6	52.27	1.00	26.01	1.00191	20
21	7,071.7	45.16	1.02	25.46	0.95644	21
22	7,754.8	42.50	1.07	22.17	0.96947	22
23	8.480.3	43.70	1.12	18.56	0.98220	23
24	8,105.2	47.88	1.10	21.32	1.00793	24
25	7,157.2	36.33	1.07	22.75	0.93810	25

*The data presented are actual values for 1951–75.

Note that the computer output provides only the results of the second-stage estimation; that is, estimation of the demand function using $\hat{P}$. Indeed, this printout indicates that a predicted price was used, since it denotes the price of copper as *PC.HAT* rather than *PC*. Note further that, since the R^2 and F values are not meaningful in 2SLS, they are not even reported.

We would predict theoretically that (1) due to a downward-sloping demand curve for copper, $b < 0$; (2) since copper is a normal good, $c > 0$; and (3) since copper and aluminum are substitutes, $d > 0$. Our estimated coefficients conform to this sign pattern:

$$\hat{b} = -66.495 < 0$$
$$\hat{c} = 13997. > 0$$
$$\hat{d} = 107.66 > 0 .$$

In order to test for the statistical significance of these parameter estimates, we calculated the t-values:

$$t_{\hat{b}} = \frac{-66.495}{31.534} = -2.11$$

$$t_{\hat{c}} = \frac{13997.}{1306.3} = 10.71$$

$$t_{\hat{d}} = \frac{107.66}{44.510} = 2.42 .$$

We estimated four parameters (a, b, c, and d), so we have $25 - 4$ degrees of freedom and the critical value of t at a 95 percent confidence level is 2.08. Since the absolute values for the calculated values of t for each of the parameter estimates exceed the critical value of t, we know that the estimated parameters are statistically significant.

Now, let's find out about the elasticities of demand. While we know that we can evaluate the elasticity at any point on the demand curve, let's use the sample means. Using the data from Table 7.1, the means of the variables under consideration are

$$\overline{QC} = 5433.63 \qquad\qquad \overline{Y} = 0.87$$

$$\overline{PC} = 37.17 \qquad\qquad \overline{PA} = 24.29 .$$

The own-price elasticity of demand evaluated at the sample mean is

$$E = -\hat{b}\,\frac{\overline{PC}}{\overline{QC}}$$

$$= -(-66.495)\left(\frac{37.17}{5433.63}\right)$$

$$= 0.45.$$

Similarly, the income elasticity of demand at the sample mean is

$$E_Y = \hat{c}\left(\frac{\overline{Y}}{\overline{QC}}\right)$$

$$= 13997\left(\frac{0.87}{5433.63}\right)$$

$$= 2.24 ,$$

and the cross-price elasticity of demand at the sample mean is

$$E_{CA} = \hat{d}\left(\frac{\overline{PA}}{\overline{QC}}\right)$$

$$= 107.66\left(\frac{24.29}{5433.63}\right)$$

$$= 0.48 .$$

In this discussion we have concentrated our attention on what we think are the two major problems that are encountered in the estimation of a demand function—specification and identification.

As we noted in Chapter 4, specification errors can result from either the selection of variables to be included or the selection of the functional form to be estimated. Obviously, the exclusion of important explanatory variables can lead to unreliability in the estimated coefficients, as can the inclusion of extraneous variables. In the case of the selection of the functional form, choosing the incorrect form can reduce the precision of the estimate in the sense that the hypothesized functional form does not "fit" the data. As we noted earlier, this might occur if the analyst uses a linear demand function when the true demand is nonlinear.

In the case of the identification problem, if the analyst fails to recognize that the observed data points are generated by the simultaneous interaction of a demand and supply function, the estimated demand function might well be a supply function or nothing at all. This problem—referred to as simultaneous equations bias—can lead to biased estimates of the parameters of the demand function.

TECHNICAL PROBLEMS

1. Cite the three major problems with consumer interviews or surveys and provide an example of each.

2. Following are four sets of demand and supply functions. For each set, determine if the demand and supply functions are identified and explain why or why not.

   a. D: $Q = \alpha + \beta P$
      S: $Q = a + bP$.
   b. D: $Q = \alpha + \beta P + \gamma Y$
      S: $Q = a + bP$.
   c. D: $Q = \alpha + \beta P$
      S: $Q = a + bP + cT$.
   d. D: $Q = \alpha + \beta P + \gamma Y$
      S: $Q = a + bP + cT + dP_F$.

3. A consulting company that wants to estimate the demand for cameras has a data set for the past 20 years that includes the quantity of cameras purchased, the price of cameras, consumers' income, and the price of film.

   a. Is this data set sufficient to identify the demand function? Why or why not? What about the supply function?
   b. The company also wants to estimate the demand for baseball bats. Their data set for this project includes the quantity of baseball bats, the price of baseball bats, consumers' income, the price of baseballs, and the price of lumber. Is this data set

sufficient to identify the demand (supply) function? Why or why
not? Explain.

4. The estimated demand for good X is:

$$Q_X = 70 - 3.5P - .6Y + 4P_R,$$

where Q_X = units of good X, P = price of good X, Y = income,
and P_R = price of related good Z. (All coefficients are statistically
significant.)

a. Is X a normal or an inferior good? Explain.

b. Are X and Z substitutes or complements? Explain.

5. In our application dealing with the world demand for copper, we
estimated the demand elasticities (at the sample means). Using
these estimates, evaluate the impact on the world consumption of
copper of:

a. The formation of a worldwide cartel in copper that increases the
price of copper by 10 percent.

b. The onset of a recession that reduces world income by 5
percent.

c. A technical breakthrough that is expected to reduce the price of
copper by 10 percent.

d. A 10 percent reduction in the price of aluminum.

6. A linear demand function of the form

$$Q_X = a + bP_X + cY + dP_R$$

was estimated using 2SLS. (Obviously, this demand function was
first identified by specifying the supply function.) The results of this
estimation are as follows:

```
SECOND STAGE STATISTICS

DEPENDENT VARIABLE: QX

OBSERVATIONS: 30

                    PARAMETER              STANDARD
    VARIABLE        ESTIMATE               ERROR

    INTERCEPT        68.38                 12.65
    PX.HAT           -6.50                  3.15
    Y                13.926                 1.306
    PR              -10.77                  2.45
```

The means of the variables are as follows:

$$\bar{Q}_X = 125$$
$$\bar{P}_X = 25$$
$$\bar{Y} = 20$$
$$\bar{P}_R = 25 .$$

a. Are the signs of $\hat{b}$ and $\hat{c}$ as would be predicted theoretically?
b. What does the sign of $\hat{d}$ imply about the relation between commodity X and the related commodity?
c. Are the parameter estimates $\hat{a}$, $\hat{b}$, $\hat{c}$, and $\hat{d}$ statistically significant?
d. Using the sample means, calculate
   (1) The own-price elasticity of demand.
   (2) The income elasticity.
   (3) The cross-price elasticity.

7. The demand for tennis balls was estimated using a linear specification:

$$Q = a + bP + cY + dP_R ,$$

where Q = cans of tennis balls (millions), P = real price of tennis balls (dollars/can), Y = consumers' income ($1,000 per capita), and P_R = real price of tennis rackets (dollars/racket). The 2SLS regression results are as follows:

```
SECOND STAGE STATISTICS

DEPENDENT VARIABLE: Q

OBSERVATIONS: 20

                      PARAMETER              STANDARD
   VARIABLE           ESTIMATE                 ERROR

   INTERCEPT            80.64                  25.03
   P.HAT              -25.93                    8.77
   Y                   10.24                    2.51
   PR                  -1.52                    0.36
```

a. Are the estimates $\hat{a}$, $\hat{b}$, $\hat{c}$, and $\hat{d}$ statistically significant?
b. Are the signs of $\hat{b}$, $\hat{c}$, and $\hat{d}$ consistent with our theory of demand?

   c. Suppose that $P = \$3$, $Y = \$15$, and $P_R = \$70$.

     (1) What is the estimated number of cans of tennis balls demanded?

     (2) What are the values of the own-price, income, and cross-price elasticities of demand?

     (3) What will happen to the number of cans of tennis balls demanded if the price of tennis balls decreases 15 percent?

     (4) What will happen to the number of cans of tennis balls demanded if consumers' income doubles?

     (5) What will happen to the number of cans of tennis balls demanded if the price of tennis rackets increases 20 percent?

8. In our examination of the world demand for copper, we used a linear specification. However, we could have estimated a log-linear specification. That is, we could have specified the copper demand function as

$$Q_c = aP_c^b\, Y^c\, P_A^d$$

or

$$\log Q_c = \log a + b \log P_c + c \log Y + d \log P_A .$$

The results of such an estimation, using the data in Table 7.1, are as follows:

```
SECOND STAGE STATISTICS

DEPENDENT VARIABLE: LOG QC

OBSERVATIONS: 25

                      PARAMETER           STANDARD
    VARIABLE          ESTIMATE             ERROR

    INTERCEPT          9.0072             0.97059
    LOG PC.HAT        -0.68233            0.30635
    LOG Y              2.5265             0.28963
    LOG PA             0.75246            0.23498
```

   a. Are the parameter estimates consistent with the theoretical predictions made about the signs of *b*, *c*, and *d*?

   b. Are the parameter estimates statistically significant?

   c. What are the values of the own-price, income, and cross-price elasticities of demand?

   d. How do these results compare with these obtained from the linear specification?

ANALYTICAL PROBLEMS

1. Suppose that you want to estimate the demand for automobiles in the United States. Specify a model that you believe might be appropriate. Check to see if your model is identified. How would the model differ if you wish to estimate the demand for a particular make of automobile?

2. Until the mid-1970s, most estimates of the demand function for automobiles did not include the price of gasoline. Why? Would this exclusion be appropriate today? What kind of an error would this be?

3. In Problem 1, we considered estimation of the demand for automobiles in the United States.
   a. Can you think of some problems—not necessarily statistical problems—involved in estimating the demand for automobiles? What are they?
   b. Is there a problem in defining what is meant by "an automobile" and "the price of an automobile"?
   c. How would you obtain data on the price of automobiles?

4. Suppose that the commodity in Problem 1 is coal rather than automobiles. How would your answers to Problems 1 and 3 differ?

5. In a recent article, a researcher reported that he had found that the demand curve for kerosene sloped upward—as the price of kerosene rose the quantity demanded of kerosene increased. What questions might you have for this researcher?

SUGGESTED ADDITIONAL REFERENCES

Intriligator, Michael D.   *Econometric Models, Techniques, and Applications*. Englewood Cliffs, N.J.: Prentice-Hall, 1978.

Kelejian, Harry H., and Wallace E. Oates.   *Introduction to Econometrics*. New York: Harper & Row, 1974.

Pindyck, Robert S., and Rubinfeld, Daniel L.   *Econometric Models and Economic Forecasts*. New York: McGraw-Hill, 1981.

Rao, Potluri, and Roger LeRoy Miller.   *Applied Econometrics*. Belmont, Calif.: Wadsworth, 1971.

Wonnacott, Ronald J., and Thomas H. Wonnacott.   *Econometrics*. New York: John Wiley & Sons, 1979.

APPENDIX: DERIVATION OF ELASTICITY ESTIMATES

As was demonstrated in Chapter 6, the own-price elasticity of demand is

$$E = -\frac{\partial Q_X}{\partial P_X} \cdot \frac{P_X}{Q_X}.$$

With the linear specification of the demand function,

$$Q_X = a + bP_X + cY + dP_R ,$$

the statistic $\hat{b}$ is an estimate of the partial derivative of quantity demanded with respect to the price of the product,

$$\hat{b} = \text{Estimate of } \left(\frac{\partial Q_X}{\partial P_X}\right).$$

Hence for any price, quantity demanded combination $(P_{X,i}, Q_{X,i})$, the estimated own-price elasticity of that point on the demand function is

$$\hat{E} = -\hat{b} \cdot \left[\frac{P_{X,i}}{Q_{X,i}}\right] .$$

With the log-linear specification of the demand function,

$$Q_X = aP_X^b Y^c P_R^d ,$$

the partial derivative of quantity demanded with respect to own price is

$$\frac{\partial Q_X}{\partial P_X} = baP_X^{b-1} Y^c P_R^d = \frac{bQ_X}{P_X} .$$

Hence, the negative of the statistic $\hat{b}$ is an estimate of own-price elasticity

$$\hat{E} = -\frac{bQ_X}{P_X} \cdot \frac{P_X}{Q_X} = -\hat{b} .$$

Using the same methodology estimates of income and cross-price elasticities can be obtained. The estimates are summarized in the following:

Elasticity	Definition	Estimate from Linear Specification	Estimate from Log-Linear Specification
Own-price	$E = -\dfrac{\partial Q_X}{\partial P_X} \cdot \dfrac{P_X}{Q_X}$	$-\hat{b} \cdot \left[\dfrac{P_{X,i}}{Q_{X,i}}\right]$	$-\hat{b}$
Income	$E_Y = \dfrac{\partial Q_X}{\partial Y} \cdot \dfrac{Y}{Q_X}$	$\hat{c} \cdot \left[\dfrac{Y_i}{Q_{X,i}}\right]$	$\hat{c}$
Cross price	$E_{XR} = \dfrac{\partial Q_X}{\partial P_R} \cdot \dfrac{P_R}{Q_X}$	$\hat{d} \cdot \left[\dfrac{P_{R,i}}{Q_{X,i}}\right]$	$\hat{d}$

Note that the elasticity estimates from the linear specification depend on the point of the demand curve at which the elasticity estimate is evaluated. In contrast, the log-linear demand curve exhibits constant elasticity estimates.

8

DEMAND FORECASTING

I n the preceding chapter, we discussed techniques which a manager can use to estimate and analyze the characteristics of demand functions. Information about prevailing demand can help managers decide about production scheduling, inventory levels, advertising, and so on. Clearly, knowledge of future market demand conditions—future market sales—can also be extremely useful to managers, particularly in predicting the individual firm's output in future periods and in making the firm's investment decisions. In this chapter, we provide some techniques that can be used to forecast future demand conditions.

The range of forecasting techniques is so wide that a complete discussion is quite beyond the scope of this text. Instead, we confine ourselves to a brief description of some of the more widely used techniques. For convenience, we divide forecasting methods into two groups—qualitative models and statistical models.

Qualitative models are more difficult to describe since there exists no explicit model or method that can serve as a reference point. There is no model that can be used to replicate the initial forecast with a given set of data, and it is this feature, above all others, that distinguishes this approach. It has been said by some that a qualitative model is essentially a "rule-of-thumb" technique. However, you should not infer from this description that qualitative forecasts are naive or unsophisticated. Indeed, it is the very complexity of this method that makes replication so difficult, since such forecasts are typically based on at least some subjective factors. In the final analysis, qualitative forecasts are often based on *expert opin-*

ion. The forecaster will examine the available data, solicit the advice of others, and then sift through this amalgamation of evidence to formulate a forecast. The weights assigned to the various bits and pieces of information are subjectively determined and, we might add, separate the neophyte from the expert.

In contrast, a statistical model employs explicit models or methods that can be replicated by another analyst. The results of statistical models can be reproduced by different researchers. An additional advantage of this approach is the existence of reasonably well-defined standards for evaluating such models. The final advantage of statistical models is the ability to use them in simulation models. (Basically, simulation models are models in which the researcher can obtain alternative forecasts for the future values of the endogenous variable, given alternative future trends in the exogenous variables.) The statistical models can be further subdivided into two categories—time-series models and econometric models.

Before we begin discussing *how* to forecast, we first take a moment to look at the question of whether forecasts are possible. We then look at some of the data that could be employed in making qualitative forecasts. Next, we consider time-series models. We then introduce econometric models and consider simulation procedures. We close this chapter with a note on some of the more important problems involved in forecasting.

8.1 SALES FORECASTS VERSUS PRICE FORECASTS

During the last half of 1984 and the first quarter of 1985, it was hard to be an economist. It seemed as if every popular publication was taking its turn at "economist bashing." Some illustrations might help you see what we mean:

THE FORECASTERS FLUNK

Poor predictions give once prestigious pundits a dismal reputation . . . "I'm thinking of quitting and becoming a hockey goalie"—Lawrence Chimerine, chairman of Chase Econometrics

Time, August 27, 1984

MAYBE ECONOMISTS SHOULD BE A LITTLE LESS POSITIVE

The Wall Street Journal, October 16, 1984

> ### ECONOMISTS ARE THIS YEAR'S ENDANGERED SPECIES
> Economists are on the run.
>
> > *Business Week,* January 14, 1985
>
> ### WHAT GOOD ARE ECONOMISTS?
> The profession is suffering from faulty forecasts and theoretical dissension.
>
> > *Newsweek,* February 4, 1985
>
> ### THE ECONOMIST'S NEW CLOTHES
> Economic forecasters have fallen into disrepute because they keep trying to do the impossible.
>
> > *Fortune,* April 1, 1985

And these articles were correct: Economists aren't very good at forecasting prices. But that leads to another question: Can anyone forecast prices?

In your finance courses you have encountered (or will encounter) a proposition referred to as *efficient markets.* The characteristics of an efficient market are very much like those of the competitive market we describe later in this text.

Definition.   An efficient market is a market characterized by:

1. *A homogeneous product.*
2. *Liquid primary and secondary (resale) markets (i.e., a large number of market participants in the primary and secondary markets and the ability of the participants to enter and exit the market freely).*
3. *The ability to contract for delivery either today or at some date in the future.*
4. *Low transactions (e.g., contracting) costs.*

In an efficient market, the price of the commodity or asset reflects all currently available, public information. In such an environment, price *changes* will be random. And, if price changes are random, there is no way to accurately forecast future prices. To see how this works, let's look at a market that has the characteristics of an efficient market.

APPLICATION

Making $1 Million Trading Wheat Futures

A recent addition to the American scene (and one we have seen nowhere else in the world) is The Weather Channel—a 24-hour cable channel devoted entirely to weather reports. From reading some of the earlier chapters of this text, you know that the market price of wheat is determined by the demand for and supply of wheat. And since the supply of wheat is in large part determined by weather conditions, shouldn't we be able to use those weather forecasts from The Weather Channel to make money?

More specifically, let's devise a trading strategy: If The Weather Channel forecasts bad wheat weather (e.g., hail in Kansas), we will buy wheat futures; that is, we will contract to buy wheat in the future at the price prevailing today. Then, when the bad weather conditions reduce the supply of wheat, the price of wheat will consequently rise. And (here comes the good part), when our futures contract matures, we will accept delivery of the wheat at the low price we contracted for today and immediately sell it at a higher price.

How much money would you expect to make on this strategy? (If you said anything greater than zero, write us because we have some land deals to offer you.) The problem with this simple trading strategy is that it is based on available public information, while today's wheat price already reflects all of the available public information. As soon as any new information relevant to wheat is available, it will be reflected in wheat prices. What then will change the price of wheat? It follows from everything we have said so far that wheat prices will change when the available information changes.

The upshot is that if we want to be able to predict wheat prices, we need to be able to predict the new information *before it is available*. And if new information is really "new," it must be random. So predicting wheat prices would require us to predict a random variable.

There are people who have made a million in the futures market. But with the strategy we proposed above—one with trades based on available, public information—the one who is making the million is the broker executing the trades.

As the preceding application indicates, you are unlikely to be successful trying to outpredict an efficient market. In an efficient market, the best forecast of the price in the future is the price today.

Principle.   In an efficient market, the price of the commodity or asset reflects all currently available, public information. In such a market, price changes are random, so the best forecast of the future price is the current market price.

The very things that economists are usually called on to predict are the prices of assets or commodities traded in markets that are very efficient—the money markets (interest rates), foreign exchange markets (foreign exchange rates), and commodity markets (the prices of gold, copper, wheat, and so on). Therefore, it is not very surprising that economists have not done very well at forecasting these prices.

But this doesn't mean that all forecasting is impossible. To the extent that the markets for consumer goods and services are less efficient than the financial or commodity markets (e.g., there are no futures markets for consumer goods and services), price forecasts are still possible. And, in any event, forecasts for total market sales (output forecasts) are possible, even in an efficient market. Indeed, it is with these output forecasts that the remainder of this chapter deals.

8.2 QUALITATIVE TECHNIQUES

As we noted, qualitative forecasting methods are very difficult to describe, due to the subjective elements involved. That is, forecasters combine available data with their knowledge of the firm and industry and, assigning subjective weights to these pieces of evidence, obtain a forecast. While qualitative forecasting may indeed be the best technique, it is difficult, if not impossible, to teach these techniques. In truth, we do not really know how people who do qualitative forecasting well do it. We can only say that those who are successful know how economics works and know a great deal about their industries.

Skillful forecasters do use data to make these forecasts. While it is impossible to set forth the manner in which their subjective weights are assigned to the data they use, we can, however, describe some of the data that may be observed and used.

It is possible that the analyst has observed through experience (or, perhaps, using regression techniques) that a relation exists between the sales of the firm and the movement in certain aggregate economic variables over time. More specifically, managers know that there are economic variables, changes in which *lead* the changes in the firm's sales. If managers know these variables, they can use these "leading indicators" as a barometer to predict changes in the sales of the firm. The problem then is the isolation of these indicators and the collection of appropriate data.

This problem of data identification and collection has been simplified immensely through the work of the National Bureau of Economic Research and the U.S. Department of Commerce. The U.S. Department of Commerce publishes, monthly, *Business Conditions Digest,* which con-

Table 8.1   The 12 Leading Indicators

1. Average workweek, production workers, manufacturing (hours).
2. Average weekly initial claims, state unemployment insurance—inverted* (thousands).
3. New orders for consumer goods and materials in 1972 dollars (billion dollars).
4. Vendor performance, companies receiving slower deliveries (percent).
5. Net business formation (index: 1967 = 100).
6. Contracts and orders for plant and equipment in 1972 dollars (billion dollars).
7. New building permits, private housing units (index: 1967 = 100).
8. Change in inventories on hand and on order in 1972 dollars, smoothed† (annual rate, billion dollars).
9. Change in sensitive materials prices, smoothed† (percent).
10. Stock prices, 500 common stocks (index: 1941–43 = 100).
11. Money supply (M2) in 1972 dollars (billion dollars).
12. Change in credit—business and consumer borrowing (annual rate, percent).

---

*This series is inverted, hence a decrease in unemployment claims will lead to an increase in the indicator.
†*Smoothed* means that irregularities in the data have been removed. The purpose in this procedure is to demonstrate the trend in the variable. Many variables exhibit considerable short-term (or seasonal) variation. In order to ascertain the trend in the variable, it is necessary to remove the effects of the short-term variation, that is, smooth the data series.

Source: U.S. Department of Commerce, *Business Conditions Digest.*

tains data on a large number of indicators. (More precisely, *Business Conditions Digest* contains almost 200 data series that could be used as indicators.) Of these, 12 variables considered particularly important as leading indicators are presented in Table 8.1.

If the forecaster can relate the firm's sales to one or more of the leading indicators, it would then be possible to generate short-term forecasts on the basis of this published data. For example, a firm that manufactures dishwashers would be very interested in the index of new building permits. An increase in building permits precedes housing starts, which precedes the purchase of dishwashers. An experienced forecaster could combine this information with personal knowledge about the firm (e.g., its share of the market) and about the market (e.g., the percentage of new houses that have dishwashers) to provide a forecast of sales for the firm. Again, it is impossible for us to determine the weights that should be assigned to these various pieces of information.

There are also more complex situations in which more than one indicator is used. In some instances, the different indicators could provide conflicting forecasts. To handle this difficulty, two multiple indicator methods are commonly employed. One method is to calculate a composite index, i.e., a weighted average of individual indicators. Indeed, the U.S. Department of Commerce itself publishes several composite indicators, one of which is the weighted average of the 12 leading indicators. In Figure 8.1, we have provided a graph of the behavior of this composite index over the period 1965–86. In this figure, it is easier to see why they are "leading" indicators. Note how the index turned down prior to the recessions of 1969–70, 1973–75, 1980, and 1981–83. Likewise, the upturn in this composite index preceded—led—the upturn in general economic activity.

Figure 8.1 Composite Index of the 12 Leading Indicators (1965–1986)

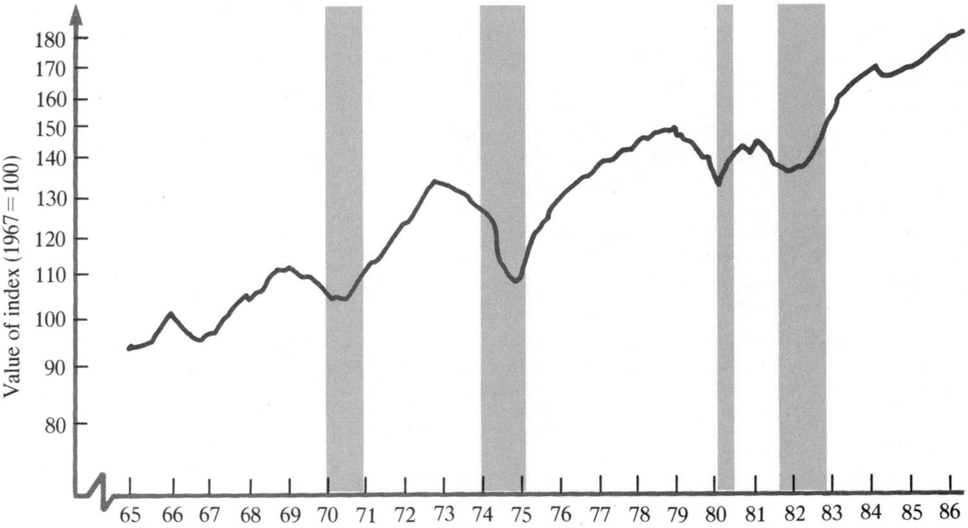

Note: Periods shaded are periods of recession as determined by the National Bureau of Economic Research (e.g., the 1969–70 recession covered the period December 1969 through November 1970).

Source: U.S. Department of Commerce, *Business Conditions Digest.*

A second way that multiple indicators are used is to calculate a diffusion index. Using this approach, one would calculate the percentage of the indicators that are rising. For example, if 5 of the 12 leading indicators were rising, the diffusion index would be $5/12$ or 42 percent. Using a diffusion index, one normally defines a critical percentage (usually 50 percent). If the diffusion index is above this critical percentage, one would say that economic activity is rising. Likewise, if the diffusion index is below the critical value, economic activity is said to be declining. In Figure 8.2 we have provided a graph of the diffusion index for the 12 leading indicators for the period 1965–86, and compared it to periods of recession.

Again, let us stress that the procedures outlined above require a great deal of subjective decisions by forecasters. The analyst must determine the appropriate indicators, then interpret them in light of the conditions that will exist in their particular markets and firms. First, these indicators do not always indicate changes in another economic variable (and there also exists some random month-to-month variation in these indicators). Second, the lead times are not necessarily constant. Third, and most important, since these leading indicators predict the *direction rather than the magnitude of changes,* the responsibility for assigning a magnitude rests with the forecaster.

Figure 8.2 Diffusion Index for the 12 Leading Indicators

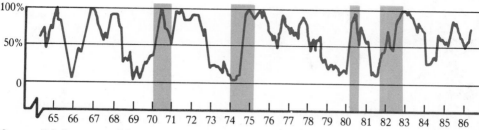

Source: U.S. Department of Commerce, *Business Conditions Digest.*

THE WALL STREET JOURNAL

APPLICATION

A Sluggish Economy*

September 1986 was a period of reassessment for many businesses in the United States. The leading indicators were giving mixed signals about the U.S. economy.

After very strong increases early in 1986, the composite index of the 12 leading indicators had posted small declines in May and June. In July (the most recent month for which data were available) the index had again risen and had risen by 1.1 percent, putting the index at an all-time high.

All other things equal, forecasters would have been optimistic, but many analysts were wary.

Industrial production had increased in the last two months but was still below the peak reached in January 1986.

Manufacturing employment was weak. (This weakness was attributed to the U.S. balance of trade deficit, with imported goods taking over traditional markets of many U.S. manufacturing firms.)

Continued to page 198

*This application contains information from several articles from *The Wall Street Journal:* "The Outlook—If Economy Is to Gain Consumers Need Help" by Lindley H. Clark, Jr., August 11, 1986; "The Outlook—The Growth in Services May Moderate Cycles" by Henry F. Myers, September 22, 1986; and "Industrial Average Declines 34.73 as Economic Data Take Their Toll" by Beatrice E. Garcia, September 26, 1986.

Particular thanks is due to Gregory P. Hoelscher, vice president, Chase Manhattan Bank. Dr. Hoelscher is active in the forecasting function of Chase and was able to provide us with the views of someone involved in forecasting.

THE WALL STREET JOURNAL

APPLICATION

Continued from page 197
And, second quarter results had certainly not pointed to an upturn.

> Inflation-adjusted GNP had risen in the second quarter at an annual rate of only 0.6 percent, down sharply from the 3.8 percent rate in the first quarter and far below the rosy predictions made at the end of 1985.

Indeed, *The Journal* reported that the mainstays of the economy so far in 1986 had been consumer spending and housing outlays. Capital spending remained in the doldrums.

And, given the most recent data, some analysts were worried about the possibility of renewed inflation.

> After half a year of price index declines (largely as a result of OPEC being unable to hold the line on oil prices), the consumer price index had risen in June at an annual rate of 5.7 percent. While the CPI remained unchanged in July, it again rose in August, this time at an annual rate of 2.5 percent.

Given the concern about inflation, the Blue Chip Economic Indicators survey was forecasting that the gain in inflation-adjusted disposable income would be much smaller in the second half of 1986 than it had been in the first half. By implication, the forecast was that consumer demand would be weaker.

In addition to the evidence provided by the monthly economic indicators and second quarter results, it had become evident by early September that the tax reform bill was going to pass in Congress. The tax bill contained provisions reducing the tax benefit to investment projects. Moreover, the tax bill was structured so that the accelerated depreciation deductions being removed would take effect on January 1, 1987, while the reduction in rates would become effective only at midyear, thereby raising the possibility of higher 1987 taxes for a significant number of taxpayers.

Two sectors of the economy would be particularly hard hit by these macroeconomic forecasts: automakers and manufacturers of business machines (particularly the so-called high technology sector). As has been noted earlier, automobiles (a consumer durable) would be particularly sensitive to income. The slow growth in consumer income would translate into lower sales for an industry already depressed. (For example, the

Continued to page 199

APPLICATION

Continued from page 198 aggressive financing incentives in place in September were able to raise sales by only 1.7 percent.) Since much of recent investment spending had been for computers and other automated office and production equipment, the reduced investment spending would be felt particularly by the business machine makers. This, coupled with the sluggish growth in consumer income, should result in smaller sales for this sector.

That was apparently the judgment of investors. During September, the S&P 500 (a broadly based measure of stock market performance) fell by 3 percent. Prices of auto stocks fell by 5 percent. The most dramatic day for the stock market was September 25 when the Dow Jones Industrial Average fell by almost 35 points. Hardest hit were auto stocks—General Motors, Ford, and Chrysler all declined—and technology issues—Hewlett-Packard led the decline, falling almost 4 points, but IBM, Burroughs, Cray Research, NCR, and Digital Equipment all declined. As the *Journal* reported, "investors seemed to be bringing their expectations on corporate profits back in line with reality."

8.3 TIME-SERIES MODELS

We now turn to the second major group of forecasting techniques—statistical forecasting. These methods lend themselves to a more analytical treatment, because the models can be replicated by another researcher. Recall that the statistical methods can be divided into two categories, time-series models and econometric models. We begin with time-series models.

As we noted in Chapter 4, a *time series* is simply a time-ordered sequence of observations on a variable. In general, forecasting via a time-series analysis uses only the time-series history of the variable of interest to develop a model for predicting future values. Time-series analyses involve the description of the process by which these historical data were generated. Thus, to forecast using time series, it is necessary to specify a mathematical model that represents the generating process.

Several characteristics of time series must be modeled if the resulting forecast is to be reliable. These are illustrated in Figure 8.3, in which the observed variable X is plotted along the vertical axis and time along the horizontal. In Panel A, we show a series that remains at a constant level over time but is subject to random variation from period to period. In

Panel B, the series exhibits a time trend in addition to the random variation. Panel C represents a series that is subject to some cyclical variation.

In the following discussion, we will provide a brief overview of some of the more basic techniques used in time-series forecasting to handle trend

Figure 8.3   Characteristics of Time Series

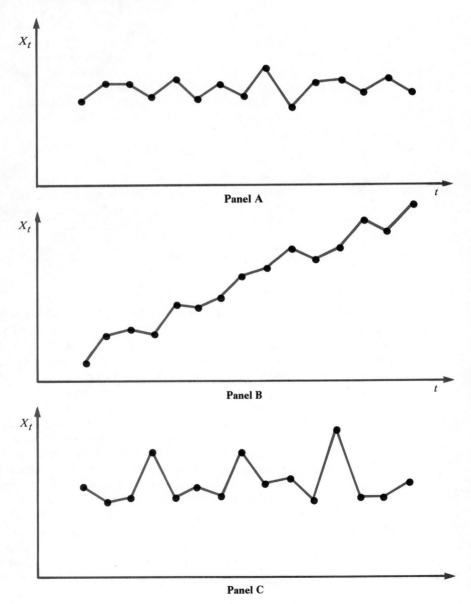

and cyclical variation. There exist other, more complicated time-series procedures, including the now widely used Box-Jenkins analysis. For those procedures we refer you to the references at the end of this chapter.

Linear Trend Forecasting

The simplest form of time-series forecasting uses a linear trend. Using this type of forecasting model, we would posit that sales—quantity demanded—increases (or decreases) linearly over time. To explain this kind of a forecast, let us use a simple example.

Suppose that, for a particular firm, sales for the period 1979–86 were as indicated by the eight data points in Figure 8.4. Using these data points, we could fit a straight line to the data scatter, as is illustrated by the solid line in Figure 8.4. Then, we would forecast sales in the future by extending this trend line and picking the forecast values of sales off this *extrapolated* trend line. We have illustrated sales forecasts for 1987 and 1992 ($\hat{Q}_{1987}$ and $\hat{Q}_{1992}$) in Figure 8.4.

This procedure is, of course, simple to accomplish using regression analysis. We have posited that there is a linear relation between sales and time,

$$Q_t = \alpha + \beta t.$$

Using available data (e.g., the eight observations for 1979 through 1986), we can use regression analysis to estimate the values of α and βt. That is, we estimate a trend line,

$$\hat{Q}_t = \hat{\alpha} + \hat{\beta} t,$$

Figure 8.4   **A Linear Trend Forecast**

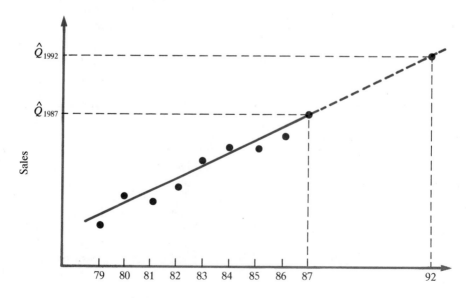

that best fits the historical data. If $\beta > 0$, sales are increasing over time, and if $\beta < 0$, sales are decreasing. However, if $\beta = 0$, sales are constant over time. (In this case, the pattern of sales might look like that in Panel A of Figure 8.3.) Hence, it is important to determine if there is indeed a *significant* trend in sales. This means that we need to determine if $\hat{\beta}$ is significantly different from zero. As always, we test for significance using a t-test.

If the estimation indicates a significant trend, we can use the estimated trend line to obtain forecasts of future sales. For example, if we wanted a forecast for sales in 1987, we simply insert 1987 into our estimated trend line:

$$\hat{Q}_{1987} = \hat{\alpha} + \hat{\beta} \times (1987).$$

Likewise, if we wanted a sales forecast for 1992,

$$\hat{Q}_{1992} = \hat{\alpha} + \hat{\beta} \times (1992).$$

Cyclical Variation (e.g., seasonal variation)

As we have indicated, time-series data may frequently exhibit regular, cyclical variation (e.g., seasonal variation) over time, and the failure to take these regular variations into account when estimating a forecasting equation would bias the forecast. Frequently, when using quarterly or monthly sales to forecast sales, seasonal variation may occur—the sales of many products vary systematically by month or by quarter. For example, in the retail clothing business, sales are generally higher around Easter and Christmas. Thus, sales would be higher during the second and fourth quarters of the year. Likewise, the sales of hunting equipment would peak during early fall, the third quarter. In such cases, you would definitely wish to incorporate the systematic variations when estimating the equation and forecasting future sales. We shall describe the technique most commonly employed to handle cyclical variation. The reader interested in additional techniques should look at the references cited at the end of this chapter.

Consider the simplified example of a firm producing and selling a product for which sales are consistently higher in the fourth quarter than in any other quarter. A hypothetical data scatter is presented in Figure 8.5. In each of the four years, the data point in the fourth quarter is much higher than in the other three. While a time trend clearly exists, if the analyst simply regressed sales against time, without accounting for the higher sales in the fourth quarter, too large a trend would be estimated (i.e., the slope would be too large). In essence, there is an upward shift of the trend line in the fourth quarter. Such a relation is presented in Figure 8.6. That is, in the fourth quarter, the intercept is higher than in the other quarters. In other words, α', the intercept of the trend line for the fourth-quarter data points, exceeds α, the intercept of the trend line

Figure 8.5 Sales with Seasonal Variation

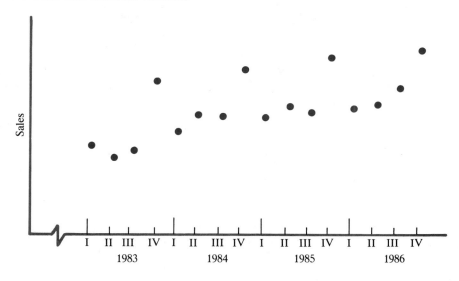

Figure 8.6 The Effect of Seasonal Variation

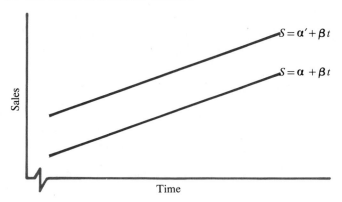

for the data points in the other quarters. One way of specifying this relation is to define α' as $\alpha' = \alpha + \delta$, where δ is some positive number. Therefore, the regression line we want to estimate will take the form:

$$Q_t = \alpha + \beta t + \delta,$$

where $\delta = 0$ in the first three quarters.

To accomplish the estimation of the preceding equation we use what is commonly referred to as a *dummy variable* in the estimating equation. A dummy variable is one that can take on only the values *zero* or *one*. In this case, we would assign the dummy variable (D) a value of one if

Table 8.2   Dummy Variable

	Q_t	t	D
	$S_{1983(I)}$	1	0
	$S_{1983(II)}$	2	0
	$S_{1983(III)}$	3	0
	$S_{1983(IV)}$	4	1
	$S_{1984(I)}$	5	0
	$S_{1984(II)}$	6	0
	$S_{1984(III)}$	7	0
	$S_{1984(IV)}$	8	1
	$S_{1985(I)}$	9	0
	$S_{1985(II)}$	10	0
	$S_{1985(III)}$	11	0
	$S_{1985(IV)}$	12	1
	$S_{1986(I)}$	13	0
	$S_{1986(II)}$	14	0
	$S_{1986(III)}$	15	0
	$S_{1986(IV)}$	16	1

the sales observation is from the fourth quarter and zero in the other three quarters. Our data observations would be as shown in Table 8.2, where S_t represents the sales figure in the tth period. Note that, since we are using quarterly data, we convert time into integers to obtain a continuous time variable. Using these data observations, we would then estimate the equation

$$Q_t = \alpha + \beta t + \delta D.$$

After this equation is estimated, we would have two equations like those shown in Figure 8.6. The estimated slope of the two equations would be the same ($\hat{\beta}$). For quarters I, II, and III the estimated intercept is $\hat{\alpha}$, while for the fourth quarter the estimated intercept is $\hat{\alpha} + \hat{\delta}$. This estimation really means that for any future period t_i, the sales forecast would be

$$Q_t = \hat{\alpha} + \hat{\beta} t_i$$

unless period t_i occurs in the fourth quarter, in which case the sales forecast would be

$$Q_{t_i} = \hat{\alpha} + \hat{\beta} t_i + \hat{\delta} = (\hat{\alpha} + \hat{\delta}) + \hat{\beta} t_i.$$

For example, going back to the data observations in Table 8.2, if we wished to forecast sales in the third quarter of 1987 we would use the equation

$$Q_{1987(III)} = \hat{\alpha} + \hat{\beta}(19).$$

If we wished to forecast sales in the fourth quarter of that year, we would use

$$Q_{1987(IV)} = (\hat{\alpha} + \hat{\delta}) + \hat{\beta}\,(20).$$

In other words, the mere fact that the forecast is for quarter IV adds the amount $\hat{\delta}$ to the sales that would otherwise be forecast.[1]

Going a step further, it could be the case that there exist quarter-to-quarter differences in sales (i.e., in Figure 8.6 there would be four trend lines). In this case, we would use three dummy variables: D_1 (equal to one in the first quarter and zero otherwise), D_2 (equal to one in the second quarter and zero otherwise), and D_3 (equal to one in the third quarter and zero otherwise).[2] Then, we would estimate the equation

$$Q_t = \alpha + \beta t + \delta_1 D_1 + \delta_2 D_2 + \delta_3 D_3.$$

In quarter I the intercept is $\alpha + \delta_1$, in quarter II it is $\alpha + \delta_2$, in quarter III it is $\alpha + \delta_3$, and in quarter IV it is α only.

To obtain a forecast for some future quarter, it is necessary to include the coefficient for the dummy variable for that particular quarter. For example, predictions for the third quarter of a particular year would take the form

$$\hat{Q}_t = \hat{\alpha} + \hat{\beta} t + \hat{\delta}_3.$$

Perhaps the best way to explain how these dummy variables can be used to account for cyclical variation is to provide an example.

APPLICATION

Use of Dummy Variables

Consider a firm with sales that are subject to seasonal variation, but which have a trend over time. We obtained sales data for 1983–86 by quarter. We wish to predict sales for all four quarters of 1987.

---

[1]Throughout this discussion, we have assumed that the trend lines differ only with respect to the intercepts—the slope is the same for all of the trend lines. We should note that dummy variables can also be used to reflect differences in slopes. This procedure is, however, beyond the scope of this text and we refer the interested reader to the references cited at the end of this chapter.

[2]Likewise, if there were month-to-month differences, we would use 11 dummy variables. Note that, in the formulation used here, one would always have one fewer dummy variable than periods considered. For further explanation, see the references at the end of this chapter.

Year	Quarter	Sales ($000)	t	D_1	D_2	D_3
	I	$ 72	1	1	0	0
	II	87	2	0	1	0
1983	III	87	3	0	0	1
	IV	150	4	0	0	0
	I	82	5	1	0	0
	II	98	6	0	1	0
1984	III	94	7	0	0	1
	IV	162	8	0	0	0
	I	97	9	1	0	0
	II	105	10	0	1	0
1985	III	109	11	0	0	1
	IV	176	12	0	0	0
	I	105	13	1	0	0
	II	121	14	0	1	0
1986	III	119	15	0	0	1
	IV	180	16	0	0	0

From the preceding discussion we know that this desired forecast requires us to estimate an equation containing three dummy variables. One such equation is

$$Q_t = \alpha + \beta t + \delta_1 D_1 + \delta_2 D_2 + \delta_3 D_3,$$

where D_1, D_2, and D_3 are, respectively, dummy variables for quarters I, II, and III.*

The data collected are presented above. (Note that, since we are using quarterly data, it is necessary to convert time into a continuous variable.) Using these data, the preceding regression equation was estimated. The results of this estimation were as follows:

---

*This is only one of the specifications that is appropriate. Equally appropriate is

$$\hat{Q}_t = \alpha + \beta t + \delta_2 D_2 + \delta_3 D_3 + \delta_4 D_4,$$
$$Q_t = \alpha + \beta t + \delta_1 D_1 + \delta_3 D_3 + \delta_4 D_4,$$

or

$$Q_t = \alpha + \beta t + \delta_1 D_1 + \delta_2 D_2 + \delta_4 D_4.$$

It is necessary only to have *any three* of the quarters represented by dummy variables.

```
DEPENDENT VARIABLE: QT        F-RATIO: 794.126

OBSERVATIONS: 16              R-SQUARE: 0.9965

                   PARAMETER          STANDARD
     VARIABLE      ESTIMATE           ERROR

     INTERCEPT     139.63             1.7436
     T               2.7375           0.12996
     D1            -69.788            1.6895
     D2            -58.775            1.6643
     D3            -62.013            1.6490
```

The first thing we might note about these results is that they indicate a positive trend in sales. That is, $\hat{\beta} > 0$. In order to be sure that there is a significant trend, we need to test for the significance of $\hat{\beta}$. The calculated t-value for $\hat{\beta}$ is $t_{\hat{\beta}} = 2.7375/0.12996 = 21.064$. With $16 - 5 = 11$ degrees of freedom, the critical value of t (using a 95 percent confidence level) is 2.201. Since $21.064 > 2.201$, we know that $\hat{\beta}$ is significant, so we do have evidence of a significant positive trend in sales.

From the preceding discussion of dummy variables we know that the estimated intercept of the trend line is, in the first quarter

$$\hat{\alpha} + \hat{\delta}_1 = 139.63 - 69.788$$
$$= 69.842,$$

in the second quarter

$$\hat{\alpha} + \hat{\delta}_2 = 139.63 - 58.775$$
$$= 80.855,$$

in the third quarter

$$\hat{\alpha} + \hat{\delta}_3 = 139.63 - 62.013$$
$$= 77.617,$$

and in the fourth quarter

$$\hat{\alpha} = 139.63.$$

Therefore, these estimates indicate that the intercepts—and thereby sales—are lower in quarters I, II, and III than in quarter IV. The question that always must be asked is: Are these intercepts *significantly* lower?

To answer this question, let's compare quarters I and IV. In quarter I, the intercept is $\hat{\alpha} + \hat{\delta}_1$; in quarter IV, it is $\hat{\alpha}$. Hence, if $\hat{\alpha} + \hat{\delta}_1$ is significantly lower than $\hat{\alpha}$, it is necessary that $\hat{\delta}_1$ be significantly less than zero. That is, if

$$\hat{\alpha} + \hat{\delta}_1 < \hat{\alpha}$$

it follows that $\hat{\delta}_1 < 0$. We already know that $\hat{\delta}_1$ is negative; to determine if it is significantly negative, we must perform a t-test. The calculated value of t for $\hat{\delta}_1$ is

$$t_{\hat{\delta}_1} = \frac{-69.788}{1.6895} = -41.307.$$

Since $|-41.307| = 41.307 > 2.201$, we know that $\hat{\delta}_1$ is significantly less than zero. Therefore, we know that the intercept—and sales—in the first quarter is less than in the fourth. Calculating the t-values for $\hat{\delta}_2$ and $\hat{\delta}_3$,

$$t_{\hat{\delta}_2} = \frac{-58.775}{1.6643} = -35.315$$

and

$$t_{\hat{\delta}_3} = \frac{-62.013}{1.6490} = -37.606,$$

we see that they are both also significantly negative. We know then that the intercepts in the second and third quarters are also significantly less than the intercept for the fourth quarter. Hence, we know that there is a significant increase in sales in the fourth quarter.

We can now proceed to forecast sales by quarters for 1987. In the first quarter of 1987, $t = 17$, $D_1 = 1$, $D_2 = 0$, and $D_3 = 0$. Therefore, the forecast for sales in 1987I would be

$$\begin{aligned}
Q &= \hat{\alpha} + \hat{\beta} \cdot 17 + \hat{\delta}_1 \cdot 1 + \hat{\delta}_2 \cdot 0 + \hat{\delta}_3 \cdot 0 \\
&= \hat{\alpha} + \hat{\beta} \cdot 17 + \hat{\delta}_1 \\
&= 139.63 + 2.7375 \cdot 17 - 69.788 \\
&= 116.3795.
\end{aligned}$$

Using precisely the same method, the forecasts for sales in the other three quarters of 1987 are as follows:

1987 II:

$$\begin{aligned}
Q &= \hat{\alpha} + \hat{\beta} \cdot 18 + \hat{\delta}_2 \\
&= 139.63 + 2.7375 \cdot 18 - 58.775 \\
&= 130.13.
\end{aligned}$$

1987 III:

$$Q = \hat{\alpha} + \hat{\beta} \cdot 19 + \hat{\delta}_3$$
$$= 139.63 + 2.7375 \cdot 19 - 62.013$$
$$= 129.6295.$$

1987 IV:

$$Q = \hat{\alpha} + \hat{\beta} \cdot 20$$
$$= 139.63 + 2.7375 \cdot 20$$
$$= 194.38.$$

In this discussion, we have confined our attention to quarterly variation. However, exactly the same techniques can be used for any type of cyclical (nonrandom) variation. It should be clear how this technique could be used for monthly data. In addition, this type of technique can be used to account for changes in sales due to forces such as wars and strikes at a competitor's facility.

8.4 ECONOMETRIC MODELS

The other method used in statistical forecasting and decision making is econometric modeling. The primary characteristic of econometric models that differentiates this approach from the preceding approaches is the use of an explicit structural model that attempts to *explain* the underlying economic relations. More specifically, if we wish to employ an econometric model to forecast future sales, it is necessary to develop a model that incorporates those variables that actually determine the level of sales (e.g., income, the price of substitutes, and so on). This approach is in marked contrast to the qualitative approach, in which a loose relation was posited between sales and some leading indicators, and the time-series approach, in which sales are assumed to behave in some regular fashion over time.

The use of econometric models has several advantages. First, econometric models require the analysts to define explicit causal relations. This specification of an explicit model helps rule out problems such as spurious (false) correlation between normally unrelated variables and may help to make the model more logically consistent and reliable.

Second, this approach allows analysts to consider the sensitivity of the variable to be forecasted to changes in the exogenous variables. Using estimated elasticities, forecasters can determine which of the variables are most important in determining changes in the variable to be forecasted.

Therefore, the analyst will know to watch the behavior of these variables more closely.

Third, this approach can easily be used in a simulation model. Basically, a simulation procedure is designed to answer "what if" questions. Whereas a single-point forecast uses actual, prevailing data on the values of or trends in the variables, a simulation model allows researchers to consider alternative projections based on hypothetical conditions. Thus, the analyst can get an idea of what could happen if market conditions change. (We will return to a consideration of simulation in the final part of this section.)

Simultaneous Equations Forecasts

The idea behind simultaneous equations forecasting is really quite simple. We illustrate this methodology using Figure 8.7. Suppose that, using regression analysis, we have estimated the demand function

$$Q_{X,t} = \hat{a} + \hat{b}P_{x,t} + \hat{c}Y_t + \hat{d}P_{R,t}$$

and the supply function

$$Q_{X,t} = \hat{e} + \hat{f}P_{X,t} + \hat{g}T_t + \hat{h}P_{F,t}.$$

(Note again that the hats on the parameters indicate that they are estimates.) Since we know the actual 1986 values for the exogenous variables Y_{1986} and $P_{R,1986}$, we know where the demand function is located in 1986. Likewise, since T_{1986} and $P_{F,1986}$ are also known, we know where the supply function is located in 1986. These demand and supply functions are illustrated in Figure 8.7. Note that their intersection indicates price and sales of X in 1986.

Suppose that in 1986 we want to forecast sales in 1989. As should be clear, in order to obtain this sales forecast, we need to know where the demand and supply functions will be located in 1989. What determines their locations?

From our discussion in Chapter 2 and in the last few chapters, the answer to this question is simple: The values of the exogenous variables determine the location of the demand and supply functions. In the case of our estimated demand function, the values of income and the price of the related good in 1989 will determine the location of the 1989 demand function. For simplicity, let's suppose that, over the period 1986–89, the price of the related good is expected to remain unchanged,

$$P_{R,1989} = P_{R,1986},$$

but income is expected to rise,

$$Y_{1989} > Y_{1986}.$$

As long as X is a normal commodity, this would mean that the 1989 location of the demand curve would be as indicated in Figure 8.7.

Figure 8.7   Simultaneous Equations Forecasting

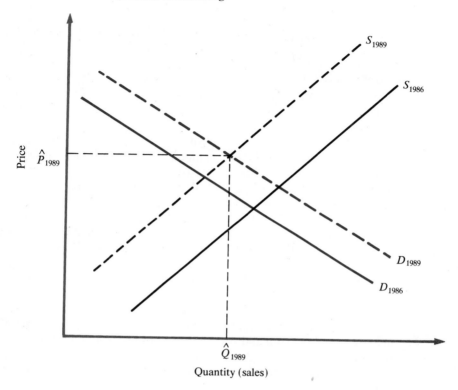

In the case of the supply function, its location is determined by the values of T and P_F. Suppose, for purposes of illustration, that comparing 1989 and 1986, we expect

$$T_{1989} = T_{1986}$$

and

$$P_{F,1989} > P_{F,1986}.$$

This set of conditions would yield a 1989 supply function like that illustrated in Figure 8.7.

Once the locations of the 1989 supply and demand functions are determined, the forecast is simple to obtain. We would find the intersection of the two functions and, from that intersection, obtain both forecasted price and forecasted sales in 1989. In Figure 8.7 these are denoted as $\hat{P}_{1989}$ and $\hat{Q}_{1989}$.

Given this graphical interpretation, let's see how we can actually obtain a forecast, using our estimated demand and supply functions:

Demand: $Q_{X,t} = \hat{a} + \hat{b}P_{X,t} + \hat{c}Y_t + \hat{d}P_{R,t}$

Supply: $Q_{X,t} = \hat{e} + \hat{f}P_{X,t} + \hat{g}T_t + \hat{h}P_{F,t}$.

Let's suppose that these functions were estimated for time periods 1,2, . . .,t and that we want a forecast for period $t + i$.

First, we need to obtain the forecasted values for the *exogenous* variables for period $t+i$. That is, we need to obtain $\hat{Y}_{t+i}, \hat{P}_{R,t+i}, \hat{T}_{t+i}$, and $\hat{P}_{F,t+i}$. There are several ways in which we might obtain these values. We might simply forecast these values using the time-series methodology described in Section 8.3.[3]

Alternatively, note that many of these exogenous variables are macroeconomic variables. In the demand function we use income (or per capita income). If we were forecasting the demand for automobiles, we might use the U.S. price of petroleum (or gasoline) as the price of the related good. In our supply function, the price of inputs, P_F, might include things like the wage rate in manufacturing. All of these aggregate (macroeconomic) variables are forecasted by many organizations. In Table 8.3 we have listed some of the more widely known macroeconomic forecasting models. Hence, we might use forecasts from one of these macroeconomic forecasting models as our $t + i$ values of the variables that are exogenous in our model.

Once we have the $t + i$ forecasts for Y, P_R, T, and P_F, we can use them to forecast the locations of the demand and supply functions. And, once the $t + i$ demand and supply functions are isolated, we can calculate the intersection of the two functions to obtain forecasted equilibrium output—sales—in period $t + i$. To see how this is accomplished, let's look at an example.

Table 8.3   Macroeconomic Forecasting Models

Public Policy Models

FRB-MIT-Penn Model
Wharton Quarterly Model
St. Louis Federal Reserve Bank Model
Michigan Quarterly Model
Department of Commerce (OBE) Model
Brookings Quarterly Model

Models Supported by Private Firms

Data Resources, Inc.
Chase Econometrics
Wharton Econometrics

---

[3]In the case of the prices, it may be necessary to consider whether these prices are determined in efficient markets. If so, some additional econometric manipulation may be necessary, an issue discussed in the references listed at the end of this chapter.

APPLICATION

A Forecast for World Copper Consumption

Returning to the copper data we presented in Chapter 7, let's forecast future copper consumption. We defined the world demand function for copper as

$$Q_{copper,t} = a + bP_{copper,t} + cY_t + dP_{aluminum,t}$$

and the supply function as

$$Q_{copper,t} = e + fP_{copper,t} + gT_t + hX_t,$$

where time is our proxy for the level of available technology and X is the ratio of consumption to production in the preceding period (to reflect inventory changes). Both of these functions are identified and can be estimated using two-stage least squares.

As you can verify, our estimate for the demand function was

$$Q_{copper,t} = -6837.8 - 66.495\, P_{copper,t} + 13997Y_t$$
$$+ 107.66\, P_{aluminum,t}.$$

We also estimated the supply function (via $2SLS$), using the data for $t = 1, 2, \ldots, 25$. The resulting estimated supply function was

$$Q_{copper,t} = 145.623 + 18.154\, P_{copper,t} + 213.88T_t + 1819.8X_t.$$

We want to forecast sales in year 26. We will obtain this forecast by proceeding with the steps outlined in our description of simultaneous equations forecasting:

Step 1—Obtain the year 26 values for the exogenous variables. Since time is our proxy for technology, the period 26 value for T is simply $\hat{T}_{26} = 26$. As previously noted, the value for X in any period is the ratio of consumption to production in the preceding period. Since both of these values are known (consumption was 7157.2 and production was 8058.0) $\hat{X}_{26} = 7157.2/8058.0 = 0.88821$. However, in the case of Y and P_R, we need forecasted values. To obtain these, we used the techniques of time-series forecasting to obtain

$$\hat{Y}_{26} = 1.13 \text{ and } \hat{P}_{R.26} = 23.79.$$

Step 2—Locate the demand and supply functions for time period 26. Using $\hat{Y}_{26}$ and $P_{R.26}$, the demand function in time period 26 is

$$Q_{copper,26} = -6837.8 - 66.495\, P_{copper,26}$$
$$+ 13997\,(1.13) + 107.66\,(23.79)$$
$$= 11540.04 - 66.495\, P_{copper,26}$$

or

$$P_{copper,26} = 173.547 - 0.0150\, Q_{copper,26}.$$

Likewise, using $\hat{T}_{26}$ and $\hat{X}_{26}$, the supply function in time period 26 is

$$Q_{copper,26} = 145.623 + 18.154\, P_{copper,26}$$
$$+ 213.88\,(26) + 1819.8\,(0.88821)$$
$$= 7322.868 + 18.154\, P_{copper,26}$$

or

$$P_{copper,26} = -403.375 + 0.0551\, Q_{copper,26}.$$

Step 3—Calculate the intersection of the demand and supply functions. Equating the two equilibrium price equations,

$$173.547 - 0.0150\, Q_{copper,26} = -403.375 + 0.0551\, Q_{copper,26}.$$

Solving for $Q_{copper,26}$,

$$0.0702\, Q_{copper,26} = 576.922,$$

and $Q_{copper,26} = 8218.3$. That is, our forecast is that sales would be 8218.3 thousand metric tons in year 26.*

---

*As we noted in Chapter 7, the data we have used for our copper market illustration are the actual data for the period 1951–75. Hence, our forecast for year 26 can be interpreted as the forecast for 1976. The actual value for copper consumption in 1976 was 8174.0, so our forecast error in this application was 0.54 percent—about ½ of 1 percent.

A Note on Simulations

As we noted earlier, the primary objective of a simulation analysis is to answer "what if" questions. This procedure can probably best be explained in the context of the preceding example.

In obtaining our forecasts for the copper market, we assumed that the exogenous variables Y and P_R would continue to follow their historical trends. However, it is quite possible that the exogenous variables will deviate from trend. For example, it may well be the case that real income will grow less rapidly than it has in the past. Thus, we might wish to obtain alternative forecasts under the assumption that the growth rate in income will be smaller than that indicated by historical trend.

Adjusting for this type of alternative is precisely what a simulation analysis is designed to do. We would provide alternative forecasts based on alternative projections about the future values of the exogenous variables. In this way, we can examine "what would happen if . . . ." Note that in this way the qualitative and quantitative forecasting techniques are brought together. In a simulation analysis, researchers can impose some subjective evaluations and employ their expertise in the market. For example, in our forecasts of copper consumption, it might be that we think that conditions in the aluminum market are such that price will rise radically. Thus, we could provide an alternate forecast that incorporates this information based on our expertise and knowledge about a particular market.

8.5 SOME FINAL WARNINGS

We have often heard it said in respect to forecasting that "he who lives by the crystal ball ends up eating ground glass." While we do not make nearly so dire a judgment, we do feel that you should be aware of the major limitations of and problems inherent in forecasting. Basically, our warnings are concerned with three issues—confidence intervals, specification, and change of structure.

To describe the issue of confidence intervals in forecasting, let's look again at the simple linear trend model,

$$Q_t = \alpha + \beta t.$$

In order to obtain our prediction model, we must estimate two coefficients, α and β. As you know, we cannot estimate these coefficients with certainty. Indeed, the estimated standard errors reflect the magnitude of uncertainty (i.e., potential error) about the values of the parameters.

In Figure 8.8, we have illustrated a situation in which we have observations on sales for period t_1 through t_n. Due to the manner in which it is calculated, the regression line will go through the mean of the distribution of data points $(\bar{Q}, \bar{t})$. In Panel A, we have illustrated as the shaded area our confidence region if there exist errors only in the estimation of the slope, β. In Panel B, the shaded area represents our confidence region if an error exists only in the estimation of the intercept, α. These two shaded areas are combined in Panel C. As you can see, the further the value of t is from the mean value of t, the wider becomes this zone of uncertainty.

Now consider what happens when we use the estimated regression line to predict future sales. At a future time period, t_{n+k}, our prediction for sales will be a point on the extrapolated regression line (i.e., $\hat{Q}$). However, note what happens to our region of uncertainty about this estimate. The further you forecast into the future, the wider is this region of uncertainty, and this region increases geometrically rather than arithmetically.

This warning applies not just to time-series models. It applies to all statistical techniques. The further the variables used in the forecasts are from the mean values used in the regression, the wider will be the region of uncertainty, and therefore, the less precise will be the forecast. For example, consider our econometric forecasting model for copper. If we attempt to forecast copper sales using a value of per capita income that is much higher than the mean in our data set, the confidence interval for our forecast will be much wider than would be the case if the value of income used in the forecast was close to the mean value in our data set.

Figure 8.8 Confidence Intervals

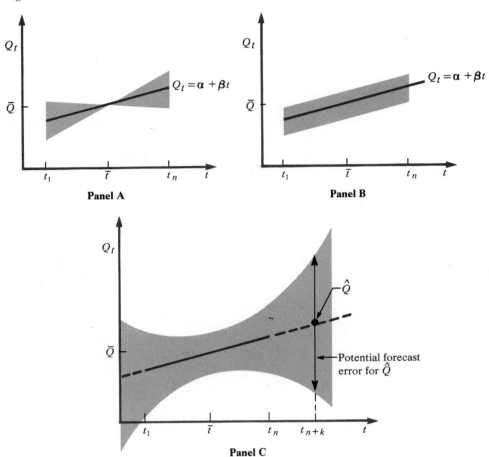

Panel A

Panel B

Panel C

We noted the problem of incorrect specification in our discussion of demand estimation, but we feel that it is important enough to deserve another mention here. In order to generate reliable forecasts, the model used must incorporate the appropriate variables. The quality of the forecast can be severely reduced if important explanatory variables are excluded or if an improper functional form is employed (e.g., using a linear form when a nonlinear form is appropriate).

We have saved what we feel to be the most important problem for last. This problem stems from potential changes in structure. Forecasts are widely, and often correctly, criticized for failing to predict "turning points"—sharp changes in the variable under consideration. If it were the case that these changes were only the result of radical changes in the exogenous variables, the simulation approach should be able to handle the problem. However, it is often the case that such changes are the result of changes in the structure of the market itself.

For example, in our consideration of the copper market, there exists the potential for a major change in structure. A major consumer of copper is the telecommunications industry. This industry has been replacing copper transmitting cables with glass fibers. As this change occurs, the demand for copper will be affected significantly. More specifically, any temporal or econometric relation estimated using data before such a change would be incapable of correctly forecasting quantity demanded after the change. In the context of a demand function, the coefficients would be different before and after the change.

Unfortunately, we know of no satisfactory method of handling this problem of "change in structure." Instead, we must simply leave you with the warning that changes in structure are likely. The further you forecast into the future, the more likely is it that you will encounter such a change. To illustrate the warning, let us give you a historical example.

APPLICATION

The Dismal Science

A classic example of a forecast made invalid by changes in structure is found in the work of Thomas Malthus, an English economist of the late 18th century. According to Malthus, food production was growing at an arithmetic rate while population was expanding geometrically. As is clear in the figure below, such a set of conditions produces a dismal forecast for the future. (Indeed, it was this forecast that led to economics being labeled "the dismal science.") Malthus predicted that population growth would outrun the available food supply, leading to periods of starvation. In the long run, he predicted only a minimum subsistence level of consumption.

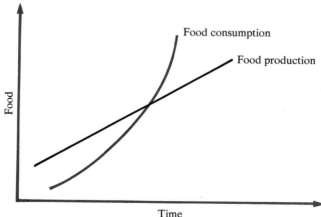

Obviously, this dire prediction did not come to pass. Where did Malthus's forecast go wrong? He was unable to foresee changes in structure—particularly in food production. Clearly, technological change in agriculture has increased the rate of growth of food production. The existing trends, which Malthus observed at the time, simply did not hold true in the future.

This example is meant to illustrate a lesson that we feel is extremely important—and one that has not been learned by many people. Compare for a moment Malthus's prediction (which appears ridiculous in retrospect) and the various predictions of doom. Simplifying, the "limits to growth" theories predict that the rate of growth in consumption will outrun the rate of growth in the production of natural resources (particularly energy), leading to depletion of natural resources and Armageddon for the developed economies—precisely the same sort of argument made by Malthus. This prediction is valid only if there are no changes in structure. However, even the most casual review of history indicates that such circumstances have led to changes in structure in the past. It seems unlikely that none will occur in the future.

TECHNICAL PROBLEMS

1. Contrast and compare qualitative and statistical forecasting methods.
2. Why is price forecasting likely to be unsuccessful in an efficient market?
3. Provide an example of a product traded in an efficient market. Provide an example of a product traded in a market that deviates substantially from the characteristics of an efficient market.
4. A linear trend equation for sales of the form

$$Q_t = \alpha + \beta t$$

was estimated for the period 1972–86 (i.e., $t = 72, 73, \ldots, 86$). The results of the regression are as follows:

```
DEPENDENT VARIABLE: QT      F-RATIO: 13.1792

OBSERVATIONS: 15            R-SQUARE: 0.8786

                 PARAMETER           STANDARD
VARIABLE         ESTIMATE            ERROR

INTERCEPT        73.7146             10.1315
T                 3.7621              1.0363
```

a. Test the estimated coefficients for statistical significance at a 95 percent confidence level. Does this estimation indicate a significant trend?

b. Perform an F-test for significance of the equation at a 95 percent confidence level.

c. Using this equation, forecast sales in 1987 and 1992.

d. Comment on the precision of these two forecasts.

5. Consider a firm subject to quarter-to-quarter variation in its sales. Suppose that the following equation was estimated using quarterly data for the period 1978–86 (the time variable goes from 1 to 36). The variables D_1, D_2, and D_3 are, respectively, dummy variables for the first, second, and third quarters (e.g., D_1 is equal to one in the first quarter and zero otherwise).

$$Q_t = \alpha + \beta t + \delta_1 D_1 + \delta_2 D_2 + \delta_3 D_3$$

The results of the estimation are presented below:

VARIABLE	PARAMETER ESTIMATE	STANDARD ERROR
INTERCEPT	51.234	7.163
T	3.127	0.524
D1	-11.716	2.717
D2	-1.424	0.836
D3	-17.367	2.112

DEPENDENT VARIABLE: QT
OBSERVATIONS: 36
F-RATIO: 761.133
R-SQUARE: 0.9761

a. Perform t- and F-tests to check for statistical significance of the coefficients and the equation.

b. Calculate the intercept in each of the four quarters. What do these values imply?

c. Use this estimated equation to forecast sales in the four quarters of 1987.

6. Supply and demand functions were specified for commodity X:

Demand: $Q_{X,t} = a + bP_{X,t} + cY_t + dP_{R,t}$
Supply: $Q_{X,t} = e + fP_{X,t} + gP_{F,t}$

Using quarterly data for the period 1980I through 1987IV, these functions were estimated (via 2SLS). The resulting parameter estimates are presented in the following estimated equations.

Demand: $Q_{X,t} = 50 - 30P_{X,t} + 0.10Y_t - 20P_{R,t}$
Supply: $Q_{X,t} = -40 + 20P_{X,t} - 10P_{F,t}$

Predicted values for the exogenous variables (Y, P_R, and P_F) for the first quarter of 1989 were obtained from a macroeconomic forecasting model. These predicted values are:

Income (Y) = 10,000
The price of the commodity related in consumption (P_R) = 20
The price of inputs (P_F) = 6.

   a. Are the signs of the estimated coefficients as would be predicted theoretically? Explain.
   b. Predict the sales of commodity X in 1989I.
7. Describe the major shortcomings of time-series models.
8. Suppose that you have an estimate of the demand function

$$Q_{X,t} = a + bP_{X,t} + cY_t + dP_{R,t}.$$

Obviously you could use historical trend to forecast the values for *all* of the right-hand side variables and thereby obtain a prediction for sales. What is the major shortcoming in such an approach?
9. In the final section of this chapter we provided warnings about three problems which frequently arise. List, explain, and provide and example of each.

ANALYTICAL PROBLEMS

1. In Technical Problem 6, you were given price forecasts for P_R and P_F. How could these price forecasts have been obtained? What problems arise in obtaining price forecasts?
2. Suppose that your firm produces refrigerators and freezers and you wish to obtain a qualitative forecast of future sales. Consider the 12 leading indicators published by the U.S. Department of Commerce. Evaluate the effect of changes in these indicators on future sales of your firm. (For example, if the average workweek of production workers in manufacturing increased, what would be the effect on your sales in the future and why?) Which of these indicators would be most important to your firm? Explain.
3. Suppose that a firm's sales are subject to cyclical variation. Describe the effect on estimated trend if the analyst does not account for this variation. Conversely, the analyst might employ a technique such as dummy variables when there exists no cyclical variation. What effect would this have on the estimation?
4. A market in which considerable sales forecasting is done is the automobile market. Clearly, if an automobile firm produces too many units, the costs from holding this inventory are substantial.

Alternatively, if too few units are produced, sales are lost and substantial profits are forgone. However, as is evident from the recent experience of U.S. automobile manufacturers, such forecasting is not yet precise.

a. If you were to provide a qualitative forecast, which of the leading indicators would be most relevant? Why? What additional information would you wish to have?

b. Comment on the applicability of time-series forecasting in the automobile market.

c. Let us consider an econometric forecasting model for this market:

   (1) Specify the demand and supply functions you think appropriate and explain why they are appropriate.

   (2) In our examination of the copper market, we forecasted the values of the exogenous variables, using historical trend. Such an approach might not be advisable in the automobile market—particularly in the case of the complementary good, gasoline. As you may be aware, the real (deflated) price of gasoline fell during most of the 1960s. Only after the mid-70s did it begin its rapid rise with its subsequent decline in the early 80s. With this circumstance in mind, suggest a methodology for forecasting automobile sales in the future.

5. As you know, the 1930s was the period of the Great Depression (although we fail to see what was so great about it). This period was followed by World War II. Many economists predicted that at the end of the war the U.S. economy would again enter a depression.

   These economists could not have been more wrong. The decade of the 1950s was one of the most productive in the history of the United States. (This fact might help to explain the TV series which extolled the 50s as the "happy days.")

   Explain why the economists' forecasts went wrong. What factors did they fail to predict correctly and what information did they exclude from their forecasts?

6. Until recently, the sale of Coors beer was rather localized. And, there are still many areas of the nation in which Coors does not distribute. We might note that recently groups such as union members and women's rights activists boycotted Coors beer. Consider the following forecasting problems.

   a. Suppose that Coors' management wishes to expand the territory in which it sells and they wish to forecast sales in a particular area in which they presently have no distributorship. How would you set up a forecasting model to predict sales in that area? What variables would you consider important in setting up the model? How important would you expect price to be?

b. Alternatively, assume that management wishes to find the best area in which to expand out of all the areas not presently served. What kind of a model would you develop in this case? What variables are important?

SUGGESTED ADDITIONAL REFERENCES

Box, G. E. P., and G. M. Jenkins. *Time Series Analysis, Forecasting and Control.* San Francisco: Holden-Day, 1970.

Granger, C. W. J. *Forecasting in Business and Economics.* New York: Academic Press, 1980.

Montgomery, D. C., and L. A. Johnson. *Forecasting and Time Series Analysis.* New York: McGraw-Hill, 1976.

Pindyck, R. C., and D. L. Rubinfeld. *Econometric Models and Economic Forecasts.* New York: McGraw-Hill, 1981.

PART THREE

PRODUCTION AND COST

THEORY OF PRODUCTION

T he theory of production is essential to understanding managerial economics. Production theory forms the foundation for the theory of supply, which, as we have seen, is one of the basic concepts in the determination of prices. Moreover, production decisions are an important part of managerial decision making.

Managers make four types of production decisions: (1) whether to produce or to shut down; (2) how much output to produce; (3) what input combination to use; and (4) what type of technology to use. This chapter is concerned primarily with the manager's choice of the input combination and choice of technology. Analysis of the shutdown and output decisions is postponed until later chapters.

We shall see that production involves the transformation of inputs— such as capital equipment, labor, and land—into output—goods or services. In this production process, the manager is concerned with *efficiency* in the use of these inputs. And, this objective of efficiency will provide us with some basic rules about the manner in which firms should utilize inputs to produce goods and services.

You will see that basic production theory is simply an application of the constrained optimization we discussed in Chapter 3. The firm attempts either to minimize the cost of producing a given level of output or to maximize the output attainable with a given level of cost. It will become clear that both optimization problems lead to the same rule for the allocation of inputs and choice of the technology. And this rule is applicable to a wide range of resource allocation problems.

We begin with a general discussion of what is meant by a production function. In this chapter we limit our attention to firms that produce a single product. We will take up the issue of multiproduct firms in Chapter 17. We then consider production in the short run, when only one input may be varied. Next we consider production and the optimal combination of inputs when two or more of the inputs are variable. To conclude our discussion, we consider the effect of an increase in all inputs on total output, and we examine the effect of changes in input prices and in technology.

9.1 PRODUCTION FUNCTIONS

A production function is the link between levels of input usage and attainable levels of output. That is, the production function formally describes the relation between physical rates of output and physical rates of input usage. With a given state of technology, the attainable quantity of output depends upon the quantities of the various inputs employed in production.

Definition. A production function is a schedule (or table, or mathematical equation) showing the maximum *amount of output that can be produced from any specified set of inputs, given the existing technology or "state of the art." In short, the production function is a catalog of output possibilities.*

Many different inputs are used in production. So, in the most general case, we can define maximum output, Q, to be a function of the level of usage of the various inputs, X. That is,

$$Q = f(X_1, X_2, \ldots, X_n).$$

But in our discussion we will generally restrict our attention to the simpler case of one output produced using either one input or two inputs. As examples of the two inputs, we will normally use capital and labor. Hence the production function we will usually be concerned with is

$$Q = f(K,L).$$

However, we must stress that the principles we will develop apply to situations with more than two inputs and, as well, to inputs other than capital and labor.

Let us emphasize that the production function shows the *maximum output* attainable from specified levels of input usage. For example, suppose the production function indicates that combining 10 units of capital and 40 units of labor yields 100 units of output per period. Clearly, 10 units of capital and 40 units of labor could produce less than 100 units of output if they are used inefficiently, but they can produce no more. If we want more output, we must increase one or both of the inputs.

Economic Efficiency

Before proceeding, we want to distinguish between *technical efficiency* and *economic efficiency*. The production function incorporates the technically efficient method of production—the latest technological processes are used. A producer cannot reduce the usage of one input and keep output the same without increasing the usage of one or more other inputs. When economists use production functions they assume that the maximum level of output is obtained from any given combination of inputs; that is, they assume that production is technically efficient.

When producers are faced with input prices, the problem is not technical but economic efficiency: how to produce a given amount of output at the lowest possible cost. To be economically efficient, a producer must determine the combination of inputs that solves this problem, given a specified production function and set of input prices. As you will recall from Chapter 3, this is a constrained optimization problem. The optimization rules we discussed there and those we develop in this chapter lead a producer to an economically efficient method of production.

We must be careful about labeling a particular production process inefficient. Certainly a process would be technically inefficient if another process can produce the same amount of output using less of one or more inputs and the same amounts of all others. If, however, the second process uses less of some inputs but more of others, the economically efficient method of producing a given level of output depends on the prices of the inputs. Even when both are technically efficient, one process might cost less—be economically efficient—under one set of input prices, while the other may be economically efficient at other input prices.

A simple example should illustrate the difference. Suppose a shoe manufacturer finds that some leather is being wasted; that is, some leather is ruined in the production process and has to be thrown out. An engineer might suggest modifying the process to eliminate the waste. An economist would probably react differently. If the price of the wasted leather is low relative to the price of the resources used to save it, economic efficiency may well involve throwing away some leather. The problem is to determine the optimal amount to waste. If the price of leather becomes quite high, less should be wasted. Economic, but not technical, efficiency is determined by input prices.

Short Run and Long Run

When analyzing the process of production, it is convenient to introduce the classification of inputs as *fixed* or *variable*. A fixed input is one for which the level of usage cannot readily be changed. To be sure, no input is ever absolutely fixed, no matter how short the period of time under consideration. However, the cost of immediately varying the use of an input may be so great that, for all practical purposes, the input is fixed. For example, buildings, major pieces of machinery, and managerial personnel are inputs that generally cannot be rapidly augmented or diminished. A variable input, on the other hand, is one for which the level of usage may be changed quite readily in response to desired changes in output. Many types of labor services as well as certain raw and processed materials would be in this category.

Given the preceding classification of inputs, economists distinguish between the *short run* and the *long run*. The short run refers to that period of time in which the level of usage of one or more of the inputs is fixed. Therefore, in the short run, changes in output must be accomplished exclusively by changes in the use of the variable inputs. Thus, if producers wish to expand output in the short run, they must do so by using more hours of labor (a variable service) and other variable inputs, with the existing plant and equipment. Similarly, if they wish to reduce output in the short run, they may discharge only certain inputs. They cannot immediately "discharge" a building or a blast furnace (even though its use may fall to zero).[1] In the context of our simplified production function, we might consider capital to be the fixed input and write the resulting short-run production function as

$$Q = f(\bar{K}, L),$$

where the bar over capital means that it is fixed. Furthermore, since capital is fixed, output depends only on the level of usage of labor, so we could write the short-run production function as simply

$$Q = f(L).$$

On the other hand, the long run is defined as that period of time (or planning horizon) in which all inputs are variable. The long run, in other words, refers to that time in the future when output changes can be accomplished in the manner most advantageous to the producers. For example, in the short run a producer may be able to expand output by operating the existing plant for more hours per day. In the long run, it may be more economical to install additional productive facilities and return to the normal workday.

Fixed or Variable Proportions

Most of our discussion in this chapter refers to production functions that allow at least some substitution of one input for one another in reaching an output target. When there is substitution we say inputs may be used in *variable* proportions. As a consequence, producers must determine not only the optimal level of output to produce but also the optimal mix of inputs. Production under variable proportions means that output can be

---

[1] Alternatively, we can say that, in the short run, the firm can vary its output but it cannot change its capacity. In the long run the firm can vary both output and capacity. We could consider a time period so short that all inputs are fixed. In this case, sometimes referred to as the *very short run,* output as well as capacity is fixed.

changed in the short run by changing the variable inputs without changing the fixed inputs. And, it means that the same output can be produced using different combinations of inputs.

Most economists regard production under conditions of variable proportions as typical of both the short and long run. There is certainly no doubt that proportions are variable in the long run. When making an investment decision, for instance, a producer may choose among a wide variety of different production processes. As polar opposites, an automobile can be practically handmade or it can be made by assembly-line techniques. In the short run, however, there may be some cases where there is little opportunity for substitution among inputs.

Fixed proportions production means that there is one, and only one, ratio or mix of inputs that can be used to produce a good. If output is expanded or contracted, all inputs must be expanded or contracted at the same rate to maintain the fixed input ratio. At first glance, this might seem the usual condition: one worker and one shovel produce a ditch; two parts hydrogen and one part oxygen produce water. Adding a second shovel or a second part of oxygen will not augment the rate of production. In such cases, the producer has little discretion about what combination of inputs to employ. The only decision is how much to produce.

In actuality, examples of fixed proportions production are hard to come by. Certainly some "ingredient" inputs are often used in relatively fixed proportions to output. Otherwise, the quality of the product would change. There is so much leather in a pair of shoes of a particular size and style. Use less leather, and we have a different type of shoe. There is so much tobacco in a cigarette, and so on. In these cases, the producer has little choice over the quantity of input per unit of output. But fixed-ingredient inputs are really only a short-run problem. Historically, when these "necessary" ingredients have become very expensive, businesses have invented new processes, discovered new ingredients, or somehow overcome the problem of a given production function and increasingly scarce ingredients. As a consequence, we will direct our attention to production when the producer has some control over the mix of inputs and concentrate on production with variable proportions.

APPLICATION

Can the West Do without South Africa's Minerals?

On August 11, 1986, *Newsweek* asked the question that is the title of this application.* As the debate over South Africa's policy of apartheid intensified, many observers worried about America's dependence on South Africa for so many "essential" minerals. P. W. Botha, the

---

*"The Mines of Apartheid," *Newsweek*, August 11, 1986, p. 80.

president of South Africa, implied he would squeeze mineral exports if more sanctions were imposed. Observers were also concerned that the rioting could turn into a civil war and produce a government hostile to the West.

At this time South Africa was the major producer of several vital minerals. Its platinum was necessary as a catalyst for many chemical and refining processes, as an agent in reducing exhaust fumes, and as a component in electronic systems. South Africa also produced a huge amount of chromium, used in stainless steel, and 15 percent of all manganese. And, the country was the shipping outlet for most of the world's cobalt, used in cutting tools and jet engines. What would happen if these supplies were cut off? The best that would happen would be that the price of these minerals would skyrocket. The worst would be that they would be unobtainable in the West.

While one solution was to find other sources of supply, *Newsweek* pointed out another: substitutes could be found for the South African minerals. For many uses, aluminum and manganese could replace chromium in making stainless steel. Other metals and ceramics, though not as efficient, could replace platinum as a catalyst. Also methods had been found to recycle much of the platinum in automobile-exhaust converters.

The point is that many of these minerals were, at the time, being used in what appeared to be fixed proportions in the production of many important products. But if these minerals were to become increasingly scarce and if their prices rose substantially, there were alternative production processes available that would use less of the minerals. As the price rose producers would find ways to decrease the proportions in which these minerals were used.

This is precisely what has happened throughout history. In the long run, no product *must* be used in fixed proportions. People found ways to use less oil as it became more expensive in the 1970s. Before that, almost no one thought that would be possible. During World War II, manufacturers learned to use synthetic rubber when natural rubber became almost nonexistent. As wood became more expensive at the turn of the century, people learned to use less wood. And there are many more such examples. For this reason, we will continue to concentrate on production under variable proportions.

9.2 PRODUCTION IN THE SHORT RUN

To simplify analysis, we begin with the two-input production function, $Q = f(K,L)$. The firm chooses the level of capital (makes its investment decision), so capital is the fixed input. The variable input, labor, can be combined with the fixed capital to produce different levels of output.

Total, Average, and Marginal Products

Suppose a firm with a production function of the form $Q = f(K,L)$ can, in the long run, choose levels of both labor and capital between 0 and 10 units. A production function giving the maximum amount of output that can be produced from every possible combination of labor and capital is shown in Table 9.1. For example, from the table, 4 units of labor combined with 3 units of capital can produce 325 units of output; 6 labor and 6 capital can produce 655 units of output; and so on. Note that with zero capital, no output can be produced regardless of the level of labor usage. Likewise, with zero labor, there can be no output.

Once we fix the level of either input, we are in the short run, and output can be changed only by varying the other input. To this end, assume that the capital stock is now fixed at two units. Since it is now in the short run, the firm can vary output only by changing the number of workers. Thus the column under 2 units of capital in Table 9.1 gives the total output, or total product of labor, for 0 through 10 workers. It is therefore the short-run production function, when capital is fixed at two units.

These total products are reproduced in column 2 of Table 9.2 for each level of labor usage. Thus columns 1 and 2 define a production function of the form $Q = f(\bar{K},L)$. In this example, total output rises with increases in labor up to a point (nine workers) and then declines.

Average and marginal products are obtained from the production function and may be viewed merely as different ways of looking at the same

Table 9.1 A Production Function

Units of Capital (K)

		0	1	2	3	4	5	6	7	8	9	10
Units of Labor (L)	0	0	0	0	0	0	0	0	0	0	0	0
	1	0	25	52	74	90	100	108	114	118	120	121
	2	0	55	112	162	198	224	242	252	258	262	264
	3	0	83	170	247	303	342	369	384	394	400	403
	4	0	108	220	325	400	453	488	511	527	535	540
	5	0	125	258	390	478	543	590	631	653	663	670
	6	0	137	286	425	523	598	655	704	732	744	753
	7	0	141	304	453	559	643	708	766	800	814	825
	8	0	143	314	474	587	679	753	818	857	873	885
	9	0	141	318	488	609	708	789	861	905	922	935
	10	0	137	316	492	617	722	809	887	935	953	967

Table 9.2   Total, Average, and Marginal Products of Labor (with capital fixed at two units)

(1) Number of Workers	(2) Total Output	(3) Average Product ($AP_L = Q/L$)	(4) Marginal Product ($MP_L = \Delta Q/\Delta L$)
0	0	—	—
1	52	52	52
2	112	56	60
3	170	56.7	58
4	220	55	50
5	258	51.6	38
6	286	47.7	28
7	304	43.4	18
8	314	39.3	10
9	318	35.3	4
10	316	31.6	−2

information. The average product of labor is the total product divided by the number of workers,

$$AP_L = Q/L.$$

In our example, average product, shown in column 3, first rises, reaches a maximum at 56.7, then declines thereafter.

The marginal product of labor (MP_L) is the additional output attributable to using one additional worker with the use of all other inputs fixed (in this case at two units of capital). That is,

$$MP_L = \Delta Q/\Delta L,$$

where Δ means "the change in." The marginal product schedule associated with the production function in Table 9.2 is shown in column 4 of the table. Because no output can be produced with zero workers, the first worker adds 52 units of output; the second adds 60 units (that is, increases output from 52 to 112), and so on. Note that increasing the amount of labor from 9 to 10 actually decreases output from 318 to 316. Thus the marginal product of the 10th worker is negative. In our example, marginal product first increases as the amount of labor increases, then decreases, and finally becomes negative. This is a pattern frequently assumed in economic analysis.

In the above example, the production function assumes that labor, the variable input, is increased one worker at a time. But we can think of the marginal product of an input when more than one unit is added. At a fixed level of capital, suppose that 20 units of labor can produce 100 units of output, and 30 units of labor can produce 200 units of output. In this case, output increases by 100 units as labor increases by 10. Thus

$$MP_L = \frac{\Delta Q}{\Delta L} = \frac{100}{10} = 10.$$

Output increases by 10 units for each additional worker hired.

Definition. The average product of an input is total product divided by the amount of the input used. Thus average product is the output-input ratio for each level of input usage.

Definition. The marginal product of an input is the change in total product attributable to using one additional unit of the input, the usage of all other inputs remaining constant.

We might emphasize that we speak of the marginal product of labor, not the marginal product of a particular laborer. We assume that all workers are the same, in the sense that if we reduce the number of workers from 8 to 7 in Table 9.2, total product falls from 314 to 304 regardless of which of the eight workers is released. Thus the order of hiring makes no difference; a third worker adds 58 units of output no matter who is hired.

Figure 9.1 shows graphically the relations among total, average, and marginal products set forth in Table 9.2. In Panel A, total product increases up to nine workers, then decreases. Panel B incorporates a common assumption made in production theory: average product first rises then falls. When average product is increasing, marginal product is greater than average product (after the first worker, at which they are equal). When average product is decreasing, marginal product is less than average product. This result is not peculiar to this particular production function; it occurs for any production function for which average product first increases then decreases.[2]

An example might help demonstrate that for any average and marginal schedule, the average must increase (decrease) when the marginal is above (below) the average. If you have taken two tests and made grades of 70 and 80, your average grade is 75. If your third test grade is higher than 75, the marginal addition is above the average, so your average grade increases. Conversely, if your third grade is less than 75—the marginal grade is below the average—your average would fall. In production theory, if each additional worker adds more than the average, average product rises; if each additional worker adds less than the average, average product falls.

As shown in Figure 9.1, marginal product first increases then decreases, becoming negative after nine workers. The maximum marginal product occurs before the maximum average product is attained. When marginal product is increasing, total product increases at an increasing rate. When

---

[2]This relation is demonstrated mathematically in the appendix to this chapter.

Figure 9.1 Total, Average, and Marginal Product (*K* = 2)

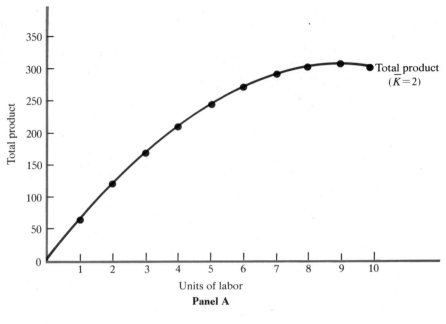

Panel A

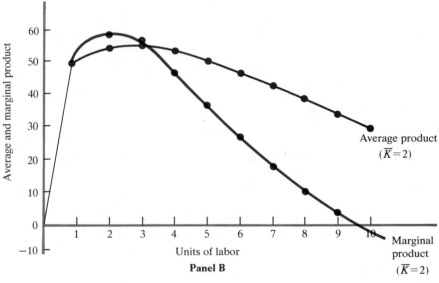

Panel B

marginal product begins to decrease (after two workers), total product begins to increase at a decreasing rate. When marginal product becomes negative (10 workers), total product declines.

We should note another important relation between average and marginal product that is not obvious from the table or the graph, but does follow directly from the discussion. If labor is allowed to vary continuously rather than in discrete units of one, as in the example, marginal product equals average product when average is at its maximum. This follows because average product must increase when marginal is above average and decrease when marginal is below average. The two, therefore, must be equal when average is at its maximum. This means that marginal product begins to decline before average product begins to fall.

Law of Diminishing Marginal Product

The slope of the marginal product curve in Figure 9.1 illustrates an important principle, the law of diminishing marginal product. As the number of units of the variable input increases, other inputs held constant, there exists a point beyond which the marginal product of the variable input declines. When the amount of the variable input is small relative to the fixed inputs, more intensive utilization of fixed inputs by variable inputs may initially increase the marginal output of the variable input as this input is increased. Nonetheless, a point is reached beyond which an increase in the use of the variable input yields progressively less additional output. Each additional unit has, on average, fewer units of the fixed inputs with which to work.

Principle. (The law of diminishing marginal product) As the amount of a variable input is increased, the amount of other (fixed) inputs held constant, a point is reached beyond which marginal product declines.

This is a simple statement concerning physical relations that have been observed in the real economic world. While it is not susceptible of mathematical proof or refutation, it is of some worth to note that a contrary observation has never been recorded. That is why it is called a law.

Shifts in Total, Average, and Marginal Products

The short-run production function in Figure 9.1 and Table 9.2 was derived from the long-run production function in Table 9.1 while holding the capital stock fixed at 2 units. But, from Table 9.1 it is clear that when different amounts of capital are used, the total product of labor changes. Thus the average and marginal products of labor change also.

For example, if the capital stock is increased from 2 to 4 units, the total product of three workers increases from 170 to 303. Thus the average

Table 9.3   Total and Marginal Product Schedules

Units of Capital

Each cell shows: MP$_L$ (top), Q (middle-left), MP$_K$ (bottom-right).

Units of Labor	1	2	3	4	5	6	7	8	9	10
1	25 / 25 / 25	52 / 52 / 27	74 / 74 / 22	90 / 90 / 16	100 / 100 / 10	108 / 108 / 8	114 / 114 / 6	118 / 118 / 4	120 / 120 / 2	121 / 121 / 1
2	30 / 55 / 55	60 / 112 / 57	88 / 162 / 50	108 / 198 / 36	124 / 224 / 26	134 / 242 / 18	138 / 252 / 10	140 / 258 / 6	142 / 262 / 4	143 / 264 / 2
3	28 / 83 / 83	58 / 170 / 87	85 / 247 / 77	105 / 303 / 56	118 / 342 / 39	127 / 369 / 27	132 / 384 / 15	136 / 394 / 10	138 / 400 / 6	139 / 403 / 3
4	25 / 108 / 108	50 / 220 / 112	78 / 325 / 105	97 / 400 / 75	111 / 453 / 53	119 / 488 / 35	127 / 511 / 23	133 / 527 / 16	135 / 535 / 8	137 / 540 / 5
5	17 / 125 / 125	38 / 258 / 133	65 / 390 / 132	78 / 478 / 88	90 / 543 / 65	102 / 590 / 47	120 / 631 / 41	126 / 653 / 22	128 / 663 / 10	130 / 670 / 7
6	12 / 137 / 137	28 / 286 / 149	35 / 425 / 139	45 / 523 / 98	55 / 598 / 75	65 / 655 / 57	73 / 704 / 49	79 / 732 / 28	81 / 744 / 12	83 / 753 / 9
7	4 / 141 / 141	18 / 304 / 163	28 / 453 / 149	36 / 559 / 106	45 / 643 / 84	53 / 708 / 65	62 / 766 / 58	68 / 800 / 34	70 / 814 / 14	72 / 825 / 11
8	2 / 143 / 143	10 / 314 / 171	21 / 474 / 160	28 / 587 / 113	36 / 679 / 92	45 / 753 / 74	52 / 818 / 65	57 / 857 / 39	59 / 873 / 16	60 / 885 / 12
9	−2 / 141 / 141	4 / 318 / 177	14 / 488 / 170	22 / 609 / 121	29 / 708 / 99	36 / 789 / 81	43 / 861 / 72	48 / 905 / 44	49 / 922 / 17	50 / 935 / 13
10	−4 / 137 / 137	−2 / 316 / 179	4 / 492 / 176	8 / 617 / 125	14 / 722 / 105	20 / 809 / 87	26 / 887 / 78	30 / 935 / 48	31 / 953 / 18	32 / 967 / 14

Cell legend:

MP$_L$	
Q	
	MP$_K$

product of three workers increases from 56.7 to 101. And the marginal product of the third worker likewise increases from 58 to 105 (i.e., $\Delta Q / \Delta L = [(303 - 198)/1 = 105]$). And, with four units of capital the total, average, and marginal products change at each level of labor usage.

Table 9.3 shows total product and the marginal product of labor for each level of capital. In each block the total product is the number on the left. The top figure on the right side of the block is the marginal product of labor, holding the capital stock fixed. These figures show that the marginal product of labor increases at every level of labor usage as capital is increased. Thus we have 10 schedules showing the total product and marginal product of labor, one for each level of capital.

Total, Average, and Marginal Products of Capital

Although we have used labor as our variable input to analyze short-run production, we should emphasize that similar relations hold for any variable input—capital, land, management, and so on. While it is customary in short-run analysis to fix capital and vary labor, we could just as easily let labor be fixed at some specified amount and allow capital to vary. This would give us total, average, and marginal product schedules and curves for capital.

The total and marginal product schedules for capital at each of the 10 levels of labor usage are shown in Table 9.3. Simply specify a given number of workers. Then going from left to right, rather than top to bottom, the total product of capital at the fixed level of labor is the number on the left side of each box. The associated marginal product of capital is the bottom number on the right side of the block.

Note that the marginal product of capital schedule behaves similarly to that of labor. At any given level of labor, the marginal product of capital first increases at low levels of capital then decreases as diminishing marginal returns set in. But, at no level of labor usage in the table does the marginal product of capital become negative. If we could increase capital beyond 10 units, it is likely that the marginal product would later become negative. Similar to labor, the marginal product of each level of capital usage increases as the number of workers is fixed at a higher level.

Summary of Short-Run Production

To this point we have used the numbers in Table 9.1 to illustrate the characteristics of short-run production. We can generalize these characteristics graphically as shown in Figure 9.2, by assuming that both output and the variable input, labor, are continuously divisible. This assumption sacrifices little realism while providing a great deal of analytical convenience.

Panel A of the figure shows a total product curve when labor is the only variable input. This curve shows the maximum amount of output that can be produced by each amount of labor when combined with the fixed inputs. The total product curve reflects the following relations:

1. No output can be produced with zero workers.
2. Output first increases at an increasing rate until L_0 workers are employed producing Q_0 units of output. Over this range marginal product is increasing.

Figure 9.2   Total, Average, and Marginal Product Curves

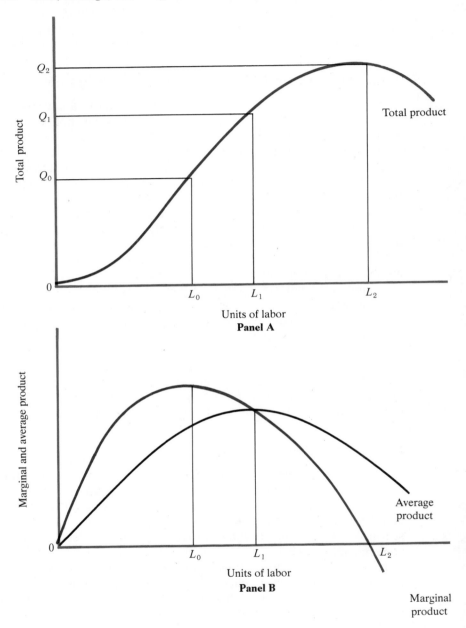

3. Total product then increases but at a decreasing rate when the firm hires between L_0 and L_2 workers. Over this range marginal product is decreasing.

4. Finally a point will be reached beyond which output will decline, indicating a negative marginal product. In Figure 9.2 this occurs for employment levels greater than L_2. The maximum possible total product is thus Q_2.

The corresponding average and marginal product curves are shown in Panel B. Note that both curves first rise, reach a maximum, then decline. Note further that marginal product attains a maximum (at L_0) at a lower input level than the level at which average product attains its maximum (at L_1). While the average product is always positive, marginal product is zero at L_2 units of labor and is negative thereafter. Beyond L_2 the firm is using so much labor (relative to the fixed inputs) that output actually falls with the addition of more units of labor. One way of looking at this is that so much labor is being used that additional workers simply get in each other's way and therefore reduce the total output that can be produced.

Note again that when marginal product is greater than average product, average product is increasing. When marginal product is less than average product, the average must be falling. When average product is at its maximum, that is, neither rising nor falling, marginal product equals average product. The reason for this was discussed previously.

The concepts of average and marginal product will become quite important later, when we analyze how firms decide how much of an input to hire—one of the four decisions a firm must make.

9.3 PRODUCTION IN THE LONG RUN

We now turn to the case of production when all inputs are variable. Although we restrict our analysis to two inputs, all of the results hold for more than two. The use of two inputs simply allows graphical analysis.

When analyzing production with more than one variable input, we cannot simply use sets of average and marginal product curves like those discussed above, because these curves were derived holding the use of all other inputs constant (fixed) and letting the use of only one input vary. As noted above, if we were to change the level of usage of the fixed input, the total, average, and marginal product curves would shift. In the case of two variable inputs, changing the use of one input would cause a shift in the marginal and average product curves of the other input. For example, an increase in capital would probably result in an increase in the marginal product of labor over a wide range of labor use.

The upshot of the preceding is that, if both labor and capital are variable, each factor has an infinite number of product curves, one for every level of usage of the other factor. Therefore, a different tool of analysis is necessary when there is more than one variable factor. This tool is the production isoquant, which is defined as follows:

Definition.   An isoquant is a curve (a locus of points) showing all possible combinations of inputs physically capable of producing a given fixed level of output.

To explain the concept of an isoquant, let us return for a moment to Table 9.1, which shows the maximum output that can be produced by combining different levels of labor and capital. Now note that several levels of output in this table can be produced in two ways. For example, 108 units of output can be produced using either 6 units of capital and 1 worker or 1 unit of capital and 4 workers. Thus these two combinations of labor and capital are two points on the isoquant associated with 108 units of output. And if we assumed that labor and capital were continuously divisible, there would be many more combinations on this isoquant.

Other input combinations in Table 9.1 that can produce the same level of output are:

$$Q = 258: \text{using } K = 2, \quad L = 5 \text{ or } K = 8, L = 2$$
$$Q = 400: \text{using } K = 9, \quad L = 3 \text{ or } K = 4, L = 4$$
$$Q = 453: \text{using } K = 5, \quad L = 4 \text{ or } K = 3, L = 7$$
$$Q = 708: \text{using } K = 6, \quad L = 7 \text{ or } K = 5, L = 9$$
$$Q = 753: \text{using } K = 10, L = 6 \text{ or } K = 6, L = 8.$$

These pairs of combinations of K and L are two of the many combinations associated with each specific level of output. They demonstrate that it is possible to increase capital and decrease labor (or increase labor and decrease capital) while keeping the level of output constant. For example, if the firm is producing 400 units of output with nine units of capital and three units of labor, it can increase labor by one, decrease capital by five, and keep output at 400. Or if it is producing 453 units of output with $K = 3$ and $L = 7$, it can increase K by two, decrease L by three, and keep output at 453. Thus, an isoquant shows how one input can be substituted for another while keeping the level of output constant.

Now let's assume that labor, capital, and output are continuously divisible in order to set forth the typically assumed characteristics of isoquants. Figure 9.3 illustrates three such isoquants. Isoquant I shows all the combinations of capital and labor that will yield 100 units of output. As shown, the firm can produce 100 units of output by using 10 units of capital and 75 of labor, or 50 units of capital and 15 of labor, or by using any other combination of capital and labor on isoquant I. Similarly, isoquant II shows the various combinations of capital and labor that can be used to produce 200 units of output. And, isoquant III shows all combinations that can produce 300 units of output. Each capital-labor combination can be on only one isoquant. That is, isoquants cannot intersect.

Figure 9.3 **Typical Isoquants**

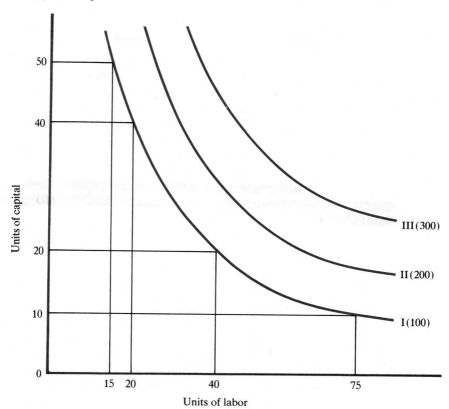

Isoquants I, II, and III are only three of an infinite number of isoquants that could be drawn. A group of isoquants is called an isoquant map. In an isoquant map, all isoquants lying above and to the right of a given isoquant indicate higher levels of output. Thus in Figure 9.3 isoquant II indicates a higher level of output than isoquant I, and III indicates a higher level than II.

We should also note that combinations other than those on a given isoquant can be used to produce the given level of output, but such combinations would not reflect the "maximum-amount-of-output" concept we introduced in our definition of a production function. In Figure 9.3 it is clear that 100 units of output *could* be produced using *more than* 10 units of capital and *more than* 75 units of labor. However, such production would "waste" inputs. In contrast, it is impossible to produce 100 units of output using less than 10 units of capital with 75 units of labor, or vice versa. For any combination along an isoquant, if the usage level of either input is reduced and the other is held constant, output must decline.

Marginal Rate of Technical Substitution

As depicted in Figure 9.3, isoquants slope downward over the relevant range of production. This negative slope indicates that if the firm decreases the amount of capital employed, more labor must be added in order to keep the rate of output constant. Or, if labor use is decreased, capital usage must be increased to keep output constant. Thus, the two inputs can be substituted for one another to maintain a constant level of output.

Great theoretical and practical importance is attached to the rate at which one input must be substituted for another in order to keep output constant. This rate at which one input is substituted for another along an isoquant is called the *marginal rate of technical substitution (MRTS)*, and is defined as

$$MRTS = -\frac{\Delta K}{\Delta L}.$$

The minus sign is added in order to make *MRTS* a positive number, since $\Delta K/\Delta L$, the slope of the isoquant, is negative.

Over the relevant range of production the marginal rate of technical substitution diminishes. That is, as more and more labor is substituted for capital while holding output constant, the absolute value of $\Delta K/\Delta L$ decreases. This can be seen in Figure 9.3. If capital is reduced from 50 to 40 (a decrease of 10 units) labor must be increased by only 5 units (from 15 to 20) in order to keep the level of output at 100 units. That is, when capital is plentiful relative to labor, the firm can discharge 10 units of capital but must substitute only 5 units of labor in order to keep output at 100. The marginal rate of technical substitution in this case is $-\Delta K/\Delta L = -(-10)/5 = 2$, meaning that for every unit of labor added two units of capital can be discharged in order to keep the level of output constant. However, consider a combination where capital is more scarce and labor more plentiful. For example, if capital is decreased from 20 to 10 (again a decrease of 10 units) labor must be increased by 35 units (from 40 to 75) to keep output at 100 units. In this case the *MRTS* is 10/35, indicating that for each unit of labor added, capital can be reduced by slightly more than one quarter of a unit.

Thus, as capital decreases and labor increases along an isoquant, the amount of capital that can be discharged for each unit of labor added declines. Or, put another way, the amount of labor that must be added for each unit of capital eliminated, holding output constant, must increase. This relation is seen in Figure 9.3. The slope of the isoquant reflects the rate at which labor can be substituted for capital. It is easy to see that the isoquant becomes less and less steep as you move downward along the isoquant. Thus *MRTS* declines along an isoquant.

Relation of MRTS to Marginal Products

For very small movements along an isoquant, the marginal rate of technical substitution equals the ratio of the marginal products of the two inputs. Let us demonstrate how this comes about.

The level of output, Q, depends upon the use of the two inputs, L and K. Since Q is constant along an isoquant, ΔQ must equal zero for any change in L and K that would remain on an isoquant. Suppose that, at a point on the isoquant, the marginal product of capital (MP_K) is 3 and the marginal product of labor (MP_L) is 6. Then, if we add 1 unit of labor, output would increase by 6 units. How much capital must be discharged to keep Q at the original level? Capital must decrease just enough to offset the increase in output generated by the increase in labor. Since the marginal product of capital is 3, 2 units of capital must be discharged. In this case the $MRTS = -\Delta K/\Delta L = -(-2)/1 = 2$, which is exactly equal to $MP_L/MP_K = 6/3 = 2$.

Or, if we were to increase capital by one unit, output would rise by 3. Labor must decrease by one half a unit to offset the increase of 3 units of output and keep output constant, since $MP_L = 6$. In this case the $MRTS = -\Delta K/\Delta L = -(1)/(-1/2) = 2$, which is again equal to MP_L/MP_K.

In more general terms, we can say that, when L and K are allowed to vary slightly, the change in Q resulting from the change in the two inputs is the marginal product of L times the amount of change in L plus the marginal product of K times its change. Put in equation form,

$$\Delta Q = (MP_L)(\Delta L) + (MP_K)(\Delta K).$$

In order that we remain on a given isoquant it is necessary to set ΔQ equal to zero. Then, solving for the marginal rate of technical substitution, we have[3]

$$MRTS = -\frac{\Delta K}{\Delta L} = \frac{MP_L}{MP_K}.$$

Using this relation, the reason for diminishing $MRTS$ is easily explained. As additional units of labor are substituted for capital, the marginal product of labor diminishes. Two forces are working to diminish labor's marginal product: (1) less capital causes a downward shift of the marginal product of labor curve, and (2) more units of the variable input (labor) cause a downward movement along the marginal product curve. Thus, as labor is substituted for capital the marginal product of labor must decline. For analogous reasons the marginal product of capital increases as less capital and more labor is used. The same two forces are present in this case: a movement along a marginal product curve and a shift in the location of the curve. In this situation, however, both forces work to

---

[3]This relation is demonstrated mathematically in the appendix to this chapter.

increase the marginal product of capital. Thus, as labor is substituted for capital the marginal product of capital increases. Combining these two conditions, as labor is substituted for capital, MP_L decreases and MP_K increases, so MP_L/MP_K will decrease.[4]

9.4 THE OPTIMAL COMBINATION OF INPUTS

We have shown that any desired level of output can be produced by a number of different combinations of inputs. But, as we noted in the introduction to this chapter, one of the four production decisions a manager must make is which input combination to use. What is the "optimal" input combination?

As you might have guessed, this decision is an application of the constrained optimization rule we discussed in Chapter 3. The firm can choose among many different input combinations to produce a given level of output. Or, faced with specified input prices, it can choose among many combinations of inputs that would lead to a given level of cost; that is, expenditure. Thus we can think of the firm as making either of two input choice decisions:

1. Choose the input combination that yields the maximum level of output possible with a given level of expenditure.
2. Choose the input combination that leads to the lowest cost of producing a given level of output.

Thus, the firm minimizes cost, subject to an output constraint, or maximizes output, subject to a cost constraint.

As we saw in Chapter 3, the solution to any constrained maximization or minimization problem is choosing the level of each activity whereby the marginal benefits from the last unit of each activity per dollar cost of the activity are equal. Thus, if there are two activities, A and B,

$$\frac{MB_A}{P_A} = \frac{MB_B}{P_B}.$$

Since the activity here is the level of usage of the input, the relevant marginal benefit is marginal product. The additional cost of each unit of input is the price of the input in question. Applying the preceding rule, the firm chooses the input combination for which the marginal product divided by input price is the same for all inputs used. This means that for

---

[4]Note that we have violated our assumption about marginal product somewhat. The marginal product of an input is defined as the change in output per unit change in the input, the use of other inputs held constant. In this case we allow the usage of both inputs to change; thus the marginal product is really an approximation. But we are speaking only of slight or very small changes in use. Thus violation of the assumption is small and the approximation approaches the true variation for small changes.

our two-input case a firm attains the highest level of output for any given level of cost or the lowest possible cost of producing any given level of output when

$$\frac{MP_L}{w} = \frac{MP_K}{r},$$

where w and r are, respectively, the prices of labor and capital. Thus the marginal rate of technical substitution (MP_L/MP_K) equals the ratio of input prices (w/r).

We can analyze the optimal input rule in a way similar to that used in Chapter 3. Suppose that the optimizing condition does not hold. Or, specifically, assume that

$$\frac{MP_K}{r} = \frac{12}{3} = 4 > 3 = \frac{6}{2} = \frac{MP_L}{w}.$$

The last unit of labor adds three units of output per dollar spent on it; the last unit of capital adds four units of output per dollar. If the firm wants to produce the maximum output possible with a given level of cost, it could spend $1 less on labor, thus reducing labor by one half a unit and hence output by three units. It could spend this dollar on capital, thus increasing output by four. Cost would be unchanged and total output would rise by one unit. And the firm would continue taking dollars out of labor and adding them to capital so long as the inequality holds. But as labor is reduced, its marginal product will increase, and as capital is increased, its marginal product will decline. Eventually the marginal product per dollar will be equal.

Or, suppose that, rather than trying to maximize the output from a given level of cost, the firm wants to minimize the cost of producing a given level of output. And suppose the above inequality holds. The firm could decrease its labor by one unit, causing output to fall by six, but saving $2 in cost. Since the marginal product of capital is 12, it must only increase capital by one half a unit to make up the lost output from the reduction in labor. This one half a unit of capital costs only $1.50, so cost falls by $2.00 − $1.50 = $0.50. And the firm continues to decrease labor and increase capital until the equality holds. If the inequality is reversed, the firm will increase labor and decrease capital.

Now that we have an intuitive grasp of the problem, let's analyze the solution graphically. For this we need a way to bring input prices into the picture.

Input Prices and Isocost Curves

As we saw above, when determining the optimal input combination, producers must pay attention to relative input prices if they are to minimize the cost of producing a given output or maximize output for a given level of cost. Input prices are determined by demand and supply in the input markets. For producers who are not "monopsonists" or "oligopsonists" (that is, the sole purchaser of, or one of a few purchasers of, an input), input prices are given by the market. We concentrate upon a producer who is a competitor in the input market facing given, market-determined input prices, so we treat the input prices as constant.

If we continue to denote the quantities of capital and labor by K and L, and their respective prices by r and w, total cost, C, is $C = rK + wL$. Total cost (total expenditure) is simply the sum of the cost of K units of capital at r dollars per unit and of L units of labor at w dollars per unit.

Let's look at a specific example. Suppose capital costs \$1,000 a month per unit ($r = \$1,000$) and labor receives a wage of \$2,500 a month per unit ($w = \$2,500$). Then our total cost function is

$$C = 1,000K + 2,500L.$$

Now suppose that the firm decides a total of \$15,000 a month is to be spent for inputs. At this cost, the equation becomes \$15,000 = \$1,000K + \$2,500L. Solving this equation for K, we can see the combinations of K and L that can be chosen: $K = 15 - 2.5L$. Similarly, if \$20,000 is to be spent on inputs, the firm can purchase combinations that adhere to the relation: $K = 20 - 2.5L$. More generally, if a fixed amount $\overline{C}$ is to be spent, the firm can choose among the combinations given by

$$K = \frac{\overline{C}}{r} - \frac{w}{r}L.$$

This equation is illustrated in Figure 9.4. If \$15,000 is spent for inputs and no labor is purchased, 15 units of capital may be bought. If \$20,000 is spent for inputs and no labor is purchased, 20 units of capital may be bought. More generally, if $\overline{C}$ is to be spent and r is the unit cost of capital, the maximum amount of capital that can be purchased is $\overline{C}/r$ units; $\overline{C}/r$ is, therefore, the vertical intercept of the line. If one unit of labor is purchased at \$2,500, two and one half units of capital must be sacrificed; if two units of labor are bought, five units of capital must be sacrificed; and so on. Thus, as the purchase of labor is increased, the purchase of capital must decrease if cost is held constant. For each additional unit of labor purchased, w/r units of capital must be foregone. In Figure 9.4, $w/r = 2.5$. Attaching a negative sign, this ratio is the slope of the line. This slope shows the market rate of trade-off between the two inputs.

The lines in Figure 9.4 are called *isocost curves* because they show the various combinations of inputs that may be purchased for a given level of expenditure. It is obvious from the figure that an increase in cost, holding input prices constant, leads to a parallel upward shift in the isocost curve. Thus the isocost curve for $C = \$20,000$ lies above the curve for $C = \$15,000$. There would exist an infinite number of isocost curves, one for each level of cost.

Figure 9.4 Isocost Curves for $r = \$1,000$ and $w = \$2,500$

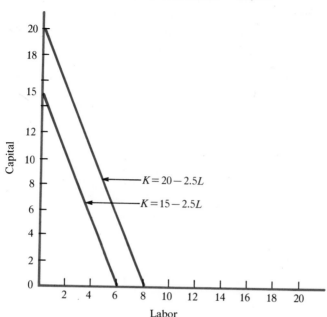

Relation. *At fixed input prices,* r *and* w *for capital and labor, a fixed outlay* $\overline{C}$ *will purchase any combination of capital and labor given by the following linear equation:*

$$K = \frac{\overline{C}}{r} - \frac{w}{r}L.$$

This is the equation for an isocost curve, whose vertical intercept $(\overline{C}/r)$ is the amount of capital that may be purchased if no labor is bought and whose slope is the negative of the input-price ratio (w/r).

If the relative input prices change, the slope of the isocost curve must change. If w rises relative to r, the isocost becomes steeper. If w falls relative to r, the isocost becomes less steep.

Production of a Given Output at Minimum Cost[5]

Whatever output a firm chooses to produce, the manager wishes to produce it at the lowest possible cost. To accomplish this objective, production must be organized in the most efficient way.

---

[5]Conditions for output maximization and cost minimization are demonstrated mathematically in the appendix to this chapter.

Suppose that at given input prices r and w a firm wishes to produce the output indicated by isoquant I in Figure 9.5. Isocost curves KL, $K'L'$, and $K''L''$ are three of the infinite number of isocost curves from which the producer can choose at the given input prices. Obviously, the firm will choose the lowest level of expenditures that enables output level I to be produced. In Figure 9.5 output level I will be produced at the cost represented by isocost curve $K'L'$. Any resource expenditure below that, for example that represented by KL, is not feasible since it is impossible to produce output I with these resource combinations. Any resource combinations above that represented by $K'L'$ are rejected because the firm wishes to produce the desired output at least cost. If combinations A or B are chosen, at the cost represented by $K''L''$, the producer can reduce cost by moving along I to point E. Point E shows the optimal resource combination: the firm should use K_0 units of capital and L_0 units of labor.

Equilibrium is attained when the isoquant representing the chosen output is just *tangent* to an isocost curve. This will be the *lowest* isocost curve that includes an input combination at which it is possible to produce the chosen output level. And the optimal input combination will be the only combination on that isocost curve capable of producing the chosen output; that is, K_0 and L_0 make up the only combination on isocost $K'L'$ that can produce the output given by I.

Recall that the slope of an isoquant is given by the $MRTS$ (which equals MP_L/MP_K), and the slope of an isocost curve is w/r. Thus at the tangency the slopes of the two curves are equal:

$$MRTS = \frac{MP_L}{MP_K} = \frac{w}{r},$$

or

$$\frac{MP_L}{w} = \frac{MP_K}{r}.$$

Put another way, the least-cost production requires that the marginal rate of technical substitution of capital for labor be equal to the ratio of the price of labor to the price of capital. The market input-price ratio tells the producer the rate at which one input can be substituted for another in the market. The marginal rate of technical substitution shows the rate at which the producer can substitute between the inputs in production. If the two are not equal, a firm can always reduce cost by moving in the direction of equality.

Principle.   To minimize the cost (expenditure) of producing a given level of output with fixed input prices, the producer must combine inputs in such quantities that the marginal rate of technical substitution of capital for labor is equal to the input-price ratio (the price of labor to the price of capital).

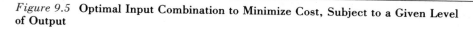

Figure 9.5 **Optimal Input Combination to Minimize Cost, Subject to a Given Level of Output**

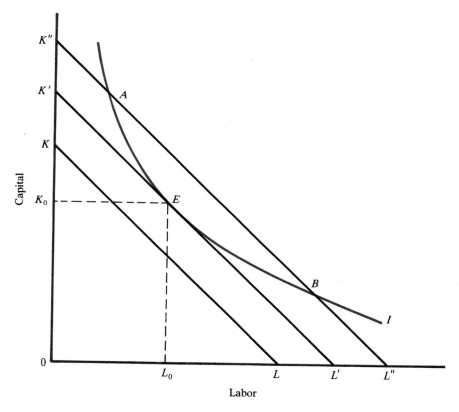

Production of Maximum Output with a Given Level of Cost

In most cases, firms will choose a level of output and then choose the input combination that permits production of that output at least cost. There may be times, however, when firms can spend only a fixed amount on production and wish to attain the highest level of production consistent with that amount of expenditure. Not too surprisingly, the results are the same in both cases.

This situation is shown in Figure 9.6. The isocost line KL shows every possible combination of the two inputs that can be purchased at the given level of cost and input prices. Four of the infinite number of possible isoquants are shown. Clearly, at the given level of cost, output level IV is unattainable. And, neither output level I nor level II would be chosen, since higher levels of output are possible with the given level of expenditure. The highest level of output attainable with the given level of cost is produced by using L_0 labor and K_0 capital. At point A, the highest

Figure 9.6   Output Maximization for a Given Level of Cost

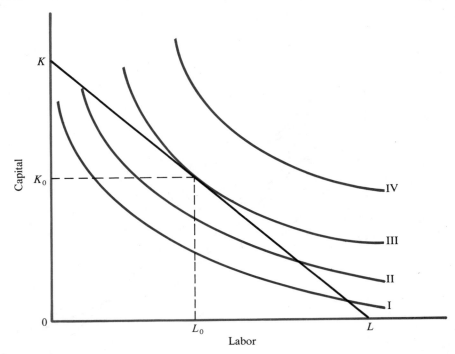

attainable isoquant, isoquant III, is just tangent to the given isocost. Thus, in the case of constrained output maximization, the marginal rate of technical substitution of capital for labor equals the input-price ratio (the price of labor to the price of capital). Or, as above, $MP_L/w = MP_K/r$.

Principle. In order either to maximize output subject to a given cost, or to minimize cost subject to a given output, the manager must employ inputs in such amounts as to equate the marginal rate of technical substitution and the input-price ratio.

The Expansion Path

In Figure 9.5 we illustrated one optimizing point for a firm. This point shows the optimal (least cost) combination of inputs for a given level of output. However, as you might expect, there exists an optimal combination of inputs for every level of output the firm might choose to produce. And, the proportions in which the inputs are combined need not be the same for all levels of output. To examine several optimizing points at once, we use the *expansion path.*

Figure 9.7 **Expansion Path**

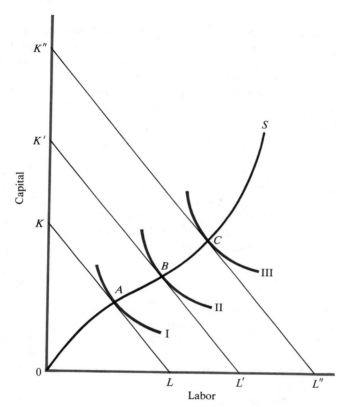

The expansion path shows how factor proportions change when output changes, with the factor-price ratio held constant. In Figure 9.7 the curves I, II, and III are isoquants depicting a representative production function. The isocosts *KL, K'L',* and *K"L"* represent the minimum costs of producing each of the three output levels, since they are tangent to the respective isoquants. Note that, since the factor-price ratio does not change, these isocosts are parallel.

Look at the three optimum points, *A, B,* and *C.* Since at each of these, (1) factor prices remain constant, and (2) the marginal rate of technical substitution is equal to the factor-price ratio, it follows that the marginal rates of technical substitution are equal at *A, B,* and *C.* Therefore, the expansion path, *OS,* is the locus of points along which the marginal rate of technical substitution is constant and equal to the input-price ratio. But it is a curve with a special feature: It is the locus along which the firm will expand output when factor prices are constant. We may accordingly formulate a definition.[6]

Definition.   The expansion path is the curve along which the firm expands (or contracts) output when factor prices remain constant. The expansion path indicates how factor proportions change when output (or expenditure) changes, input prices remaining constant. Since it is made up of points of efficient (least cost) input combinations, the expansion path is the locus of efficient combinations of the inputs. On the expansion path, the marginal rate of technical substitution is constant, since the factor-price ratio is constant.

As we shall see in Chapter 10 the expansion path gives the firm its cost structure. That is, the expansion path shows the optimal (least cost) combination of inputs to be used to produce each level of output. The sum of the quantities of each input used times the respective input price gives the minimum cost of producing every level of output. This in turn permits us to relate cost to the level of output produced.

9.5 RETURNS TO SCALE

Let us now consider the effect of a proportional increase in all inputs on the level of output produced. For example, if we were to double the firm's usage of all inputs, output would increase. But, the question is: By how much? To address this question, we need the concept of returns to scale.

Consider a 25 percent increase in the usage of all inputs. If output increases by exactly 25 percent, we say that the production function exhibits *constant returns to scale*. If, however, output increases by more than 25 percent, we say that the production function exhibits *increasing returns to scale*. Alternatively, if output increases by less than 25 percent, we say that the production function is characterized by *decreasing returns to scale*.

These relations can be illustrated using Figure 9.8. We begin with an arbitrary level of usage of capital and labor at K_0 and L_0. This combination of capital and labor produces some level of output, Q_0. For purposes of illustration, let us define Q_0 to be 100 units. Now, we double our level of

---

[6]We should note that thus far in our discussion of the expansion path we have assumed that as the firm expands output, it increases its usage of all inputs. This need not be the case. It is possible that as a firm expands, it actually decreases the usage of one or more— though not all—inputs over the relevant range. For example, in the two-input case, a firm may increase output by using more capital and less labor. In this case, labor would be called an *inferior input*. An input is said to be inferior if, over a range, increased output causes less of the input to be used. In such cases, the expansion path curves backward if the quantity of the inferior input is plotted along the horizontal axis, or curves downward if the quantity of the inferior input is plotted along the vertical. Since this phenomenon is not of particular theoretical importance, we will not consider it further in our analysis.

Figure 9.8 Returns to Scale

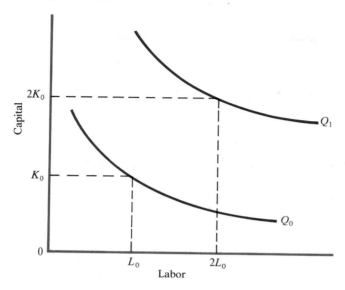

input usage to $2K_0$ and $2L_0$. Output will increase to Q_1. The question is the magnitude of the increase. Input usage has increased by 100 percent. Has output increased by 100 percent, more than 100 percent, or less than 100 percent? If Q_1 is equal to 200, output would have exactly doubled in response to the doubling of input usage, so constant returns to scale are indicated. If Q_1 is greater than 200 units (say, 215), increasing returns to scale are indicated. If Q_1 is less than 200 units (say, 180), the production function exhibits decreasing returns to scale.

We can define returns to scale more analytically by first writing the production function in functional form as

$$Q = f(L,K).$$

Suppose we increase the inputs by a constant proportion (say, λ) and observe the proportionate change (z) in output. We have

$$zQ = f(\lambda L, \lambda K).$$

Again remember that λ and z represent proportionate increases in the level of input usage and level of output, respectively.

We have noted, in the case of constant returns to scale, that if inputs are increased by a given percent, output rises by the same percent, that is, $z = \lambda$. More generally, if all inputs are increased by a factor of λ and output goes up by a factor of z, then a firm experiences:

1. Increasing returns to scale if $z > \lambda$. (Output goes up proportionately more than the increase in input usage.)

2. Constant returns to scale if $\lambda = z$. (Output goes up by the same proportion as the increase in input usage.)
3. Decreasing returns to scale if $\lambda > z$. (Output goes up proportionately less than the increase in input usage.)

Do not deduce from this discussion of returns to scale that firms with variable-proportions production functions actually expand output by increasing their usage of every input in exactly the same proportion. As we have seen above, the very concept of variable proportions means that they do not necessarily expand inputs in the same proportions. The expansion path may twist and turn in many directions.

9.6 CHANGES IN INPUT PRICES AND TECHNOLOGICAL CHANGE

We have derived the expansion path under one set of input prices and a given technology. But, it should be clear that changes in input prices change the slope of the isocost curves and therefore change the expansion path. Since the isoquant map is determined by a given level of technology, technological change may shift the entire isoquant map and, therefore, change the expansion path also. This section will address such changes.

Changes in Relative Prices

To see the effect of a change in input prices, let's begin with a firm producing a given level of output with the most efficient—cost minimizing—combination of labor and capital. From the above analysis we know that at this combination

$$\frac{MP_L}{w} = \frac{MP_K}{r}.$$

Now suppose that the price of labor rises while the price of capital is unchanged. Since r is unchanged and, at the original combination of inputs, MP_L and MP_K are unchanged, the increase in w makes

$$\frac{MP_L}{w} < \frac{MP_K}{r}$$

at the original combination of labor and capital.

If the firm wishes to continue producing the same level of output, it will increase capital and decrease labor as it moves along the isoquant. This substitution of capital for labor keeping output constant, after a wage increase, is called the substitution effect.

Conversely, if r rather than w increases, the marginal product per dollar of capital will become smaller than the marginal product per dollar of labor. In this case the substitution effect will mean an increase in labor and a decrease in capital along the isoquant. And it follows that if the

Figure 9.9 Expansion Paths with Changed Input Prices

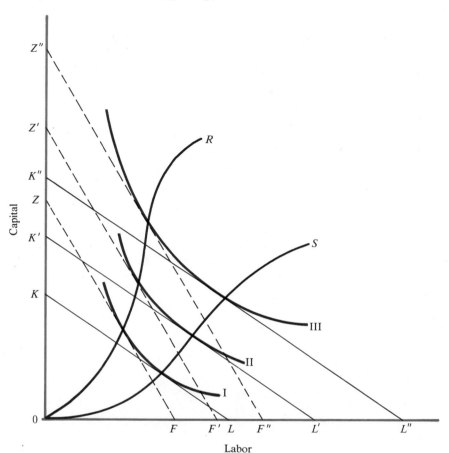

price of labor (capital) decreases, the firm will substitute labor (capital) for capital (labor).

If the substitution effect of a change in relative prices occurs at any given level of output (on any isoquant), it takes place over the entire isoquant map. This then causes the expansion path to change.

To see this effect, consider first the expansion path $0S$ in Figure 9.9. The relative price of labor and capital, w/r, is given by the slope of KL, $K'L'$, and $K''L''$. The tangencies of these isocosts to isoquants I, II, and III indicate the optimal quantities of capital and labor used to produce each of these three levels of output, and $0S$, of course, gives the optimal combination for every other level of output over the range.

Next let the price of labor increase relative to the price of capital. Since the ratio w/r increases, the slope of the isocost curves must become steeper. These new isocosts are shown as *ZF, Z'F'*, and *Z"F"*. Now the tangency on each isoquant occurs at a lower amount of labor and a greater amount of capital. These new optimal input combinations indicate that the firm substitutes capital for labor to produce each level of output when the price of labor rises relative to the price of capital. The new expansion path, *0R,* now gives the new optimal combination of inputs for each level of output.

If input prices change again, the firm would substitute once more. The direction of substitution depends upon the direction of the relative change in input prices. If the price of labor rises relative to the price of capital, the firm substitutes capital for labor at each level of output. If the price of capital rises relative to the price of labor, the firm substitutes labor for capital. Firms will always substitute away from the input that becomes relatively more expensive and toward the input that becomes relatively less expensive. These relations can be summarized in the following:

Relation.   If the input-price ratio changes, firms substitute toward the input that becomes relatively less expensive and away from the input that becomes relatively more expensive. In the case of labor and capital, if w/r increases (decreases), K/L increases (decreases) at each level of output. This change in the K/L ratio is called the substitution effect.

THE WALL STREET JOURNAL

APPLICATION

Firms Adapt to Higher Wage Rates

The Wall Street Journal reported in the fall of 1986 that young workers were becoming increasingly scarce.* During the late 1960s and early 1970s the birthrate in the United States had fallen sharply. In 1981 over 24 million young people between 16 and 24 years old were in the civilian labor force. By 1986 the number had fallen by over 2 million and was expected to continue to drop. But the number of jobs traditionally filled by young workers was increasing rapidly. The Bureau of Labor Statistics predicted that the number of jobs created between 1984 and 1990 would be a million higher than the number of people added to the labor force.

Continued on page 257

*Martha Brannigan, "A Shortage of Youths Brings Wide Changes to the Labor Market," September 2, 1986. Adapted by permission of *The Wall Street Journal*. © Dow Jones and Company, Inc., 1986. All rights reserved.

APPLICATION

Continued from page 256
As you would expect, when the supply of young, unskilled workers decreased while the demand for them increased, their wage rate was rising rapidly. The *WSJ* noted that the $3.35 an hour minimum wage rate was becoming irrelevant in many areas. Inexperienced cooks' assistants were receiving over $6 an hour. Several types of businesses were hard hit by the dearth of young workers: hotels and restaurants (especially fast-food restaurants), convenience stores and other retailers, and businesses needing beginning computer and clerical skills. As the wage rate for the young workers they typically hired rose, their costs rose also.

What would you do if you managed a business that depended on young, inexperienced, but low-wage workers? Let's look at the way some businesses were adapting during this period.

Some companies increased their employment of older people in jobs previously held by youths. McDonald's Corp. started job-training programs for senior citizens. Other companies tried day care as a way of attracting more young mothers. U.S. Restaurants, Inc., a Pennsylvania restaurant chain, began finding and subsidizing child care for workers, especially during busy lunch hours.

Burger King Corp. offered grants of up to $2,000 over two years to fast-food workers attending college or vocational school. Atlanta Marriott Northwest provided bus transportation from downtown for maids and other help. Other firms began to substitute inner-city youths. For example, Abraham and Straus, a Federated Department Stores division, hired high school dropouts and others from disadvantaged backgrounds. In New York, that company hired poor teenagers from the slums, trained them, and offered transportation to suburban stores that needed entry-level help during peak sales periods. In Philadelphia, Southland Corp., which franchises 7-Eleven Food Stores, began recruiting and training retarded people at special stores for jobs ranging from maintenance to bookkeeping.

These are only a few examples of firms that substituted one type of labor, which they previously did not employ, for another type after the wages of their traditional workers rose. Firms will find ways to substitute after changes in relative prices.

Technological Change

Another factor that can affect input usage is a change in technology. Technological change is simply an improvement in the state of knowledge—the knowledge about how to organize factors of production. An improvement in technology means that any given set of inputs in the relevant range can produce more output than was possible under the old technology.

This then means that a given level of output can be produced using fewer inputs than before. For example, suppose that the firm was using 10 units of capital and 9 units of labor to produce 100 units of output. If, after technological change, 10 units of capital and 9 units of labor can produce more than 100 units of output, it must be the case that the 100 units of output can be produced using less of both labor and capital. Thus technological change causes the isoquant representing 100 units to shift downward toward the origin. And, after this shift in the isoquant, at a given set of input prices 100 units can be produced at a lower cost (on a lower isocost curve) than was previously possible.

The technological change not only causes the 100-unit isoquant to shift downward but also shifts the entire isoquant map downward. Thus, each level of output can be produced at a lower cost.

This cost-reducing shift in the isoquant map is shown in Figure 9.10. Suppose the firm originally produces 1,000 units of output, given by isoquant I. With the given input prices it produces at point A, using L_1 labor and K_1 capital. After technological change shifts the isoquant map downward, isoquant I, associated with 1,000 units of output, moves to I'. The new cost-minimizing combination of inputs is L_2 and K_2, point B on I'. Since input prices have not changed, $R'Z'$ is parallel to the original isocost RZ. But $R'Z'$ represents a lower cost of producing the same level of output. And, every other level of output can be produced at a lower cost.

In the case shown in Figure 9.10, the cost-minimizing *ratio* of capital to labor remains the same after the technological change; the ray from the origin, K_1/L_1, passes through points A and B. When the ratio remains constant, the technological change is called *neutral*. But this need not be the case.

Technological change is biased if at any level of output the cost-minimizing ratio of inputs is changed. With two inputs, capital and labor, the change is said to be capital using (or labor saving) if the ratio of capital to labor increases. It is labor using (or capital saving) if the ratio of capital to labor decreases.

Figure 9.11 shows biased technological change. In both panels, the firm begins as before, producing at point A on isoquant I, using L_1 and K_1 units of labor and capital. Panel A shows capital using (labor saving) technological change. After the change, the original isoquant I shifts to I'. Since input prices do not change, the cost-minimizing isocost curve is now $R'Z'$. Now the cost-minimizing combination to produce the original

Figure 9.10 **Neutral Technological Change**

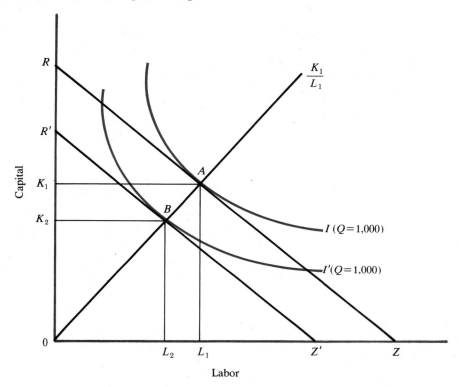

Figure 9.11 **Biased Technological Change**

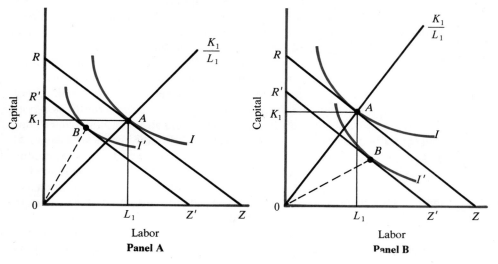

Panel A

Panel B

level of output is at point *B*. Both labor and capital are reduced, but the ratio of capital to labor increases, as shown by the ray from the origin to point *B*.

Panel B of Figure 9.11 shows labor using (capital saving) technological change. We begin at the original equilibrium at *A* on isoquant *I*. This isoquant shifts to *I'* after the change. The new cost-minimizing equilibrium is at *B*. As shown by the ray from the origin to point *B*, the ratio of capital to labor decreases. In this case, the firm actually increases its use of labor, but it could be the case that both inputs decrease, as in Panel A. The important point in classifying technological change is not the effect on the absolute amounts of the inputs used, but the change in the ratio or proportion of the inputs.

Input Price Changes and Technological Change

To this point, we have treated changes in input prices and changes in technology independently. But often a change in one will lead to a change in the other.

For example, suppose we have a period of widespread capital using (labor saving) technological change throughout much of the economy. Many industries are undertaking this technological change and are in the process of substituting capital for labor. During this process one would expect the demand for capital to increase while the demand for labor decreases. This shift in demand may well cause the price of capital to rise and the price of labor to fall. Then, as firms see the change in relative prices they would be induced, to some extent, to substitute labor for capital in the manner discussed previously.

This effect may, however, be offset because technological change reduces firms' costs. This reduction in cost will induce firms to expand output and increase their usage of both inputs.

Technological change frequently follows a change in relative input prices. Suppose, for example, that labor is becoming increasingly scarce, and consequently the price of labor is rising relative to the price of capital. We would expect firms to respond initially by attempting to substitute capital for labor to the extent permitted by the existing technology.

Firms would also be induced to undertake research and development in order to find new ways to produce using more capital and less labor; that is, they would try to discover ways to bring about capital using (labor saving) technological change. This effect is called induced technological change. The technological change does not come about because someone happened to discover new methods of production—firms are induced to try to find new technologies in order to conserve the more expensive input. Once again it is difficult to separate the effect of the change in technology from the effect of the change in relative input prices.

Many observers believe that important technical advances are often a response to increased scarcity of natural resources or some other inputs into the production process. Certainly the 1970s saw a great deal of technological change that enabled people to conserve an increasingly more expensive resource, oil. As oil prices rose, manufacturers found ways to make automobiles more fuel efficient and to substitute other sources of energy for oil. Many argue that the present modernization of U.S. manufacturing, in which capital is being substituted for labor, is in response to higher wage rates for U.S. labor.

THE WALL STREET JOURNAL
APPLICATION

Is a Change in Technology Always Good?

Critics of U.S. manufacturing industry believe that many manufacturing plants are out of date. They believe that automation and new technology will enable U.S. firms to cut production costs and compete much more successfully in the international marketplace. And many U.S. firms are likewise convinced. But as *The Wall Street Journal* pointed out, changing technology can be tricky.

On May 13, 1986, the *Journal* reported that the General Motors Corp. and the Ford Motor Co. were spending billions to automate their plants in an effort to compete with their Japanese rivals.* The story went on, however, to show that high technology does not always mean lower costs. Let's see why.

GM had recently opened a plant in Hamtramck, Michigan,

intended to be a state-of-the-art, high technology production facility for welding, assembling, and painting cars. The plant used robots to perform such tasks as applying sealants to car joints, welding, and painting. However, technical problems were soon apparent. The assembly line frequently stopped while software corrections were made; production was only 30 to 35 cars an hour, rather than the projected 60 per hour; and the robot painting system broke down so often that several hundred cars had to be repainted with handheld spray guns.

GM certainly had a high technology plant, but it had not experienced technological change in the sense we have discussed. Recall that technological change occurs when a firm can produce more output with the same set of inputs than was possible with the old technology. Thus when

Continued on page 262

*Amal Nag, "Tricky Technology: American Car Makers Discover 'Factory of the Future' Means Headaches Just Now." Adapted by permission of *The Wall Street Journal.* © Dow Jones & Company, Inc., 1986. All rights reserved.

THE WALL STREET JOURNAL

APPLICATION

Continued from page 261
technological change occurs, a firm can produce the same level of output at a lower cost. GM's new automated production line had not at that time led to technological change, because the new technologies hadn't improved productivity—technological change is *always* cost reducing.

One auto analyst argued that GM wasn't trying to reduce cost in the first place. Quotas on Japanese imports over the past few years had protected domestic car makers and led to record profits. These profits fueled U.S. auto makers' plunge into robotics and other new technologies. The analyst pointed out, however, that "GM thought in terms of automation rather than replacing the current system with a better system."

Ironically, the Japanese car makers appeared to have avoided the trap of technology for its own sake. Mazda Motor Corp., for example, had also recently built a new assembly plant in the United States. Mazda's plant did not, however, have the sophisticated high-technology equipment used at the new GM plant. Nevertheless, Mazda would use 3,500 workers to produce 240,000 cars a year in their new plant, while the GM plant would have 5,000 workers and an annual output of 220,000 cars. The problem, as an auto industry consultant noted, is to select "just the right amount of technology."

In spite of the problems, GM and other U.S. auto makers were convinced that automation was the wave of the future. Ford, which was making mistakes similar to those made by GM, argued that the malfunctions were just the result of trying to do too much too soon. Auto industry officials contended that automation would cut costs and increase quality in the long run. They also believed that automation was the most efficient method for providing the production line flexibility necessary to respond quickly to changing market conditions.

Time will be the test of the new technologies in the auto industry. If the technical difficulties are ironed out and production costs fall, then technological change will have occurred, and the U.S. auto industry will be more profitable and more able to respond quickly to changing consumer desires.

9.7 SUMMARY

This chapter has set forth the basic theory of production and the optimal combination of inputs under a given set of input prices. The basic concepts upon which production theory is based are given in the following definitions:

Definition. A production function is a schedule, table, or equation showing the maximum output that can be obtained from any given combination of inputs.

Definition. An isoquant is the locus of points showing combinations of inputs physically capable of producing a given level of output. The slope of the isoquant, the marginal rate of technical substitution, shows the rate at which one input can be substituted for another while maintaining the same level of output.

Definition. An isocost curve shows all combinations of inputs that can be purchased at some given level of cost. The slope of the isocost curve, the ratio of the input prices, shows the rate at which the market allows inputs to be substituted.

The optimal combination of inputs is determined by the following:

Relation. The firm minimizes the cost of producing any given level of output or maximizes the output that can be produced at any given level of cost when the marginal rate of technical substitution equals the ratio of the input prices. This requires that for all inputs used, the ratios of the marginal product to the price of the input are equal.

After a change in relative input prices or in technology, the firm adapts according to the following principles:

Principle. When input prices change, firms use more of the now relatively less expensive input and less of the now relatively more expensive input to produce any given level of output. This is called the substitution effect.

Principle. Technological change shifts the isoquant map toward the origin and allows each relevant level of output to be produced at a lower cost. The change may or may not change the input ratio.

TECHNICAL PROBLEMS

1. Fill in the blanks in the following table.

Units of Labor	Total Product	Average Product	Marginal Product
1	_____	40	_____
2	_____	_____	48
3	138	_____	_____
4	_____	44	_____
5	_____	_____	24
6	210	_____	_____
7	_____	29	_____
8	_____	_____	−27

2. The following table shows the amount of total output produced from various combinations of labor and capital.

Units of Labor	Units of Capital			
	1	2	3	4
1	50	120	160	180
2	110	260	360	390
3	150	360	510	560
4	170	430	630	690
5	160	480	710	790

   a. Calculate and graph the marginal product and average product of labor when capital is held constant at two units. When the average product of labor is increasing, what is the relation between the average product and marginal product? What about when the average product of labor is decreasing?
   b. Calculate and graph the marginal product of labor for each level of the capital stock. How does the marginal product of the second unit of labor change as the capital stock increases? Why?

3. Explain precisely why *MP* is greater than (less than) *AP* when *AP* is rising (falling).

4. A publishing house is using 400 printers and 200 printing presses to produce books. The printers' wage rate is $20, and the price of a printing press is $100. The last printer added 20 books to total output, while the last press added 50 books to total output. Is the

publishing house making the optimal input choice? Why or why not? If not, what should the firm do?

5. A business executive claims that a company should never hire another worker if the new person causes diminishing returns. Explain why this statement is wrong.

6. An expansion path can be derived under the assumption either that firms attempt to produce each output at minimum cost or that they attempt to gain maximum output at each level of cost. The paths are identical in both cases. Explain.

7. In the graph below, *LZ* is the isocost and I is an isoquant. Explain precisely why combinations *A* and *B* are not efficient. Explain in terms of the relation of the ratio of the marginal products to the ratio of the input prices. Explain, in these terms, why the direction of substitution in each case, labor for capital or capital for labor, is optimal. Using the ratio of input prices given by *LZ*, find and label the least cost combination of labor and capital that can produce the output designated by I. In the above terms, explain why this combination is optimal.

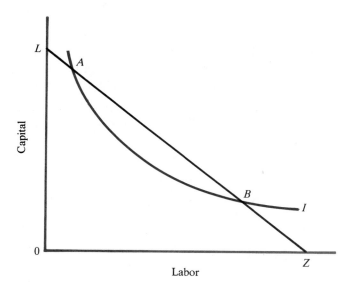

8. In the graph on the following page, the price of capital is $100 per unit.
   a. What is the price of labor?
   b. How many units of each input are used to produce each level of output at the least cost?
   c. What is the minimum cost of producing each level of output?
   d. Construct the expansion path.

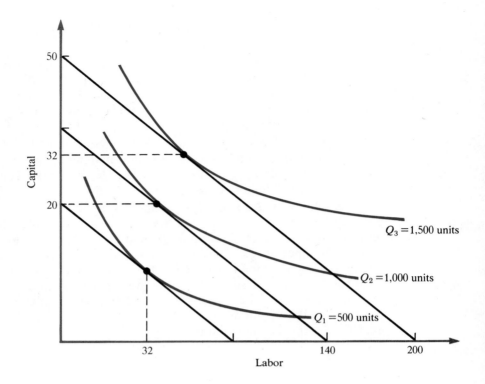

9. In the graph below, the isoquants I, II, and III are associated, respectively, with 1,000, 2,000, and 3,000 units of output. The price of capital is $2 a unit and the price of labor is $1 a unit.

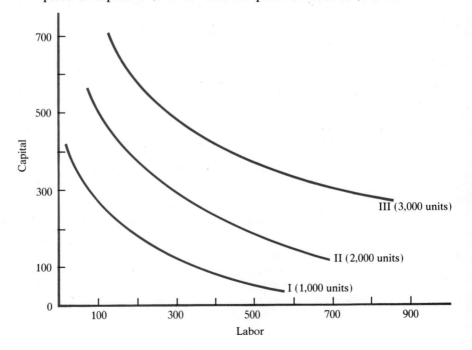

a. How many units of each input are used to produce each level of output efficiently?

b. Construct the expansion path.

c. What is the minimum cost of producing each level of output?

d. Answer each question under the assumption that the price of labor is now $2 a unit and the price of capital is $1 a unit.

10. In the graph below, show the effect of technological change that increases the capital/labor ratio.

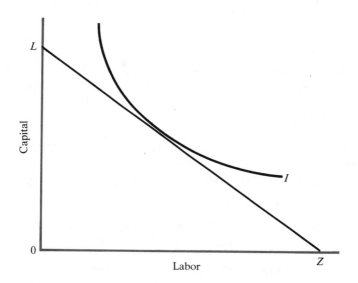

ANALYTICAL PROBLEMS

1. Explain why the marginal product of any input might become negative. That is, why would additional units of the input cause output to fall? (Do not answer that the firm hires inferior inputs. Assume all units of the input are alike.)

2. Over the past two decades, more and more firms have begun using computers. (We might say that the computer-labor ratio has risen.) Provide the economic rationale for this trend.

3. What types of changes do you believe will occur because of the rapid expansion of sales and fall in prices of personal computers?

4. Explain the following statement: "It is possible for a producer to be technically efficient and not economically efficient, but it is impossible for a producer to be economically efficient without being technically efficient."

5. *Business Week,* in an article dealing with management (October 22, 1984, p. 156), wrote "When he took over the furniture factory three years ago . . . [the manager] realized almost immediately that it was

throwing away at least $100,000 a year worth of wood scrap. Within a few weeks, he set up a task force of managers and workers to deal with the problem. And within a few months, they reduced the amount of scrap to $7,000 worth.'' Was this necessarily an *economically efficient* move?

6. How would our theory of efficient production or cost minimization relate to managers of government bureaus or departments that are not run for profit? How about nonprofit private clubs that collect just enough dues from their members to cover the cost of operation?

7. Explain why firms that find the average product or productivity of their labor force falling will probably find that their costs are rising.

8. Why do you think that in the long run there are probably no fixed-proportion production functions? What about in the short run?

APPENDIX

1. The marginal rate of technical substitution (*MRTS*) along an isoquant is the ratio of the marginal products of the two inputs.
   Define the two-input production function as

   $Q = f(K,L)$.

   The marginal products of the two inputs are

   $MP_L = \partial Q/\partial L$ and $MP_K = \partial Q/\partial K$.

   Take the total differential of the production function and set $dQ = 0$ to force output to remain constant along a particular isoquant:

   $$dQ = \frac{\partial Q}{\partial K}\, dK + \frac{\partial Q}{\partial L}\, dL = 0.$$

   Solving for the *MRTS*,

   $$MRTS = -\frac{dK}{dL} = \frac{\partial Q}{\partial L}\Big/\frac{\partial Q}{\partial K} = \frac{MP_L}{MP_K}.$$

2. Cost minimization requires that the MRTS equals the input-price ratio.
   The firm wants to minimize cost, $C = rK + wL$, subject to the constraint that output is fixed at a specified level, $\bar{Q} = f(K,L)$. It is necessary to set up the Lagrangian function

   $\mathcal{L} = rK + wL + \lambda[\bar{Q} - f(K,L)]$,

   where λ is the Lagrangian multiplier. Minimization with respect to the usage of capital and labor requires that the partial derivatives be equal to zero:

$$\frac{\partial \mathcal{L}}{\partial K} = r - \lambda \frac{\partial Q}{\partial K} = 0$$

$$\frac{\partial \mathcal{L}}{\partial L} = w - \lambda \frac{\partial Q}{\partial L} = 0.$$

Combining these two conditions, it follows that the necessary condition for minimizing the cost of producing a given level of output is

$$\frac{r}{w} = \frac{\partial Q / \partial K}{\partial Q / \partial L},$$

or

$$\frac{\partial Q}{\partial L} \bigg/ \frac{\partial Q}{\partial K} = \frac{MP_L}{MP_K} = MRTS = \frac{w}{r}.$$

3. Output maximization requires that the *MRTS* equals the input-price ratio.

   In this case, the firm wishes to maximize output, $Q = f(K,L)$, subject to a given level of expenditure, $\bar{C} = rK + wL$. We set up the Lagrangian function

   $$\mathcal{L} = f(K,L) + \lambda(\bar{C} - rK - wL).$$

   Maximization requires that the partial derivatives with respect to the choice variables, K and L, be set equal to zero:

   $$\frac{\partial \mathcal{L}}{\partial K} = \frac{\partial Q}{\partial K} - \lambda r = 0$$

   $$\frac{\partial \mathcal{L}}{\partial L} = \frac{\partial Q}{\partial L} - \lambda w = 0.$$

   Combining these necessary conditions, we obtain precisely the same result we obtained for cost minimization,

   $$\frac{\partial Q / \partial K}{\partial Q / \partial L} = \frac{r}{w}.$$

4. When average product is increasing, marginal product is greater than average product. Marginal product equals average product when average product attains its maximum. When average product is decreasing, marginal product is less than average product.

   Differentiating average product with respect to L yields

   $$\frac{d(AP_L)}{dL} = \frac{d(Q/L)}{dL} = \frac{L(dQ/dL) - Q}{L^2} = \frac{1}{L}(MP_L - AP_L).$$

   If AP_L is rising, $d(AP_L)/dL > 0$; thus $MP_L > AP_L$. If AP_L is falling, $d(AP_L)/dL < 0$; thus $MP_L < AP_L$. And if average product is at its maximum, $d(AP_L)/dL = 0$; thus $MP_L = AP_L$.

10

THEORY OF COST

T he theory of cost is important to a manager because it provides the foundation for two important production decisions made by managers: whether or not to shut down and how much to produce. As such, the theory of cost provides the framework for the theory of supply.

We will develop the theory of cost from the underlying theory of production. Recall from Chapter 9 that production theory shows how to determine the least cost method of producing a given level of output with a specific set of input prices. Therefore, just as cost theory will provide the foundation of supply, production theory provides the foundation for the theory of cost. That is, the production function and input prices determine the cost of producing any specific level of output.

After discussing a few basic concepts, we set forth the theory of cost in the short run, when the level of usage of some inputs is fixed. In this case some costs are fixed also. We then analyze cost in the long run, when all inputs are variable.

10.1 SOME BASIC CONCEPTS

Fixed and Variable Costs

Recall from Chapter 9 that we divide production into the short run and the long run. Since cost is derived from production, we make the same distinction in the theory of cost. In the long run, all inputs are variable;

hence all costs are variable. As we shall see, we treat cost in the long run as the firm's planning horizon.

In the short run some inputs are fixed. Since these inputs have to be paid regardless of the level of output produced, these payments to the fixed factors of production remain constant no matter what output is produced. This payment is called fixed cost. An example would be monthly payments on a loan outstanding on the firm's plant. These payments must be made even if the firm ceases production during a given period.

The payments to variable factors of production are called variable costs. Producing more output requires more inputs. Thus, variable cost increases as the level of output increases. Examples of variable cost would be payments for many types of labor, ingredient inputs or raw materials, and some types of capital.

Explicit and Implicit Costs

When most people think of cost, they think only of the explicit cost—the actual payment by firms to labor, capital, and other factors of production. Whether these costs are fixed or variable, they are straightforward; they are the amounts that firms must pay to owners of the resources in order to bid these resources away from alternative uses.

Producers also incur some costs referred to as implicit costs and, in a complete analysis, implicit costs must be taken into consideration. To aid in understanding the nature of implicit costs, consider two firms that produce a particular good and are in every way identical, with one exception. Both use identical amounts of the same resources to produce identical amounts of the good. The owner of one firm rents the building in which the good is produced. The owner of the other firm inherited the building the firm uses and therefore pays no rent. Whose costs are higher? For decision-making purposes, the costs for both are the same even though the second firm makes lower payments to outside factors of production. The reason the costs are the same is that using the building to produce goods costs the second firm the amount of income that could have been earned had it been leased at the prevailing rent. Since these two buildings are the same, presumably the market rentals would be the same. In other words, a part of the cost incurred by the second firm is the (implicit) payment from firm owners to themselves as the owners of a resource (the building) used by the firm. Thus, one implicit cost would include what firm owners could make from selling or leasing the capital they own if they were not using it in their firms.

Another implicit cost would be the value of the firm owner's time that is used to manage the business. Presumably, if the owner of a firm were not managing the business or working for the firm in another way, he or she could obtain a job with some other firm, possibly as a manager. The salary that could be earned in this alternative occupation is an implicit cost that should be considered as part of the total cost of production. These implicit costs are just as real as explicit costs.

Definition.   The implicit costs incurred by firms in producing a commodity consist of the amounts that could be earned in the best alternative use of the owner/manager's time and of any other of his or her resources currently used to produce the commodity in question. Implicit costs must be added to explicit costs in order to obtain total costs.

With this definition in mind, we can turn to the analysis of short-run then long-run costs.

10.2 COST IN THE SHORT RUN

A firm uses resources to produce its output. Since these resources must be paid, the firm must bear a cost. As noted above, in the short run the levels of use of some inputs are fixed, and the costs associated with these fixed inputs must be paid regardless of the level of output produced.[1] Other costs vary with the level of output. The sum of these costs—fixed and variable—is short-run total cost.

Definition.   Total fixed cost is the sum of the short-run fixed costs that must be paid regardless of the level of output. Total variable cost is the sum of the amounts spent for each of the variable inputs used. Total cost in the short run is the sum of total variable and total fixed cost.

We now turn to the relation between the production function and cost.

Short-Run Total Cost

To examine the relation between production and cost in the short run, let's look at the simplest case. Suppose that the firm uses two inputs, capital and labor, to produce output. The amount of capital is fixed at three units—for example, three machines. The firm must make a fixed payment of $2,000 per period for each of the three units of capital. Thus its fixed cost is $6,000 per period.

---

[1]As was noted in Chapter 9, it is not quite precise to say that the usage of some resources cannot be changed. Certainly the firm could scrap a very expensive piece of capital equipment, buy another one twice as large, and have it installed before lunch, if it is willing to pay the price. In fact, the firm can probably change any input rather rapidly, given, once more, its willingness to pay. It is frequently helpful in analyzing problems to assume that some inputs are fixed for a period of time. Moreover, it does not deviate too much from reality to make this assumption, since firm owners often consider certain resources as fixed over a period of time. You should not be overly concerned about the time factor in the short and long run. The fixity of resources is the important element.

With one of the two inputs fixed, the only way the firm can vary its output is by changing the amount of labor it uses. In Table 10.1, columns 1 and 2 show the firm's short-run production function when capital is fixed at three units. In this case output (*Q*) is changed in increments of 100 by varying labor. Column 1 shows the amount of labor (*L*) required to produce each level of output between 0 and 600. Column 3 shows the average product of labor (*Q/L*) at each level of output. The marginal product of labor for each change in labor usage is shown in column 4. The associated average and marginal product curves are depicted graphically in Figure 10.1.

Note that from the table and figure, average and marginal products conform to the theoretical pattern discussed in Chapter 9. Both rise at low levels of labor usage then fall thereafter. Marginal product equals average product when the latter is at its maximum, 33.33.

To obtain total variable cost (*TVC*) we must know the price of the variable input, labor. Assume that the wage rate (*w*) is $1,000 per period. Since *TVC* is the amount spent on labor at each level of output, it is simply $1,000 times the amount of labor used to produce that output (*w* × *L*). The total variable cost of producing each output is given in column 5. The total cost of producing each output (*TC*) is the sum of the constant fixed cost (*FC*, in column 6) and the total variable cost of that output. Column 7 gives the total cost of producing each level of output.

Figure 10.2 is the graph of the total cost schedules in columns 5, 6, and 7. Since fixed cost does not change with output, it is simply a hori-

Figure 10.1 **Average and Marginal Product Curves**

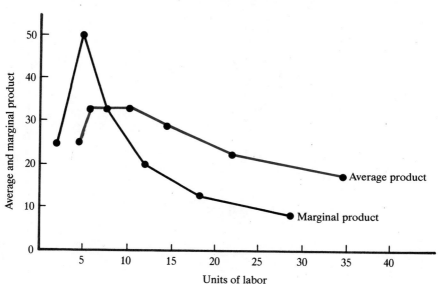

Table 10.1 Production and Cost Functions when $K = 3$, $r = \$2,000$, and $w = \$1,000$

(1) Labor (L)	(2) Output (Q)	(3) Average Product $\left(\frac{Q}{L}\right)$ (AP)	(4) Marginal Product $\left(\frac{\Delta Q}{\Delta L}\right)$ (MP)	(5) Total Variable Cost ($1,000 × L) (TVC)	(6) Fixed Cost ($2,000 × 3) (FC)	(7) Total Cost (TVC + FC) (TC)	(8) Average Fixed Cost $\left(\frac{FC}{Q}\right)$ (AFC)	(9) Average Variable Cost $\left(\frac{TVC}{Q}\right)$ (AVC)	(10) Average Total Cost $\left(\frac{TC}{Q}\right)$ (ATC)	(11) Marginal Cost $\left(\frac{\Delta TVC}{\Delta Q}\right)$ (SMC)
0	0	—		0	$6,000	$ 6,000	—	—	—	
			25							$ 40
4	100	25		$ 4,000	6,000	10,000	$60	$40	$100	
			50							20
6	200	33.33		6,000	6,000	12,000	30	30	60	
			33.33							30
9	300	33.33		9,000	6,000	15,000	20	30	50	
			20							50
14	400	28.57		14,000	6,000	20,000	15	35	50	
			12.50							80
22	500	22.73		22,000	6,000	28,000	12	44	56	
			8.33							120
34	600	17.65		34,000	6,000	40,000	10	56.67	66.67	

Figure 10.2 **Total Cost Curves**

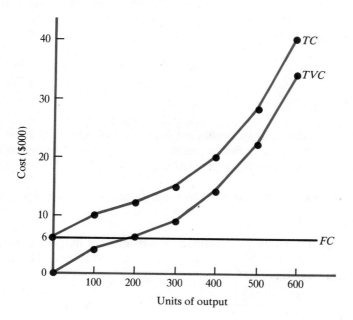

Units of output

zontal line at $6,000. Total variable cost and, therefore, total cost must increase as output increases, because increased output can result only from using more labor. From the graph we can see that variable cost first increases at a decreasing rate until 200 units of output then increases at an increasing rate. This is the "typically assumed" cost structure and, as we shall see, follows from our assumptions about the short-run production function. Since *TC* is *TVC* plus *FC*, the total cost curve in Figure 10.2 is simply *TVC* plus $6,000. At zero output *TC* is $6,000, because variable cost is zero.

Average and Marginal Cost

Another way of examining to the firm's cost structure is to analyze the behavior of short-run average and marginal costs. First, consider average fixed cost (*AFC*), given in column 8 of the table.

Definition. *Average fixed cost is total fixed cost divided by output,*

$$AFC = FC/Q.$$

Note that average fixed cost is obtained by dividing the fixed cost (in this case $6,000) by output. Thus *AFC* is high at relatively low levels of output; since the denominator increases as output increases, *AFC* decreases over the entire range of output. If output would continue to increase, *AFC* would approach zero as output became extremely large.

Next, consider average variable cost (*AVC*).

Definition. Average variable cost is total variable cost divided by output,

$$AVC = TVC/Q.$$

The average variable cost of producing each level of output in Table 10.1 is shown in column 9. *AVC* at first decreases to $30 then increases thereafter.

Next consider average total cost (*ATC*).

Definition. Average total cost is short-run total cost divided by output,

$$ATC = TC/Q.$$

The average total cost of producing each level of output is given in column 10 of Table 10.1. Since total cost is total variable plus total fixed cost,

$$ATC = \frac{TC}{Q} = \frac{TVC + FC}{Q} = AVC + AFC.$$

The average total cost in the table has the same general structure as average variable cost. It first declines, reaches a minimum at $50, then increases thereafter. The minimum *ATC* is attained at a larger output (between 300 and 400) than that at which *AVC* attains its minimum (between 200 and 300). This result is not peculiar to the cost schedules in Table 10.1; as we shall show later, it follows for all average cost schedules of the general type shown here.

Finally, short-run marginal cost (*SMC*) is defined as follows:

Definition. Short-run marginal cost is the change in either total variable cost or total cost per unit change in output; or

$$SMC = \frac{\Delta TVC}{\Delta Q} = \frac{\Delta TC}{\Delta Q}.$$

The two definitions are the same because, when output increases, total cost increases by the same amount as the increase in total variable cost. Thus, since $TC = FC + TVC,$

$$SMC = \frac{\Delta FC}{\Delta Q} + \frac{\Delta TVC}{\Delta Q} = 0 + \frac{\Delta TVC}{\Delta Q} = \frac{\Delta TVC}{\Delta Q}.$$

The short-run marginal cost is given in column 11 of Table 10.1. It is the per unit change in cost resulting from a change in output when the use of the variable input changes. For example, when output increases from 0 to 100, both total and variable costs increase by $4,000. The change in cost per unit of output is, therefore, $4,000 divided by the increase in output, 100, or $40. Thus the marginal cost is $40. It can be seen that *MC* first declines, reaches a minimum of $20, then rises. Note that minimum marginal cost is attained at an output (between 100 and 200) below those at which either *AVC* or *ATC* attains its minimum. Marginal cost equals *AVC* and *ATC* at their respective minimum levels. We shall return to the reason for this result below.

The average and marginal cost schedules in columns 9, 10, and 11 are shown graphically in Figure 10.3. Average fixed cost is not graphed because it is a curve that simply declines over the entire range of output and because, as we shall see, it is irrelevant for decision making. The curves in Figure 10.3 depict the properties of the cost schedules we have discussed. All three curves decline at first, then rise. Marginal cost equals *AVC* and *ATC* at each of their minimum levels. Marginal cost is below *AVC* and *ATC* when they are declining and above them when they are increasing. Since *AFC* decreases over the entire range of output and since *ATC* = *AVC* + *AFC*, *ATC* becomes increasingly close to *AVC* as output increases.

As we show below, these are the general properties of typically assumed average and marginal cost curves. But, before we turn to these

Figure 10.3 **Average and Marginal Cost Curves**

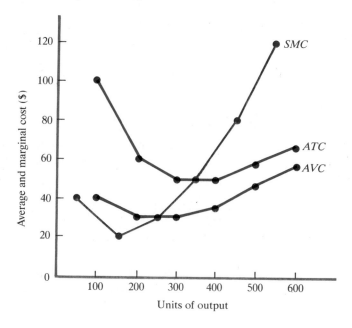

general cost curves, let's look at the relation between production and cost once again.

Relations between Average Variable and Marginal Costs and Average and Marginal Products

To show the relation between production and cost, let's return once more to Table 10.1. Recall that the wage rate paid each worker is $1,000. From the production function, four workers can produce 100 units of output. Thus the total variable cost is the price per worker, $1,000, times the number of workers. Since the average product of four workers is 25, we can write total product, 100, as the average product, 25, times the number of workers, four. Thus we can see that average variable cost at 100 units of output is

$$AVC = \frac{\$1,000 \times 4}{25 \times 4} = \frac{\$1,000}{25} = \frac{w}{AP} = \$40,$$

the figure shown in column 9.

By calculation you can see that the average variable cost at each level of output is the wage rate divided by the average product, and this holds for any production function with one variable input, since

$$AVC = \frac{TVC}{Q} = \frac{w \times L}{AP \times L} = \frac{w}{AP}.$$

A similar relation exists between marginal cost and marginal product. The additional cost of moving from 100 to 200 units of output is $1,000 times the number of additional workers needed, two (an increase from four to six). Thus $\Delta TVC = \$1,000 \times 2 = w \times \Delta L$. The change in output is the marginal product per additional worker, 50, times the number of additional workers, two. Thus $\Delta Q = MP \times \Delta L = 50 \times 2 = 100$. So

$$SMC = \frac{\Delta TVC}{\Delta Q} = \frac{\$1,000 \times 2}{50 \times 2} = \frac{w}{MP} = \$20,$$

the figure shown in column 11. Again by calculation, for each change in output given in the table, marginal cost is the wage rate divided by the marginal product. And this holds for every production function with one variable input, since

$$SMC = \frac{\Delta TVC}{\Delta Q} = \frac{\Delta(w \times L)}{\Delta Q} = w\left(\frac{\Delta L}{\Delta Q}\right) = \frac{w}{MP}.$$

The relations between cost and production determine the slopes of average and marginal cost. From Chapter 9 and Figure 10.1, we know that average product first increases, reaches a maximum, then declines thereafter. Since $AVC = w/AP$ for a one-input production function, when average product increases, average variable cost must decrease. As *AP* decreases, *AVC* must increase. Thus, when *AP* attains its maximum, *AVC* reaches its minimum.

And, since $SMC = w/MP$, marginal cost falls as marginal product increases and rises as *MP* decreases; *SMC* is at a minimum when *MP* attains its maximum. Also, since *MP* reaches its maximum before the maximum *AP*, the minimum marginal cost comes at a lower output than the minimum average variable cost. All these relations are evident in Table 10.1 and in Figures 10.1 and 10.3.

Furthermore, the minimum *ATC* is reached at a larger output than that at which *AVC* attains its minimum. This relation is shown in Table 10.1 and Figure 10.3 for the specified numerical cost function. But, it is easily shown that this result holds in general. We know that

$$ATC = AFC + AVC$$

and that average fixed cost declines over the entire range of output. Thus, *ATC* declines at first because both *AFC* and *AVC* are falling. Even when *AVC* begins to rise, the decrease in *AFC* continues to drive down *ATC* as output increases. However, an output is finally reached at which the increase in *AVC* overcomes the decrease in *AFC,* and *ATC* begins to rise.[2]

The relations between marginal and average products and marginal and average costs may be generalized to several variable inputs. Suppose that *n* variable inputs are used with fixed amounts of other inputs. Let $X_1, X_2, X_3, \ldots, X_n$ denote the quantities of these variable inputs used, and let $w_1, w_2, w_3, \ldots, w_n$ be the prices of these inputs. Thus

$$AVC = \frac{w_1X_1 + w_2X_2 + w_3X_3 + \cdots + w_nX_n}{Q}$$

$$= \frac{w_1X_1}{Q} + \frac{w_2X_2}{Q} + \frac{w_3X_3}{Q} + \cdots + \frac{w_nX_n}{Q} = \sum_{i=1}^{n} \frac{w_i}{AP_i},$$

where AP_i is the average product of the *i*-th input. Again the falling average products of the inputs must, after a point, cause *AVC* to rise.

Under the same conditions, marginal cost can be written as

$$MC = \frac{w_1\Delta X_1 + w_2\Delta X_2 + w_3\Delta X_3 + \cdots + w_n\Delta X_n}{\Delta Q}$$

$$= \frac{w_1\Delta X_1}{\Delta Q} + \frac{w_2\Delta X_2}{\Delta Q} + \frac{w_3\Delta X_3}{\Delta Q} + \cdots + \frac{w_n\Delta X_n}{\Delta Q} = \sum_{i=1}^{n} \frac{w_i}{MP_i}.$$

As was the case for *AVC,* the declining marginal products of the inputs must, after a point, cause marginal cost to increase.

---

[2]This relation is derived mathematically in the appendix to this chapter.

THE WALL STREET JOURNAL

APPLICATION

Are Costs and Productivity Related?

During the summer of 1986, *The Wall Street Journal* reported that General Motors, the largest car manufacturer in the world (in fact the largest firm in the world) was having cost problems.* GM was no longer drawing closer to Japanese car manufacturers in terms of cost after a period of narrowing the gap. GM's chairman conceded that GM had stopped gaining on the Japanese. The chairman of the Chrysler Motor Corp. said, "They [GM] aren't the low cost producer. The industry no longer marches to their tune."

The relative profit margins of GM, Ford, and Chrysler were evidence that GM's average costs had risen. The three U.S. firms were charging essentially the same prices for their auto-mobiles, but, during the preceding year, GM earned only 4.1 cents on every dollar's worth of goods sold, compared to 4.8 cents for Ford and 7.7 cents for Chrysler. Thus GM's cost must have been higher.

But what about productivity? Was it related to cost? It appears so. During the preceding year, both Ford and Chrysler produced 18 automobiles per auto employee in North America while General Motors produced only 12. Thus labor's average product at GM was considerably below that of its U.S. competitors. This appears to be an important reason for GM's higher average cost of producing automobiles. And this is what cost theory predicts: when average product decreases, average cost increases.

*Doron P. Levin, "In a High Tech Drive, GM Falls Below Rivals in Auto Profit Margins," *The Wall Street Journal*, July 22, 1986. Adapted by permission of *The Wall Street Journal*. © Dow Jones and Company, Inc., 1986. All rights reserved.

General Short-Run Cost Curves

Most of the properties of cost curves set forth thus far in this section were derived using the specific production and cost functions in Table 10.1. These properties also hold for general cost curves when output and therefore cost vary continuously rather than discretely, as assumed above. These typical average and marginal cost curves are shown in Figure 10.4. These curves show the following:

Figure 10.4 **Short-Run Average and Marginal Cost Curves**

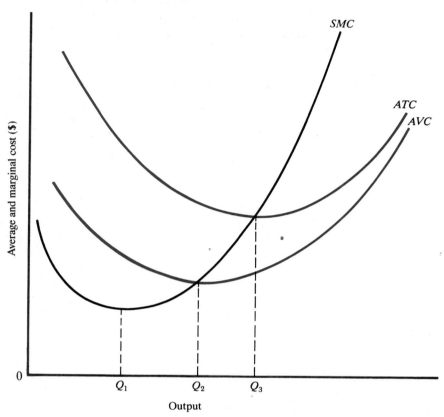

Relations. *(1)* **AFC** *declines continuously, approaching both axes asymptotically (as shown by the decreasing distance between* **ATC** *and* **AVC**). *(2)* **AVC** *first declines, reaches a minimum at* Q_2, *and rises thereafter. When* **AVC** *is at its minimum,* **SMC** *equals* **AVC**. *(3)* **ATC** *first declines, reaches a minimum at* Q_3, *and rises thereafter. When* **ATC** *is at its minimum,* **SMC** *equals* **ATC**. *(4)* **SMC** *first declines, reaches a minimum at* Q_1, *and rises thereafter.* **SMC** *equals both* **AVC** *and* **ATC** *when these curves are at their minimum values. Furthermore,* **SMC** *lies below both* **AVC** *and* **ATC** *over the range in which these curves decline;* **SMC** *lies above them when they are rising.*

In general, the reason marginal cost crosses *AVC* and *ATC* at their respective minimum points follows from the definitions of the cost curves. If marginal cost is below average variable cost, each additional unit of output adds less to cost than the average variable cost of that unit. Thus average variable cost must decline over this range. When *SMC* is above *AVC*, each additional unit of output adds more to cost than *AVC*. Thus, in this case, *AVC* must rise.

So, when *SMC* is less than *AVC*, average variable cost is falling; when *SMC* is greater than *AVC*, average variable cost is rising. Thus *SMC* must equal *AVC* at the minimum point on *AVC*.[3] Exactly the same reasoning would be used to show that *SMC* crosses *ATC* at the minimum point on the latter curve.

Short-run cost is closely related to production. With only one variable input,

$$SMC = \frac{w}{MP} \text{ and } AVC = \frac{w}{AP}.$$

Thus the following relations must hold:

Relations. When marginal product (average product) is increasing, marginal cost (average variable cost) is decreasing. When marginal product (average product) is decreasing, marginal cost (average variable cost) is increasing. When marginal product equals average product at maximum AP, marginal cost equals average variable cost at minimum AVC. Similar but not identical relations hold when more than one input is variable.

As noted in Chapter 9, when the fixed inputs are allowed to change, the short-run production function changes. This, of course, will shift the short-run cost curves. In this case, the firm is in the long run, to which we turn after examining why profit-maximizing decisions depend on marginal cost, not fixed cost.

APPLICATION

Irrelevance of fixed cost

Marginal cost is by far the *most important* cost function for decision-making purposes. And, fixed cost is the *least important*. As you will recall, we emphasized in Chapter 3 that decision making involves comparing the marginal benefits from a particular activity with its marginal costs. This is frequently called benefit-cost analysis.

To see the irrelevance of fixed costs for this type of analysis, consider the following hypothetical example. The manager of a restaurant that is open from 6:00 A.M. to 10:00 P.M. is considering

---

[3]This relation is derived mathematically in the appendix to this chapter.

keeping the restaurant open 24 hours a day. Under the current 16-hour-per-day operation, the restaurant averages $1,700 a day in revenues with total costs of $1,600 a day. Of this, $240 a day is fixed cost—interest payments on capital.

Based upon market surveys, the manager believes that keeping the restaurant open the additional eight hours would increase average daily total revenue to $2,150 and average daily cost to $2,000. Thus the marginal revenue from remaining open all night is expected to be $450; the expected marginal cost is $400. Should the restaurant be opened the additional eight hours? Certainly. The marginal revenue exceeds the marginal cost by $50, so $50 a day, on average, would be added to profit.

Note that in making the decision the manager considers only *marginal cost*. Fixed cost should not be considered. To see this, suppose that the manager had allocated a proportion of fixed cost to the additional eight hours. If this were done, one third of the fixed cost, $80, would be added to the cost of staying open the extra time. Thus the manager would compute the total cost of remaining open the additional time as $400 + $80 = $480. Since this amount exceeds the additional revenues that would be generated, the decision would be to remain closed at night. But, as we have seen, staying open adds $50 a day to profit. Taking fixed cost into consideration would have led to an incorrect decision. Marginal changes are all that matter when making such types of decisions.

To illustrate the point further, we might consider why airlines sometimes put on flights that cause losses to occur when all costs are considered, or why trucking companies sometimes make seemingly unprofitable hauls. The reason is that the marginal benefit exceeds the marginal cost. It may be that a particular flight has so little passenger and freight demand that the total cost of the flight exceeds the total revenue when the fixed cost of the plane is spread over this extra flight. But if the plane would be idle otherwise, the real cost of the additional flight is the added labor and fuel costs, the added wear and tear on capital, and any other costs that would not be encountered if the flight was not made. In other words, only the marginal costs matter. If these marginal costs are expected to be less than the expected additional revenues from making the additional flight, the trip will be made. Exactly the same rationale applies to the decision of trucking companies about additional hauls.

Employees who manage departments or divisions of firms frequently use the same line of reasoning. Say you manage a department in a large department store. How do you convince your store manager that you need more advertising? You know more advertising will increase sales and therefore your revenues. Convince the manager that the additional returns from the additional sales will exceed the additional cost of increased advertising. Use the same argument when you wish more sales help or more of any resource, like floor space, that will increase sales. Managers of offices or branches of plants can use much the same type of argument.

The point is, therefore, when making decisions about changes, only marginal cost should be considered. Fixed cost is irrelevant.

10.3 LONG-RUN COSTS: THE PLANNING HORIZON

Recall from Chapter 9 that the long run is not some date in the future. The long run simply means that all inputs are variable to the firm. Therefore, one of the first decisions to be made by the owner and/or manager is the scale of operation, that is, the size of the firm. To make this decision the manager must know the cost of producing each relevant level of output. As we will see, just as short-run cost is derived from the short-run production function, long-run cost is derived from the long-run expansion path.

Derivation of Cost Schedules from a Production Function

Let us assume for analytical purposes that the firm's levels of usage of the inputs will not affect the price that must be paid for the inputs. Further, assume that the only two inputs are labor (L) and capital (K). The price of labor (w) is $5 per unit, and the price of capital (r) is $10. Figure 10.5 shows a portion of the firm's expansion path. Isoquants I, II, and III are associated, respectively, with 100, 200, and 300 units of output.

For the given set of input prices, the isocost curve with intercepts of 12 units of capital and 24 units of labor, which clearly has a slope of $-5/10$ $(= -w/r)$, shows the least cost method of producing 100 units of output: use 10 units of labor and 7 units of capital. If the firm wants to produce 100 units, it spends $50 ($5 $\times$ 10) on labor and $70 ($10 $\times$ 7) on capital, giving it a total cost of $120.

Similar to the short run, we define long-run average cost as

$$LRAC = \frac{\text{Long-run total cost } (LRTC)}{\text{Output } (Q)},$$

and long-run marginal cost as

$$LRMC = \frac{\Delta(LRTC)}{\Delta Q}.$$

Therefore at an output of 100,

$$LRAC = \frac{\$120}{100} = \$1.20.$$

Figure 10.5 Long-Run Expansion Path

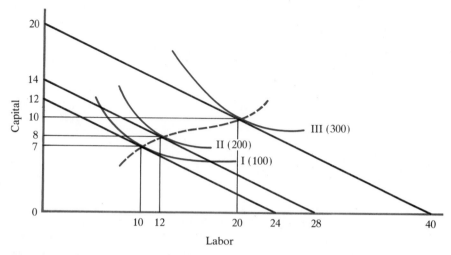

Since there are no fixed inputs in the long run, there is no fixed cost when output is zero. Thus the long-run marginal cost of producing the first 100 units is

$$LRMC = \frac{\$120 - 0}{100 - 0} = \$1.20.$$

The level of output, the least cost combination of labor and capital that can produce that output, and long-run total, average, and marginal costs when output is 100 units are given in the first row of Table 10.2.

Returning to Figure 10.5, we see that the least cost method of producing 200 units of output is to use 12 units of labor and 8 units of capital. Thus producing 200 units of output costs $140 (= $5 × 12 + $10 × 8). The average cost is $0.70 (= $140/200) and, since producing the additional 100 units increases total cost from $120 to $140, the marginal cost is $0.20 (= $20/100). These figures are shown in the second row of Table 10.2, and they give us additional points on the firm's long-run total, average, and marginal cost curves.

Figure 10.5 shows that the firm will use 20 units of labor and 10 units of capital to produce 300 units of output. Using the same methods as before, we calculate total, average, and marginal costs, which are given in row 3 of Table 10.2.

Figure 10.5 shows only three of the possible cost-minimizing choices. But, if we were to go on, we could obtain additional least cost combinations, and in the same way as above, we could calculate the total, average, and marginal costs of these other outputs. This information is shown in the last four rows of Table 10.2 for output levels from 400 through 700.

Table 10.2 Derivation of Long-Run Cost Schedules

(1) Output	(2) Labor (units)	(3) Capital (units)	(4) Total Cost at $5 per Unit of Labor, $10 per Unit of Capital	(5) Average Cost	(6) Marginal Cost
	Least Cost Combination of				
100	10	7	$120	$1.20	$1.20
200	12	8	140	0.70	0.20
300	20	10	200	0.67	0.60
400	30	15	300	0.75	1.00
500	40	22	420	0.84	1.20
600	52	30	560	0.93	1.40
700	60	42	720	1.03	1.60

Thus at the given set of input prices and with the given technology, column 4 shows the long-run total cost schedule, column 5 the average cost schedule, and column 6 the marginal cost schedule. The corresponding long-run total cost curve is given in Panel A, Figure 10.6. This curve shows the least cost at which each quantity of output in Table 10.2 can be produced when no input is fixed. Its shape depends exclusively on the production function and the input prices.

This curve reflects three of the commonly assumed characteristics of long-run total cost. First, because there are no fixed costs, LRTC is zero when output is zero. Second, cost and output are directly related; that is, LRTC has a positive slope. It costs more to produce more, which is to say that resources are scarce or that one never gets something for nothing. Third, LRTC first increases at a decreasing rate, then increases at an increasing rate. This implies that marginal cost first decreases then increases.

Turn now to the long-run average and marginal cost curves derived from Table 10.2 and shown in Panel B of Figure 10.6. These curves reflect the characteristics of typical LRAC and LRMC curves. They have essentially the same shape as in the short run—but, as we shall see below, for different reasons. Long-run average cost first decreases, reaches a minimum (at 300 units of output), then increases. Long-run marginal cost first declines, reaches its minimum at a lower output than that associated with minimum LRAC (between 100 and 200 units), then increases thereafter.

In Figure 10.6, marginal cost crosses the average cost curve at approximately the minimum of average cost. As we will show below, when output and cost are allowed to vary continuously, LRMC crosses LRAC at exactly the minimum point on the latter. (It is only approximate in Figure 10.6 because output varies discretely.)

The reasoning is the same as that given for short-run average and marginal cost curves. When marginal cost is less than average cost, each

Figure 10.6 **Long-Run Total, Average, and Marginal Cost**

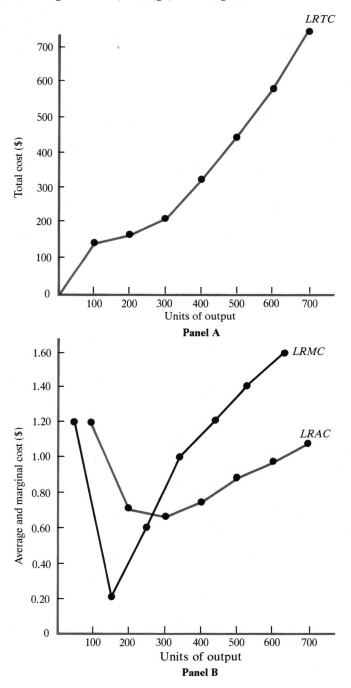

additional unit produced adds less than average cost to total cost, so average cost must decrease. When marginal cost is greater than average cost, each additional unit of the good produced adds more than average cost to total cost, so average cost must be increasing over this range of output. Thus marginal cost must be equal to average cost when average cost is at its minimum.

Figure 10.7 shows long-run marginal and average cost curves that reflect the typically assumed characteristics when output and cost can vary continuously. These characteristics are summarized in the following:

Relations.   (1) Long-run average cost, defined as

$$LRAC = \frac{LRTC}{Q},$$

first declines, reaches a minimum (here at Q_2 units of output), then increases. (2) When LRAC is at its minimum, long-run marginal cost, defined as

$$LRMC = \frac{\Delta LRTC}{\Delta Q},$$

equals LRAC. (3) LRMC first declines, reaches a minimum (here at Q_1, less than Q_2), then increases. LRMC lies below LRAC over the range in which LRAC declines; it lies above LRAC when LRAC is rising.[4]

It is important to note that in the long run the firm may use different amounts and combinations of inputs to produce different levels of output. Nothing is fixed except the set of technological possibilities (the state of the art) and the prices at which the firm can purchase inputs. Thus, completely different production processes may be used to achieve minimum cost at, say, Q_1 and Q_2 units of output. This "planning horizon" in which nothing is fixed except factor prices and technology is called the long run, and the associated curve that shows the minimum cost of producing each level of output is called the long-run total cost curve.

Economies and Diseconomies of Scale

Thus far we have concentrated exclusively upon describing the generally assumed shapes of the long-run cost curves. But we have not yet analyzed the economic forces behind these shapes. These forces are economies and diseconomies of scale.

Recall from Chapter 9 our discussion of increasing and decreasing returns to scale: When all inputs are increased in the same proportion

---

[4]This result is derived mathematically in the appendix to this chapter.

Figure 10.7 **Long-Run Average and Marginal Cost Curves**

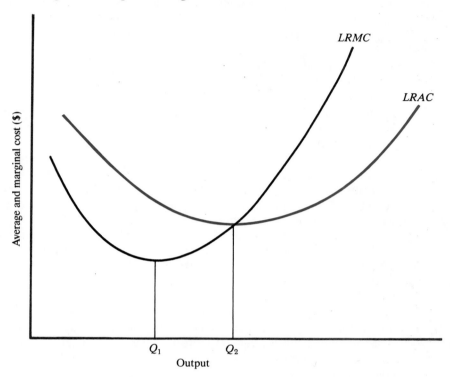

and output increases in a smaller proportion, the result was referred to as decreasing returns to scale. Alternatively, when all inputs are increased in the same proportion and output increases in a greater proportion, we referred to that as increasing returns to scale.

In the preceding section, we told you about the relation between the short-run production function and short-run cost curves. As you have probably guessed, there also exists a specific relation between returns to scale (a production concept) and the shape of the long-run cost curves. With constant input prices, increasing returns to scale require that the average cost curve decline. This case is referred to as *economies of scale*. Over the range of decreasing returns to scale, the long-run average cost curve is rising and we say that the cost function is characterized by *diseconomies of scale*.

A simplified example might help to demonstrate this point. Suppose there exist increasing returns to scale. Doubling output requires less than twice as much of each input, so the increase in cost is less than double (again assuming constant input prices) and average cost falls. Conversely, in the range of decreasing returns to scale, doubling output requires more than twice as much of each input. In this case, cost will more than double, so average cost will rise. (This example assumes fixed proportions, but it should be noted that the relation holds in the case of variable proportions when inputs are not increased in the same proportion.)

In any case, increasing returns to scale lead to economies of scale which in turn cause long-run average cost to decline. As the size of plant and the scale of operation become larger, certain economies of scale are usually realized. That is, after adjusting all inputs optimally, the unit cost of production is reduced as the firm produces more output.

One reason for this phenomenon is specialization and division of labor. When the number of workers is expanded, with a fixed stock of capital equipment, the opportunities for specialization and division of labor are rapidly exhausted. The marginal product curve rises, to be sure, but not for long. It very quickly reaches its maximum and declines. But, in the long run, when workers and equipment are expanded together, very substantial gains may be reaped by division of jobs and the specialization of workers in one job or another.

Proficiency is also gained by concentration of effort. If a plant is very small and employs only a small number of workers, each worker will usually have to perform several different jobs in the production process. In doing so he or she is likely to have to move about the plant, change tools, and so on. Not only are workers not highly specialized but a part of their work time is consumed in moving about and changing tools. Thus, important savings may be realized by expanding the scale of operation. A larger plant with a larger work force may permit each worker to specialize in one job, gaining proficiency and decreasing or eliminating time-consuming interchanges of location and equipment. There naturally will be corresponding reductions in the unit cost of production.

Technological factors constitute a second force contributing to economies of scale. If several different machines, each with a different rate of output, are required in a production process, the operation may have to be quite sizable to permit proper "meshing" of equipment. Suppose only two types of machines are required, one that produces and one that packages the product. If the first machine can produce 30,000 units per day and the second can package 45,000 units per day, output will have to be 90,000 units per day in order to utilize fully the capacity of each type of machine.

Another technological element is the fact that the cost of purchasing and installing larger machines is usually proportionately less than the cost of smaller machines. For example, a printing press that can run 200,000 papers per day does not cost 10 times as much as one that can run 20,000 per day—nor does it require 10 times as much building space, 10 times as many people to work it, and so forth. Again, expanding size tends to reduce the unit cost of production.

A final technological element is perhaps the most important of all: as the scale of operation expands there is usually a qualitative, as well as a quantitative, change in equipment. Consider ditchdigging. The smallest scale of operation is one laborer and one shovel. But as the scale expands beyond a certain point the firm does not simply continue to add workers and shovels. Shovels and most workers are replaced by a modern ditch-digging machine. In like manner, expansion of scale normally permits the introduction of various types of automation devices, all of which tend to reduce the unit cost of production.

Thus two broad forces, (1) specialization and division of labor and (2) technological factors, enable producers to reduce unit cost by expanding the scale of operation.[5] These forces give rise to the negatively sloped portion of the long-run average cost curve.

But why should the long-run average cost curve ever rise? After all possible economies of scale have been realized, why doesn't the curve become horizontal?

The rising portion of *LRAC* is usually attributed to decreasing returns to scale, causing diseconomies of scale, which generally implies limitations to efficient management. Managing any business entails controlling and coordinating a wide variety of activities—production, transportation, finance, sales, and so on. To perform these managerial functions efficiently, the manager must have accurate information, otherwise the essential decision making is done in ignorance.

As the scale of plant expands beyond a certain point, top management necessarily has to delegate responsibility and authority to lower echelon employees. Contact with the daily routine of operation tends to be lost, and efficiency of operation declines. Red tape and paperwork expand; management is generally not as efficient. Thus, the cost of the managerial function increases, as does the unit cost of production.

It is very difficult to determine just when diseconomies of scale set in and when they become strong enough to outweigh the economies of scale. In businesses where economies of scale are negligible, diseconomies may soon become of paramount importance, causing *LRAC* to turn up at a relatively small volume of output. Panel A of Figure 10.8 shows a long-run average cost curve for a firm of this type. In other cases, economies of scale are extremely important. Even after the efficiency of management begins to decline, technological economies of scale may offset the diseconomies over a wide range of output. Thus the *LRAC* curve may not turn upward until a very large volume of output is attained. This case (typified by the so-called natural monopolies) is illustrated in Panel B of Figure 10.8.

---

[5]This discussion of economies of scale has concentrated upon physical and technological forces. There are financial reasons for economies of scale as well. Large-scale purchasing of raw and processed materials may enable the buyer to obtain more favorable prices (quantity discounts). The same is frequently true of advertising. As another example, financing of large-scale businesses is normally easier and less expensive: a nationally known business has access to organized security markets, so it may place its bonds and stocks on a more favorable basis. Bank loans also usually come easier and at lower interest rates to large, well-known corporations.

Figure 10.8 Various Shapes of *LRAC*

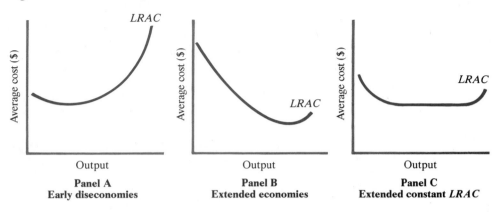

Panel A	Panel B	Panel C
Early diseconomies	Extended economies	Extended constant *LRAC*

In many actual situations, however, neither of these extremes describes the behavior of *LRAC*. A very modest scale of operation may enable a firm to capture all of the economies of scale, and diseconomies may not be incurred until the volume of output is very great. In this case, *LRAC* would have a long horizontal section as shown in Panel C of Figure 10.8. Some economists and business executives feel that this type of *LRAC* curve describes many production processes in the American economy. For analytical purposes, however, we will assume a "representative" *LRAC*, such as that illustrated earlier in Figure 10.7.

THE WALL STREET JOURNAL

APPLICATION

An Airline Runs into Trouble

The Wall Street Journal, August 11, 1986, reported that: "In its early days, People Express Inc.'s maverick management style inspired admiration and emulation. Executives, consultants, and academics swarmed to the airline, seeking insight into the methods that were credited with its initial success."* Students at the Harvard Business School studied the company's philosophy.

But the philosophy didn't work very long. In 1986 the five-

Continued on page 293

*"Airline's Ills Point out Weaknesses of Unorthodox Management Style," by Amanda Bennett. Adapted by permission of *The Wall Street Journal*. © Dow Jones & Company, Inc., 1986. All rights reserved.

THE WALL STREET JOURNAL

APPLICATION

Continued from page 292
year-old airline was in trouble. It was "experiencing huge losses and the possibility of bankruptcy." According to the *Journal*, many observers felt that the People's experiment ". . . that once demonstrated the potential of an increasingly popular style of management is now betraying its limitations." Let's look at what happened.

People Express was divided into operating groups of 250 people who decided how they would carry out their assigned tasks. Employees moved from job to job, sometimes daily. Flight attendants would track lost bags; pilots would take tickets and tend computer operations. Everyone had to deal with customers. Donald C. Burr, the airline's founder and chairman wrote, "The next time you fly People Express, your coffee may be served by People's chief financial officer, Bob McAdoo, who is a certified flight attendant and flies weekly."

People Express basically shunned formal lines of authority and standard reporting proce- dures. Mr. Burr ". . . once boasted that no People official was more than three levels away from him or a managing director, so that problems could be dealt with in person."

But, as the *WSJ* noted, many observers felt that the lack of tighter organization had detrimental effects. As any company grows bigger, a system such as People's can get unwieldy. "When employees are more numerous, it becomes increasingly difficult to depend on telephone calls and face-to-face meetings to keep information flowing, and on shared ideals to keep company goals in sight." Moreover, management specialists were saying, at the time, that the system of rotating employees through various assignments was reducing productivity.

To summarize, People Express had become so large that managerial diseconomies of scale had set in, and it was consequently losing money. As the company grew so rapidly, it was not realizing the gains from specialization. These managerial diseconomies are real and must be overcome if any company is to avoid losses. The chairman of a software company, which in four years had grown from 8 employees to 1,300, summed up the problem: "Managing a company with 1,200 employees isn't twice as difficult as one with 600. There's a multiplier effect."

Continued on page 294

THE WALL STREET JOURNAL

APPLICATION

Continued from page 293
People Express was a loosely managed firm that was efficient when the company was small. But as a vice president of a New York consulting firm said, "With a system of shared responsibility, when things aren't going well

where do you push the button to make it right? You can't push on 500 or 1,000 people."

Another management consultant commented, "If People wanted to remain a small counterculture airline, they could have gotten away with it longer." People Express was taken over by Texas Air a few months later.

Although managerial diseconomies of scale are a serious problem in rapidly growing firms, they can be overcome by changes in the managerial structure. In an earlier article, *The Wall Street Journal* described how the Minnesota Mining and Manufacturing Co. (3M) had offset the problem of large size during the 1970s.† The article noted that 3M was trying to "think small."

The top personnel officer at 3M said, "We are keenly aware of the problems of large size. We make a conscious effort to keep our units as small as possible because we think it keeps them flexible and vital. When one gets too large, we break it apart. We like to say that our success in recent years amounts to multiplication by division."

Even though 3M employed some 87,000 workers, its average manufacturing plant employed only 270 people. Many product management groups consisted of only five people. Despite the declining role of many of the largest firms, 3M's earnings grew almost fourfold during the 1970s, while its work force increased 40 percent. Thus it appears that 3M had successfully overcome the problems brought about by large size by breaking its huge production facility into many smaller, more manageable divisions.

What works for one company, however, may not work for another. The point is that when firms become so large that their average cost begins to rise, sometimes a managerial restructuring of one type or another may be the solution.

†"Some Fight Ills of Bigness by Keeping Employment Units Small," by Frederick C. Klein, *The Wall Street Journal,* February 5, 1982. Adapted by permission of *The Wall Street Journal.* © Dow Jones & Company, Inc., 1982. All rights reserved.

10.4 RELATIONS BETWEEN SHORT-RUN AND LONG-RUN COSTS

We can summarize our discussion of cost thus far by noting that firms *plan* in the long run and *operate* in the short run. Indeed, we call the long run the firm's planning horizon. The long-run cost function gives the most efficient (the least cost) method of producing any given level of output, because all inputs are variable. But once a particular firm size is chosen and the firm begins producing, the firm is in the short run. Plant and equipment have already been constructed. Now if the firm wishes to change its level of output, it can't vary the usage of all inputs. Some inputs, the plant and so forth, are fixed to the firm. Thus the firm cannot vary all inputs optimally and therefore cannot produce this new level of output at the lowest possible cost.

Such a situation is shown in Figure 10.9, where *LRAC* is the firm's long-run average cost curve. Suppose that, when making its plans, the firm had decided that it wanted to produce Q_0 units of output per period. It chooses the optimal combination of inputs to produce this output at the lowest possible cost. At this least cost, the average cost of producing Q_0 units is AC_0 in the figure. Since it would not wish to vary any of its inputs so long as it continues to produce Q_0—and so long as input prices and technology remain the same—the short-run average total cost of producing Q_0 is the same as the long-run average cost.

Thus the short-run average total cost, *SRAC*, equals and is tangent to *LRAC* at Q_0. But, since some inputs are fixed in the short run, if the firm wants to vary its output in the short run, it cannot produce this new output at the lowest possible cost. At any output other than Q_0, the short-run input combination is less efficient—would result in a higher total, and hence average, cost—than the combination that would be chosen if all inputs were variable.

Suppose, for example, that the firm wants to increase its output from Q_0 to Q_1. If all inputs were variable, it could produce this output at an average cost of AC_L. But if plant and some other inputs are fixed, *SRAC* gives the average cost of producing Q_1. This average cost is AC_S, which is clearly higher than AC_L because total cost is greater in the short run than in the long run. And, because total cost is greater in the short run than in the long run, at any output other than Q_0, *SRAC* will be higher than *LRAC*. Only at Q_0 are the two average costs the same.

Figure 10.10 shows the typical relation between short- and long-run average and marginal cost curves. In this figure, *LRAC* and *LRMC* are the long-run average and marginal cost curves. Three short-run situations are indicated by the three sets of curves: $SRAC_1$, MC_1; $SRAC_2$, MC_2; and $SRAC_3$, MC_3.

Let's look at $SRAC_1$ and MC_1. These are the short-run curves for the plant size designed to produce output Q_S optimally. The long-run and short-run average cost curves are tangent at this output. Since marginal cost,

Figure 10.9   **Long-Run and Short-Run Average Cost Curves**

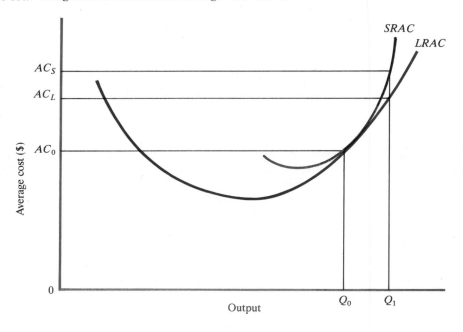

Figure 10.10   **Long-Run and Short-Run Average and Marginal Costs**

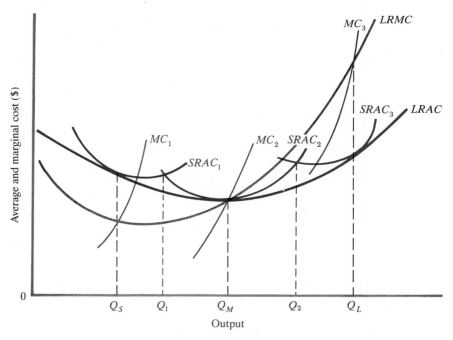

$\Delta C/\Delta Q$, is given by the slope of the total cost curve, long-run marginal cost equals short-run marginal cost at the output given by the point of tangency, Q_S. Finally, short-run marginal cost crosses short-run average cost at the latter's minimum point. Note that because Q_S is on the decreasing portion of *LRAC*, $SRAC_1$ must be decreasing also at the point of tangency.

$SRAC_3$ and MC_3 show another short-run situation—a different plant size. Here tangency occurs at Q_L on the increasing part of *LRAC*. Thus $SRAC_3$ is increasing at this point also. Again the two marginal curves are equal at Q_L, and MC_3 crosses $SRAC_3$ at the minimum point on the latter.

Finally, $SRAC_2$ is the short-run average cost curve corresponding to the output level—plant size—at which long-run average cost is at its minimum. At output level Q_M the two average cost curves are tangent. The two marginal cost curves, MC_2 and *LRMC*, are also equal at this output. And, since both average cost curves attain their minimum at Q_M, the two marginal cost curves must intersect the two average cost curves. Thus all four curves are equal at output Q_M. That is, at Q_M, $LRAC = SRAC_2 = MC_2 = LRMC$.

If the firm is limited to producing only with one of the three short-run cost structures shown in Figure 10.10, it would choose the cost structure— plant size—given by $SRAC_1$ to produce outputs from zero to Q_1, because the average cost, and hence the total cost, of producing each output over this range is lower under this cost specification. If it wishes to produce any output between Q_1 and Q_2, it would choose the plant size given by $SRAC_2$. This average cost curve lies below either of the other two for any output over this range. It would choose the cost structure shown by $SRAC_3$ for any level of output greater than Q_2.

But typically the firm is not limited to three sizes—large, medium, or small. In the long run it can build the plant whose size leads to lowest average cost. The long-run average cost curve is a planning device, because this curve shows the least cost of producing each possible output. Managers therefore are normally faced with a choice among a wide variety of plant sizes.

The long-run planning curve, *LRAC*, is a locus of points representing the lowest possible unit cost of producing the corresponding output. The manager determines the desired size of plant by reference to this curve, selecting the short-run plant that yields the lowest unit cost of producing the volume of output desired.

Relations. (1) LRMC intersects LRAC when the latter is at its minimum point. There exists some short-run plant size for which the minimum SRAC coincides with minimum LRAC. (2) At each output where a particular SRAC is tangent to LRAC, the relevant SRMC equals LRMC. At outputs below (above) the tangency output, the relevant SRMC is less (greater) than LRMC. (3) For all SRAC curves, the point of tangency with LRAC is at an output less (greater) than the output of minimum SRAC if the tangency is at an output less (greater) than that associated with minimum LRAC.

THE WALL STREET JOURNAL

APPLICATION

Oil Drillers Cut Costs

One fifth of the U.S. oil production comes from a tundra in Alaska, 250 miles inside the Arctic Circle. The nation's largest field, Prudhoe Bay, and second largest, Kuparuk River, are located in this tundra. But in 1986, the oil companies drilling there had fallen upon hard times. The price of oil had dropped from above $30 a barrel to below $15. And it costs so much to get the Alaskan crude to market that its price at the well had fallen to barely $4 a barrel, less than a third the world price.

The Wall Street Journal described how one oil company, Atlantic Richfield (Arco), which operated the Kuparuk River field, was coping with the situation.* "Alaska's oil producers are facing on a vast scale a problem vexing companies all across the country: how to extract oil as efficiently and cheaply as possible from existing fields. By cutting production costs, U.S. companies can better compete with foreign petroleum. . . . To . . . keep in production fields that might otherwise be abandoned, companies now are scrutinizing production expenses, which loom large in their costs."

One expert in oil economics said, "It's surprising how costs that everyone says are absolutely fixed can come down." Arco's costs of producing a barrel of oil from Kuparuk had been cut 40 percent from a year earlier.

The *Journal* noted that the cost reduction at Kuparuk affected every aspect of the field's operation, from the kitchen of its luxurious dormitory to the giant compressor in its processing facilities. The president of Arco's Alaska unit said, "You realize that there are some things you can do without, and you learn to live without."

What did they learn to live without? Janitorial staff was reduced. Many contract electricians, welders, and specialists in instrumentation were replaced by Arco's own employees. Unskilled laborers were earning $8 an hour, down from $24 an hour the year before. Arco decreased the number of employees at a new enhanced recovery facility from a projected 107 workers to 59. Well operators were inspecting 48 wells per shift, up from 32 previously. The company made significant decreases in its preventive maintenance, betting that machinery would continue to work without it. Even repairs were sometimes delayed.

Continued on page 299

*Frederick Rose, "Weakness in Oil Prices Is Forcing Economies in Alaskan Oil Field," *The Wall Street Journal,* October 21, 1986. Adapted by permission of *The Wall Street Journal.* © Dow Jones & Company, Inc., 1986. All rights reserved.

APPLICATION

Continued from page 298

Clearly, the changes troubled many workers. Some kitchens were closed. Housekeepers scrubbed dormitories every other day rather than every day. Lobster and crab were eliminated from the menu; hot lunches were replaced by sandwiches. But as the *WSJ* noted, "employees seem to have accepted the changes, partly because they are happy to still have jobs." An oil field foreman stated, "everybody reads the paper, and we know why the push is there."

Does all of this mean that Arco and other oil firms were not trying to minimize their costs of production before the sharp decline in oil prices, but then were? Not necessarily. Certainly the oil producers did not have the incentive to search for those significant cost reductions when oil prices were high and business was booming. The slump induced them to search for cost-reducing changes. But there were two other aspects of the situation.

Many of the cost-reducing changes, such as reduced maintenance and repair, were strictly temporary or short-run measures. The firms could not continue to neglect maintenance indefinitely. And the reductions in workers' wage rates and the deterioration in working conditions would not have been possible during the boom in the oil industry. As we noted, jobs in the oil fields were difficult to find during the oil slump. But when business was booming and oil workers were in great demand, it was necessary to pay high wages and provide luxurious living facilities to attract workers to such a remote location. In 1986, when so many oil workers were looking for a job, these were not necessary.

So the point is this: Just as a change in relative input prices induces firms to search for ways to change the technology, a deterioration of business conditions induces them to find ways to cut costs. It would not necessarily have been economical to use resources to search out cost-reducing measures when business was good; these resources were better used in exploration for new deposits and development of these deposits. And, as we noted, many of the cost-reducing changes were strictly short run and could not have been carried out under other, more favorable, business conditions. Thus it is reasonable to continue to assume that firms attempt to achieve the least cost method of production, or at least something close to it. And these costs frequently depend upon business conditions.

10.5 SUMMARY

The physical conditions of production and input prices jointly determine the cost of production. If the set of technological possibilities changes, the cost curves change. Or if the prices of some factors of production change, the firm's cost curves change. Therefore, it should be emphasized that cost curves are generally drawn under the assumptions of constant factor prices and a constant technology.

We have distinguished between cost in the short run and in the long run. Except for one output level, cost is always higher in the short run than in the long run for every short-run situation.

While the cost of production is important to business firms and to the economy as a whole, it is only half the story. Cost gives one aspect of economic activity; it is the obligation to pay out funds. The other aspect is revenue or demand. To the individual manager, revenue constitutes the flow of funds from which the obligation may be met.

Thus both demand and cost must be taken into consideration. After considering empirical estimation of production and cost in the next chapter, we will combine our theories of demand and cost to analyze firms' supply decisions.

TECHNICAL PROBLEMS

1. The first two columns in the table below give a firm's short-run production function when the only variable input is labor, and capital, the fixed input, is held constant at 5 units. The price of capital is $2,000 per unit and the price of labor is $500 per unit.

Units of Labor	Units of Output	Average Product	Marginal Product	Cost Fixed	Cost Variable	Cost Total	Average Cost Fixed	Average Cost Variable	Average Cost Total	Marginal Cost
0	0									
20	4,000									
40	10,000									
60	15,000									
80	19,400									
100	23,000									

a. Complete the table.

b. Graph the average variable cost, average total cost, and marginal cost curves.

c. What is the relation between average variable cost and marginal cost? Between average total cost and marginal cost?

d. What is the relation between average product and average variable cost? Between marginal product and marginal cost?

2. Fill in the blanks in the following table.

Output	Total Cost	Total Fixed Cost	Total Variable Cost	Average Fixed Cost	Average Variable Cost	Average Total Cost	Marginal Cost
100	260		60				
200							.30
300					.50		
400						1.05	
500			360				
600							3.00
700					1.60		
800	2,040						

3. Assume that labor—the only variable input of a firm—has the average and marginal product curves shown in the following figure. Labor's wage is $2 per unit.

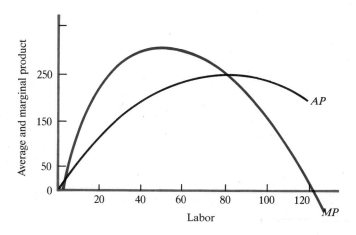

a. When the firm attains minimum average variable cost, how many units of labor is it using?
b. What level of output is associated with minimum average variable cost?
c. What is the average variable cost of producing this output?
d. Suppose the firm is using 100 units of labor. What is marginal cost? What is average variable cost?

4. Suppose that a firm is currently employing 20 workers, the only variable input, at a wage rate of $60. The average product of labor is 30, the last worker added 12 units to total output, and total fixed cost is $3,600.

      a. What is marginal cost?
      b. What is average variable cost?
      c. How much output is being produced?
      d. What is average total cost?
      e. Is average variable cost increasing, constant or decreasing? What about average total cost?

5. The graph below shows five points on a firm's expansion path when the price of labor is $25 per unit and the price of capital is $100 per unit.

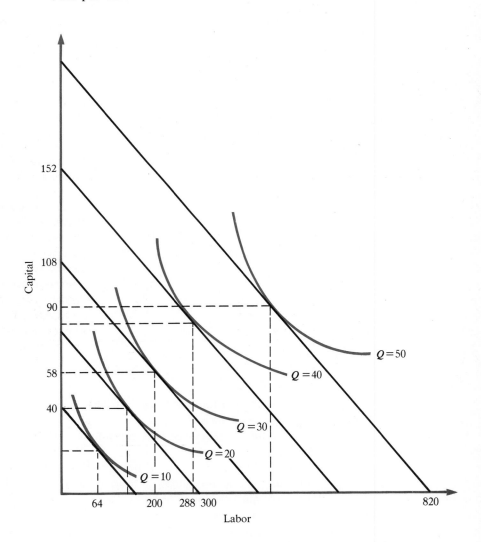

    a. Prepare a table showing long-run total cost, long-run average cost, and long-run marginal cost.

    b. Graph these cost functions.

    c. Over what range of output do economies of scale exist? Over what range are there diseconomies of scale?

6. Until recently you worked as an accountant, earning $30,000 annually. Then you inherited a piece of commercial real estate bringing in $12,000 in rent annually. You decided to leave your job and operate a video rental store in the office space you inherited. At the end of the first year, your books showed total revenues of $60,000 and total costs of $30,000 for video purchases, utilities, taxes, and supplies. What is your economic profit for the year?

7. Explain why long-run average cost first falls, then rises. Why does short-run average variable cost first fall, then rise?

8. Explain why short-run marginal cost increases at a greater rate than long-run marginal cost beyond the point at which they are equal.

9. Explain why short-run average cost can never be less than long-run average cost.

10. Suppose average variable cost is constant over a range of output. What is marginal cost over this range? What is happening to average total cost over this range?

11. Economists frequently say that the firm plans in the long run and operates in the short run. Explain.

ANALYTICAL PROBLEMS

1. Explain why it would cost Boris Becker or Martina Navratilova more to leave the professional tennis tour and open a tennis shop than it would for the coach of a university tennis team.

2. You are the adviser to the president of a university. A wealthy alumnus buys, then gives a plot of land to the university to use as an athletic field. The president says that, as far as the land is concerned, it does not cost the university anything to use the land as an athletic field. What do you say?

3. We frequently hear several terms used by businesspersons. What do they mean in economic terminology?

    a. Spreading the overhead.

    b. A break-even level of production.

    c. The efficiency of mass production.

4. How much does it cost you to keep money in a checking rather than a savings account? If there is this cost, why do people keep money in a checking account? What would cause people to keep less in a savings account and more in checking?

5. Suppose that you manage a business and have to make business trips of two to four days at least once a month. What factors determine the total cost of a trip? What factors would you consider when deciding whether your salespeople should travel by automobile or airplane? Are these necessarily the same factors that determine the cost of your own travel?

6. Recently a large number of steel manufacturers have closed down or disposed of a large number of steel mills. What factors must they have considered in making this decision?

7. This question anticipates material in the next chapter, but it should be worthwhile to think about it now.
    a. Why would managers want to have estimates of costs?
    b. What costs would be the most important?
    c. How would you go about having costs estimated?
    d. What might be some of the problems you would encounter?

8. Fixed costs are very real in the sense that the firm must pay them. Then why do we say that managers should totally ignore fixed cost when making decisions?

9. In line with Problem 8, suppose you have gone to school two years. In two more years you can obtain your degree, but someone offers you a well-paying job now. What factors would you consider when making the choice whether or not to leave school and take the job? How would the fact that you have already put in two years toward your degree affect your decision?

10. It is clear that, at least theoretically, the average product of labor and cost are inversely related. And in our application we saw that this relation was true for General Motors. Explain why this relation would hold in general.

11. In the application concerning People Express and the managerial diseconomies it encountered, we mentioned another firm that overcame that problem by breaking up into small units. What types of firms would be most likely to take such an approach? What types would not?

12. In the application "Oil Drillers Cut Costs," the *WSJ* pointed out that Alaskan drillers, facing hard times with low oil prices, were trimming costs in ways they never did before. Why wouldn't these firms have done this before in order to make even more profits when times were good? Could they, in fact, have undertaken all the measures they did when oil prices were high?

APPENDIX

Define short-run total cost as

$$TC = C(Q) + F,$$

where $C(Q)$ is variable cost and F is fixed cost. Thus short-run marginal cost is

$$MC = \frac{dTC}{dQ} = \frac{dC(Q)}{dQ},$$

and short-run average total cost is

$$ATC = \frac{TC}{Q} = \frac{C(Q)}{Q} + \frac{F}{Q}.$$

1. Minimum average total cost is attained at the output at which the increase in AVC just offsets the decrease in AFC. ATC reaches its minimum when

$$\frac{dATC}{dQ} = \frac{dAVC}{dQ} + \frac{dAFC}{dQ} = 0.$$

Since

$$\frac{dAFC}{dQ} = \frac{-F}{Q^2},$$

this term must be negative. Thus when $d(ATC)/dQ = 0$, $d(AVC)/dQ$ must be positive (AVC is increasing) and equal in absolute value to $d(AFC)/dQ$.

2. When AVC is increasing (decreasing), MC is above (below) AVC. $MC = AVC$ at minimum AVC. The same relation holds for ATC.

    Average cost (either total or variable) reaches its minimum when

$$\frac{dAC}{dQ} = \frac{dTC}{dQ} Q - \frac{TC}{Q^2} = 0.$$

Rewriting this condition as

$$\frac{dAC}{dQ} = \frac{1}{Q} \left(\frac{dTC}{dQ} - \frac{TC}{Q}\right) = 0,$$

it follows that, when average cost is at a minimum, $MC = AC$. Also, when $d(AC)/dQ > 0$, average cost is increasing and $MC > AC$. When $d(AC)/dQ < 0$, average cost is decreasing and $MC < AC$. These relations hold for both ATC and AVC.

11

EMPIRICAL PRODUCTION AND COST FUNCTIONS

I n Chapters 9 and 10, we provided the theoretical foundations of production and cost. In making real-world managerial decisions—such as deciding how much to produce—it will be necessary to obtain estimates of these functions, particularly estimates of the cost function. In this chapter, we present techniques that can be used to obtain these estimates.

Corresponding to the order in which the theoretical relations were discussed, we begin by looking at the empirical production functions. We concentrate on estimating a production function using regression analysis. The need to have a specification which conforms to the properties of a production function, as described in Chapter 9, leads us to the Cobb-Douglas production function, the mathematical properties of which are described in Appendix A to this chapter. In our discussion, we concentrate on estimating the production function and on determining whether it exhibits increasing or decreasing returns to scale. However, our empirical production function can also be used to investigate the efficiency of input usage as described in Chapter 9, a topic that is more complex than the other material in this chapter and is therefore relegated to Appendix B.

We then turn to estimation of a cost function. While we do describe an engineering cost function, we again concentrate on estimates obtained via regression analysis. We begin our discussion of empirical cost functions by looking at some general issues relating to the estimation of short-run versus long-run cost functions and some potential data problems. We then show how to estimate the short-run cost functions described in Chapter 10: average variable cost *(AVC)*, marginal cost *(MC)*, and total variable cost *(TVC)*. In our discussion of estimates of a long-run cost function, we will concentrate on determining whether there are economies or diseconomies of scale.

11.1 ESTIMATION OF PRODUCTION FUNCTIONS

To obtain estimates of production functions, we use the techniques of regression—described in Chapter 4—to estimate the relation between output and the levels of input usage. We continue to consider the case of two inputs—capital and labor. The technique can, however, be used to consider several inputs.

Consider the general production function we employed in Chapter 9,

$$Q = f(K,L).$$

In order to estimate this function, it is first necessary to express the production relation in *explicit* functional form. Given our discussion of regression techniques, the form that might first come to mind is a simple linear form. For example, we could specify output as

$$Q = \alpha K + \beta L.$$

There are, however, three major problems with this linear functional form.

First, in this form, it is not necessary to use positive amounts of both inputs in order to produce output. For instance, let K equal zero. Output would then be equal to βL, which is positive if L is positive. Therefore, production could take place without using any capital. (The same is true for labor.)

Second, with this formulation, the isoquants are straight lines. While they still slope downward, they are not concave from above. Hence, we do not have a diminishing marginal rate of technical substitution *(MRTS)*.

Third, given the linear isoquants, the marginal products are constant. Consider, for example, the marginal product of labor that would exist in this linear specification,

$$MP_L = \Delta Q/\Delta L = \beta.$$

Holding capital usage constant, the marginal product of labor is constant. Hence, the law of diminishing marginal product is violated.

These three problems indicate that the linear form does not conform to the necessary theoretical characteristics of a production function. Therefore, these problems effectively eliminate the simple linear specification as an appropriate form to use for estimating a production function.

Given the problems with the linear specification, it is necessary to choose a more complex functional form; that is, a nonlinear specification. As we described in Chapter 4, a tractable nonlinear form is a log-linear specification. Let's use this specification and define our production function to be

$$Q = AK^\alpha L^\beta.$$

This form of an empirical production relation was developed in the 1920s by Charles W. Cobb and Paul H. Douglas and is now commonly referred to as the *Cobb-Douglas production function.* The mathematical properties of this function are summarized in Appendix A to this chapter.

Note first that, in this functional form, both inputs are required in order to produce output. If either capital or labor usage equals zero, output equals zero. That is, $f(K,0) = f(0,L) = 0$. Furthermore, this form exhibits the required concave isoquants; so, the *MRTS* will diminish as required by the theory of production.

Also, with a Cobb-Douglas production function, the marginal products of capital and labor are:

$$MP_K = \alpha(Q/K) \text{ and } MP_L = \beta(Q/L).$$

These marginal products are not constant, but vary with the level of input usage. Recall from Chapter 9 that the marginal products must be positive. In the context of this production function, that requirement implies that α and β be positive. Further, the law of diminishing marginal product requires, in this specification, that α and β be less than one. Hence, in order that the properties of the Cobb-Douglas specification conform to the properties of the production relation discussed in Chapter 9, it is required that

$$0 < \alpha < 1 \text{ and } 0 < \beta < 1.$$

If these requirements are satisfied, we can say that the Cobb-Douglas specification conforms to the theoretical properties described in Chapter 9.

In a Cobb-Douglas production function, the coefficients α and β measure, respectively, the output elasticities of capital and labor,

$$E_K = \alpha \text{ and } E_L = \beta.$$

Using these coefficients, we can evaluate the impact of changes in capital or labor usage on output.

In Chapter 9 we introduced the concept of returns to scale. To summarize that discussion, we will denote the percentage increase in input usage as λ and the corresponding percentage increase in output as z. Then, we can determine returns to scale by the following:

$$\text{If} \begin{Bmatrix} z > \lambda \\ z = \lambda \\ z < \lambda \end{Bmatrix} \text{the production function exhibits} \begin{Bmatrix} \text{increasing} \\ \text{constant} \\ \text{decreasing} \end{Bmatrix} \text{returns to scale.}$$

In a more quantitative manner, we can consider the question of returns to scale by looking at a measure called *the function coefficient.* Basically, this measure is an elasticity reflecting the percentage change in output in response to a given percentage change in the level of usage of all inputs. We define the function coefficient, $\mathcal{E}$, as

$$\mathscr{E} = \frac{\text{Percentage change in output}}{\text{Percentage change in input usage}}.$$

From the preceding, it follows that, if there exist constant returns to scale, $\mathscr{E} = 1$. If the production function exhibits increasing returns to scale, $\mathscr{E} > 1$. And, if there exist decreasing returns to scale, $\mathscr{E} < 1$. The function coefficient can be decomposed further. Since the increase in output is attributable to increases in the levels of usage of the individual inputs, we can write it in terms of the inputs themselves. For example, in our two-input case,

$$\mathscr{E} = \frac{\text{Percentage change in output}}{\text{Percentage change in } K} + \frac{\text{Percentage change in output}}{\text{Percentage change in } L}.$$

Hence, the function coefficient is equal to

$$\mathscr{E} = E_K + E_L.$$

That is, the function coefficient is equal to the sum of the output elasticities.

Therefore, in the case of our two-input, Cobb-Douglas production function, the function coefficient is simply

$$\mathscr{E} = \alpha + \beta.$$

If $\alpha + \beta$ is greater than one, we know that the production function exhibits increasing returns to scale. Conversely, if $\alpha + \beta$ is less than one, there exist decreasing returns to scale.

Testing for Increasing or Decreasing Returns to Scale

In determining whether a production function exhibits increasing or decreasing returns to scale, we must, as always, consider the question of statistical significance. It is not sufficient that the sum of the estimates of α and β is greater (less) than one. Rather, we must determine whether this sum is *significantly* greater (less) than one. If $\alpha + \beta$ is not significantly greater (less) than one, we cannot reject the existence of constant returns to scale. As was the case with the tests of significance of individual coefficients described in Chapter 4, this will require that we perform a t-test.

When testing the significance of an individual estimated coefficient as described in Chapter 4, we determined whether the estimate is significantly different from *zero*. For example, looking at $\hat{\alpha}$, we calculated a t-statistic that we wrote as

$$t_{\hat{\alpha}} = \frac{\hat{\alpha}}{S_{\hat{\alpha}}},$$

where $S_{\hat{\alpha}}$ is the standard error of $\hat{\alpha}$. Since we were testing "different from zero," the more correct way of writing this t-value is

$$t_{\hat{\alpha}} = \frac{\hat{\alpha} - 0}{S_{\hat{\alpha}}}.$$

The zero is the value we are testing "different from." Then, we compare (the absolute value of) this calculated t-value with the critical value of t from the t-table at the end of the book.

However, in this case, we must determine whether the sum, $\alpha + \beta$, is significantly different from *one*. In this case, our t-statistic becomes

$$t_{\hat{\alpha}+\hat{\beta}} = \frac{(\hat{\alpha} + \hat{\beta}) - 1}{S_{\hat{\alpha}+\hat{\beta}}},$$

where the value 1 indicates what we are testing "different from" and $S_{\hat{\alpha}+\hat{\beta}}$ is the estimated standard error of the sum of the estimated coefficients (parameters). After calculating this statistic, we compare it with a critical t-value in precisely the manner described in Chapter 4. Again note that, since this calculated t-statistic can be negative (if $\hat{\alpha} + \hat{\beta} < 0$), we compare the *absolute value* of the calculated t with the critical t obtained from the table.

The only problem involved in performing this test is that of obtaining the estimated standard error of $\hat{\alpha} + \hat{\beta}$. The available regression packages will provide the user with variances and covariances of the regression coefficients, $\hat{\alpha}$ and $\hat{\beta}$, in a variance-covariance matrix.* Let us denote the variances of $\hat{\alpha}$ and $\hat{\beta}$ as Var($\hat{\alpha}$) and Var($\hat{\beta}$) and the covariance between $\hat{\alpha}$ and $\hat{\beta}$ as Cov($\hat{\alpha},\hat{\beta}$). As you may remember from your statistics course, Var($\hat{\alpha} + \hat{\beta}$) = Var ($\hat{\alpha}$) + Var ($\hat{\beta}$) + 2 Cov ($\hat{\alpha},\hat{\beta}$); so, the estimated standard error of $\hat{\alpha} + \hat{\beta}$ is

$$S_{\hat{\alpha}+\hat{\beta}} = \sqrt{\text{Var}(\hat{\alpha}) + \text{Var}(\hat{\beta}) + 2\text{Cov}(\hat{\alpha},\hat{\beta})}.$$

---

*As with any other variance measure, the variance of the regression coefficient provides a measure of the dispersion of the variable about its mean. The covariance of the regression coefficients provides information about the joint distribution—that is, the relation between the two regression coefficients.

Using a Cobb-Douglas production function, we can estimate the production function; and, as demonstrated above, we can obtain estimates of

Marginal products of the inputs,
Output elasticities, and
Returns to scale.

As we noted in Chapter 4, in order to estimate this Cobb-Douglas production function, it is necessary to convert it into logarithms. Thus, the equation that will actually be estimated is

$$\log Q = \log A + \alpha \log K + \beta \log L.$$

To see how such an estimation can be used, let us now turn to an example.

APPLICATION

Production in U.S. Electric Utility Firms

To illustrate the estimation of production functions, let's look at a production function for electric utility firms in the United States. We use this example for two reasons. First, the methodology used is illustrative of the technique described above.

Second, the results have interesting implications. The fact that governments allow electric utilities to operate as monopolies is predicated on the existence of increasing returns to scale. If the firms exhibit substantial increasing returns to scale, they are referred to as "natural monopolies" (a subject to which we will return in a later chapter). Therefore, an important question relating to electric utilities is whether or not increasing returns to scale actually exist. The existence of increasing returns to scale in this industry has been questioned. While we will not replicate the more complicated studies, we can use our Cobb-Douglas production function to illustrate the manner in which you may test for increasing returns to scale.

To simplify the problem, let's continue to consider only two inputs—capital and labor. We will employ a Cobb-Douglas specification; so our production function will be

$$Q = AK^{\alpha}L^{\beta}.$$

In order to estimate this production function we must have data for output, capital input, and labor input. A sample of 20 privately owned electric utility firms was selected. The data collected for each firm were:

Output: Total generation and transmission of electric power, expressed in million kilowatt-hours.

Capital: Stock of physical capital held by the firm, expressed in million dollars.

Labor: Total number of employees, expressed in thousand workers.

The data set is shown below.

Firm	Q	K	L
1	4.612	321.502	1.019
2	8.297	544.031	2.118
3	1.820	156.803	0.448
4	5.849	250.441	1.265
5	3.145	247.983	0.603
6	1.381	82.867	0.665
7	5.422	366.062	0.962
8	7.115	485.406	1.435
9	3.052	99.115	0.829
10	4.394	292.016	1.501
11	0.248	21.002	0.145
12	9.699	556.138	2.391
13	14.271	667.397	2.697
14	17.743	998.106	3.625
15	14.956	598.809	3.085
16	3.108	118.349	0.714
17	9.416	423.213	1.733
18	6.857	468.897	1.406
19	9.745	514.037	2.442
20	4.442	236.043	1.497

In order to estimate our production function, we first convert it to logarithms,

$$\log Q = \log A + \alpha \log K + \beta \log L.$$

We then used a regression program to estimate this equation, using the preceding data. The computer output we obtained is reproduced on page 313. Note that in this regression "run" we also requested the variances and covariances for the regression coefficients. On our printout, these values appear in the matrix following the estimates of the coefficients.

The values for the F-ratio and R^2 are both quite acceptable. (As you can confirm, the critical value for F at a 95 percent confidence level is 3.59; so the equation is significant.) From the printout, we know that the estimated values for the parameters are

$$\log \hat{A} = -1.5416$$
$$\hat{\alpha} = 0.53296$$
$$\hat{\beta} = 0.65384.$$

```
DEPENDENT VARIABLE: LOG Q    F-RATIO: 241.261

OBSERVATIONS: 20                R-SQUARE: 0.9660

                   PARAMETER        STANDARD
       VARIABLE    ESTIMATE         ERROR

       INTERCEPT   -1.5416          0.6560
       LOG K       0.53296          0.12071
       LOG L       0.65384          0.14248

            VARIANCE-COVARIANCE MATRIX FOR
                ESTIMATED COEFFICIENTS

                INTERCEPT        LOG K        LOG L

    INTERCEPT    0.43029       -0.07900      0.08476
    LOG K       -0.07900        0.01457     -0.01575
    LOG L        0.08476       -0.01575      0.02030
```

Taking the antilog of log $\hat{A}$ (as described in Chapter 4), the estimated value of A is 0.214; so, the estimated Cobb-Douglas production function could be written as

$$\hat{Q} = (0.214) \, K^{0.53296} \, L^{0.65384}.$$

And, since $\hat{\alpha}$ and $\hat{\beta}$ both lie between zero and one, the estimated function will have properties that conform to those described in Chapter 9.

Testing for Positive and Decreasing Marginal Products

The estimates themselves suggest that these properties are satisfied. That is,

$$0 < 0.53296 < 1 \quad \text{and} \quad 0 < 0.65384 < 1.$$

But, to determine if these conditions are really satisfied, we must perform t-tests for these estimated coefficients. With 20 observations and 3 estimated coefficients we have $20 - 3 = 17$ degrees of freedom. Thus, from the t-table at the end of this book, the critical value of t for a 95 percent confidence level is 2.110.

We first need to see if the marginal products are significantly positive—if $\hat{\alpha}$ and $\hat{\beta}$ are significantly greater than zero. This requires that we calculate the t-values:

$$t_{\hat{\alpha}} = \frac{\hat{\alpha}}{S_{\hat{\alpha}}} = \frac{0.53296}{0.12071} = 4.415$$

$$t_{\hat{\beta}} = \frac{\hat{\beta}}{S_{\hat{\beta}}} = \frac{0.65384}{0.14248} = 4.589$$

Since both of these exceed the critical value, we can say that $\hat{\alpha}$ and $\hat{\beta}$ are both significantly greater than zero.

To test for decreasing marginal products, we must determine if $\hat{\alpha}$ and $\hat{\beta}$ are significantly less than one.* Using the method described in our discussion of the estimation of returns to scale, this test requires that we calculate

$$t_{\hat{\alpha}} = \frac{\hat{\alpha} - 1}{S_{\hat{\alpha}}} = \frac{0.53296 - 1}{0.12071} = -3.869$$

$$t_{\hat{\beta}} = \frac{\hat{\beta} - 1}{S_{\hat{\beta}}} = \frac{0.65384 - 1}{0.14248} = -2.430.$$

Since the *absolute values* of both of these calculated t-statistics exceed the critical t, we can say that both $\hat{\alpha}$ and $\hat{\beta}$ are significantly less than one. Thus, our estimated function does indeed satisfy the properties of a production function.

---

*We should note that, throughout this text, we employ what are referred to as "two-tailed" t-tests. In this case, a single-tail test would be more appropriate, but such a distinction could confuse our primary objective. The interested reader should see the references listed at the end of Chapter 4.

Remember that the coefficients $\hat{\alpha}$ and $\hat{\beta}$ are the estimates of the output elasticities of capital and labor. Thus, our estimates indicate that a 10 percent increase in capital usage will lead to a 5.3 percent increase in output. That is,

$$E_K = \frac{\text{Percentage change in output}}{\text{Percentage change in capital usage}}.$$

So,

Percentage change
in output = (Percentage change in capital usage) $\times$ (E_K)
$= 10 \times 0.53296$
$= 5.3296$ percent.

Likewise, our estimates indicate that a 10 percent increase in labor usage would result in a 6.5 percent increase in output.

We now turn to the question of the existence of increasing returns to scale. As we showed earlier, the function coefficient is equal to the sum of the output elasticities

$$\mathcal{E} = E_K + E_L$$
$$= \alpha + \beta.$$

If $\mathcal{E}$ is greater than one, we would say that there exist increasing returns to scale. In our case, the estimate of the function coefficient is

$$\hat{\mathcal{E}} = \hat{\alpha} + \hat{\beta}$$
$$= 0.53296 + 0.65384$$
$$= 1.1868,$$

which *suggests* that increasing returns to scale do exist.

However, we must determine whether this estimate is *significantly* greater than one. As we showed earlier, this requires an additional *t*-test, where the calculated t is

$$t_{\hat{\alpha}+\hat{\beta}} = \frac{(\hat{\alpha} + \hat{\beta}) - 1}{S_{\hat{\alpha}+\hat{\beta}}}.$$

The standard error of $\hat{\alpha} + \hat{\beta}$ is

$$S_{\hat{\alpha}+\hat{\beta}} = \sqrt{\text{Var}(\hat{\alpha}) + \text{Var}(\hat{\beta}) + 2\text{Cov}(\hat{\alpha},\hat{\beta})}.$$

From the variance-covariance matrix provided, Var $(\hat{\alpha}) = 0.01457$ as it has to be.* Likewise, Var$(\hat{\beta}) = 0.02030$. And, Cov$(\hat{\alpha},\hat{\beta}) = -0.01575$. Hence

$$S_{\hat{\alpha}+\hat{\beta}} = \sqrt{0.01457 + 0.02030 + 2(-0.01575)}$$
$$= \sqrt{0.00337}$$
$$= 0.05805.$$

It follows that the calculated *t*-statistic will be

$$t_{\hat{\alpha}+\hat{\beta}} = \frac{1.1868 - 1}{0.05805} = 3.2179.$$

Since this value exceeds the critical *t*-value (2.110), we can say that $\hat{\alpha} + \hat{\beta}$ is significantly greater than one. Thus, for this sample, the data indicate that increasing returns to scale do exist.

---

*Since Var$(\hat{\alpha}) = (S_{\hat{a}})^2$, it follows that Var$(\hat{\alpha})$ must be $(0.12071)^2$, which is 0.01457.

11.2 REGRESSION ANALYSES OF COST— SOME GENERAL CONSIDERATIONS

If we can assume that firms have been operating efficiently, that is, minimizing cost, we can use the techniques of regression analysis to obtain an estimate of the cost function. As we demonstrated in Chapter 10, cost is defined to be a function of output. That is,

$$C = f(Q).$$

Or, more generally, we can say that total cost is determined by the level of output and a set of additional characteristics, X, including such things as the prices of the inputs:

$$C = f(Q;X).$$

It follows then that our basic task is to estimate the relation between cost and the level of output.

Short-Run versus Long-Run Estimation

Before we describe the estimation procedures, we should note that there exist several methodological differences between short-run and long-run cost estimation, and the differences are substantial. Indeed, even the objectives of the two types of estimations are quite different.

In the case of estimates of short-run cost functions, the resulting estimates would be used in the firm's pricing decision. More specifically, such estimates would be used to determine the marginal cost associated with producing additional units of output.

Conversely, since we defined the long run to be the firm's planning horizon, it follows that estimates of the long-run cost function would be used in the firm's investment decisions. More specifically, a primary objective of long-run cost estimation is to determine the extent of economies and diseconomies of scale, in order that the manager can select the optimal plant size.

With this basic difference in the objectives of short- and long-run estimation in mind, let us turn now to some more specific differences. We begin with a consideration of short-run cost estimation.

To estimate a short-run cost function, the data must be such that the usage level of one (or more) of the inputs is fixed. (In the context of the simple, two-input production function we employed in Chapter 9, this restriction could be interpreted to mean that the firm's capital stock is fixed while labor usage is allowed to vary.) The most widely accepted method for obtaining such a data set is to use time-series data for a specific firm. That is, the analyst could collect cost and output data for a firm over a period sufficiently short that the firm's level of usage of one (or more) of its inputs is fixed. For instance, the analyst might collect monthly observations over a two-year period in which the firm did not change its basic plant (i.e., capital stock). Thus, the analyst could obtain 24 observations on cost and output. With such a time-series data set, there exists a potential data problem. While output is expressed in physical units, cost is expressed in nominal dollars. Hence the nominal cost data would include the effect of inflation. That is, over time, inflation would cause reported costs to rise, even if output remained constant. Such a situation is depicted in Figure 11.1. As you can see in this figure, estimation based upon such a data set would indicate that the cost function has an extremely large positive slope—even if the slope of the true cost function is zero or negative. Hence, it is necessary to eliminate the effects of inflation. As we will demonstrate below, such an elimination can be accomplished by deflating the cost data by an appropriate price index.

In the case of long-run cost estimation, the analyst would want to have a data set in which the usage level of all inputs is variable. While it might be possible to obtain such a data set from time-series observations on an individual firm, the most generally used method is to collect a cross-section data set. That is, observations are collected from several different firms at a given point in time. In this kind of a data set, the objective is to include firms that use different levels of the inputs and produce different levels of output. The primary difficulty encountered in such data sets is that it is possible—particularly if the firms are separated geographically—that the input prices paid by the various firms in the data set are different. For example, consider the following hypothetical situation: Suppose that two firms produce the same level of output using the same amounts of capital and labor. However, the input prices for Firm 1 are twice those facing Firm 2. This situation is depicted graphically in Figure 11.2. As was the situation in the short-run problem, estimation using such a data

Figure 11.1   **Problem of Inflation**

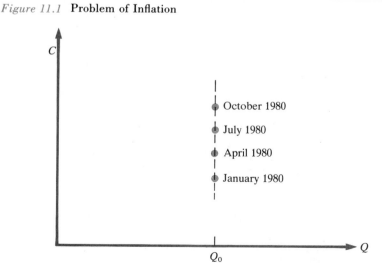

Figure 11.2   Problem of Differing Input Prices

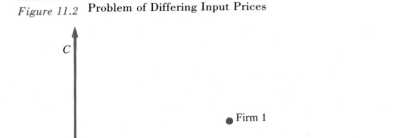

set would indicate that the cost function is rising steeply, even if the true cost function (i.e., abstracting from different input prices) does not exhibit such a relation. Hence, it will be necessary to eliminate the effect of the input price differences.

While it is theoretically possible to use some sort of an index for input price differences (similar to the price index approach used in short-run estimation), the calculation of such an index may not be practical. Instead, the approach normally used in long-run cost estimation is to adjust for different input prices in the regression equation itself. In the context of the two-input production process we have been considering, such an adjustment would imply that the cost function to be estimated is

$$C = f(Q, w, r),$$

where w and r are, respectively, the prices of labor and capital. That is, in order to estimate the long-run cost function (using cross-section data), it may be necessary to include, as independent variables, not only output but also the prices of the inputs.

Data Problems

A potentially troublesome problem can also result from the difference between the accounting definition of cost and the economic definition of cost. As we stressed in Chapter 10, the economist's definition of cost is based on opportunity cost. However, since accounting data are of necessity based on expenditures, opportunity cost may not be reflected in the firm's accounting records. Let's use an example to illustrate this problem. Suppose a firm owns its own machinery. The opportunity cost of this equipment is the income that could be derived if the machinery were leased to another firm. However, this cost would not be reflected in the accounting data.

In a two-input setting, total cost may be defined as

$$C = wL + rK.$$

The wage rate should reflect the opportunity cost of labor to the firm; so, expenditures on labor, wL (including any additional compensation not paid as wages), would reflect opportunity cost. The problem is the calculation of the firm's opportunity cost of capital. We need to calculate the cost of capital, r, in such a way that it reflects the *user cost* of capital. User cost must include not only the acquisition cost of a unit of capital but also (1) the return foregone by using the capital rather than renting it, (2) the depreciation charges resulting from the use of the capital, and (3) any capital gains or losses associated with holding the particular type of capital. Likewise, the measurement of the capital stock, K, must be such that it reflects the stock actually owned by the firm. For example, you might want the capital variable to reflect the fact that a given piece of capital has depreciated physically or embodies less technology than a new piece of capital. While these problems are difficult, they are not insurmountable. The main thing we want you to remember is that such opportunity cost data would be expected to differ greatly from the reported cost figures in accounting data.

An additional data problem relates to the matching of output and cost data. Using accounting data, it is often difficult to relate cost to the corresponding output. For example, it could be the case that a firm enters a constant depreciation charge, while in fact the machinery depreciates more rapidly in earlier periods than in later periods (or vice versa).

11.3 ESTIMATION OF A SHORT-RUN COST FUNCTION

We need first to specify a short-run cost function. As we have already noted, cost is a function of output,

$$C = f(Q).$$

As with our estimation of the production function, it is necessary to convert this general function into an explicit functional form. And, in selecting the functional form to be employed, we want to be sure that our empirical cost function conforms to the properties and relations described in Chapter 10.

To this end, let's look again at the short-run cost function we developed. (Recall that these cost functions embody the characteristics of production theory which we discussed in Chapter 9.) In Figure 11.3, we illustrate again the total variable cost, average variable cost, and marginal cost curves. We want our empirical cost function to reflect the properties shown in these graphs.

Figure 11.3   **Representative Cost Curves**

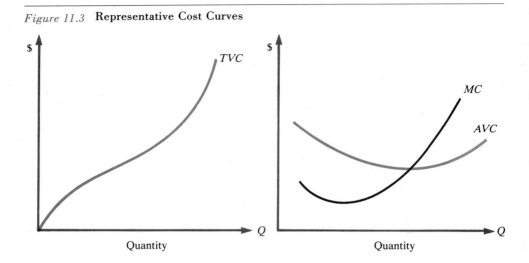

Since the shape of any one of these three curves will uniquely identify the shape of the remaining two, let's begin with the average variable cost curve. We know that this curve should be U-shaped. What does this imply about the functional form of the average variable cost function? Let's first consider the simplest possible form—a linear specification,

$$AVC = a + bQ.$$

Since the intercept of the average variable cost curve on the vertical axis must be positive, it is necessary that $a > 0$. If b is positive, this function is an upward-sloping straight line. Likewise, if b is negative, this function is a downward-sloping straight line; and, if b is zero, it is a horizontal line. Therefore, under no circumstances could this function exhibit the desired U-shape. That is, this simple linear specification would be inappropriate.

Since the simplest form won't work, let's consider a slightly more complex specification,

$$AVC = a + bQ + cQ^2.$$

Again, we know that a must be positive. If b is negative and c is positive, the following relations would hold: At low levels of output, the negative coefficient b could dominate, in the sense that the absolute value of bQ is larger than that of cQ^2 and the average variable cost curve would slope downward. However, as output increases, Q^2 gets much larger than Q and the positive coefficient c would dominate, thus causing the average variable cost curve to begin to slope upward. Hence, if $a > 0$, $b < 0$, and

$c > 0$, the specification proposed above indeed results in a U-shaped average variable cost curve.[1]

Given our specification for average variable cost, what can we say about the corresponding total and marginal cost functions? Specification of total cost is straightforward. Since $AVC = TVC/Q$, it follows that

$$TVC = AVC \cdot Q.$$

Marginal cost is slightly more difficult to derive. However, after some manipulation, it can be shown that[2]

$$MC = a + 2bQ + 3cQ^2.$$

If $a > 0$, $b < 0$, and $c > 0$, the marginal cost curve will also be U-shaped.

Notice that all three of these cost functions employ the same three parameters, a, b, and c. It follows that it is necessary only to estimate any one of the three functions in order to obtain estimates of all three. For example, if we were to estimate the total variable cost function, we would obtain estimates of the parameters a, b, and c. Then, using the preceding specifications, the marginal and average variable cost functions can be generated.

As to the estimation itself, ordinary least squares estimation of the total (or average) variable cost function is usually sufficient. Once the estimates of a, b, and c are obtained, it is necessary to determine whether the parameter estimates are of the hypothesized signs and statistically significant. The tests for significance are again accomplished using t-tests.

Using the estimates of a total or average variable cost function, we can also obtain an estimate of the output at which average cost is a minimum. Remember that when average variable cost is at its minimum, average variable cost and marginal cost are equal. Thus we can define the minimum of average variable cost as that output at which

$$AVC = MC.$$

Using the specifications of average variable cost and marginal cost that we presented above, we can write this condition as

$$a + bQ + cQ^2 = a + 2bQ + 3cQ^2$$

---

[1]The demonstration of this requires the use of calculus: The slope of the average variable cost function is $\partial AVC/\partial Q = b + 2cQ$. Average variable cost is at its minimum when this derivative is equal to zero (i.e., $Q = -b/2c$). However, to guarantee a minimum, the second derivative must be positive. That is, $\partial^2 AVC/\partial Q^2 = 2c > 0$; so, c must be positive. Therefore, if the slope of the average variable cost curve is ever to be negative, it is necessary that b be negative.

[2]As in footnote 1, demonstration of this relation requires the use of calculus:

$$MC = \frac{\partial TVC}{\partial Q} = \frac{\partial(aQ + bQ^2 + cQ^3)}{\partial Q} = a + 2bQ + 3cQ^2.$$

or

$$bQ + 2cQ^2 = 0.$$

Solving for Q, the level of output at which average cost is minimized is

$$Q = -b/2c.$$

A Potential Data Problem

Suppose that the data for average variable cost are clustered
around the minimum point of the average variable cost curve,
as in the following figure.

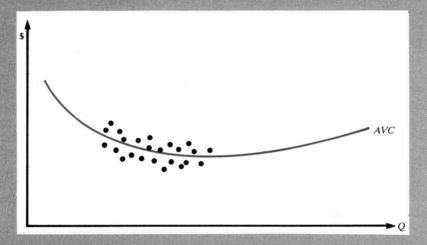

If we estimate the average variable cost function, using these
data points, the result would be that, while $\hat{a}$ would be positive
and $\hat{b}$ would be negative, the coefficient $\hat{c}$ would not be
statistically significant. That is, the t-test would indicate that c
is not statistically different from zero. Does this result mean
that the average cost curve is not U-shaped, since c must be
treated as equal to zero? Not necessarily. The problem is that
since we do not have observations for the larger levels of
output, our estimation simply cannot tell us whether or not
average cost is rising over that range of output.

APPLICATION

A Short-Run Cost Function

Suppose that the date is January 1987 and that the capital stock of our firm had remained unchanged since the fourth quarter of 1984. We could then collect quarterly observations on cost and output over this period and use the resulting data set to estimate a short-run cost function for our firm.

Data on output and average variable cost were collected from this firm over this period. These data are as follows:

Quarter	Output (000 units)	Average Variable Cost
1984IV	30	$112
1985I	10	116
1985II	15	86
1985III	25	86
1985IV	40	145
1986I	20	100
1986II	35	135
1986III	45	178
1986IV	50	202

At this point, you probably recognize the problem we told you about earlier: while output is measured in physical units, average variable cost is measured in nominal (i.e., current) dollars. Hence, the reported cost data are subject to the effects of inflation. That is, over the period considered, reported costs have increased due to the effects of inflation. We wish to eliminate the influence of inflation. The most common method for accomplishing this is to "deflate" the nominal costs. Such a deflation involves the use of a price index. In order to convert nominal cost into a constant dollar cost, we divide the nominal cost by the appropriate price index for that period. For purposes of illustration, we will use the consumer price index (CPI). Following are the values for this index for the period under consideration. These values were obtained from the *Survey of Current Business* (U.S. Department of Commerce).

Quarter	Consumer Price Index (1967 = 1.0)
1984IV	3.121
1985I	3.139
1985II	3.177
1985III	3.197
1985IV	3.224
1986I	3.230
1986II	3.216
1986III	3.237
1986IV	3.260

For example, to obtain the constant dollar average variable cost for the 30,000 units produced in the fourth quarter of 1984, we would divide $112 by 3.121 to obtain $35.89. Doing the same thing for each of the cost figures, we obtain the following data set:

Quarter	Output (000 units)	Deflated Average Variable Cost
1984IV	30	$36
1985I	10	37
1985II	15	27
1985III	25	27
1985IV	40	45
1986I	20	31
1986II	35	42
1986III	45	55
1986IV	50	62

Given these transformed data, we can now proceed to the estimation of the cost function. As we have shown, it is sufficient to estimate any one of the three cost curves. In this example, we have elected to estimate the average variable cost function. Remember that the form of this function is

$$AVC = a + bQ + cQ^2.$$

The computer printout obtained from the estimation of this equation is reproduced on page 325. (Note that, in the printout, $Q2$ stands for the variable Q^2.)

We first must determine whether the signs of the estimated coefficients are as hypothesized. Recall that the theoretical analysis requires $a > 0$, $b < 0$, $c > 0$. Inspection of the regression output indicates that our estimated coefficients do conform to this sign pattern. However, we must also ensure that these coefficients are

```
DEPENDENT VARIABLE: AVC      F-RATIO: 51.404

OBSERVATIONS: 9              R-SQUARE: 0.9449

                PARAMETER              STANDARD
    VARIABLE    ESTIMATE               ERROR

    INTERCEPT    44.35                  6.17
    Q            -1.44                  0.46
    Q2            0.04                  0.008
```

statistically significant. As always, this determination of significance is made using a *t*-test. In this example, since there are nine observations and three estimated parameters, we have 9 − 3 = 6 degrees of freedom; thus, from the T-value table at the end of the book, the critical value of *t* (at a 95 percent confidence level) is 2.447. Calculation of the test statistics for the individual coefficients yields

$$t_{\hat{a}} = 7.19$$
$$t_{\hat{b}} = -3.13$$
$$t_{\hat{c}} = 5.0.$$

Clearly, the absolute values for these calculated *t*-statistics all exceed the critical value of *t*. Hence, all of the coefficients are of the hypothesized sign and are statistically significant. Thus, our estimates will yield a short-run cost function with the shape of those described in Chapter 10.

A primary objective of short-run cost estimation is to obtain an estimate of the marginal cost function. Suppose that the firm desires to produce 27,000 units of output. What is the marginal cost associated with this level of output?*

As we have shown, the marginal cost function associated with the average cost function above is

$$MC = a + 2bQ + 3cQ^2.$$

Using our estimates of *a, b,* and *c,* our estimated marginal cost function is

$$MC = 44.35 + 2(-1.44)Q + 3(0.04)Q^2$$
$$= 44.35 - 2.88Q + 0.12Q^2.$$

---

*Normally, the marginal cost refers to the cost of producing the last unit—the 27,000th unit. However, since our data were expressed in 1,000 units, the marginal cost is interpreted as the additional cost per unit for producing the last 1,000 units—the cost per unit for the 26,001th through 27,000th unit.

And, the marginal cost associated with 27,000 units of output is, therefore,

$$MC = 44.35 - 2.88(27) + 0.12(27)^2$$
$$= 44.35 - 77.76 + 87.48$$
$$= \$54.07.$$

Average variable cost for this level of output is

$$AVC = 44.35 - 1.44(27) + 0.04(27)^2$$
$$= 44.35 - 38.88 + 29.16$$
$$= \$34.63.$$

Then, total variable cost for 27,000 units of output is

$$TVC = AVC \times Q$$
$$= 34.63 \times 27,000$$
$$= \$935,010.$$

Finally, we can calculate the output level at which average variable cost is minimized. As we have shown, this output is

$$Q = -b/2c.$$

In our example, this becomes

$$Q = \frac{1.44}{2 \times 0.04} = 18.$$

That is, average variable cost reaches its minimum at an output level of 18,000 units.

11.4 ESTIMATION OF A LONG-RUN COST FUNCTION

Earlier we argued that the general form for the long-run cost function in a two-input setting is

$$C = f(Q, w, r).$$

That is, using cross-section data, we must include as independent variables the prices of the inputs. Hence, it is necessary to specify a cost function that includes the input prices.

At first glance, it would appear that the solution would be simply to add the input prices as additional explanatory variables in the cost function developed above. That is, total cost would be

$$TC = aQ + bQ^2 + cQ^3 + dw + er.$$

However, such a function fails to satisfy a basic characteristic of cost functions. A total cost function can be written as $TC = wL + rK$. And, if we double both of the input prices, holding output constant, input usage will not change, but total cost will double. That is,

$$TC' = (2w)\,L + (2r)K$$
$$= 2(wL + rK)$$
$$= 2TC.$$

The long-run cost function suggested above does not satisfy this requirement. For a given output, if we were to double the input prices,

$$TC' = aQ + bQ^2 + cQ^3 + d(2w) + e(2r)$$
$$= aQ + bQ^2 + cQ^3 + dw + er + (dw + er)$$
$$= TC + dw + er.$$

Clearly, TC' is not equal to $2TC$.

Therefore, we must consider an alternative form for estimating a long-run cost function. The most commonly employed form is a log-linear specification like the Cobb-Douglas specifications used for production functions. With this type of specification, the total cost function would be expressed as

$$TC = \alpha Q^\beta w^\gamma r^\delta.$$

Using this functional form let's see what happens if we double input prices while holding output constant:

$$TC' = \alpha Q^\beta (2w)^\gamma (2r)^\delta$$
$$= 2^{(\gamma + \delta)}(\alpha Q^\beta w^\gamma r^\delta)$$
$$= 2^{(\gamma + \delta)}TC.$$

If $\gamma + \delta = 1$, doubling input prices will indeed double the total cost of producing a given level of output—the required characteristic of a cost function. Hence, it is necessary to *impose* this condition on the log-linear cost function we proposed. We do so by defining δ as $1 - \gamma$; so

$$TC = \alpha Q^\beta w^\gamma r^{1-\gamma}$$

or

$$TC = \alpha Q^\beta (w/r)^\gamma r.$$

At this point, we encounter an estimation problem. If we convert the preceding equation to logarithms in order to estimate it, we have

$$\log TC = \log \alpha + \beta \log Q + \gamma \log \left(\frac{w}{r}\right) + 1 \log r.$$

While we can estimate the parameters log α, β, and γ, this formulation requires that the coefficient for log r be *precisely* equal to one. If we were to estimate this equation, such a value cannot be guaranteed; so, we must impose this value. This is done simply by moving log r to the left-hand side of the equation:

$$\log TC - \log r = \log \alpha + \beta \log Q + \gamma \log (w/r).$$

In this way, the coefficient on log r is forced to be equal to one. Finally, using the rules of logarithms, we can rewrite this equation as

$$\log \left[\frac{TC}{r}\right] = \log \alpha + \beta \log Q + \gamma \log (w/r).$$

It is this equation that we will actually estimate in order to obtain an estimate of the long-run cost function.

Once we have this function estimated, what can we do with it? As we have noted earlier, the primary use of the long-run cost function is in the firm's investment decision; so a primary objective of long-run cost estimation is to determine the extent of economies of scale. From the discussion of log-linear functions in Chapter 4, we know that the coefficient β indicates the elasticity of cost with respect to output. That is, β is interpreted as

$$\beta = \frac{\text{Percentage change in cost}}{\text{Percentage change in output}}.$$

Note that, when $\beta > 1$, cost is increasing more than proportionately to output (e.g., if the percentage change in output is 25 percent and the percentage change in cost is 50 percent, β would be equal to 2); therefore long-run average cost would be increasing. Hence if $\beta > 1$, the estimates would indicate diseconomies of scale. Conversely, if $\beta < 1$, economies of scale would be indicated. Furthermore, note that the magnitude of the estimate of β will indicate the "strength" of the economies or diseconomies of scale. The statistical significance of β can be tested in the manner outlined earlier.

APPLICATION

Costs in the U.S. Electric Utility Industry

In order to illustrate the techniques of long-run cost estimation, let's return to the data for the electric utility firms that we used to illustrate the estimation of a production function. Again, in order to keep our example simple, we limit our attention to two inputs—capital and labor.

In the earlier application we reported data for output, capital usage, and labor usage for 20 firms. However, for long-run cost estimation, the required data are total cost, output, and the input prices. Since total cost is

$$C = rK + wL,$$

we can calculate total cost using the capital usage and labor usage data already presented and the input prices.* The data set to be employed is shown below.

---

*See Appendix B for a description of how the input prices were calculated.

Firm	C	Q	r	w
1	30.8923	4.612	0.06903	8.5368
2	58.5825	8.297	0.06903	9.9282
3	15.1205	1.820	0.06754	10.1116
4	32.8014	5.849	0.07919	10.2522
5	22.7768	3.145	0.06481	11.1194
6	11.9176	1.381	0.06598	9.6992
7	34.4028	5.422	0.06754	10.0613
8	47.5209	7.115	0.06565	10.9087
9	18.9136	3.052	0.10555	10.1954
10	36.0902	4.394	0.06572	11.2585
11	3.2401	0.248	0.07919	10.8759
12	62.0032	9.699	0.06903	9.8758
13	74.7206	14.271	0.06789	10.9051
14	96.0053	17.743	0.06903	7.4775
15	63.4357	14.956	0.06572	7.8062
16	15.9901	3.108	0.07919	9.2689
17	42.3249	9.416	0.06565	8.3906
18	44.6781	6.857	0.06565	9.8826
19	59.2520	9.745	0.06860	9.8235
20	38.7337	4.442	0.08206	12.9352

The function to be estimated is

$$\log (TC/r) = \log \alpha + \beta \log Q + \gamma \log (w/r).$$

The computer output obtained from this estimation is[†]

```
DEPENDENT VAR: LOG (TC/R) F-RATIO: 324.328

OBSERVATIONS: 20          R-SQUARE: 0.9745

                 PARAMETER        STANDARD
VARIABLE         ESTIMATE

INTERCEPT        -0.41600         1.03943
LOG Q             0.83830         0.03315
LOG (W/R)         1.05435         0.20939
```

Returns to scale = 1.893

[†]A user of the first edition of this text pointed out a troublesome point in this estimation: In the log-linear specification, both γ and δ would be expected to be between 0 and 1. In this estimation, γ was estimated to be $1.05435 > 1$. However, the estimate of γ is not significantly greater than (different from) one. The t statistic in this case is

$$t = \frac{1.05435 - 1}{0.20939} = 0.260.$$

Clearly $0.260 < 2.110$. So, although troublesome, these estimates do not conflict with the required theoretical properties.

As we have shown, the coefficient β is of primary importance since it indicates the existence of economies or diseconomies of scale. In our estimation $\beta < 1$, so economies of scale are indicated. However, it is necessary to determine if this coefficient is statistically significant. Using the methodology described earlier in this chapter, the appropriate test statistic is

$$
\begin{aligned}
t_{\hat{\beta}} &= \frac{\hat{\beta} - 1}{S_{\hat{\beta}}} \\
&= \frac{0.83830 - 1}{0.03315} \\
&= -4.87783.
\end{aligned}
$$

We then compare the absolute value of this test statistic with the critical *t*-value. In this example, since we have $20 - 3 = 17$ degrees of freedom, the critical value of t (at a 95 percent confidence level) is 2.110. Since 4.87783 exceeds 2.110, it follows that $\hat{\beta}$ is statistically significant and that there is indeed evidence of economies of scale.[‡]

[‡]Note that these results are consistent with the results from the estimation of the production function we presented earlier—both indicate the existence of increasing returns to, or economies of, scale. However, such a result is to be expected. Since the cost function is itself derived from a production function, both should reflect the same characteristics. If the production function indicates increasing returns to scale, the cost should, under fairly normal circumstances, show economies of scale.

Before we conclude this section, we should note a limitation of the technique illustrated in the preceding example and suggest a possible extension. The preceding methodology is capable of indicating either economies or diseconomies of scale, but not both. That is, this technique could indicate either a rising or a falling long-run average cost curve, but it would not, in its present form, provide an estimate of a U-shaped long-run average cost function. Since one objective of any long-run analysis is to determine the plant size at which long-run average cost is at a minimum, an estimate of a U-shaped average cost curve is definitely desired.

One possible way to handle this limitation is to segment the available data. To illustrate this procedure, let us suppose that the true long-run average cost curve is as illustrated by *LAC* in Panel A of Figure 11.4. What the manager of the firm wants to know is the smallest plant size for which long-run average cost is a minimum (Q^*). Suppose that the analyst has data relating to outputs between Q_1 and Q_3. If the analyst were to estimate the cost function described above using all of these data points, it is quite likely that the result would be an estimated long-run average cost function similar to that shown by the dashed line $L\hat{A}C$ in Panel A of

Figure 11.4

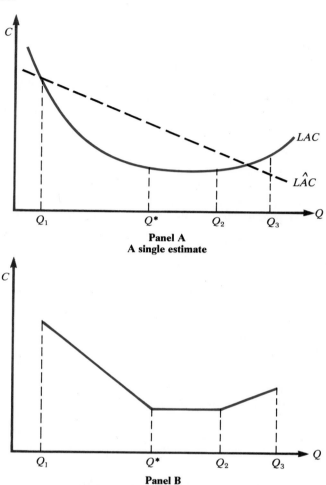

Panel A
A single estimate

Panel B
Estimates from segmented samples

Figure 11.4. Alternatively, the analyst could obtain three estimates of the cost function. In the first, the analyst would want to use data relating to outputs between Q_1 and Q^*. The second estimate would use data between Q^* and Q_2, and the third, data between Q_2 and Q_3. Combining these estimates, the analyst would then obtain an estimate of the long-run average cost curve that would look something like that illustrated in Panel B of Figure 11.4. From such an estimation, the analyst could obtain an estimate of the minimum optimal plant size, Q^*.

Obviously, the problem is determining the proper manner of segmenting the data. If you knew beforehand the proper data to include in each of the individual estimations, such estimation would be redundant: if you knew the value of Q^*, why estimate it? Thus, the segmenting of the data must be made on the basis of estimation results. That is, in reality, numerous estimates must be made using alternative data segmentations. Then, the most appropriate manner of segmenting the data would be the one that provides the "best" estimations. One criterion that could be used would be to employ that segmentation of the data that maximizes the R^2 values for the individual estimated cost functions.

11.5 AN ALTERNATIVE APPROACH—
THE ENGINEERING TECHNIQUE

Given the problems associated with the regression methodologies described in the preceding sections, several alternative approaches to the analysis of cost have been suggested. In this section, we will briefly describe the most widely used alternative approach—the engineering technique.

The engineering approach to cost analysis represents an attempt to avoid a problem we mentioned earlier—accounting costs may not reflect opportunity costs. In this approach, the analyst begins with what we might call an engineering production function. That is, a function that determines the optimal input combinations for producing any given level of production is identified. Then, given these *technologically efficient* input levels, cost can be obtained by multiplying each level of input usage by the current price of the input and summing over the inputs. This methodology should be more clear in an example to follow.

The engineering technique has several obvious advantages: (1) Since it avoids the difficulties encountered when we attempt to obtain a measure of cost from accounting data, it reduces the probability of errors from measurement. (2) Using such an approach, the analyst can eliminate many extraneous factors that might tend to complicate the problem without increasing precision. (3) This approach fits well with our theoretical analysis, since it involves current technology and current input prices.

APPLICATION

An Engineering Cost Function in Petroleum Refining*

An industry in which the engineering technique is apparently widely used is petroleum refining. If a firm is considering the construction of a new refinery, it needs some estimates for the investment (fixed) and operating (variable) costs associated with the proposed refinery. Since the refinery does not exist at the time these evaluations must be made, the firm must resort to the engineering technique. In this application,

*This application is adapted from J. H. Gary and G. E. Handwerk, *Petroleum Refining* (New York: Marcel Dekker, 1975), pp. 214–27.

we present a simplified example of the manner in which these estimates are obtained.

At the outset, note that petroleum refineries are designed to handle a specific type and quantity of crude oil. In this example, let's assume that the refinery is designed to process 30,000 barrels per day (bpd) of a particular crude oil or mix of crude oils. The first process used in refining the crude oils is atmospheric distillation. On the basis of physical evaluation of the specific crude oils to be processed, the engineers estimate that this process will result in 8,000 bpd of finished products (e.g., gasoline and fuel oils) and 22,000 bpd of materials that require further processing. Part of the materials requiring further processing (18,000 bpd) can be processed via vacuum distillation to yield final products. The remainder (4,000 bpd) must be sent through a hydro-desulfurizer. As a result of this process, the engineers estimate an output of 561 pounds per day of sulfur, 1,000 bpd of finished products, and 2,900 bpd of materials that require still further processing. These 2,900 bpd are processed in a catalytic reformer to yield 2,700 bpd of finished products. The complete processing flow is described in the figure below.

An Engineering Production Flow

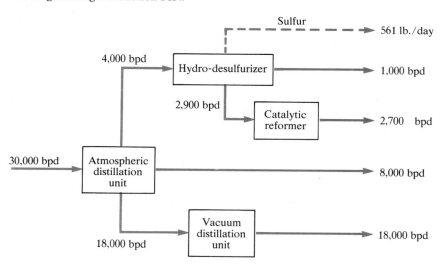

Given this knowledge of the production process, the firm knows what types of capital are required and the necessary capacities for each (e.g., this refinery will require a catalytic reformer with a capacity of 2,900 bpd). The firm can then use available industry sources to obtain the cost of such capital equipment. In this way, the firm will be able to obtain estimates of the capital costs associated with this proposed refinery. These capital costs, summarized below, result in a total fixed cost of $11,050,000.

Item	Required Capacity (bpd)	Cost
Atmospheric distillation unit	30,000	$ 3,800,000
Vacuum distillation unit	18,000	2,400,000
Hydro-desulfurizer	4,000	1,250,000
Catalytic reformer	2,900	3,600,000
		$11,050,000

The next task is to obtain an estimate of the variable costs associated with this refinery. These are normally calculated on an annual basis, assuming that the refinery is operating at capacity. The major variable inputs are crude oil, labor, cooling water, electric power, royalties, and catalyst replacement. Assuming that the refinery operates 340 days per year, the refinery will require 10,200,000 barrels of crude oil. If the crude oil to be used sells for $15 per barrel, crude oil costs will be $153,000,000. Using data obtained from other plants, the engineers calculate that this refinery will require a staff of 22 workers. Assuming an average annual wage of $36,000, annual labor costs would be $792,000. Required cooling water and electric power are determined from data on comparable refineries. Multiplying these requirements by the average current costs of the inputs, annual expenditures are obtained. Let us assume that these are, respectively, $50,000 and $320,000. Royalties are paid to patent owners on the basis of the throughput of the refinery. For example, if the royalty rate on the catalytic reformer is 9 cents per barrel, the annual royalty is $88,740 $(0.09 \times 2,900 \times 340 = 88,740)$. Let us assume that total royalties amount to $132,000 annually. Finally, catalyst replacement is also determined by the amount of crude oil processed. We assume that the annual expenditures for catalyst replacement are $56,000. Combining these, the annual variable costs associated with this refinery are

Crude oil	$153,000,000
Labor	792,000
Cooling water	50,000
Electric power	320,000
Royalties	132,000
Catalyst replacement	56,000
	$154,350,000

As the preceding application indicates, an engineering approach to cost estimation is straightforward and useful. But, we must point out that this approach involves several problems. An obvious difficulty is that the engineering production function may be based on the operation of a pilot plant and the production function may not prove to be valid when the firm expands to a full-scale production facility.

However, we feel that there is an even more serious problem. This problem results from the difference between the engineer's and the economist's view of efficiency. An example should illustrate our concern. Consider a very simple production process: Coal is moved from river barges to the loading hopper for a plant by means of a crane. Suppose that in this process some coal is dropped into the river. It is very likely that the engineer and the economist would differ as to their concept of the efficiency of this process. While the engineer might suggest modifying or replacing the crane to eliminate the "waste," the economist might take a very different view. If the price of coal is low relative to the price of capital, it could be efficient (in the economic sense) to drop coal into the water. The real problem is to determine the optimal amount to drop. The point is that the technologically efficient combination of inputs need not be the economically efficient combination.

In spite of these difficulties, engineering cost functions are widely used. In many instances the manager will obtain estimates of the cost function from the production or engineering division of the firm. And, in these instances, it is very likely that the forthcoming estimates are based on an approach like the one we have described above. (To provide you with a feel for this, in some of our subsequent applications we will use an engineering cost function.)

TECHNICAL PROBLEMS

1. Consider the linear production function

$$Q = \alpha K + \beta L.$$

Calculate the marginal rate of technical substitution and explain why this functional form does not adhere to the theoretical properties of a production function.

2. We estimated a Cobb-Douglas production function

$$Q = AK^\alpha L^\beta.$$

The resulting computer output is

```
DEPENDENT VARIABLE: LOG Q          F-RATIO: 146.53

OBSERVATIONS: 30                   R-SQUARE: 0.9278

                 PARAMETER               STANDARD
VARIABLE         ESTIMATE                 ERROR

INTERCEPT         -3.0                     0.5
LOG K              0.60                    0.15
LOG L              0.55                    0.20

           VARIANCE-COVARIANCE MATRIX FOR
               ESTIMATED COEFFICIENTS

                 INTERCEPT      LOG K      LOG L

INTERCEPT          0.25        -0.03       0.10
LOG K             -0.03         0.023     -0.02
LOG L              0.10        -0.02       0.04
```

The values for output and input usage (all in thousand units) for the firm under consideration are

$$Q = 100.0$$
$$K = 150.0$$
$$L = 1.0.$$

a. Determine if these estimates indicate:
   (1) Positive marginal products.
   (2) Diminishing marginal products.
b. Calculate the marginal products for capital and labor. (Use the values provided for Q, K, and L.)
c. Suppose capital usage increases by 10 percent. By what percentage would output be expected to increase? What would be expected to happen to output if labor usage increased by 5 percent?
d. Determine whether these estimates indicate increasing, constant, or decreasing returns to scale. (Make sure you test for statistical significance.)

3. A consulting firm estimated the production function for newspaper printing using a Cobb-Douglas specification:

$$Q = AK^\alpha L^\beta,$$

where Q = number of newspapers printed per hour, K = number of printing presses, and L = number of workers. They obtained the following results:

```
DEPENDENT VARIABLE: LOG Q          F-RATIO: 24.06

OBSERVATIONS: 43                   R-SQUARE: 0.723

VARIABLE      PARAMETER ESTIMATE   STANDARD ERROR

INTERCEPT           0.22                0.07
LOG K               0.87                0.04
LOG L               0.68                0.12
```

a. Are the estimates log $\hat{A}$, $\hat{\alpha}$, and $\hat{\beta}$ statistically significant?
b. Do these results imply positive and diminishing marginal products for the two inputs?
c. If a firm uses 20 printing presses and 500 workers, how many newspapers can they expect to print per hour?
d. If a firm is printing 1,000 newspapers an hour using 10 printing presses, how many newspapers would another printing press add to estimated output?
e. What would happen to the number of newspapers produced if a firm increases the number of printing presses by 20 percent?
f. If a firm is printing 500 newspapers an hour and the marginal product of labor is 2, how many workers is the firm using?
g. What would happen to the number of newspapers produced if a firm decreases the number of workers by 15 percent?

4. Compare and contrast short-run and long-run cost estimation with respect to:
a. Objectives.
b. Type of data employed.

5. Describe the data problems involved in cost estimation using:
a. Time-series data.
b. Cross-section data.

6. The chief economist for a large appliance manufacturer estimated the firm's short-run cost function for vacuum cleaners using an average variable cost function of the form:

$$AVC = a + bQ + cQ^2,$$

where AVC = dollars per vacuum cleaner and Q = number of vacuum cleaners (millions). Total fixed cost is $30 million. The following results were obtained:

```
DEPENDENT VARIABLE: AVC          F-RATIO: 39.428

OBSERVATIONS: 19                 R-SQUARE: 0.736

VARIABLE      PARAMETER ESTIMATE    STANDARD ERROR

INTERCEPT            81.93              17.81
Q                    -3.05               0.94
Q2                    0.24               0.08
```

a. Are the estimates $\hat{a}$, $\hat{b}$, and $\hat{c}$ statistically significant?
b. Do the results indicate that the average variable cost curve is U-shaped? How do you know?
c. If the firm produces 3 million vacuum cleaners, what is estimated average variable cost? Marginal cost? Total variable cost? Total cost?
d. Answer part *(c)* assuming that the firm produces 10 million vacuum cleaners.
e. At what level of output will average variable cost be minimum? What is minimum average variable cost?

7. Consider the cost function

$$TC = \alpha Q^{\beta} w^{\gamma} r^{\delta}.$$

What condition is necessary in order that doubling input prices will double the total cost of producing a given level of output? Explain.

8. Following are the results of an estimation of the cost function

$$(TC/r) = \alpha Q^{\beta}(w/r)^{\gamma}$$

```
DEPENDENT VAR: LOG (TC/R)   F-RATIO: 265.690

OBSERVATIONS: 35            R-SQUARE: 0.9432

                PARAMETER        STANDARD
VARIABLE        ESTIMATE         ERROR

INTERCEPT         -0.5             0.4
LOG Q              1.6             0.2
LOG (W/R)          0.7             0.3
```

What do these estimates indicate with respect to economies or diseconomies of scale?

9. Return to our application dealing with an engineering cost function in petroleum refining.
   a. Disregarding the output of sulfur, calculate the average variable cost associated with a barrel of finished products.
   b. In such an approach, maintenance expense is normally calculated as a percent of total capital cost. Would such a cost be fixed or variable?
   c. Note that fuel is not included as a cost of operation. This is because the firm does not purchase any fuel oils; rather, it simply burns some of its own output. Comment on such a practice. How should this be treated in cost estimation?

ANALYTICAL PROBLEMS

1. Suppose the firm you manage is faced with an investment decision. It can either expand its existing plant or build another plant of the same size. Under what conditions would one or the other of these options be preferred? How would you go about obtaining the necessary data to make the decision?

2. Suppose that your firm is interested in constructing a new production facility and that you must choose among several alternative plant sizes. What type of cost estimation is required? What type of data are necessary? Explain.

3. Why is a linear specification unacceptable for estimating an average variable cost function?

4. It could be argued that a publicly owned utility (e.g., a water system or a mass transportation system) should operate at that level of output at which average cost is minimized. How would such a firm go about determining this output level? How could regulators check to see if the utility is actually operating at this output level?

5. Suggest a methodology by which an analyst can obtain a measure of the opportunity cost of capital to a firm that owns (rather than leases) its capital stock.

6. We have argued that engineering cost functions may not reflect the economically efficient combinations of inputs. Could this be the case in the instance of the engineering cost function for petroleum refining described in an application? Note that, in this production process, crude oil is completely utilized. Might there exist a circumstance in which it would be economically efficient to "waste" crude oil? Suggest the way in which this wastage would most likely occur.

SUGGESTED ADDITIONAL REFERENCES

Intriligator, M. D. *Economic Models, Techniques, and Applications*. Englewood Cliffs, N.J.: Prentice-Hall, 1978.

Miller, R. L. *Intermediate Microeconomics: Theory, Issues, and Applications*. New York: McGraw-Hill, 1978.

Theil, H. *Introduction to Econometrics*. Englewood Cliffs, N.J.: Prentice-Hall, 1978.

APPENDIX A: THE COBB-DOUGLAS PRODUCTION FUNCTION

In Chapter 11, we introduced the Cobb-Douglas production function:

$$Q = AK^\alpha L^\beta.$$

This functional form has been widely used in business economics applications. In this appendix we will describe the mathematical properties of this function.

Input Usage   In order to produce output, both inputs are required.

$$Q(0,L) = A0^\alpha L^\beta = Q(K,0) = AK^\alpha 0^\beta = 0.$$

Marginal Products   The marginal product functions for capital and labor are

$$Q_K = \alpha AK^{\alpha-1}L^\beta = \alpha \frac{Q}{K}$$

and

$$Q_L = \beta AK^\alpha L^{\beta-1} = \beta \frac{Q}{L}.$$

In order that the marginal products be positive, α and β must be positive. The second derivatives,

$$Q_{KK} = \alpha(\alpha - 1)\, AK^{\alpha-2}L^\beta$$

and

$$Q_{LL} = \beta(\beta - 1)\, AK^\alpha L^{\beta-2},$$

demonstrate that, if the marginal products are diminishing (i.e., Q_{KK} and $Q_{LL} < 0$), α and β must be less than one.

Marginal Rate of Technical Substitution   From Chapter 9, the *MRTS* of L for K is Q_L/Q_K. In the context of the Cobb-Douglas function,

$$MRTS = \frac{Q_L}{Q_K} = \frac{\beta}{\alpha} \cdot \frac{K}{L}.$$

Note first that the *MRTS* is invariant to output,

$$\frac{\partial MRTS}{\partial Q} = 0.$$

Hence, the Cobb-Douglas production function is *homothetic*—the production function has a straight line expansion path and changes in the output level have no effect on relative input usage. Moreover, the *MRTS* demonstrates that the Cobb-Douglas production function is characterized by concave isoquants. Taking the derivative of the *MRTS* of *L* for *K* with respect to *L*,

$$\frac{\partial MRTS}{\partial L} = -\frac{\beta}{\alpha} \cdot \frac{K}{L^2}.$$

Hence, the *MRTS* diminishes as more and more capital is replaced with labor: the isoquants are concave.

Output Elasticities   Output elasticities are defined as

$$E_K = \frac{\partial Q}{\partial K} \cdot \frac{K}{Q} = Q_K \cdot \frac{K}{Q}$$

and

$$E_L = \frac{\partial Q}{\partial L} \cdot \frac{L}{Q} = Q_L \cdot \frac{L}{Q}.$$

Using the Cobb-Douglas specification

$$E_K = \left(\alpha \frac{Q}{K}\right) \cdot \frac{K}{Q} = \alpha$$

and

$$E_L = \left(\beta \frac{Q}{L}\right) \cdot \frac{L}{Q} = \beta.$$

The Function Coefficient   Begin with an implicit production function, $Q = Q(K,L)$. Suppose that the levels of usage of both inputs are increased by the same proportion (λ); i.e., $Q = Q(\lambda K, \lambda L)$. The definition of the function coefficient $(\mathcal{E})$ is

$$\mathcal{E} = \frac{dQ/Q}{d\lambda/\lambda}.$$

Take the total differential of the production function

$$dQ = Q_K dK + Q_L dL$$

and rewrite this as

$$dQ = Q_K K \frac{dK}{K} + Q_L L \frac{dL}{L}.$$

Since K and L were increased by the same proportion, $dK/K = dL/L = d\lambda/\lambda$. Thus,

$$dQ = \frac{d\lambda}{\lambda} (Q_K K + Q_L L).$$

Using this expression, the function coefficient is

$$\mathcal{E} = Q_K \cdot \frac{K}{Q} + Q_L \cdot \frac{L}{Q} = E_K + E_L.$$

In the context of the Cobb-Douglas production function, it follows that

$$\mathcal{E} = \alpha + \beta.$$

APPENDIX B: THE EFFICIENCY CRITERION

The estimates of a production function can also be used to determine whether or not the firm (or industry) is using the optimal combination of inputs. As we showed in Chapter 9, if the firm is minimizing cost for a given output or maximizing output for a given expenditure, the optimality condition is

$$MP_L/MP_K = w/r.$$

If

$$MP_L/MP_K < w/r$$

the firm is overutilizing labor—using too much labor relative to capital. Likewise, if

$$MP_L/MP_K > w/r$$

the firm is overutilizing capital.

The optimal level of use of its inputs is an important consideration for the firm, so the relation between the marginal rate of technical substitution and the input-price ratio is one that should be estimated.

In the context of the Cobb-Douglas production function, we know that the marginal rate of technical substitution is

$$\frac{MP_L}{MP_K} = \frac{\beta}{\alpha} \cdot \frac{K}{L}.$$

and we can write the optimally condition as

$$\frac{\beta}{\alpha} \cdot \frac{K}{L} = \frac{w}{r} \qquad \text{or} \qquad \frac{\beta}{\alpha} \cdot \frac{K}{L} - \frac{w}{r} = 0$$

Then, multiplying by α, the efficiency criterion becomes

$$\beta \frac{K}{L} - \alpha \frac{w}{r} = 0.$$

In this form,

$$\beta \frac{K}{L} - \alpha \frac{w}{r} < 0$$

implies that the firm is overutilizing labor, since this inequality implies that $(MP_L/MP_K) < (w/r)$. Likewise,

$$\beta \frac{K}{L} - \alpha \frac{w}{r} > 0$$

implies that the firm is overutilizing capital.

To observe this relation empirically, we obtain estimates of α and β from the estimation of the production function. We can then obtain the values of $K, L, w,$ and r that are relevant for the particular firm under consideration. Using these values, we can calculate the value for the expression presented above, which we will denote as $\hat{\psi}$. That is,

$$\hat{\psi} = \hat{\beta}(K/L) - \hat{\alpha}(w/r).$$

It is highly unlikely that the calculated value of ψ will be exactly equal to zero. Instead, the question is whether or not the calculated $\hat{\psi}$ is *significantly* different from zero. The answer to this question will require yet another t-test. As in the preceding t-tests, it is necessary to form this calculated t value by dividing the estimate by its own standard error. In this case, the t-statistic would be

$$t = \frac{\hat{\psi}}{S_{\hat{\psi}}}.$$

The problem, as you might expect, is obtaining an estimate of the standard error for $\hat{\psi}$. Using more advanced statistical techniques, it can be shown that the estimated variance of $\hat{\psi}$ can be calculated as*

$$\text{Var}(\psi) = \left(\frac{K}{L}\right)^2 \text{Var}(\beta) + \left(\frac{w}{r}\right)^2 \text{Var}(\alpha) - 2\left(\frac{K}{L}\right)\left(\frac{w}{r}\right) \text{Cov}(\alpha,\beta).$$

---

*In the most general terms, let us define ψ to be simply a function of the estimated parameters α and β,

$$\psi = f(\alpha,\beta).$$

Then, the asymptotic variance of ψ is

$$\text{Var}(\psi) = \left(\frac{\partial \psi}{\partial \alpha}\right)^2 \text{Var}(\alpha) + \left(\frac{\partial \psi}{\partial \beta}\right)^2 \text{Var}(\beta)$$
$$+ 2\left(\frac{\partial \psi}{\partial \alpha}\right)\left(\frac{\partial \psi}{\partial \beta}\right) \text{Cov}(\alpha,\beta).$$

Note that, in our calculations, we treat the values of $K, L, w,$ and r as constants.

The estimated standard error of $\hat{\psi}$ is then

$$S_{\hat{\psi}} = \sqrt{\hat{\psi})}.$$

Given this value, the t-value for $\hat{\psi}$ may be calculated, and, if the absolute value of the calculated t exceeds the critical value of t, we can say that $\hat{\psi}$ is significantly different from zero. We illustrate this technique with an application.

APPLICATION

Input Efficiency in the U.S. Electric Utility Industry

Another question of considerable interest for electric utilities, and of course for other firms, is whether or not the firms are efficiently utilizing inputs. It has been argued that, as a result of the regulation imposed on electric utilities, such firms would overutilize capital. From the preceding discussion, this would imply that

$$MP_L/MP_K > w/r$$

or, for a Cobb-Douglas production function,

$$\beta \frac{K}{L} - \alpha \frac{w}{r} > 0.$$

Let us use the sample of 20 firms provided in the preceding example to examine this question.

As you can verify, we already have everything we need to calculate the marginal products. We also need data on the input prices for labor, w, and capital, r. For the 20 firms in our sample these data are in the table that follows.*

---

*In this example, the input price for labor, w, was obtained simply by dividing total salaries and wages by the number of employees, giving us the average annual payment per worker expressed in thousand dollars. Calculation of the input price for capital is somewhat more complicated. In general, the user price of capital can be expressed as

$$r = q_K(i + \delta),$$

where q_K is the unit acquisition cost of the capital stock, i is the real rate of interest, and δ is the rate of depreciation (assuming that the relative prices of different capital goods do not change). In our case, capital is measured in dollars, so the unit acquisition cost is by definition equal to one. However, it is necessary to account for differences in the price level at the time of acquisition by using a price index. The real rate of interest was estimated using a rational expectations approach. Finally, a straight-line rate of depreciation was employed.

Firm	r	w
1	0.06903	8.5368
2	0.06903	9.9282
3	0.06754	10.1116
4	0.07919	10.2522
5	0.06481	11.1194
6	0.06598	9.6992
7	0.06754	10.0613
8	0.06565	10.9087
9	0.10555	10.1954
10	0.06572	11.2585
11	0.07919	10.8759
12	0.06903	9.8758
13	0.06789	10.9051
14	0.06903	7.4775
15	0.06572	7.8062
16	0.07919	9.2689
17	0.06565	8.3906
18	0.06565	9.8826
19	0.06860	9.8235
20	0.08206	12.9352

We could examine the input efficiency condition for any of the 20 firms. But, since the question posed is whether the industry is overutilizing capital, let's evaluate the efficiency condition at the mean values for this sample of firms. Using the preceding data and that presented in the earlier application, we calculated the mean values of K, L, w, and r as:

$$\bar{K} = 372.411$$
$$\bar{L} = 1.529$$
$$\bar{w} = 9.966$$
$$\bar{r} = 0.072.$$

Using these means and the estimates of α and β from the earlier application, we calculated our variable ψ,

$$\hat{\psi} = \hat{\beta} \cdot \left(\frac{\bar{K}}{\bar{L}}\right) - \hat{\alpha} \cdot \left(\frac{\bar{w}}{\bar{r}}\right)$$
$$= 0.65384 \cdot \left(\frac{372.411}{1.529}\right) - 0.53296 \cdot \left(\frac{9.966}{0.072}\right)$$
$$= 85.482.$$

As hypothesized, $\hat{\psi} > 0$. It would *appear* that the firms are overutilizing capital. However, we must determine whether this overcapitalization is statistically significant.

As we have demonstrated, the test for significance of ψ involves a *t*-test, in which we calculate the *t*-value

$$t = \frac{\hat{\psi}}{S_{\hat{\psi}}}$$

and compare it to our critical *t*-value, in this case 2.110. It is first necessary to calculate the variance of $\hat{\psi}$.

$$\text{Var}(\hat{\psi}) = \left(\frac{\bar{K}}{\bar{L}}\right)^2 \text{Var}(\hat{\beta}) + \left(\frac{\bar{w}}{\bar{r}}\right)^2 \text{Var}(\hat{\alpha}) - 2\left(\frac{\bar{K}}{\bar{L}}\right)\left(\frac{\bar{w}}{\bar{r}}\right)\text{Cov}(\hat{\alpha},\hat{\beta})$$

$$= (243.565)^2(0.02030) + (138.417)^2(0.01457)$$

$$- 2(243.565)(138.417)(-0.01575)$$

$$= 2,545.402.$$

Then, the standard error of $\hat{\psi}$ is

$$S_{\hat{\psi}} = \sqrt{\text{Var}(\psi)} = 50.452.$$

It follows then that the *t*-value is

$$t = \frac{85.482}{50.452}$$

$$= 1.694.$$

Comparing this calculated *t*-value with the critical value, we see that ψ is not statistically significant (at the 95% confidence level). Thus, for this sample, they hypothesized overcapitalization cannot be confirmed empirically. That is, since ψ is not significantly different from zero, this data set does not indicate that there exists any significant overutilization of capital. We can not reject the hypothesis that the firms in this sample are using the optimal amounts of capital and labor.

PART FOUR

PERFECT
COMPETITION

12

THEORY OF PERFECTLY COMPETITIVE FIRMS AND INDUSTRIES

N ow that we have analyzed both demand and cost, we are prepared to consider the question posed by every manager: What can I do to maximize my firm's profits? The answer to this question depends on the type of industry in which the firm operates. There are many possible variations of industry structure. On one extreme, an industry could consist of a very large number of firms producing a homogeneous product. On the other extreme, an industry could consist of only one firm. And there are several structures between these two extremes. In this chapter, we consider the first structure, called perfect competition.

We will consider an industry consisting of so many firms that each firm takes the market-determined price as given—no one firm can influence market price. We assume that each firm in the industry attempts to maximize its profit. Certainly managers may have other goals, but, other things equal, managers would prefer more profit to less. In any case, we use the assumption of profit maximization because it works well and because it provides a reasonably good description of the way firms actually behave.

Within this framework of profit maximization under perfect competition, the manager looks at the demand and cost conditions facing the firm in order to answer three fundamental questions: (1) Should I produce or shut down? (2) If I produce, what is the appropriate level of production? (3) What amounts of each input should I use? (Since, as we noted, the perfectly competitive firm must take market price as given, the manager is not faced with the decision concerning what price to charge.)

We should emphasize at the outset that the exacting characteristics of perfect competition are met by few real-world markets. Although markets *approach* perfect competition, we know of no market that meets *all* of the assumptions. You might therefore ask why such a theory should be considered.

The answer can be given in as much or as little detail as desired. For our purposes, the answer is brief. First, generality can be achieved only by means of abstraction. Hence, no theory can be perfectly descriptive of real-world phenomena. Furthermore, the more accurately a theory describes one specific real-world case, the less accurately it describes all others. Thus, these theories are used in many cases because what is lost in realism is substantially compensated for by the gain in generality.

A second point of great importance is that the conclusions derived from the model of perfect competition (and the theory of pure monopoly to be introduced in Chapter 14) have, by and large, permitted accurate explanation and prediction of real-world phenomena. That is, these models frequently work well as theoretical models of economic processes even though they do not accurately describe any specific firm or industry. Thus the fundamentals of the theories are useful not only to theoretical economists but also to managerial decision makers.

To summarize, no market is perfectly competitive, but the behavior of many markets closely approximates the model. Thus, we can use the model for a first approximation. If necessary, we can revise the predictions of the model to reflect the significant characteristics of the market in question.

12.1 SOME PRINCIPLES

The basic principles of profit maximization are straightforward and follow directly from the discussion of optimization in Chapter 3. The firm will increase any activity so long as the additional revenue from the increase exceeds the additional cost of the increase. The firm will decrease the activity if the additional revenue is less than the additional cost. Thus the firm will choose the level of the activity at which the additional revenue just equals the additional cost.

Suppose that the activity or choice variable is the firm's level of output. As the firm increases its level of output, each additional unit adds to the total revenue of the firm. The change in revenue per unit change in output is, as you will recall, called marginal revenue. As the firm increases its level of output, each unit increase in output increases the firm's total cost. As you will recall from Chapter 10, the added cost per unit increase in output is called marginal cost.

Thus, the firm will choose to expand output so long as the added revenue from the expansion (marginal revenue) is greater than the added cost of the expansion (marginal cost). The firm will decrease output if marginal cost is greater than marginal revenue. Profit maximization is, therefore, based upon the following principle:

Principle. *Profit is the difference between revenue and cost. If an increase in output adds more to revenue than to cost, the increase in output adds to profit. If the increase in output adds less to revenue than to cost, the increase in output subtracts from profit. The firm, therefore, chooses the level of output at which marginal revenue equals marginal cost. This level maximizes total profit.*

In this chapter, we are concerned with the special case in which the price of the produced commodity is given to the firm by the market. In this special case, marginal revenue equals price. For example, if the firm produces plywood, and the market price of plywood is $200 per 1,000 square feet, the marginal revenue from each additional thousand square feet is $200. The owner of the firm would increase plywood production as long as the marginal cost of each additional thousand square feet is less than $200. It would not increase production if each additional thousand square feet costs more than $200 to produce.

Of course, as we mentioned above, we can also analyze profit maximization through the firm's choice of the level of input usage. Again the principle is simple and follows directly from the analysis in Chapter 3. The firm will expand its usage of any input (or factor of production) so long as additional units of the input add more to the firm's revenue than to cost. The firm would not increase the usage of the input if hiring more units increases the firm's cost more than its revenue. From the input side, profit maximization is, therefore, based upon the following principle:

Principle. *If an increase in the usage of an input in the production process adds more to revenue than to cost, the increase in input usage adds to profit. If the increase in usage of the input adds less to revenue than to cost, the increase in usage reduces profit. The firm, therefore, chooses the level of input usage at which the additional revenue per unit change in the input—called marginal revenue product (MRP)— equals the additional cost per unit of the input added—called marginal factor cost (MFC).*

Here, we are interested in the case in which the price of the input is given to the firm by the market. In this case the input's marginal factor cost is the market-determined price of the input. For example, suppose that a manufacturing firm can hire all of the labor it wishes at $10 an hour or $80 a day. The firm would increase labor usage so long as it expects each additional laborer hired to add more than $80 a day to the firm's revenue. It would not increase the number of laborers hired if an additional laborer would add less than $80 a day to revenues. It would follow the same procedure when hiring all other inputs. The marginal revenue product of each must equal its price. In this way profit is maximized.

Let us stress that the term *profit* means return over and above all costs, including implicit costs. Recall from Chapter 10 that implicit costs are included in total cost. Therefore, if the owner manages the firm, the wages that would be paid to an equally qualified manager must be included as a cost of operation. Or, suppose that the owner has invested personal resources in purchasing the capital used in the firm's production process. The return that could be earned elsewhere from the use of the capital is an opportunity cost and is an implicit cost to the firm.

Economists frequently refer to the opportunity cost of using the owner's capital as a "normal return." Any return over and above the "normal" return is called "pure profit" or "economic profit." To illustrate, suppose the owner has $1 million invested in the firm. Suppose also that the normal return in the economy is 6 percent per year. If the firm earns 10 percent per year, the normal profit, included in cost, is 6 percent; the pure or economic profit is the additional 4 percent return. In this text, when we use the term *profit,* we mean pure or economic profit; that is, profit over and above the normal return on the owner's resources.

12.2 CHARACTERISTICS OF PERFECT COMPETITION

Perfect competition forms the basis of one of the most important and widely used models of economic behavior. The essence of perfect competition is that neither buyers nor producers recognize any competitiveness among themselves; that is, no direct competition among economic agents exists.

Thus, the theoretical concept of competition is diametrically opposed to the generally accepted concept of "competition." One might maintain that the automobile industry or the cigarette industry is quite competitive, since each firm in these industries must consider what its rivals will do before it makes a decision about advertising campaigns, design changes, quality improvements, and so forth. However, that type of market is far removed from the theory of perfect competition, which permits no personal rivalry. ("Personal" rivalry is personal in the sense that firms consider the reactions of other firms in determining their own policy.) In perfect competition all relevant economic magnitudes are determined by impersonal market forces.

Several important conditions define perfect competition:

1. The product of each firm in a perfectly competitive market must be identical to the product of every other firm. This condition ensures that buyers are indifferent as to the firm from which they purchase. Product differences, whether real or imaginary, are precluded under perfect competition. Thus, the market is characterized by a homogeneous (or perfectly standardized) commodity.

2. Each firm in the industry must be so small relative to the total market that it cannot affect the market price of the good it produces by changing its output. If all producers act together, changes in quantity will definitely affect market price. But, if perfect competition prevails, each producer is so small that individual changes will go unnoticed. Neither is any individual firm able to affect the price of any input by its usage of that input.

Again all producers could, under certain conditions, change their usage of an input and affect its price. In other words, the actions of any individual firm do not affect the market supply of the product produced or the market demand for any input.

3. There exists unrestricted entry into and exit from the industry. Hence there can be no artificial restrictions on the number of firms in the industry.

4. Each firm has full and complete knowledge about the product and the market. Thus each firm knows the best—least cost—method of production, the price of the output, and input prices. Even potential entrants not in the market know whether or not firms in the industry are making economic profits.

The model can be summarized by the following:

Characteristics. Perfect competition is an economic model of a market possessing the following characteristics: each economic agent is so small relative to the market that it can exert no perceptible influence on product or input prices; the product is homogeneous; there is unrestricted and easy entry and exit of business firms into and out of the industry; and each firm has perfect knowledge.

APPLICATION

Financial Markets as [Super] Competitive Markets

Of all the markets we are familiar with, none is more competitive than the financial markets—the stock markets, the markets for foreign exchange, the bond markets, and so on. Consider the characteristics listed above:

Homogeneous Product   The assets traded on financial markets are as homogeneous as products can be. The share of GM stock sold by one brokerage house is identical to that sold by another.

Individual Traders Small Relative to the Market   While one trader may hold a large percentage of the shares of a particular firm (T. Boone Pickens and Carl Ichan come to mind), the holdings of an individual trader relative to the total market are still small.

Unrestricted Entry and Exit   In the financial markets, entry occurs on the demand side. (The supply of GM stock is effectively fixed, and it is the demand for GM stock that determines its price.) And there are no barriers to entry. It is an easy matter to enter the market and buy or sell the financial assets. Indeed, in the financial markets, you can even sell securities you don't own—sell short—if you believe the price is too high.

In addition to these characteristics, the financial markets have special features that make them more than simply competitive:

A Centralized Marketplace   While the traders need not travel any further than the computers on their desk tops, there is one central marketplace, rather than several smaller markets. Hence, every buyer has access to every seller, and vice versa.

Widespread Information   There are well-established institutions for collecting and distributing information; for example, *The Wall Street Journal,* the S&P Manuals, Moody's Bond Rating Service, Value Line, and the Dow Jones Broad Tape. Indeed, these markets come about as close to perfect knowledge as markets are going to get.

No Constraints on Rapid Price Adjustment   If the market participants in the financial markets determine that the price is too high, it will change immediately. There are no long-term contracts that tend to constrain the adjustment of price.

12.3 THE DEMAND CURVE FACING AN INDIVIDUAL FIRM

The marginal revenue of a perfectly competitive firm is the market-determined price of the product it produces and sells. Each firm believes that it can sell all it wishes at the prevailing market price. Thus, the marginal revenue curve is a horizontal line at the market-determined price. This horizontal marginal revenue curve is also the demand facing the firm—demand is said to be perfectly elastic. This condition does not contradict the fact that the demand for the output of the *industry* is negatively sloped. Certainly the law of demand holds in that case.

A perfectly competitive firm faces a horizontal demand because of two of the conditions that must exist in a perfectly competitive market. First, each firm in the industry produces a homogeneous product. Therefore, the product of any firm in the industry is a perfect substitute for the product of every other firm. Second, each firm is small relative to the size of the total market for the product. Thus, no firm acting alone can affect market price and each firm takes the market price, set by total industry supply and demand, as given.

Any firm can sell all it wants at the going market price. For example, if the market price of the product is $10 per unit, the marginal revenue from each additional unit sold is $10. So the marginal revenue curve and hence the demand curve is a horizontal line at $10. Such a curve is shown in Figure 12.1, where marginal revenue equals the price, $10, at any relevant output.

Figure 12.1 **Marginal Revenue-Demand Facing a Perfectly Competitive Firm**

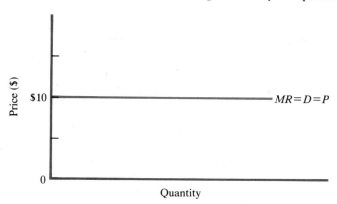

The firm would have no reason to charge any higher or any lower price. Since it can sell all it wants at $10, there would be no reason to lower the price. If the firm raised its price, the availability of perfect substitutes from other firms at $10 means it could sell nothing at the higher price.

Figure 12.2 illustrates the relation between the individual firm's demand and the market-determined price. Panel A shows equilibrium in the market. Supply and demand have the "typically" assumed shapes. Equilibrium price is p_0 and quantity demanded and supplied is q_0. The marginal revenue, and hence demand, for any firm in this perfectly competitive industry is shown in Panel B. Each producer knows that changes in the firm's output will have no perceptible effect upon market price. A change in the rate of sales per period of time will change the firm's revenue, but it will not affect market price.

The producer in a perfectly competitive market, therefore, does not have to reduce price in order to expand the rate of sales. Any number of units (per period of time) can be sold at the market equilibrium price.

Relation. The demand curve facing a producer in a perfectly competitive market is a horizontal line at the level of the market equilibrium price. The output decisions of the individual seller do not affect market price. In this case, the demand and marginal revenue curves are identical (i.e., D = MR). Demand is perfectly elastic and the coefficient of price elasticity approaches infinity.

12.4 PROFIT MAXIMIZATION IN THE SHORT RUN

Let us turn now to the output decision of a competitive firm in the short run. Recall from Chapter 10 that, in the short run, the firm has two types of costs—fixed costs, a fixed amount that must be paid regardless of output, and variable costs, which vary with the level of output. In the

Figure 12.2 Derivation of Demand for a Perfectly Competitive Firm

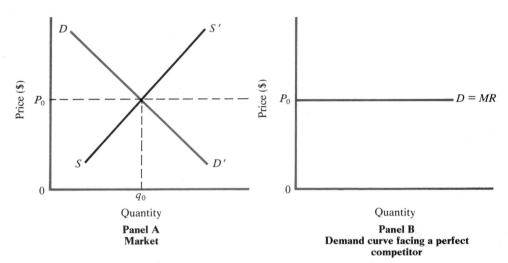

Panel A
Market

Panel B
Demand curve facing a perfect
competitor

short run, the firm must make two decisions. The first decision is whether to produce or to shut down (produce zero output). If the first decision is to produce, the second decision concerns the proper level of output. (As we noted earlier, the firm has no control over price, which is determined in the market, so the individual firm does not have a pricing decision.)

Once the decision to produce is made, the output decision is straightforward. The firm wishes to increase its output as long as the marginal revenue from another unit sold (price) exceeds the marginal cost of producing that unit. Suppose that the firm is producing 200 units of output which it can sell at a price of $100 per unit and the marginal cost of unit 201 is $80. Thus selling unit 201 would add $100 to revenue, but it would add only $80 to cost, so profit would increase by $20. And the firm would increase profit by increasing output over the entire range of output at which *MR* is greater than *MC*.

If, on the other hand, the firm has made a mistake and is producing an output at which price (marginal revenue) is less than marginal cost, it can increase its profit by reducing output. For example, suppose that the marginal cost of producing unit 401 is $130, while the price is still $100. The firm could decrease its output by one unit and reduce its cost by $130. The lost sale of that unit would reduce revenue by $100. So the firm's profit would increase $30. And it would continue to reduce output as long as *MC* is greater than price (*MR*). Thus the firm would maximize its profit by producing and selling the output at which marginal cost equals price (*MR*).

We obviously don't mean to imply that the firm begins with zero output then expands by actually producing and selling the first unit, then the second, and so on until it produces and sells that last unit, at which *MR*

Figure 12.3 **Short-Run Equilibrium**

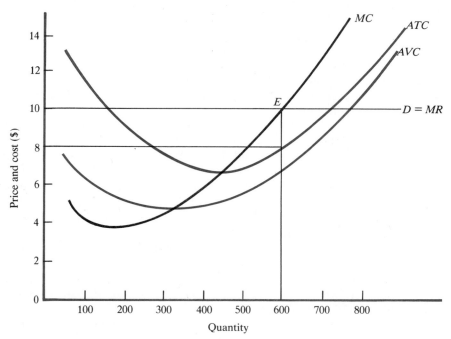

equals *MC*. The firm makes its short-run production decision after it looks at its price and cost structure. It then chooses the optimal level of output and produces it.

This situation is illustrated graphically in Figure 12.3. In this figure we have a typical set of short-run cost curves—marginal cost (*MC*), average total cost (*ATC*), and average variable cost (*AVC*). (Average fixed cost is omitted for convenience and because it is irrelevant for the output decision.) Suppose that the market-determined price, and therefore the marginal revenue, is $10 per unit. Marginal revenue equals marginal cost at point *E,* with 600 units of output being produced and sold.

The firm would not produce less than 600 units. At any lower output, an additional unit sold would add $10 to the firm's revenue, but, since marginal cost is less than $10 for this unit of output, the cost of producing this additional unit is less than the additional revenue. Thus, at any output lower than 600 units, producing and selling an additional unit of output would increase profit. Likewise, the firm would not produce more than 600 units. Beyond 600 units, a reduction in output would increase profit because one less unit of output would reduce cost by more than $10, the lost revenue. Thus producing any output less than or greater than 600 units is not profit maximizing.

Therefore the firm maximizes profit by producing and selling 600 units of output per period of time. From the figure, we can see that the average total cost of producing 600 units is $8 per unit. Thus the total cost of production is average total cost times quantity or $8 × 600 = $4,800. Total revenue, price times quantity, is $10 × 600 = $6,000. The maximum possible profit is therefore $6,000 − $4,800 = $1,200.

Looking at Figure 12.3, suppose that the market price is higher than $10. The demand facing the firm would rise and the profit-maximizing level of output would also rise. If price is higher, the firm will produce a greater output. Conversely, if price is lower, the firm will produce a lower output. It follows then that output varies directly with price. For example, if price is $12, the firm would produce almost 700 units; if price is $8, it would produce slightly more than 500 units.

The equality of price and short-run marginal cost guarantees either that profit is a maximum or that loss is a minimum. Whether a profit is made or a loss incurred can be determined only by comparing price and average total cost at the equilibrium rate of output. If price exceeds unit cost, the firm enjoys a short-run profit. On the other hand, if unit cost exceeds price, a loss is suffered.

Figure 12.4 illustrates four possible short-run situations for the firm. First, if the market-established price is p_1, the demand and marginal revenue facing the firm are D_1 and MR_1. The optimal point for the firm is at point A, where $MC = p_1$, and the firm will produce q_1 units of output. Since ATC is less than price, the firm makes a profit.

Next let the market price fall to p_2. MC now equals price at point B; the firm produces q_2. Since B is the lowest point on ATC, price just equals average total cost, and the firm makes neither a profit nor a loss. It does cover its opportunity cost, which is included in ATC.

If price falls further to p_3, the firm produces q_3. Price equals MC at point C. Because average total cost is greater than price at this output, total cost is greater than total revenue, and the firm suffers a loss. The amount of loss is the loss per unit (CR) times the number of units produced (q_3).

When price is p_3 and demand is $D_3 = MR_3$, there is simply no way the firm can earn a profit. At every output level, average total cost exceeds price. The firm will continue to produce if, and only if, it loses less by producing than by closing the plant entirely. Recall that there are two types of costs in the short run: fixed costs and variable costs. The fixed costs cannot be changed and are incurred whether the plant is operating or not. Fixed costs are unavoidable in the short run and are the same at zero output as at any other.

If the firm produced zero output, total revenue would also be zero and total cost would be the total fixed cost. The loss would thus be equal to total fixed cost. If the firm can produce where $MC = MR$ and if at this output total revenue is greater than total variable cost, a smaller loss is suffered when production takes place than if the firm were shut down. The firm covers all of its variable cost and some revenue is left over to cover a part of fixed cost. The loss is that part of fixed cost not covered and is clearly less than the entire fixed cost.

Figure 12.4 Profit, Loss, or Ceasing Production in the Short Run

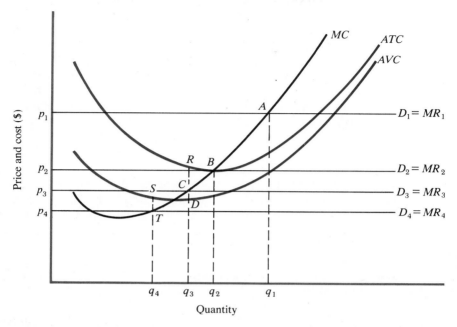

Returning to Figure 12.4 you can see more easily why if price is p_3 the firm in the short run would produce at C and not shut down. The firm loses CR dollars per unit produced. However, not only are all variable costs covered but there is an excess of CD dollars per unit sold. The excess of price over average variable cost, CD, can be applied to fixed costs. Thus, not all of the fixed costs are lost, as would be the case if production were discontinued. The amount CD times q_3 can be applied to fixed costs. Although a loss is sustained, it is smaller than the loss associated with zero output.

To be sure, the firm would not and could not go on for a very long time suffering a loss in each period. In the long run, the firm would leave the industry if it could not cover total costs. However, we shall postpone long-run analysis until we complete our discussion of the short run.

Finally, in Figure 12.4, suppose that the market price is p_4. Demand is given by $D_4 = MR_4$. If the firm were to produce, its equilibrium would be at T where $MC = p_4$. Output would be q_4 units per period of time. However, since the average variable cost of production exceeds price, not only would the firm lose all of its fixed costs, it would also lose ST dollars per unit on its variable costs as well. The firm could improve its earnings situation by producing nothing and losing only fixed cost. Thus when price is below average variable cost at every level of output, the short-run, loss-minimizing output is zero.

As shown in Chapter 10, average variable cost reaches its minimum at the point at which marginal cost and average variable cost intersect. If price is less than the minimum average variable cost, the loss-minimizing output is zero. For any price equal to or greater than minimum average variable cost, equilibrium output is determined by the intersection of marginal cost and price.[1]

Principles.   (1) Average variable cost tells whether to produce; the firm ceases to produce—shuts down—if price falls below minimum AVC. *(2) Marginal cost tells how much to produce; if* P > *minimum* AVC, *the firm produces the output at which* MC = P. *(3) Average total cost tells how much profit or loss is made if the firm decides to produce; profit equals the difference between* P *and* ATC *multiplied by the quantity produced and sold.*

From the preceding discussion you probably have seen that the short-run marginal cost curve above the intersection with average variable cost is the firm's short-run supply curve. That is, marginal cost above average variable cost indicates the quantity the firm would be willing and able to supply at each price in a list of prices per period of time, which is the definition of supply. For market prices lower than minimum average variable cost, quantity supplied is zero.

In contrast to market demand curves of consumers, described in Chapter 6, the industry supply curve cannot always be obtained by simply summing (horizontally) the marginal cost curves of each producer. The reason is that the short-run supply curve for each firm is derived assuming that the prices of variable inputs are given. No change in input usage by an individual firm acting alone can change an input's unit cost to the firm, because a single competitive firm is so small, relative to all users of the resource. But if all producers in an industry were to simultaneously expand output and thereby their usage of inputs, there may be marked effects in resource markets. When all firms attempt to increase output, the prices of some variable inputs may be bid up and the increase in these input prices causes an increase in all firms' cost curves, including marginal cost. As a consequence, the industry's short-run supply curve usually is somewhat more steeply sloped and somewhat less elastic when input prices increase in response to an increase in industry output than when input prices remain constant (as would be the presumption if we simply summed the marginal cost curves). In any case, in the short run quantity supplied by the industry does vary directly with price.

Any change that shifts the firm's marginal cost curve shifts the firm's supply curve and hence the industry's supply curve. For example, an increase in the wage rate would increase (shift upward) each firm's marginal cost curve, since labor is probably a variable input. With the higher wage the marginal cost of producing each additional unit of output would rise, so each firm would supply less at each price of the product.

---

[1]This will be demonstrated mathematically in the appendix to this chapter.

We can summarize the theory of the competitive firm in the short run as follows: In the short run, some costs are fixed regardless of the level of production. The firm will produce in the short run so long as the price is high enough that it can cover all of its variable cost and at least some portion of its fixed cost. For the individual firm, market price is equal to marginal revenue because each unit sold adds an amount equal to the market price to the firm's revenue. Equilibrium output is that at which marginal revenue equals marginal cost. The firm's short-run supply curve is its marginal cost above average variable cost.

If price equals marginal cost above average total cost, a pure economic profit is earned. Profit is price minus *ATC* times output. If price equals marginal cost between *ATC* and *AVC,* the loss to the firm is *ATC* minus price times output. If price falls below minimum *AVC,* the firm produces nothing and loses all of its fixed cost.

THE WALL STREET JOURNAL

APPLICATION

Insurance and Litigation Expenses: A Different Type of Production Cost

The Wall Street Journal, May 5, 1986, reported that the rising cost of lawsuits was disrupting the economy.* More and more consumers were suing more and more producers and receiving higher and higher awards. Over the past decade paid claims and defense costs had risen from under 1.4 percent of total gross national product to almost 1.8 percent, an increase of almost 30 percent. One analyst estimated that liability costs rose 61 percent from 1980 to 1986.

The Chief Justice of the Supreme Court, Warren Burger, said litigation has become "too costly, too painful, and too inefficient." There was certainly evidence of a dramatic increase in tort cases—cases of injury or damage to persons or property over which one can file a civil suit. Product liability cases had increased 370 percent from 2,886 to 13,554. All tort cases had increased 62 percent.

Some lawyers pointed to changing legal theories that expanded liability and drove up insurance premiums. For example, a victim's negligence no longer prevented the recovery of damages. Cases once thought of as frivolous were now permitted. Three states allowed people to sue for emotional injury allegedly caused by the mere witnessing of a car accident. And the awards were becoming higher and higher.

Continued on page 362

*"The Costs of Lawsuits, Growing Ever Larger, Disrupts the Economy," by Stephen Wermiel, *The Wall Street Journal,* May 15, 1986. Adapted by permission of *The Wall Street Journal.* © Dow Jones and Company, Inc., 1986. All rights reserved.

THE WALL STREET JOURNAL

APPLICATION

Continued from page 361

All of this clearly drove up the insurance rates firms had to pay. More litigation and higher settlements raised the risk the insurance companies had to take when they insured a client against such claims. This in turn increased the costs of insurance companies. They wanted to supply less insurance at each rate. Thus insurance rates were driven up.

The higher insurance rates increased the costs of firms that would be liable to lawsuits, and, according to the *Journal,* this was a large segment of the business and even the public sector. Hotel rates were increased because of the increased cost of liability insurance. A director of the Philadelphia transit system, wanting to raise the fare from $1 to $1.25, said that 22 cents of each fare, up from 14 cents, would go to defending claims and paying insurance premiums. Almost one tenth of the members of the American College of Obstetricians and Gynecologists had stopped delivering babies because of the malpractice threat. The insurance premiums of many obstetricians had doubled or tripled over two

Continued on page 363

"Business is OK but I'm gonna have to shut down. I can't get any insurance!"

From *The Wall Street Journal,* with permission of Cartoon Features Syndicate.

APPLICATION

Continued from page 362
years. And the same thing was happening in many manufacturing industries. The above cartoon shows one typical small business that was affected.

Anytime prices go up, people look for someone to blame. This time was no exception. Some were blaming the lawyers; others blamed the insurance companies; still others blamed those who sued for damages. A Washington, D.C., lawyer and former law professor went so far as to say, "Consumers don't realize that when they sue the 'deep pockets,' who can afford to pay, they're picking their own pockets."

Now we know this can't be the case. Certainly the increased number of lawsuits and the higher awards drove up the costs of insurance companies. Thus insurance rates were driven up, in turn increasing the costs of the

firms buying insurance. This increased cost then led to an increase in the prices paid by consumers. This is what our theory would predict. Consumers ultimately paid in the form of higher prices.

But the lawyer was wrong in blaming the consumers who sued for not realizing that they were "picking their own pockets." Just as no single firm in a competitive industry can affect product price by its own output, no single consumer can affect insurance rates by filing a suit against a producer. In this sense, consumers are like perfect competitors. They maximize subject to the constraint that they have no effect on any prices. It was all consumers acting together that increased the number of cases and caused prices to rise. This is different from the conclusion that individuals were to blame.

12.5 PROFIT MAXIMIZATION IN THE LONG RUN

In the short run the firm is limited by past decisions, i.e., its fixed costs. In the long run all inputs are variable; the firm is not bound by the past. The long run may be viewed as the planning stage, prior to the firm's entry into the industry. In this stage the firm is trying to decide how large a production facility to construct, i.e., the optimal amount of fixed cost. Or, if a firm is operating in the short run at a scale such that it is not obtaining maximum possible profits, the long run is the period of time necessary for the firm to readjust its scale. Once the plans have congealed, the firm operates in a short-run situation again. It operates in the short run until it makes another long-run change in the scale of operation.

In the long run, just as in the short run, the firm attempts to maximize profits. We use exactly the same approach, except in this case there are no fixed costs; all costs are variable. As before, the firm takes a market-determined price as given. This market price is again the firm's marginal revenue. As in the preceding section, the firm would increase output as long as the marginal revenue from each additional unit is greater than the marginal cost of that unit. It would contract output when marginal cost exceeds marginal revenue. The firm will maximize profit by equating marginal cost and marginal revenue.

Profit-Maximizing Equilibrium

Suppose that an entrepreneur is considering entering ·a competitive industry in which the firms already in the industry are making economic profits. The prospective entrant, knowing the long-run costs and the product price, expects to make an economic profit also. Since all inputs are variable, the entrant can choose the scale or plant size for the new firm. Let's examine the decision graphically.

In Figure 12.5, *LAC* and *LMC* are the long-run average and marginal cost curves. The demand curve (*D*) indicates the equilibrium market price (p_0) and is equal to marginal revenue. As long as price is greater than long-run average cost, the firm can make a profit. Thus any output between q_0 and q_1 yields some profits. These levels of output are sometimes called break-even points.

Maximum profit occurs at point *S* where marginal revenue equals long-run marginal cost. The firm would want to select the plant size to produce q_m units of output. Note that the firm would not, under these circumstances, try to produce at point *M,* the minimum point of long-run average cost. At *M,* marginal revenue exceeds marginal cost, so the firm can gain by producing more output. In Figure 12.5 total revenue (price times quantity) is given by the area of the rectangle Op_0Sq_m. The total cost (average cost times quantity) is the area Oc_0Rq_m. The potential total profit is the shaded area c_0p_0SR.

Thus the firm would plan to operate at a scale (or plant size) such that long-run marginal cost equals price. This would be the most profitable situation under the circumstances. But, as we shall see, these circumstances will change. If the prospective firm in Figure 12.5 is free to enter the industry, so are other prospective entrants. And this entry will drive down the market price. Let's see how this will happen.

Long-Run Competitive Equilibrium

If firms in a competitive industry are making above-normal returns (i.e., pure profit), there is strong reason to believe that the market price will fall. Profits attract new firms into the industry and the new firms will

Figure 12.5   Profit Maximization in the Long Run

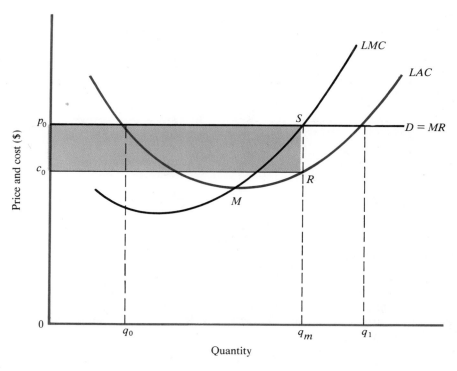

increase industry supply. This increased supply drives down price. In fact, price may even be driven below long-run average cost and cause temporary losses. But if losses occur, some firms would leave the industry, thereby reducing supply and driving up price. As we shall show, unrestricted entry and exit will result in a long-run equilibrium at which each firm produces at the minimum point on its long-run average cost curve. All pure profits are eliminated, and only a normal rate of return is earned.

The adjustment process is shown in Figure 12.6. In Panel A, DD' is the market demand for the product and S_1S_1' is the original market supply with a given number of firms in the industry.[2] Suppose that all firms are alike and have identical cost curves as illustrated by those shown in Panel B. Demand and supply in the market result in a market price of p_1. Taking this price as given, each firm produces q_1 and makes a pure profit.

---

[2]We ignore for now the problem that firms would exit if price falls below minimum average cost, and assume the firm's supply curve is its marginal cost. We could simply let this supply be marginal cost above average cost. We will assume for now that the industry's usage of any input does not affect the price of that input. S_1S_1' is therefore the horizontal summation of the long-run marginal cost curves of all firms in the industry at the time.

Figure 12.6 Long-Run Equilibrium Adjustment in a Perfectly Competitive Industry

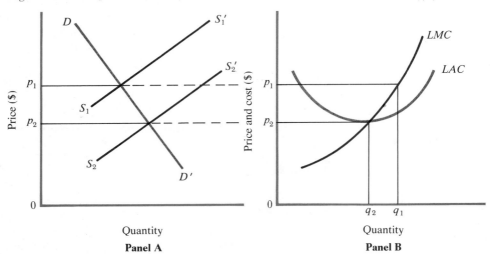

Panel A   Panel B

This profit induces entry, which causes supply to increase as more firms enter the industry, thereby driving down price in the market. Entry will continue as long as firms are earning economic profit, and price will continue to decline. In other words, entry will continue until supply increases to $S_2 S_2'$ and price falls to p_2. At this price each firm will produce q_2. Price will equal long-run average cost at its minimum point (where $LAC = LMC$). Each firm covers all of its costs, including implicit costs, but no firm makes an economic profit. This situation is called long-run competitive equilibrium.

Definition. In long-run competitive equilibrium, price equals long-run marginal cost, which equals long-run average cost at its minimum point. No firm makes an economic profit.

If too many firms enter and price falls below each firm's long-run average cost, the opposite situation occurs. All firms make losses and exit occurs. As firms exit, supply decreases and price increases. Exit would continue until supply rises to $S_2 S_2'$ and price to p_2. The same equilibrium results and all losses are competed away. Each firm is in long-run competitive equilibrium.

The long-run equilibrium is summarized in Figure 12.7. The point of long-run equilibrium occurs at point E in this figure. Each firm in the industry makes neither economic profit nor loss. Each firm is earning a normal return. There is no incentive for further entry because the rate of return in this industry is the same as in the best alternative. For the same reason, there is no incentive for a firm to leave the industry. The number of firms stabilizes, each firm operating with a plant size represented by *SAC* and *SMC*.

Figure 12.7 Long-Run Equilibrium for a Firm in a Perfectly Competitive Industry

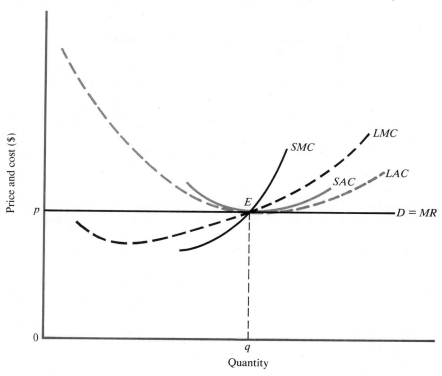

We should note in closing this section that the assumption that all firms have identical cost curves is not necessary for obtaining long-run competitive equilibrium in which no firm is making an economic profit. The cost curves can differ because of different productivity of some resources, and an identical equilibrium will occur.

THE WALL STREET JOURNAL

APPLICATION

How Profits Get Competed Away: The Miniwarehouse Industry

Miniwarehouses rent out small storage spaces, usually to individuals and small businesses.

The renters do their own moving, so each warehouse usually needs only one employee, a resident caretaker.

Continued on page 368

THE WALL STREET JOURNAL

APPLICATION

Continued from page 367

The business began in the 1960s in the Southwest, where people move frequently between apartments or houses without attics or basements. By 1986, there were between 12,000 and 20,000 miniwarehouses in the United States.

On June 6, 1986, *The Wall Street Journal* reported, "When it comes to locking up profits, miniwarehouses have been a good place to put investment dollars. In recent years, annual pretax returns have often reached 20 percent. Losses have been infrequent."* The *WSJ* went on to point out, "Their opportunities are likely to grow even more. But that may not be good news. Profits are growing slimmer for the industry, and potential pitfalls more numerous." The director of the industry trade group noted that it was not an easy business to make money in anymore, nor was there an assured return any longer.

At the same time the industry was undergoing a change in the ownership structure. Larger chains or syndicators were buying or building large numbers of miniwarehouses, then selling shares of the partnerships to relatively small investors. The *WSJ* said, "The industry may be in the midst of a fundamental change, from isolated mom-and-pop operations to centrally managed chains."

It went on to note that the development of the chains makes it easier to invest in the warehouses, although as the number of warehouses has grown so has the prospect of market saturation. Oklahoma City, Houston, and Dallas, all in the Southwest, were already overbuilt. So were Denver, Orange County, California, and other areas.

In other words, the miniwarehouse industry was moving toward long-run competitive equilibrium. The economic profits were being competed away by an increased number of firms. And in many places these profits had already been competed away.

This example shows that even if an industry does not meet all of the assumptions of perfect competition, the theory explains industry behavior. Certainly the assumption of perfect knowledge was not met. Since the warehouses differed in their location, the product, or in this case the service, was not identical for all firms. But unrestricted entry, led to the elimination of economic profit in the long run.

*Frederick Rose, "Room to Profit? Storage Spaces Lure Investors," *The Wall Street Journal*, June 6, 1986. Adapted by permission of *The Wall Street Journal*. © Dow Jones & Company, Inc., 1986. All rights reserved.

12.6 PROFIT-MAXIMIZING INPUT USAGE

Thus far, we have analyzed the firm's profit-maximizing decision in terms of the output decision. But, as noted in the introduction, we can also consider profit maximization from the input side. Of course, when we determine the profit-maximizing level of output, we implicitly have determined the input usage of the firm. Recall from Chapter 10 that the cost function is directly related to the production function. Thus, when we determine a unique profit-maximizing level of output, we also determine the quantity of each input that is used in the production process.

But, it is possible to determine a profit-maximizing equilibrium directly from the input decision. In this way, we are able to develop the firm's demand for factors of production.

Value of Marginal Product

Recall that in the introduction to this chapter we argued that the firm would increase its usage of an input so long as the addition to total revenue per unit of the input, which we called marginal revenue product, exceeds the price of the input. The firm would decrease input usage if its price is greater than its marginal revenue product.

For a perfectly competitive firm the marginal revenue product of an input is called the value of marginal product, defined as follows:

Definition. The value of marginal product (VMP) of a factor of production is the additional revenue that one additional unit of the input contributes to the firm. For a competitive firm, VMP is therefore the price of the output produced times the marginal product of the input.

For example, if one additional unit of an input, say labor, has a marginal product of 10 and the price of the product being produced is $5, the value of marginal product for that input is $50.

As we showed in Chapter 9, the "typical" marginal product curve first increases, reaches a maximum, then declines thereafter. Therefore, the *VMP* curve, which is simply price times marginal product, also rises then declines. At the level of input usage at which marginal product becomes negative, the value of marginal product becomes negative also. Since an input's marginal product depends upon the usage of the other inputs, the value of marginal product also changes when the quantities of other inputs change.

A "typical" *VMP* schedule for a single variable input is given in Table 12.1, assuming that the price of the product is $10. This schedule shows the value of marginal product first rising, reaching a maximum, then declining and becoming negative at 9 units of the input. If the price of the product increases, *VMP* will increase for each level of input usage. If the price of the product falls, *VMP* falls also.

Table 12.1 VMP Schedule (price = $10)

Units of Variable Input	Output	Marginal Product	Value of Marginal Product
1	20	20	$200
2	50	30	300
3	90	40	400
4	120	30	300
5	138	18	180
6	150	12	120
7	155	5	50
8	158	3	30
9	154	−4	−40

VMP and the Hiring Decision

As would be expected from our previous discussion, the quantity of an input the firm will hire depends on the marginal benefit and the marginal cost of the input. The marginal benefit is the value of marginal product—the addition to total revenue. The marginal cost is the amount that must be paid to hire another unit of the input—the addition to total cost. If the *VMP* of an additional unit of the input is greater than the price of the input, the firm will increase its usage of that input. If the *VMP* of the last unit hired is less than the price of the input, the firm will decrease its usage of the input.

Suppose that labor is the input whose *VMP* schedule is shown in Table 12.1. If the wage rate of labor is $100 per period, each additional unit of labor hired up to the sixth adds more to revenue than it adds to cost. Each unit after the sixth adds less than the wage rate to revenue. Thus, with the given *VMP* schedule and wage, the firm will hire six units of labor.

If the firm is hiring only five units, it could add the sixth unit of labor and revenue would rise by $120 while cost would increase by $100; thus profit would increase $20. If the firm makes a mistake and hires the seventh, it should increase profit by reducing labor usage by one unit: eliminating the seventh worker would decrease revenue $50 as cost falls $100; profit would increase $50. Thus we have the following principle:

Principle. If the **VMP** *of an additional unit of a variable input is greater than the price of that input, that unit will be hired. If the* **VMP** *of an additional unit adds less than its price, that unit will not be hired. If the usage of the variable input varies continuously, the firm will employ the amount of the input at which*

VMP = Input price.

This general rule for a continuously variable input is illustrated graphically in Figure 12.8. In this example, labor is the only variable input. If

Figure 12.8 **A Competitive Firm's Demand for Labor**

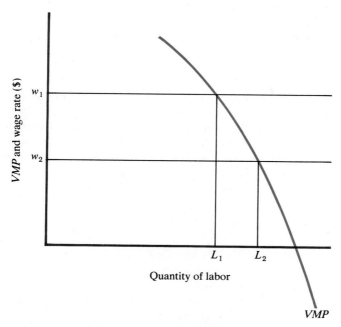

the wage rate is w_1, the firm would wish to hire L_1 units of labor. The firm would not stop short of L_1, because up to employment level L_1 an additional unit of labor would add more to revenue than to cost. It would not hire more than L_1, because beyond L_1 the added cost would exceed the added revenue. If the wage rate falls to w_2, the firm would increase its labor usage to L_2 units.[3] Hence, if labor is the firm's only variable input, the firm will maximize profit or minimize loss by employing the amount of labor for which the value of the marginal product of labor equals the wage rate:

$$VMP_L = w.$$

This result holds for any variable input.

This result is equivalent to the condition that the profit-maximizing, perfectly competitive firm will produce the level of output at which $P = MC$. Recall from Chapter 10 that

$$MC = \frac{w}{MP_L}.$$

---

[3]Note that we did not include the upward-sloping portion of the *VMP* curve, because this segment is not relevant to the hiring decision. If the wage equals *VMP* and *VMP* is increasing, the firm could hire additional units, and the value of the marginal product of these added inputs would be greater than the wage. Thus this would not be a profit-maximizing decision.

Thus the optimizing condition when one input is variable is

$$P = MC = \frac{w}{MP_L},$$

or

$$P \cdot MP_L = VMP_L = w.$$

Thus, $VMP = w$ is equivalent to $P = MC$ when only one input is variable.

We can also define the relevant range over which the use of the variable input could vary. Clearly the firm would never hire labor beyond the point at which VMP is negative. Furthermore, the firm would hire no labor if, at the point where $VMP = w$, average product is less than marginal product. If $AP < MP$, the value of the average product is less than the value of the marginal product, which is equal to the wage rate;

$$VAP = P \cdot \frac{Q}{L} < VMP = w.$$

Thus the total revenue ($P \cdot Q$) is less than the total cost of labor ($w \cdot L$). In terms of our previous analysis, price would be less than average variable cost, and the firm would shut down.[4]

The demand for a single variable input by the competitive firm is the positive portion of the VMP curve over the range of input usage over which AP is greater than MP. This portion of VMP gives the quantity of the variable input that will be hired at each price of the input.

When there is more than one variable input, the firm's demand function for a particular input is slightly different. For example, if the quantities of other inputs are also variable, when wages fall from w_1 to w_2 in Figure 12.8, the firm will use more labor but it may use more or less of the other variable inputs. For this reason, the VMP curve of labor may shift—either outward or inward. Thus, the firm may use more than or less than L_2 units of labor at wage w_2, but not less than L_1. The firm's demand for any variable imput is negatively sloped.

Nevertheless, two things are certain: (1) the firm will hire more labor when the wage falls, and (2) it will hire labor up to quantity at which the wage equals the value of marginal product, even though VMP may shift. Thus, for every variable input, the firm will hire the quantity of the input at which its VMP equals its price. If, for example, the firm has two variable inputs, denoted I and J, the firm will maximize profits by using both inputs at such levels that[5]

$$VMP_I = P_I$$
$$VMP_J = P_J.$$

---

[4]This result is demonstrated mathematically in the appendix to this chapter.

[5]It can be shown that when these results hold, the price of the output equals marginal cost.

Since the marginal product of either input shifts according to the level of usage of the other, these conditions must hold *simultaneously*.

Input Demand by a Competitive Industry

Any one competitive firm can vary its level of use of an input in response to a change in the input price and can therefore vary output without affecting the price of the commodity produced. However when all firms respond to a change in the price of an input by changing the level of usage of the input, commodity price (i.e., the price of their output) does change. Since each firm's demand for the input is derived holding commodity price constant, all firms' input demands shift when all firms change simultaneously.

To illustrate the process, we use labor as the variable input (although all of the following holds for any input). Let's suppose that a typical firm having only labor as a variable input is depicted in Figure 12.9, Panel A. At the existing market price of the commodity produced, d_1d_1' is the firm's demand curve for labor. If the market wage rate is w_1, the firm uses l_1 units of labor. Aggregating over all the firms in the industry, L_1 units of labor are employed. Thus, point A in Panel B is one point on the industry demand curve for labor.

Next, suppose that the price of labor declines to w_2. Other things equal, the individual firm would move along d_1d_1' to point b' and would employ l_2' units of labor. But, other things are *not* equal. When all firms expand their use of the input, total output expands. Stated differently, the market supply curve for the commodity shifts to the right because of the decline in the input's price. For a given commodity demand, commodity price must fall; when it does, the individual firm's demand curve for labor— the *VMP* curve—also falls.

In Panel A, the decline in individual input demand attributable to the decline in commodity price is represented by the shift leftward from d_1d_1' to d_2d_2'. At wage rate w_2, b is now the equilibrium point, with l_2 units employed. Aggregating for all employers, L_2 units of labor are used (point B is obtained in Panel B). Any number of points such as A and B can be generated by varying the market price of the input. Connecting these points, you can obtain DD', the industry demand for the input, which must be negatively sloped.

Thus the wage rate that firms in the industry must pay for any type of input is determined by supply and demand in the market for that input. The demand for the input is the industry's demand plus the demand or demands of all other industries using that input. Since each industry's demand is negatively sloped, the total demand for the input must be negatively sloped also.

The supply of the input in the market would be positively sloped. Since additional units of the input—say, some type of labor—must be bid away from other occupations, presumably a higher price must be paid to obtain

Figure 12.9 Derivation of the Industry Demand for a Variable Input

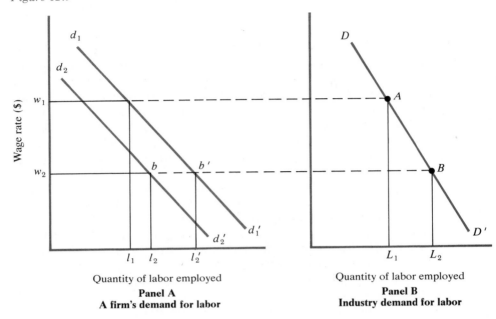

Panel A
A firm's demand for labor

Panel B
Industry demand for labor

additional units of the input in the market. For example, if the construction industry in a particular area wants to hire more electricians, the added electricians must be bid away from other areas—at a higher wage.

Demand and supply in the market, therefore, determine the wage rate that firms in the industry must pay. Anything that increases (decreases) the demand for the input must increase (decrease) the price that firms must pay for the input. To see this effect, let's look at the following application.

APPLICATION

Supply and Demand in High-Wage Labor Markets*

In our theoretical discussion of wage determination we used the example of labor markets. We do not want to give the impression that the theory applies solely to low-wage, relatively unskilled labor. The

*The information for this application is from "The New Dealmakers," *Newsweek,* May 26, 1986, pp. 47–52.

same type of analysis applies equally well to occupations paying extremely high salaries.

To see this, we look at what was happening to the salaries of investment bankers in 1986. According to *Newsweek*, ". . . investment bankers can move up faster and make more money than almost any other kind of businessman. They make money the new-fashioned way: they do deals."

And that was exactly why their salaries were rising so rapidly—Wall Street was making more deals. A wave of firm mergers and acquisitions was taking place in the United States, and the investment bankers were the ones putting together or organizing these deals. One transaction could bring in $10 million to the firm handling the merger or acquisition. The Wall Street firms wanted people who could handle the deals, but there were few people who had the training or experience for the job.

In other words, as the demand for people to carry out the "deals" increased, the fees for the brokerage firms and the productivity of the "dealers" increased also.† For these reasons the demand for investment bankers had increased dramatically.

And this increase in demand had the effect that we would expect. Experienced investment bankers were earning $1 million or more a year as were some who were not quite so experienced. The "superstars" earned over $3 million. The typical starting income for a new investment banker who had just graduated from one of the nation's top business schools was $80,000 a year, almost $10,000 a year higher than beginning management consultants and $30,000 higher than new stock and bond traders.

But the salaries had to be high to bid these new graduates away from other occupations, despite the glamour of investment banking. The typical work schedule for a recent graduate was over 70 hours a week, compared with 45 to 60 in most of the other popular job choices. More experienced bankers spoke of 80- to 100-hour weeks when putting together a deal. Clearly such a schedule allowed little time for family and leisure.

The huge salaries had the desired effect. The percentage of Harvard Business School graduates choosing investment banking rose from less than 10 percent in 1978 to over 25 percent in 1986. Over the same period those choosing manufacturing, other than high technology and electronics, fell from 30 percent to 15 percent.

---

†This is not quite productivity in the sense we have been using it; that is, producing a product. In fact, many observers were worried that the best young business graduates were being attracted to dealmaking, which, they said, contributed nothing to American industry and its ability to compete against foreign competition. Yet, in a sense, these people produced a service, which the brokerage firms were able to sell to others. Saying whether this was good or bad would simply be a value judgment.

Thus the market for high-wage employees behaves like the market for all types of labor. An increase in the demand for the product—in this case the increase in mergers and acquisitions—increased the demand for workers—investment bankers. This increase in demand increased salaries as firms bid among themselves for available employees. But as *Newsweek* pointed out, "investment banking won't be in fashion forever." Mergers come in waves, and the 1986 wave was tapering off. This would lead one to predict that the demand for investment bankers would level off and stop the rapid rise in salaries.

12.7 SUMMARY

Perfectly competitive markets exist when there are a large number of buyers and sellers, identical products, unrestricted entry and exit by producers, perfect knowledge, and prices freely determined by the interaction of supply and demand. In the short run, the firm produces the quantity at which short-run marginal cost equals price, so long as price exceeds average variable cost. Therefore, marginal cost above average variable cost is the firm's short-run supply curve. If all input prices are given to the industry, industry short-run supply is the horizontal summation of all marginal cost curves. If the industry's (although not the individual firm's) use of the inputs affects the prices of some inputs, industry supply is less elastic than this horizontal summation.

In the long run, the entry and exit of firms force each firm to produce at minimum *LAC*. That is, the firm will produce where $LAC = LMC = SAC = SMC$. Economic or pure profit is zero at this output. (Although each firm earns a normal profit.)

The salient feature of perfect competition is that, in long-run market equilibrium, market price equals minimum average cost. This means that each unit of output is produced at the lowest possible cost, either from the standpoint of money cost or of resource use. The product sells for its average (long-run) cost of production; each firm, accordingly, earns the going rate of return in competitive industries, nothing more or less.

It should be emphasized that firms do not choose to produce the quantity with the lowest possible long-run average cost simply because they believe this level of production is optimal for society and they wish to benefit society. The firms are merely trying to maximize their profits. Given that motivation, the market forces firms to produce at that point. If society benefits, it is not through any benevolence of firms, but through the functioning of the market.

Finally, no matter how many factors of production are variable, the firm hires each variable input so that the value of the marginal product of the input equals its price. If only one input is variable, the firm's demand for that input is its *VMP* curve.

It should be emphasized that the theory of perfect competition is not designed to describe specific real-world firms. It is a theoretical model that is frequently useful in explaining real-world behavior and in predicting the economic consequences of changes in the different variables contained in the model. The conclusions of the theory, not the assumptions, are the crucial points when analyzing economic problems.

TECHNICAL PROBLEMS

1. Consider the following cost curves for a perfectly competitive firm:

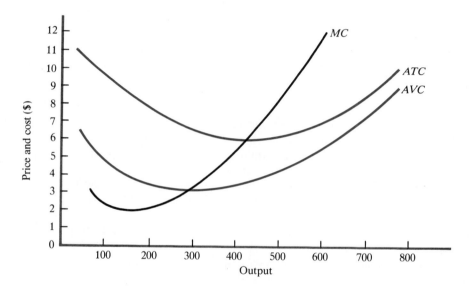

a. If price is $9 per unit of output, the firm should produce ___ units.

b. Since average total cost is $___ for this output, total cost is $___.

c. The firm makes a profit of $___.

d. Price falls to $5. The firm now produces ___ units.

e. Total revenue is now $___ and total cost is $___. The firm makes a loss of $___.

f. Total variable cost is $___, leaving $___ to apply to fixed cost.

g. If price falls below $___ the firm will produce zero output. Explain why.

2. Describe a position of long-run competitive equilibrium for a perfectly competitive firm and industry. How and why does such an equilibrium come about?

3. The following figure shows a perfectly competitive firm's short-run cost structure.

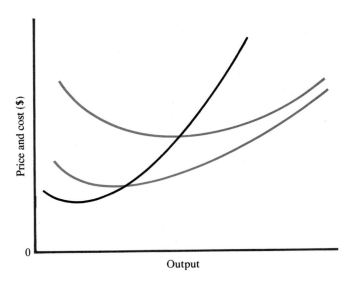

a. Label the three curves.
b. Show a price at which the firm would make a pure profit. Show the quantity it would produce and the amount of pure profit that would be earned.
c. Show a price at which the firm would continue to produce in the short run but would suffer losses. Show the output and losses at this price.
d. Show the price below which the firm would not produce in the short run.

4. Explain why the short-run supply curve of a perfectly competitive industry could be less elastic than the horizontal summation of the supply curves of all the firms in the industry.

5. The MidNight Hour, a local nightclub, earned $100,000 in accounting profit last year. This year the owner, who had invested $1 million in the club, decided to close the club. What can you say about economic profit (and the rate of return) in the nightclub business?

6. Firm A and Firm B both have total revenues of $100,000 and total fixed costs of $50,000; Firm A has total variable costs of $80,000, while Firm B has total variable costs of $110,000.
   a. How much profit or loss is each firm earning? Should Firm A operate or shut down? What about Firm B? Why?
   b. Firm C and Firm D both have total revenues of $200,000 and total costs of $250,000; Firm C has total fixed costs of $40,000, while Firm D has total fixed costs of $70,000. How much profit or loss is each firm earning? Should Firm C operate or shut down? What about Firm D? Why?

7. In a perfectly competitive industry the market price is $12. A firm is currently producing 50 units of output; average total cost is $10, marginal cost is $15, and average variable cost is $7.

   a. Draw a graph of the demand and cost conditions facing the firm and show where the firm is currently producing.

   b. Is the firm making the profit-maximizing decision? Why or why not? If not, what should the firm do?

   c. Answer (a) and (b) when market price is $25, the firm is producing 10,000 units of output, and average total cost, which is at its minimum value, is $25.

8. A typical firm in a perfectly competitive market made positive economic profits last period. What will happen this period to:

   a. The number of firms in the market.

   b. The market demand curve.

   c. The market supply curve.

   d. Market price.

   e. Market output.

   f. The firm's output.

   g. The firm's profit.

9. Suppose that a perfectly competitive industry is in long-run competitive equilibrium. Then the price of a substitute good decreases. What will happen in the short run to:

   a. The market demand curve.

   b. The market supply curve.

   c. Market price.

   d. Market output.

   e. The firm's output.

   f. The firm's profit.

   What will happen in the long run?

10. The supply of labor to all firms in a perfectly competitive industry is reduced. Explain the effects on the wage rate, the quantity of labor employed, total industry supply of the commodity produced, and the price of the output.

11. The following figure shows the relevant portion of the marginal product curve for labor (the only variable input) of a perfectly competitive firm.

   a. In a separate graph draw the associated marginal revenue product curve (value of marginal product) over the relevant range of labor usage. The price of the product produced is $2 per unit.

   b. At a wage rate of $30 how much labor will the firm hire? What if the wage rate falls to $25?

   c. Suppose the price of the product falls to $1. Draw the new *VMP* curve.

   d. How much labor is hired now at each of the two wage rates?

12. Explain why the industry's demand for an input is less elastic than the horizontal sum of all firms' demands for the input.

13. Explain why, when there is more than one variable input, the firm's demand for one of the inputs is not the *VMP* curve, but every input is hired so that its *VMP* equals its price.

ANALYTICAL PROBLEMS

1. Grocery stores and gasoline stations in a large city would appear to be an example of perfectly competitive markets—there are numerous sellers, each seller is relatively small, and the products sold are quite similar. How could we argue that these markets are not perfectly competitive (leaving out the assumption of perfect knowledge)? Could each firm have some monopoly power? How do you think the theory of perfect competition would permit us to make predictions about the behavior of such firms?

2. Insurance agents receive a commission on the policies they sell. Many states regulate the rates that can be charged for insurance. Would higher or lower rates increase the incomes of agents? Explain, distinguishing between the short run and long run.

3. Suppose that an excise tax is placed on the products sold in a perfectly competitive market. That is, for every unit sold, each firm must pay the state $k per unit. What would be the effect on each firm's marginal cost? Output? Industry supply? The price of the product?

4. If all of the assumptions of perfect competition hold, why would firms in such an industry have little incentive to carry out technological change or much research and development? What conditions would encourage research and development in competitive industries?

5. Suppose you manage a small manufacturing firm that has been making short-run losses for almost two years. The board of directors directs you to remedy the situation. What steps would you try to take? What information would you want to get?

6. At the present time the oil business is somewhat depressed. Suppose that oil prices increase rather rapidly over the next few years. What will happen to the salaries of petroleum engineers and oil geologists? Distinguish between the short run and long run.

7. In the miniwarehouse market, there are many firms but most firms are small, and the product being sold (rental storage space) is similar across firms. Suppose that the pretax rate of return on investment in this market has been 20 percent for the last two years. What changes would you expect to observe in the market over the next few years?

8. Most agriculture fits the competitive model relatively well. However, many crops have support prices above the price that would prevail in the absence of controls. Many farmers argue that they can't make a profit even with these support prices. Explain why. Explain why even higher support prices would not help.

9. Notwithstanding the facts in Question 8, some farmers are making huge incomes. Explain why.

10. Suppose that the workers in a competitive industry are unionized, and the union obtains a large wage increase. What will happen to the number of workers hired? To profits? To the number of firms? To the method of production?

APPENDIX

1. A perfectly competitive firm will maximize profit by producing the output at which price equals marginal cost if $P \geq AVC$.

Let F = fixed cost, $C(Q)$ = variable cost, Q = output, and P = price. Thus profit is

$$\pi = P \cdot Q - C(Q) - F.$$

Maximizing profit with respect to output requires

$$\frac{d\pi}{dQ} = P - \frac{dC}{dQ} = 0.$$

Since dC/dQ is marginal cost for very small changes in Q, price equals marginal cost.

To analyze whether the firm should operate or shut down, write the profit function as

$$\pi = P \cdot Q - \frac{C(Q)}{Q}Q - F = \left(P - \frac{C(Q)}{Q}\right)Q - F$$
$$= (P - AVC)Q - F.$$

If profit is positive when $P = MC$, the firm clearly would choose to operate. But suppose that profit is negative (the firm is making a loss) when $P = MC$. Should the firm produce or shut down?

The firm must pay the fixed cost, F, at any output, including zero. First, suppose that $P > AVC$ when $P = MC$. In this case, since $(P - AVC)Q - F > -F$, the firm should continue to produce. Its loss is less than $-F$, the fixed cost it would lose if it shuts down. That is, the positive term in the profit function, $(P - AVC)Q$, partially offsets the negative term, $-F$. But, if $P = MC$ and $P < AVC$, $(P - AVC)Q < 0$, and $(P - AVC)Q - F < -F$. Thus, the firm should shut down and lose only $-F$, its fixed cost. It loses less by shutting down than by operating.

2. The firm will hire a variable input at the point where the price of the input, w, equals the value of the input's marginal product. Let the only variable input be labor, L. The production function is $Q = f(L)$. Thus profit would be

$$\pi = P \cdot f(L) - w \cdot L - F,$$

where P is product price and F is fixed cost. Profit maximization requires

$$\frac{d\pi}{dL} = P \frac{dQ}{dL} - w = 0,$$

where dQ/dL is labor's marginal product. Since the value of the marginal product is $P \cdot MP_L$,

$$VMP_L = w,$$

if the firm produces a positive output.

The firm will shut down if at the point where $w = VMP_L$, $MP_L > AP_L$. Write the profit function as

$$\pi = P \cdot \frac{Q}{L} L - wL - F = (P \cdot \frac{Q}{L} L - P \cdot MP_L \cdot L - F$$
$$= PL(AP_L - MP_L) - F.$$

If $AP_L < MP_L$, the firm will lose only $-F$ if $L = 0$; that is, if it shuts down. It will lose $(P \cdot Q/L - w)L - F$, if $L > 0$. If, where $w = VMP_L$, $MP_L < AP_L$, the firm will produce even though it is making a loss, because it would lose less than $-F$.

13

PROFIT MAXIMIZATION IN COMPETITIVE MARKETS— IMPLEMENTATION OF THE THEORY

I n the preceding chapter, we described in theoretical terms how a firm in a perfectly competitive market maximizes profit in the short run. As we demonstrated, the firm can attain maximum profits through the selection of either the optimal level of output or the optimal level of usage of its inputs.

In this chapter, we will show you ways the manager of a firm can actually *implement* these theoretical relations. Using what we have already learned about the estimation and forecasting of production, cost, and demand functions, we can estimate (forecast) the levels of output or input usage that will maximize the firm's profit in the short run. In essence, this chapter is the first "payoff" from all the discussions we have presented in preceding chapters: We have spent a lot of time describing the estimation of the various functions; now we can use these techniques to answer the primary question in the mind of the manager: What can I do to maximize profit?

Following the outline we set forth in Chapter 12, we will first describe the profit-maximizing output decision. Then, we will turn to a brief description of the profit-maximizing input decision.

13.1 PROFIT-MAXIMIZING OUTPUT

As we described in Chapter 12, the manager of a firm must answer two questions. Let's begin by restating these questions and the answers we found in our theoretical discussion:

1. Do I produce or shut down? *The firm should produce as long as the market price exceeds the minimum of average variable cost—P > AVC.*
2. If I produce, how much should I produce? *The output that will maximize profit or minimize loss is that at which market price is equal to marginal cost—P = MC.*

It follows that in order to be able to determine or forecast the profit-maximizing level of output for the firm, we need estimates of or forecasts for the market price of the commodity being produced by the firm, the firm's average cost function, and the firm's marginal cost function. Let's first review how we are able to obtain these components before showing you how we can obtain actual answers to the questions facing the manager.

Price Forecasts

As we described in Chapter 8, price forecasts are what cause economists' hair to become prematurely gray. However, the message of that discussion was not that we can't forecast prices but rather that we are unlikely to be able to outforecast an efficient market. In an efficient market, the current price reflects all available public information, so the best price forecast is the market price.

THE WALL STREET JOURNAL

APPLICATION

Futures Prices as Price Forecasts

As reported in *The Wall Street Journal,* the November 12, 1986 price per bushel of corn was $1.58, up 7 cents from the day before and down 76 cents from the year before. If a manager needs to make a decision for which corn prices on November 13 are a factor, the best available price forecast is $1.58 per bushel. Likewise, if November 20 or November 30 prices are needed, the best available forecast is $1.58.

CASH PRICES

Wednesday November 12, 1986.
(Quotations as of 4 p.m. Eastern time)
GRAINS AND FEEDS

	Wed	Tues	Yr. Ago
Alfalfa Pellets, dehy. Neb., ton	76.00	75.00	69.50
Barley, top-quality Mpls., bu	2.05	1.95-2.05	2.27½
Bran, (Wheat middling) KC ton ...	57.00	57.00	76.00
Brewer's Grains, Milw. ton	100.00	100.00	70.00
Corn, No. 2 yel. Cent-Ill. bu	bp1.58	1.51	2.34

For dates further in the future, the best forecast is still the market price. But, instead of the current price—the spot price—the most appropriate price is the futures price. The futures price is the price of a contract for

Continued on page 385

THE WALL STREET JOURNAL

APPLICATION

Continued from page 384
delivery of a specified amount of a specified commodity (or asset) on a specified date in the future. The corn futures contracts traded on the Chicago Board of Trade (CBT) are for delivery of 5,000 bushels of corn at a Chicago warehouse. CBT corn futures contracts are available for deliveries in March, May, July, or December. Below are the

FUTURES PRICES

Wednesday, November 12, 1986.
Open Interest Reflects Previous Trading Day.

	Open	High	Low	Settle	Change	Lifetime High	Lifetime Low	Open Interest
-GRAINS AND OILSEEDS-								
CORN (CBT) 5,000 bu.; cents per bu.								
Dec	170¾	174½	170¼	173¼	+ 2¾	235½	161	74,322
Mar87	179	182¾	179	182	+ 2¾	242½	172½	41,095
May	185½	188¼	185¼	187¼	+ 1¾	242	180	15,671
July	187¼	189½	187¼	189¼	+ 1½	227	182¾	18,824
Sept	189¼	191¼	189	190½	+ 1¼	201½	182½	2,185
Dec	193	194¾	192½	194¾	+ 1¼	197	183	7,490
Mar88	200	202¼	200	202¼	+ 1½	203¾	195	228

Est vol 25,000; vol Tues 29,729; open int 160,015, +1,939.

November 12 prices for available futures contracts as they appeared in the November 13 *Wall Street Journal*. If, on November 12, 1986, a manager needs to make a decision for which May 1987 corn prices are a factor, the best forecast is the futures price for the May 1987 contracts. On November 12, this contract settled at 187.25 cents per bushel (or $1.87 per bushel). This table of prices also reminds us that this price is a forecast. The open/high/low prices indicate the volatility of May 87 corn futures prices during the day of November 12. The lifetime high/low prices provide a measure of historic volatility in this May 87 price.

In the same way, forecasts for corn prices through March 1988 can be obtained. However, as we already know, the further in the future the manager looks, the less precise will be the forecast. In the futures market this is also reflected in the number of outstanding contracts—the open interest. As the contracts mature further in the future, forecasts are less precise, and, all other things equal, the volume of futures contracts declines.

In the preceding application, the November 13 and November 20 forecasts would both be the same: $1.58 per bushel. But, doesn't this neglect the random price movements that we know go on in an efficient market? Couldn't the November 20 price be substantially higher or lower than the November 13 price?

And the same situation exists between September and December 1987. From the futures price data, the best price forecast for corn on November

2, 1987 is the same as for September 29, 1987: 190.5 cents per bushel.

As should be evident, the price forecasts for nearby dates and distant dates are not identical. Price forecasts in an efficient market will reflect the random movement inherent in such prices. This random movement is summarized by the variance of the historic price series. To illustrate this, let's look at copper again.

APPLICATION

A Random Walk Forecast

Suppose that, on January 1, 1987, copper was being traded at 59 cents per pound. Suppose further that, from historical data, it had been determined that (1) there was no trend in copper prices and (2) the monthly variance in copper price (expressed as a percentage of the copper price) was one-half of 1 percent (0.005).

Since there is no trend—no drift—in copper prices, the point forecast for copper prices on February 1, 1987, would be 59 cents per pound as would be the forecast for March, April, and so on. These point forecasts are illustrated with the solid line in the following figure.

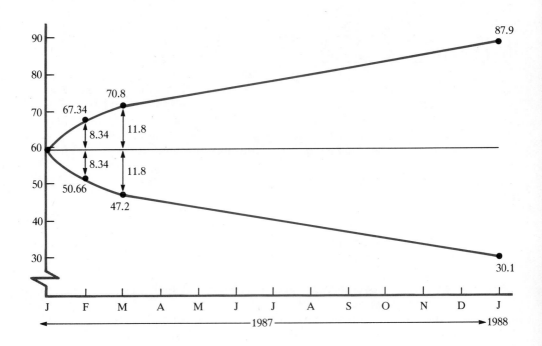

However, if the analyst wanted a 95 percent confidence interval for these forecasts, it would be necessary to consider the variance of copper prices. From statistics, the analyst knows that 95 percent of the actual values lie within two standard deviations of the mean—in this case, within two standard deviations of the point forecast. Since February is only one month out, the variance for February is simply the monthly variance and the 95 percent confidence interval for February is

$$59 \pm 2 (\sqrt{1 \times 0.005} \times 59) = 59 \pm 8.34.$$

Since March forecasts have two months to run, the variance for the March estimates is twice the monthly variance (2×0.005) and the 95 percent confidence interval is

$$59 \pm 2 (\sqrt{2 \times 0.005} \times 59) = 59 \pm 11.8.$$

Continuing, the point estimate for January 1, 1988 would still be 59 cents per pound. However, since this forecast is 12 months hence, the variance is 12 times the monthly variance and the 95 percent confidence interval becomes

$$59 \pm 2 (\sqrt{12 \times 0.005} \times 59) = 59 \pm 28.9.$$

Put another way, we can summarize our forecasts for copper prices on January 1, 1988 in terms of three forecasts:

High: 87.9 cents per pound
Best: 59.0 cents per pound
Low: 30.1 cents per pound

The point of the preceding application can be summarized as follows: If the price of a commodity traded in an efficient market has no drift, the 95 percent confidence interval for a forecast n months in the future is

$$P_t \pm 2 (\sqrt{n\sigma^2} \times P_t),$$

where P_t is the current price of the commodity and σ^2 is the monthly variance in the price. If the price exhibits drift, e.g.,

$$P_{t+n} = P_t + \theta_n,$$

the 95 percent confidence interval for a forecast of price in n months is

$$P_{t+n} \pm 2 (\sqrt{n\sigma^2} \times P_{t+n}).$$

That is, the 95 percent confidence interval is placed around the drift—trend—line.

Hence, for commodities (or assets) traded in efficient markets, the futures markets and random walk forecasts provide forecasts for future prices. However, for commodities traded in markets that are less efficient, more traditional forecasting techniques are useful. For example, in the following application we will consider an apparel market—the market for men's shirts. There is no futures market for ready-to-wear shirts, nor is there a low-cost means of contracting for delivery in the future. The apparel market does not conform to the characteristics of an efficient market. Hence, current price and expected future price can diverge significantly. To forecast future shirt prices, the manager of a firm could use a qualitative forecast or a time-series forecast. Or, if the manager wanted to incorporate explicitly the effects of changes in things such as consumer income and input prices on the price of shirts, an econometric model might be employed.

APPLICATION

An Econometric Price Forecast

The manager of Beau Apparel, Inc.—a manufacturer of men's clothing—was preparing the firm's production plan for the first quarter of 1988. One of the firm's divisions produces moderately priced men's shirts and the manager wanted to obtain a price forecast for this product for 1988I that would subsequently be used in making the production decision for this division.

The manager realized that, in this particular segment of the shirt market, Beau Apparel was only one of many firms that produced a fairly homogeneous product and that none of the firms in this "moderate price shirt market" engaged in any significant advertising. Hence, this market approximated the conditions of a perfectly competitive market. Therefore, the manager specified a simplified demand-supply system for the market:

$$\text{Demand: } Q_t = a + bP_t + cY_t$$
$$\text{Supply: } Q_t = e + fP_t + gP_{F,t}.$$

Using quarterly data for the period 1981I–1987IV, these equations were estimated. The estimated demand and supply functions were as follows:

$$\text{Demand: } Q_t = 125 - 2P_t + 12.5Y_t$$
$$\text{Supply: } Q_t = 250 + 8P_t - 5P_{F,t}.$$

In this estimation, sales (Q) were expressed in thousand units, the price of the product (P) in dollars per unit and income (Y) and the price of factors (P_F) in $1,000.

To obtain 1988I forecasts for the exogenous variables, the manager purchased forecasts of income and input prices from a large econometric forecasting firm. The 1988I forecast for the price of inputs was $10,000. So, in the model, the forecasted 1988I value for P_F was 10.

However, in the case of an income forecast for 1988I, the forecasting firm was less sure. Indeed, the firm provided three different forecasts, each predicated on different assumptions about legislation pending in Congress. These income forecasts were as follows:

> High = $22,000
> Best = $18,000
> Low = $14,000.

In forecasting the price of shirts in the first quarter of 1988, the manager of Beau Apparel would then have three alternative values of $\hat{Y}_{1988I}$: 22, 18, and 14.

To obtain price forecasts for shirts, it was then necessary for the manager to insert the forecasted values for the exogenous variables into the estimated demand and supply functions. Using the high forecast for income,

$$\text{Demand: } Q_{1988I} = 125 - 2P_{1988I} + 12.5(22)$$
$$= 400 - 2P_{1988I}$$
$$\text{Supply: } Q_{1988I} = 250 + 8P_{1988I} - 5(10)$$
$$= 200 + 8P_{1988I}.$$

Calculating an equilibrium solution, that is, setting quantity demanded equal to quantity supplied,

$$400 - 2\hat{P}_{1988I} = 200 + 8\hat{P}_{1988I}.$$

Solving this equation for price,

$$\hat{P}_{1988I} = 20.$$

Hence, the manager of Beau Apparel found that the 1988I forecast for the price of shirts, assuming the high-income forecast, is $20 per unit.

In precisely the same way, using the "best" forecast for income in 1988I, the forecasted price of shirts in the first quarter of 1988 would be $15 per unit. And, using the low-income forecast, the 1988I price forecast would be $10 per unit. So, the manager of Beau Apparel has three price forecasts for shirts for the first quarter of 1988:

> High = $20
> Best = $15
> Low = $10.

Estimation of Average Variable Cost

To obtain an estimate of the firm's average variable cost curve, several methods can be used. However, let us continue with regression analysis and employ the technique we described in Chapter 11. Using time-series data for a period short enough that the firm's fixed costs (e.g., the firm's capital stock) have not changed, we can estimate the function

$$AVC = a + bQ + cQ^2.$$

To remind you of the way this function is used, let's return to our application dealing with a competitive firm.

APPLICATION

An Average Variable Cost Function

The manager of Beau Apparel also wanted to obtain an estimate of the shirt division's average variable cost function. The manager knew that the last major change in the division's capital stock had occurred in the second quarter of 1985, so using quarterly data for the division for 1985III through 1987IV, the function

$$AVC = a + bQ + cQ^2$$

was estimated. Again output was expressed in thousand units and average variable cost was expressed in dollars per unit. The estimated *AVC* function obtained from the computer printout was

$$AVC = 20 - 3Q + 0.25Q^2.$$

The value for R^2 was 0.8952 and the F value was 29.897. All of the estimated coefficients ($\hat{a}$, $\hat{b}$, and $\hat{c}$) were of the required sign and were statistically significant.

Derivation of the Marginal Cost Function

As we demonstrated in Chapter 11, if the average variable cost function is

$$AVC = a + bQ + cQ^2,$$

the marginal cost function is

$$MC = a + 2bQ + 3cQ^2.$$

Hence, once the analyst has estimated the average variable cost function, it is a trivial matter to obtain the corresponding marginal cost function. Let's see how our shirt manufacturer did this.

APPLICATION

A Marginal Cost Function

In the preceding application, the manager of Beau Apparel had estimated an average variable cost function for the shirt division as

$$AVC = 20 - 3Q + 0.25Q^2.$$

Therefore, the marginal cost function for shirts is

$$MC = 20 + 2(-3)Q + 3(0.25)Q^2$$
$$= 20 - 6Q + 0.75Q^2.$$

The Shutdown Decision

We are now in a position to answer the manager's first question: Do I produce or should I shut down? As we know from Chapter 12, the firm should produce as long as price exceeds minimum average variable cost.

We already know forecasted price. Hence, to consider the shutdown decision, we need only find the minimum average variable cost. As we demonstrated in Chapter 11, the average variable cost curve will be at its minimum when $AVC = MC$, so the output at which AVC is a minimum is $\tilde{Q} = -b/2c$. Then, to find minimum average variable cost, we simply substitute this output level into the estimated average variable cost function:

$$AVC_{MIN} = a + b\tilde{Q} + c(\tilde{Q})^2.$$

The firm should produce as long as $P \geqq AVC_{MIN}$. If $P < AVC_{MIN}$, the firm should shut down—produce zero output. To see how this decision is implemented, let's return to our application.

APPLICATION

Should I Produce?

As we noted earlier, the manager of Beau Apparel estimated the average variable cost function for shirts to be

$$AVC = 20 - 3Q + 0.25Q^2.$$

Therefore, the manager knows that this average variable cost curve is at its minimum when output is

$$\tilde{Q} = -(-3)/2(.25) = (3)/(0.5) = 6$$

(i.e., an output of 6,000 units). Substituting this output level into the estimated average variable cost function, the minimum average variable cost is

$$AVC_{MIN} = 20 - 3(6) + 0.25(6)^2 = 11.$$

That is, minimum average variable cost is $11 per unit.

The manager of Beau Apparel then compares this minimum average variable cost with the three price forecasts described in an earlier application. With the high forecast,

$$\hat{P} = \$20 > \$11 = AVC_{MIN},$$

so the firm should produce. Likewise, with the "best" forecast

$$\hat{P} = \$15 > \$11 = AVC_{MIN}$$

and the firm should again produce. However, if it turns out that the low forecast is correct, the firm should shut down—produce zero output—since

$$\hat{P} = \$10 < \$11 = AVC_{MIN}.$$

The Output Decision

If price exceeds minimum average variable cost, we know that the firm will produce, but the question is: how much? We can answer this question easily, since we know that the firm will maximize its profit or minimize its loss if it produces that output at which $P = MC$.

In the context of the average variable cost function we have been using (i.e., $AVC = a + bQ + cQ^2$), the profit-maximizing (or loss-minimizing) output is determined by setting forecasted price equal to estimated marginal cost:

$$\hat{P} = \hat{a} + 2\hat{b}Q + 3\hat{c}Q^2.$$

Solving this equation for Q gives us the optimal output for the firm. To see how this would work in the context of actual estimates, we return to our shirt manufacturer.

APPLICATION

How Much Should I Produce?

The manager of Beau Apparel found that the firm's shirt division should produce if the market price is $20 (the high forecast) or $15 (the "best" forecast). The next question is, of course: How much should I produce at either of these two prices?

Looking first at the high forecast, optimal output is that at which the price forecast is equal to marginal cost. That is

$$20 = 20 - 6Q + 0.75Q^2.$$

Solving this equation for Q (by factoring), the optimal—profit-maximizing or loss-minimizing—output is $Q = 8$. Since output was expressed in thousand units, this gives an output of 8,000 units. That is, if the price is expected to be $20 per unit, the optimal level of output is 8,000 units.

With the "best" forecast, the optimal output is again determined by equating the price forecast with the estimated marginal cost function:

$$15 = 20 - 6Q + 0.75Q^2$$

or

$$0.75Q^2 - 6Q + 5 = 0$$

As luck would have it, the solution to this equation is not as simple as was the preceding case. To solve this equation, we must resort to the quadratic formula:*

$$Q = \frac{-(-6) \pm \sqrt{(-6)^2 - 4(0.75)\,(5)}}{2(0.75)} = \frac{6 \pm 4.6}{1.5}.$$

Using the quadratic formula, the equation has two solutions—$Q = 0.93$ and $Q = 7.1$. Which is correct? That is, which one of these is the optimal output for a price of $15 per unit? If you look again at Figure 12.3, you should be able to see that the correct output is the higher output, 7.1. However, an alternate way of checking is to look at the average variable costs for the two outputs:

$$AVC_{Q=0.93} = 20 - 3(0.93) + 0.25(0.93)^2 = \$17.43$$
$$AVC_{Q=7.1} = 20 - 3(7.1) + 0.25(7.1)^2 = \$11.30.$$

Since $17.43 exceeds the price of $15 per unit, the output level of $Q = 0.93$ cannot be optimal, so the optimal level of output for a price of $15 is 7.1. That is, if the price is expected to be $15 per unit, the firm would produce 7,100 units.

---

*For an equation of the form $aY^2 + bY + c = 0$ the solutions for Y are found as
$$Y = \frac{-b \pm \sqrt{b^2 - 4ac}}{2a}.$$

Total Profit or Loss

Once the firm's output decision is made, the calculation of total profit or loss is very simple. Total profit (loss) is simply total revenue minus total cost.

Total revenue for a competitive firm is price times quantity sold. Total cost is the sum of total variable cost and total fixed cost, where total variable cost is average variable cost times the number of units sold. Hence, total profit (loss) is

$$\text{Profit} = TR - TC$$
$$= (P \times Q) - [(AVC \times Q) + TFC].$$

APPLICATION

What's the Bottom Line?

In the applications in this section, the manager of Beau Apparel has been attempting to determine the optimal production level for the firm's shirt division for 1988I. So far, this manager has looked at the shutdown and production questions. As you might expect, the final question this manager has is: What is the profit or loss associated with each of the alternative price forecasts?

$$\text{Profit} = (P \times Q) - [(AVC \times Q) + TFC].$$

Based on actual costs in the fourth quarter of 1987, the manager expects total fixed costs for the shirt division for 1988I to be $30,000. The values for total revenue and total variable cost depend on the price forecast and corresponding optimal output. Let's look at each of the three price forecasts in turn:

High forecast—$\hat{P} = 20: In this case, the manager has determined the optimal level of production to be $Q = 8$, i.e., 8,000 units. The average variable cost associated with the production of 8,000 units is

$$AVC_{Q=8} = 20 - 3(8) + 0.25(8)^2 = \$12.$$

Therefore, profit will be

$$\text{Profit} = (\$20)(8,000) - [(\$12)(8,000) + \$30,000] = +\$34,000.$$

That is, if price is $20 per unit, the shirt division would be expected to earn a profit of $34,000 in the first quarter of 1988.

Best forecast—$\hat{P} = 15: We have seen that, with a price of $15 per unit, the optimal output is $Q = 7.1$, that is, 7,100 units. The average variable cost for this output level is

$$AVC_{Q=7.1} = 20 - 3(7.1) + 0.25(7.1)^2 = \$11.30$$

and total profit is

$$\text{Profit} = (\$15)(7,100) - [(\$11.30)(7,100) + \$30,000] = -\$3,730.$$

That is, if price is $15 per unit, the shirt division of Beau Apparel will be expected to suffer a *loss* of $3,730 in the first quarter of 1988. However, the firm will continue to produce since, as should become more clear in the next case, this is the minimum loss that would be possible in the short run.

Low forecast—$\hat{P} = \$10$: In an earlier application, we showed that with this price, the division should shut down—produce zero output. Hence,

$$\text{Profit} = 0 - [0 + \$30,000] = -\$30,000.$$

In this case, the division would be expected to suffer a loss equal to its fixed costs ($30,000) in the first quarter of 1988.

In the applications presented in this section we have looked at the way the manager of a competitive firm would make decisions when faced with three alternative price forecasts. Our purpose in using the three price forecasts was to reinforce the material presented in Chapter 12. As we showed there, in the short run, a firm would make one of the choices below.

1. Produce a positive level of output and earn an economic profit (if $P > ATC$).
2. Produce a positive level of output and suffer an economic loss less than the amount of total fixed cost (if $AVC < P < ATC$).
3. Produce zero output and suffer an economic loss equal to total fixed cost (if $P < AVC$).

Thus, the applications presented here have mirrored the discussion and graphical exposition of Chapter 12.

However, by confronting the manager with three price forecasts we have also introduced uncertainty. How can a manager make a profit-maximizing decision when confronted by uncertainty? We defer this issue for now, but we will return to this question in Chapter 19.

13.2 PROFIT-MAXIMIZING LEVELS OF INPUT USAGE

A firm can also attain profit maximization through selection of the optimal level of employment of its inputs. That is, a firm can maximize profits by selecting the optimal value for *either* output *or* input usage.

To show how profit maximization can be attained by selection of the optimal level of input usage, we look at the case of a single variable input. The more complex situation in which a firm has several inputs that are variable is handled in the appendix to this chapter.

To be consistent with our discussion in Chapter 12, let the variable input be labor, although the techniques shown can be used for any input. We know that the firm will maximize profit if it employs labor at the level at which the value of the marginal product of labor equals the wage rate,

$$VMP_L = w.$$

As was described in Chapter 12, for a firm in a competitive market, VMP_L is equal to the price of the firm's output times the marginal product of labor. The wage rate is determined in the aggregate labor market, so an individual firm treats the wage rate as given (parametric).

Therefore, to implement this decision, the firm needs three pieces of information: (1) the market wage rate, (2) the price of its output, and (3) the marginal product function for labor. The market wage rate can be determined directly by the firm or forecasted using the techniques we described in Chapter 8. The price of the firm's output can be determined or forecasted by the firm in precisely the manner we described in section 13.1. Hence, the only potential difficulty is in finding the marginal product function for labor.

Essentially, as we described in Chapter 9, we have a production function with a single variable input, $Q = f(L)$. For the reasons described in Chapter 11, an appropriate empirical production function would be a log-linear function,

$$Q = AL^\beta,$$

where $0 < \beta < 1$. With this short-run production function, the marginal product function for labor is

$$MP_L = \beta AL^{\beta-1}.$$

Once we have obtained the price forecast for the firm's output ($\hat{P}$), the forecasted wage rate ($\hat{w}$), and estimates of the parameters of the production function ($\hat{\beta}$ and $\hat{A}$), we can express the profit-maximizing condition as

$$(\hat{P}) \times (\hat{\beta}\hat{A}L^{\hat{\beta}-1}) = \hat{w}.$$

To obtain the profit-maximizing employment level for labor, the analyst then needs to solve this equation for L. To show you how this is done using estimates and forecasts, let's turn to the following application.

APPLICATION

How Many Workers Should I Hire?

We have already seen how the manager of Beau Apparel selected the optimal output level for the firm's shirt division. Now let's see how the manager selected the optimal level of use of the variable factor of production—labor.

In order to determine the profit-maximizing (or loss-minimizing) level of usage of labor in 1988I, the manager needs to know three things:

1. *Forecasted price for the firm's output—the market price of output—in 1988I.* In an earlier application, we saw how such a forecast was obtained. For this application, let's use only the high forecast; so, $\hat{P}_{1988I} = \$20$.

2. *Forecasted wage rate in 1988I.* As with price, various forecasting techniques could be used to obtain a forecast for the wage rate. In this case, the manager of Beau Apparel purchased a wage forecast for the geographic region in which its plant is located from an economic forecasting firm. The forecast provided by the consulting firm was $16 per hour, so $\hat{w}_{1988I} = \$16$.

3. *The firm's short-run production function.* Using the available quarterly data for the division for the period 1985II–87IV, the manager estimated a production function of the form

   $$Q = AL^{\beta}.$$

More specifically, the manager used the 10 quarterly observations to estimate

$$\log Q = \log A + \beta \log L,$$

where output (Q) was expressed in thousand units and labor usage (L) was in thousand hours. Using the estimated coefficients from the computer printout, the estimated production function was

$$\log Q = 1.004 + 0.6 \log L.$$

This equation had an R^2 of 0.9210 and an F value of 93.266. The appropriate t-tests were performed to determine that the estimate of β was significantly greater than zero and less than one.

Rewriting the estimated production function in its exponential form, the empirical production function was

$$Q = (2.73)L^{0.6}.$$

From this estimated production function, the marginal product function for labor was

$$MP_L = (0.6)(2.73)L^{0.6-1.0} = (1.638)L^{-0.4}.$$

Using the price and wage forecasts and the estimated marginal product function, the profit-maximization condition ($P \times MP_L = w$) can be expressed as

$$(20) \times (1.638L^{-0.4}) = 16$$

or

$$L^{-0.4} = 0.4884$$

Taking logarithms of both sides of the preceding equation,

$$-0.4 \log L = -0.717,$$

so $\log L = 1.792$ and it follows that (using natural logs) $L = 6.0.*$ That is, the profit-maximizing level of labor usage in the first quarter of 1988 is 6,000 hours. (This is the equivalent of 12 full-time employees.)

As we noted in Chapter 12, the firm would actually hire this amount of labor—6,000 hours—only if the average product of labor exceeds the marginal product. If $AP_L < MP_L$, the firm would shut down. Hence, in order to make sure that $L = 6.0$ is indeed optimal, we must be sure that $AP_L \geq MP_L$. Using $L = 6.0$ in the estimated marginal product function, $MP_L = 0.8$. The average product of labor is

$$AP_L = Q/L = [(2.73)L^{0.6}]/L = (2.73)L^{-0.4}.$$

Using $L = 6.0$ in this average product function, $AP_L = 1.33$. Hence, at $L = 6.0$, $AP_L > MP_L$ and 6,000 hours of labor usage is indeed optimal.

Using this optimal employment level in the estimated production function, the profit-maximizing output level is

$$Q = (2.73)6^{0.6} = 8.$$

That is, the profit-maximizing output level is 8,000 units.

Further, since the level of labor usage and the wage rate are both known, the manager can calculate total variable cost:

$$TVC = w \times L = \$16 \times 6,000 = \$96,000.$$

And, since total fixed cost in 1988I is \$30,000, the expected profit for the shirt division of Beau Apparel is:

$$\text{Profit} = (\$20 \times 8,000) - [\$96,000 + \$30,000] = \$34,000.$$

This is precisely the same result that was obtained via the optimal output determination.†

---

*In this application, natural logarithms were used. Therefore, if $\log L = 1.792$,

$$L = e^{\log L} = e^{1.792} = 6.001.$$

†The results in this application correspond precisely to those obtained by equating $P = \$20$ to marginal cost in an earlier application. This correspondence was accomplished via a "judicious" selection of the parameters of the short-run production function, that is, A and β. However, since the production function exhibits only diminishing returns to the variable factor, it would not generate a U-shaped average variable cost curve and this correspondence is not guaranteed for other prices. (We return to this issue in Analytical Problem 8.)

TECHNICAL PROBLEMS

1. In a perfectly competitive market, under what condition will a firm produce rather than shut down in the short run? If the decision is to produce, how is the optimal level of production determined?

2. Look again at the copper price forecast. Suppose that copper prices exhibited a downward trend, falling by one-fifth of a cent per month. Using the same January 1987 price (59 cents per pound) and the same monthly variance (0.005), calculate 95 percent confidence intervals for copper price forecasts for
   a. February 1987
   b. March 1987
   c. January 1988.

3. Suppose that the manager of a firm operating in a perfectly competitive market has estimated the firm's average variable cost function to be

$$AVC = 10.0 - 3.0Q + 0.5Q^2,$$

where AVC was expressed in dollars per unit and Q was measured in 100 units. Suppose that total fixed cost is $600.
   a. What is the corresponding marginal cost function?
   b. At what output is AVC a minimum?
   c. What is the minimum value for AVC?

If the forecasted market price of the firm's output is $10 per unit,
   d. How much output will this firm produce in the short run?
   e. How much profit (loss) is this firm expected to earn?

If the forecasted market price of the firm's output is $5 per unit,
   f. How much output will this firm produce in the short run?
   g. How much profit (loss) is this firm expected to earn?

4. The production manager of the ABC Co., a perfectly competitive firm, has just returned from a trade convention. On the basis of the presentations there, he believes that market price next period will be somewhere between $15 and $25, with $20 being the best guess.
   The firm's average variable cost function is

$$AVC = 30 - 10Q + Q^2,$$

where AVC is dollar per unit, Q = number of units (1,000), and total fixed cost is $10,000.
   a. How much output should the firm produce and how much profit (loss) will it earn if price is $15? $20? $25?
   b. What is the shutdown price? How likely is it that the firm will have to shut down to minimize losses?
   c. If the manager's predictions are accurate, what is the range of expected profit?

5. To find the optimizing level of usage of a single variable input, what condition must be satisfied for a firm in a perfectly competitive market? In order that this level of usage actually be optimal, what must be the relation between the average and the marginal products?

6. Suppose that a firm operating in a perfectly competitive market has only one variable input—labor. The manager of the firm estimated a short-run production function for the firm of the form

$$Q = AL^\beta.$$

The resulting estimated function was

$$\log Q = 1.176 + 0.7 \log L,$$

where Q was measured in 1,000 units and L was measured in 1,000 hours of labor input.

   a. Using the estimates obtained, rewrite the production function in the form $Q = AL^\beta$.
   b. What is the marginal product of labor function?

The manager has forecasted the price of the firm's output to be $10 per unit and the price of labor (the wage rate) to be $14 per hour.

   c. What is the firm's value of the marginal product function?
   d. What is the indicated optimal level of usage of labor?
   e. Ensure that this level of usage is indeed optimal (i.e., compare AP_L and MP_L at this level of usage of labor).

7. Using your results in Problem 6,
   a. How much output will this firm produce?
   b. What is the firm's total revenue?
   c. What is the firm's total variable cost?

If total fixed cost for the firm is $50,000,

   d. How much profit (loss) will the firm earn?
   e. If the firm had elected to shut down, how much profit (loss) would it have earned?

ANALYTICAL PROBLEMS

1. Suppose that you are the manager of a firm. If you wanted to determine the profit-maximizing level of output or input usage for your firm, how might you decide whether or not the competitive model is appropriate?
2. How does a manager decide how to obtain a price forecast for the firm's output?
3. In our application dealing with the futures market we noted that "As the contracts mature further in the future . . . all other things equal, volume will decline." Open interest on corn futures contracts does not decline regularly. Why might this be so?
4. In this chapter, we used estimates of the cost function obtained from regression analysis. Could the manager use estimates obtained using the engineering cost function approach? Defend your answer.

5. If a firm is suffering losses (or is shut down) in the short run, what decisions must it make for the long run? What are the firm's alternatives? What kind of data would the manager need to look at to make the necessary decision?

6. "The most a firm could ever lose is the amount it has invested (its fixed cost)." Is this true or false? Explain.

7. Given the kind of production functions we used in this chapter,

$$Q = AL^\beta, 0 < \beta < 1,$$

the average product of the input is guaranteed to exceed the marginal product. Why?

8. In our application titled "How Many Workers Should I Hire?" we obtained precisely the same results for a forecasted price of $20 that we obtained earlier by equating price to marginal cost. As you might wish to verify, this correspondence does not hold for other prices (e.g., $15 per unit). The reason for this is that the form of the average variable cost function we estimated,

$$AVC = a + bQ + cQ^2,$$

does not "match" the form of the production function we estimated,

$$Q = AL^\beta.$$

In what sense do these two functions not "match"?

APPENDIX: THE PROFIT-MAXIMIZING LEVELS OF INPUT USAGE WHEN SEVERAL INPUTS ARE VARIABLE

If the firm hires several variable inputs, the profit-maximization condition remains unchanged. However, the profit-maximization conditions for the inputs must be solved simultaneously, so the computation is somewhat more complex.

Let's look at a case in which the firm has two variable inputs—capital and labor. The profit-maximization conditions require that the value of the marginal products for the inputs be equal to the respective input prices. That is,

$$P \times MP_L = w \text{ and } P \times MP_K = r,$$

where r is the user cost of capital; i.e., the cost to the firm of using a unit of capital.

We have already talked about the way in which the firm can obtain its price forecast ($\hat{P}$). And, the firm can obtain forecasts of the price of capital ($\hat{r}$) in much the same way it obtains forecasts for the wage rate ($\hat{w}$). Hence, the remaining question is the determination of the marginal product functions for labor and capital.

In this case, we have a two-input production function, $Q = f(K,L)$. As we described in Chapter 11, we can use a Cobb-Douglas production function, so we can write our empirical production function as

$$Q = AK^\alpha L^\beta,$$

where $0 < \alpha, \beta < 1$. As we noted in Chapter 11, with this production function, the marginal product functions are

$$MP_K = \alpha\frac{Q}{K} = \alpha AK^{\alpha-1}L^\beta$$

$$MP_L = \beta\frac{Q}{L} = \beta AK^\alpha L^{\beta-1}.$$

Once the production function has been estimated (i.e., we have the estimates $\hat{A}$, $\hat{\alpha}$, and $\hat{\beta}$), it can be used in conjunction with the forecasts of the output price and the prices of inputs to express the two profit-maximizing conditions as

$$(\hat{P}) \times (\hat{\beta}AK^{\hat\alpha}L^{\hat\beta-1}) = \hat{w}$$

and

$$(\hat{P}) \times (\hat{\alpha}AK^{\hat\alpha-1}L^{\hat\beta}) = \hat{r}.$$

To determine the profit-maximizing levels of wage of labor and capital, we need to solve these two equations simultaneously for L and K. To show you how this is done, let's go to an example.

APPLICATION

A More Complicated Employment Decision

Phoenix Manufacturing produces a small machine part sold in a market that approximates perfect competition. In its short-run production process, Phoenix is able to vary not only its usage of labor but also the usage of a portion of its capital, since it leases some of its machinery on a short-term basis. The firm does, however, have some inputs, e.g., its building, that are not variable in the short run.

The manager of Phoenix Manufacturing wanted to determine the profit-maximizing (or loss-minimizing) levels of usage of the two variable inputs in 1988. From an econometric forecasting firm, the manager obtained a forecast for the market price of the firm's output in 1988 of $18 per unit.

From the same consulting firm, the manager obtained forecasts for the wage rate in the region in which the plant is located and the rental price of capital in 1988. The wage rate was forecasted to be $16 per hour. The forecast for the 1988 rental price (user price) of capital was 12 percent, that is, the annual cost of using $1 worth of capital for one year is 12 cents, so $\hat{r} = 0.12$.

The manager collected historical data for Phoenix Manufacturing on the firm's levels of usage of labor and the variable capital input and the resulting output. Using these data, a production function of the form

$$Q = AK^\alpha L^\beta$$

was estimated in which Q was expressed in thousand units, K in thousand dollars, and L in thousand hours of labor usage. The resulting estimate was

$$\log Q = -1.6 + 0.5 \log K + 0.4 \log L$$

or

$$Q = (0.2)K^{0.5}L^{0.4}.$$

From this production function, the marginal product functions for labor and capital were

$$MP_L = (0.4)(0.2)K^{0.5}L^{(0.4-1.0.)} = (0.08)K^{0.5}L^{-0.6}$$

and

$$MP_K = (0.5)(0.2)K^{(0.5-1.0)}L^{0.4} = (0.1)K^{-0.5}L^{0.4}.$$

Since the manager knew that profit maximization occurs when the levels of usage of the inputs are such that the values of the marginal products are equal to the input prices, the profit-maximizing conditions for Phoenix Manufacturing in 1988 are

$$(18) \times [(0.08)K^{0.5}L^{-0.6}] = 16$$
$$(18) \times [(0.1)K^{-0.5}L^{0.4}] = 0.12.$$

After performing some arithmetic and taking logarithms, these equations can be written as

$$0.5 \log K - 0.6 \log L = 2.41$$
$$-0.5 \log K + 0.4 \log L = -2.71.$$

Solving these equations for $\log K$ and $\log L$,

$$\log K = 6.62$$
$$\log L = 1.5;$$

it follows then that $K = 750$ and $L = 4.5$. That is, the profit-maximizing levels of use of the two inputs are 4,500 hours of labor and $750,000 of capital.

In the preceding discussion and application we have confined ourselves to two inputs. However, this technique can be expanded to any number of variable inputs. The methodology will not change. The only thing that happens when you add more inputs is that the computation of the solution becomes more complex.

PART FIVE

FIRMS WITH
MARKET POWER

14

THE THEORY
OF MONOPOLY

J ust as perfect competition lies at one extreme of the spectrum of market structures, pure monopoly lies at the other. A pure monopoly exists if and only if a single firm produces and sells a particular, well-defined commodity or service. Since the monopoly is the only seller in the market, it has neither rivals nor direct competitors. Furthermore, no new sellers can enter the market. Therefore, the demand function facing a monopolist is the market demand for the product.

Monopoly is similar to perfect competition in the sense that it provides a useful analytical framework, even though all of the exacting conditions of the model seldom are met in the real world. It is difficult to pinpoint a true monopolist in real-world markets. Yet many markets closely approximate monopoly organization, and many real-world firms—both large and small—possess a considerable amount of monopoly power, in the sense of having no, or few, relatively close substitutes for the products they sell (e.g., local utility companies).

Although monopolists have no *direct* close competitors who sell the same product, they do have indirect competition. Certainly all goods and services compete for a place in the consumer's budget. Thus, to some extent, the monopolist's product competes with all other goods and services.

Furthermore, every product has some substitutes, even though these substitutes may not be particularly close. For example, before 1982, American Telephone and Telegraph (AT&T) was, because of its government franchise, the only firm providing long-distance telephone service in the United States. Nonetheless, there were substitutes: telegrams, mail, personal visits, and no communication at all. And, as we shall see, other goods can become much closer substitutes for a monopolist's product as its price is increased. The presence of monopoly therefore depends to some extent on the relative prices of the monopoly product and other "poor" substitutes.

The theory of monopoly is important for two reasons. First, many firms approach a pure monopoly, and, therefore, the monopoly model is useful for analyzing their behavior. Second, the monopoly model gives an insight into how all firms with monopoly power make decisions in order to maximize their profit.

Monopoly power simply means that a firm can increase its price without losing all of its sales. All firms other than perfect competitors possess some monopoly power. Recall that a perfect competitor, facing a horizontal demand, would lose all of its sales if it raised its price. A public utility in a well-defined market approaches pure monopoly. It could raise its price and lose some, but not all, of its sales. It would have considerable monopoly power.

But other firms have monopoly power also, even though they are not pure monopolies. For example, Ford competes with several other automobile manufacturers, but Ford could raise its price without losing all of its sales. Even a single grocery store in a large city possesses some monopoly power. We will analyze more thoroughly the behavior of firms that are not pure monopolies but do possess monopoly power in the next chapter. The theory to be developed in this chapter will give an insight into how such firms behave.

We will begin our analysis by examining some characteristics of monopoly and discussing some reasons for its existence. Then we will analyze a monopolist's short- and long-run profit-maximizing decisions. In this discussion we shall emphasize two major points: (1) the mere existence of monopoly does not guarantee economic profit, and (2) just as the perfect competitor does, a monopolist maximizes profit by producing the output at which marginal revenue equals marginal cost. But, unlike the perfect competitor, the monopolist's price is not the marginal revenue. We end the chapter with an analysis of the monopolist's choice of input usage.

14.1 CHARACTERISTICS OF MONOPOLY

As we stressed above, no absolutely pure monopoly exists because every product has some substitutes. Even a single bank in a small town has substitutes: people can bank in a nearby city. Or if, for example, Coca-Cola was the only soft drink manufacturer, it would be a monopolist only if people would accept no other beverage, regardless of the price of Coke. Certainly Coca-Cola and the bank would have considerable monopoly power, or market power, but they would not be pure monopolists. Therefore, we typically characterize monopoly by the amount of monopoly power the firm possesses. So let's look at what determines the amount of monopoly power.

If a firm produces and sells 100 percent of the total output of a well-defined product, it has substantial monopoly power and would approach a pure monopoly. Other firms with a smaller percent of the market, say 90, 80, or even 65, would probably have considerable monopoly power but would not be pure monopolies. So a firm's market share is one way of determining how much monopoly power it has.

A problem with this method of determining monopoly power is defining the relevant market. We alluded to this question above when discussing the single bank in a small town and the soft drink market. Is the relevant market for banking services local, regional, statewide, or nationwide? Is the relevant market the soft drink market or the beverage market? These questions also have arisen during antitrust cases, with no clear consensus. Therefore, classifying monopoly or determining monopoly power by share of the market remains rather imprecise.

Another way of determining how much monopoly power a firm possesses is to consider how substitutable other products are for the product it sells. Recall from Chapter 6 that how substitutable other products are is the most important determinant of the product's demand elasticity and cross-price elasticity. Thus these two elasticities can give an insight into how much monopoly power a firm has and how closely it approaches a pure monopoly.

As demand becomes less elastic, fewer consumers would switch away from the product after a given price increase. This means that consumers view the product as less substitutable with other products. Thus the less elastic is demand, the more monopoly power the firm possesses; that is, the fewer customers it loses after a price increase.[1] Conversely, as demand becomes more elastic, monopoly power declines.

Thus a rough scale measuring monopoly power may be set up using the seller's elasticity of demand at a given level of output or price. When demand is perfectly elastic (horizontal), the firm has zero monopoly power. As demand becomes less horizontal and elasticity declines, monopoly power increases until the firm's elasticity is equivalent to the market elasticity of demand. Note that we do not say that demand becomes inelastic at the profit-maximizing output; it does not. The firm's demand elasticity approaches the market demand elasticity as monopoly power becomes large. At this point the firm would be considered the only seller in the market (however defined) and would have the maximum monopoly power possible.

---

[1]Using own-price elasticity to determine the extent of monopoly power does not mean that a firm would choose to produce and sell a level of output on the inelastic portion of its demand. That is, monopoly power does not imply $|E| < 1$; it simply means the less elastic is demand, the less monopoly power. We will show that a monopolist always chooses to produce and sell on the elastic portion of its demand when we develop the monopoly model in section 14.3.

Another helpful measure of monopoly power is a firm's cross-price elasticity of demand. Recall from Chapter 6 that this elasticity measures the sensitivity of the quantity purchased of one good to a change in the price of another good. It therefore tells us directly whether two goods are good substitutes and thus in the same market. A large, positive cross-price elasticity means that consumers consider the goods to be easily substitutable. Monopoly power in this case is likely to be weak. If a firm produces a product for which we cannot find other products with a high cross-price elasticity, we can be reasonably sure that the firm is alone in its market, and there are no good substitutes available.

Therefore, although no firm is a pure monopolist in the sense of having no substitutes, we can use the monopoly model to explain and analyze the behavior of firms with considerable monopoly power. Such firms can be giants or relatively small, depending upon the size of the market.

APPLICATION

Is the National Football League a Monopoly?

During the summer of 1986 a jury in Room 318 of the federal courthouse in Manhattan answered the question that is the title of this application. The answer was yes. Let's see if we agree.

The United States Football League (USFL), a recently formed league that until 1986 played its games in the spring, sued the old established National Football League (NFL), which played in the fall, for $1.69 billion damages. The USFL charged the NFL with using "unfair" practices to hold its monopoly of professional football. It based its case on the fact that the new league planned to switch to fall games in direct competition with the NFL and, according to the USFL, the NFL used unfair pressure on the major TV networks to keep the USFL from obtaining a TV contract for the fall season. The jury said that the NFL was indeed a monopoly. But it did not believe that the defendant unfairly kept the USFL from competing and awarded the plaintiff $1, which was automatically tripled to $3 under antitrust law. The NFL won a huge victory, and the USFL suspended play for the season.

Some sports observers felt that the jury was unclear because it found that the NFL was a monopoly and then did not award the USFL damages. Monopoly is illegal, however, only if firms use unfair means to attain it. The jury found that this was not true.

And on the foremost charge that the NFL had monopolized the pro football TV market, and on seven other charges, the NFL was absolved. In other words, the jury believed the NFL had not significantly harmed the USFL. The television issue was extremely important because over 60 percent of the NFL's revenue is from TV.

Let's look at the issues involved. First, if the TV market for professional football was the relevant market and if an overwhelming share of the market was the relevant criterion for monopoly, the NFL was clearly a virtual monopolist. But, by awarding the USFL such insignificant damages, the jury must have believed that this was not the relevant market.

What was the relevant market? Most would say it was the sports TV market or perhaps even the TV market as a whole. In the sports TV market the NFL must compete with the baseball playoffs and World Series until well into October. Then college and professional basketball, as well as some other sports, become popular. College football is a major competitor throughout the fall, although the two seldom compete on the same day or night. Nonetheless, professional football is a dominant television sport in the fall and early winter.

So what about the NFL's alleged monopoly in the TV market? Clearly, a cross-price elasticity between the NFL and the USFL would show considerable monopoly power for the NFL. The new league was willing to sell its games to the networks for considerably less than the NFL, but the major networks were not willing to buy. They obviously thought that USFL games were not a particularly good substitute for NFL games. More important, they thought the fans and the advertisers didn't think they were good substitutes either.

But, could other programs have been a close substitute? To examine this issue, one must look at the own-price elasticity of demand for NFL games. In 1986, the NFL still had one year left on its $2.1 billion contract with the networks. During his 26-year term as NFL commissioner, Pete Rozelle had obtained significant increases in the prices charged the networks for TV games, indicating a relatively inelastic demand.

But, the TV contract would have to be renegotiated in one year. *The Wall Street Journal* was not optimistic for the NFL. The *Journal* reported that Mr. Rozelle was facing a TV market in chaos. Sports ratings in general, and NFL ratings in particular, had suffered during recent years. The NFL's performance rebounded slightly in 1985, but the appetite of advertisers for sports programs had not. A former network executive and sports-television consultant wondered where the NFL would make up the shortfall if it got less income from the networks—all of which said they were losing money on the telecasts. He noted that putting more games on television would only glut the market—advertising rates would fall and networks would pay less for NFL broadcast rights. Thus it remains to be seen how much monopoly power the NFL really has, even though it is a true monopolist in the professional football market.

Sources: "The Award Was Only Token," by Craig Neff, *Sports Illustrated*, August 11, 1986, and "Despite Court Victory, NFL Faces Major Obstacles in Months Ahead," by Hal Lancaster, *The Wall Street Journal*, August 6, 1986.

14.2 BARRIERS TO ENTRY

Before analyzing monopoly behavior, we need to first examine why some industries approach a monopoly structure while others are considerably more competitive. The question to be addressed is: Why in some industries does the largest firm produce a large percentage of total output while in other industries no one firm has a substantial share of the total market?

We can explain why a firm would continue to have a monopoly position or considerable monopoly power by looking at various barriers to entry. A barrier to entry exists when an established firm (or firms) has some advantages over potential entrants, making it difficult for other firms to enter the industry. It is impossible to enumerate every reason a potential producer might not be able to enter a market, since what constitutes a barrier depends on the market in which it arises. Instead we simply cite several examples of how barriers to entry can lead to monopoly.

Economies of Scale

An extremely important barrier to entry is created when the long-run average cost curve of a firm decreases over a wide range of output, relative to the demand for the product. Thus economies of scale can erect a barrier to the entry of new firms. This case is frequently called a "natural" monopoly. A natural monopoly exists when the minimum average cost of production occurs at a rate of output so large that one firm can supply the entire market at a price covering full cost. To illustrate this situation, suppose there exists a market in which one firm supplies the entire market and enjoys a pure profit. Because of the existence of substantial economies of scale, the average cost at smaller rates of output is so high that entry is not profitable for small-scale firms. On the other hand, the entry of another large-scale producer is also discouraged because the added production of this firm would increase the quantity supplied and drive price below the pure-profit level for all firms. Therefore, entry is discouraged and a natural monopoly exists.

If a smaller firm enters the market, it would, because of higher costs, have to charge a higher price than the monopolist, in order to make even a normal profit. For identical, or even similar, products, the entrant will not make any sales. At the higher price the entrant might attempt to convince buyers its product is better, but this usually means either increased costs for advertising or higher production costs. In both circumstances costs will be higher, and this makes successful entry all the more difficult.

When these long-run economies exist it is difficult to maintain a competitive market, even if a number of producers begin at a small scale. In fact, competition could only exist if producers were strictly prohibited from expanding. Imagine what would happen if they were not. Every firm would have the incentive to expand and move down the *LRAC* curve where unit costs would be lower, and, as a consequence, prices could be lower. A larger firm could always undersell smaller firms and drive them out of business. Bigger firms would continue getting bigger until only the largest firm remained. Pervasive economies of scale are not conducive to the existence of perfect competition, because profit-maximizing incentives naturally lead each firm to try to dominate the industry. Eventually the largest firm will drive the smaller ones out of the market. This, of course, leads to a natural monopoly.

Barriers Created by Government

An obvious entry barrier is government. Licensing and franchises are ways monopolies are created by government decree. For example, licenses are granted to radio and television stations by the Federal Communications Commission (FCC), and only those stations possessing a license are allowed to operate. Locally, this confers immense monopoly power on those stations that have FCC approval. Entrants can petition the FCC for a license to operate, but if those stations who are operating protest to the commission, the petition is usually denied. Governments also grant exclusive franchises for city, county, and state services. For example, local telephone and cable television utilities have a great deal of monopoly power in that they are the only regional producer of the product. By law, no other producer can exist.

Another legal barrier to competition lies in the patent laws. These laws make it possible for a person to apply for and obtain the exclusive right to produce a certain commodity, or to produce a commodity by means of a specified process that provides an absolute cost advantage. E. I. du Pont de Nemours & Company enjoyed patent monopolies over many commodities, cellophane being the most notable. The Eastman Kodak Company continues to hold numerous patents on its camera equipment.

Despite examples to the contrary, holding a patent on a product or production process may not be quite what it seems in many instances. In the first place, a patent has only a limited life span. It is meant to reward innovative activities. Second, the holder of a product patent may choose not to exploit the monopoly position in the production of the product. If diseconomies of scale set in at a low level of production, the patent holder may find it more profitable to sell production rights to a few firms, or to many. Third, a firm that owns a patented lower-cost production process may have a cost advantage over other firms in the market, but sell only a small part of the industry's total output at the equilibrium position. The new technique will lead to patent monopoly only if the firm has the capability to supply the entire market, or finds it profitable to do so. Fourth, a patent gives one the exclusive right to produce a particular, meticulously specified commodity, or to use a particular, meticulously specified process to produce a commodity. A patent does not preclude the development of closely related substitute goods or closely allied production processes.

International Business Machines (IBM) has the exclusive right to produce their patented computers, but many other computers are available and there is competition in the computer market.

Input Barriers

Historically, an important reason for monopoly power has been the control of raw-material supplies. If one firm (or perhaps a few firms) controls all of the known supply of a necessary ingredient for a particular product, the firm or firms can refuse to sell that ingredient to other firms at a price low enough for them to compete. Since no others can produce the product, monopoly results. For many years the Aluminum Company of America (Alcoa) owned almost every source of bauxite, a necessary ingredient in the production of aluminum, in North America. The control of resource supply, coupled with certain patent rights, provided Alcoa with an absolute monopoly in aluminum production. It was only after World War II that the federal courts effectively broke Alcoa's monopoly in the aluminum industry.

Another frequently cited input barrier arises in capital markets. Established firms, perhaps because of a history of good earnings, are able to secure financing at a more favorable rate than new firms. Imagine how far a typical person would get by walking into a bank and requesting a loan for $20 million to start a mainframe computer company. Most bankers would take a very dim view of this new company's survival. Knowing that you would be in the same market as IBM and other well-established companies, bankers would probably turn down the loan application. If the loan was made available, the interest rate for a new company would be above that paid by established firms. Capital markets pose a barrier for new firms when a large investment is necessary to enter a market.

Brand Loyalties

On the demand side, older firms may have, over time, built up the allegiance of their customers. New firms might find this loyalty difficult to overcome. For example, no one knows what the service or repair policy of a new firm may be. The preference of buyers can also be influenced by a long successful advertising campaign; established brands, for instance, allow customers recourse if the product should be defective or short of its advertised promises. Although technical economies or diseconomies of scale may be insignificant, new firms might have considerable difficulty establishing a market organization and overcoming buyer preference for the products of older firms. A classic example of how loyalty preserves monopoly power can be found in the concentrated lemon juice market. ReaLemon lemon juice has successfully developed such strong brand loyalties among consumers that rival brands evidently cannot survive in the market. The situation was so serious that the courts forced ReaLemon to license its name to would-be competitors.

The role of advertising as a barrier to entry has been a source of controversy. Some argue that advertising acts as a barrier to entry by strengthening buyer preferences for the products of established firms. On the other hand, consider the great difficulty of entering an established industry without access to advertising. A good way for an entrenched monopoly to discourage entry would be, in fact, to get the government to prohibit advertising. The reputation of the old firm would enable it to continue its dominance. A new firm would have difficulty informing the public about the availability of a new product unless it was able to advertise. Thus advertising may be a way for a new firm to overcome the advantages of established firms. The effect of advertising on entry remains a point of disagreement among economists.

The purpose of this discussion is to expose you to several of the most common types of entry barriers and to illustrate the diversity of factors that prevent entry into a market and, consequently, foster monopoly power. It is noteworthy that several of the barriers mentioned are somewhat influenced by the monopolist. The control of inputs and the development of consumer loyalties are effective barriers essentially erected by firms already producing in the market.

Yet despite the existence of barriers to entry, firms can lose and have lost their positions of extensive monopoly power. Even quite strong barriers to entry can be overcome. The monopolist can become complacent in its protected position and allow inefficiencies to enter the production process. This raises the cost, and hence the price, and allows new, more efficient firms to enter the market. Or some potential entrants are ingenious enough to find ways to lower cost, or (as noted above) get around patent protection, or overcome brand loyalty to the established firm. Thus barriers to entry do protect the established firm with great monopoly power, but not completely.

THE WALL STREET JOURNAL

APPLICATION

Advantages of Established Firms and Strategic Behavior*

We emphasized that brand loyalty and the reputation enjoyed by a dominant firm can erect barriers to the entry of new firms into a market. But the strength of these barriers depends in large part on the behavior of the dominant firm. Let's look at the strategic behavior of two firms that dominated their markets. They reacted differently to the threat

Continued on page 416

*"Higher Quality IBM 'Clones' Put Pressure on Computer Prices," by Brenton R. Schender, *The Wall Street Journal*, May 15, 1986 and "Calling Long Distance: User Vote Shows Strong Support for AT&T," by Francine Schwadel, *The Wall Street Journal*, August 22, 1986. Adapted by permission of *The Wall Street Journal*. © Dow Jones and Company, Inc., 1986. All rights reserved.

THE WALL STREET JOURNAL

APPLICATION

Continued from page 415 of entry with markedly different results.

In 1981, International Business Machines Corp. (IBM) introduced its Personal Computer (PC) for $2,205. Although other companies made similar computers, undoubtedly IBM's PC dominated the market, particularly the business market.

One reason for IBM's domination was name identification—the advantage of the established firm. As long as the name IBM was on the box, people weren't intimidated. Also, IBM used a copyrighted basic input output system (BIOS) chip to control the way the computer talks to the screen and peripheral equipment. So IBM had two of the barriers to entry discussed above: the advantage of being established and a patent. But these barriers didn't stand very long.

In 1984 IBM had approximately 80 percent of the personal computer market. But by March 1986, IBM's share of the market had, for the first time, fallen below 50 percent (to 45%). New entrants had reduced IBM's market share significantly. Dozens of IBM clones—machines virtually identical to IBM's standard PC—were readily available and selling for as little as $500 (less than one fourth of

IBM's suggested retail price). These clones were made from parts manufactured in the Far East and assembled in the United States. Many of the parts were practically identical to those used by IBM.

Some people did think that the clones were inferior to IBM's machines, but far more did not. And certainly the clones were much cheaper, even though many dealers were cutting the price on IBM's PC. Not only did the clones cut heavily into IBM's share of the home computer market, but its share of the business market declined as well.

What happened to IBM's barriers to entry? *Newsweek* suggested two reasons for the decline.[†] One reason was, in part, that IBM was a victim of its own success. Its PC was so popular at first that competitors realized they would have to build machines that could use software and peripheral equipment made for the PC. Also, as more PCs were sold, people became more computer literate, and IBM no longer had its original mystique. And, of course, there were the lower prices of the competition.

But, the only way to make a true IBM clone was to develop a basic input output system chip that acted like IBM's without

Continued on page 417

[†]"Dog-Eat-Dog Shakeout," *Newsweek,* May 19, 1986, p. 55.

THE WALL STREET JOURNAL

APPLICATION

Continued from page 416 violating the copyright. Compaq developed such a compatible chip and became a half-billion dollar company.

Nevertheless, IBM would probably have been able to hold on to most of its share of the market had it been willing to cut its prices while it still dominated the market. As *The Wall Street Journal* reported, "Judging from the rock-bottom prices of the 'no-name' clones, both manufacturers and retailers have been operating on sales margins often exceeding 50 percent." Entry would have been discouraged by lower IBM prices. People would have been willing to pay some premium for the IBM PC, but many were not willing to pay the premium that existed in the market.

So, barriers to entry, such as those enjoyed by IBM, can protect a dominant firm with considerable market power for only so long. In the absence of strict licensing restrictions, to maintain a dominant position in a market a firm must generally continue to improve its product and keep its price low enough to discourage entry.

We turn now to another firm, American Telephone and Telegraph (AT&T), that dominated its market, but reacted differently to a severe threat of competition. From 1984 until September 1986, millions of Americans cast their ballots to decide which long-distance telephone company they would choose. Before the breakup of the AT&T Bell system in 1984, AT&T had a market share of 90 percent. Many analysts predicted that the company would suffer a drubbing in the balloting, some predicting a decline in share to as low as 60 percent. The theory was that people would desert AT&T in droves once federally mandated "equal access" enabled them to enjoy cheaper service without having to dial extra digits.

It didn't happen. AT&T held an estimated 80 percent of the market. Competitors such as MCI and Sprint made some penetration into AT&T's market share, but not nearly as much as predicted. It appears that two factors were responsible for AT&T's success: brand name familiarity and the company's marketing strategy.

One half of the respondents, in a poll conducted by *The Wall Street Journal*/NBC News, who expressed a preference for one of the phone firms cited familiarity with AT&T as the most influential element in their choice. The poll indicated that quality of service was the most

Continued on page 418

THE WALL STREET JOURNAL

APPLICATION

Continued from page 417 important factor in choosing a long-distance company for 47 percent of the respondents; cost of service came in second with 25 percent. A research analyst with the Gartner Group concluded, "People will pay an extra buck or two a month for a known commodity."

So AT&T succeeded to a large extent because of its advantage of being established for so long and its reputation for quality. But, according to the chairman of MCI, ". . . most of AT&T's competitors failed to make the capital investments necessary to wrest large chunks of business away from AT&T." The *Journal* pointed out, however, ". . . AT&T didn't succeed solely because of the weakness of its competitors. To the amazement of naysayers, it transformed itself into a marketing powerhouse. . . ."

AT&T went after heavy users with special pricing packages and such incentives as discounts on restaurant meals and exercise classes. It took to the airwaves with a series of TV commercials featuring the actor Cliff Robertson, who stressed AT&T's quality and reliability and suggested that its competitors weren't up to snuff. The company went so far as to prepare special materials to appeal to such diverse markets as military personnel, people in the process of moving, and various ethnic groups.

Certainly AT&T lost some customers in the balloting. Some reacted like one person who picked MCI, "I don't like AT&T. I think it's a monopoly." One analyst described many people who switched as "people who hate the corporate giant" or "people who drive foreign cars." She described people who stuck with AT&T as "risk averse," "traditionalists," or "those who drive American cars."

In addition to its marketing blitz, AT&T kept its price low enough to reduce the gap between its price and competing companies. At one time it was possible to lower a family's long-distance bill by as much as 50 percent a month by using another company. By 1986, AT&T narrowed the price difference to the 10 percent range. This wasn't enough to offset the brand loyalty and reputation for quality for a large number of people.

Thus AT&T had a great advantage over its competitors from being the old, established firm. But it was not content to rest on its laurels and exercise its

Continued on page 419

14.3 PROFIT MAXIMIZATION UNDER MONOPOLY—THE OUTPUT AND PRICE DECISIONS

As was the case for the perfectly competitive firm, we assume that the monopolist wishes to maximize profit, given prevailing cost and demand conditions. As you know, *any* firm can increase profit by expanding output so long as the marginal revenue from the expansion exceeds the marginal cost of expanding output. The firm would reduce output if marginal revenue is less than marginal cost. The basic principle of profit maximization—profit is maximized by producing and selling the output at which marginal cost equals marginal revenue—is the same for the monopoly as for the perfectly competitive firm.

The fundamental difference is that, for the monopolist, marginal revenue is not equal to price. Instead, the marginal revenue for additional units sold is less than the price at which these units sell. Unlike the firm in a perfectly competitive market, the monopoly firm cannot sell all it desires to sell at the prevailing market price. Since a monopolist is the only firm selling in the market, the demand facing the monopolist is the market demand. Additional sales by a competitive firm do not lower the market price, but a monopoly firm can sell more only by lowering the price charged. Therefore, the marginal revenue from additional units sold is the price of those units *less* the reduction in the price of those units that could have been sold at the higher price.

Demand and Marginal Revenue

As we showed in Chapter 6, if the demand curve is downward sloping, the marginal revenue from each additional unit sold is less than price (beyond the first unit). Thus the marginal revenue curve lies below the demand curve. As we noted above, the demand function facing a monopolist is the market demand for the product. The market marginal revenue curve is, therefore, the marginal revenue curve of the monopolist.

A typical demand curve and marginal revenue curve are shown in Figure 14.1. As we showed in Chapter 6, when marginal revenue is positive, demand is elastic (at outputs between zero and q). When marginal revenue is negative, demand is inelastic (at outputs greater than q). We might note that in the case of a straight-line demand curve (as in Figure 14.1), the marginal revenue curve has the same vertical intercept as demand and is twice as steep.

As we discussed above, we can ascertain the amount of market power possessed by a firm by looking at the effect of changes in the prices of other products upon the firm's demand function. All firms, except for perfect competitors, possess some monopoly power. That is, they do not face horizontal demand curves. But the point at which a firm with monopoly power is called a monopolist is somewhat arbitrary. In any case we can analyze the profit-maximizing decision of most firms with monopoly power using the model of pure monopoly.

A Numerical Example

Before examining monopoly behavior graphically, we can illustrate two basic principles with a numerical example.

Principles.   If the marginal revenue from selling additional units of output exceeds the marginal cost of producing those units, a profit-maximizing monopolist increases its output. If the marginal revenue from selling additional units of output is less than the marginal cost of producing them, the monopolist does not produce these additional units.

From these two principles it logically follows that when output is continuously divisible a monopolist maximizes profit by producing and selling the level of output at which marginal revenue equals marginal cost.

Figure 14.1 Demand and Marginal Revenue Facing a Monopolist

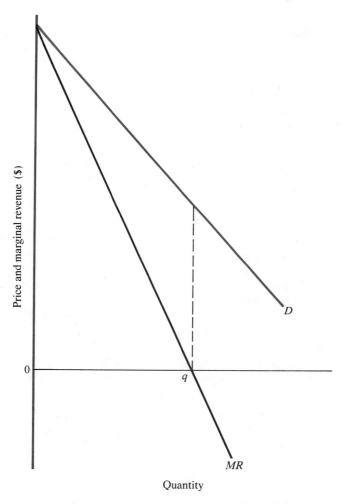

Quantity

In Table 14.1, columns 1 and 2 give the demand schedule facing a monopolist, for 10 through 70 units of output in discrete intervals of 10. Column 3 shows the associated total revenue schedule (price times quantity). The total cost of producing each level of output is given in column 4. We obtain the profit or loss from producing and selling each level of output by subtracting total cost from total revenue (shown in column 7). Examination of the profit (loss) column indicates that the maximum profit ($70) occurs when the firm sells 40 units of output at a price of $6.00.

We reach the same conclusion using the marginal revenue-marginal cost approach. The marginal revenue from selling additional units of output exceeds the marginal cost of producing the additional units until 40 units are produced and sold. After 40 units the marginal revenue of the

Table 14.1   Monopoly Profit Maximization

(1) Output	(2) Price	(3) Total Revenue	(4) Total Cost	(5) Marginal Revenue	(6) Marginal Cost	(7) Profit (loss)
0	$8.00	0	$ 50			− $50
				>$7.50	>$4.00	
10	7.50	$ 75	90			− 15
				> 6.50	> 2.00	
20	7.00	140	110			30
				> 5.50	> 2.50	
30	6.50	195	135			60
				> 4.50	> 3.50	
40	6.00	240	170			70
				> 3.50	> 4.50	
50	5.50	275	215			60
				> 2.50	> 5.50	
60	5.00	300	270			30
				> 1.50	> 6.50	
70	4.50	315	335			− 20

next 10 units is $3.50 per unit; the marginal cost of the next 10 units is $4.50 per unit. Clearly, increasing output and sales from 40 to 50 would lower profit, as would any additional units beyond 40. Thus profit must increase until 40 units then decreases thereafter. We reach the same conclusion that we obtained by subtracting total cost from total revenue—an output of 40 units maximizes profit.

The example in Table 14.1 is shown graphically in Figure 14.2. Since marginal revenue and marginal cost are per-unit changes in revenue and cost over the discrete changes in output, we plot these in the middle of the interval. For example, the marginal cost of increasing output from zero to 10 ($4.00) and the marginal revenue from increasing sales from zero to 10 ($7.50) are plotted midway between zero and 10, at five units of output. Marginal cost equals marginal revenue at 40 units of output which, as we saw from the table, is the profit-maximizing level of output. The demand curve shows the price the firm will charge for the 40 units, $6.00.

We turn now from a specific numerical example of profit maximization for a monopolist to a more general graphical analysis of a monopolist in the short run. In this case, we will assume, for analytical convenience, that output and price are continuously divisible.

Short-Run Equilibrium: Profit Maximization

The short-run cost curves confronting a monopolist are derived in exactly the same fashion as those faced by a perfectly competitive firm. From the theory of cost developed in Chapter 10, we know that cost depends upon the production function and input prices. The chief difference between a monopolist's cost curves and those for a perfect competitor is found in the potential impact of output changes on factor prices.

In the theory of perfect competition we assumed that each firm is very small relative to the total factor market and can, therefore, change its

Figure 14.2 Monopoly Profit Maximization

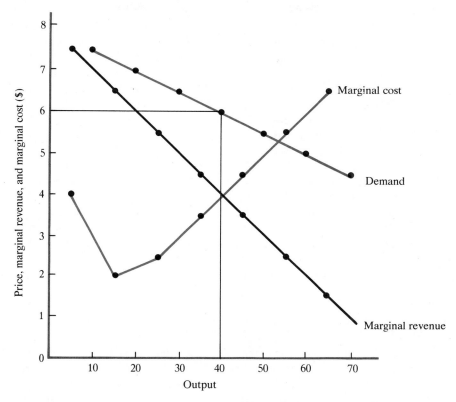

own rate of output without affecting factor prices, just as any one consumer can change the amount of a good purchased without affecting its price. But recall that, if all firms in the industry change output and, therefore, the use of all inputs, the prices of some of those inputs may change. The output of the monopolist, the sole firm in the industry, is accordingly the output of the industry. Certainly a monopolist, just as a competitive industry, may be so small relative to the demand for all inputs that its input use will have no effect on the price of any input. To be sure, even a very large monopolist will purchase some inputs, such as unskilled labor, the prices of which are not affected by the monopolist's rate of use. On the other hand, there is a possibility that a monopoly firm will purchase certain inputs for which the firm's rate of purchase will have a definite effect on the prices of these factors of production.

Notwithstanding the monopolist's possible effect upon factor prices, the cost curves for a monopoly firm are typically assumed to have the general shapes described in Chapter 10. The primary implication of rising supply prices of variable inputs is that the average and marginal cost curves rise more rapidly or fall less rapidly than if input prices were constant. Thus, for example, marginal cost may rise not only because of diminishing marginal productivity, but also because input prices rise with increased use.

A monopolist, just as a perfect competitor, attains maximum profit (or minimum loss) by producing and selling that rate of output for which the positive (negative) difference between total revenue and total cost is greatest (least). This condition occurs when marginal revenue equals marginal cost.[2]

Using this proposition, the position of short-run equilibrium is easily described graphically. Figure 14.3 shows the relevant cost and revenue curves for a monopolist. (Since *AVC* and *AFC* are not necessary for exposition, they are omitted.) The profit-maximizing monopolist produces q_0 units of output, since at this level of production $MC = MR$. From the demand curve we see that price must be p_0 in order to ration the q_0 units among those who wish to buy the commodity. Total revenue is p_0 times q_0, or the area of the rectangle Op_0Bq_0. The unit cost of producing this amount of output is c_0. Total cost is then c_0 times q_0, or the area Oc_0Dq_0. Profit is $TR - TC$, or the shaded area c_0p_0BD. Since price is greater than average total cost at the equilibrium output, the firm earns an economic profit over and above its opportunity cost or normal return. But, this need not be the case.

Short-Run Equilibrium: Loss Minimization

People somehow have the idea that anyone with monopoly power can charge any price desired and make a profit. For example, several famous country and western musicians recently put on a benefit concert, called Farm Aid, to raise money for farmers. One of the best-known performers said, "These people can't take care of themselves. If you earn 87 cents for a bushel of corn, and it costs you $1.25 to put it in the ground, why even plant it. If you and I made a guitar, we could charge whatever we wanted to for it. These people can't."

The singer's motives were good, but his economic analysis wasn't. Certainly the farmer must take the market-determined price as given. And, if he made a guitar, the famous singer could charge any price he wanted. But there is no guarantee that anyone would buy his guitar at that price. And there may not be any price someone would pay that is high enough to cover the cost of making the guitar.

So it is a misconception that any monopoly is assured a profit. If demand is sufficiently low, a monopolist may incur a loss in the short run, just as

---

[2]This result is derived mathematically in the appendix to this chapter.

Figure 14.3 **Short-Run Equilibrium under Monopoly**

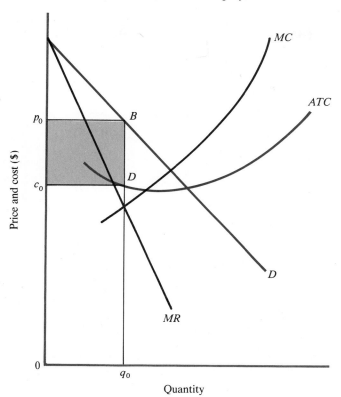

a pure competitor may. Figure 14.4 shows a loss situation. Marginal cost equals marginal revenue at output q_1, which can be sold at a price p_1. Average cost is c_1. Total cost, Oc_1Dq_1, exceeds total revenue, Op_1Bq_1; hence the firm suffers a loss shown as the shaded area p_1c_1DB.

Note that in Figure 14.4 the monopolist would produce rather than shut down in the short run, since total revenue (Op_1Bq_1) exceeds total variable cost ($OvNq_1$). After all variable costs have been covered, there is still some revenue (vp_1BN) left to apply to fixed cost. However, if demand decreases so that the monopolist cannot cover all of variable cost at any price, the firm would shut down and lose only fixed cost. This situation is analogous to that of the perfect competitor.

In the short run, the primary difference between a monopoly and a perfect competitor lies in the slope of the demand curve. Either may earn a pure profit; either may incur a loss.

Figure 14.4 **Short-Run Losses under Monopoly**

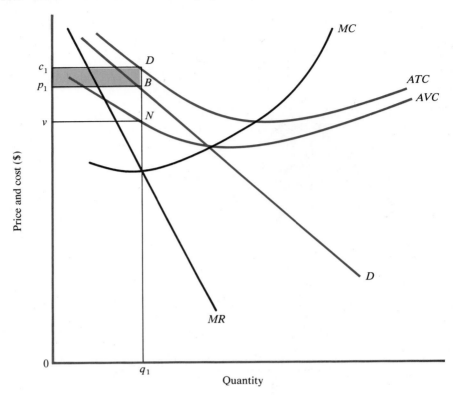

Principle. *In the short run a monopoly will produce a positive output
if some price on the demand curve exceeds average variable cost. It
maximizes profit or minimizes loss by producing the quantity for which*
MR = MC. *The price for that output is given by the demand curve. If
the price exceeds average total cost the firm makes a pure economic
profit. If price is less than average total cost but exceeds average
variable cost, the firm suffers an economic loss, but continues to
produce in the short run. If demand falls below average variable cost
at every output, the firm shuts down in the short run and loses only its
fixed cost. If the firm produces a positive output, equilibrium price
exceeds marginal cost, since the monopolist's demand curve is above
its marginal revenue curve at every output.*[3]

---

[3]We should note that a monopolist would never choose a situation in which it was
producing and selling an output on the inelastic portion of its demand. When demand is
inelastic, marginal revenue is negative. Since marginal cost is always positive, it must equal
marginal revenue when the latter is also positive. Thus the monopolist will always be on
the elastic portion of demand.

Long-Run Equilibrium

We have said that a monopoly exists if there is only one firm in the market. Among other things, this statement implies that entry into the market is closed. Thus, if a monopolist earns a pure profit in the short run, no new producer can enter the market in the hope of sharing whatever pure profit potential exists. Therefore, economic profit is not eliminated in the long run, as was the case under perfect competition. The monopolist will, however, make adjustments in plant size as demand conditions warrant, even though entry is prohibited.

Clearly, in the long run, a monopolist would use the plant size designed to produce the quantity at which long-run marginal cost equals marginal revenue. Profit would be equal to the product of output times the difference between price and long-run average cost. New entrants cannot come into the industry and compete away profits—entry will not shift the demand curve facing the monopolist.

But demand conditions can change for reasons other than the entry of new firms, and such changes will cause the monopolist to make adjustments. Suppose that demand for the product changes, due perhaps to a change in consumer's incomes. At first the firm will adjust without changing plant size. It will produce the quantity at which the new marginal revenue curve equals short-run marginal cost, or it will shut down in the short run if it cannot cover variable costs. In the long run, however, the monopolist can adjust to the change in demand by changing plant size.

Long-run equilibrium adjustment for a monopoly firm must take one of two possible courses: (1) If the monopolist incurs a short-run loss and if there is no plant size that will result in pure profit (or, at least, no loss), the monopoly will go out of business; or (2) If it suffers a short-run loss or earns a short-run profit with the original plant, the manager must determine whether a plant of different size (and thus a different price and output) will lead to a larger profit. If the latter course of action is followed, the firm will select the plant size designed to produce the output at which the new marginal revenue equals long-run marginal cost.

Generalizing, we have the following:

Principle. A monopolist maximizes profit in the long run by producing and selling that level of output for which long-run marginal cost equals marginal revenue. The optimal plant is the one whose short-run average cost curve is tangent to the long-run average cost curve at the point corresponding to long-run equilibrium output. At this point, short-run marginal cost also equals marginal revenue.

This proposition is illustrated in Figure 14.5. The monopolist would build a plant to produce the quantity at which long-run marginal cost equals marginal revenue. In each period, Q units are produced, costing c per unit and selling at a price of p per unit. Long-run profit is $cpBE$. By the

Figure 14.5 **Long-Run Equilibrium under Monopoly**

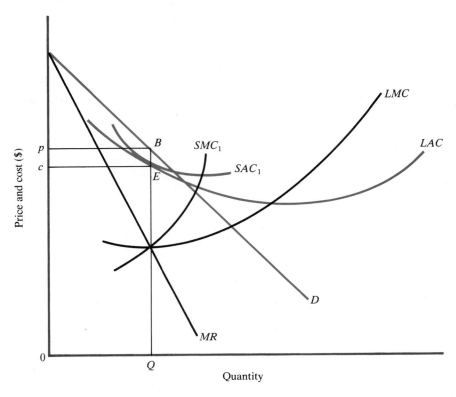

now familiar argument, this is the maximum profit possible under the given revenue and cost conditions. The monopoly operates in the short run with the plant size indicated by SAC_1 and SMC_1. This is the best the monopolist can attain, and it can be attained because in the long run plant size is variable and the market is effectively closed to entry.

THE WALL STREET JOURNAL

APPLICATION

What Can a Giant Do When It's Losing Money?

In this section we have emphasized that even firms with considerable market power can make losses; that is, make below-

normal profits in the short run. And, if it is covering its variable costs, the firm will continue producing. *The Wall Street Journal,* April 28, 1986, described

Continued on page 429

THE WALL STREET JOURNAL

APPLICATION

Continued from page 428 what was happening to one such firm and what it was doing.*

The *Journal* reported that for five years Firestone Tire & Rubber Co. made a lot of moves applauded by securities analysts, but the company's bottom line didn't show the results. Long before corporate restructuring became a manager's buzzword, John J. Nevin, Firestone's chairman and chief executive, closed aging plants and slashed the number and sizes of Firestone tires. He sold a profitable polyvinyl chloride resins business after deciding that it would never become a force in the industry. In his six years at the helm, he rigorously pruned management ranks and reduced the payroll from 107,000 to 50,000.

But, during the 1985 fiscal year, Firestone earned a minuscule 1.3 percent rate of return. After the plant-closing charges were deducted, it earned an even lower return. Clearly, this was nowhere close to a normal profit for the stockholders. So Firestone was losing money even though its sales revenue for the year was a whopping $3.84 billion.

The problem was that while costs had risen 4 percent since mid-1981, prices had fallen 7 percent over the same period because of declining demand. Tire buyers, not stockholders, reaped the benefits. Even a firm as large as Firestone couldn't simply increase prices and make a profit.

So what was Firestone to do? As the *Journal* noted, even though it couldn't earn acceptable (normal) profits on invested assets, it also couldn't cut investment in its basic businesses without sinking hopelessly behind rivals technologically. The company couldn't sell aging tire factories that no one wanted. And it couldn't even afford the employee severance costs and facilities write-downs involved in closing plants. In other words, the loss from shutting down was greater than the loss from continuing to produce.

But Firestone was trying to do something about the problem. Mr. Nevin said, "For many companies, the question is whether to go belly-up slowly or focus on certain parts of the industry where they can compete." Firestone was focusing on radial tires for *Continued on page 430*

*"Many Companies Find They Can't Pass Along Rising Costs to Buyers," by Ralph E. Winter. Adapted by permission of *The Wall Street Journal*.

THE WALL STREET JOURNAL

APPLICATION

Continued from page 429
passenger cars and light trucks
and on maintaining its strong
position in farm tires. He
suggested that Firestone might
even gradually limit its U.S. tire
production primarily to tires for
new cars and trucks and to
practically identical tires in the
replacement market. He noted
that U.S. producers enjoy an
advantage in the new-car market
because auto makers demand a
product meeting the specific
needs of their vehicles. Commodity grade replacement tires,
for which price is more important
than performance, would come
from Firestone plants abroad or
foreign licensees. Firestone
would retail the imports through
company-operated service
centers and wholesale them
through its dealer network.

The complex world of
Firestone and the even more
complex restructuring plans may
seem far removed from our
abstract, theoretical world of cost
and demand curves. But it isn't.
Certainly our abstract model
cannot capture all the complexities of the problem. It isn't
meant to. It does provide a
framework for analyzing not only
the problem of Firestone but also
the problems of firms in similar
situations, all of which would
differ. Firestone was not earning
a normal return even though its

accounting profit was positive.
But it was at least covering
variable cost, so shutting down
would have been more costly.
And the top management was
planning to move into the long
run, when they could completely
reorganize its production facilities
and its product lines, and, they
hoped, make an economic profit.

You may wonder why we
generally use as real-world
examples and applications only
stories about corporate giants,
such as Firestone, AT&T, and
IBM. The reason is that *The Wall
Street Journal* and other major
business publications typically
don't do stories about what small
local firms are doing.

For example, Pooh's Park in
College Station, Texas, for almost
20 years was the only roller
skating rink in a county of over
100,000 people. As such, we
would call it a monopoly. For
many years Pooh's Park was
quite successful. Then it began
losing money, yet continued to
stay open for several years
despite its losses. In the fall of
1986, Pooh's Park went into the
long run. It closed down. Pooh's
Park suffered many of the same
problems as Firestone, primarily
declining demand because of a
sluggish economy. As far as we
know, *The Wall Street Journal*
did not send a reporter to cover
the closing.

14.4 INPUT DEMAND FOR A MONOPOLIST

Thus far we have analyzed profit maximization for a monopoly firm in terms of the output decision. As was the case for perfectly competitive firms, we can also analyze profit maximization in terms of input usage. We will first look at the monopoly firm's input decision assuming that it faces given (constant) prices for the inputs it purchases. Then, given our earlier discussion of the possibility that the monopoly firm's employment decision may affect the prices of some inputs, we will look at input decisions with an upward-sloping supply function for an input.

Input Prices Given

The analytical principles underlying the demand for a single variable input for a monopolist are the same as those for perfectly competitive firms. But, since price does not equal marginal revenue for a monopoly, there is one methodological difference.

To illustrate this difference, let's assume a monopoly hires a single variable input and faces a market-determined price for that input. As in the case of competition, when a monopoly employs an additional unit of the input, output increases by an amount equal to the marginal product of the input. However, to sell the larger output, commodity price must be reduced. Hence, total revenue is not augmented by price times the marginal product of the input. Instead, total revenue changes by marginal revenue times marginal product. We call this the *marginal revenue product* of the input.

Definition.   Marginal revenue product for a monopolist is the additional revenue attributable to the addition of one unit of the variable input (V). It is equal to per-unit marginal revenue times marginal product:

$$MRP_v = \Delta TR/\Delta V = MR \times MP_v.$$

Since price is greater than marginal revenue, marginal revenue product is less than the value of the marginal product (price times marginal product).

In the case of a competitive firm, *VMP* declines because marginal product declines. For a monopolist, marginal revenue product declines with increases in the usage of the input not only because marginal product declines but also because marginal revenue declines as output is increased.

For example, assume that increasing the usage of the variable input by one unit increases output from 30 to 38 units; thus $MP = 8$. Suppose that the firm could sell 30 units at a price of $25 each, but to sell 38 units, price must fall to $22.

Thus the *gross* addition to total revenue from hiring the additional unit of the input is 8 (the added production) times $22 (the new selling price) or $8 \times \$22 = \$176$. But to sell the additional 8 units, the price of the 30 units that could have been sold at $25 must fall by $3. Thus the lost revenue from the price reduction is $\$3 \times 30 = \$90$. This loss must be subtracted from the gross gain to give a *net* gain of $\$176 - \$90 = \$86$. This net gain—$86—is the marginal revenue product of the input.

A monopolist's demand for a single variable input is the positive, negatively sloping portion of the *MRP* curve. Since both *MP* and *MR* decline, the input demand function must also decline.

In Figure 14.6, the relevant portion of *MRP* is shown. Begin with the price of the input at w_0. The firm will hire v_0 units of the input at this price. It would not hire fewer than v_0, because an additional unit of input would add more to the firm's revenue (*MRP*) than it costs (w_0). Clearly it would not hire more than v_0, because an additional unit of the input would add less to revenue than it costs the firm to hire that unit.

If the price of the input rises to w_1, the firm decreases its usage of the input to v_1 units, the level at which *MRP* equals w_1. Thus we see that within the relevant range the *MRP* curve is the monopolist's demand curve for a single factor of production.[4]

Principle. A monopolist who purchases a variable productive resource or input in a perfectly competitive input market (the price of the input is given to the firm) will employ that amount of the input for which marginal revenue product equals the price of the input. Consequently, the marginal revenue product curve, within the relevant range, is the monopolist's demand curve for the variable input when only one variable input is employed. Marginal revenue product declines for two reasons: (1) the marginal product of the input declines as more units of the variable input are added, and (2) to sell the additional output, the monopoly must lower the price of its output.

Recall that, for a perfect competitor, the condition that input price equals the value of marginal product of that input is equivalent to the profit-maximizing condition that product price equals marginal cost. For a monopolist, the condition that input price equals *MRP* is equivalent to the profit-maximizing condition that $MR = MC$.

To see this result, recall from Chapter 10 that cost minimization requires

$$MC = w/MP_v,$$

where V is the variable input and w is its price. The monopolistic firm chooses the output level at which

$$MR = MC = w/MP_v.$$

---

[4]In the appendix to this chapter we show that a monopolist would not choose a level of a variable input at which the average revenue product is less than the marginal revenue product.

Figure 14.6 **Marginal Revenue Product and Input Demand**

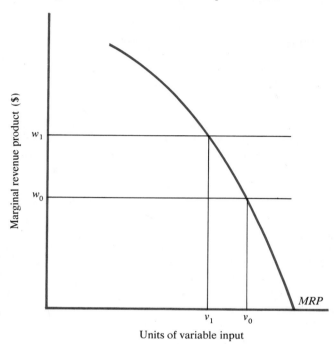

Units of variable input

Thus,

$$MR \times MP_v = MRP_v = w,$$

and $MRP_v = w$ is equivalent to $MR = MC$.

As was the case for perfect competition, the derivation of input demand curves is more complicated when production involves more than one variable input. The *MRP* curve is no longer the demand for the productive service, because the inputs are interdependent in the productive process. A change in the price of any one input leads to a change not only in the usage of that input but also in the use of other inputs as well. Recall that the marginal product curve for an input is derived assuming the usage of all other inputs is held constant. Thus changes in the rates of usage of other inputs shift the *MRP* curve.

Nonetheless, the monopolist's demand for an input is still downward sloping. And, most important, the monopolist still uses the amount of each variable input at which its marginal revenue product equals its price.[5] For instance, if the monopoly firm uses three variable inputs—v_1, v_2, and v_3—which have given, market-determined prices—w_1, w_2, and w_3—the firm will maximize profit (or minimize loss) by employing each input so that

[5]The mathematical derivation of this result is given in the appendix to this chapter.

$$MRP_{v_1} = w_1$$
$$MRP_{v_2} = w_2$$
$$MRP_{v_3} = w_3.$$

Since the inputs are interdependent in the production process, these conditions must hold simultaneously; the optimal levels of usage of the inputs must be determined simultaneously.

Thus, if an input's price is given to the monopoly we have the following:

Principle. A monopolist's demand for a variable productive resource must be negatively sloped. Even though input demand, when more than one input is variable, is not the MRP *curve, at every point on the demand curve the price of the input equals its marginal revenue product.*

Upward-Sloping Input Supply

Thus far we have assumed that the price of an input is determined by supply and demand in the resource market and is independent of how much of the input is used by an individual firm. But, as we noted earlier in this chapter, a monopoly firm may well be large enough to have an effect upon the prices of some of the inputs it uses.

In such instances, the firm must pay a higher price if it wishes to hire more units of the input. And, it not only has to pay more to the additional units of the resource hired but also must pay the higher price for those units that it could have hired (or was hiring) at the lower price. Thus the addition to cost is the cost of the added units hired plus the cost of paying more to the other units already being used. This added cost is called the *marginal factor cost* of an input. Marginal factor cost is greater than the price of the input. Therefore, if the monopoly firm faces an upward-sloping input supply function, it will make its employment decision by equating the marginal revenue product of the input with the marginal factor cost of the input (rather than the input price):

$$MRP = MFC.$$

In this case, the input price will be less than *MFC*.

APPLICATION

Monopoly Power of Another Sort

When most people think of monopoly, the first examples that come to mind are corporate giants like AT&T and IBM. While you may not become the CEO of such a company, you are quite likely to meet with another type of monopoly power, that of labor unions. Although only

20 percent of the labor force is unionized and this figure has been declining, unions are still quite important in many sectors of the economy.

Established labor unions can be thought of as the single seller of particular types of labor service to a firm. Once a labor contract is put into effect, the firm can hire only union labor under the conditions specified by the labor contract.

In essence, unions can use their monopoly power to do one of two things: (1) they can set a wage rate (or a package of wage rates), then let the firm or industry determine the amount of labor hired; or (2) they can set the number of workers available to the firm or industry, and then let market forces determine the wage rate (or rates). These actions are shown in the figure below. The firm's (or industry's) demand for labor is DD'. If the pre-union wage rate is w_0, L_0 units of labor are hired.

Suppose a labor union is organized, and it sets a higher wage rate of w_1. At this wage, L_1 units of labor are hired. Obviously, given the downward-sloping demand for labor, fewer workers will be hired at the higher wage.

Alternatively, if the union wants to establish a wage of w_1, it could make available only L_1 units of labor. No more workers are permitted

The Effect of Unions

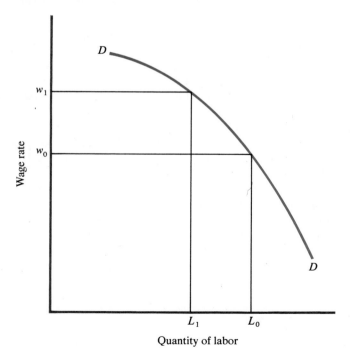

to join the union, and under the contract only union labor can be employed. The reduction in the amount of available labor drives the wage up to w_1.

In this simplified analysis, if the union wishes to obtain increased wages, it can do so only with a reduction in the number of workers hired. Increased wages would be obtained only by reducing employment.

This is not to say that workers as a group cannot be made better off by the formation of a union that increases wages. If the demand for labor is inelastic over the range L_0 to L_1, the increase in the wage rate from w_0 to w_1 would increase the total amount of wage income received by labor. The union could decrease the number of hours worked by each union member and keep all L_0 workers employed. (Of course, if demand is elastic, the wage bill would decrease. Those workers who keep their jobs would be better off, but some workers would have to find employment elsewhere.)

While the union possesses monopoly power, it might not be able to obtain as high a wage as desired. The union can always use the threat of a strike if the firm's management does not accept the wage asked for. But, although a strike generally causes the firm to suffer losses, workers also suffer reduced incomes during a strike. These reduced incomes may well offset any wage increases.

In addition, the union must also consider the reduction in employment associated with a higher wage. If too many workers are forced into unemployment, there is the possibility that this unemployed labor could cause the union to break up.

The effect on wages alone is not the entire story of the effect of labor unions. In fact, there is considerable controversy among economists about the overall impact of unions on productivity and costs.

No one denies that when unions obtain wage increases above the level that would otherwise exist, firms substitute other resources—most notably capital—for labor, and employment declines. But one group of economists argues that unions increase labor productivity through decreased turnover and the establishment of grievance procedures, seniority systems, work rules, and so on. They also argue that unions somehow shock management into becoming more efficient.[*]

Opponents of this view argue that unions lead to an inefficient input mix, reduce management flexibility, bring about inefficient work rules, and limit competition based upon individual productivity.[†] Thus far the evidence is somewhat inconclusive. So the jury is still out on the effects of unions on productivity; further research is required.

---

[*]A summary of the evidence may be found in Barry T. Hirsch and Albert N. Link, "Unions, Productivity, and Productivity Growth," *Journal of Labor Research*, Winter, 1984, pp. 29–37.
[†]See Morgan O. Reynolds, *Power and Privilege* (New York: Universe Books, 1984), pp. 83–88.

14.5 SUMMARY

A pure monopoly is a firm that is the sole seller of a well-defined product. The demand curve facing the monopolist is the market demand curve for the product. The monopolist faces no direct competition but does have indirect competition. We frequently speak of monopoly in terms of the amount of *monopoly power* possessed by a firm. The degree of monopoly power is determined by the extent of lost sales from an increase in price. Monopoly power is measured by the share of the market possessed by a single firm, the cross-price elasticity of demand with other products, and the firm's own-price elasticity of demand.

If a firm possesses monopoly power over an extended period of time, it must be protected by one or more barriers to the entry of other firms. Some of these barriers are economies of scale over a large range of output, governmental restrictions on entry, and other advantages of established firms.

A monopoly maximizes profit by choosing the level of output at which marginal revenue equals marginal cost. The price is determined by the demand curve at that level of output. Since demand is downward sloping, the equilibrium price is greater than marginal cost. A monopolist will produce and sell a positive level of output as long as some portion of demand is greater than average variable cost. The firm may make an economic profit or, in the short run, make a loss. In its hiring decision a monopolist purchases each variable input so that the marginal revenue product of the input equals its price (or marginal factor cost).

Although pure monopolists are rare, the monopoly model is useful for analyzing firms that approach monopoly. It is also useful as a first approximation for analyzing all firms with monopoly power. But, as we shall see in the next chapter, some additional complications arise in market structures between perfect competition and pure monopoly.

TECHNICAL PROBLEMS

1. Consider a monopoly firm with the demand and cost curves shown in the following figure. Assume that the firm is operating in the short run with the plant designed to produce 400 units of output optimally.

   a. What output should be produced?

   b. What will be the price?

   c. How much profit is made?

   d. If the firm can change plant size and move into the long run, what will be output and price?

   e. Will profit increase? How do you know?

   f. Draw in the new short-run average and marginal cost curves associated with the new plant size.

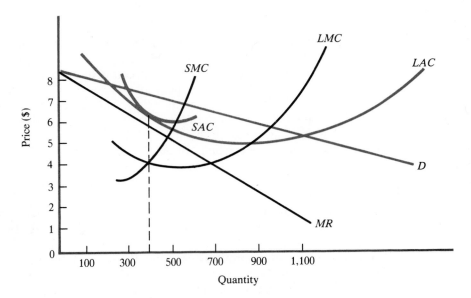

2. Explain why a profit-maximizing monopolist always produces and sells on the elastic portion of the demand curve. If costs are zero what output will the monopolist produce?

3. A monopolist faces the short-run cost structure shown below.

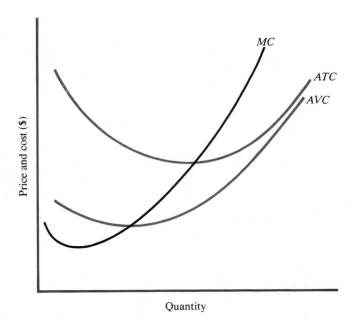

a. Show a demand curve (and associated marginal revenue curve) with which the monopolist earns a short-run economic profit. Show the price, quantity, and amount of profit being earned.

b. Show a demand curve (and associated marginal revenue curve) with which the monopolist earns losses but continues to operate in the short run. Show the price, quantity, and amount of loss. What will the firm do in the long run?

c. Show a demand curve (and associated marginal revenue curve) with which the monopolist shuts down in the short run. What will the firm do in the long run?

4. Compare the perfectly competitive firm and the monopolist as to how each makes the following decisions:

a. How much to produce.

b. What to charge.

c. Whether or not to shut down in the short run.

5. If a monopolist is not making enough profit, it can simply raise price until it does. Comment.

6. A monopolist is producing a level of output, 500 units, at which price is $8, marginal revenue is $5, average total cost is $6, and marginal cost is $10.

a. Draw a graph of the demand and cost conditions facing the firm.

b. Is the firm making the profit-maximizing decision? Why or why not? If not, what should the firm do?

7. A monopolist faces the following demand and cost schedules.

Price	Quantity	Total Cost
$20	7	$36
19	8	45
18	9	54
17	10	63
16	11	72
15	12	81

a. How much output should the monopolist produce?

b. What price should the firm charge?

c. What is the maximum amount of profit that this firm can earn?

8. How might advertising to make the demand curve less elastic be useful to a firm that desires to raise the price of the product it sells without encouraging entry?

9. Discuss the difference between a monopolist's demand for an input and the input demand for a perfectly competitive firm.

Contrast this with input demand for a perfectly competitive industry.

10. How can we say that when more than one input is variable, the monopolist's demand for an input is not its marginal revenue product curve, yet in equilibrium the monopolist hires each input so that its *MRP* equals its price?

11. The demand for a factor of production depends to a certain extent on the demand for the product produced by the input. Explain the connection.

12. In the following table, columns 1 and 2 make up a portion of the production function of a monopolist for a single variable input, labor. Columns 2 and 3 make up the demand function facing the monopolist over this range of output.

(1) Labor	(2) Quantity	(3) Price
9	50	$21
10	100	20
11	140	19
12	170	18
13	190	17
14	205	16
15	215	15

a. Derive and graph *MP, MR,* and *MRP* over this range.

b. If the wage rate is $60, how much labor would the firm hire? Why? What if the wage falls to $40?

13. Why would a monopolist's demand for a single variable input decline more rapidly than that of a perfectly competitive firm?

ANALYTICAL PROBLEMS

1. A monopolist sells a product, which is a normal good, and is making an economic profit in the long run. Per capita income decreases. What will happen to the firm's output, price, employment of labor, and profit in the short run? In the long run?

2. A monopolist is making a profit in the long run. The wage rate decreases. What will happen to the firm's output, price, employment of labor, and profit?

3. What incentives would a pure monopoly have to advertise when it has no direct competition? What type of advertising might it choose to use? Why?

4. Why would labor unions seek restrictive work rules? Given your answer, can you think of other types of rules a union might desire? Why would management agree to such rules?

5. Discuss the argument that unionization somehow "shocks" management into becoming more efficient. Some evidence is that after unionization, firms frequently purchase more capital to use with labor. Comment.

6. You are attempting to unionize the workers in a particular plant. What economic conditions would make your job easier? What would make your job harder? Analyze the case of an entire industry; an entire trade or profession; a government employees union.

7. The patent system conveys monopoly rights to some good or process. It is often claimed to be beneficial to economic growth because it encourages research. But, in general, it is asserted that monopolies result in inefficient resource allocation. Discuss.

8. Neighborhood grocery stores in a large city would appear to be an example of a perfectly competitive market—there are numerous sellers, each seller is small, and each store carries generally the same products (i.e., homogeneous outputs). However, it can be argued that these are monopolies. Comment.

9. In what sense is the only bank in a small town a monopoly? In what sense is it not? In what sense is GM or Exxon a monopoly? In what sense is it not? How about the U.S. Postal Service or your local electric company? If you were an adviser to a Supreme Court justice, how would you decide what does or does not constitute a monopoly? How could cross-price elasticity of demand help you decide?

10. In 1945, ALCOA was found guilty of attempting to monopolize the aluminum market. Up to that time, the company maintained low markups and had a modest profit rate. Ironically, if ALCOA had set high markups and realized a high profit rate before World War II, it probably would not have been found guilty. Can you explain why?

11. Oil companies advertise that they are very pollution conscious. Why do they do so? Why don't individual farmers advertise that they use pollution-free insecticide?

12. Firms and their unions frequently agree on public policy issues. Why would the big-three auto manufacturers and the United Automobile Workers both lobby for tariffs and quotas on foreign cars?

13. In the Firestone application, we said that the CEO was planning to go into the long run. Explain.

14. Hindsight is great. What could IBM have done to hold on to their huge share of the personal computer market? The person with the best answer gets to become CEO of IBM.

15. How was AT&T's entrenched position in the long-distance market an advantage when people chose their long-distance service? How was it a disadvantage?

APPENDIX

1. A monopolist produces and sells the level of output at which marginal revenue equals marginal cost, as long as price exceeds average variable cost. The monopolist's profit function is

$$\pi = R(Q) - C(Q) - F,$$

where $R(Q)$ and $C(Q)$ are, respectively, revenue and variable cost as functions of output, Q, and F is fixed cost.

Profit maximization requires

$$d\pi/dQ = dR/dQ - dC/dQ = 0.$$

Since dR/dQ is marginal revenue and dC/dQ is marginal cost, $MR = MC$ in equilibrium.

Let $P = P(Q)$ be the monopolist's demand function, and let Q^* be the output at which $MR = MC$. If

$$\pi = P(Q^*)Q^* - C(Q^*) - F > 0,$$

the firm makes an economic profit. If

$$P(Q^*) - C(Q^*)/Q^* > 0,$$

that is, if price in equilibrium exceeds average variable cost, and if π at Q^* is negative,

$$|P(Q^*)Q^* - C(Q^*) - F| < F.$$

Thus the firm produces Q^*. If price is less than average variable cost, the firm minimizes its loss by producing nothing and loses only fixed cost.

2. A monopolist would not employ any amount of a variable input at which the average revenue product is less than the marginal revenue product. By definition,

$$ARP = (Q/V) \times P$$

and, in equilibrium,

$$MRP = w,$$

where w is the price of the variable input, V, and P is the price of the product. If

$$ARP = (Q/V) \times P < MRP = w,$$
$$P \times Q < w \times V.$$

Thus, total revenue is less than total variable cost, and the firm would shut down, losing only its fixed cost.

3. A monopolist using several variable inputs uses the amount of each variable input at which its marginal revenue product equals the price of that input.

Let the production function be

$$q = f(V_1, V_2, \ldots, V_n),$$

where q is output and V_i is the quantity used of the i-th input. The monopolist faces a demand for its product of

$$p = p(q) = p[f(V_1, V_2, \ldots, V_n)],$$

where $p' < 0$. Let w_i be the price of the i-th input. The firm's profit function is therefore

$$\pi = p[f(V_1, V_2, \ldots, V_n)] \ f(V_1, V_2, \ldots, V_n) - \sum_{i=1}^{n} w_i V_i.$$

The firm maximizes π with respect to the n variable inputs, which requires

$$(dp/dq \ q + p) f_1 = w_1$$
$$(dp/dq \ q + p) f_2 = w_2$$

$$\cdot$$
$$\cdot$$
$$\cdot$$

$$(dp/dq \ q + p) f_n = w_n.$$

Since total revenue is $p(q)q$, marginal revenue is

$$dTR/dq = dp/dq \ q + p.$$

From above, profit maximization requires that for each input, V_i, $(dp/dq \ q + p) f_i = w_i$. Since f_i is the marginal product of the i-th input, profit maximization requires

$$MR \times MP_i = MRP_i = w_i = \text{input price}.$$

15

IMPERFECT COMPETITION

P erfect competition and pure monopoly are the two extremes of the broad range of existing market structures. Most nonagricultural markets and firms fall somewhere between the extremes. This is not to say that these two polar models do not provide useful tools for analyzing the behavior of real-world firms and markets. As we have emphasized, they *are* useful tools of analysis.

Nonetheless, certain complications do, at times, arise in the analysis of the intermediate market structures, which are frequently referred to as *imperfect competition*. In order to deal with these complications, economists divide these imperfectly competitive structures into two categories: monopolistic competition and oligopoly.

Under monopolistic competition, just as in perfect competition, the market consists of a large number of firms. But, unlike perfect competition, the products produced under monopolistic competition are differentiated rather than homogeneous. Each firm in the market produces a product that is distinguishable in one way or another from the products sold by other firms in the market. But, these products, while different, are quite closely related. The products of the other firms in the market are good, but not perfect, substitutes for the product sold by a monopolistically competitive firm.

Monopolistic competition is monopolistic in the sense that each firm has some monopoly (market) power. No firm produces exactly the same product as that produced by a rival firm. But there is competition because other firms produce close substitutes. Like perfect competition, there is unrestricted entry into and exit from a monopolistically competitive market. If economic profits are being earned, firms can freely enter the market, selling a similar, though slightly differentiated, product. Likewise, if losses occur, firms can freely exit the market.

Oligopoly, the other intermediate market, lies closer to monopoly. It differs from monopolistic competition in that the number of firms is not so large as to render negligible the contribution of each firm. Thus an oligopolist has more market power than a monopolistic competitor because the number of firms is small enough that each firm has a substantial share of the market.

How small must the number of firms be to make a market oligopolistic? The answer is that a market has few enough sellers to be considered oligopolistic if the firms recognize their *mutual interdependence*. In all of the other market structures, firms make decisions without considering how their actions will affect other firms and how, in turn, other firms' reactions will affect them. Oligopolists must take these reactions into account in their decision-making process.

For example, when contemplating a price change, a design innovation, or a new advertising campaign, Ford Motor Company must anticipate how General Motors and the Chrysler Corporation will react because, without doubt, Ford's actions will affect the demand for Chevrolets and Chryslers. Likewise, Dow Chemical must consider how DuPont will react when making price, output, and research decisions.

This, in short, is the central problem in oligopoly analysis. The oligopolistic firm is large enough to recognize (*a*) the mutual interdependence of the firms in the oligopoly market and (*b*) that its decisions will affect the other firms, which in turn will react in a way that affects the initial firm. The great uncertainty is how one's competitors will react.

Many real-world industries satisfy the general description of oligopoly. However, there as yet exists no *general* theory of oligopoly behavior. The problem in developing oligopoly theory is the oligopoly problem itself. Mutual interdependence and the resulting uncertainty about reaction patterns of rivals make it necessary for economists to make specific assumptions about behavioral patterns—how oligopolists believe their competitors will react and how their competitors actually react.

Therefore, as we shall see, the decisions made in the oligopoly model (e.g., price and output) depend critically upon the assumptions made about the behavioral reactions of rival managers. Since many different assumptions can and have been made, many different solutions can and have been reached. Thus, there is no single "theory of oligopoly."

This chapter will analyze decision making under both of these market structures. We first discuss profit maximization under monopolistic competition, then turn to oligopoly. Keep in mind throughout the discussion that both types of firms have the same goal as that of perfect competitors and monopolists—to maximize profit. And, to maximize profit, each type of firm tries to equate marginal revenue and marginal cost. But complications arise under each structure. The complication under monopolistic competition is the combination of unrestricted entry and exit with some market power. The complication under oligopoly is the mutual interdependence of firms.

15.1 MONOPOLISTIC COMPETITION

The theory of monopolistic competition is designed to explain the behavior of firms selling in markets characterized by: (1) a large number of firms that are small relative to the total market, (2) unrestricted entry and exit of firms in the market, and most important (3) a product for each firm that is similar to, but somewhat different from, the products sold by every other firm in the market. Thus, the only important difference between perfect competition and monopolistic competition is the differentiated products in the latter structure. We will see that this modest change in the assumptions of perfect competition has a significant effect on the behavior of sellers in the market.

The reason for this change in behavior is that product differentiation in monopolistic competition will prevent the firm's demand from becoming horizontal. Real or perceived differences between goods, though slight, will make them less than perfect substitutes. For example, toothpastes are similar, but they taste different, have different colors, and, presumably, clean your teeth differently. Because consumers can identify these differences, toothpastes aren't perfect substitutes, and every producer will have some, though not much, market power.

Gasoline stations across the road from each other are good, but not perfect, substitutes. Drivers traveling east may find one more convenient; westbound drivers may prefer the other. In fact, gasoline stations in a city are monopolistically competitive. Your car would run on gasoline from any of them. But they differ in location; some people prefer Exxon, some prefer Gulf; some prefer the service at Joe's, others prefer Julie's service. And the differentiating characteristics go on and on. The most important point is that although the products are similar, they are differentiated, causing each firm to have a small amount of market power.

Because of this market power, each firm in a monopolistically competitive market faces a downward-sloping demand, which is relatively elastic but not horizontal. A firm could raise its price slightly without losing all its customers; it could lower its price slightly without gaining the entire market.

As we shall see, the theory of monopolistic competition is essentially a long-run theory; in the short run there is virtually no difference between monopolistic competition and monopoly.

Short-Run Equilibrium

Because a monopolistically competitive firm produces and sells a differentiated product, the demand curve facing the firm is downward sloping.

And, because the firm's output is so small relative to the total quantity sold in the market, it believes that its price and output decisions will go unnoticed by other firms in the market. It therefore acts independently. With the given demand, marginal revenue, and cost curves, the firm maximizes profit or minimizes loss by equating marginal revenue and marginal cost.

Figure 15.1 illustrates the short-run, profit-maximizing equilibrium for a firm in a monopolistically competitive market. Profit is maximized by producing an output of Q and selling it at price P.

In the situation illustrated, the firm will earn an economic profit, shown as the shaded area *PABC*. However, as was the case for perfect competition and monopoly, in the short run the firm could operate with a loss, if the demand curve was below *ATC* but above *AVC*. If the demand curve was below *AVC*, the firm would shut down.

So far as the short run is concerned, there appears to be very little competition in monopolistic competition. Indeed, Figure 15.1 is virtually identical to a figure illustrating short-run equilibrium under monopoly. But when a longer view is taken, one essential element of monopoly is

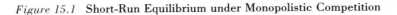

Figure 15.1 Short-Run Equilibrium under Monopolistic Competition

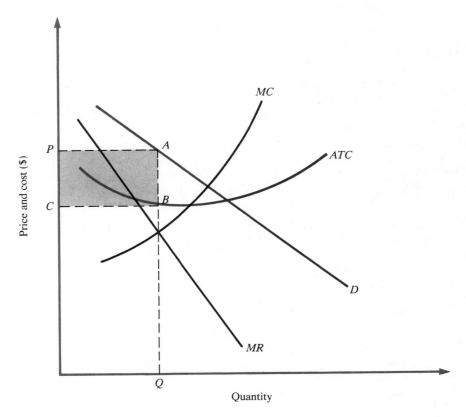

missing. In particular, a monopoly cannot be maintained if there is unrestricted entry. If pure profit is present in the short run, other firms will enter and produce the product, and they will continue to enter until all pure profits are eliminated. This feature leads us to a discussion of the long-run equilibrium for a monopolistically competitive firm.

Long-Run Equilibrium

While the short-run equilibrium for a firm under monopolistic competition is similar to that under monopoly, the long-run equilibrium is more closely related to the equilibrium position under perfect competition. Because of unrestricted entry, all economic profit must be eliminated in the long run. Such a zero-profit equilibrium can only occur at an output at which price equals long-run average cost. This occurs when the firm's demand is tangent to long-run average cost. The only difference between this equilibrium and that for perfect competition is that, for a firm in a monopolistically competitive market, the tangency cannot occur at minimum average cost. Since the demand curve facing the firm is downward sloping under monopolistic competition, the point of tangency must be on the downward-sloping range of long-run average cost. Thus, the long-run equilibrium output under monopolistic competition is less than that forthcoming under perfect competition in the long run.

This result is shown in Figure 15.2. *LAC* and *LMC* are the long-run average and marginal cost curves for a typical monopolistically competitive firm. Suppose that the short-run demand curve is given by D_m. In this case the firm would be making substantial economic profits, and if this firm is making profits, we would expect that other firms in the market are also earning economic profits. Thus we would expect these profits to attract new firms into the market. While the new firms would not sell exactly the same products as existing firms, their products would be very similar. So as new firms enter, the number of substitutes would increase and the demand facing the typical firm will shift backward and probably become more elastic (though not perfectly elastic). Entry will continue as long as there is some economic profit being earned. Thus entry causes each firm's demand curve to shift backward until a demand curve such as *D* in Figure 15.2 is reached. This long-run demand curve, *D*, is tangent to *LAC* at a price of $\bar{P}$ and output of $\bar{Q}$.

In such an equilibrium either an increase or a decrease in price by the firm would lead to losses. No more entry would occur since there are no pure profits to be earned in this market.

If "too many" firms enter the market, each firm's demand curve would be pushed so far back that demand falls below *LAC*. Firms would be suffering losses and exit would take place. As this happened, the demand curve would be pushed back up to tangency with *LAC*. Free entry and exit under monopolistic competition must lead to a situation where demand is tangent to *LAC*—where price equals average cost—and no economic profit is earned.

Figure 15.2   Long-Run Equilibrium under Monopolistic Competition

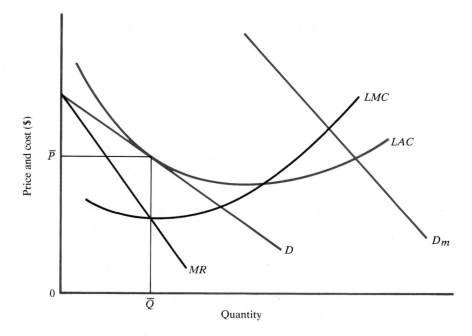

The equilibrium in Figure 15.2 must also be characterized by the intersection of *LMC* and *MR*. Only at output $\bar{Q}$ can the firm avoid a loss, so this output must be optimal. But we also know that the optimal output requires marginal cost to equal marginal revenue. Thus, at $\bar{Q}$, it must be the case that *MR* = *LMC*.

Principle. Long-run equilibrium in a monopolistically competitive market is attained when the demand curve for each producer is tangent to the long-run average cost curve. Unrestricted entry and exit lead to this equilibrium. At the equilibrium output, price equals long-run average cost and marginal revenue equals long-run marginal cost.

We might note that short of getting the government to prevent entry, there is nothing the firms in a monopolistically competitive market can do about having their profits competed away. Even if the firms were to conspire to fix a price, new firms would enter. Each firm would find its demand decreased and its sales reduced until price equaled average cost and economic profits were zero, although possibly at a higher price than would occur in the absence of the price-fixing agreement.

We have emphasized that, under monopolistic competition, profits are competed away in the long run. While this is certainly correct in general, we do not mean to imply that there is no opportunity for astute managers to postpone this situation into the future by innovative decision making.

THE WALL STREET JOURNAL

APPLICATION

How Quickly Are Profits Competed Away?

An article in *The Wall Street Journal* emphasized how rapidly a new product can be imitated and, consequently, how rapidly the profit of the firm introducing the new product could disappear.* The article also pointed out that small firms were becoming increasingly aware that this would happen and described what some firms were doing about it.

For example, the *Journal* noted that, "Every new product is a gamble, but Sara Lee Corp. is being unusually gutsy with a major frozen-food introduction. . . . The company is rolling out a line of fruit muffins nationally without running them through a test market." Why the rush? Nancy Dixon, senior product manager, said, "We didn't want to let the muffin trend crest before we got into the national market. And while we were busy testing it in a few cities, someone would have taken our idea and run with it." Sara Lee was already competing against the established Pepperidge Farm brand and a new muffin from Pillsbury.

Most new products undergo rigorous test marketing before

going national, but a growing number of firms were taking shortcuts. Companies were testing products on a few consumers and combining the results with other marketing data to predict sales. Previously, they had sold the products in several selected cities before going national.

Chester Kane, president of a new-product development firm, told the *Journal,* "Companies want to grab as much time on the shelves as possible. You're lucky if you get three or four years out of a new shampoo, and if you go into test, you might lose one of those years." Marketing consultants said that product life cycles are shortening every year as record numbers of new products and extremely crowded shelves are forcing retailers to weed out slow movers more quickly than ever before.

Companies like to go national quickly with a distinctive new product in a competitive, crowded market. Ralston Purina Co., for example, didn't bother with test markets for its Sun Flakes, the only cereal with 100 percent Nutrasweet. Frito-Lay skipped test marketing for its new Topples cheese snack so

Continued on page 451

*"Companies Get on Fast Track to Roll out Hot New Brands," by Ronald Alsop, July 10, 1986. Adapted by permission of *The Wall Street Journal*. © Dow Jones & Company, Inc., 1986. All rights reserved.

THE WALL STREET JOURNAL

APPLICATION

Continued from page 450
competitors wouldn't have time to study the ingredients and copy them. A spokesman for Frito-Lay said, "We felt very strongly we had a winner and didn't want to tip our hand."

So firms are well aware that their new products can and will be copied. When that happens, there go the profits. The object is to get the new products out quickly and keep the profits for a little longer.

Another monopolistically competitive market in which profits were rapidly eliminated was video rentals. On July 14, 1986, *The Wall Street Journal* reported, "The sign in the window of many video stores these days reads 'For Sale.' "[†] According to an industry publication, the number of video stores for sale more than doubled from 1985 to 1986. The magazine found 118 video stores advertised in the newspapers of seven major metropolitan areas in May, up from 52 only a year earlier. A company that bought and resold inventory of failed video stores doubled its revenue from 1985 to 1986.

A few owners said they were merely cashing in. But the *Journal* noted that competition

was by far the most important reason for selling out. Owners of stores all over the nation were pointing to the increasing number of stores. The competition came from three sources: large video chains, franchises, such as 7-Eleven Food Stores, that began renting videos, and mass merchandisers, such as K mart, that sell inexpensive tapes.

According to a professor of marketing at Babson College in Boston, "This is another example of how almost every idea in retailing in the last two years has started with entrepreneurs and ended up in the hands of major retailers."

It is also an example of the way monopolistic competition works in the long run. And it doesn't take long to reach the long run.

Exactly the same thing was happening in the retail flower business in 1986. *The Wall Street Journal* reported, "Americans were buying many more flowers than ever before, but the number of retail outlets was rising far more rapidly than revenues."[‡] A once tranquil industry was growing increasingly competitive

Continued on page 452

[†]"Now Playing at Video Stores: 'For Sale.' " Adapted by permission of *The Wall Street Journal.* © Dow Jones & Company, Inc., 1986. All rights reserved.
[‡]"Smaller Flower Retailers Wilt as Competition Grows Intense," by Steven P. Galante, August 4, 1986. Adapted by permission of *The Wall Street Journal.* © Dow Jones & Company, Inc., 1986. All rights reserved.

THE WALL STREET JOURNAL

APPLICATION

Continued from page 451
as Americans, particularly younger people, were becoming "European flower conscious."

Business skill became more important than an eye for artistic flower arrangements. "Far from being a bed of roses the industry these days is more like the War of the Roses."

And the biggest competitors to the florists were the mass merchandisers, particularly supermarket chains. One florist said, "Their prices are similar, but they're offering convenience, longer hours, and bigger floral displays." All of a sudden the place where the florists had been buying their groceries was their competition.

So in monopolistically competitive industries we find that new products get copied more rapidly and the profitable period is becoming shorter; when the demand for a product increases, entry and profit elimination are rapid.

What does a manager do? Rick Whitaker, in *The Wall Street Journal* column, "Manager's Journal," had some suggestions:[§]

1. Grab enough information on consumers and competitors to become market driven. Ask "Why would anyone buy this product?" Then test it.
2. Narrow your focus. New companies usually can do only one thing well.
3. Push a new product into the market quickly.
4. Use outsiders as sources of information. Hire professionals in marketing and sales as soon as they can be afforded.

No matter what a firm may do, its economic profit does have a tendency to be eliminated, or at best reduced, in the long run if it sells in a monopolistically competitive market. But innovative managerial practices can make the long run longer.

[§]"Push Your Innovation before Someone Else Does," July 23, 1986. Adapted by permission of *The Wall Street Journal*. © Dow Jones & Company, Inc., 1986. All rights reserved.

15.2 CHARACTERISTICS OF OLIGOPOLY

Firms selling in each of the other three market structures we have analyzed had the same characteristics as all other firms selling in the same structure. For example, all firms in a perfectly competitive market produce a homogeneous product and take market price as given. All firms in a monopolistically competitive market produce a differentiated product and take product demand as given. Such simplicity is not the case in oligopolistic markets, even though all oligopolists do have some of the same characteristics.

Similar Characteristics

One characteristic of all oligopoly markets is that there are few enough firms that each firm recognizes its mutual interdependence with the other firms. This is the most important characteristic, and the one that makes the analysis of oligopoly so complicated. An oligopolist knows that if it changes the price of its product, its rivals will notice the price change. And, accordingly, they may change their price, or they may not. This then leads to uncertainty. If rivals change their prices, sales after the original price change will differ from sales if the rivals do not change their prices. This uncertainty about competitors' reactions leads to uncertainty about the oligopolist's demand and marginal revenue curves.

Firms in other market structures do not worry about rivals' reactions. They can set marginal revenue equal to marginal cost and maximize profit, even though in two of the other structures we have analyzed, this profit is competed away in the long run. This absence of mutual interdependence makes these other structures easier to analyze. The oligopolist would like to equate marginal revenue to marginal cost. But since it is uncertain about the reactions of rivals, it is uncertain about its marginal revenue. And the mutual interdependence and uncertainty are present in other oligopoly decisions, such as advertising campaigns, product design, and marketing strategies.

Another characteristic common to all oligopolies is that each firm has a certain amount of monopoly or market power. If an oligopolist increases its price, it won't lose all of its sales; if it lowers its price, it won't gain the entire market. But, we must stress that how much sales are gained or lost depends on rivals' behavior.

Finally, oligopoly markets are characterized by moderate to high barriers to entry. Just as a monopoly must be protected by entry barriers to maintain its monopoly position, oligopolists must be similarly protected from entry. Otherwise the market would become much more like competition.

Although the barriers to entry in a monopoly market may be stronger, entry barriers for oligopoly are practically identical in their form. Just as was the case for monopoly, economies of scale over a large range of output are probably the most important barrier in oligopoly markets. But in an oligopoly market the extent of these economies permits a few firms, rather than only one, to sell in the market without making losses. New firms would be forced to enter the market at a large size in order to compete with existing firms. This case is called "natural oligopoly."

Other oligopoly entry barriers similar to monopoly are control of an essential raw material or the possession of protective patents by a few firms. Brand loyalty is quite an important barrier to entry in many, though not all, oligopoly markets. Buyer allegiance for durable goods can be built by establishing a reputation for service. No one knows what the service or repair policy of a new firm may be. Or, the allegiance of buyers can be built by a long, successful advertising campaign. (This type of allegiance is also probably more prevalent for durable goods.) New firms might have considerable difficulty establishing a market organization and overcoming buyer preferences for the established firms.

Differing Characteristics

Oligopolies can be classified by the type of product produced. In some oligopoly markets the products are homogeneous. Unless a buyer knows which firm sold the product, it would be impossible to determine the seller solely from the characteristics of the product itself. Some examples are markets such as steel, aluminum, and nickel. Other oligopoly markets are characterized by differentiated products. In varying degrees it is possible to determine who produced the product from the product itself or its package. Some examples are automobiles, major home appliances, breakfast cereals, and cigarettes. As we shall see, the type of product produced can affect the oligopolist's strategic behavior.

Broadly speaking, economists refer to two contrasting patterns of behavior for oligopolists: cooperative or noncooperative. Cooperative oligopolists tend to follow changes made by rival firms. For example, if a rival raises price, a cooperative oligopolist would go along with the move and raise price also. Noncooperative behavior, on the other hand, does not accommodate such changes. If a rival firm raises price, other firms would keep prices low in order to attract sales away from the higher price producer.

But, oligopolists have ways other than price to compete. Some oligopolistic markets are characterized by a great deal of price competition. In others, firms don't compete extensively by price changes but do compete in other ways, such as advertising, product quality, and other marketing strategies.

Because of the differences in oligopoly markets, there are four general oligopolistic market structures. These are, first, a few noncooperative firms producing either (1) a homogeneous product or (2) related but differentiated products; and, second, a few cooperative firms producing either (3) a homogeneous product or (4) related but differentiated products.

In general, the price and output decisions of an oligopolist depend to some extent on the market structure. If an oligopolist produces a homogeneous product and does not cooperate, the market tends toward the perfectly competitive solution. Each firm's demand elasticity will be high because of the availability of close substitutes. If each firm's output exhausts all economies of scale, price will be close to minimum long-run average cost.

On the other hand, as we shall see, cooperative oligopolists producing identical products tend to behave much like a monopoly. Firms tend to act as one; since buyers cannot distinguish among products, when price rises it appears as though a monopoly actually controlled production.

Differentiated products make cooperation more difficult. In a cooperative agreement, price differences would have to be negotiated to account for quality differences. Added to the increased difficulty of setting prices is the opportunity to compete for sales by quality changes. This type of competition is difficult to control. The most visible sort of cooperation when products are differentiated is leadership by a dominant firm in price or model changes.

Oligopoly behavior is also determined by other factors. For example, if entry barriers are relatively moderate and new firms would find it relatively easy to enter, the gains from cooperation are small. High prices encourage new firms to enter the market. Prices in such oligopoly markets tend to be low and cooperation to increase profit minimal. When entry is extremely difficult, firms have a greater incentive to reach a cooperative agreement. Prices will tend to be higher in such markets.

The history of the industry and even the personalities of the top executives tend to affect oligopoly behavior. Over time firms learn something about how their rivals will react to changes. Some industries are characterized by a "live and let live" attitude. In others, firms compete far more aggressively and competitively. As noted above, in some markets competition takes the form of price cutting. In others, firms compete much more by advertising and marketing strategy.

Again, the distinguishing characteristic of oligopoly is the recognition by each firm that its actions will have a noticeable effect upon other firms and that these rivals will react accordingly. Thus the potential reactions of other firms must be taken into account when an individual firm makes decisions, especially decisions about price and output. This is why we have no general theory of oligopoly. Oligopoly behavior depends on so many things that its forms are as numerous as the number of oligopolistic industries. Thus the best we can do in one short chapter is give you a feel for some of the more important aspects of this market structure.

APPLICATION

Oligopoly Interdependence in the Airplane Market*

There are only two manufacturers of large commercial jet airplanes in the United States—Boeing and McDonnell Douglas. They fit all of the characteristics of oligopoly described above. But, in 1983, the two giants faced a new type of competition from a different source. Let's look at what happened and what the two giants planned to do about it.

*"The Hot Market in Used Jets," *Newsweek*, December 5, 1983, p. 90.

In 1979 the commercial airlines were deregulated. Many cut-rate carriers, such as People Express, entered the market. These low-cost airlines generally flew used airplanes. And, with fuel prices falling, older, less fuel-efficient airplanes were becoming more economical than new planes that used less fuel. These two events spawned a new market—the used jet industry. Previously, used airplanes had been purchased from airlines that were switching to new planes.

Several new firms became the airplane industry's newest phenomenon—firms devoted to reconditioning and selling used commercial aircraft. The president of one such company, Evergreen Air Center in Arizona, said that they had never been busier or more prosperous. The firm's sales had gone from $3 million to $19 million in two years. Another company expected sales to reach $54 million in 1983, compared with $43 million the previous year. Even more revealing, Boeing estimated that of the 400 or so airlines flying its planes, only 16 percent bought them new, compared with 65 percent five years before.

Clearly, the two giant manufacturers couldn't continue to sit back and wait for the market for new airplanes to pick up. They didn't. *Newsweek* reported, "That development has forced both Boeing and McDonnell Douglas, the two domestic plane-makers, to jump into the used-plane business themselves."

The shrinking domestic market for new planes caused the two aerospace giants to react. They entered a new market. And they had an advantage in selling and servicing used airplanes. James Blue, director of used-plane sales for Boeing, said, "We're still supporting them [cut-rate airlines] because *someday* they're going to buy a *new* Boeing aircraft. We're convinced of it." The decision was seen as a sound investment for the future.

It appears that both Boeing and McDonnell Douglas had to go into the used-plane market. First, they were losing some business to the new brokers and they felt that they had to react. Second, one firm could not stay out of the used-plane market if the other entered it. When "someday" came and the airlines began buying new, rather than used, jets, the manufacturer with its foot in the door of the "cut-rate" market would have an edge on the firm that stayed out. Each firm recognized its mutual interdependence and acted accordingly.

15.3 NONCOOPERATIVE OLIGOPOLY BEHAVIOR

In spite of the uncertainty about the reactions of rivals, the managers of oligopolies do use the marginal benefit-marginal cost rule when making decisions. A firm would reduce price and increase output as long as expected marginal revenue exceeds expected marginal cost. It would increase price and reduce output if expected marginal revenue is less than expected marginal cost.

The problem is, of course, accurately forecasting marginal revenue and marginal cost; that is, how to form accurate expectations. Any change in price and output by one firm will have a noticeable effect upon the sales of other firms. These rival firms may react by changing *their* prices and levels of output. Or, it is possible they may not react at all. In any case, the firm making the price and output decisions must take into consideration these potential changes by rivals, because any price changes by rival firms would be expected to shift the firm's demand curve and therefore its marginal revenue curve.

This differs from the cases of monopoly and monopolistic competition. Firms in those two types of markets can change price and output under the assumption that their demand and marginal revenue functions will remain constant. Oligopolists cannot make changes under the same assumption. There is a good chance that these curves will not stay put for very long.

So there is the problem. The oligopolist equates marginal revenue to marginal cost, but must consider what will happen to demand when rivals react to the change. In making price and output decisions, the oligopolist's expectations about the reactions of other firms depend, as noted, upon several factors, including the way rivals have reacted to past changes, the market share of the firm, and the type of product sold. Thus we have a large number of ad hoc analyses of specific industries and their pricing policies, rather than a general theory of oligopoly.

Price Rigidity under Oligopoly

Some economists have argued that the very nature of the oligopoly problem—the expected reaction of rivals—causes oligopoly markets to be characterized by a great deal of price rigidity. That is, prices under oligopoly would not be very responsive to changes in demand or cost conditions.

Many theories have been set forth to explain why prices are supposedly inflexible in an oligopoly market structure. The most frequently cited hypothesis took the following form: If one oligopolist increases its price, competing oligopolists will hold their prices constant, so the oligopolistic firm that raises its price will lose considerable sales to rivals. On the other hand, if one oligopolist lowers its price, the rival firms, fearing substantial losses in sales, will also lower their prices. Thus, the oligopolist that lowers the price will experience only an insignificant increase in sales, because of the price competition.

The nature of the problem is shown in Figure 15.3. Suppose that a firm in a noncooperative oligopolistic market structure has been producing 400 units of output per period and selling them at $5 each. Its total revenue is therefore $2,000. Also suppose that the firm is considering changing its price.

Figure 15.3 Price Rigidity under Oligopoly

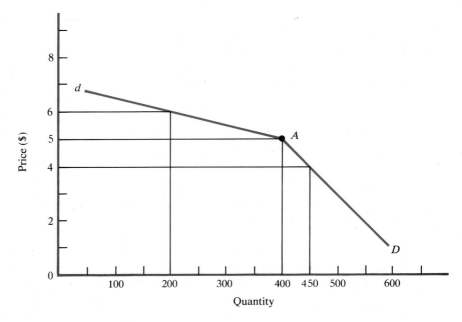

The firm believes that if it increases its price to $6, its rivals will not change their prices and the firm will lose a great deal of sales to them after the price increase. Thus it thinks it will be able to sell only 200 units after raising its price to $6. Its revenue would fall to $1,200. For any price increase that is unmatched by the other firms, this firm's demand is segment *dA*, which is quite elastic as is shown by the fall in revenue after the price increase.

But, suppose the firm decreases price from $5 to $4. Now the firm expects its rivals to match the price decrease so as not to lose sales. Thus the firm would gain few, if any, additional sales from its rivals by decreasing price. Sales would increase some, because of the downward-sloping market demand for the products of all the firms, but not by much. In the figure sales increase only to 450 units when price is reduced to $4. Thus revenue decreases to $1,800. For any reduction in price from $5, the firm's demand is the inelastic segment *AD*, when rivals match the decrease. Thus the firm expects revenue to decline if price is changed in any direction, under its assumption about its rivals' behavior.

If the preceding hypothesis is true, oligopolists would have little motivation to change prices. Thus oligopoly is sometimes claimed to be less adaptable than other market structures, since prices are rigid. This theory is supposed to explain why oligopoly markets are characterized by "sticky" prices, but of course it cannot explain why price is where it is in the first place. It must, therefore, be regarded as an ex post rationalization of market behavior rather than an ex ante explanation of market behavior.

Furthermore, there is a certain amount of contradictory empirical evidence. Several studies have shown that, in general, oligopoly markets are characterized by as many price changes as both more competitive markets and markets characterized by monopoly.

There are many other theories designed to explain oligopoly price and output decisions, dating as far back as 1836. Yet none is accepted as a good general explanation of oligopoly price behavior when the firms are noncooperative. Nevertheless, we can say a good bit more about other aspects of noncooperative oligopolistic markets.

THE WALL STREET JOURNAL

APPLICATION

Oligopolists Do Use Price Competition—But They Don't Like It

Since the airlines were deregulated in 1979, the industry has been in a turmoil. The transition was painful to the major carriers, and even fatal to some. New lines instigated fare wars that the majors were forced to enter. Service competition became severe, adding to the cost of service. Most major airlines lost money. Clearly they had to do something.

By the fall of 1986, some airlines thought they had found a solution to their problems—mergers. Mergers would decrease the number of airlines in important hub cities. Mergers would reduce competition. Reduced competition would allow the carriers to increase fares, decrease service, and increase profits.

The Wall Street Journal reported what had happened and what was expected to happen.* The prediction is summarized in one sentence: "Air travelers can expect higher fares as the big fish in the airline industry keep gobbling up the little ones."

Industry executives and regulatory officials saw "immediate changes in ticket prices and levels of service." The head of the Justice Department section that reviews airline mergers said, "There's little question that we're going to see higher fares in some markets. . . . The only question is over how much change there will be."

All observers felt that the primary objective of the airlines, when they merged or took over other lines, was to reduce price competition. A former airline

Continued on page 460

*"Increased Fares, Fewer Flights Are Likely Results of Airline Mergers," by John Koten, September 17, 1986. Adapted by permission of *The Wall Street Journal.* © Dow Jones & Company, Inc., 1986. All rights reserved.

THE WALL STREET JOURNAL

APPLICATION

Continued from page 459 executive summed up, "It's obvious that a major motive behind many of the airline mergers is to eliminate the competition. Carriers are trying to achieve the market dominance that, among other things, will give them better control over prices."

It appears that the objective of many of the mergers was to give one or two carriers predominance in major U.S. hub cities. Northwest acquired Republic and gained most of Minneapolis. It immediately reduced the number of departures 15 percent. (It said the purpose was to reduce noise pollution.) After Texas Air took over People Express, only two carriers served Denver.

The point is that oligopolists do resort to price competition, but they don't like it. They do it because they are forced to. And it doesn't take many firms to bring on price competition. An analysis by the Civil Aeronautics Board showed that the ideal competitive balance at an airport was three carriers with full flight schedules. But the airlines didn't want an ideal competitive balance. The solution was to get two or even one airline serving a major city in order to reduce price competition.

Nonprice Competition in Oligopoly Markets: Advertising

Although the preceding discussion indicates that there is a certain amount of debate among economists as to the amount of price competition in industries characterized by oligopoly, most would agree that oligopoly is characterized by considerable nonprice competition, particularly when the product is differentiated. The alternative forms of nonprice competition are as diverse as the minds of inventive managers can make them. Yet there is one central feature: an oligopoly frequently attempts to attract customers to its own product (and, therefore, away from that of rivals) by some means other than a price differential.

Nonprice competition accordingly involves differentiating a product, even when the product is fundamentally homogeneous. The ways of differentiating are diverse, but the two principal methods of nonprice competition are advertising and product quality.

Using advertising and product quality, the firm wishes to increase the demand for its product and make it less elastic. As we know, the firm chooses the amount of advertising and product quality at which the marginal cost of advertising (quality) equals the marginal revenue from increased advertising (quality). The oligopolist then allocates its advertising budget so that the marginal revenue per dollar spent is the same for all media.

These choices, however, are not as simple for oligopolists as for firms in a monopolistically competitive market. The problem is the same as we have for price and quantity choices: Any one firm's change in its advertising or quality will have a noticeable effect on the sales of other firms, and these rivals would be expected to react by changing their own advertising or quality. Thus each firm has to take into account the reactions of other firms when making its decisions. As was the case for price, this interdependence complicates the decision considerably.

In the case of advertising, oligopolistic interdependence has an additional complicating effect. It can lead to excessive—greater than the optimal—amounts of advertising. In such cases, it is possible that sellers in an oligopolistic market could increase their profits if they could cooperate and reduce the amount of advertising done by each. Advertising is, in certain cases, excessive (to advertisers) because it is frequently a defensive measure taken to counteract the advertising of rival firms.

How rivalry leads to unprofitable amounts of advertising can be illustrated by a model known as "the prisoner's dilemma." The model is best described by the story for which it is named. Suppose that a crime is committed and two suspects are apprehended and questioned by the police. Unknown to the suspects, the police do not have enough evidence to convict them unless one of them confesses. So the police separate them and make each one an offer known to the other. The offer is, if one suspect confesses to the crime and turns state's evidence, the one who confesses receives only a 2-year sentence, while the other (who does not confess) gets 10 years. If both prisoners confess, each receives a 2-year sentence. If neither confesses, the probability is very high both will go free. Thus, each prisoner could receive 2 years, 10 years, or go free, depending upon what the other does.

Figure 15.4 shows the four possibilities. The upper-left and lower-right cells show the results if both, respectively, do not confess or confess. The upper-right and lower-left cells show the consequences if one confesses and the other does not.

The problem is that the suspects cannot collude. If they could, it is clear that neither would confess. However, they must make their decisions independently. The suspect who pleads innocent stands a chance of 10 years in prison if the other confesses. However, the worst that could happen if a suspect confesses to the crime is two years imprisonment regardless of what the other does.

Whether or not the crime was committed by these suspects, the less each knows about the other, the more likely he or she will confess to the

Figure 15.4 The Prisoner's Dilemma

		Suspect 1	
		Does not confess	*Confesses*
Suspect 2	*Does not confess*	A 1: 0 years 2: 0 years	B 1: 2 years 2: 10 years
	Confesses	C 1: 10 years 2: 2 years	D 1: 2 years 2: 2 years

crime. In other words, the less information these accused criminals possess about each other, the less certainty they have about going free—settling in cell A. Each wants to avoid cells B and C. Each can get two years in prison with certainty by confessing. Thus, the safest tactic is for both to confess, and they end up in cell D.

Oligopolists are often caught in a similar dilemma in the case of nonprice competition—particularly with advertising. Suppose there are only two choices: spend a small amount of money on advertising or spend a lot. If all firms are spending a small amount on advertising, a single firm could increase its profits at the expense of the other firms if it increased its advertising while the others do not. Conversely, if any firm does little or no advertising while the other firms advertise heavily, that firm loses a substantial share of the market. However, as in many imperfectly competitive markets, the total amount of advertising by all firms has little effect on total sales in the market. That is, market demand is relatively inelastic with respect to advertising.

To illustrate this situation, let's assume that there are only two rival firms. As with the prisoner's dilemma, each firm has two choices, so there are four possible outcomes for the rival firms. We have provided a hypothetical example in Figure 15.5. In cells A through D of the figure, the profitability (π) of each outcome is shown for the firms. If both firms have low advertising budgets, profits are $100 for each firm. But you can see that there is a big temptation for one firm to increase its advertising relative to that of the rival. If only one firm switches to high advertising expenditures, its profits jump to $150, largely because it attracts business away from the firm with a low advertising budget—whose profits fall to $60. (Note that, to a small extent, total market profits also rise because the total market expands as a result of more total advertising.) However, neither outcome B nor C is an equilibrium. The low advertiser can at least raise profits to $80 by matching its rival's high advertising budget. In the long run, both firms end up with high advertising expenditures,

Figure 15.5 The Advertiser's Dilemma

		Firm 1	
		Low expenditures	High expenditures
Firm 2	Low expenditures	A π_1: 100 π_2: 100	B π_1: 150 π_2: 60
	High expenditures	C π_1: 60 π_2: 150	D π_1: 80 π_2: 80

slightly increased sales, and lower profits. From each seller's perspective, there is too much advertising.

Once a firm decides to increase advertising, it is very difficult to avoid cell D in Figure 15.5. And it is quite unlikely that, without an explicit agreement, firms will return to cell A. The uncertainty inherent in an oligopoly market will result in lower profits than might otherwise be earned.

THE WALL STREET JOURNAL

APPLICATION

An Advertiser's Dilemma: Baby Food and Burger Wars

For many years, baby food was one of the sleepiest categories in the supermarket. Although price-cutting promotions were rampant, there was little innovation in new products and little money spent on marketing. Gerber controlled most of the market.*

In 1984, Beech-Nut, a Nestlé subsidiary, introduced a new product called Stages—four groups of products for babies at different ages. At the same time Heinz developed an instant baby food (just mix with water). As *The Wall Street Journal* reported, "Those products were merely the beginning of what has turned out to be a vicious and still escalating war with Gerber Products Co. over the $700 million baby-food market." Heinz and Beech-Nut gained market share at Gerber's

Continued on page 464

*The material dealing with the baby food portion of this application is from "Baby-Food Fight: Beech-Nut, Heinz Put the Heat on Gerber," by Ronald Alsop, *The Wall Street Journal,* July 24, 1986. Adapted by permission of *The Wall Street Journal.* © Dow Jones & Company, Inc., 1986. All rights reserved.

THE WALL STREET JOURNAL

APPLICATION

Continued from page 463
expense, but the total market grew very little. The number of births was growing at only 1 to 2 percent a year, and babies eat baby food for only a limited period of time, even though Beech-Nut was trying to extend that period. There was really no way to substantially increase the total market.

So the three oligopolists were caught in a dilemma. The total market was relatively fixed, but each had to increase its advertising to hold on to its share of the market, or possibly to increase that share. Beech-Nut reported it would spend $22 million on marketing in 1986, more than double its previous expenditures. Gerber increased its advertising and promotion outlays 50 percent, to $36 million. Heinz would not disclose its budget.

Gerber, for the first time in years, began advertising on network TV. Because only about 4 percent of U.S. households have babies, broadcast TV is not a particularly efficient advertising medium for these firms. But as the director of product management at Gerber said, ". . . our competitors went on TV, and we want to be certain our voice is the loudest in the

market." This is truly an advertiser's dilemma.

The three big hamburger chains were, at about the same time, caught in a similar dilemma. According to *Newsweek,* McDonald's, Burger King, and Wendy's control about one third of the $47 billion fast-food market.[†] During the first part of 1986 McDonald's reported "soft sales" and Burger King said its earnings for the same period were "disappointing." Analysts said Wendy's profits were down 40 percent for the first quarter of the year.

The president of McDonald's, speaking before an audience of restauranters, was blunt in telling them that they all were going to have to be more efficient. But, *Newsweek* pointed out, "Marketing—and more marketing—has been the classic response to such admonitions."

Burger King's chairman put his finger on the real problem: "Advertising [in the hamburger business] is like the arms race. Once you start, there's no way to stop." All together, Wendy's, McDonald's, and Burger King planned to spend more than a half-billion dollars to *out-advertise the competition.* Another advertiser's dilemma in the Burger Wars.

[†]The material for the burgers portion of this application is from "Burgers: The Heat Is On," *Newsweek,* June 16, 1986, p. 53.

Nonprice Competition in Oligopoly Markets: Product Quality

As we noted, oligopolists also can use changes in product quality as a means of nonprice competition—that is, to differentiate their product from those of rival firms. The product quality change may be real or perceived. In either case, such decisions are made employing the same process as that used in the case of advertising—evaluating marginal revenue and marginal cost.

As was true for advertising, the firm must take into consideration the reaction of its rivals to any quality changes. Thus, quality changes that will be noticed by consumers but cannot be quickly copied by rivals are frequently attempted. A wine that is aged longer to give it a better taste, a few added inches between seats on an airplane, or fewer defective parts in a large shipment of equipment are quality changes not easily copied by rivals.

Product-quality competition is particularly intense in service oligopolies, where product quality is difficult to judge. Doctors and dentists, for instance, do not usually compete via the prices they charge patients, but the quality of their services and the waiting time in their offices vary a great deal.

The annual style change made by manufacturers of consumer durables is another method of product quality competition. We see such changes in automobiles, household appliances, TVs, stereos, and sporting goods. Until the new models are put on the market, these style changes are closely guarded secrets. If other firms do not know what the new model is going to look like, it may take a year or more for the rivals to copy. (If, in fact, the style change is successful.)

We could go on with many other examples, but we are sure you have seen our point. The types of quality competition are practically as numerous as the oligopolistic industries themselves.

But oligopolists have another way of using product quality as a method of competition, other than by simply improving the real or perceived quality of their product. Products can be thought of as a collection of attributes or characteristics. For example, an automobile can be described by its engine size, brakes, transmission, suspension, fuel efficiency, tires, head and trunk room, number of doors, color, and so on. These product features can differ among products and can be altered by the manufacturers to differentiate their products from others. How a producer selects these attributes determines the quality and nature of the product and the product's substitutability with other products in the market. A manufacturer who produces an automobile with most of the attributes that characterize a Cadillac Sedan DeVille will make a car that is an unlikely substitute for a Ford Mustang.

To see how product attributes can serve as a competitive tool, let's look at a hypothetical example. The basic idea is captured by letting all of the possible preferences consumers may have for a particular attribute be measured along a scale with end points 0 and 1, as shown in Figure 15.6. Let us say that this product attribute is sugar on breakfast cereal; 0 is cereal with no sugar and 1 is cereal of virtually pure sugar cubes. The value 1/4, 1/2, and 3/4 mark equal distance points along this scale. Suppose that those who buy breakfast cereal are evenly distributed along this scale so that the number of individuals who want no sugar on their cereal is equal to the number who want their cereal half-sugared and is equal to the number who want all sugar.

In the case of the first firm to produce cereal, it does not matter how much sugar is put on its product. It is the only cereal consumers can buy. Thus, we arbitrarily locate firm A on the scale at A_1. Since sugar is expensive, we place A_1 on the lower end of the scale. We subscript the location because the firm may later want to change the sugar content of its cereal when other firms enter the market.

Rivalry begins when firm B decides to enter the market. The new seller knows the preferences of consumers, that is, the scale in Figure 15.6, and how much sugar A has on its product. The question is, how much sugar should B use to capture the largest share of the market? Market share is very important to profit maximization. The larger a firm's market share, the fewer the substitutes, and hence the less elastic is demand. Consequently, the higher is price. Also, if there are economies of scale, increased sales allow a producer to move down the *LRAC* curve and realize a lower average cost of production. Of course, at the margin, higher prices and lower production costs must be balanced against the marginal cost of increasing market share, which may, for example, involve advertising, or, in this case, using more sugar.

In Figure 15.6, we can see that with constant prices firm B could capture most of the market by using a little more sugar than A. The best thing for B to do is enter with a product that is just to the right of A_1. We label this point B_1. Firm B captures all of the market to the right of A_1 in sugar content.

Firm A will, of course, not tolerate this for long. Its market share has been reduced to a very small part of the total market. Only those buyers with preferences between 0 and A_1 remain loyal to A's cereal. The firm could lower price or think about countering B's product by putting more sugar on its cereal. It can regain much of its lost market by moving just to the right of B_1. But then B will move to the right of A again, and A will then move to the right of B a second time. The leapfrogging will continue until one firm drops out of the market, or both firms end up with equal market shares at the midpoint of the preference scale. After a large number of moves, we will find both firms putting approximately the same amount of sugar on their cereal and supplying the amounts desired by the average buyer; that is, at A_n and B_n.

The situation gets more complicated when a third firm enters the market. With a little experimenting, you will discover that firms will not find

Figure 15.6 **Product Quality Measure**

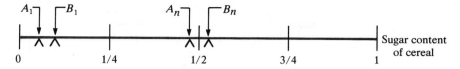

an equilibrium; they continually change the amount of sugar on their cereals. This is not uncommon in the real world—think how many "new" and "improved" labels producers put on their products. Often these improvements are nothing more than a slight adjustment in a product attribute, a change the marketing personnel hope will place them near their rival, but on the side of the preference scale that gives them the largest market share.

We have oversimplified things a great deal by allowing product differentiation for only one product variable and assuming price competition does not take place at the same time. Realistically, there are all sorts of ways attributes can be mixed. Discovering the attributes that capture the largest share of the market requires sophisticated marketing techniques and, at times, just plain luck. The point of our simple model, though, is that product differentiation is a competitive tool that firms use to maximize profits. Differentiation can be as much a part of competition as price.

You might be asking whether people care about product attributes. Who cares how much sugar a firm puts in its product? Well, in at least one case a great many people cared.

APPLICATION

Who Cares about a Little Bit of Sugar?

On Wednesday, July 10, 1985, Coca-Cola announced that it was bringing back its old Coke with a little less sugar, now called Classic Coke, after switching to a sweeter version almost three months before. ABC interrupted its soap opera, "General Hospital," to break the news. Dan Rather, Peter Jennings, and Tom Brokaw had news stories on the CBS, ABC, and NBC evening news. ABC featured the story on "Nightline." Senator David Pryor expressed jubilation on the Senate floor during a debate on South Africa. *Time* covered the story in a prominent article.* What was all the fuss about?

---

*Material in this application is from "Coca-Cola's Big Fizzle," *Time*, July 22, 1985, pp. 48–52.

It began April 23, 1985, when Coca-Cola announced that, after extensive testing, it was changing the flavor of Coke for the first time in its 99-year history. In essence, Coca-Cola had added a little more sugar to the recipe, making Coke taste much more like Pepsi, which celebrated the occasion by declaring a company holiday. Coke's advertising agency reported that two thirds of the nation heard the news within 24 hours.

The change caused a national furor. Coke had merely tried to move its product closer to its largest competitor on the flavor spectrum, much like the hypothetical cereal firms we previously analyzed. But people thought it was like tampering with a national institution. Coca-Cola received as many as 1,500 phone calls a day as well as a multitude of protesting letters. "Save Coke" clubs were formed. And all of this was after by far the most extensive market testing program in the company's history.

After almost three months of protest, Coca-Cola decided to keep the new, sweeter Coke on the market but bring back the old flavor of Coke and call it Classic Coke.

Was it one of the dumbest marketing moves in history? Some thought so. Or was it a giant hoax? Did Coke plan all along to reintroduce the Classic Coke and reap the benefits of all the publicity? After all, Coke had Pepsi almost surrounded in the sugar battle. How are Coke and Pepsi going to come out of the battle? Only time will tell.

Donald R. Keough, the president of Coca-Cola denied the stories that the new Coke was a deliberate plot to create support for the old product, saying, "Some critics will say Coca-Cola has made a marketing mistake. Some cynics say that we planned the whole thing. The truth is, we're not that dumb, and we're not that smart."

Thus far we have reached the conclusion that noncooperative oligopolists compete in many ways. Although they don't like price competition, they use it. And they don't like nonprice competition much better, but they use it also. They are forced into these many forms of competitive behavior because of the mutual interdependence of demand and the resulting uncertainty. And we have barely touched the surface on ways oligopolists compete for sales. As we pointed out earlier, the methods of competition depend not just on the structure of the market, but on the history of the industry and even on the personalities of the managers. So there are many, many patterns of competition that oligopolies can follow.

We should mention in closing this section that oligopolists do not consist only of the industrial giants—the GMs and Fords and the Coca-Colas and Pepsis. Markets served by much smaller firms can be just as oligopolistic. They can compete in as many different ways and with just as much ingenuity as the industrial giants—even though they probably would not make the CBS evening news and *Time*. Some examples would be the major banks that serve a city, the large department stores, and manufacturers of baby food, as discussed above. All have similar problems. Yet the solutions turn out quite different. The one conclusion we can draw is, if oligopolists cooperate they can be better off than if they don't. But, even with cooperation, to which we now turn, problems can arise.

15.4 COOPERATIVE OLIGOPOLY BEHAVIOR

So far we have discussed oligopoly behavior under the assumption that rival firms do not cooperate or collude. But firms do, at times, cooperate and reach agreements to raise price and reduce output or to limit competition in other areas, even though explicit price fixing and other collusive behavior is illegal in the United States. Yet antitrust litigation still flourishes, indicating that such behavior is still thought to continue. In other countries collusion is legal and, in some cases, even encouraged by government.

In the preceding section we saw the effect of a price increase by an oligopolist when its rivals did not change their prices. The firm lost a great deal of its sales. But suppose all the other firms increase their prices by approximately the same amount. With the prices of its rivals set higher, we would expect the demand of an individual firm to be much less elastic. Thus if a firm could somehow convince its rivals to follow, it could increase its price without a substantial reduction in sales. Since total cost always falls when output falls, the firm could, it hopes, increase its profit.

Thus it is possible for all firms to make themselves better off by cooperative agreements, even though these agreements may be illegal. Such cooperative arrangements are called collusive agreements. The most extreme form of collusion is a cartel.

Cartel Profit Maximization

A cartel is a group of firms whose objective is to limit the competitive forces within a market. It may take the form of open collusion, with the member firms entering into contracts about price and other market variables. Or, the cartel may involve secret collusion among members with no explicit contract. At this time, the most famous cartel is OPEC (Organization of Petroleum Exporting Countries), an "association" of the major oil-producing nations.

Let's consider an *ideal* cartel. Suppose a group of firms producing a homogeneous commodity forms a cartel. A central management body is appointed, its function being to determine the uniform cartel price. The task, in theory, is relatively simple, as illustrated in Figure 15.7. Market demand for the homogeneous commodity is given by *DD'*, so marginal revenue is given by the dashed line *MR*. The marginal cost curve for the cartel must be determined by the management body. If all firms in the

Figure 15.7   Cartel Profit Maximization

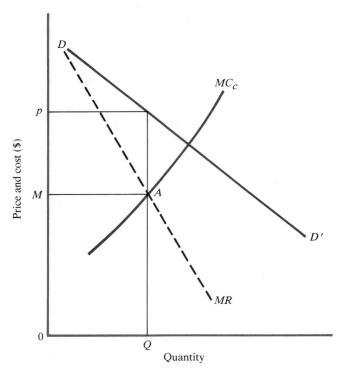

cartel purchase their inputs in perfectly competitive markets, the cartel marginal cost curve (MC_c) is simply the horizontal sum of the marginal cost curves of the member firms. Otherwise, allowance must be made for the increase in input price accompanying an increase in input usage; MC_c will be steeper than would be the case if all input markets were perfectly competitive. (Recall the discussion of short-run supply in Chapter 12.)

In either case, once the management group determines the cartel marginal cost curve (MC_c), the problem is the simple one of determining the price that maximizes cartel profit—the monopoly price. In Figure 15.7 marginal cost and marginal revenue intersect at A. This gives the level of output, Q, and the price, p, that maximize total profit for the cartel.

Once the profit-maximizing price and output are determined, the problem confronting cartel management is how to allocate the output among the member firms. Two fundamental methods of allocation are possible: market sharing (or quotas) and nonprice competition.

There are several possible variants of market sharing or quotas. Indeed there is no uniform principle by which quotas can be determined. In practice, the bargaining ability of a firm and the importance of the firm to the cartel are likely to be extremely important elements in determining a quota. However, one method of allocating the market is to use either the relative sales of each firm in some pre-cartel period or the "productive capacity" of the firm as a basis for allocating shares of the cartel sales. As a practical matter, the choice of which pre-cartel period or what measure of capacity to use is a matter of bargaining among the members. The most skillful bargainer is likely to come out best.

While market sharing or quota agreements may be difficult in practice, some guidelines can be set forth. If the cartel produces a homogeneous product, a reasonable objective for the cartel is to produce the optimal output at the minimum total cost. In this way, total cartel profit is maximized.

Minimum cartel cost is achieved when each firm produces that output for which its marginal cost equals the common cartel marginal cost and marginal revenue. Returning to Figure 15.7, we see that each firm would produce the amount at which its marginal cost is equal to M. Summing to obtain MC_c, total cartel output will be Q, and total profit is maximized.

To reinforce this conclusion, suppose that two firms in the cartel are producing at different marginal costs, that is, assume

$$MC_1 > MC_2$$

for firms 1 and 2. In this case the cartel manager could transfer sales from the higher cost firm 1 to the lower cost firm 2. So long as the marginal cost of producing in firm 2 is lower, total cartel cost can be lowered by transferring production. For example, suppose MC_1 equals \$20 and MC_2 equals \$10. One unit of output taken away from firm 1 lowers the cartel's cost \$20. Producing that unit in firm 2 increases cartel cost by \$10. Thus the total cost of production falls \$10. And the cartel would continue taking output away from firm 1 and increasing the output of firm 2, thus lowering total cost, until $MC_1 = MC_2$. This equality would result because MC_1 would fall as the output of firm 1 decreases, and MC_2 would increase as the output of firm 2 increases. Thus in equilibrium the marginal costs will be equal for all firms in the cartel.[1]

The difficulty involved with this method of allocation is that, if firms differ in their cost structures, the lower-cost firms obtain the bulk of the market and therefore the bulk of the profits. To make this method of allocation acceptable to all members, a profit sharing system, more or less independent of sales quota, must be devised.

In some cases, it will be easy for the member firms to agree upon the share of the market each is to have. This is illustrated in Figure 15.8 for an "ideal" situation. Suppose only two firms are in the market and they decide to divide the market evenly. The market demand curve is DD', so the half-share curve for each firm is Dd. The marginal revenue curve for

---

[1]This point is demonstrated mathematically in the appendix to this chapter.

Figure 15.8 **Ideal Market Sharing**

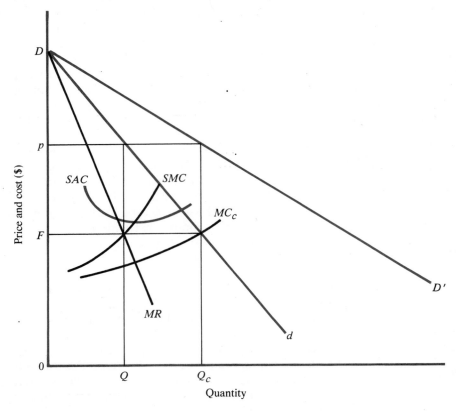

Dd is the line MR, the half-share marginal revenue for each firm. Suppose each firm has identical costs, represented by SAC and SMC.

With these individual marginal revenue, marginal cost, and demand curves, each firm will decide to produce Q units of output, where MR and SMC intersect. A uniform price of p is established on each firm's demand. At p a total output of Q_c is supplied (Q_c is twice Q, the output of each firm). This is a tenable solution because the market demand is consistent with the sale of Q_c units at a price of p.

To see this, let's go the other way around. Suppose a cartel management group is formed and given the task of maximizing cartel profit. With the demand curve DD', the cartel management views Dd as the marginal revenue curve; Dd lies halfway between market demand, DD', and the vertical axis. Next, summing the identical marginal cost curves, it obtains cartel marginal cost MC_c. The intersection of cartel marginal cost and cartel marginal revenue occurs at the level F, corresponding to output Q_c and price p. Since this is the same solution arrived at by the identical firms, the firms' decision to share the market equally is consistent with the objective of the cartel.

In this example we have assumed firms with identical cost functions. The solution is more complex when cost conditions differ, as we noted above. Nonetheless, cartel profit is maximized when total cartel output is chosen so that market marginal revenue equals the horizontal sum of all firms' marginal costs—the cartel's marginal cost curve. Price is determined from the market demand curve at the chosen output. Output is allocated to the firms so that each firm's marginal cost equals market marginal revenue (which is also equal to the cartel's marginal cost) at the chosen level of output.

Ideal situations like the one described above are rare. More likely, cost conditions will differ among firms. Yet another problem arises when firms produce a differentiated product. In such cases a cartel frequently allocates sales through nonprice competition. This type of allocation is frequently associated with "loose" cartels.

In such cases, a uniform price is fixed and each firm is allowed to sell all it can at that price. The only requirement is that firms do not reduce price below the cartel price. There are many examples of this type of cartel organization in the United States today. For instance, in many localities both medical doctors and lawyers have associations whose code of ethics is frequently the basis of price agreement. The patient market, for example, is divided among the various doctors on the basis of nonprice competition: each patient selects the doctor of his or her choice. Similarly, the generally uniform prices of haircuts, major brands of gasoline, and movie tickets do not result from perfect competition within the market. Rather, they result from tacit, and sometimes open, agreement upon a price. The sellers compete with one another in various ways, but not by price variations. This type of cartel arrangement is rather common in the sale of services. We will discuss tacit collusion after pointing out the major problem facing all cartels, both formal and informal. This is the problem of cheating.

The Problem of Cheating

Unless backed by strong enforcement mechanisms, cartel agreements are quite likely to collapse from internal pressure. That is, cartel members, particularly in times of weakened demand, have a strong incentive to cheat on the agreement in an effort to increase profits. A few large, geographically concentrated firms producing a relatively homogeneous commodity may form a successful cartel and maintain it, at least during prosperous times. But the greater the number of firms in the cartel, the more the products are differentiated, and the greater the geographical dispersion of the firms, the greater is the incentive to cheat on the cartel agreement. When profits are low or even negative, firms have an increased incentive to increase output and reduce price.

A typical cartel is characterized by a high (perhaps monopoly) price, a relatively low output, and a sales distribution that causes most firms to produce an output less than that associated with minimum long-run average cost. In this situation, any one firm, acting alone, can profit tremendously from secret price concessions leading to increased sales. As we shall see, this incentive to cheat on the agreement typically causes the cartel to break up.

The incentive of a cartel member to cheat can be explained using our previously developed theory of sticky prices. Figure 15.9 shows the potential gain for a single member of the cartel. Assume the price is fixed at P_0; the cartel member, in this case, sells Q_0, but output may vary among members.

The firm knows that if it reduces price slightly, say to P_1, and other cartel members do not detect the reduced price, it can increase its own sales tremendously. In this case, the firm believes that an unmatched price reduction to P_1 would increase sales to Q_2 and mean a substantial increase in profit. Thus the firm believes that the segment of its demand for an *undetected* price reduction is Ad.

This demand segment is quite elastic, because the firm knows that an unmatched price reduction would allow it to gain sales from the other, obedient members of the cartel. This situation is most likely when the number of members in the cartel is large and the product is differentiated.

But the price reduction is unlikely to go unmatched for very long. In the first place, even in a cartel with a large number of firms, other members are likely to notice their decrease in sales and find out that a rival has lowered price. A reasonable reaction would be to match the lower price. This would protect their market share and punish the cheater by reducing its sales. In most cartels that is the only means of enforcement. In the second place, if this firm has the incentive to reduce price and increase sales, so do all of the other firms in the cartel. And this incentive is increased because every firm knows that every other firm has the same incentive. So there is the tremendous temptation to be the first to reduce price and gain at least a temporary increase in sales and profits before the others begin to cheat.

If rivals match the price cut or they all cheat on the agreement, the firm's demand is the inelastic segment AD. Customers would have no reason to change sellers if they all sell at the lower price, P_1. Thus the firm's gain in sales is small; output increases from Q_0 to Q_1 rather than to Q_2. This increase is due mainly to increased total market sales because of the lower price charged by everyone in the cartel.

The increase in sales from Q_1 to Q_2 represents sales that would have been attracted away from rivals. A substantial increase in the output of one firm while others are losing sales at the cartel price is, however, a strong signal of cheating. Rivals will suspect that someone has lowered the price. So a potentially large increase in sales from an undetected price cut is the incentive for cheating, but, at the same time, it is the signal to others that someone is cheating.

For these reasons, even strong cartels are likely to break up, particularly during times when the economy is weak. All have the incentive to

Figure 15.9 The Incentive to Cheat

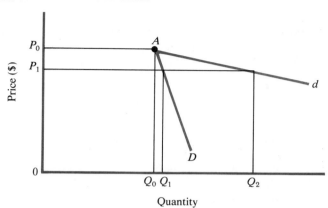

cheat on the agreement, and firms generally do. To see what one famous cartel did about cheating, let's look at the following application.

APPLICATION

Is Cheating a Problem for Cartels?

On August 26, 1985, *Time* reported that Lloyd's of London, the 297-year-old insurance exchange had a new and unusual client.* The ancient company had insured unusual clients in the past, including ships against sinking, actresses against breaking their legs, and at least one rock star (David Lee Roth) against paternity suits. Their latest unusual client was the Organization of Petroleum Exporting Countries (OPEC).

OPEC, a once powerful, 13-country oil cartel, attempted to raise prices and keep them up by limiting production. According to *Time,* Saudi Arabia and Kuwait, two giants of the cartel, had long thought that many members were cheating on their quotas. This additional supply on the market would drive down the price of oil. So cheating was a problem for those who stuck by the agreement.

Time reported that OPEC hired Lloyd's of London to help find out which countries in the cartel were exceeding their quotas and thus depressing the price of oil. "Some 1,000 Lloyd's insurance agents worldwide keep track of all ship movements in and out of major ports, and the exchange stores the information in its central computer in

*The material in this application is from "Slippery Job for Lloyd's," *Time,* August 26, 1985, p. 46.

England." Lloyd's task was to report any suspicious tanker movements by oil producers to OPEC's Vienna headquarters. The Saudis and Kuwaitis had found it difficult to prove what they suspected. "But now they may be able to confront the offenders with hard evidence that they were out of line." *Time* didn't report what else they might do to punish the guilty parties.

Tacit Collusion

A less extreme form of cooperation among oligopoly firms is tacit collusion—agreement without communication. For instance, the producers in a market may restrict their sales to specific geographical regions without meeting and explicitly designating marketing areas on a map. One firm's market area is understood from the ongoing relations it has had with its rivals. As opposed to the formation of a cartel in an attempt to monopolize a market, tacit collusion is not per se (categorically) illegal. However, evidence of agreement would quickly tip the legal balance against accused participants.

Examples consistent with tacit collusion are evident among manufacturers of consumer durables. For instance, oligopolists will often act together (cooperatively) by changing their models annually at the same time. Washing machines, refrigerators, cooking ranges, and lawn mowers have annual model changes that are announced by manufacturers at nearly the same time. Without any known agreement, there is a surprising amount of uniformity in such behavior. The same holds true for fashions, that is, when spring and fall designs are announced. Why do makers of soft drinks and beer all use the same size cans and bottles (or makers of breakfast cereal package their product in the same size boxes)? Certainly, all consumers do not have a preference for the 12-ounce size. But, as far as anyone knows, cereal makers and bottlers have no explicit agreement that only certain container sizes are allowable.

Probably the strongest evidence consistent with tacit collusion is found in the prices oligopolists charge. Particularly in the service sector of our economy, there is surprising price uniformity, even though there is a wide variance in the quality of services. For instance, lawyers and real estate agents by and large charge the same prices for their services even though the quality of services varies from lawyer to lawyer and broker to broker. Explicit collusion is illegal in these industries and presumably does not take place, but a substantial amount of price uniformity exists.

How does tacit collusion arise? What makes oligopolists cooperate without an explicit arrangement? The answer lies in the consequences of noncooperation. As we know, each oligopolist realizes that what it does will cause its rivals to react. The expected reaction is likely to leave sellers no better off than they were before the move. Oligopolists know that they are related to rivals in what we referred to earlier as the prisoner's dilemma. A new style or a lower price may increase profits in the short run, but may reduce profits in the long run.

Thus, whether or not an oligopolist makes a change depends upon the relative expected costs and benefits of making the change. Profits may increase substantially at first as a result of a change, but decrease after rivals react. How quickly rivals react in large measure determines how profitable a change will be. Moreover, since each oligopolist knows that its rivals may have the same motivation to make a change, there is the temptation to move first.

In many cases "patterns of behavior" are established among rivals. Oligopolists cooperate because, given the expected reaction of rivals to one firm's attempt to raise profits, long-run profits are more likely maximized by stable behavior. This is particularly true because other behavior in the long run will raise the costs to producers, and revenues are not likely to go up after rivals have adjusted.

APPLICATION

Tacit Collusion and Market Sharing

From 1951 until 1972, the market for steam turbine generators in the United States was extremely concentrated, consisting of two firms— General Electric and Westinghouse. From 1951 until 1959, the industry was characterized by a cartel. This cartel was eliminated in 1959. But there is strong evidence of tacit collusion during the period 1963–72. Let's look at this evidence.

First consider prices over this period. In the table below the quoted prices of comparable generators are presented. There is, to say the least, a remarkable degree of consistency. It would appear, at the very least, that the firms were following some common course of conduct.

Prices of Comparable Generators, 1963–1971

Date	Quoted Price ($000)	
	General Electric	**Westinghouse**
May 1963	$10,722	$10,722
January 1964	11,286	11,286
June 1964	11,004	11,851
November 1964	11,817	11,817
July 1966	12,566	12,566
October 1966	13,306	13,306
May 1967	14,245	14,245
August 1968	14,858	14,858
June 1969	15,733	15,733
February 1970	16,659	16,659
December 1970	17,584	17,584
August 1971	18,201	18,201

Given this agreement on price, it would then be necessary for the firms to agree on the manner in which output will be allocated. As we have described, allocation of a market could be accomplished through either nonprice competition or some form of market sharing. In the case of steam turbine generators, the firms apparently resorted to some sort of market sharing. The relative shares of the two firms are presented in the following table. While the shares are not constant, there does not appear to be any evidence of a significant shift in favor of one or the other. Thus, it would appear that these firms applied a policy of sharing the market rather than competing on some nonprice basis, even without overt collusion.

Relative Shares, 1963–1972

	General Electric	**Westinghouse**
1963–64	55%	45%
1964–65	67	33
1965–66	56	44
1966–67	56	44
1967–68	61	39
1968–69	55	45
1969–70	59	41
1970–71	64	36
1971–72	60	40

Source: This application is taken from Bruce T. Allen, "Tacit Collusion and Market Sharing: The Case of Steam Turbine Generators," *Industrial Organization Review*, vol. 4 (1976).

Price Leadership

Another cooperative solution to the oligopoly problem is price leadership. This solution does not require open collusion, but the firms in the market must tacitly agree to the solution. Price leadership has been quite common in certain industries. It was characteristic of the steel industry some time ago. At times it has characterized the tire, oil, and cigarette industries.

Any firm in an oligopoly market can be the price leader. While it is frequently the dominant firm in the market, it may be simply the firm with a reputation for good judgment. There could exist a situation in which the most efficient—the least cost—firm is the price leader, even though this firm is not the largest. In any case, the price leader sets a price that will maximize industry profits, and all firms in the industry compete for sales through advertising and other types of marketing. The price remains constant until the price leader changes the price, or one or more other firms break away.

Possibly the simplest form of price leadership is "barometric" price leadership. In this case the price leader is a firm with a reputation for good decision making. (In reality, most price leaders have been one of the larger firms.) The price leader acts as a barometer for prevailing market conditions and sets the price so as to maximize profits under these conditions. For example, if consumers' incomes increase (and the commodity in question is normal), the price leader would note an increase in demand and would respond by raising price. If all of the other firms in the industry follow with price increases, the result will be that the industry moves to a new position of equilibrium with a minimum of interfirm competition. It is important to note that, in this case, the price leader has no power to coerce the other firms into following its lead. Instead, the rival firms will follow this lead only so long as they believe that the price leader's behavior accurately and promptly reflects changes in market conditions.

A much more structured form of price leadership is *dominant firm* price leadership. In this case, there is one firm in the oligopoly market that has the capability of becoming a monopoly. Hence the market is composed of one dominant firm and numerous small ones.

The dominant firm could possibly eliminate all its rivals by a price war. But in addition to being costly, this would establish the firm as a monopoly, with its attendant legal problems. Possibly a more desirable course of action for the dominant firm is to become the price leader and set the market price so as to maximize its own profit, at the same time letting the small firms sell all they wish at that price. Note that, given the size of the dominant firm, in this type of price leadership the price leader— the dominant firm—does have the ability to enforce the price it sets. It does not have to rely on its reputation or the trust of the smaller firms. The small firms, recognizing their position, will behave as do perfectly competitive firms. That is, they will regard their demand curve as a horizontal line at the price set by the dominant firm and sell that amount for which marginal cost equals price. Notice, however, that this does not necessarily entail the long-run, zero-profit solution for the smaller firms, because the dominant firm may set price above the (minimum) average cost of some firms.

There are many variations of dominant firm price leadership. One may allow for the existence of two or more dominant firms, for product differentiation, for geographically separated sellers, for transportation costs, and so on. In all cases, however, the dominant firm is allowed to set price, since it controls such a large share of the market.

15.5 SUMMARY

The key feature of monopolistic competition is that in the long run the firm's economic profit is competed away even though each firm has some market power. The firm's demand is downward sloping because each firm sells a product that is somewhat differentiated from that of every other firm in the market. In the short run a monopolistic competitor acts like a monopolist.

As we have tried to demonstrate, while the oligopoly market structure is perhaps more "realistic" than perfect competition or monopoly, this increase in realism cannot be gained without a cost. The increased complexity of the firm's decisions in an oligopoly market effectively precludes straightforward solutions.

We have emphasized that the primary feature differentiating oligopoly from the other market structures is that the *firms recognize their mutual interdependence*. In contrast to the other market structures, it is not sufficient for a firm in an oligopoly market to make its output and pricing decisions on the basis of its own demand and cost conditions. In addition, an oligopolist must consider the potential reactions of its rivals. In this chapter we discussed some possible ways in which the oligopoly firms could resolve this difficulty. However, as you have seen, the determination of the profit-maximizing levels of output and price for a specific firm becomes extremely difficult. (Furthermore, as we have shown, oligopolistic firms would be expected to compete frequently with one another on a nonprice basis.) Typically, the best solution for oligopolists is to collude with each other, but this is frequently impossible, illegal, or both.

The important point then is that, for the oligopoly market structure, we are unable to provide a simple profit-maximization rule of the type presented in Chapters 12 and 14. In the oligopoly market, the answer to the question of the profit-maximizing levels of output and price is: "It depends." In the cases of perfect competition and monopoly we could show you the forest. In our discussion of the oligopoly market, the best we have been able to do is to bump into several of the trees.

TECHNICAL PROBLEMS

1. Describe the features of monopolistic competition:
    a. How is it similar to monopoly?
    b. How is it similar to perfect competition?
    c. What are the characteristics of short-run equilibrium?
    d. What are the characteristics of long-run equilibrium?
    e. How is long-run equilibrium attained?
2. The figure below shows the long-run average and marginal cost curves for a monopolistically competitive firm.
    a. Assume the firm is in the short run and making profits. Draw in the demand and marginal revenue curves. Show output and price.
    b. Now let the firm reach long-run equilibrium. Draw in the new demand and marginal revenue curves. Show output and price.

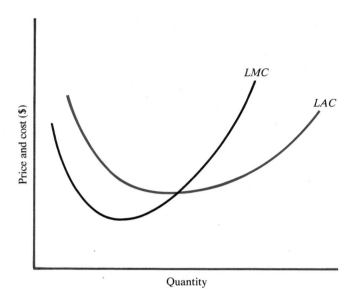

3. A monopolistic competitor is producing a level of output, 750
   units, at which price is $80, marginal revenue is $40, average total
   cost is $100, marginal cost is $40, and average fixed cost is $10.
   a. Draw a graph of the demand and cost conditions facing the
      firm.
   b. Is the firm making the profit-maximizing decision? Why or why
      not? If not, what should the firm do?

4. Suppose that a monopolistically competitive industry is in long-run
   equilibrium. Then consumers' incomes increase (the firms are
   producing a normal good).
   a. In the short run, what will happen to:
      (1) The demand facing a typical firm.
      (2) The amount of output produced by a typical firm.
      (3) The amount of profit earned by a typical firm.
   b. What will happen in the long run?

5. Compare a monopolistic competitor's short-run demand with that
   of a monopolist (discussed in Chapter 14).

6. Compare and contrast oligopoly with perfect competition, pure
   monopoly, and monopolistic competition. What is the principal
   distinguishing characteristic of oligopolies?

7. What types of barriers to entry might permit a profitable oligopoly
   to last a long time?

8. What forms of nonprice competition might exist in an oligopoly
   market?

9. An oligopoly firm, which knows its demand and marginal revenue curves, is producing 1,000 units of output; price is $13, marginal revenue is $9, and average total cost, which is at its minimum value, is $7.

    a. Draw a graph of the demand and cost conditions facing the firm.

    b. Is the firm making the profit-maximizing decision? Why or why not? If not, what should the firm do?

10. An oligopolist faces known demand and marginal revenue curves and has the short-run cost structure shown below.

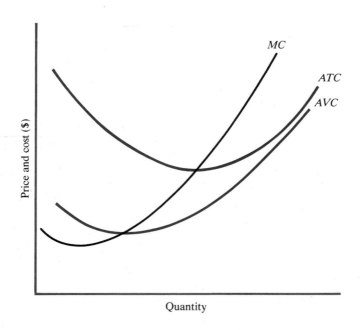

a. Show a demand curve (and associated marginal revenue curve) with which the oligopolist earns a short-run economic profit. Show the price, quantity, and amount of profit being earned. What will the firm do in the long run?

b. Show a demand curve (and associated marginal revenue curve) with which the oligopolist makes losses but continues to operate in the short run. Show the price, quantity, and amount of loss. What will the firm do in the long run?

c. Show a demand curve (and associated marginal revenue curve) with which the oligopolist shuts down in the short run. What will the firm do in the long run?

11. In the graph below MC_1 and MC_2 are the marginal cost curves for two firms that have formed a cartel. D and MR represent the

market demand and marginal revenue for the cartel and MC_T is the cartel's marginal cost curve.

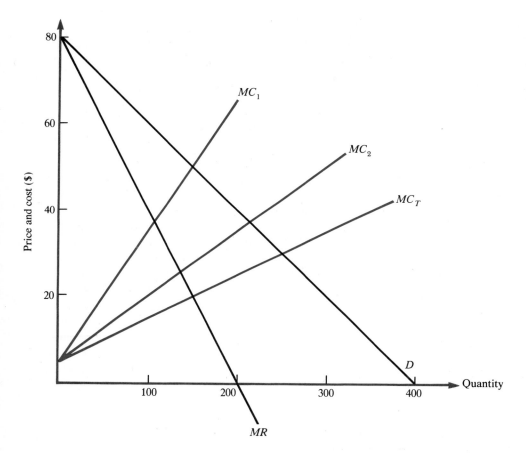

a. What is the profit-maximizing level of cartel output? How should it be allocated between the two firms? What price should the cartel set?

b. Suppose the firms are each producing and selling 75 units of output. What is marginal cost for each firm? Is this optimal? Why or why not? If not, what should the firms do instead?

12. Consider the bituminous coal industry to be a competitive industry in long-run equilibrium. Suppose that the firms in the industry were able to form a cartel.

a. What will happen to the equilibrium output and price of coal? Why?

b. How might the output be allocated among the individual firms?

c. After the cartel is operating, are there incentives for the individual firms to cheat? Why (or why not)?

13. What is "tacit collusion"? How would the behavior of the firms differ from that of members of a cartel? Why would tacit collusion exist?

14. Would you expect the competitive strategies of oligopolists who produce a homogeneous product to differ from the strategies of oligopolists producing a differentiated product? Explain.

ANALYTICAL PROBLEMS

1. "One sure test that an industry is competitive is the absence of any economic profit." Comment.

2. An industry said to be characterized by monopolistic competition is the apparel industry. Suppose you were hired as a consultant by a firm in this industry. How would you advise the firm as to the levels of output, price, input usage, and levels of advertising? What problems might you encounter?

3. In monopolistic competition, the entry of new firms eliminates economic profit. Obviously, firms in such a market would desire to maintain these profits. What policies might be suggested to keep profits from being eliminated? Why would it be impossible to implement such policies in a perfectly competitive market?

4. Many states have had laws restricting the sale of most goods on Sunday. Consumers, by and large, oppose such laws because they find Sunday afternoon a convenient time to shop. Paradoxically, retail trade associations frequently support the laws. Discuss the reasons for merchants supporting these laws. (You may find the prisoner's dilemma useful.)

5. Restaurants in large cities seem to fit the model of monopolistic competition. But some make substantial profits while others are going broke or just breaking even. Is this consistent with the theory? Why or why not?

6. Why would firms like Sara Lee and others in the application on profits being competed away introduce new products without extensive testing? Discuss the pros and cons of this strategy.

7. Suppose you were attempting to establish a price-fixing cartel in an industry.
   a. Would you prefer many or few firms? Why?
   b. How could you prevent cheating (price cutting) by cartel members? Why would members have an incentive to cheat?
   c. Would you keep substantial or very few records? What are the advantages and disadvantages of each?
   d. How could you prevent entry into the industry?
   e. How could government help you prevent entry and even cheating?

    f. How would you try to talk government into helping? Under what conditions might this work?

8. In one application, we cited the behavior of General Electric and Westinghouse as a possible case of collusive market sharing. Could this behavior be instead a case of price leadership? Explain.

9. Many economists argue that more research, development, and innovation occur in the oligopolistic market structure than in any other. Why might this conclusion be true?

10. In the absence of long-run economies of scale, what conditions would cause an oligopoly structure to evolve and be maintained over a long period of time?

11. In the application on used jets, we noted that the two giant jet manufacturers would have an advantage over other firms selling used jets. Why might that be so?

12. In the Coca-Cola application, some observers thought the firm's strategy would hurt Coke in the long run; others thought it would help. Make a case for each conclusion. Why was Pepsi so jubilant when Coke brought its product's taste so close to that of Pepsi?

APPENDIX

If a cartel is maximizing total profit, the marginal costs of all firms are equal.

Assume two firms in a cartel. Their outputs are Q_1 and Q_2; the respective cost functions are $C_1(Q_1)$ and $C_2(Q_2)$. The industry demand is $P = P(Q_1 + Q_2) = P(Q)$. Total industry profit is

$$\pi_T = P(Q_1 + Q_2) \times (Q_1 + Q_2) - C_1(Q_1) - C_2(Q_2).$$

Maximizing π with respect to the outputs of the two firms gives the first order conditions:

$$\frac{\partial \pi_T}{\partial Q_1} = \frac{\partial P}{\partial Q}(Q) + P - \frac{\partial C_1}{\partial Q_1} = MR_T - MC_1 = 0$$

$$\frac{\partial \pi_T}{\partial Q_2} = \frac{\partial P}{\partial Q}(Q) + P - \frac{\partial C_2}{\partial Q_2} = MR_T - MC_2 = 0.$$

It therefore follows that, for maximizing total industry profit,

$$MR_T = MC_1 = MC_2.$$

16

PROFIT MAXIMIZATION FOR FIRMS WITH MARKET POWER— IMPLEMENTATION OF THE THEORY

N ow that we have described in theoretical terms how firms with market power can maximize profit (or minimize loss), we are in a position to show how these relations can actually be implemented. In this chapter, we will describe how the manager of the firm can use estimates of the firm's production function, cost function, and demand function to determine the firm's optimal levels of outout, price, and input usage.

As was the case in Chapter 13, the objective of this chapter is to show how a manager can combine the principles of microeconomic theory and some relatively simple empirical estimates to obtain forecasts or estimates that will aid in maximizing the firm's profits. While this discussion will get a little technical, our objective is *not* to turn you into a "technocrat"; rather, we want you to understand how the theoretical principles of profit maximization can be and are implemented.

We will begin by looking at the output and price decisions for a monopoly firm. Following this, we look at the modifications/complications that are involved in the same decision for a firm in a monopolistically competitive market. Then we will turn to the alternative manner in which the firm can attain profit-maximization—the selection of the optimal levels of usage of its inputs.

We should note that, although we do not specifically address the case of oligopoly, the basic principles of profit maximization apply in this market structure also. The oligopolist determines its output and price by equating marginal revenue and marginal cost. You will recall, however, that oligopolists have the additional problem of not knowing their marginal revenue unless they know how their rivals will react to changes in their price and output. In this chapter we will ignore the problem of how to estimate demand for an oligopolist and concentrate on monopoly and monopolistic competition. When oligopolists know their rivals' reactions, they behave like monopolists.

16.1 MONOPOLY OUTPUT AND PRICE

From the discussion in Chapter 14, we know that the profit-maximizing or loss-minimizing output for a monopoly firm is that at which marginal revenue is equal to marginal cost. Once this output level is determined, we know that the unit price of the output is taken directly from the demand curve. And, we know that the monopoly firm will *actually* produce in the short run—rather than shut down—as long as this price exceeds average variable cost at the output level selected. Let's see how a monopoly firm might actually go about implementing these decisions.

In order to determine the optimal output for the firm, the manager must employ the condition $MR = MC$. We have already had a great deal to say about the estimation of a firm's marginal cost function and there is nothing unusual about the marginal cost function for a monopoly firm. However, obtaining an estimate of the marginal revenue function for a monopoly differs from the case of perfect competition we described in Chapter 13. As we stressed in Chapter 14, the monopoly firm does not face a horizontal demand curve, but instead faces a down-sloping market demand function.

Let's write the estimated demand function facing the monopoly firm as a linear function

$$Q = a + bP + cY + dP_R.$$

As before, in order to isolate the demand curve that is relevant for the period in question, we must have forecasts for (or estimates of) the values of the exogenous variables, Y and P_R, in that period. If we denote these forecasts as $\hat{Y}$ and $\hat{P}_R$, we can rewrite the demand function for the specific period in question as

$$Q = a' + bP,$$

where $a' = a + c\hat{Y} + d\hat{P}_R$.

If we solve this demand function for P, we obtain what is referred to as the *inverse demand function:*

$$P = \frac{-a'}{b} + \frac{1}{b}Q.$$

Total revenue for the firm is simply price times quantity sold, so in terms of our estimated demand function,

$$TR = \frac{-a'}{b}Q + \frac{1}{b}Q^2.$$

Finally, since $MR = \Delta TR / \Delta Q$, it follows that

$$MR = \left(\frac{-a'}{b}\right) + 2\left(\frac{1}{b}\right)Q.$$

To make this procedure somewhat more clear, let's look at a stylized example.

APPLICATION

Estimation of a Marginal Revenue Function

By virtue of its patents, Aztec Electronics possesses substantial monopoly power in the product it manufactures. The manager of Aztec wished to determine the optimal values for output and price for 1988.

The demand for the firm's product was specified as a function of the price of the product, income of the customers, and the price of a complementary good,

$$Q = f(P, Y, P_R).$$

Using data available for the period 1978–87, a linear form of this function was estimated. The resulting estimated demand function was

$$Q = 41 - 0.5P + 1.5Y - 0.4P_R,$$

where output (Q) was measured in 100,000 units, average annual family income (Y) in thousand dollars, and the two prices (P and P_R) in dollars per unit.

From an economic consulting firm, the manager obtained 1988 forecasts for income and the price of the complementary good as, respectively, \$18,000 and \$45. Using these values—$\hat{Y} = 18$ and $\hat{P}_R = 45$—the estimated (forecasted) demand function in 1988 was

$$Q = 50 - 0.5P.$$

The corresponding inverse demand function was obtained by solving for P,

$$P = 100 - 2Q.$$

And, from this inverse demand function, the manager was able to identify the marginal revenue function:

$$MR = 100 - 4Q.$$

Once you have obtained the marginal revenue function, the determination of the optimal level of output is made by equating marginal revenue and marginal cost, then solving for Q. It's been our experience that it is much easier to see this with an example, so let's return to our application.

APPLICATION

How Much Do I Produce?

The manager of Aztec Electronics also obtained an estimate of the firm's average variable cost function:

$$AVC = 28 - 5Q + 1Q^2.$$

In this estimation, AVC was measured in dollars per unit and Q was again measured in 100,000 units. Given this average variable cost function, the marginal cost function is

$$MC = 28 - 10Q + 3Q^2.$$

In order to determine the optimal level of production, the manager equated the 1988 marginal revenue function with the firm's marginal cost function

$$100 - 4Q = 28 - 10Q + 3Q^2.$$

Solving this equation for Q, two solutions were obtained: $Q = 6$ and $Q = -4$. Since $Q = -4$ is an irrelevant solution (we cannot have negative outputs), the optimal level of production is $Q = 6$. That is, the profit-maximizing (or loss-minimizing) output level for 1988 is 600,000 units.

Given that you know the optimal level of production, determination of the optimal price is really nothing more than finding the price on the demand curve that corresponds to the optimal output level. In terms of the functions we have been working with, this means that the optimal output—let's call it Q^*—is plugged into the inverse demand function to give the optimal price,

$$P^* = \left(\frac{-a'}{b}\right) + \frac{1}{b}Q^*.$$

To see how this works, let's continue with our example.

APPLICATION

What Price Do I Charge?

In the preceding application, we saw that the manager of Aztec Electronics had determined the optimal output in 1988 to be 600,000 units (i.e., $Q^* = 6$). Inserting this value into the inverse demand function,

$$P^* = 100 - 2(6) = 88,$$

the optimal price for 1988 was found to be $88 per unit.

Remember that nothing *guarantees* that a monopoly firm will make a profit in the short run. It is possible, as we showed in Chapter 14, for a monopoly firm to suffer a loss in the short run if the optimal price is below average total cost. However, if the optimal price is above average variable cost, it is still in the best interest of the firm to continue producing, since the loss will be smaller than the loss would be if the firm simply shut down—produced zero output. Only if the optimal price is below average variable cost at that output level should the firm shut down.

APPLICATION

The Shutdown Decision

In the preceding applications, we have seen that the manager of Aztec Electronics found the optimal 1988 output to be 600,000 units, which would be priced at $88 per unit. But, isn't it possible that this price would yield a total revenue that is less than variable cost and that the best policy is to shut down? To consider this, the manager compared the optimal price with the average variable cost of producing the 600,000 units.

Using the estimated average variable cost function, AVC per unit for 600,000 units was calculated as

$$AVC = 28 - 5(6) + 1(6^2) = \$34.$$

Since $88 > $34, the manager knows that all of the variable costs will be covered and the best policy is to produce.

Put another way, the firm's expected total revenue in 1988 was $52.8 million (i.e., $88 × 600,000$) and total variable cost was forecasted to be \$20.4 million (i.e., \$34 × 600,000). Since total revenue exceeds total variable cost, the firm should continue to produce.

On the basis of actual 1987 data, the manager of Aztec Electronics would have had a very good estimate of the firm's fixed costs in 1988. Suppose that projected 1988 fixed costs were \$27 million. In this case, with an output of 600,000 units priced at \$88 per unit, the expected profit is \$5.4 million. Clearly, the firm should continue to produce since it can earn an economic profit.

If, on the other hand, projected fixed costs for 1988 were \$35 million, the firm would be expected to suffer a loss of \$2.6 million. Should the firm continue to produce? Yes. If it produces the 600,000 units, its loss would be \$2.6 million. But, if it shuts down, the loss in 1988 would be \$35 million. (If it shuts down, Aztec would have a loss equal to its fixed costs.)

In the preceding, we have considered only a linear demand function. Given the form of the marginal cost function, a linear demand function is somewhat easier to use in determining the optimal level of production. However, we could use a log-linear demand function. Let's look briefly at how we would obtain the marginal revenue function.

We begin by estimating a log-linear demand function

$$Q = aP^b Y^c P_R^d.$$

Once we have estimates of a, b, c, and d, we can obtain forecasts for the exogenous variables—$\hat{Y}$ and $\hat{P}_R$—to give us a forecasted demand function for some future period; for example, the demand function for 1988. We can write this forecasted demand function as

$$Q = BP^b,$$

where $B = a\hat{Y}^c \hat{P}_R^d$.

Solving for the price of the commodity (P), the inverse demand function is

$$P = B^{-1/b} Q^{1/b}.$$

Then, total revenue ($P \times Q$) is

$$TR = B^{-1/b} Q^{(1/b)+1}.$$

From this total revenue function, the marginal revenue function is

$$MR = \left(\frac{b+1}{b}\right) B^{-1/b} Q^{1/b}.$$

Let's look at an example using this log-linear form of the demand function.

APPLICATION

Marginal Revenue for a Log-Linear Demand Function

In preparation for forecasting the optimal level of service and the optimal monthly service fee for 1988, the manager of Allied Cable TV, Inc., elected to estimate a demand function of the form

$$Q = aP^b Y^c.$$

The manager was able to obtain a cross-section data set in which Q was measured as the number of households served (in thousands), P as the (monthly) service fee, and Y as the average annual family income of households in the service area (in thousand dollars). Using these data, the estimated demand function was

$$\log Q = 2.785 - 2.0 \log P + 3.0 \log Y.$$

Since the antilog of 2.785 is 16.2, the estimated demand function can be expressed as

$$Q = 16.2P^{-2}Y^3.$$

From an economic consulting firm, the manager obtained an estimate of average annual family income for Allied's service area in 1988 of $20,000; that is, $\hat{Y} = 20$. Using this forecast in the estimated demand function, the forecasted demand function for Allied Cable TV in 1988 was

$$Q = 16.2P^{-2}(20)^3 = 129,600P^{-2}.$$

Solving this equation for P, the inverse demand function for 1988 was

$$P = 360Q^{-1/2}.$$

Forecasted total revenue is $P \times Q = 360Q^{1/2}$, so the forecasted marginal revenue function was

$$MR = 180Q^{-1/2}.$$

16.2 OUTPUT AND PRICE FOR MONOPOLISTICALLY COMPETITIVE FIRMS

In Chapter 15 we noted that there is essentially no difference in the short-run analysis of monopoly and monopolistic competition: A firm in a monopolistically competitive market faces a downward-sloping demand curve. So, the firm maximizes profit or minimizes losses by producing the output at which marginal revenue equals marginal cost. Once this output is selected, the price to be charged is taken directly from the firm's demand curve.

Therefore a monopolistically competitive firm will follow the steps we outlined in the preceding section to determine its optimal output level and price:

1. Given an estimate of the demand function facing the firm, obtain the inverse demand function and the marginal revenue function.
2. From the estimated average variable cost function, obtain the marginal cost function.
3. Determine the optimal output level by equating the marginal revenue and marginal cost functions.
4. Use the optimal output level in the inverse demand function to obtain the optimal price.
5. To make sure that the firm should actually produce, compare the optimal price and average variable cost at the optimal output level. The firm should continue to produce as long as the optimal price is greater than average variable cost and would shut down only if average variable cost exceeds price.

Complications

In general, the implementation of the output and pricing decision is the same for a monopolistically competitive firm as for a monopoly firm. However, a complication arises in the estimation of the demand function facing the individual firm. For any one firm, demand is determined not only by the firm's own price, the income of the consumers, the price of related goods, and the firm's level of advertising, but also by the prices charged by its competitors and their advertising. That is, the demand function facing firm i may be written as

$$Q_i = f(P_i, Y, P_R, A_i, P_j, A_j, P_k, A_k, \ldots),$$

where

$$Q_i = \text{The sales of firm } i$$
$$P_i = \text{The price charged by firm } i$$
$$Y = \text{Income of the consumers}$$
$$P_R = \text{The price of related goods}$$
$$A_i = \text{Advertising by firm } i$$
$$P_j, P_k, \ldots = \text{The prices charged by competitors}$$
$$A_j, A_k, \ldots = \text{Advertising by competitors.}$$

Thus, to obtain estimates of the individual firm's demand function, a substantial amount of data is required.

And, in order for this technique to be useful, we need to forecast demand in the future. As you are aware, in order to do this, we need the future values for the competitors' prices and advertising. A precise prediction is simply impossible. These values are not constant, nor do they follow some trend. Hence, in order to obtain an accurate forecast of future demand, the manager must be able to predict the pricing and advertising policies of its competitors.

The upshot of all this is simply that it is much more difficult to obtain an accurate estimate of and forecast for an individual firm's demand function in a monopolistically competitive market. On a practical basis, this would suggest that the firm might consider doing simulation analyses like those outlined in Chapter 8. That is, given the best estimate of its demand function from historical data, the firm might consider several different demand forecasts based on alternative assumptions about the policies of the other firms in the market.

Cost-Plus Pricing

It should be clear to you that the short-run pricing decision based on the equality of marginal revenue and marginal cost is the one that will give maximum profit (or minimum loss). However, there is considerable evidence to suggest that many firms—particularly those in monopolistically competitive markets—use a pricing technique based on average rather than marginal cost. This technique is called cost-plus pricing.

The basic concept is deceptively simple. In cost-plus pricing, the firm determines its average total cost then adds a percentage markup (or margin). Thus, price is

$$P = ATC + (m \cdot ATC)$$
$$= (1 + m) \cdot ATC,$$

where m is the markup on cost. For example, if the markup is 20 percent, price would be $(1.2) ATC$.

This very basic description of cost-plus pricing glosses over two major difficulties. First, how does the firm determine average total cost? Second, how does the firm select the "appropriate" markup (or margin)?

Given that costs vary with the level of output produced, determination of average cost requires that the firm first specify the level of output that will be produced. Obviously, a precise determination of this output would require consideration of the prevailing demand conditions—a feature not incorporated in cost-plus pricing. Instead, firms typically specify a "standard" volume of production, based on some assumption about the percentage of the firm's capacity that will be utilized. Furthermore, the costs used are derived from accounting data. As we have noted in earlier chapters, the use of accounting data may not be valid, since accounting costs do not always reflect opportunity costs. Also, such historical data would not reflect recent or potential changes in input prices.

Notwithstanding the difficulties involved in determining average cost, a potentially more troublesome problem is the selection of the markup percentage. While the firm might arbitrarily select some target rate of return on invested capital, recent empirical evidence suggests that the firms use a more subjective approach. It appears that the markups for different products differ according to such factors as the degree of competitiveness in the market and the price elasticity of demand. Apparently, the manager employs knowledge about the market to determine the markup that maximizes profits.

Cost-plus pricing has been criticized on two grounds. First, it employs average rather than marginal cost. As we know from Chapter 3, marginal (or incremental) cost rather than total cost should be used in making any optimizing decision. Second, cost-plus pricing does not incorporate a consideration of prevailing demand conditions. Using the $MR = MC$ pricing rule, demand conditions enter explicitly through the marginal revenue function, but cost-plus pricing does not embody this information.

These criticisms are valid. However, it should be noted that, *under certain circumstances,* cost-plus pricing may approximate $MR = MC$ pricing. Let us show you how this can occur. As we have shown in an earlier chapter, marginal revenue may be written as

$$MR = P\left(1 - \frac{1}{E}\right),$$

where E is the own-price elasticity of demand. Setting marginal revenue equal to marginal cost, our optimization condition may be written as

$$P = \left(\frac{E}{E - 1}\right)MC.$$

If the firm has a flat average cost curve (e.g., if the firm's long-run cost relation is characterized by constant returns to scale), average cost is constant and is equal to marginal cost. In this case, we could write the preceding condition as

$$P = \left(\frac{E}{E - 1}\right)AC.$$

Note the similarity between this equation and the equation for cost-plus pricing, $P = (1 + m)AC$. Setting these equations equal (i.e., assuming that cost-plus pricing is equivalent to $MR = MC$ pricing), the markup would be

$$m = \frac{1}{E - 1}.$$

That is, if firms are using cost-plus pricing as an approximation to pricing based on profit maximization, the markup would be determined by the price elasticity of demand—precisely the relation indicated in the empirical investigations mentioned earlier. While we are limited to the elastic portion of the demand function (i.e., where $E > 1$), this formulation indicates that, as the demand curve is more elastic (i.e., as E increases), the profit-maximizing markup decreases. For example, if $E = 2$, the profit-maximizing markup would be 100 percent. However, if the demand curve were more elastic, say, $E = 5$, the profit-maximizing markup would fall to 25 percent. The point is that if the firm's average cost is constant, cost-plus pricing *could* be equivalent to pricing based on profit maximization. Moreover, the size of the markup would depend on the own-price elasticity of demand, which of course depends upon the availability of good substitutes for the product. The better the substitute, the lower the markup.

16.3 PROFIT-MAXIMIZING INPUT USAGE

Firms with market power can also make their profit-maximizing (or loss-minimizing) decision via the selection of the optimal levels of usage of their inputs. To see how this can be done—and to demonstrate that this situation is very similar to the situation we described for a perfectly competitive firm—we consider the case where the firm employs a single variable input and pays a fixed (constant) price for that input. Implementation of the more complicated cases—multiple variable inputs and an upward-sloping supply function for inputs is covered in the appendix to this chapter.

Consider a firm that has market power in its output market—it faces a downward-sloping demand function for its output. However, the firm is one of many purchasers of the input, so its employment decision will have no effect on the input price. As an example, you might think of the single electric utility firm or cable TV firm in your city. This kind of a firm has substantial market power (albeit in its own small market) so it faces a downward-sloping demand curve. The firm uses a variable input—labor—in conjunction with its fixed capital stock to produce its output. But, since it is only one of many firms hiring labor in the city, its employment decision—how much labor it hires—would not be expected to change the citywide wage rate.

As we know from Chapter 14, in this case, the optimum level of employment for the firm is that at which the marginal revenue product of the input is equal to the price of the input. Since we are using labor as an example, we can express this condition as

$$MRP_L = w,$$

where MRP_L is the marginal revenue product of labor and w is the market-determined wage rate. From Chapter 14 we know that, for a firm with market power, MRP is equal to the product of the firm's marginal revenue function and the marginal product function for the input,

$$MRP_L = MR \times MP_L.$$

As in Chapter 13, let's use a one-input (short-run) production function of the form

$$Q = AL^\beta,$$

where $0 < \beta < 1$. As we know, the marginal product function for labor is

$$MP_L = \beta AL^{\beta-1}.$$

To "match" this log-linear production function, let's also use a log-linear demand function,

$$Q = aP^b Y^c P_R^d.$$

As we demonstrated earlier in this chapter, after we have estimated this demand function and obtained forecasts for the exogenous variables—$\hat{Y}$ and $\hat{P}_R$—the forecasted demand function may be written as

$$Q = BP^b,$$

and the marginal revenue function as

$$MR = \left(\frac{b+1}{b}\right) B^{-1/b} Q^{1/b}.$$

If, however, we want to solve for the optimal level of usage of labor, the marginal revenue function must be expressed in terms of L rather than Q. To accomplish this, let's substitute the production function ($Q = AL^\beta$) into our MR function. After this substitution, the marginal revenue function becomes

$$MR = \left(\frac{b+1}{b}\right) B^{-1/b} (AL^\beta)^{1/b}$$

$$= \left(\frac{b+1}{b}\right) B^{-1/b} A^{1/b} L^{\beta/b}.$$

We can obtain the marginal revenue product function as

$$MRP_L = MR \times MP_L,$$

where the MR and MP_L functions are those derived above. Then, to determine the optimal level of usage of labor, we equate this marginal revenue product function to the price of labor, w, and solve for L. To make this somewhat complicated procedure more understandable, let's look at an example.

APPLICATION

The Employment Decision

Allied Cable TV, Inc., is a firm that (1) has substantial monopoly power in its local market, (2) uses a single variable input—labor, and (3) faces a fixed, market-determined price for labor. The manager of Allied wants to determine the optimal level of labor usage for 1988. As we know, in order to make this determination, the manager must have estimates/forecasts of the marginal product function for labor, the firm's marginal revenue function, the marginal revenue product function for labor, and the wage rate. Let's take these in order.

Marginal Product
The manager used available historical data to estimate a short-run production function of the form

$$Q = AL^\beta.$$

Measuring output in thousand households served and labor usage in thousand hours per month, the estimated function was

$$\log Q = 3.892 + 0.4 \log L.$$

Rewriting this function in its exponential form, the short-run production function was

$$Q = 49L^{0.4}$$

and the corresponding marginal product function was

$$MP_L = (0.4)(49)L^{0.4-1} = 19.6L^{-0.6}.$$

Marginal Revenue
We introduced the forecasted 1988 marginal revenue function for Allied Cable TV in an earlier application. As we saw, the forecasted inverse demand function in 1988 was

$$P = 360Q^{-1/2},$$

(where price was expressed in dollars per household per month and output was expressed in thousand households serviced per month) and the marginal revenue function was

$$MR = 180Q^{-1/2}.$$

Substituting the estimated production function into this marginal revenue function,

$$MR = 180(49L^{0.4})^{-1/2}$$
$$= 25.714L^{-0.2}.$$

Marginal Revenue Product

Using the preceding estimates/forecasts of MP_L and MR, the manager of Allied Cable TV calculated the marginal revenue product of labor as

$$MRP_L = (25.714L^{-0.2}) \times (19.6L^{-0.6}) = 504L^{-0.8}.$$

Wage Rate

From an econometric forecasting firm, the manager obtained a forecast for the 1988 wage rate of $18 per hour.

Optimization

To determine the optimal monthly employment level for Allied Cable TV in 1988, the manager equated the forecasts for MRP_L and w:

$$504L^{-0.8} = 18.$$

Solving this equation for L,

$$L^{-0.8} = 0.0357,$$

Therefore, $L = 64.4$. That is, the optimal monthly level of labor usage in 1988 is forecasted to be 64,400 hours, or an annual level of usage of 772,800 hours. (This is approximately 386.4 full-time employees.)

Given $L = 64.4$, the output of the firm in 1988 would be obtained from the production function as

$$Q = 49(64.4)^{0.4} = 259.3.$$

Then, the price of the output is, from the inverse demand function,

$$P = 360(259.3)^{-1/2} = 22.36.$$

That is, these estimates indicate that Allied should serve 259,300 households and charge a monthly fee of $22.36.

16.4 SUMMARY

The optimal output level for a monopoly firm—for a firm with market power—is that at which marginal revenue is equal to marginal cost. Given an estimated demand function,

$$Q = f(P),$$

we can solve for the inverse demand function,

$$P = f^{-1}(Q)$$

From this inverse demand function, we can obtain the estimated marginal revenue function. For example, if the inverse demand function is linear,

$$P = a - bQ,$$

the marginal revenue function will be of the form

$$MR = a - 2bQ.$$

The marginal cost function can be obtained from an estimated average variable cost curve or from a linear program or from an engineering cost function. In any case, the marginal cost function will be of the form

$$MC = \alpha + \beta Q + \gamma Q^2.$$

Equating the marginal revenue and marginal cost functions, we can solve for the optimal level of output.

Given the optimal output level, the price to charge is determined from the inverse demand function. That is, the optimal output level is plugged into the inverse demand function to yield the optimal price.

The calculated optimal output is the profit-maximizing output only if the corresponding price exceeds average variable cost; if price is less than average variable cost at the optimum output level, the profit-maximizing (loss-minimizing) decision is to shut down. To check this condition, it is necessary only to calculate the average variable cost for the optimum output level and compare this with the price indicated from the inverse demand function.

The profit-maximizing output decision for a monopolistically competitive firm follows the same rules. It is complicated, however, by the fact that it is much more difficult to obtain estimates of the demand function facing a monopolistically competitive firm. Faced with these difficulties, monopolistically competitive firms have resorted to alternative pricing rules. One of the most common of these is cost-plus pricing, where the price charged represents a markup (margin) over average total cost:

$$P = (1 + m) \, ATC.$$

Two problems exist with this approach: (1) the appropriate output level at which to measure ATC is unknown, and (2) the appropriate margin (m) is unknown. However, when the firm's cost curve is relatively flat, cost-plus pricing can approximate profit maximization if the markup is equal to $1/(E - 1)$, where E is the own-price elasticity of demand.

A monopolistic firm—or a firm with market power—can also maximize profit by selecting the optimal level of input usage. The rule for optimization is to equate the marginal revenue product of the input with its price (e.g., in the case of labor),

$$MRP_L = w.$$

To implement this rule, we note that the marginal revenue product is equal to the product of the marginal revenue and the marginal product functions.

$$MRP_L = MR \times MP_L.$$

From an estimated demand function, we can solve for the inverse demand function and then the marginal revenue function. In the case of a log-linear demand function and a Cobb-Douglas production function, the resulting marginal revenue function will take the form

$$MR = AL^b.$$

The marginal product function will be of the type

$$MP_L = CL^d.$$

Multiplying the two functions together, the marginal revenue product function will be of the form

$$MRP_L = (AC)L^{b+d} = \alpha L^\beta.$$

Then, equating the marginal revenue product function with the cost of the input,

$$\alpha L^\beta = w,$$

We can solve for L^*, the optimal level of usage of the input.

TECHNICAL PROBLEMS

1. The manager of a monopoly firm obtained the following estimate of the market demand function for its output:

    $$Q = 26 - 1P + 2Y - 5P_R,$$

    where Q was measured in 100 units, prices in dollars per unit, and income (Y) in thousand dollars. From an econometric forecasting firm, the manager obtained forecasts for the 1988 values of Y and P_R as, respectively, \$20,000 and \$2. For 1988, what is
    a. The forecasted demand function?
    b. The inverse demand function?
    c. The marginal revenue function?

2. For the firm in Problem 1, the manager estimated the average variable cost function as

    $$AVC = 20 - 7Q + 1Q^2,$$

    where AVC was measured in dollars per unit and Q was measured in 100 units.
    a. What is the estimated marginal cost function?
    b. What is the optimal level of production in 1988?
    c. What is the optimal price in 1988?
    d. Check to make sure that the firm should actually produce in the short run rather than shut down.

    In addition, the manager expects fixed costs in 1988 to be \$22,500.
    e. What is the firm's expected profit or loss in 1988?

3. The Ali Baba Co. is the only supplier of a particular type of Oriental carpet. The estimated demand for their carpets is

$$Q = 112 - .5P + 5Y,$$

where Q = number of carpets (1,000), P = price of carpets (dollars per unit), and Y = consumers' income per capita ($1,000). The estimated average variable cost function for Ali Baba's carpets is

$$AVC = 200 - 12Q + 2Q^2.$$

Consumers' income per capita is expected to be $20,000 and total fixed cost is $100,000.

a. How many carpets should the firm supply in order to maximize profit?
b. What is the profit-maximizing price of carpets?
c. What is the maximum amount of profit that the firm can earn selling carpets?
d. Answer (a) through (c) if consumers' income per capita is expected to be $30,000 instead.
e. Answer (a) through (c) if total fixed cost is expected to be $2 million instead.

4. The manager of a monopoly firm estimated a demand function of the form

$$Q = aP^b Y^c P_R^d.$$

The estimated function was

$$\log Q = 2.303 - 2.0 \log P + 2.0 \log Y - 0.5 \log P_R.$$

The manager obtained forecasts for the 1988 values of the exogenous variables as $\hat{Y}_{1988} = 20$ and $\hat{P}_{R,1988} = 100$.
a. What is the forecasted demand function for 1988?
b. What is the inverse demand function?
c. What is the marginal revenue function?

5. Under what condition(s) would cost-plus pricing be equivalent to profit-maximization; that is, $MR = MC$ pricing?

6. If the condition(s) in Problem 5 are satisfied and if the own-price elasticity of the demand function facing the firm is equal to 1.5, what is the profit-maximizing markup? What is the profit-maximizing markup if the own-price elasticity is equal to 3?

7. Return to the firm introduced in Problem 4. The manager of the firm estimated the short-run production function as

$$\log Q = 4.605 + 0.6 \log L.$$

Using these results with the marginal revenue function obtained in Problem 4, obtain the firm's marginal revenue product function for labor.

8. Use your results from Problem 7 and suppose that the expected wage rate for 1988 is $20,
   a. What is the optimal level of usage of labor?
   b. What are the values of output and price that correspond to that level of usage of labor?

ANALYTICAL PROBLEMS

1. In this chapter, we used both linear and log-linear demand function estimates in our applications. On a practical basis, how would the analyst choose between these specifications? (In what situation would one or the other be easier to work with?)

2. In our discussion of monopolistic competition, we noted that a monopolistically competitive firm is faced with much more uncertainty. What kind of uncertainty might a monopolistically competitive firm face?

3. Suppose a manager wanted to use cost-plus pricing. How might he or she determine if the characteristics of the firm are such that cost-plus pricing can approximate profit maximization? How might the manager obtain the estimate of own-price elasticity necessary to determine the optimal markup?

4. In our discussion of the employment decision, we used estimates of the production relation obtained from regression analysis. Could the manager use some other method of estimating the production relation, for example, linear programming? Explain your answer.

APPENDIX: PROFIT-MAXIMIZING LEVELS OF INPUT USAGE—COMPLICATIONS

Several Variable Inputs with Fixed Input Prices

If the firm has several variable inputs, the optimizing condition for each input remains unchanged. However, as in the case of the input decision for a perfectly competitive firm, there is an additional complication: the optimizing conditions must be solved simultaneously.

Without going into a great deal of detail, let's look at how the firm might approach the input decision if it employs two variable inputs— capital and labor. From our discussion thus far we hope you can see that, if the production function is of the Cobb-Douglas form,

$$Q = AK^\alpha L^\beta,$$

and the forecasted demand function is log-linear,

$$Q = BP^b,$$

the marginal revenue product of labor will take the form

$$MRP_L = ZK^\theta L^\phi,$$

where Z, θ, and ϕ are known parameters. Likewise, the marginal revenue product of capital will take the form

$$MRP_K = WK^\delta L^\eta,$$

where W, δ, and η are also known parameters.*
  Then, the optimizing conditions for the two inputs are

$$ZK^\theta L^\phi = w$$
$$WK^\delta L^\eta = r.$$

To obtain the optimal levels of input usage, these conditions must be solved simultaneously for K and L. As in the appendix to Chapter 13, such a solution involves substantial mathematical manipulation. But, the primary point is that, given estimates of the production function and the demand function, a determination of the optimal values can be obtained. And, this same technique could be extended to consider three or more variable inputs.

Upward-Sloping Input Supply

Thus far, we have presumed that the individual firm's employment decision will have no effect on the price it will have to pay for the inputs it employs. We have been considering a labor market sufficiently large that the individual firm can hire as much or as little of the input as it desires at a constant input price. However, as we noted in Chapter 14, it is possible that a firm with market power may be large enough that its employment decision will affect the market price of the input. In this case, if the firm wishes to employ more of the input, it will be required to pay more for the input—the price of the input will rise.

  To see how this complication influences the employment decision, let's look at a firm that employs only a single variable input, labor. In this case, the price of the input (the wage rate) is not constant. Instead, the wage rate depends on the amount of labor the firm hires,

$$w = f(L).$$

As the firm hires more labor, the wage rate rises, so we would want our function—the labor supply function—to reflect this positive relation. The

---

*Specifically, the marginal revenue products of the inputs are

$$MRP_L = \left(\frac{b+1}{b}\right)\beta B^{1/b}A^{1+1/b}K^{\alpha/b+\alpha}L^{\beta/b+\beta-1}$$

$$MRP_K = \left(\frac{b+1}{b}\right)\alpha B^{-1/b}A^{1+1/b}K^{\alpha/b+\alpha-1}L^{\beta/b+\beta}.$$

simplest such function is a linear function, $w = m + nL$, where m and n are both positive. With this function, total factor (labor) cost is $w \times L = mL + nL^2$ and the marginal factor cost function is $MFC = m + 2nL$.

The linear specification is completely acceptable. But, given the way in which we have calculated our marginal revenue product function, a more convenient specification of the firm's labor supply function is a log-linear form,

$$w = mL^{n\cdot}$$

With this form, the total factor cost function ($w \times L$) is

$$TFC = mL^{n+1}$$

and the marginal factor cost function is

$$MFC = (n + 1)mL^n.$$

Equating this marginal factor cost function with the firm's marginal revenue product function for labor, the manager can determine the firm's optimal level of usage of labor. To show you how this can be done, let's look at an example.

APPLICATION

The Employment Decision with an Upward-Sloping Labor Supply

In an earlier application we looked at Allied Cable TV's employment decision presuming that the firm faced a constant wage rate for labor. Alternatively, suppose that the manager had discovered that the labor required by Allied was specialized and in limited supply in the city. Therefore, if Allied were to increase its employment, it would have to raise the wage rate it paid.

To reevaluate the employment decision under this altered situation, the manager obtained an estimate of the labor supply function facing Allied. The estimated labor supply function was

$$w = 8.55L^{0.17},$$

where the wage rate was measured in dollars per hour and labor usage was measured in thousand hours per month. From this estimated labor supply function, the marginal factor cost function for Allied is

$$MFC = 10L^{0.17}.$$

Equating this marginal factor cost function with the firm's marginal revenue product function for labor (as obtained in the earlier application), the profit-maximization condition is obtained:

$$504L^{-0.8} = 10L^{0.17}.$$

Then, the manager was able to solve this equation to determine the optimal level of usage of labor. That is,

$$L^{0.97} = 50.4,$$

so $L = 56.9$. That is, with this upward-sloping supply curve for labor, the optimal monthly labor usage for Allied in 1988 was forecasted to be 56,900 hours (on an annual basis, 341.4 full-time employees).

17

MULTIPLE PLANTS, MARKETS, AND PRODUCTS

U ntil now we have only considered—at least implicitly—a very simple firm. We have been looking at a firm that has a single plant in which it produces a single product that is sold in a single market. Clearly, this is frequently not the situation actually faced by real-world firms or corporations, even though the models give great insight into a firm's decision process.

In this chapter, we want to show how some complications—multiple plants, multiple markets, and multiple products—affect the profit maximization principles we have described. The discussion of each of these topics will of necessity be brief. It is not our intention to provide an exhaustive discussion of these complications; such a discussion could and does form the basis for entire courses. Rather, it is our intention to show that these complications do not alter the principles of profit maximization we have set forth: The firm continues to produce that output at which marginal revenue equals marginal cost (or choose the level of input usage at which marginal revenue product is equal to marginal factor cost). The effect of these complications does, however, make the implementation of these principles more computationally complex: "The rule's the same but the arithmetic is a little harder."

In this discussion, we limit our attention to firms with market power, so we will be looking at monopoly, oligopoly, and monopolistic competition. Since we will be concerned with the firm's output and pricing decision—the firm's short-run decisions—we know that these market structures are analytically the same. Hence, in our discussion, we will normally consider a monopoly firm, but the conclusions also apply to monopolistic competition and oligopoly.

We begin with a discussion of multiplant firms. This will be followed by a discussion of firms that sell in multiple markets and then a discussion of firms that produce multiple products.

We should note that we treat these extensions of the theory as separate topics without trying to integrate them. But keep in mind that firms, frequently, can and do fall in two or even all three of the categories. That is, a firm such as an automobile manufacturer would produce several different products in several different plants and may well sell in several different markets. This extension would, however, further complicate an already somewhat complex analysis. We do, however, end with a discussion of why firms would want to produce multiple products.

17.1 MULTIPLANT FIRMS

A firm with market power often produces output in more than one plant. In this situation, it is likely that the various plants will have different cost conditions. The problem facing the firm is, therefore, how to allocate the firm's desired level of production among these plants.

For simplicity, let's assume there are only two plants, A and B. Suppose at the desired level of output, the following situation holds:

$$MC_A < MC_B.$$

Clearly the firm should transfer output from the higher cost Plant B to the lower cost Plant A. If the last unit produced in Plant B costs $10, but one more unit produced in Plant A adds only $7 to A's cost, that unit should be transferred from B to A. The transfer results in a cost reduction of $3. In fact, output should be transferred from B to A until

$$MC_A = MC_B.$$

Equality eventually occurs because of increasing marginal cost. As output is transferred out of B into A, the marginal cost in A rises, and the marginal cost in B falls. It is simple to see that exactly the opposite occurs in the case of

$$MC_A > MC_B.$$

Output is taken out of A and produced in B until

$$MC_A = MC_B.$$

The total output decision is easily determined. The horizontal summation of all plants' marginal cost curves is the firm's total marginal cost curve. This total marginal cost curve is equated to marginal revenue in order to determine the profit-maximizing output and price. This output is

Figure 17.1 Multiplant Firm

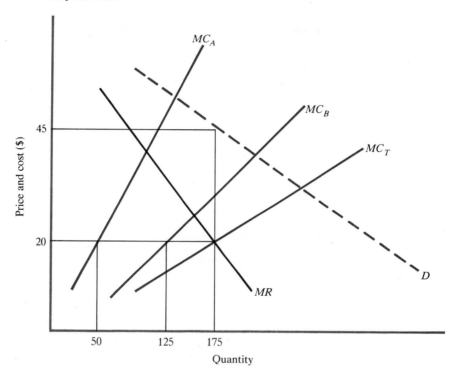

divided among the plants so that the marginal cost is equal for all plants.[1] The solution is identical to that for a cartel dividing production among firms.

The two-plant case is illustrated in Figure 17.1. Demand facing the firm is *D,* and marginal revenue is *MR.* The marginal cost curves for Plants A and B are respectively MC_A and MC_B. The total marginal cost curve for the firm is the *horizontal summation* of MC_A and MC_B, labeled MC_T. Profit is maximized when this curve equals marginal revenue, giving an output of 175 units and a price of $45. Marginal cost at this output is $20. Equalization of marginal costs requires Plant A to produce 50 units and Plant B to produce 125 units, which of course sums to 175 since MC_T is the horizontal summation of MC_A and MC_B. This allocation equalizes marginal costs and is consequently the least cost method of production for the desired level of output.

---

[1] For a mathematical demonstration, see the appendix to this chapter.

Hence, in this case, the principle of profit maximization has been expanded to include the allocation decision: The firm with plants A and B will maximize profit if it produces the level of output and allocates production between the plants so that

$$MR = MC_T = MC_A = MC_B.$$

This principle can certainly be expanded to consider production in three or more plants. But, in order to see how this principle could be implemented by a firm, let's look at a simple, two-plant numerical example.

APPLICATION

Allocation of Production between Two Plants

Mercantile Enterprises—a firm with some degree of market power—produces its product in two plants. Hence, when making production decisions, the manager of Mercantile must decide not only how much to produce but also how to allocate the desired production between the two plants.

The production engineering department of Mercantile was able to provide the manager with simple, linear estimates of the incremental (marginal) cost functions for the two plants:

$$MC_A = 28 + 4Q_A \qquad MC_B = 16 + 2Q_B,$$

where the marginal costs were measured in dollars per unit and output was measured in thousand units. Note that the estimated marginal cost function for Plant A (a plant built in 1948) is higher for every output than that for Plant B (a plant built in 1967); Plant B is more efficient. Summing horizontally (and, after some algebraic manipulation), the total marginal cost function for $Q = Q_A + Q_B$ is

$$MC_{TOTAL} = 20 + \frac{4}{3} Q,$$

when output is more than 6,000 units. (We will discuss the total marginal cost function for outputs less than 6,000 units below.)

Suppose that the estimated demand curve for Mercantile's output is

$$Q = 114 - 3P,$$

where output was measured in thousand units and price was measured in dollars per unit. Using techniques described earlier in this text, the corresponding marginal revenue function is

$$MR = 38 - \frac{2}{3}Q.$$

Equating marginal revenue and total marginal cost,

$$38 - \frac{2}{3}Q = 20 + \frac{4}{3}Q,$$

the profit-maximizing output for the firm is $Q = 9$ (i.e., 9,000 units). At this level of output, marginal revenue and total marginal cost are both $32. In order to maximize profit, the production of the 9,000 units should be allocated between Plants A and B so that the marginal cost of the last unit produced in either plant is $32:

$$MC_A = 28 + 4Q_A = 32 \qquad MC_B = 16 + 2Q_B = 32.$$

Hence, for Plant A, $Q_A = 1$. That is, 1,000 units will be produced in Plant A. Likewise, for Plant B, $Q_B = 8$; 8,000 units will be produced in Plant B.

Now, suppose that forecasted demand decreases. Let's suppose that a new forecast of the demand for Mercantile's output is

$$Q = 96 - 3P.$$

Given that the corresponding marginal revenue function is

$$MR = 32 - \frac{2}{3}Q,$$

the firm's profit-maximizing output declines to 6,000 units. At this output, marginal revenue and marginal cost are both $28. Equating MC_A and MC_B to $28, the manager found that for Plant A, $Q_A = 0$, and for Plant B, $Q_B = 6$. That is, Plant A will be shut down and all of the output will be produced in Plant B.

As you can verify, were demand to decline any further, Mercantile would produce using only Plant B. So, for output levels less than 6,000 units, the total marginal cost function is MC_B. That is, for outputs less than 6,000 units, Mercantile becomes a single-plant firm.

From the preceding discussion and application, you should be able to see how a firm decides to allocate production among multiple plants. As we have seen, the allocation is determined both by the marginal cost functions of the various plants and the demand function facing the firm. It may be the case that a firm will use several plants to produce its output. But, it can also be the case that if demand declines, the firm may shut down one or more of its plants.

THE WALL STREET JOURNAL

APPLICATION

Firms Close Inefficient Plants

So far we have seen that a multiplant firm will produce a larger percentage of its output in those plants that are more efficient; that is, have lower marginal cost curves. We have also seen that if demand declines sufficiently, the firm will be induced to shut down its less efficient plants. This is apparently what happened to U.S. Steel Corporation (now USX) and what GM was considering in 1986.

In December of 1983, *The Wall Street Journal* reported that U.S. Steel had undertaken still another retrenchment of its steel operations.* The firm had announced the closing of nearly one fifth of its steel-making capacity and 23 finishing and fabricating mills. The closings were expected to affect a total of more than 15,000 employees.

This behavior is entirely predictable given the preceding discussion of profit maximization in a multiplant firm. The demand facing U.S. Steel had declined, due in part to the lower price charged for imported steel. This decline in demand led to a decline in output, and the

facilities that bore the brunt of the cuts were the least efficient plants. Indeed, that is what the *WSJ* article concluded: The plants closed were those that had higher (marginal) costs at a given level of output.

In 1986, General Motors was experiencing similar difficulties.† Although GM was still the largest auto manufacturer, its market share had fallen from its traditional 45 percent to 42.5 percent the year before. Ford had made inroads into GM's share with its extremely popular Ford Taurus and Mercury Sable. Also foreign manufacturers were taking bigger chunks of the U.S. market.

GM had planned capital spending of between $9 and $10 billion a year through 1990. But heavy spending on overhauling old plants had depressed earnings for several quarters. GM then announced that it would cut its proposed capital spending budget to between $6 and $7 billion annually. Cuts in plant modification and other projects were being considered, and the

Continued on page 513

*"U.S. Steel to Trim Output Capacity by Almost 20 Percent," by Thomas F. O'Bayle and J. Ernest Beasley, *The Wall Street Journal*, December 28, 1983. Adapted by permission of *The Wall Street Journal*. © Dow Jones and Company, Inc., 1983. All rights reserved.

†"GM Begins Cuts in New Projects, Other Spending," by Dale D. Buss and Amal Kumar Naj, July 14, 1986. Adapted by permission of *The Wall Street Journal*. © Dow Jones and Company, Inc., 1986. All rights reserved.

APPLICATION

Continued from page 512
WSJ indicated that some might be scrapped altogether. One GM source said, "Maybe we can get the [right] amount of products from fewer plants."

The point is that the multiplant theory we have described is basically a short-run theory. The firm allocates its output among its plants so that the marginal cost of production in each plant is equal. In the long run, however, the firm would close down less efficient (higher cost) plants as U.S. Steel did and GM is

probably going to do. And, in the long run, the firm can completely modify and modernize the less efficient plants and lower its overall costs, as GM has done and was planning to continue to do. Or firms can replace the high-cost plants with completely new ones, again as GM had done. Nonetheless, once the new plants have been built or old plants modified, the firm will still allocate production so as to equalize marginal cost for all plants.

17.2 FIRMS WITH MULTIPLE MARKETS— PRICE DISCRIMINATION

Thus far our analysis has assumed that market demand is simply the horizontal summation of the demands of all consumers and every consumer is charged the same price for the product. But, since consumers are different, we would expect their demands to differ. At times, firms can take advantage of these differences in demand in order to increase their profit. Price discrimination—pricing in multiple markets—is the method through which this is accomplished. Basically, price discrimination means that the firm charges different consumers different prices (when there are no corresponding differences in costs). For example, price discrimination can occur when a firm charges different prices in its domestic and foreign markets or perhaps when a doctor charges one fee for an operation to low-income patients and another fee for the same operation to high-income patients.

Certain conditions are necessary for the firm to be *able* to price discriminate. First, the firm must possess some market power. We normally think of price discrimination in the context of a monopoly firm, but, since they have market power, monopolistic competitors and oligopolists may also be able to price discriminate. Second, the demand functions for the individual consumers or groups of consumers must differ. (As we will demonstrate later, this statement can be made more specific to require that the own-price elasticities must be different.) Third, the different markets must be separable. The firm must be able to identify the individuals or groups of individuals and separate them into submarkets. This leads to the final requirement. Purchasers of the product must not be able to resell it to other customers. If consumers could buy and sell the product among themselves, there is no way that the firm can keep the submarkets separated. (You don't want the low-price buyers to sell your product to the high-price buyers.)

Normally, economists speak of three degrees of price discrimination. However, because we only want to provide a brief overview of this topic, we will limit our discussion to what is referred to as "third-degree" price discrimination. This is the form most commonly observed and is the form that best illustrates our primary concern in this section: profit maximization with multiple markets.

Allocation of Sales in Two Markets

The analysis of price discrimination is a straightforward application of the *MR = MC* rule. As a first step in that analysis, let us assume that a firm has two separate markets for its product. Demand conditions in each market are such that the marginal revenues from selling specified quantities are as given in Table 17.1. Assume also that the firm has decided to produce 12 units. How should it allocate sales between the two markets?

Consider the first unit; the firm can increase revenue by $45 by selling it in Market 1 or by $34 by selling in Market 2. Obviously, the firm will sell the first unit in Market 1. So, the first unit (1) is sold in Market 1. The second unit is also sold in Market 1 since its sale there increases revenue by $36, whereas it would only increase revenue by $34 in Market 2. Since $34 can be gained in 2 but only $30 in 1, unit three is sold in Market 2. Similar reasoning shows that the fourth unit goes to 1 and the fifth to 2. Since unit six adds $22 to revenue in either market, it makes no difference where it is sold; six and seven go one to each market. Eight and 9 are sold in 1 because they yield higher marginal revenue there; 10 goes to 2 for the same reason. Unit 11 can go to either market, since the additional revenues are the same, and unit 12 goes to the other. Thus we see that the 12 units will be divided so that the marginal revenue is the same for the last unit sold in each market; the firm sells seven units in Market 1 and five in Market 2. Thus, the price discriminating firm allocates a given output in such a way that the marginal revenues in each market are equal.[2]

The results from Table 17.1 indicate that the firm will maximize profit if it allocates its output such that

---

[2] For a mathematical demonstration, see the appendix to this chapter.

Table 17.1 Allocation of Sales between Two Markets

Quantity	Marginal Revenue Market 1	Order of Sales	Marginal Revenue Market 2	Order of Sales
1	$45	(1)	$34	(3)
2	36	(2)	28	(5)
3	30	(4)	22	(7)
4	22	(6)	13	(10)
5	17	(8)	10	(12)
6	15	(9)	8	
7	10	(11)	7	
8	7		4	
9	4		2	
10	0		1	

$$MR_1 = MR_2.$$

This condition should not be surprising since it is nothing more than another application of the principle of constrained optimization that we presented in Chapter 3: If the firm wants to maximize profit subject to the constraint that there is only a limited number of units to sell, the firm will allocate sales so that the marginal revenues (marginal benefits) per unit are equal in the two markets. (The marginal cost of selling one unit in Market 1 is the unit not available for sale in Market 2.)

Although the marginal revenues in the two markets are equal, the prices charged are not. The higher price will be charged in the market with the less elastic demand; the lower price will be charged in the market having the more elastic demand. In the more elastic market, price could be raised only at the expense of a large decrease in sales. In the less elastic market higher prices bring less reduction in sales.

This assertion can be demonstrated as follows. Let the prices in the two markets be P_1 and P_2. Likewise, let E_1 and E_2 denote the own-price elasticities. As we know from Chapter 6, we can express marginal revenue as

$$MR = P\left(1 - \frac{1}{E}\right).$$

We noted above that the firm will maximize profit if it allocates output so that $MR_1 = MR_2$. That is,

$$P_1\left(1 - \frac{1}{E_1}\right) = P_2\left(1 - \frac{1}{E_2}\right).$$

Now, suppose Market 1 has the more elastic demand:

$$E_1 > E_2.$$

It follows that

$$\left(1 - \frac{1}{E_1}\right) > \left(1 - \frac{1}{E_2}\right).$$

So,

$$\frac{P_1}{P_2} = \frac{\left(1 - \frac{1}{E_2}\right)}{\left(1 - \frac{1}{E_1}\right)} < 1.$$

That is,

$$P_1 < P_2.$$

Therefore, if a firm price discriminates, it will always charge the lower price in the market having the more elastic demand curve.

Profit Maximization with Price Discrimination

Thus far we have assumed that the price discriminating firm wishes to allocate a given level of output among its markets in order to maximize the revenue from selling that output. Now we turn to how the firm determines the profit-maximizing level of output and the prices to charge in the different markets.

As you by now probably expect, the decision involves equating marginal revenue with marginal cost. The firm's marginal cost curve is no different from that of a nondiscriminating firm with market power. So the problem is to derive the marginal revenue curve.

With discrete data such as in Table 17.1, we would simply increase sales as discussed above, then determine the total marginal revenue from the allocation of each unit of output to the market with the higher marginal revenue. Thus total marginal revenue from Table 17.1 would be \$45 for the first unit sold, \$36 for the second (both in Market 1), \$34 for the third (in Market 2), \$30 for the fourth, and so on.

For continuous demand and marginal revenue curves in each submarket, the total marginal revenue curve for a price discriminating firm is simply the horizontal summation of the marginal revenues in each market. Assume that the firm sells in two markets, 1 and 2. The demand and marginal revenue curves in Markets 1 and 2 are shown respectively as D_1 and MR_1 in Panel A of Figure 17.2 and as D_2 and MR_2 in Panel B. In Panel C of the figure the total marginal revenue, MR_T, is the horizontal summation of MR_1 and MR_2.

From the above discussion, we know that the firm will allocate any given output between the two markets so that MR_1 equals MR_2. For example, if the firm produces 300 units of output at which MR equals \$30,

Figure 17.2 Deriving Total Marginal Revenue

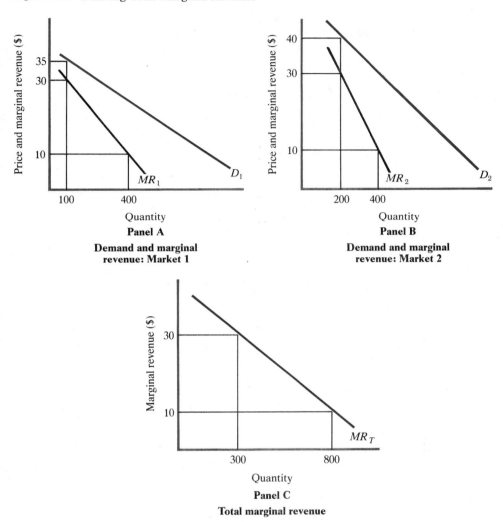

Panel A
Demand and marginal revenue: Market 1

Panel B
Demand and marginal revenue: Market 2

Panel C
Total marginal revenue

it will sell 100 units in Market 1 and 200 in Market 2. At 100 units of output (from Panel A), MR_1 equals $30. At 200 units of output (from Panel B), MR_2 also equals $30. Thus, no matter which market unit 300 is sold in, the firm's marginal revenue is $30, as shown in Panel C. And this is the only allocation of 300 total units that equates the marginal revenues in the two markets. Likewise, if the firm wants to sell 800 units, it will sell 400 in Market 1 and 400 in Market 2; as shown in the figure, the marginal revenue is $10 in each market. Thus for 800 units of output the total marginal revenue is $10. At every other output, the marginal revenue in Panel C (MR_T) is obtained in the same way.

For each level of output the price in each market is given by the demand in that market. For example, if 300 units are sold, we see from D_1 that the price of the 100 units sold in Market 1 is \$35; from D_2 we see that the price of the 200 units sold in Market 2 is \$40. (We did not graph the horizontal sum of D_1 and D_2 since that curve is irrelevant for the price discriminating firm.)

Now the only decision left is how much total output the firm should produce to maximize its profits. All of the relations are generalized graphically in Figure 17.3. Again the firm is selling a product in two markets. D_1 and MR_1 are demand and marginal revenue in Market 1; D_2 and MR_2 are demand and marginal revenue in Market 2. MR_T is the horizontal summation of the two marginal revenue curves. For convenience, all these curves are shown on the same graph, along with the firm's average cost (AC) and marginal cost (MC).

As always, the firm maximizes profit by producing the output at which marginal revenue equals marginal cost. In this case Q_T, where MC equals MR_T, is the total output. The marginal revenue and marginal cost are both equal to the dollar amount M in Figure 17.3.

The market allocation rule, previously determined, requires that marginal revenue be the same in each submarket. Since the total market marginal revenue is the added revenue from selling the last unit in either submarket, $MR_1 = MR_2 = M$. At a marginal revenue of M, the quantity sold in Market 1 is Q_1; in Market 2, Q_2. Since MR_T is the horizontal summation of MR_1 and MR_2, $Q_1 + Q_2 = Q_T$, the total output. Furthermore, from the relevant demand curves, the price associated with output Q_1 in Market 1 is p_1, the price associated with Q_2 in Market 2 is p_2.

Summarizing these results, if the aggregate market for a firm's product can be divided into submarkets with different price elasticities, the firm can profitably practice price discrimination. Total output is determined by equating marginal cost with aggregate marginal revenue. The output is allocated among the submarkets so as to equate marginal revenue in each submarket with aggregate marginal revenue at the profit-maximizing level of output. That is, with two markets, the profit-maximization criterion for the firm is expanded to become

$$MR_T = MC = MR_1 = MR_2.$$

Finally, price in each submarket is determined from the submarket demand curve.

Examples of price discrimination are not hard to find. Many drugstores offer discounts on drugs to persons 65 and over. Thus, the drugstores price discriminate. Retired persons probably have a more elastic demand for drugs, because the market value of their time is lower. Retired persons would tend to shop around more for lower prices, and differences in price among different age-groups can be explained by different price elasticities, resulting from different evaluations of time.

Figure 17.3 Profit Maximization with Two Markets

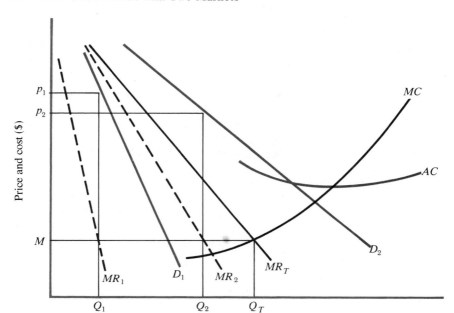

Movies, plays, concerts, and similar forms of entertainment practice price discrimination according to age. Generally, younger people pay lower prices. Supposedly, in this case, younger people have more elastic demands for such tickets, possibly because of the availability of more substitute forms of entertainment. (It is not correct to say that different ticket prices for afternoon and evening performances are evidence of price discrimination. These are different products in the eye of the consumer.)

Airlines frequently discriminate between vacation and business travel. Vacation travelers would have a more elastic demand than business travelers, probably because the value of time in business travel is greater. Other examples of price discrimination are electric companies that charge lower rates to industrial users than to households (although this may be, in part, due to differences in costs), and university bookstores that charge lower prices to faculty than to students. On the other hand, students frequently are charged a lower price for subscriptions to newspapers and magazines.

Manufacturers and sellers of durable goods, such as automobiles and large appliances, sometimes practice price discrimination also. Automobiles with exactly the same characteristics all have the same window or sticker price (excluding the shipping charge). But as you probably know, dealers generally discount these prices on many models. Except for extremely "hot sellers," people seldom pay the listed price. However, everyone does not pay the same price for the same vehicle. Ms. Jones may pay a lower price than Mr. Smith because Ms. Jones is willing to hold out longer or possibly the dealer recognized that Mr. Smith is more sold on the car. Perhaps Mr. Smith came into the showroom, saw the list price, and said, "Wow, is that all you're charging for that great car!" In any case, Mr. Smith probably has the less elastic demand. We should note, however, that this is a slightly different form of price discrimination than that discussed above. In this case the dealer treats each potential consumer as a separate market, and charges as much as the consumer is willing to pay, if possible.

In order to implement profit maximization with multiple markets, it would be necessary for the manager to estimate demand functions for each of the markets. After summing to obtain a total demand function, total output would be that at which total marginal revenue is equal to marginal cost. Then, this output would be allocated to the various markets so that the marginal revenues are all equal to total marginal revenue at the profit-maximizing output. Let's illustrate this procedure with a simple example.

APPLICATION

Profit Maximization with Multiple Markets

The manager of Galactic Manufacturing—a firm with substantial monopoly power—knows that the firm faces two distinct markets. Using the techniques described earlier in this text, the demand curves for these two markets were forecasted to be

$$\text{Mkt 1: } Q_1 = 100 - 2P_1 \text{ and Mkt 2: } Q_2 = 50 - .5P_2,$$

where output is measured in thousand units and price in dollars per unit. Solving for the inverse demand functions in the two markets,

$$\text{Mkt 1: } P_1 = 50 - .5Q_1 \text{ and Mkt 2: } P_2 = 100 - 2Q_2.$$

The marginal revenue functions associated with these inverse demand functions are:

$$\text{Mkt 1: } MR_1 = 50 - 1Q_1 \text{ and Mkt 2:} MR_2 = 100 - 4Q_2.$$

From the inverse demand function in Market 1, Q_1 equals zero when P_1 equals \$50. Since at any price above \$50 nothing will be purchased in Market 1, at any price from \$50 to \$100 the market quantity demanded is the quantity demanded in Market 2. Thus, at outputs below 25 units, the demand and marginal revenue in Market 2 are the market demand and marginal revenue. After 25 units of output (below a price of \$50) the market marginal revenue for $Q = Q_1 + Q_2$ is the horizontal sum of MR_1 and MR_2, which, after a certain amount of algebraic manipulation, is

$$\text{Total } MR = MR_T = 60 - .8Q.$$

The manager obtained from the engineering department a linear estimate of the firm's marginal cost function per 1,000 units:

$$MC = 10 + .2Q.$$

Equating these estimates of marginal cost and marginal revenue,

$$60 - .8Q = 10 + .2Q,$$

gives the profit-maximizing level of output, $Q^* = 50$ (i.e., 50,000 units). At this level of output total marginal revenue and marginal cost both equal \$20. To determine the allocation of the 50,000 units between the two markets, the marginal revenue in each market must be equal to total marginal revenue; that is, \$20. The manager must, therefore, solve the two equations

$$\text{Mkt 1: } 20 = 50 - 1Q_1 \text{ and Mkt 2: } 20 = 100 - 4Q_2.$$

Hence for Market 1, $Q_1 = 30$ (i.e., 30,000 units), and for Market 2, $Q_2 = 20$ (i.e., 20,000 units). Finally, substituting these quantities into the respective demand functions, the profit-maximizing prices will be \$35 in Market 1 and \$60 in Market 2.

17.3 FIRMS WITH MULTIPLE PRODUCTS

To this point, we have assumed that the firm produces a single product. However, even a very cursory survey of the existing firms in the United States would show that many produce and sell several different products or at least several different models. While it is possible that the firm's products could be unrelated, it is more likely that the products produced are related either in consumption or production. When the products are related, the firm's output and pricing decision must incorporate the interrelations.

In this section we provide a brief overview of profit maximization for a multiple-product firm. We consider three possibilities: First, we examine the case of products that are related in consumption. We then turn very briefly to a consideration of products that are complements in production. (This topic is discussed more extensively in the appendix to this chapter.) We conclude this section with a discussion of products that are substitutes in production.

Multiple Products Related in Consumption

Recall that the demand for a particular commodity depends not only on the price of the product itself but also on the prices of any related commodities, incomes, tastes, and so on. For simplicity, let us ignore the other factors and write our demand function as

$$Q_x = f(P_X, P_Y),$$

where Q_X is the quantity demanded of commodity X, P_X is the price of X, and P_Y is the price of a related commodity Y—either a substitute or complement.

In our discussion so far, we have treated P_Y as if it were given to the firm. That is, we assumed P_Y to be a parameter (i.e., a constant) determined outside of the firm. Thus, the firm would maximize its profits by selecting the appropriate level of production and price for X. If, however, the firm in question produces *both* commodities X and Y, the price of the related commodity Y is no longer parametric—exogenous—but is controlled by the firm. The profitability of X would then depend on the price of Y and vice versa.

In order to maximize the profit of the firm, the levels of output and prices for the related commodities must be determined *jointly*. Hence, for a two-product firm, the profit-maximization conditions remain the same,

$$MR_X = MC_X \text{ and } MR_Y = MC_Y.$$

However, the marginal revenue of X will be a function of the quantities of both X and Y, as will the marginal revenue of Y. Hence, these marginal conditions must be satisfied *simultaneously*. (Note that in this case the products are not related in production, so MC_X and MC_Y depend on, respectively, the output of X and the output of Y.) To see how a firm would maximize profit under these circumstances, let's look at another stylized example. (In this example we will look at a firm that produces products that are substitutes in consumption, but the same technique would apply for products that are complements in consumption.)

APPLICATION

Profit Maximization with Substitutes in Consumption

Zicon Manufacturing produces two types of automobile vacuum cleaners. One, which we denote as product X, plugs into the cigarette lighter receptacle; the other—product Y—has rechargeable batteries. Assuming that there is no other relation between the two products other than the apparent substitutability in consumption, the manager of

Zicon wanted to determine the profit-maximizing levels of production and price for the two products.

Using the techniques described in this text, the demand functions for the two products were forecasted to be

$$Q_X = 80 - 8P_X + 6P_Y \text{ and } Q_Y = 40 - 4P_Y + 4P_X,$$

where the outputs were measured in thousand units and the prices in dollars per unit. Solving these two forecasted demand functions simultaneously, the manager obtained the following functions in which prices are a function of both quantities:

$$P_X = 70 - \frac{1}{2}Q_X - \frac{3}{4}Q_Y \text{ and } P_Y = 80 - 1Q_Y - \frac{1}{2}Q_X.$$

So, the marginal revenue functions were

$$MR_X = 70 - 1Q_X - \frac{3}{4}Q_Y \text{ and } MR_Y = 80 - 2Q_Y - \frac{1}{2}Q_X.$$

From the production manager, estimates of the incremental cost (marginal cost) functions were obtained:

$$MC_X = 10 + \frac{1}{2}Q_X \text{ and } MC_Y = 20 + \frac{1}{4}Q_Y,$$

where output was again measured in thousand units.

To determine the outputs that will maximize profit, the manager of Zicon equated *MR* and *MC* for the two products,

$$70 - 1 Q_X - \frac{3}{4}Q_Y = 10 + \frac{1}{2}Q_X$$

$$80 - 2 Q_Y - \frac{1}{2}Q_X = 20 + \frac{1}{4}Q_Y.$$

Solving these equations simultaneously, the profit-maximizing outputs were found to be $Q_X = 30$ (i.e., 30,000 units) and $Q_Y = 20$ (i.e., 20,000 units). Finally, using these outputs in the price functions, the manager of Zicon found that the profit-maximizing price for X was \$40 and for Y was \$45.

From the preceding discussion and illustration, the point we wish to stress is that if a firm produces products that are related in consumption, profit maximization requires that output levels and prices be determined jointly. Specifically, in such a firm, the profit-maximizing price for a particular commodity will be determined not only by the demand and cost conditions for that commodity, but also by those of any related commodities the firm produces.

Multiple Products that Are Complements in Production

In the preceding section we considered products that are related in consumption. To examine products that are related in production, we begin by considering a firm that produces outputs that are complements in production.

Complementarity in production typically occurs when an ingredient input is used to produce two or more products. The classic example is that of beef carcasses and hides. Clearly these products are complements in production. Furthermore, the joint production of the two products is characterized by fixed proportions—for each additional beef carcass produced, one additional hide is produced also.

Petroleum refining has similar characteristics. With an existing refinery and a given mix of input crude oils, production of an additional barrel of one of the lighter distillates, such as gasoline, requires that the refinery produce some additional amount of the heavy distillates, like fuel oil. Complementarity in production can also be observed in mineral extraction. Frequently, two or more metals are found together in the same ore deposit. When the ore goes into the smelter, more than one metal is produced. For example, since nickel and zinc frequently are in the same deposit, the smelters are designed to produce both metals from the same ore.

Since complements in production frequently result from one raw material producing two or more products, this type of joint production results in the product being produced in fixed proportions from the ingredient. If the firm produces outputs that are complements in production and characterized by fixed proportions production, the profit-maximizing firm will select the level of output of the joint product at which total marginal revenue equals total marginal cost. Given this level of production, the prices for the individual products would be taken from the individual demand curves. However, it is possible that, at the profit-maximizing level of output for the joint product, the marginal revenue for one or more of the individual products is negative. In such an instance, the firm would sell that product only to the point at which marginal revenue becomes zero and destroy the excess. (This principle is illustrated in the appendix to this chapter.)

The principles and implementation for products that are complements in production can be expanded to consider products that are complements but are not produced in fixed proportions. The principles remain the same but the solution becomes more complex.

Multiple Products that Are Substitutes in Production

While the case of products that are complements in production is clearly possible, a more common situation is the multiproduct firm that produces outputs that are substitutes in production. This situation is most easily seen in the case of a firm that produces several models of the same basic product. These different models compete for the limited production facilities of the firm and are therefore substitutes in the firm's production process. In the long run, the firm can adjust its production facility in order to produce the profit-maximizing level of each product. However, in the short run, the firm must determine how to allocate its limited production capacity among the competing products in order to maximize profit.

As you should recognize, the short-run case is still another example of constrained optimization. The firm must maximize profit subject to the constraint imposed by the limited production facility. For simplicity, let us consider a firm that produces only two products, which we will denote as X and Y. Further, we assume that the two products are produced using the same production facility and that the cost of operating this facility is invariant to the product produced. The marginal benefit accrued from producing an additional unit of either product is the marginal revenue that is generated. In the case of product X, this is MR_X. The marginal cost of producing an additional unit of one product is the reduction in output of the competing product. For product X, the marginal cost is the corresponding reduction in the production of Y, ΔY. Conversely, the marginal cost of producing an additional unit of Y is ΔX. As we demonstrated in Chapter 3, a firm will maximize its objective function subject to a constraint when the ratios of marginal benefit to marginal cost are equal for all decision variables. In the case in question, this means that profit will be maximized when the levels of production of the two products are such that

$$\frac{MR_X}{\Delta Y} = \frac{MR_Y}{\Delta X}.$$

To see how this condition can be utilized, let's look at a very simplified example.

APPLICATION

The Allocation of Assembly Line Time

A division of Surefire Products, Inc., manufactures two products, X and Y, that are unrelated in consumption but are substitutes in production. More specifically, these two products are produced on the same assembly line, so they compete for the limited time available. The question facing the manager of the parent company—Surefire Products—is: How should an eight-hour production day be allocated between the production of X and the production of Y?

The demand functions for the two products were forecasted to be

$$Q_X = 60 - \frac{1}{2} P_X \text{ and } Q_Y = 40 - \frac{2}{3} P_Y,$$

where the quantities were the number of units demanded per day and the prices were expressed in dollars per unit. From these forecasted demand functions, the marginal revenue functions were

$$MR_X = 120 - 4Q_X \text{ and } MR_Y = 60 - 3Q_Y.$$

Discussions with the plant supervisor indicated that, in one hour of production time, either two units of X or four units of Y could be produced. In a sense, the "production functions" for the two products are

$$Q_X = 2H_X \text{ and } Q_Y = 4H_Y,$$

where H_X and H_Y denote, respectively, one hour of assembly line time in the production of X and Y. From this, the marginal cost of using an additional hour in the production of X is $\Delta Y = 4$. That is, if this plant devotes an additional hour to the production of X, it must forgo the production of four units of Y. Likewise, the marginal cost of an additional hour in the production of Y is $\Delta X = 2$.

Hence, the firm will maximize profit subject to the limitation of the eight-hour production day if it produces amounts of X and Y such that the condition

$$\frac{120 - 4Q_X}{4} = \frac{60 - 3Q_Y}{2}$$

is satisfied. This condition requires that $Q_X = \frac{3}{2} Q_Y$. Using the "production functions" above, this profit-maximization condition can be rewritten in terms of the hours devoted to the production of the two products; that is, since $Q_X = \frac{3}{2} Q_Y, \frac{3}{2} Q_Y = 2H_X$ and $Q_Y = 4H_Y$, so

$$H_X = 3H_Y.$$

For profit maximization, the firm should devote assembly line time to X and Y in the ratio 3:1.

Using this optimality condition with the time constraint (i.e., $H_X + H_Y = 8$), it follows that to maximize profits, six hours will be devoted to product X and two hours to product Y. That means that Surefire Products will produce 12 units of X per day and 8 units of Y; so, from the demand functions, the optimal prices are $96 per unit for X and $48 per unit for Y.

As you may have guessed from the preceding application, there is another way of expressing the optimization condition for the allocation of the production facility between the production of X and Y. Suppose we define F as the level of usage of the production facility. Thus $\Delta X/\Delta F$ is the marginal product of the production facility in the production of X (MP_X). Likewise $\Delta Y/\Delta F$ is the marginal product of the production facility in the production of Y (MP_Y). Now, we divide both sides of the previous optimization condition,

$$\frac{MR_X}{\Delta Y} = \frac{MR_Y}{\Delta X},$$

by ΔF to obtain the new optimization condition,

$$(MR_X) \times (MP_X) = (MR_Y) \times (MP_Y),$$

or

$$MRP_X = MRP_Y,$$

where MRP_X and MRP_Y are, respectively, the marginal revenue products of F in the production of X and Y. With a given level of usage of the production facility, the firm will maximize profit by allocating the facility so that its marginal revenue product in producing each good is the same.

If, in the long run, the firm can vary its usage of its production facilities, we can generalize this condition. In Figure 17.4 the horizontal axis measures the level of usage of the limited production facilities. We have illustrated the marginal revenue product curves for the production facility in the production of the two products and, summing horizontally, the total marginal revenue product curve. In this situation, we continue to consider a single marginal cost curve—that is, we assume that costs depend only on the level of usage of the production facility and are not affected by the type of product produced. We know that profit will be maximized at the point at which marginal cost is equal to total marginal revenue product. Thus, the usage level of the production facility will be F_{TOTAL}. The question then becomes how this level of usage (e.g., machine-hours) is to be divided between the two products.

From our discussion to this point, the answer is probably obvious. If the allocation were such that $MRP_X > MRP_Y$, profit could be increased by reallocating from the production of Y to the production of X. This would reduce MRP_X and increase MRP_Y. Such a reallocation would continue until the marginal revenue products are equal, $MRP_X = MRP_Y$. Further, since the total marginal revenue product curve is simply the horizontal sum of the two individual curves, the profit-maximizing condition is

$$MRP_{TOTAL} = MC = MRP_X = MRP_Y.$$

Figure 17.4   Profit-Maximizing Allocation of Production Facilities

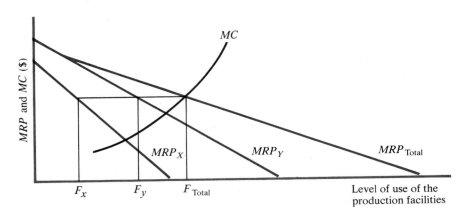

Thus, profits will be maximized when production is allocated such that the marginal additions to revenue are the same for the two products; F_X is devoted to the production of X and F_Y to the production of Y. To show how this decision rule could be implemented, let's return to our example.

APPLICATION

Optimal Usage of a Production Facility

The manager of Surefire Products, Inc., also wanted to consider changing the daily production schedule for the plant producing X and Y from a strict eight-hour-per-day schedule. That is, the manager wanted to know the answers to two questions: (1) What is the optimal level of usage (hours of operation) of the plant? (2) How should this level of usage be allocated between the production of the two products?

Using the demand forecasts and the estimates of the "production functions" provided by the plant supervisor, estimates of the marginal revenue product of the production facility in the production of X and Y were

$$MRP_X = [120 - 4\,(2H_X)] \times (2)$$
$$= 240 - 16H_X$$

and

$$MRP_Y = [60 - 3\,(4H_Y)] \times (4)$$
$$= 240 - 48H_Y.$$

To obtain the total marginal revenue production function, these two curves were summed horizontally, that is, these functions were inverted to find H_X and H_Y, then the hours were summed ($H_T = H_X + H_Y$). The resulting total MRP was

$$MRP_T = 240 - 12H_T.$$

Working with the engineers for Surefire, the plant supervisor was able to come up with an estimate of the additional cost of operating the plant an additional hour—an incremental (marginal) cost for usage of the plant. This estimate was

$$MC = 72 + 2H_T.$$

Equating the total marginal revenue product of an hour's usage of the plant with the marginal cost of an additional hour's usage,

$$240 - 12H_T = 72 + 2H_T,$$

the manager of Surefire Products found that the optimal level of usage of the plant was 12 hours per day. At this level of usage, $MRP_T = MC = \$96$. To allocate these hours between the production of X and Y, the marginal revenue products for the production facility in the production of X and Y must both be equal to $96:

$$240 - 16H_X = 96 \text{ and } 240 - 48H_Y = 96.$$

So, the optimal allocation would be nine hours in the production of X and three hours in the production of Y.

17.4 WHY MULTIPLE PRODUCTS?

The preceding discussion simply assumed that firms produce not one, but several products, then described the conditions of production under several sets of product characteristics. We did not attempt to answer why firms would want to produce multiple products. In some cases the answer is obvious, in others it is not so obvious. Certainly firms produce multiple products for a multitude of reasons. We can only summarize a few of these reasons, which are among the most common.

Complements in Consumption

It is rather easy to see why a firm would produce and sell two or more products that are complements in consumption. These products are used together and are frequently purchased together. The firm would be able to set prices and quantities that maximize the total profit from the products.

For example, we see single firms manufacturing razors and the blades that fit the razors. The firm has control over both design and prices. It may well want to set a very low price for the razor to increase sales and extend the future market for its blades. It can also advertise the two together.

Another example is a firm such as Coleman, which produces several commodities that are complementary—tents, lanterns, stoves, ice chests, and so forth. Consumers of outdoor recreational equipment frequently wish to purchase this "bundle" of commodities. Therefore, we would expect the sales of, say, lanterns to depend to some extent on the price charged for goods that are used in conjunction; for example, tents. It follows that the price charged for tents would affect the profits of the division producing lanterns, and those of the firm as a whole. And, even if the goods are not purchased at the same time, buyer loyalty can carry over for the next purchase. A family that was well satisfied with a Coleman tent would be likely to choose a Coleman product when it purchased a stove.

Similar examples of complementary goods produced and sold by the same firm are golf clubs and golf balls, tennis rackets and tennis balls, and baseball equipment. In all such cases the firm will set output and price to maximize total profits rather than the profit from a single item. Therefore, as stressed in section 17.3, the firm must determine the output and price for all the products simultaneously.

Complements in Production

Our discussion of complements in production in section 17.3 and in the appendix deals specifically with the fixed proportions production of two or more products from the same ingredient input. We mentioned as examples the production of beef carcasses and hides, a refinery that produces several final products from crude oil, and a smelter that obtains different minerals from the same ore. But there are more subtle examples of complementarity in production. In these examples the final products need not be produced in fixed proportions.

Less obvious examples arise from capital expenditures that contribute to the production of more than one product. Railroads, for instance, offer both freight and passenger transportation over the same tracks and between the same depots. These inputs are shared. The postal service shares its capital in sorting and delivering parcels and letters. Finally, telephone companies use the same lines and switching gear to place local and long-distance calls. In these instances, a single investment contributes to the production of more than one product. This is a common phenomenon among multiproduct firms.

Whenever it is less costly to produce products together rather than separately, costs are said to be "subadditive." Define $C(X)$ as the total cost of producing X, $C(Y)$ as the cost of producing Y, and $C(X,Y)$ as the cost of producing goods X and Y together. Cost is subadditive, if, for any amount of X and Y, $C(X) + C(Y)$ is greater than $C(X,Y)$. Thus if a single firm produces X and another firm produces Y, a firm that produces both goods could undersell both of the other firms.

Subadditivity can create barriers to entry. Suppose we have three products, X, Y, and Z, with the following costs of production for a specified number of units:

1. X, Y, or Z produced alone has a total cost of $10 for the specified number of units of each good.
2. Any two products produced together have the cost of $16 for the specified number of units.
3. All three products produced together in the specified amounts have a total cost of $23.

Thus we see that

$$C(X) + C(Y) + C(Z) = \$30$$
$$C(X,Y) + C(Z) = C(X,Z) + C(Y) = C(Y,Z) + C(X) = \$26$$
$$C(X,Y,Z) = \$23.$$

Costs are subadditive because it is less costly to produce two together rather than all three separately, and all three together rather than just two. Notice that the firm producing X, Y, and Z together can undersell any firm that is not. For instance, the seller with a cost of $23 could set $p_X = p_Y = p_Z = 8.66 ($25.98) and not be undersold by anyone in the long run. Those producers making two or fewer products together would be driven out of business. A firm must, therefore, produce all three products to successfully enter any one market, thus creating a barrier to entry. Generally, it is more costly to enter all three markets and produce all three products than it is to just enter one.

There are other examples of the production of goods that are complementary in production. But we can summarize the majority of such cases simply by saying that when such complementarity exists it is less costly to produce the goods together than to produce them separately.

Substitution in Consumption and Production

The reason firms produce products that are good substitutes for other products they sell is less obvious, particularly when these products compete for time and space on the firm's production facilities. But we do see a multitude of firms doing just that. Automobile manufacturers sell a range of cars, many of which are quite similar. We see the same thing in firms that make TVs, stereos, home appliances, food products, soap, and an array of products.

Recall that we discussed in Chapter 15 how oligopolists compete by changing product quality or altering the characteristics of the product they sell. We used the example of two cereal manufacturers changing the amount of sugar. But, we see that cereal manufacturers produce several brands of cereal. Kellogg, for example, sells All Bran and Bran Flakes, extremely close substitutes. You might recall also that in the Coke application, some observers thought that Coke might be better off after it brought back Old Coke. They felt that Coca-Cola would then have a product highly competitive with Pepsi while keeping its old market. (We might note that the two Cokes are substitutes in production for the approximately 500 independent bottlers that use the syrup to make Coke, then distribute it. At the time they were not set up to handle two syrups, and many were, therefore, a bit apprehensive about the move.)

So sometimes a firm can block entry or gain a competitive advantage over its rivals by introducing new substitutes for its own product in the market. Such a maneuver is greatly preferred to seeing new entrants or old rivals introduce them. Producing related products crowds the market with choices. As choices proliferate, the demand for each individual product decreases and becomes more elastic. This makes it more difficult for a firm to enter that segment of the market, since it would have a smaller demand. Price and sales would be lower than would be the case if the original firm had not introduced so many substitutes. It therefore becomes less likely under these conditions that total costs will be covered.

Historically, there are some interesting cases where firms with market power sold multiple products expressly for the purpose of blocking entry. In the 1940s, American Tobacco, Liggett and Myers (L&M), and Reynolds, after being found guilty of conspiring to monopolize the cigarette industry, began independently introducing multiple cigarette brands to protect their respective market shares. Before the antitrust suit, the companies were purchasing low-grade tobacco at auctions in an effort to keep new entrants from introducing a low-grade, inexpensive cigarette. Apparently it was not used in cigarette production and nothing was done with the tobacco after it was purchased. When the suit was settled, the companies were ordered to cease and desist from this practice. Soon thereafter, the companies began developing their own inexpensive brands.

A more recent example of brand proliferation to block entry can be found in the ready-to-eat cereal industry. In the mid-70s the Federal Trade Commission (FTC) began investigating the big three cereal makers—Post, Kellogg, and General Mills—for possible anticompetitive behavior. The accusation made by the FTC was that these companies had generated multiple brands of cold cereal to deter entry. They had introduced a sufficient number of brands to cover the spectrum of tastes consumers had for cold cereals. No new firm could come into the market and carve itself a niche, because any type of cereal the firm could develop would have a close substitute from one of the other makers. Nothing came of the FTC investigation, largely because it was very difficult to prove the intentions of the established cereal makers, but the strategy, for whatever reason it was pursued, was a very effective deterrent to entry.

Certainly not all, not even most, firms that produce multiple products that are substitutes in consumption do so to maintain a monopoly position. Many oligopolists are caught in a "product quality" dilemma, similar to the advertiser's dilemma discussed in Chapter 15. If they don't enter a particular segment of the market, they will lose a considerable market share to their rivals. It is possible that each of the oligopolists would be better off if each offered fewer products.

In spite of this possible problem, producing a variety of differentiated yet similar products that are substitutes is simply another way that firms, particularly oligopolists, compete among themselves. We turn now to an application showing how one firm was extremely successful in expanding across a wide segment of its market.

APPLICATION

Gallo Spans the Wine Market: If Gallo Sells It, It's Number One*

The E. & J. Gallo winery has grown from a shed in 1933 to the largest winery in the world. The owners, Ernest and Julio Gallo, accomplished this through a shrewd marketing strategy and by producing a broad range of wines that are substitutes in a sense but are to some extent in different segments of the market. As you probably know, wine varies from the cheapest jug wines and wine coolers to extremely expensive French champagne and burgundy. Gallo has established a dominant position in practically every submarket in the low- to middle-priced range.

Its latest success is the Bartles & Jaymes wine cooler, a combination of wine and juice. California Cooler, which introduced this extremely successful product in 1981, was the largest seller of wine coolers until 1985. Less than one year after Gallo introduced Bartles & Jaymes with an advertising and marketing campaign that the president of California Cooler called a "blitzkrieg," Gallo had the largest share of the wine cooler market. California Cooler had fallen to second place.

This was only the latest such move by Gallo, which produces 25 percent of all the wine drunk in the United States, including imports. The winery's major product is a relatively inexpensive table wine, typically sold in jugs. Its Gallo brand is the number one seller in this market and its Carlo Rossi brand is number two.

Gallo entered the brandy market, and its E & J brandy became the best seller in the United States. Its André champagne is the nation's best-selling sparkling champagne. Gallo is the largest producer of low-priced, flavored wines with its Thunderbird and Boone's Farm brands. And Gallo is the largest seller of the higher priced varietal wines— wines made from a single type of grape and named after the grape, for example, Cabernet Sauvignon. This latter success is despite the fact that Gallo has the reputation of producing a lower priced wine.

*The information in this application is from "Another Coup for the Fighting Gallos," by Andrew Pollack, *The New York Times*, July 6, 1986.

Not all of Gallo's introductions have been such overwhelming successes. The first introduction of varietals in 1974 flopped, as did its 1970 introduction of a champagne under the Gallo name. But enough were successes that Gallo's sales have been estimated at between $650 million and $1 billion. This is a large volume for a family-owned, family-run business, which produces 40 percent of the wine made in California.

Consumption patterns in the wine market during the 1980s and Gallo's response illustrate the benefits to a firm from selling several products. During that period, American wine producers were hurt by a drop in total alcohol consumption in the United States along with the large increase in the sales of imported wine—up from 14 percent in 1975 to 23.4 percent in 1985. But, in large part because of its highly successful wine cooler, Gallo's wine shipments rose 7.4 percent in 1985 and were up 19 percent in the first half of 1986. So its overall sales rose as sales in the U.S. wine industry were falling. This illustrates how a firm can protect itself to some extent by producing multiple products, even though these products are substitutes.

17.5 SUMMARY

In this chapter we have looked at a lot of "special cases." While it might seem that we have introduced a lot of new conditions, we really haven't. Essentially, all we have done is apply the basic principles of profit maximization to instances in which the firm has more than one plant or market or product. To see that the resulting roles for profit maximization have much in common, let's review them briefly:

1. Multiple Plants   If a firm produces in two plants, A and B, it should allocate production between the two plants so that $MC_A = MC_B$. The optimal total output for the firm is that at which $MR = MC_{TOTAL}$. Hence, for profit maximization, the firm should produce the level of output and allocate the production of this output between the two plants so that

$$MR = MC_{TOTAL} = MC_A = MC_B.$$

2. Multiple Markets   If a firm sells in two distinct markets, 1 and 2, it should allocate output (sales) between the two markets such that $MR_1 = MR_2$. The optimal level of total output for the firm is that at which $MR_{TOTAL} = MC$. Hence, for profit maximization, the firm should produce the level of output and allocate the sales of this output between the two markets so that

$$MR_{\text{TOTAL}} = MC = MR_1 = MR_2.$$

3. Multiple Products/Related in Consumption
Defining the two products to be X and Y, the firm will produce and sell those levels of output for which

$$MR_X = MC_X \text{ and } MR_Y = MC_Y.$$

Since the products are related in consumption, MR_X is a function not only of Q_X but also of Q_Y, as is MR_Y. Therefore, the marginal conditions for the two products must be satisfied simultaneously.

4. Multiple Products/Substitutes in Production
If a firm produces two products, X and Y, that compete for the firm's limited production facilities, the firm should allocate the production facility so that the marginal revenue product of the production facility is equal for the two products, $MRP_X = MRP_Y$. If in the long run the firm can vary its usage of or size of the production facility, the optimal level of usage of the facility is that at which $MRP_{\text{TOTAL}} = MC$. Hence, for profit maximization the firm should select the level of usage of its production facility and allocate this level of usage between the production of the two products so that

$$MRP_{\text{TOTAL}} = MC = MRP_X = MRP_Y.$$

Note, in particular, the similarities between cases 1, 2, and 4. All of these are allocation problems, so they share a common solution. Case 3 requires only that the basic profit-maximization conditions for the related products be solved simultaneously.

So, the view we want to leave you with is that the complications introduced in this chapter do not change the basic rules of profit maximization. As we noted at the outset, the only thing these real-world complications do is to make profit maximization a little more computationally complex.

TECHNICAL PROBLEMS

1. In the graph on following page, D represents the demand for dishwashers facing the Allclean Company. The firm manufactures dishwashers in two plants; MC_1 and MC_2 are their marginal cost curves.

   a. How many dishwashers should the firm produce?

   b. What price should the firm set?

   c. How should the output be allocated between the two plants so as to maximize profit?

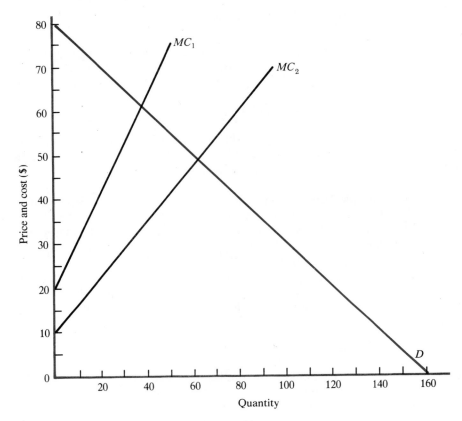

2. A firm with two factories, one in Michigan and one in Texas, has decided that it should produce a total of 500 units in order to maximize profit. The firm is currently producing 200 units in the Michigan factory and 300 units in the Texas factory. At this allocation between plants, the last unit of output produced in Michigan added $5 to total cost, while the last unit of output produced in Texas added $3 to total cost.

   a. Is the firm maximizing profit? If so, why? If not, what should it do?

   b. If the firm produces 201 units in Michigan and 299 in Texas, what will be the increase (decrease) in the firm's total cost?

3. Look again at Mercantile Enterprises—our example of a multiplant firm.

   a. Suppose the forecasted demand function is

   $$Q = 78 - 1.2P.$$

   How many units will be produced? How will these units be allocated between Plants A and B?

b. Suppose the forecasted demand function is

$Q = 88 - 3P$.

How many units will be produced? How will these units be allocated between Plants A and B?

4. What conditions are necessary for a firm to be able to price discriminate?

5. A hotel serves both business and vacation travelers. D_1 is the demand for business travelers and D_2 is the demand for vacation travelers in the figure below. The firm wishes to price discriminate. Suppose that the total marginal revenue for the firm is \$20 at the profit-maximizing level of *total* output.

   a. What is the profit-maximizing number of business travelers to serve? Vacation travelers?

   b. What price should be charged to each?

   c. Answer (*a*) and (*b*) assuming that \$30 is the marginal revenue at the profit-maximizing level of *total* output.

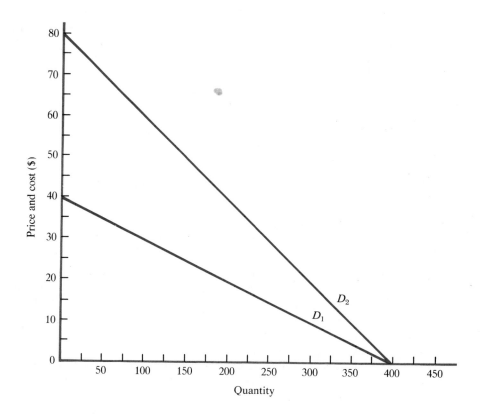

6. A financial newspaper is purchased by both businesses and students. MR_1 is the marginal revenue for students and MR_2 is the marginal revenue for businesses in the figure below. MC is the marginal cost curve of producing the newspaper.
   a. What is the profit-maximizing level of total output?
   b. How should this output be allocated between students and business?
   c. Draw the relevant demand in each market. What price should be charged to each?

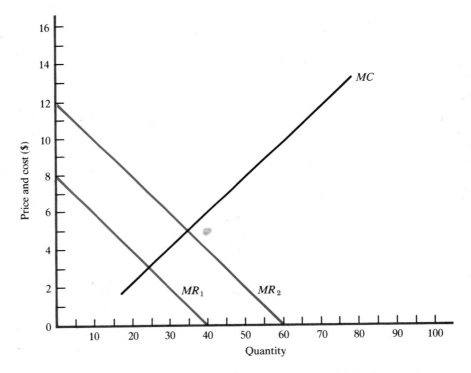

7. A bar offers female patrons a lower price for a drink than male patrons. The bar will maximize profit by selling a total of 200 drinks (a night). At the current prices, male customers buy 150 drinks, while female customers buy 50 drinks. At this allocation between markets, the marginal revenue from the last drink sold to a male customer is $1.50, while the marginal revenue from the last drink sold to a female customer is $0.50.
   a. What should the bar do about its pricing?
   b. If the bar sells 151 drinks to males and 49 to females instead, what will be the increase (decrease) in total revenue?

8. Using our application dealing with profit maximization in multiple markets (Galactic Manufacturing), what price would be charged if

the firm does not price discriminate? Demonstrate that the firm will have a higher profit if it price discriminates than if it charges the same price in both markets.

9. Suppose a firm serves two distinct markets. The forecasted demand functions in the two markets are

$$\text{Mkt 1: } Q_1 = 50 - 0.25P_1 \text{ and Mkt 2: } Q_2 = 100 - 1.0P_2,$$

and the firm's incremental (marginal) cost function has been estimated to be

$$MC = 20 + 0.4Q.$$

   a. What is the profit-maximizing total level of output?
   b. How should this output be allocated between the two markets?
   c. What are the profit-maximizing prices in the two markets?
   d. Which market has the more elastic demand?

10. How would the profit-maximizing decision for a firm that produces two products that are related in consumption differ from that for a firm whose two products are unrelated?

11. Look again at Zicon Manufacturing—a firm that produces products that are substitutes in consumption. Suppose that the production manager changed the estimates of the incremental (marginal) cost functions to

$$MC_X = 20 + \frac{1}{4} Q_X \text{ and } MC_Y = 16 + \frac{1}{2} Q_Y.$$

   Calculate the new profit-maximizing levels of output and price for the two products.

12. Look again at the division of Surefire Products, Inc., that produces two products that are substitutes in production. Suppose that the forecasted demand function for X was changed to

$$Q_X = 76 - \frac{1}{2} P_X.$$

   a. How will an eight-hour production day be allocated between the production of the two products?
   b. What will be the daily outputs?
   c. What prices will be charged?

13. In our application dealing with the optimal usage of a production facility (Surefire Products, Inc.), suppose that the plant supervisor changes the estimate of the incremental (marginal) cost for usage of the plant to

$$MC = 150 + 3H_T.$$

   a. What is the optimal level of usage for the plant (hours per day)?

    b. How will this level of usage be allocated between the production of the two products?

    c. What will be the daily outputs?

    d. What prices will be charged?

ANALYTICAL PROBLEMS

1. Consider a monopoly firm with two plants. One of the plants has a distinct cost advantage in the sense that, at every output, average cost per unit is lower. Why would the firm elect to produce any output from the plant with the higher average costs? What would the firm probably do in the long run?

2. Do price differences always indicate price discrimination? Put another way, could there exist a situation in which two groups of consumers were being charged different prices yet the firm was not price discriminating?

3. Although there exists relatively little difference in the cost of producing hardcover and paperback books, they sell for very different prices. Explain this pricing behavior.

4. In 1980, *The Wall Street Journal* reported on dating services, noting that the fees were $300 for men and $250 for women. The owner of the service said that the differences in fees was to compensate for inequalities in pay scales for men and women. Can you suggest any alternative reasons for this difference?

5. In the case of substitutes in production, we assumed that production costs, for example, cost of running the assembly line, were invariant to the product produced. How would the problem and the optimization condition change if production costs were different for the different products?

6. Can you think of examples of firms that produce products that are both related in consumption and substitutes in production? In general, how would this additional complication affect the optimization condition?

7. In 1986, many observers of the automobile industry were saying that GM was producing cars that were too much alike. Many GM executives agreed. Why would this be a problem for GM?

8. *The New York Times* article on which our Gallo application was based noted that Gallo was considering entering a much more expensive segment of the wine market, possibly in competition with fine French imports. What problems would Gallo likely encounter if it did enter this market?

APPENDIX

Mathematical Demonstration of Results

1. To maximize profit, a multiplant firm will produce the level of output at which the horizontal sum of each plant's marginal cost equals marginal revenue. Each plant will produce the output at which the marginal costs of all plants are equal.

Assume the firm has two plants, A and B, whose total cost functions are respectively $C_A(Q_A)$ and $C_B(Q_B)$. The firm's total revenue function is $R(Q_A + Q_B) = R(Q)$. Thus the firm's profit function is

$$\Pi = R(Q) - C_A(Q_A) - C_B(Q_B).$$

Maximizing profit with respect to Q_A and Q_B requires

$$\frac{\partial \Pi}{\partial Q_A} = \frac{\partial R}{\partial Q} - \frac{\partial C_A(Q_A)}{\partial Q_A} = 0$$

$$\frac{\partial \Pi}{\partial Q_B} = \frac{\partial R}{\partial Q} - \frac{\partial C_B(Q_B)}{\partial Q_B} = 0.$$

Combining these conditions, profit is maximized when

$$MR = MC_A = MC_B.$$

2. A price-discriminating firm maximizing profit will produce the level of output at which marginal revenue in each market equals marginal cost. The price in each market is given by the demand in that market.

Assume the firm sells its output in two markets. The demands in these markets are

$$P_1(Q_1) \text{ and } P_2(Q_2).$$

Cost is a function of total output:

$$C = C(Q_1 + Q_2) = C(Q).$$

The firm maximizes profit,

$$\Pi = P_1(Q_1)Q_1 + P_2(Q_2)Q_2 - C(Q),$$

with respect to the levels of output sold in the two markets.

Thus the first-order conditions for profit maximization are

$$\frac{\partial P_1}{\partial Q_1} Q_1 + P_1 - \frac{\partial C}{\partial Q} = MR_1 - MC = 0$$

$$\frac{\partial P_2}{\partial Q_2} Q_2 + P_2 - \frac{\partial C}{\partial Q} = MR_2 - MC = 0.$$

Thus, profit maximization requires that the marginal revenues in the two markets be equal and equal to marginal cost. Once Q_1 and Q_2 are determined, P_1 and P_2 are given by the demand functions.

Multiple Products that Are Complements in Production

In the text we discussed rather briefly how a firm would maximize profit when producing products that are complements in production and are produced in fixed proportions from an ingredient input. We did not develop the profit-maximizing conditions in the text because the graphical analysis is more complex than that in the rest of the chapter and because this type of multiproduct firm is not as widely encountered as the others. We will examine these conditions here.

Again assume that the firm produces only two products, X and Y, in fixed proportions. Our problem is to determine the level of output and the price for each of these complementary products.

In Figure 17.A1, we have provided a graphical analysis of this problem. In this figure, the demand curves for the two products are denoted as D_X and D_Y and the corresponding marginal revenue curves are shown as the dashed lines MR_X and MR_Y. The marginal cost curve shown is the marginal cost of producing the joint product.

In order to determine how much of the joint product to produce, we need to obtain the demand curve and the marginal revenue curve for the joint product. To obtain the joint product demand curve, we sum the individual demand curves *vertically:* For example, given some level of production of beef carcasses and hides, the total price received is equal to the sum of the prices received for the carcasses and hides, since the number of carcasses must equal the number of hides.

The marginal revenue curve for the joint product is also obtained via the *vertical* summation of MR_X and MR_Y, but there is one major difference. In Figure 17.A1, note that MR_Y becomes zero at an output we have denoted as Q_Y. For sales of commodity Y in excess of Q_Y, the marginal revenue for Y would be negative. Clearly, no firm would wish to sell a unit of a product for which the marginal revenue is negative, so the maximum amount of Y the firm will *sell* is Q_Y. Therefore, the marginal revenue curve for the joint product is the vertical sum of MR_X and MR_Y until MR_Y equals zero. For outputs in excess of Q_Y, the excess units of Y would be discarded and, only commodity X would be sold; the joint marginal revenue curve corresponds to MR_X. The result is the "kinked" joint product marginal revenue curve shown in Figure 17.A1.

The profit-maximizing level of production for the firm is determined at that level of output at which the joint marginal revenue is equal to the joint marginal cost. In Figure 17.A1, this means that the firm will produce Q units of the joint product. The firm will then sell Q units of product X at a price of P_X and Q units of product Y at a price of P_Y.

Figure 17.A1 **Profit Maximization with Joint Products**

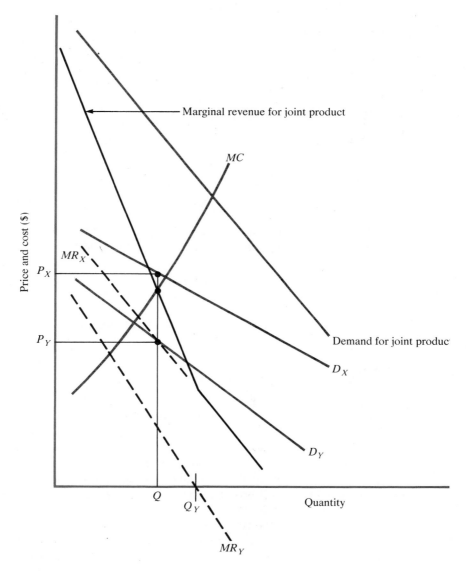

To see how the firm can implement profit maximization with joint products, let's turn to another stylized example.

A firm produces refined chemicals. In one of its divisions a joint product is produced. That is, as it refines the raw chemical input, the processes will yield equal amounts of two products, which we will denote simply as products X and Y. The question facing the manager is, of course, how much of products X and Y should the firm sell and at what prices?

The demand functions for the two products had been forecasted as

$$Q_X = 285 - P_X \text{ and } Q_Y = 150 - 2P_Y,$$

where the outputs were measured in thousand pounds and the prices in cents per pound. The marginal revenue curves associated with these demand functions are

$$MR_X = 285 - 2Q_X \text{ and } MR_Y = 75 - Q_Y.$$

Note that the marginal revenue function for Y is equal to zero at an output of 75 (i.e., 75,000 pounds). So, for output levels of the joint product less than or equal to 75, the marginal revenue function for the joint product is the vertical summation of the two marginal revenues,

$$MR = 360 - 3Q.$$

For output levels in excess of $Q = 75$, the joint product marginal revenue function is the same as MR_X.

Given the existing capital stock, the incremental (marginal) cost function for refining the raw chemical input was estimated to be

$$MC = 10 + 2Q,$$

where marginal cost is measured in cents per pound and output (Q) is in thousand pounds.

Equating marginal revenue and marginal cost for the joint product,

$$360 - 3Q = 10 + 2Q,$$

the profit-maximizing level of production of the joint product is $Q = 70$ (i.e., 70,000 pounds). Using $Q = 70$ in the two demand curves, the manager determined that the firm should sell 70,000 pounds of X at \$2.15 per pound and 70,000 pounds of Y at \$0.40 per pound.

So far, our results have indicated that the firm will produce *and sell* equal amounts of the two products. This need not always be the case. The joint product nature of the production relation we have been considering does require that the firm will always *produce* equal amounts of the two products. (You can't produce an additional beef carcass without producing an additional hide.) But, there is nothing that requires the firm to *sell* equal amounts of the two products.

We have illustrated this situation in Figure 17.A2. The only difference between this figure and Figure 17.A1 is the location of the marginal cost curve for the joint product. In this case, the firm will *produce Q'* units of the joint product. And, since MR_X is positive at Q', the firm will *sell Q'* units of X at the price P'_X. However, at Q', MR_Y is negative. Clearly the firm will not sell Q' units of Y. Instead, the firm will *sell* only Q_Y units of commodity Y at the price of P'_Y. Since it has produced Q' units of Y but only sells Q_Y units, what will the firm do with the remainder (i.e., $Q' - Q_Y$ units of Y)? The answer is simple: the firm will destroy the remainder, since marketing these units would reduce the firm's revenues.

Figure 17.A2 **Profit Maximization with Joint Products—Destruction of One Product**

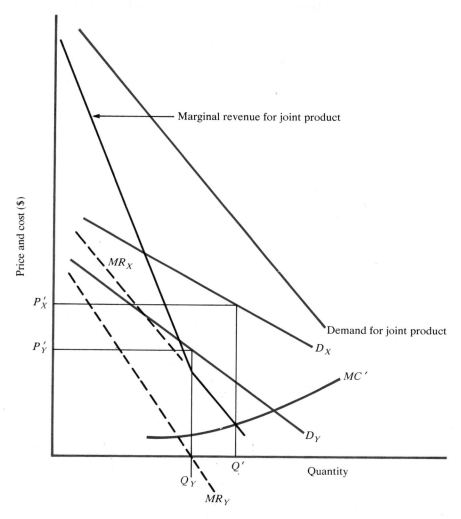

Look again at the decision faced by the manager in the above numerical example. Suppose that the engineers had instead estimated the incremental (marginal) cost of refining the joint product to be

$$MC = 80 + \frac{1}{2}Q.$$

How would this alternative marginal cost function affect the firm's decisions?

Setting this marginal cost function equal to the joint product marginal revenue function used before,

$$360 - 3Q = 80 + \frac{1}{2} Q,$$

the *implied* optimal output would be $Q = 80$. However, as the manager is aware, at this production level, the marginal revenue for product Y would be negative. Hence, in this range of production, the joint product marginal revenue function coincides with MR_X, so to determine optimal production, the manager must equate marginal cost to the marginal revenue for product X,

$$285 - 2Q = 80 + \frac{1}{2} Q.$$

Hence, in this situation, the optimal level of production of the joint product is $Q = 82$. That is, the firm will produce 82,000 pounds of chemicals X and Y.

Since MR_X is positive at $Q = 82$, the firm will sell the 82,000 pounds of X. From the demand function for X, the price charged will be $2.03 per pound.

However, Horizon will sell chemical Y only to that point at which its marginal revenue is zero. That is, since $MR_Y = 0$ when $Q = 75$, the firm will sell only 75,000 pounds of chemical Y and will destroy the remaining 7,000 pounds. From the demand function for Y, the price that will be charged for the 75,000 pounds of Y that is sold is 37.5 cents per pound.

TIME AND UNCERTAINTY

18

PROFIT MAXIMIZATION OVER TIME

T o this point in our analysis, we have employed a simplified model of a firm. The firm we have considered so far is one that is owned and managed by a single entrepreneur, has only a single-period horizon, and faces no uncertainty. In essence, it is like the firm is formed at the start of the period by the entrepreneur who knows with certainty the demand and cost conditions that will prevail in the coming period. Using this certain knowledge, the entrepreneur selects the output level (or, in the case of multiproduct firms, levels) that will maximize the single-period profit. Then, at the end of the period, the entrepreneur liquidates the firm, pockets the profit, and has the capital available to form yet another firm next period.

Although that is an extremely useful framework for analysis, it clearly is not the way the "real world" operates. In the remainder of this text we will eliminate these simplifications to describe the behavior of an indefinitely lived, shareholder-owned firm, which operates in an uncertain environment.

That seems like a very tall order for only three chapters. And, in some ways it is. Given our three-chapter limitation, we will only be able to scratch the surface of a number of issues. However, in other ways, the order is not very tall at all. For someone who understands the principles in the optimization chapter (see Chapter 3), this material should be nothing new. What we have seen so far are applications of the marginal benefit = marginal cost rule, and that is what you will see in this section as well.

In the remainder of this text, we will consider more explicitly a share-holder-owned firm, with particular attention to the conflicts that can arise between competing groups of shareholders or between the shareholders and the managers. In this chapter, we will consider the effect of adding a time dimension to our optimization problem. Chapter 19 adds uncertainty. Then, in Chapter 20, we combine the two to look at the investment decision, an intertemporal (i.e., over time) decision the firm must make under uncertainty.

Our experience has been that, once the time dimension is added to an economics problem, a lot of fuzzy thinking occurs. It's not too hard to see that, in a single-period world, a profit-maximizing firm should produce that output at which marginal revenue is equal to marginal cost. But, once we add the time dimension and the problem looks more like a "real-world" situation, there seem to be a lot of suggestions for the optimal behavior of the firm, including things like maximizing market share or maximizing the return on the shareholders' equity. In this section we hope to convince you that the situation isn't as complex as it sometimes seems and that there is one simple rule for a profit-maximizing firm to follow: *maximize the present value of the firm.*

18.1 NET PRESENT VALUE

How much would you be willing to pay today for a project that will return $100 in one year? (Remember that there is as yet no uncertainty in our world; the $100 is a sure thing.) As an alternative to this risk-free project, you could invest in other riskless activities, the best example of which is U.S. government securities. Suppose that one-year government bonds are paying 6 percent annually. How much would you have to invest in these bonds to get $100 at the end of the year? If I invest X today at an interest rate of 6 percent, in one year my investment will return $X(1.06)$. And, if this investment is worth $100 at the end of one year,

$$X(1.06) = \$100,$$

it follows that the amount I must invest today is $94.34. That is, the present value of $100 in one year with an interest rate—a discount rate—of 6 percent is $94.34.

Now suppose that the project would return the $100 not in one year, but in two years. How much would it be worth then? For the time being, suppose that the annual interest rate on two-year U.S. government bonds is also 6 percent. If I invested X at 6 percent, I would have at the end of year one $X(1.06)$ and at the end of year two $[\$X(1.06)](1.06) = \$X(1.06)^2$. Thus, for my investment to have been worth $100 in two years,

$X(1.06)^2 = \$100$,

it follows that the amount I must invest today is $89.00. The present value of $100 in two years with a discount rate of 6 percent is $89.00.

By this point, you should be seeing the pattern emerge: The present value of $100 in one year at 6 percent is

$$PV = \frac{\$100}{(1.06)}.$$

The present value of $100 in two years at 6 percent is

$$PV = \frac{\$100}{(1.06)^2}.$$

Therefore, the present value of $100 to be received in t years with a discount rate of 6 percent is

$$PV = \frac{\$100}{(1.06)^t}.$$

In the following principle, this relation is made even more general to determine the present value of some net cash flow (*NCF*) to be received in t years at a prevailing interest rate of r. (Note that if the interest rate is 6 percent, r is 0.06.)

Principle. The present value of $NCF to be received in t *years at a discount rate of* r *is*

$$PV = \frac{\$NCF}{(1 + r)^t}.$$

As was illustrated above, the present value of a cash flow declines the further in the future it is to be received—for example, the present value of $100 at 6 percent was $94.34 in one year and only $89.00 in two years. As should be evident from the more general statement of present value, the present value of a cash flow is inversely related to the discount rate—for example, the present value of $100 to be received in two years is $89.00 with a discount rate of 6 percent, but only $85.73 with a discount rate of 8 percent. And obviously the present value of a cash flow increases as the size of the cash flow increases—for example, using one year to maturity and a discount rate of 6 percent the present value of $200 is $188.68, rather than the $94.34 for a $100 cash flow. These relations are summarized in the following principle. The first two of which are also illustrated graphically in Figure 18.1.

Figure 18.1   The Present Value of $100: Changes in the Discount Rate and Time to Maturity

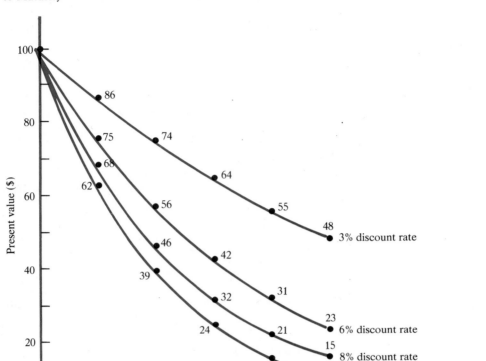

Principle.   There exists an inverse relation between the present value of a cash flow and the time to maturity—the present value of cash flow $NCF to be received in t years is greater than that for the same cash flow to be received in t + i years.

There exists an inverse relation between the present value of a cash flow and the discount rate—the present value of cash flow $NCF discounted at r is greater than that for the same cash flow discounted at r + j.

There exists a direct relation between the present value of a cash flow and the size of the cash flow—using the same times to maturity and discount rates, the value of cash flow $NCF is less than that for cash flow $(NCF + k).

So far we have considered the present value of an investment which makes a single payment. What about the value of an investment project that makes a number of payments? For example, what is the value of a riskless project that pays $100 in one year and $100 in two years? As we know from the preceding, the present values of each of these payments depends on the relevant discount rates; and, since the project is riskless, the discount rate is interest rate for government securities. Suppose that the annual interest rate for a one-year government security is 6 percent and that for a two-year security is 7 percent. The present value of the first payment would then be

$$\frac{\$100}{(1.06)} = \$94.34$$

and the present value of the second payment would be

$$\frac{\$100}{(1.07)^2} = \$87.34.$$

Thus, the present value of the project is

$$PV = \frac{\$100}{(1.06)} + \frac{\$100}{(1.07)^2} = \$181.68.$$

From the preceding, you should be able to see that the present value of a project which has a number of cash flows is equal to the sum of the present values of the net cash flows. Let us put this a little more precisely.

Principle. The present value of a stream of cash flows, where $\$NCF_t$ is the cash flow received or paid in period t, is given by

$$PV = \sum_{t=0}^{T} \frac{\$NCF_t}{(1 + r_t)^t},$$

where r_t is the discount rate for period t, and T is the life span of the stream of cash flows.

To see how this principle works, let's look at an application.

APPLICATION

The Value of an Asset

At the end of 1986, the management of Metroplex Properties was offered participation in a six-year limited partnership on a new office building. Construction was to begin on January 1, 1987 with completion on December 31, 1987. Scheduled occupancy, income, and expenses were as follows: (Remember these cash flows are known with certainty.)

Year	Occupancy Rate (percent)	Rental Income	Expenses	Net Cash Flow
1988	60	$325,000	$200,000	+ $125,000
1989	80	425,000	250,000	+ 175,000
1990	100	525,000	300,000	+ 225,000
1991	100	525,000	300,000	+ 225,000
1992	100	525,000	325,000	+ 200,000

Note: For simplicity, we assume that payments and receipts occur at the end of the year.

At the end of 1992, the value of the building would be $1,000,000.

Clearly, the management of Metroplex needed to determine the value of the project. From *The Wall Street Journal*, they found the annual interest rates for one-, two- , . . . , six-year government securities as

Maturity	Interest Rate (percent)
Dec. 1987	5.75
Dec. 1988	6.00
Dec. 1989	6.25
Dec. 1990	6.50
Dec. 1991	6.75
Dec. 1992	7.00

And, using these rates, they calculated the present value of the project as

$$PV = \frac{\$125,000}{(1.06)^2} + \frac{\$175,000}{(1.0625)^3} + \frac{\$225,000}{(1.065)^4} + \frac{\$225,000}{(1.0675)^5} + \frac{\$200,000}{(1.07)^6} + \frac{\$1,000,000}{(1.07)^6}$$

$$= \$111,250 + \$145,899 + \$174,898 + \$162,309 + \$133,268 + \$666,342$$

$$= \$1,393,966.$$

Once we have the present value of a project, calculation of the net present value is simple:

Principle.   The net present value of a project (asset) is the difference between the present value of the net cash flows of the project and its current cost:

$$NPV = PV - \text{Cost of project.}$$

APPLICATION

The Net Present Value of an Asset

The management of Metroplex Properties had been offered a 33 percent share of the six-year agreement described in the preceding application for $450,000. The net present value of this asset is

$$NPV = (0.33)(\$1,393,966) - \$450,000 = \$10,009.$$

18.2 MAXIMIZING THE VALUE OF THE FIRM—YET ANOTHER MARGINAL RULE

We have seen in the preceding section that present value is additive. For example, the present value of a project returning $100 after one year and $125 after two years is equivalent to the sum of the present values of a project returning $100 in one year and another project returning $125 in two years. Or, in more general terms, if I have two projects (assets), A and B, the present value of the portfolio of projects, $A + B$, is equal to the sum of the present values of Projects A and B: $PV(A + B) = PV(A) + PV(B)$.

Going a step further, a firm is really nothing more than a portfolio of projects (assets). How much is the firm worth? What price would it bring if it were sold? The worth of the firm is simply its present value. And, the present value of this portfolio of projects is simply the sum of the present values of the individual projects.

If the objective is to maximize the present value of the firm, what behavior is required? Think about the firm as a portfolio of n projects. Should it grow by acquiring an additional (marginal) project, the $n + 1$th project? From the principles of optimization, we know that the present value of the firm will increase if the marginal benefit (the present value of the additional project) exceeds the marginal cost (the cost of the additional project). Put another way, an additional project will increase the value of the firm if the present value of the additional project is greater than its cost (i.e., if the net present value of the project is positive).

Principle.   The value of the firm will increase if it undertakes additional projects or acquires additional assets for which the net present value is positive.

Could the firm be better off by shrinking? Could the value of a firm increase by selling off a project? Using the optimization principles, the value of the firm would rise as a result of selling off a project if the present value of the divested project was less than its market value (the price the firm could get for it). That is, the value of the firm will rise if it sells projects that have negative net present values.

Principle.   The value of the firm will increase if it divests projects or assets for which the net present value is negative.

This principle seems right in theory, but it may sound a little strange to you. Why would someone else be willing to pay more for an asset/project/subsidiary than it is worth to the firm itself? The reason has to be that the project fits better with the portfolio of projects of the acquiring firm than with the divesting firm, most likely because of product complementarities like those we looked at in Chapter 17.

In the jargon of the investment banker, an asset worth more to a third party than to the firm itself is referred to as the firm's "crown jewels." Recently, the managers of many firms have sold the crown jewels to raise the value of the firm and thereby the value of the firm's stock in order to avoid a takeover.

THE WALL STREET JOURNAL

APPLICATION

Selling off the Crown Jewels

Perhaps the most widely cited instance of selling the crown jewels is Brunswick Corporation's sale of its Sherwood Medical Industries Division.* In January 1982, the Whittaker Corporation made a takeover bid for Brunswick (apparently motivated by a desire to acquire Sherwood). Brunswick responded by selling Sherwood to American Home Products (for $425 million) and distributing the value directly to its shareholders.

Continued on page 557

*See Michael C. Jensen's "Takeovers: Folklore and Science," *Harvard Business Review*, November/December 1984.

THE WALL STREET JOURNAL

APPLICATION

Continued from page 556
The total value to Brunswick's shareholders of the proceeds of the sale of Sherwood plus the remaining value of Brunswick was greater than Whittaker's bid for the entire company. Put another way, Sherwood Medical Industries was worth more to American Home Products than it was to Brunswick (or to Whittaker). Not surprisingly, Whittaker's takeover bid was withdrawn in March.

And the Brunswick case is not an isolated instance. In 1986, almost every issue of *The Wall Street Journal* had a similar story. For example, the October 9 issue reported that Lucky Stores Inc. (a Dublin, California-based supermarket and chain store concern) was contemplating selling its Gemco discount department store division to avoid a takeover by investor Asher Edelman.[†] According to the *Journal*, Dayton Hudson Corp.'s Target discount department store unit was the most likely buyer of Gemco's assets, because with 70 of its 80 stores located in California, Gemco would make a good fit for Target, which had recently moved into the Southern California market. Indeed, an analyst with Drexel Burnham Lambert indicated that Gemco's 50 Southern California stores could give Target a 50 percent share in that region.

A similar story appeared in the November 4, 1986 issue. Faced with a takeover threat from Sir James Goldsmith, The Goodyear Tire & Rubber Co. was looking for a buyer for its Celeron Corp. subsidiary.[‡] Celeron Corp. is an oil and gas concern currently building a $900 million pipeline to transport crude from California to Texas refineries. As the *Journal* reported, "Goodyear's move was intended to bolster the price of Goodyear stock." And, if this move was to be successful, it must be that Celeron was worth more to someone else than its present value as part of the Goodyear portfolio of projects and assets.

[†]"Lucky Is Selling Gemco Division, Edelman Says," by James B. Stewart and Steve Werner, *The Wall Street Journal*, October 9, 1986. Adapted by permission of *The Wall Street Journal*. © Dow Jones and Company, Inc., 1986. All rights reserved.

[‡]"Goodyear, Responding to Takeover Bid, Seeks Buyer for Its Oil and Gas Unit," by Ralph E. Winter and Gregory Stricharchuk, *The Wall Street Journal*, November 4, 1986. Adapted by permission of *The Wall Street Journal*. © Dow Jones and Company, Inc., 1986. All rights reserved.

Combining the two preceding principles we have a general rule for the behavior of a value-maximizing firm.

Principle. The Net Present Value Rule *for maximizing the value of the firm is to accept projects (acquire assets) for which the net present value is positive and reject projects for which the net present value is negative.*

APPLICATION

Metroplex Properties Again

In an earlier application, we saw that, if the price for the investment project was $450,000, the net present value for the project was $10,009. Clearly, Metroplex should accept this project. This project will increase the value of Metroplex.

However, if the price Metroplex had been offered for the 33 percent share in the office building project was $470,000, the net present value of the project would be negative: $NPV = (0.33)(\$1,393,966) - 470,000 = -\$9,991$. In this instance, the management of Metroplex should reject the project. Accepting a project with a negative net present value would reduce the value of the firm.

18.3 MAXIMIZING THE VALUE OF THE FIRM VERSUS SINGLE-PERIOD PROFIT

After adding the time dimension to our problem, we have proposed that the proper objective of the firm is the maximization of value. In section 18.4 to follow, we will show you why this objective is desired by the shareholders. But, before that, since we have spent so much time on the principles of single-period profit maximization, let's see how the two objectives fit together.

In our review of present value, we defined present value as the sum of discounted net cash flows,

$$PV = \Sigma \frac{NCF_t}{(1 + r_t)^t}.$$

However, as was demonstrated in our real estate application, the cash flow in period t can be decomposed into the difference between the revenue in that period (R_t) and the costs in period t (C_t). Hence, we can write present value as

$$PV = \Sigma \frac{R_t - C_t}{(1 + r_t)^t}.$$

And, since $R_t - C_t$ is profit in period t, it appears that the maximum present value will be attained by maximizing profit in each period. That is, the preceding indicates that single-period profit maximization and maximizing the value of the firm are equivalent means to the same end: maximizing profit in each period will result in the maximum value of the firm and maximizing the value of the firm requires maximizing profit in each period.

In most cases, the two approaches are consistent. However, inconsistencies between single-period profit maximization and maximizing the value of the firm do arise when revenues and/or costs are not independent over time. This somewhat complicated statement might best be explained using some examples. The simplest case we know is when the firm's output decision in one period affects costs in subsequent periods.

APPLICATION

Maximizing the Value of a Mine[†]

In the 1970s, the "energy crisis" led to a lot of interest in exhaustible resources. As it turns out, the principal difference between exhaustible resources such as oil or copper and other products and commodities is in the cost functions. For a "normal" commodity, the marginal cost of production today depends only on today's output level,

$$MC_t = f(Q_t).$$

But, think about a copper mine. The cost today of extracting another ton of refined copper from existing deposits depends not only on how much ore we extract today, but also on the amount of ore we extracted yesterday, and the day before, and the day before that, and so on,

$$MC_t = f(Q_t, Q_{t-1}, Q_{t-2}, \ldots).$$

The more copper we have extracted from the deposit—whether today or in the past—the more costly it is to extract another unit.

This effect is illustrated in the following figure. The curve labeled MC_t is the traditional, single-period marginal cost of production which reflects only the effect of production in period t on costs in period t. If we include the impact of today's production on costs in the future, the marginal cost curve rises to MC'_t.[‡]

[†]For more on this topic, see our text, *The Economics of Mineral Extraction* with Gerhard Anders and Phil Gramm (New York: Praeger Publishers, 1980).

[‡]We ignore the fact that extraction now means there is less in the deposit to extract in the future. This is called a user cost.

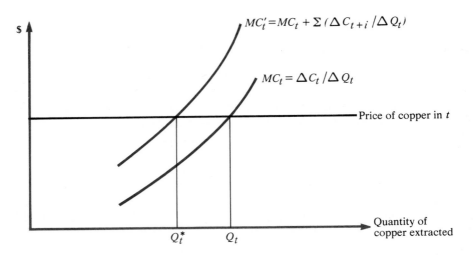

Since copper is traded in a competitive market, let's see how single-period profit maximization and maximization of the value of the firm compare. A manager of the mine who ignored the time effects and simply maximized profit in each period would equate the market price of copper with single-period marginal cost, MC, and extract Q_t. If, however, the effects of today's extraction on future costs were included, the amount extracted would be Q_t^*.

Hence, single-period profit maximization and maximization of the value of the firm would not be consistent for this mine. The output from single-period profit maximization is larger than that which would maximize the value of the mine.

The preceding application was an example of a situation in which the firm's costs were not independent over time. It could be the case that revenues are not independent over time. Suppose a firm used the $MR = MC$ rule to determine the price that will maximize profit in the current period. However, if this price is high enough to encourage the entry of new firms, profits will decline over time as these additional competitors enter the market. Thus, the existing firms may be willing to forgo some profit in the current period in order to maintain their market power and have a larger stream of profits in the future. Consequently, these firms may be willing to set a price below the short-run profit-maximizing level in order to discourage new entrants, thereby maximizing the value of the firm. This behavior, referred to as limit pricing, is illustrated in the following application.

APPLICATION

Limit Pricing

Zephyr Products—a firm providing industrial services—was the first firm to enter a new market and therefore enjoys the position of being the "established firm." The manager of Zephyr has determined the single-period profit-maximizing price to be $2,000. With this price, annual profit is $80,000.

However, the manager of Zephyr knows that, if price is set at $2,000, additional firms will enter the market. Entry would eventually drive price to $1,200 and Zephyr's annual profit to $30,000. Using experience in other markets, Zephyr's profits over its five-year planning horizon would be

Year:	1	2	3	4	5
Profit:	$80,000	$50,000	$40,000	$30,000	$30,000

Alternatively, Zephyr can limit price. The manager of Zephyr Products believes that if price were set at $1,400, no firms would enter the market. With this price, Zephyr's annual profit would be $50,000, and this level of profit could be maintained over the five-year planning horizon.

Hence, the manager of Zephyr is faced with a choice of two strategies—two income streams. Which would be chosen? The manager will select that stream of income that has the higher present value. Using the prevailing U.S. Treasury rates provided earlier in this chapter, the present values are as follows:

Maximize single-period profit and permit entry

$$PV = \frac{\$80,000}{(1.0575)} + \frac{\$50,000}{(1.06)^2} + \frac{\$40,000}{(1.0625)^3} + \frac{\$30,000}{(1.065)^4} + \frac{\$30,000}{(1.0675)^5}$$
$$= \$75,650 + \$44,500 + \$33,348 + \$23,320 + \$21,641$$
$$= \$198,459.$$

Limit price

$$PV = \frac{\$50,000}{(1.0575)} + \frac{\$50,000}{(1.06)^2} + \frac{\$50,000}{(1.0625)^3} + \frac{\$50,000}{(1.065)^4} + \frac{\$50,000}{(1.0675)^5}$$
$$= \$47,281 + \$44,500 + \$41,685 + \$38,866 + \$36,069$$
$$= \$208,401.$$

In this case, the value of Zephyr Products is maximized by limit pricing. Hence, the management of Zephyr would *desire* to limit price. The remaining question is whether they are *able* to do so.*

For a firm to maintain a stream of profit in the future, the price set must exceed its own average cost. But, if entry is to be discouraged, the price must be less than the average cost of potential entrants. Consider Zephyr's situation as illustrated below. Although Zephyr's single-period profit maximum occurs with a price of $2,000, we know that this price will attract entrants—that is, $2,000 exceeds the minimum of the potential entrant's average total cost curve.† The management of Zephyr has proposed a limit price of $1,400. For this limit price to be maintained, the minimum of the potential entrant's *ATC* must lie above $1,400. If the minimum of the potential entrant's *ATC* was lower than $1,400, Zephyr's limit price would have to drop

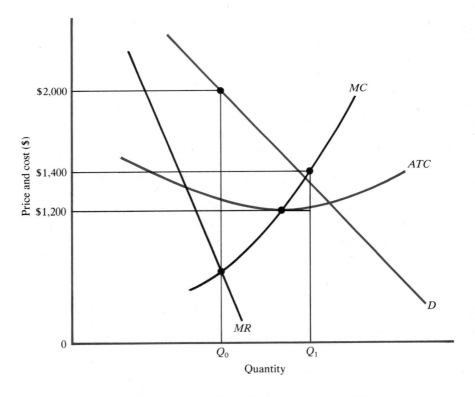

*In this discussion we limit our attention to the case in which there exist established firms operating with the optimal plant size and potential entrants that would use much smaller plants. Thus, we will ignore the impact of the output of the potential entrants on market price.
†If entry was deterred at the profit-maximizing price—if the minimum *ATC* for potential entrants was above $2,000—we would say that entry is blockaded: Zephyr could maximize single-period profit without attracting entrants.

(and Zephyr's per-period profit from limit pricing would also drop). If the minimum *ATC* for the potential entrant occurred at $1,200, Zephyr would be unable to limit price. In order to discourage entry, price would have to be set below its own average total cost curve. Thus, Zephyr would be suffering a loss—a situation that is clearly not in its own best interests.

Hence, limit pricing is *possible* if the minimum of the average total cost curve of Zephyr lies below that of potential entrants. The question then becomes why average costs might be lower for existing firms than for new entrants. While there are several alternative explanations, including such things as the ownership of raw materials or possession of the best locations, a more general explanation is the existence of substantial economies of scale. Suppose, as is illustrated below, that there do exist substantial economies of scale. We might expect that the existing, established firms have used these economies of scale to their advantage and are using relatively large plants as is shown by the location of Zephyr's average total cost curve. If new firms enter with relatively small plants, their average total cost curves will be above those of the existing firms and limit pricing could be possible for the existing firms like Zephyr.

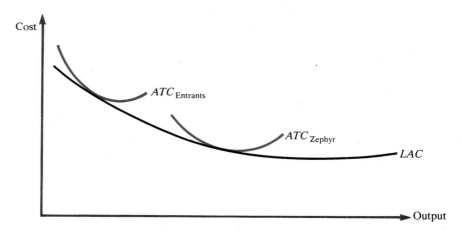

18.4 MAXIMIZING THE VALUE OF THE FIRM AND SHAREHOLDER CONFLICTS

In the introduction to this chapter, we mentioned the conflicts that can occur among shareholders or between shareholders and the managers of the firm. How does an objective of maximizing the value of the firm affect these conflicts?

Figure 18.2 Indifference Maps for Current and Future Consumption

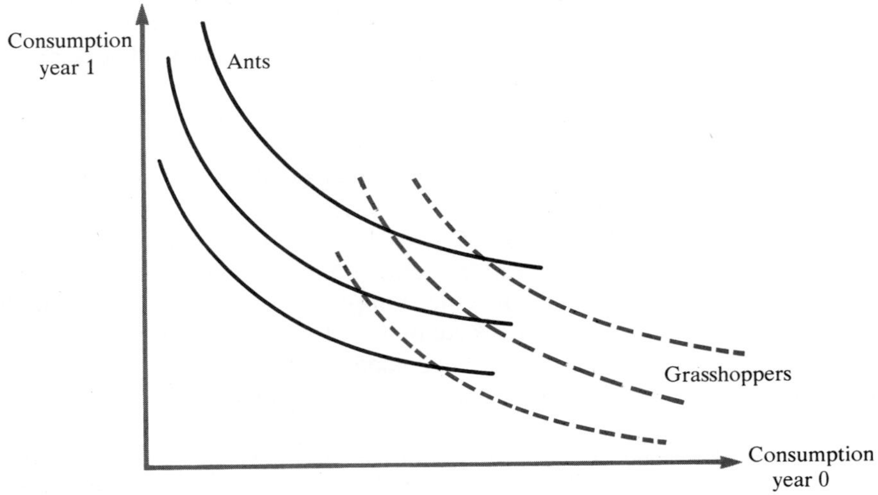

Conflicts among Shareholders In the 1930s, Irving Fisher first pointed out that an objective of maximizing the value of the firm will effectively eliminate those conflicts among shareholders that are based on differences in their individual preferences for current and future consumption. Using an example adapted from texts by Eugene F. Fama and Merton H. Miller and by Richard Brealey and Stewart Myers (see additional references), let's see what Fisher meant.

There are different types of investors (and we don't mean big and little ones). Investors differ as to their marginal rates of substitution between current and future consumption. Figure 18.2 shows the preferences of two types of investors for consumption this year (plotted on the horizontal axis) and consumption next year (plotted on the vertical axis). We can call the investors with the dashed indifference curves "grasshoppers" and those with the solid indifference curves "ants." Using the techniques developed in Chapter 5, we see that grasshoppers have a higher marginal rate of substitution of consumption today for consumption next year than ants; that is, grasshoppers must get a larger increase in future consumption than ants in order to be willing to give up the same amount of current consumption. Thus, grasshoppers place a higher value than ants on current consumption. How can we get both of these types of investors to cooperate in the same enterprise? Put another way, how can a firm have both types of shareholders without continual conflict?

Using Panel A of Figure 18.3, let's suppose that our two investors are both endowed with W_0 dollars in year 0 and W_1 dollars in year 1. However, they also have access to the credit market, in which they can borrow or lend at the annual interest rate, r. Thus, they can consume more than W_0

Figure 18.3 **The Credit Market**

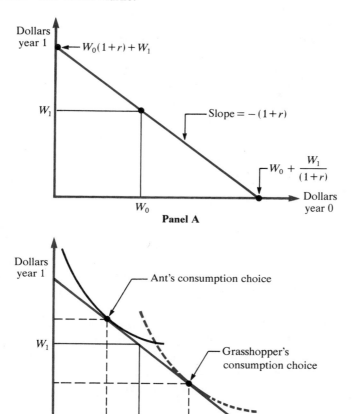

Panel A

Panel B

in year 0, repay the loan plus interest in year 1, and consume less than W_1 in the future. Or they can consume less than W_0 in the present and more than W_1 in the future. Or they can consume only their incomes in each year.

The budget line in Panel A shows how grasshoppers and ants can redistribute consumption between the years. People who choose to consume nothing in year 0 can, in year 1, consume W_1 plus $(1 + r)W_0$, the principal and interest payment for lending the first year's income, W_0. Those who want to consume as much as possible in year 0 and nothing in year 1 can consume W_0 plus the present value of W_1, which is $W_1/(1 + r)$. That is, they can borrow an amount equal to $W_1/(1 + r)$, then pay back this amount with interest when they receive W_1 next year, because $(W_1/(1 + r))(1 + r) = W_1$. The budget line connecting these two points shows every possible combination of current and future consumption,

Figure 18.4 **Investment Possibilities**

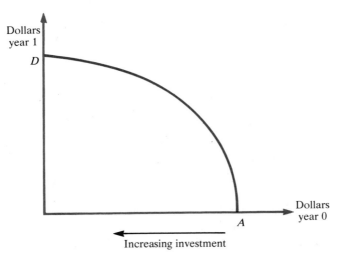

given the interest rate, r. The absolute value of the slope of this line is $(1 + r)$. The cost of $1 worth of consumption today is $(1 + r)$, since $1 in year 0 is worth $1(1 + r)$ in year 1.

If they have access only to the credit market, both grasshoppers and ants chose the combination that maximizes their utility under the constraint. As illustrated in Panel B of Figure 18.3, the grasshopper, who places a higher value on current consumption, maximizes utility by borrowing from next year's income to consume more than W_0 today. The ant lends today in order to consume more than W_1 next year.

Now suppose that, in addition to the credit market, the grasshopper and the ant can also purchase shares in riskless investment projects or assets. The trade-off between current and future dollars with these riskless investments is illustrated in Figure 18.4. The potential investor has A dollars in year 0 to either spend or invest. As consumption in year 0 is reduced and income is put into investment projects, income in period 1 rises. The "investment possibilities" curve is DA. The greater the investment (the lower the consumption) in year 0, the greater the income next year.

The slope of this curve implies that the return on the first group of investments is substantially more than the interest rate in the credit market. But as consumption is reduced and more and more investments are undertaken, the rate of return on these additional investments decreases; that is, there are diminishing marginal returns to investments. Thus as more and more dollars are invested, the additional income in year 1 from an additional dollar invested in year 0 falls.

Now let's look at how the grasshopper and the ant will behave under these circumstances. The grasshopper's behavior is illustrated in Panel A

Figure 18.5 **Maximizing Behavior**

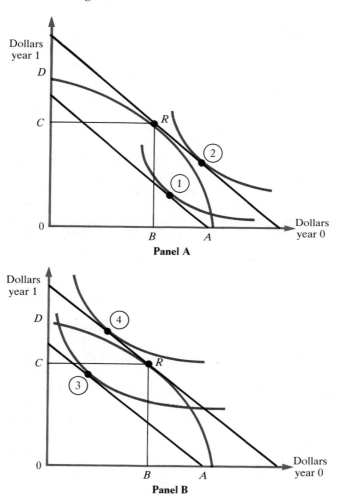

of Figure 18.5. Without the investment possibilities, the utility-maximizing consumption choice is shown at ①. However, given the availability of investment opportunities, the grasshopper can be made better off.

The grasshopper's investment possibilities curve is illustrated as DA, where A equals W_0 plus $W_1/(1 + r)$, the maximum amount available to spend or invest in year 0. Note that the intercept in period 1, D, is greater than $(W_1 + W_0 (1 + r))$, because the grasshopper can do better by investing than by loaning in the credit market. The objective is to choose the level of investment that maximizes the consumption possibilities; that is, the level of investment that leads to the highest possible budget line given the current interest rate, r. In effect, the grasshopper wishes to maximize his income. (Don't forget, though, that once the income is maximized the grasshopper can still borrow or lend at r to obtain the optimal timing of consumption.)

With the investment possibilities curve DA, the grasshopper's highest budget line with slope $(1 + r)$ is attained at R. The maximum possible income thus is earned when the market interest rate, r equals the rate of return (ROR) on the marginal investment—that is, the slope of the budget line must be equal to the slope of the investment possibilities curve. Consider what could happen if this was not true: if $ROR > r$, the grasshopper can borrow \$1, put it in investments, and have \$1 ($ROR - r$) after the loan is repaid.

So, with the ability to invest in riskless projects, the grasshopper will: (1) borrow the present value of next year's income to obtain a current income of OA, and (2) invest the amount AB in riskless assets, implying a current income of OB and an income next year of OC.

Recall, however, that after investing the grasshopper still has access to the credit market for either borrowing or lending along the new budget line. In this case the grasshopper can now borrow more than the present value of W_1, since with the investments, next year's income will exceed W_1. Thus the grasshopper borrows against next year's income, OC, and reaches equilibrium at ②, which clearly represents a higher level of utility than ①.

The behavior of the ant is illustrated in Panel B of Figure 18.5. Without riskless investment projects, the ant's consumption choice is at ③. However, with those projects available, the ant will behave exactly like the grasshopper in steps (1) and (2), moving to R. The ant also wants to maximize the consumption possibilities; that is, move to the highest possible budget line. But, the difference is that the ant will use the credit market to lend part of this year's income, OB, to attain the consumption choice set at ④.

The important point is that, even with their different consumption preferences, each will invest the same amount in assets or projects—AB in Figure 18.5. Although they have different consumption preferences, both are income maximizers with respect to their investment decisions. Their differing consumption preferences come into play when they reallocate the income to maximize utility.

So, the upshot of all this is that these very different investors can cooperate. These investors can be shareholders of the same firm, without imposing different constraints on the firm's management (e.g., regarding dividend policies). The instructions they will give the management of the firm will be identical: *maximize the present value of the firm*. This simple rule will avoid conflicts among the shareholders.

Conflicts between Shareholders and Managers In the simple firm we described in the early part of this text, the entrepreneur was both the owner (the shareholder) and the manager; what was good for the owner was, by definition, good for the manager. However, if this owner/manager identity does not exist, conflicts are likely between the shareholders and the managers they have appointed to operate the firm. In general, these conflicts are based on differences in the objectives of the shareholders and the managers. More specifically, the conflicts can most often be traced to the contracts made between the shareholders and their agents—the management team. Referred to as *the agency problem,* these conflicts between shareholders and managers are currently receiving a great deal of attention from economists.

As we have tried to demonstrate, the shareholders have a straightforward objective: maximize the value of the firm. Managers need not share this objective. While any number of possible managerial objectives could be proposed, a fairly common situation is illustrated in the following application.

APPLICATION

What Happened to the Golden Boys at EasTex Oil?*

EasTex Oil has been in the oil business a long time. When the firm was changed from a partnership to a corporation in 1954, the board of directors looked at a number of possibilities for compensating the management. They decided that, since the major problem facing the oil industry was cheap oil coming in from the Middle East, the best compensation plan was one that would guarantee EasTex's continued presence in the oil business. Hence, a compensation plan was set up that used a complicated ratio based on net operating income, growth in sales, and the rank of the firm when compared to other oil producers.

The net result was that, if there were monies available after paying the dividend to the shareholders, the management of EasTex would plow these free cash flows into new exploration projects. After all, only if EasTex got larger would the management team get bigger bonuses.

In the late 1950s, 60s, and the early 70s, this plan worked well. EasTex got larger and its value got higher, so both the shareholders and the managers were happy. And, in 1973, the management was golden: EasTex was sitting on huge reserves when the world price of crude quadrupled. The value of EasTex shot up. The press proclaimed the president of EasTex to be a genius.

Throughout the 1970s and into the 80s, the management of EasTex continued to do as they had in the past: all free cash flows were plowed into new exploration projects, not paid to stockholders.

---

*This application is a stylized representation of data presented by Michael C. Jensen, "The Takeover Controversy: Analysis and Evidence," *Midland Corporate Finance Journal,* Summer 1986.

However, in the late 1970s (particularly following the beginnings of deregulation in 1979), the oil business had started changing— consumption of oil had declined; forecasts of future oil prices were lower than they had been in the mid-70s; the costs of exploration had increased dramatically; and interest rates were approaching record highs.

The result of these changes was a decrease in the net present value of oil exploration projects. Indeed, exploration ventures that would have been positive net present value projects in 1975 became projects with negative net present value by 1980. Hence, since the management of EasTex was investing all free cash flows in exploration projects, they were undertaking projects for which the net present value was negative.

The management team was happy; their compensation was tied to sales and growth and they were accomplishing both. But, the shareholders were not happy. With the management undertaking negative net present value projects, the value of EasTex (and therefore the value of shares of EasTex) was declining. The business section of one of the statewide papers even ran a story asking "What happened to the golden boys of EasTex oil?", which pointedly referred to the decline in the value of the firm. But, since their bonuses were secure, the management of EasTex shrugged the story off as just the ramblings of someone who really didn't know the oil game.

The point of this application is that the shareholders' objective of maximizing the value of the firm can lead to conflicts between shareholders and managers. However, the same simple objective can provide a way to resolve the conflict. The problem for the stockholders of EasTex was that they had given their managers a compensation plan that induced the managers to maximize sales (or size) rather than maximize the value of the firm. Resolving the conflict then requires that the compensation system be changed to one that will induce the managers to maximize the value of the firm. The simplest approach is to change the compensation plan from one based on accounting revenues to one based on economic profitability.

It's easy for us to propose a sweeping change in compensation plans. In the real world of corporate politics, it may not be so easy to implement. It could well be the case that the management team likes the compensation system they have and have enough clout with the board of directors to keep it in place.

If this is the case, the objective of maximizing the value of the firm still provides guidance. If the value of the firm is less with one set of managers than it would be with another, there is a profit to be made by acquiring the firm and replacing the management team. And that has been a common occurrence in the 1980s.

APPLICATION

Goodbye to the Golden Boys at EasTex Oil

In May of 1984, CentOkla Oil company announced plans to take over EasTex Oil. In its Securities and Exchange Commission filing, the management of CentOkla said that it had purchased 14 percent of EasTex's outstanding shares.

In a press conference in New York City, the Tulsa-based CentOkla let it be known that it planned to operate EasTex as a division under the direction of CentOkla's management team. On the announcement of the acquisition plan, EasTex's share price rose by 40 percent. This time it was the shareholders who were happy.

In this stylized application, it is clear that the shareholders—the owners of EasTex—will benefit from the takeover. However, it should also be clear that, in any takeover motivated by maximizing the present value of the firm, the shareholders of the target firm will benefit. Indeed, it has been estimated that, for $239 billion of merger and acquisition deals in 1984 and 1985, the shareholders of the target firms realized increases of $75 billion in the value of their holdings. Hence, it is not surprising to find articles like the following.

THE WALL STREET JOURNAL

APPLICATION

A Value Determined Tender

On November 4, 1986, *The Wall Street Journal* reported that Celanese Corp. had agreed to be acquired by Hoechst AG, a West German chemicals and pharmaceuticals giant.* American Hoechst Corp. (the American subsidiary of Hoechst AG) would pay $245 for each common share of Celanese, a $27.50 premium over the price of the share one day prior to the announcement.

*"Celanese Gets $2.72 Billion Bid from Hoechst," by Patricia Bellew Gray and Terence Roth, *The Wall Street Journal*, November 4, 1986. Adapted by permission of *The Wall Street Journal*. © Dow Jones and Company, Inc., 1986. All rights reserved.

18.5 SUMMARY

The value today of a cash flow to be received in the future is its *present value*. The present value of a net cash flow, $NCF, to be received with certainty in t periods is

$$PV = \frac{\$NCF}{(1 + r)^t},$$

where r is the t-period riskless interest rate—the discount rate. Note that the present value increases as (1) the size of the cash flow increases, (2) the time to receipt decreases, or (3) the discount rate decreases.

For a project/asset with a stream of cash flows, over its T-period lifetime, the present value is

$$PV = \sum_{t=0}^{T} \frac{\$NCF_t}{(1 + r_t)^t},$$

where NCF_t is the net cash flow received in period t and r_t is the t-period discount rate. The *net present value* of a project/asset is the difference between its present value and its cost,

$$NPV = PV - \text{Cost of project/asset.}$$

A firm is nothing more than a portfolio of projects/assets. Hence, the value of the firm is the sum of the present values of those projects/assets. In order to maximize the value of the firm, the manager need only follow a simple rule:

NPV Rule - Accept projects with positive NPVs and reject projects with negative NPVs.

As long as revenues and costs are independent over time, single-period profit maximization is equivalent to maximizing the value of the firm. Inconsistencies occur when the firm's output decision in one period affects costs in subsequent periods (as in the case of resource extraction) or revenues in subsequent periods (as in the case of limit pricing).

In addition to providing a simple decision rule for maximizing the value of the firm, the NPV rule effectively eliminates conflicts within the firm. Although shareholders may differ with respect to trade-offs between current and future consumption, all shareholders send the same message to the manager: accept positive *NPV* projects and reject negative *NPV* projects. Indeed, the principal conflict between shareholders and managers is when managers fail to maximize the value of the firm and turn instead to alternative objectives. When such conflicts arise, the most straightforward method of dealing with the conflict is to adjust management compensation plans to reward managers for maximizing value. If this fails to occur, outsiders can see that the current value of the firm is less than that possible with different management objectives and a takeover becomes likely.

TECHNICAL PROBLEMS

In the following problems, use the term structure of U.S. Treasury securities for the riskless interest rates below:

Time to Maturity (years)	Interest Rate (percent)
1	5.75
2	6.00
3	6.25
4	6.50
5	6.75

1. Calculate the present value of $1,000 to be received in
   a. One year.
   b. Two years.
   c. Three years.
   d. Four years.
   e. Five years.

2. What is the present value of the following income stream from a project? (Treat all cash flows as paid or received at year-end.)

Year	Net Cash Flow
1	− $10,000
2	$20,000
3	$50,000
4	$75,000
5	$50,000

3. If the purchase price of the project described in Problem 2 is $125,000, what is the project's net present value? What is the project's net present value if its purchase price is $150,000?

4. If the purchase price of the project outlined above is $125,000, should the firm undertake the project? What if the price is $150,000? What is the maximum the firm should pay for this project?

5. Look again at the application dealing with Zephyr Products' decision about whether to limit price. Reevaluate this decision if
   a. Entry occurred slower than originally presumed—that is:

Year	1	2	3	4	5
Profits	$80,000	$60,000	$50,000	$40,000	$30,000

b. The limit price annual profits were $45,000 rather than $50,000.

c. The U.S. Treasury interest rates were 1 percent higher—that is:

Years to maturity interest rate	1	2	3	4	5
	6.75%	7.0%	7.25%	7.5%	7.75%

6. The Environmental Protection Agency (EPA) is charged with regulating the amount of pollutants that firms can emit into the environment. The EPA can force firms to cease polluting beyond some acceptable level or it can impose fines upon polluting firms. The Hardrock Mining Co. operates a metal refining plant—a smelter—near a small city. In the process of refining the ore, the smelter is emitting sulfur dioxide (SO_2) into the air at the rate of 10 parts per million (molecules). The EPA regulation states that the firm will be fined $50,000 a year for every part per million in excess of five parts per million. The chief executive officer of Hardrock Mining asks his engineering department to investigate the problem and propose some solutions.

    In their report, the engineering department notes that the firm will have an entirely new plant in five years, so the solution to the present problem will be short run. They report that there are two possible solutions. The first is to put in a new air purification process, which will reduce the sulfur dioxide below five parts after it is installed. The cost will be $1,050,000, payable now. The second solution is to install scrubbers—that is, modify the present plant and equipment. This will reduce pollution to eight parts the first two years, and to seven parts thereafter. This will cost $250,000 at the end of the first year and $250,000 at the end of the second. Of course, the firm would have to pay a fine each year.

    The CEO adds a third alternative by noting that the firm could do nothing and pay the fine. The fine would be $250,000 a year, since five parts of sulfur dioxide above the maximum would be emitted each year.

    Prepare a report for the CEO ranking the three alternatives using the interest rates provided.

ANALYTICAL PROBLEMS

1. Financial assets (e.g., shares of stock) are said to be "zero net present value projects." Why?

2. If an asset like a share of stock is a zero *NPV* project (see Problem 1), noninterest-bearing checking accounts look like negative *NPV* projects. However, firms do hold such assets. Why?

3. If all costs are considered, the owner of a monopoly earns only a normal profit. Explain why this is true.

4. Taxicabs in New York City are licensed—in order to pick up passengers in the five boroughs of NYC, you must have a "medallion" displayed on the hood of your taxi. There are no new medallions available. If you want a medallion, you have to buy it from someone who owns one.

   If you were to purchase an NYC taxicab company, what is it you are purchasing? How would you calculate the value of the taxicab company?

   In October 1986, Mayor Ed Koch suggested that the number of NYC taxicab medallions be increased. What was the reaction to this suggestion? Why?

5. "Crown jewels" are assets/projects/subsidiaries for which market value exceeds present value for the firm that owns them. Explain how this can occur: Why would a project be worth more to one party than to another?

6. What types of firms would you expect to be able to use limit pricing? What types either could not or would not use this strategy? Provide some examples of industries in which you might expect limit pricing and some for which limit pricing would not be expected.

7. Different investors have different utility functions—particularly with respect to the trade-off between current and future consumption. It seems therefore that a firm could cater to these differences in order to attract miserly (or spendthrift) investors and thereby raise its value. Why is this not possible?

8. By acquiring EasTex, CentOkla Oil bought oil reserves cheaper than it could have acquired the reserves via exploration and drilling. Our hypothetical application illustrates a situation that occurred frequently during the early 1980s: one oil company acquired another—and its reserves—at "bargain basement prices."

   These (often hostile) takeovers led to a great deal of criticism of takeover activity. As many press reports put it, Wall Street was undervaluing oil reserves and was wasting resources in nonproductive merger and acquisition activity. Comment.

SUGGESTED ADDITIONAL REFERENCES

For an extremely clear exposition of the present value and the net present value optimization rules see:

Brealey, Richard, and Stewart Myers. *Principles of Corporate Finance*. New York: McGraw-Hill, 1984.

A more in-depth coverage can be found in:

Fama, Eugene F., and Merton H. Miller. *The Theory of Finance*. Hinsdale, Ill.: Dryden Press, 1972.

The agency problem discussion in section 18.4 was drawn from a number of sources. Some of the original work on the agency problem is collected in:

Jensen, Michael C., and Clifford W. Smith, Jr. *The Modern Theory of Corporate Finance*. New York: McGraw-Hill, 1984.

For more specific references to takeovers, some of the best sources are some nontechnical papers by Michael Jensen:

Jensen, Michael C. "Takeovers: Folklore and Science," *Harvard Business Review*, November/December 1984.

————. "The Takeover Controversy: Analysis and Evidence," *The Midland Corporate Finance Journal*, Summer 1986. (Indeed, this entire issue, which was devoted to takeovers, is an excellent introduction to the topic of takeovers.)

19

PROFIT MAXIMIZATION UNDER UNCERTAINTY

T
he manager of a firm faces uncertainty in a number of ways. In the case of single-period profit maximization, we know that uncertainty exists about demand: future prices or marginal revenues are forecasts based only on information currently available, information about the future period is yet unknown. Uncertainty about costs also exists. For example, if the firm is using a new production plant or process, it has no data—only forecasts about the costs it will incur for various production levels. Likewise, if the firm is to produce a level of output far different from one it has produced previously, uncertainty about the costs of production increases.

For profit maximization over time, uncertainty means that the manager does not know the net cash flow that will occur in some future period. Instead, the manager knows that there is some range of outcomes for net cash flows: there exists a distribution of outcomes for the future net cash flows.

To describe some of the techniques used by a manager to deal with uncertainty, we begin by looking at uncertainty as summarized by a probability distribution. Using the tools provided by statistics, the manager can make use of the expected value and variance of the probability distribution in making profit (value)-maximizing decisions. We then move on to uncertainty in decisions made over time and look at how a manager can value risky cash flows. The present value concept set forth in Chapter 18 must be modified to incorporate risk. Indeed, for the present value formula, both the numerator (net cash flows) and the denominator (the discount rate) must be adjusted to reflect the riskiness of future cash flows. And, of the two, the modification to the discount rate is the more complicated and the one that will receive the majority of our attention.

19.1 DECISION MAKING UNDER UNCERTAINTY

When, in Chapter 13, we discussed the decision-making process for a firm in a competitive market, we introduced uncertainty. As you may recall, the manager of Beau Apparel faced three price forecasts—a high, a best, and a low forecast. And, as summarized below, these different forecasts would lead to very different outcomes for the firm.

Price Forecast	Should the Firm Shut Down?	Optimal Output Level	Profit (Loss)
$20	No	8,000	$34,000
15	No	7,100	(3,730)
10	Yes	0	(30,000)

How does this manager of Beau Apparel or any other manager make decisions when confronted with such uncertainty? What tools and techniques are available to assist the manager in evaluating decisions?

Probability Distributions   The most straightforward way of dealing with uncertainty about a parameter is to look at its probability distribution, which provides information about the likelihood of a particular event occurring.

Definition. A probability distribution lists (or graphs) all possible outcomes and the corresponding probabilities of occurrence.

A probability distribution of particular interest to a plant manager is that for machine breakdown. For example, the probability distribution for at least one machine breaking down might look as follows:

Outcome	Probability of Occurrence during One 8-Hour Shift (percent)
At least one machine breaks down	20%
No machine breaks down	80

Figure 19.1

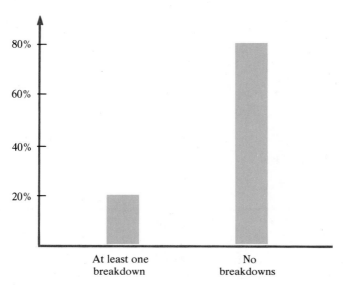

This probability distribution for machine breakdown can also be displayed graphically as in Figure 19.1.

Instead of only two possible outcomes, as in the case of machine breakdowns, the probability distribution could have several outcomes. For example, the director of advertising might have posited five potential outcomes for a new set of ads:

Outcome	Probability (percent)
Sales decline by 5% to 47,500 units	10%
Sales remain unchanged at 50,000 units	20
Sales rise by 5% to 52,500 units	30
Sales rise by 10% to 55,000 units	25
Sales rise by 15% to 57,500 units	15

This probability distribution is represented graphically in Figure 19.2.

The probability distribution (either in tabular or graphical form) does provide a summary of the degree of uncertainty. But, the manager may wish an even more concise summary. For example, the question posed to the advertising director might be "How many additional units do you expect these new ads to generate?" To answer this question, the adver-

Figure 19.2

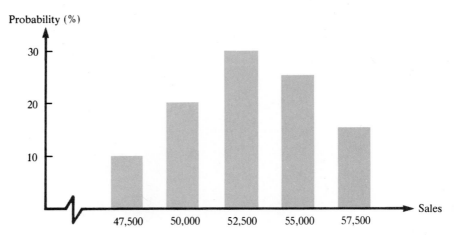

tising director will have to obtain expected sales; that is, the *expected value* of the probability distribution.

Definition. **Given a probability distribution which relates various outcomes (X_i) to their probabilities of occurrence (P_i), the expected value *is the probability-weighted sum,***

$$E(X) = \sum_{i=1}^{n} X_i P_i \cdot$$

The expected value of the distribution is the mean of the distribution.

Using the preceding definition and the probability distribution in Figure 19.2, the expected level of sales for the new ad campaign is

$$\begin{aligned}
E(\text{Sales}) &= (47,500)(0.1) + (50,000)(0.2) + (52,500)(0.3) \\
&\quad + (55,000)(0.25) + (57,500)(0.15) \\
&= 4,750 + 10,000 + 15,750 + 13,750 + 8,625 \\
&= 52,875.
\end{aligned}$$

And, given this summary statistic, the advertising director can respond that the new ads are expected to generate an additional 2,875 units of sales.

Expected values can be used by the manager to select between or among different projects/techniques/ad campaigns/and so on. For example, if the advertising director is choosing between two ad campaigns, both of which require the same level of total expenditures, the expected sales for the two campaigns could be used to decide which one to use. Suppose the probability distributions for sales for the two ad campaigns are as illustrated in Figure 19.3.

Figure 19.3

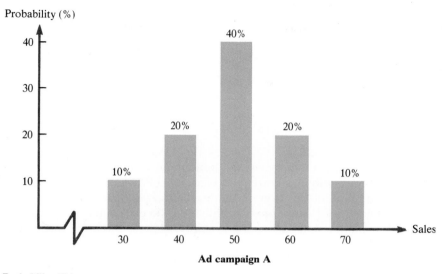

Ad campaign A

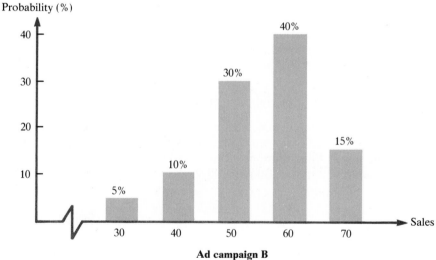

Ad campaign B

The expected values for the two campaigns are

$$E(\text{Sales}_A) = (30)(.1) + (40)(.2) + (50)(.4) + (60)(.2) + (70)(.1)$$
$$= 3 + 8 + 20 + 12 + 7$$
$$= 50$$
$$E(\text{Sales}_B) = (30)(.05) + (40)(.1) + (50)(.3) + (60)(.4) + (70)(.15)$$
$$= 1.5 + 4 + 15 + 24 + 10.5$$
$$= 55.$$

Hence, on the basis of expected value calculations, ad campaign B dominates campaign A.

A slightly more complex expected value approach can be used by the
manager of Beau Apparel.

APPLICATION

Beau Apparel Again

The price uncertainty faced by Beau Apparel was the result of
uncertainty about legislation pending in Congress and the impact of
that legislation on per capita income in 1988I. By collecting some
additional information on the legislation pending in Congress, the
manager of Beau Apparel eliminated the econometric forecasting firm's
low-income forecast as a possibility. Hence, the price forecast of $10
was ignored.

The manager then had two options remaining: Option 1—use the
price forecast of $15 and produce 7,100 units. Option 2—use the $20
price forecast and produce 8,000 units. If the manager selects option 1
and it turns out that $15 is, in fact, the true price, we know that the
firm will lose $3,730. However, if the manager selects option 1 and the
true price turns out to be $20, the firm will earn a profit of $31,770.
That is,

$$(\$20) \times (7,100) - [(\$11.30) \times (7,100) + \$30,000] = \$31,770.$$

Likewise, if the firm selects option 2, the firm will earn a profit of
$34,000 if $20 is the true price or suffer a loss of $6,000 if $15 is the
true price. Thus there are four possible outcomes, which are
summarized in the following table.

	Profit (Loss) When 1988I Price Is	
	$15	$20
Option 1: Produce 7,100 units	−3,730	+31,770
Option 2: Produce 8,000 units	−6,000	+34,000

The economic consulting firm used by Beau Apparel was able to assign
probabilities to the passage of the legislation and was therefore able to
assign probabilities to the two prices:

Outcome	Probability (percent)
Price = $15	40
Price = $20	60

Using these probabilities, expected profits from the two options can be calculated as

Option 1: E(Profit) $= (-3,730)(0.4) + (31,770)(0.6)$
$= -1,492 + 19,062$
$= \$17,570.$

Option 2: E(Profit) $= (-6,000)(0.4) + (34,000)(0.6)$
$= -2,400 + 20,400$
$= \$18,000.$

On the basis of these probabilities, option 2 would be selected: Beau Apparel would produce 8,000 units for 1988I.

So far, we have talked only about the expected value of a probability distribution; that is, the mean of the distribution. However, as you may know from any statistics classes you have taken, distributions are generally classified by two parameters: the mean and the variance. The variance measures the dispersion of the distribution about its mean. In Figure 19.4 we have illustrated two profit distributions which have the same means—expected values—but different variances. The larger variance associated with distribution B is illustrated with a larger dispersion (a wider spread of the values around the mean).

Since distribution A has a more compact distribution, there is less "risk" for distribution A than for distribution B. Hence, in making decisions under uncertainty, some consideration of variance must be included.

As noted above, variance is a measure of the dispersion of the distribution about its mean. More specifically,

Definition. The variance of the distribution of outcomes X_i (denoted σ_x^2) is the probability-weighted sum of the squared deviations from the expected value (mean),

$$Variance\ (X) = \sigma_x^2 = \sum_{i=1}^{n}(X_i - E(X))^2 P_i$$

Figure 19.4

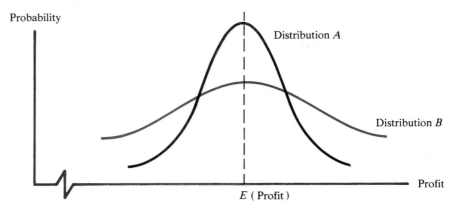

As an example, consider the distributions illustrated in Figure 19.5. As is evident from the graphs and demonstrated below, the two distributions have the same mean. However, their variances differ significantly. Distribution A is substantially less risky—has a smaller variance—than B.

	Distribution A			Distribution B		
Profit X	Probability P	$(X)(P)$	$[X - E(X)]^2(P)$	Probability P	$(X)(P)$	$[X - E(X)]^2(P)$
30	.05	1.5	20	.1	3	40
40	.2	8	20	.25	10	25
50	.5	25	0	.3	15	0
60	.2	12	20	.25	15	25
70	.05	3.5	20	.1	7	40
		$E(X) = 50$	$\sigma_A^2 = 80$		$E(X) = 50$	$\sigma_B^2 = 130$

Since variance is a squared term, it is quite likely to be numerically much larger than the mean. To avoid this scaling problem, the standard deviation (the square root of the variance) is commonly used.

Definition.   **The standard deviation of a probability distribution, denoted as σ_x, is the square root of the variance,**

$$\sigma_x = \sqrt{Variance(X)}.$$

The standard deviations of the distributions illustrated in Figure 19.5 are $\sigma_A = 8.94$ and $\sigma_B = 11.40$.

The point of this discussion has been to provide some rules for decision making under uncertainty. The manager needs to be able to choose be-

Figure 19.5

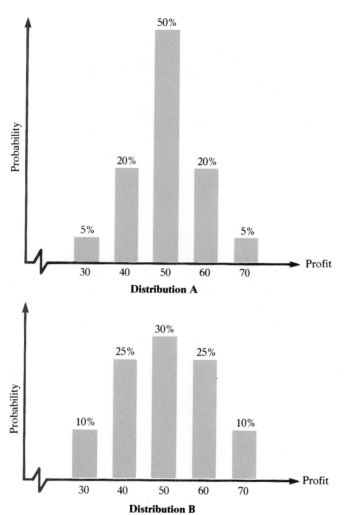

Distribution A

Distribution B

tween (or among) competing projects/techniques/output levels/ad campaigns/and so on. For simplicity let's consider Projects A and B where we know the expected profit for each, $E(\text{Profit}_A)$ and $E(\text{Profit}_B)$, and the standard deviations of the two distributions, σ_A and σ_B.

If $E(\text{Profit}_A) = E(\text{Profit}_B)$ and $\sigma_A < \sigma_B$, the choice is simple: Select Project A, the project with the smaller variance.

If $E(\text{Profit}_A) > E(\text{Profit}_B)$ and $\sigma_A < \sigma_B$, the choice is again simple: Project A dominates Project B, that is, Project A has a higher expected profit and lower "risk," so Project A will always be selected.

If $E(\text{Profit}_A) > E(\text{Profit}_B)$ but $\sigma_A > \sigma_B$, the problem faced by the manager is more complex, involving the trade-off between risk and return we discussed in Chapter 5.

When confronted by a situation involving a trade-off between risk and return, the manager could explicitly incorporate a measure of risk in the decision-making process, as we will in section 19.2. Or, the manager could resort to various kinds of strategic behaviors. One of the best-known strategies, adapted from the mathematical area of game theory, is known as MiniMax. Rather than explain the mechanics of this behavior, let's look at how the manager of Beau Apparel used it.

APPLICATION

A Minimax Strategy

When last we considered Beau Apparel, we saw that option 2 (produce 8,000 units) has a higher expected profit than option 1 (produce 7,100 units). However, as is illustrated in the following figure, the profit distribution for option 2 is more dispersed than is the distribution for option 1. Moreover, it can be demonstrated (and you will be asked to demonstrate in Technical Problem 4) that option 2 has a larger standard deviation than option 1.

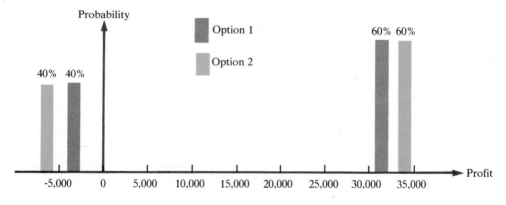

The upshot is that, while option 2 has a higher expected profit, it is riskier than option 1. Because of this, the manager of Beau Apparel decided to use a MiniMax approach. Reproduced below is the profit matrix for the two options facing the manager and the two possible prices for shirts in 1988I.

With option 1, the worst the firm could do is to lose $3,730. With option 2, the worst the firm could do is lose $6,000. If the manager of

| | Profit (Loss) When 1988I Price Is | | Worst Possible Outcome |
	$15	$20	
Option 1	− 3,730	+ 31,770	− 3,730
Option 2	− 6,000	+ 34,000	− 6,000

Beau Apparel followed the MiniMax strategy, the option selected would be that which provides the minimum of the worst possible outcomes—option 1 would be selected. Using the MiniMax strategy, the manager selects the option that maximizes the minimum profits (or minimizes the maximum loss).

Although MiniMax is an ad hoc solution to a situation in which the manager must trade off between risk and expected profit, it is, nonetheless, widely used. In essence, this strategy formalizes a common strategy of "making the best out of the worst possible outcome." It is important to note that, using the MiniMax strategy, the decision made previously to use option 2 was reversed.

19.2 VALUING RISKY CASH FLOWS

When we discussed the valuation of a *riskless* project (asset) in Chapter 18, we determined that the value of the project was given by its present value. As you will remember, to obtain the present value of some specific project, j, we employ the valuation equation

$$PV_j = \sum_{t=0}^{T} \frac{NCF_{j,t}}{(1 + r_t)^t},$$

where $NCF_{j,t}$ is the net cash flows generated by project j in year t and r_t is the riskless discount rate in year t (the interest rate on U.S. government securities). The question we must now turn to is: How will this valuation equation change if project j is a *risky* project?

Uncertain Cash Flows   The obvious change is that the numerator of the equation must change. The cash flows from project j are no longer known with certainty. Instead of a single, known value for $NCF_{j,t}$, there exists a probability distribution for the cash flow from project j in year t, a stylized illustration of which is provided in Figure 19.6.[1]

---

[1] A normal distribution is illustrated for simplicity. All of the results also follow for a nonsymmetric distribution.

Figure 19.6 **Cash Flows from a Risky Project**

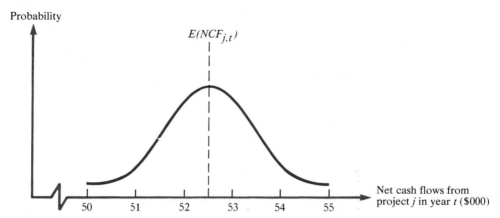

How can we summarize this probability distribution in our valuation equation? As we know from the preceding section, the expected value of a probability distribution provides a summary statistic for the distribution. Hence, instead of referring to the net cash flow from project j in period t, we can consider the *expected* net cash flow, $E(NCF_{j,t})$.

A Discount Rate Reflecting Risk   Less obvious is the change required in the denominator of the valuation equation. For the riskless project, the appropriate discount rate was *the* riskless rate. Since there was no question about how large the cash flow would be, the only thing that mattered was when the cash flows would be received (paid).

However, as is clear from Figure 19.6, the probability distribution for the cash flows from the risky project j has some nonzero variance. In section 19.1, we defined variance as a measure of risk, so the cash flows from this project are risky in the sense that the size of the cash flow varies. And projects that have larger variances (standard deviations) for their cash flows will be riskier.[2]

Since this risk associated with the variance in the probability distribution for cash flows is not accounted for in the numerator of the valuation equation, it must be accounted for in the denominator. Thus, this risk must be reflected in the discount rate used. The riskless rate is clearly not appropriate; neither is some common "discount rate for risky projects." Project j has some level of risk associated with the probability distribution of its cash flows and this risk is not necessarily the same as the risk for some other project k—even if the two projects had the same

---

[2]The risk discussed here deals with variation in the size of the cash flow. It should not be confused with default (performance) risk which is imbedded in the numerator: $E(NCF)$ will incorporate any probabilities of default.

expected net cash flows. Therefore, there will exist a specific discount rate that reflects the risk associated with project j. Let's denote this specific discount rate for cash flows received (paid) from project j in year t as $r_{j,t}$.

Expected Present Value Combining the preceding discussions of uncertain cash flows and a risk-adjusted discount rate, it should be clear that, for a risky project j, we will calculate the *expected* present value as:

$$E(PV_j) = \sum_{t=0}^{T} \frac{E(NCF_{j,t})}{(1 + r_{j,t})^t}.$$

Just as the present value equation provides the value of a riskless project, the equation above can be used to value a risky project.

At this point, it should be clear how the firm could estimate a probability distribution for the cash flows from a project and determine the expected net cash flows.

APPLICATION

Estimating Expected Net Cash Flows

The managers of Zeus Manufacturing are considering the acquisition of machinery to produce a new product line. The machinery has a five-year time horizon. (At the end of five years, the project has no scrap value). After extensive consultations and review of similar projects, they obtained low, best, and high estimates for the net cash flows from the project in each of its five years. The resulting table of outcomes is presented below:

Year	Net Cash Flow Estimates ($ million)		
	Low	Best	High
1	−2	0	4
2	1	3	5
3	4	5	6
4	4	5	6
5	2	4	5

The management team subjectively assigned probabilities to these outcomes as low—20 percent, best—70 percent, high—10 percent.

Using these probabilities, the expected net cash flow in year 1 is zero

$$E(NCF_1) = (-2)(0.2) + (0)\,(0.7) + (4)(0.1)$$
$$= -.4 + 0 + .4 = 0$$

Similarly, the expected net cash flows for years 2 through 5 are

$$E(NCF_2) = 2.8$$
$$E(NCF_3) = 4.9$$
$$E(NCF_4) = 4.9$$
$$E(NCF_5) = 3.7.$$

19.3 THE APPROPRIATE DISCOUNT RATE FOR A RISKY PROJECT

Thus far we have seen that, to discount the expected net cash flows from a risky project j, we will need to use a discount rate different than the riskless rate. Indeed, to compensate the firm for bearing the additional risk, the discount rate will need to be higher than the riskless rate. Thus, we could express the appropriate discount rate for cash flows from risky project j in year t as

$$r_{j,t} = r_t + (\text{risk premium})_j,$$

where r_t is the riskless rate and the second term is the appropriate risk premium for project j.

Hence, our task is to find a way to determine the appropriate risk premium. There exist a number of rules of thumb. Let's look at two that are used most often:

Risk-Adjusted Discount Rates   The preceding equation displays our problem very clearly; we need to attach a risk premium to the riskless rate. The risk-adjusted discount rate approach does that directly, adding a risk premium directly to the riskless rate.

APPLICATION

Using Risk-Adjusted Discount Rates

The managers of Zeus wanted to determine the expected present value of the project introduced in the application above. Their policy had been to attach a risk premium based on their evaluation of how risky the project is. The risk premiums they use are

Project Riskiness	Risk Premium (percent)
Low-risk project	3
Average-risk project	6
High-risk project	9

In their judgment, the project being considered was an average-risk project. Hence, the rates used to discount the expected cash flows are obtained by adding this risk premium to the riskless rate (the interest rate for U.S. government securities):

Years to Maturity	Riskless Rate (percent)	Risk Premium (percent)	Risk-Adjusted Discount Rate (percent)
1	5.75	6	11.75
2	6.00	6	12.00
3	6.25	6	12.25
4	6.50	6	12.50
5	6.75	6	12.75

Using these risk-adjusted discount rates, the expected present value of the project was

$$E(PV_j) = \frac{0}{(1.1175)^1} + \frac{2.8}{(1.12)^2} + \frac{4.9}{(1.1225)^3} + \frac{4.9}{(1.125)^4} + \frac{3.7}{(1.1275)^5}$$
$$= 0 + 2.232 + 3.464 + 3.059 + 2.031$$
$$= 10.786$$

That is, the expected present value of the new machinery is $10,786,000.

Apparently simple, the risk-adjusted discount rate methodology is complicated by an obvious problem: How does the manager determine the appropriate risk premium? Elegant mathematical formulas have been presented by Franco Modigliani and Merton Miller and by J. Miles and R. Ezzell.[3] However, the risk-adjusted discount rates remain rules of thumb.

Weighted-Average-Cost-of-Capital The weighted-average-cost-of-capital (WACC) approach reflects prevailing market conditions more than the

---

[3]See the references at end of chapter.

preceding approach. In essence, the WACC approach implies that the appropriate discount rate for new projects is the rate currently paid by the firm in the market; i.e., a weighted average of the rate at which the firm can borrow and the rate of return required by the firm's shareholders. Specifically, the weighted-average-cost-of-capital for a firm (let's denote this r_{WACC}) is given by[4]

$$r_{WACC} = r_D\left(\frac{D}{D+E}\right) + r_E\left(\frac{E}{D+E}\right),$$

where D and E are the current market values of the firm's outstanding debt and equity and r_D and r_E are, respectively, the current rate at which the firm can borrow and the rate of return on equity required by the firm's shareholders to induce them to hold the shares of stock.

APPLICATION

Using Weighted-Average-Cost-of-Capital

To calculate the weighted-average-cost-of-capital for Zeus Manufacturing, the managers first needed the current market value of Zeus's debt and equity. The market value of Zeus's equity was the easier of the two: there were 1,200,000 shares of stock currently selling at $27.25 per share, so

$$E = 1{,}200{,}000 \times \$27.25 = \$32{,}700{,}000.$$

Zeus had issued debt with a face value of $95 million. Currently, these corporate bonds are being traded at 92 percent of their face (par) value, so

$$D = 0.92 \times \$95{,}000{,}000 = \$87{,}400{,}000.$$

The managers also needed Zeus's current borrowing rate and the rate of return required by its shareholders. Using data on the general performance of the stock market and a subjective assessment of the riskiness of Zeus, the finance director has estimated that Zeus's shareholders require a return of 18 percent,

$$r_E = 0.18.$$

---

[4]This formula neglects corporate taxes. If corporate taxes were included,

$$r_{WACC} = (1-CTR)\, r_D\left(\frac{D}{D+E}\right) + r_E\left(\frac{E}{D+E}\right),$$

where CTR is the marginal corporate income tax rate.

Using the market valuation of Zeus's debt issues and prevailing interest rates, the finance director calculated that the current yield on Zeus's debt—the interest rate Zeus would have to pay to borrow money today—is 7 percent,

$$r_D = 0.07.$$

Hence, the weighted-average-cost-of-capital for Zeus Manufacturing is

$$r_{\text{WACC}} = 0.07\left(\frac{87.4}{87.4 + 32.7}\right) + 0.18\left(\frac{32.7}{87.4 + 32.7}\right)$$
$$= 0.05 + 0.05 = 0.10.$$

Using this discount rate to discount the expected net cash flows of the project under consideration,

$$E(PV_j) = \frac{0}{(1.1)^1} + \frac{2.8}{(1.1)^2} + \frac{4.9}{(1.1)^3} + \frac{4.9}{(1.1)^4} + \frac{3.7}{(1.1)^5}$$
$$= 0 + 2.314 + 3.681 + 3.347 + 2.297$$
$$= 11.639.$$

That is, the expected present value of the project is $11,639,000.

The weighted-average-cost-of-capital approach is intuitively appealing, and, in some cases, it works. Specifically, the WACC approach works (1) if the project being considered is just like the rest of the firm, and (2) if the project is to be financed with the same mix of debt and equity prevailing in the rest of the firm. The WACC approach does *not* work for projects that are more or less risky than the firm's existing portfolio of projects. Likewise, the WACC approach is not appropriate if acceptance of the project would cause the firm's debt/equity ratio to change.

Perhaps because it is more intuitively appealing than the risk-adjusted discount rate approach, the weighted-average-cost-of-capital approach is widely used. For example, in 1978, almost half the firms surveyed used WACC as the appropriate discount rate.[5] However, like the risk-adjusted discount rate approach, weighted-average-cost-of-capital is a rule-of-thumb approach. An analytical method of determining the appropriate discount rate is the capital asset pricing model, to which we now turn.

Capital Asset Pricing Model   The capital asset pricing model has its origins in portfolio theory, a topic we alluded to in Chapter 5. As developed by

---

[5]See Harold Bierman, Jr., *Implementation of Capital Budgeting Techniques–Survey & Synthesis* (New York: Financial Management Association, 1986), p. 25.

Figure 19.7   The Impact of Diversification on an Individual Investor's Portfolio Risk

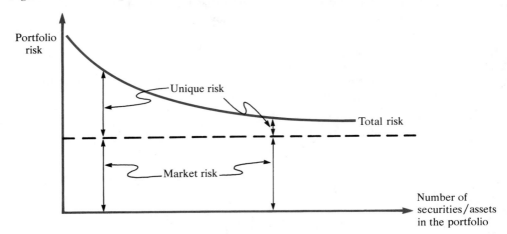

Harry Markowitz (1952), the core of portfolio theory is deceptively simple: as more securities are added to the investor's portfolio, the portfolio risk (the standard deviation of portfolio returns) declines. This principle is illustrated in Figure 19.7: as more securities are added to the portfolio, the unique risk associated with a particular security is diversified away, leaving the investor with only market risk—the risks faced due to economy-wide changes. Hence, as more and more securities (assets) are added to the investor's portfolio, the total portfolio risk declines toward market risk—the risk associated with a portfolio which contains some of all of the securities (assets) available in the market. The security's unique risk is diversified away.

Therefore, from the perspective of the investor—the ultimate owner of a shareholder-owned firm—the only thing that matters is market risk. When evaluating an individual security, the only thing that matters is its contribution to market risk. Likewise, the instruction from the shareholder to a firm's management is simple:

> When evaluating a project, consider only its contribution to
> market risk. Ignore its unique risk since I can effectively eliminate
> this risk by holding a well-diversified portfolio.

APPLICATION

The Benefits of Diversification

Suppose that, during the first quarter of 1986, an individual investor wanted to hold a portfolio of shares of stock. How is the riskiness of the portfolio influenced by its composition?

Suppose that the investor had held only one stock. For example, suppose that the investor had bought a share of stock in Chase Manhattan Bank on December 27, 1985 and held the share until March 28, 1986 (i.e., 13 weeks). The weekly returns on this single stock portfolio would have been as illustrated below.

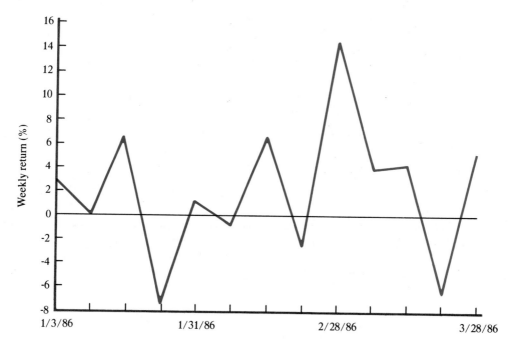

Instead, suppose that the investor had held a portfolio made up of two stocks: a portfolio of one share of Chase and one share of General Motors. Illustrated on the following page are the weekly returns for the two stocks and for the portfolio. Note that by diversifying her holdings, the investor would have been able to reduce the variability of returns. Holding the portfolio made up of one share of stock in each firm results in a lower level of risk (as measured by the standard deviation of returns) than would result if either of the shares were held individually:

$$\sigma_{CHASE} = 5.58\%, \ \sigma_{GM} = 2.88\%, \ \sigma_{(1 \ CHASE + 1 \ GM)} = 2.57\%.$$

It is important to note that the volatility (the standard deviation) of the portfolio is not simply the average of the components: *the volatility of the portfolio is lower than the average of the volatilities of the individual shares.*

And, the investor can further reduce the riskiness of her portfolio. Indeed, if she were to hold a *market portfolio* containing shares of all available securities and assets, the investor could reduce the risk to only market risk. To approximate this market portfolio, suppose that

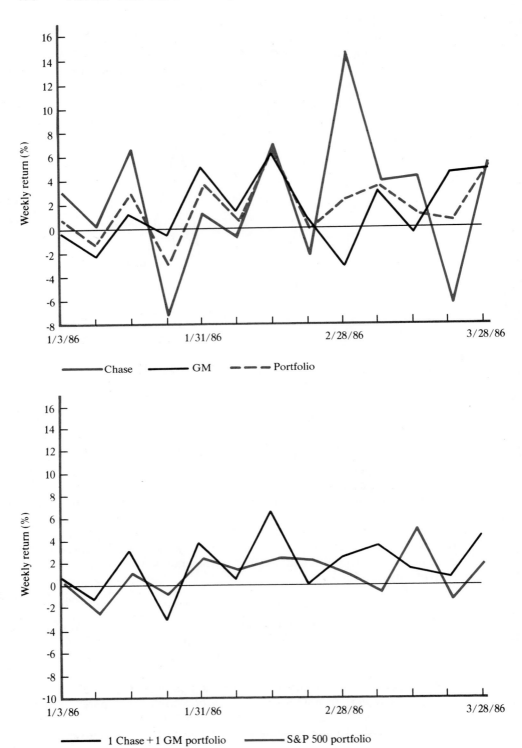

she had held the portfolio which makes up the S&P 500*. The weekly returns for the S&P 500 portfolio and for the 1 Chase + 1 GM portfolio are displayed on the facing page. Note that, by diversifying further, the volatility of returns has declined. The standard deviation of the S&P 500 returns was 1.84 percent as compared with 2.57 percent for the 1 Chase + 1 GM portfolio.

Finally, suppose that a new project (or asset or share) becomes available for inclusion in the investor's portfolio. This project is risky, but what risk is important? The investor can diversify away the unique risk of the project by combining it with the S&P 500 portfolio. Therefore the only risk that matters—and consequently the only risk used in the decision about whether or not to undertake the project—is its contribution to market risk.

---

*Standard & Poor's 500 Stock Index (the S&P 500) reflects the behavior of a portfolio of 500 important stocks. Rather than having a portfolio made up of one share of each (an equally weighted portfolio like the 1 Chase + 1 GM portfolio), each of the 500 stocks is weighted by the market value of the share.

Before going on, let's summarize the principles of portfolio theory.

Principle. Portfolio theory demonstrates that, as the investor combines more projects (or assets or securities) in a portfolio, the portfolio risk— the standard deviation of portfolio returns—declines.

Principle. The total risk—standard deviation of returns—of a project (or asset or security) can be decomposed into unique risk and market risk. Since portfolio theory indicates that unique risk can be eliminated by holding the project in a well-diversified portfolio, the only risk that matters is the project's market risk: specifically, the project's contribution to market risk.

The upshot of the preceding is that, for our project j, the only risk that will be priced by investors is the project's contribution to market risk. But, if we are going to implement this approach we need some *measure* of market risk. How do we obtain such a measure?

As it turns out, we have already shown you how to obtain such a measure. (We just didn't tell you at the time why we were doing it.) In Chapter 4, we looked at the *market model,*

$$r_j = \alpha + \beta r_m,$$

where r_j is the rate of return for project (or asset or security) j and r_m is the rate of return for the market portfolio. Looking at this equation in the light of the preceding discussion, the parameter β measures the market risk of project j.

A Reminder about Regression Coefficients

In the market model, the parameter β provides a measure of the relation between the return on project j and the return on the market portfolio,

$$\beta = \frac{\Delta r_j}{\Delta r_m}.$$

If $\beta = 1$, the variability of returns to project j is exactly equal to that of the market portfolio, so project j would contribute no additional risk when added to the market portfolio. If $\beta < 1$, the variability of the returns to project j is less than that for the market portfolio, so if project j is added to the existing market portfolio, portfolio risk will decline. If $\beta > 1$, the variability of the returns to project j is greater than that for the market portfolio, so portfolio risk will increase if project j is added to the market portfolio.

Principle. The market risk of a project (or asset or security) is measured by β in the market model,

$$r_j = \alpha + \beta r_m.$$

Using the estimate of β, project j is

$$
\left.
\begin{array}{l}
\textit{More risky than} \\
\textit{As risky as} \\
\textit{Less risky than}
\end{array}
\right\}
\textit{ the market portfolio if } \beta
\left\{
\begin{array}{l}
> 1 \\
= 1. \\
< 1
\end{array}
\right.
$$

To this point, we have seen that the relevant risk for a project is its contribution to market risk. And we have seen how we could measure market risk. But, we haven't yet seen how this is going to answer the question we started with: If the appropriate discount rate for project j in period t is

$$r_{j,t} = r_t + (\text{risk premium})_j,$$

how do we obtain a measure of the risk premium?

In the mid-1960s Jack Treynor, William Sharpe, and John Lintner provided an answer to this question with what has come to be called the capital asset pricing model (CAPM). They noted that two points are already known:

Point 1 Riskless Securities: $r_{j,t} = r_t$ **and** $\beta = 0$ By definition, the discount rate on riskless securities is the risk-free rate (r_t), and, since the return on securities like U.S. Treasury bills is fixed regardless of what happens to the market, $\Delta r_{\text{TREASURY BILLS}}/\Delta r_m = \beta = 0$.

Point 2 The Market Portfolio: $r_{m,t} = r_{m,t}$ **and** $\beta = 1$

These two points—the two benchmarks—are plotted in Figure 19.8.

The solution provided by the CAPM is both simple (after the fact) and elegant. Treynor, Sharpe, and Lintner proposed that the expected return, and therefore the risk premium, is a linear function of β. This linear relation is illustrated in Figure 19.9.

We know that the risk premium for a riskless security is zero,

$$r_t = r_t + 0,$$

and that the risk premium for the market portfolio is $r_{m,t} - r_t$,

$$r_{m,t} = r_t + (r_{m,t} - r_t);$$

so, the risk premium for project (or asset or security) j is proportional to its β,

$$r_{j,t} = r_t + \beta(r_{m,t} - r_t).$$

A project with a β of 0.5 will have a risk premium half as large as the risk premium on the market. A project with a β of 2 will have a risk premium twice as large as that for the market portfolio.

Figure 19.8 The Benchmarks: A Riskless Security and the Market Portfolio

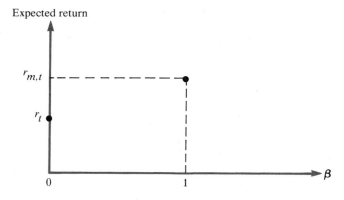

Figure 19.9 **Capital Asset Pricing Model**

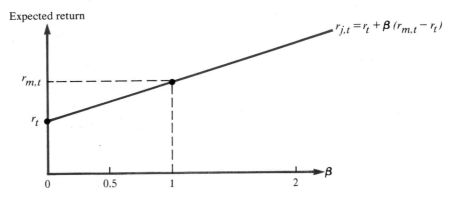

Principle. *The appropriate discount rate for project* j *in year* t *is the risk-free rate plus a risk premium:*

$$r_{j,t} = r_t + (\text{risk premium})_j.$$

Using the capital asset pricing model, the risk premium is proportional to the β from the market model. That is,

$$r_{j,t} = r_t + \beta (r_{m,t} - r_t),$$

where β is obtained from the market model,

$$r_{j,t} = \alpha + \beta r_{m,t}.$$

In order to implement the capital asset pricing model and to determine the appropriate discount rate, we need to know three values: r_t, β, and $(r_{m,t} - r_t)$. The risk-free rate, r_t, can be observed in the market. As we have seen, β can be estimated. The remaining value—the market risk premium, $(r_{m,t} - r_t)$—can also be estimated using historical data. For example, R. G. Ibbotson and R. A. Sinquefield looked at the market risk premium over the period 1926–1981 and found it to be 8.3 percent.

APPLICATION

Using the Capital Asset Pricing Model

In Chapter 4, we estimated the market model for Chase Manhattan Bank stock. The estimated equation was

$$r_{\text{CHASE}} = 0.00183 + 1.36926 r_{\text{MARKET}}.$$

Hence for Chase, $\beta = 1.369$.*

If we wish to determine the present value of future Chase cash flows, the discount rate is calculated using

$$r_{\text{CHASE},t} = r_t + 1.369(r_{m,t} - r_t).$$

If we use Ibbotson and Sinquefield's market risk premium (8.3 percent), Chase's risk premium is $(1.369)(8.3\%) = 11.36$ percent. Then, given the risk-free rates, we can calculate the appropriate discount rate for Chase Manhattan Bank cash flows. For example, suppose we wish to discount a \$10 million cash flow expected from Chase in three years. If the risk-free rate for a three-year maturity is 6.25 percent, the discount rate for Chase is $6.25\% + 11.36\% = 17.61\%$. Hence, the expected present value of the expected \$10 million in three years is

$$E(PV) = \frac{\$10,000,000}{(1.1761)^3} = \$6,147,057.$$

---

*Actually this β is Chase's *equity* β. In this application, we will treat this equity β as equal to the asset β. In fact, however, the calculation of the asset β would have to reflect the firm's debt-equity ratio:

$$\beta_{\text{ASSET}} = \beta_{\text{EQUITY}} \left(\frac{E}{D+E}\right) + \beta_{\text{DEBT}} \left(\frac{D}{D+E}\right).$$

If we presume the β for debt is zero, Chase's asset β becomes

$$\beta_{\text{CHASE ASSETS}} = 1.369\left(\frac{E}{D+E}\right).$$

Once the appropriate discount rate has been obtained, the expected present value of a project is obtained in the standard way.

APPLICATION

Valuing a Risky Project with the CAPM

The managers of Zeus Manufacturing also used the capital asset pricing model to evaluate the expected present value of the project described in the applications in this chapter. Using data from similar projects, the managers of Zeus estimated the market model for this project as

$$r_{j,t} = 2.35 + 0.88r_{m,t}.$$

From currently available market data, the managers estimated the market risk premium to be 9.3 percent. Hence, the risk premium for this project was $(0.88)(9.3) = 8.18\%$.

Given the current risk-free rates, the discount rates for the project were determined as

Years to Maturity	Riskless Rate (percent)	Risk Premium (percent)	Discount Rate (percent)
1	5.75	8.18	13.93
2	6.00	8.18	14.18
3	6.25	8.18	14.43
4	6.50	8.18	14.68
5	6.75	8.18	14.93

And, using these discount rates,

$$E(PV_j) = \frac{0}{(1.1393)^1} + \frac{2.8}{(1.1418)^2} + \frac{4.9}{(1.1443)^3} + \frac{4.9}{(1.1468)^4} + \frac{3.7}{1.1493)^5}$$
$$= 0 + 2.148 + 3.270 + 2.833 + 1.845$$
$$= 10.096.$$

That is, the expected present value of the project was $10,096,000.

19.4 SUMMARY

When confronted with uncertainty, the manager must consider a *probability distribution* relating outcomes (X_i) to their probability of occurrence (P_i). A measure of the central tendency of a probability distribution is the *expected value* (mean), which is the probability-weighted sum

$$E(X) = \sum_{i=1}^{n} X_i P_i.$$

The *variance* of the distribution reflects the dispersion around the mean and therefore provides a measure of risk: More compact distributions—distributions with smaller variances—are less risky. (An alternative measure is the *standard deviation,* the square root of the variance.)

A problem faced by all firms is the valuation of net cash flows generated by risky (in the sense of nonzero variance) projects/assets/securities. In this case the manager must consider the *expected present value* of the project,

$$E(PV_j) = \sum_{t=0}^{n} \frac{E(NCF_{j,t})}{(1 + r_{j,t})^t},$$

where $E(NCF_{j,t})$ is the *expected net cash flows* generated by this *j*th project in period *t* and $r_{j,t}$ is the *t* period discount rate which reflects the riskiness of project *j*.

The difficulty in evaluating the expected present value of a project is the determination of the *appropriate discount rate for a risky project.* Put another way, the problem is the determination of the *risk premium* for the *j*th project,

$$r_{j,t} = r_t + \text{(Risk premium)}_j.$$

We first considered two rules of thumb. With a *risk-adjusted discount rate,* some premium associated with the [total] variability in returns to the project is used. With the *weighted-average-cost-of-capital* approach, the firm's borrowing and equity costs are weighted by their relative shares to provide the discount rate for the firm,

$$r_{\text{WACC}} = r_D\left(\frac{D}{D+E}\right) + r_E\left(\frac{E}{D+E}\right).$$

The *capital asset pricing model* approach to the determination of the appropriate risk premium is based on *portfolio theory.* Portfolio theory demonstrates that (1) an investor can reduce risk by holding a well-diversified portfolio, and (2) the risk that matters is not total risk (total variability), but rather is the project's contribution to market risk. In the estimation of the *market model,*

$$r_j = \alpha + \beta r_m,$$

the parameter β measures the market risk of project (or asset or security) *j*:

$$\text{Project } j \text{ is } \begin{Bmatrix} \text{more risky than} \\ \text{as risky as} \\ \text{less risky than} \end{Bmatrix} \text{ the market portfolio as } \beta \begin{Bmatrix} > \\ = \\ < \end{Bmatrix} 1.$$

Using the estimate of β, the risk premium for project *j* is $\beta(r_{m,t} - r_t)$, where $r_{m,t} - r_t$ is the market risk premium. Hence, using the capital asset pricing model, the appropriate discount rate is

$$r_{j,t} = r_t + \beta(r_{m,t} - r_t).$$

TECHNICAL PROBLEMS

In Problems 1 and 2, consider two probability distributions for sales:

Sales (in 1,000 units)	Distribution 1 Probability (percent)	Distribution 2 Probability (percent)
50	10	10
60	20	15
70	40	20
80	20	30
90	10	25

1. Graph the two distributions. What are expected sales for the two probability distributions?
2. Calculate the variance and standard deviation for both of the distributions. Which distribution is more "risky?"
3. Look again at the application "Beau Apparel Again." Suppose that the probabilities had been reversed:

Outcome	Probability (percent)
Price = $15	60
Price = $20	40

Reevaluate the two options. What would the probabilities have to be to make the manager indifferent between the two options?

4. Look again at the application "A MiniMax Strategy." Demonstrate that option 2 has a larger standard deviation than option 1.

For Problems 5 through 8, consider a risky project being evaluated by Ajax Industries. The project will provide a single net cash flow in one year. The probability distribution for the net cash flow is

Net Cash Flow ($ million)	Probability (percent)
7.5	5
8.0	10
8.5	15
9.0	35
9.5	25
10.0	10

5. What is the expected net cash flow for this project?
6. From *The Wall Street Journal,* determine the appropriate risk-free interest rate. Using this rate as the discount rate, calculate an expected present value for the project. Is this expected present value "too high" or "too low" (or is it "just right")? Why?
7. By examining the current market price of its bonds, the managers know that the market value of Ajax's debt is $47 million and that Ajax's current borrowing rate is 8 percent. There are 1.7 million shares of Ajax currently selling for $43 per share. The expected return on Ajax's stock is 12 percent.

What is Ajax's weighted-average-cost-of-capital? Using this measure, what is the expected present value of the project?

8. The managers of Ajax used data from similar projects to estimate the market model for the project under consideration. The estimated equation was

$$r_{\text{NEW MACHINERY}} = 0.51 + 1.2r_{\text{MARKET}}.$$

They estimated the current market risk premium to be 8 percent.

Using the capital asset pricing model, what is the risk premium for this project? What is the appropriate discount rate? What is the expected present value of the project?

9. Why does diversification of the portfolio reduce the risk faced by an individual investor?

If diversification is good for the investor, isn't it also good for the firm? Put another way, does portfolio theory provide a rational motive for firms to diversify?

ANALYTICAL PROBLEMS

1. A project which has a large variance (standard deviation) in returns is said to be a "risky" project. In what sense is it risky? What kinds of risk are not captured by this definition of risk?

2. Using the strategy known as MiniMax, the manager "makes the best out of the worst possible outcome." Criticize this strategy.

3. Suppose that a firm used a single discount rate—the firm's cost of capital—to discount all projects. What error is the firm making?

4. "A portfolio manager needs to pick 'winners'—stocks or assets or securities that have high expected returns and low variances."
   What is wrong with this statement?

5. There could exist projects for which the weighted-average-cost-of-capital approach and the capital asset pricing model approach are equivalent. What kind of projects are these?

6. The managers of Lone Star Enterprises decided to use the capital asset pricing model to evaluate a new venture. To this end, they
   a. Obtained risk-free rates from the current market prices of U.S. Treasury securities.
   b. Estimated the market model using the rate of return on shares of Lone Star Enterprises.
   c. Obtained an estimate of the current market risk premium.
   d. Estimated the risk premium on this new venture by multiplying the current market risk premium by the β obtained in (b).
   e. Added the resulting risk premium to the risk-free rates to obtain discount rates for the new venture.
   Critique Lone Star's managers.

7. The core of the capital asset pricing model is the β estimate. What then is one of the primary criticisms of the CAPM?

   (After answering this question, you might like to see what the experts have to say. Richard Brealey and Stewart Myers suggest "Risk-Return Classes of New York Stock Exchange Common Stocks, 1931–1967" by W. F. Sharpe and G. M. Cooper in *Financial Analysts Journal* [March-April 1972].)

8. *For Discussion Only.* A survey made in 1976 indicated that less than 5 percent of the firms surveyed used the CAPM. By 1982, survey results indicated that this percentage had risen, but only to 20 percent.

   Why do you think that firms have been unwilling to adopt this analytical methodology?

SUGGESTED ADDITIONAL REFERENCES

A comprehensive overview of the topics covered in this chapter can be found in:

Brealey, Richard, and Stewart Myers. *Principles of Corporate Finance.* New York: McGraw-Hill, 1984.

The formulae for calculating risk-adjusted discounted rates are contained in the Brealey & Myers text noted above and in more detail in:

Miles, J., and R. Ezzell. "The Weighted Average Cost of Capital, Perfect Capital Markets and Project Life: A Clarification." *Journal of Financial and Quantitative Analysis,* September 1980, pp. 719–30.

Miller, M. H., and F. Modigliani. "Some Estimates of the Cost of Capital to the Electric Utility Industry: 1954–1957." *American Economic Review,* June 1966, pp. 333–91.

Modigliani, F., and M. H. Miller. "Corporate Income Taxes and the Cost of Capital: A Correction." *American Economic Review,* June 1963, pp. 433–43.

A concise discussion of some alternative discount rates for risky projects—including the risk-free rate, the borrowing rate, the weighted-average-cost-of-capital, and the capital asset pricing model—appears in:

Bierman, Harold, Jr. *Implementation of Capital Budgeting Techniques—Survey & Synthesis.* New York: Financial Management Association, 1986.

The original work in portfolio theory was:

Markowitz, H. M. "Portfolio Selection." *Journal of Finance,* March 1952.

The capital asset pricing model is also referred to as the Sharpe-Lintner-Treynor model. Treynor never published his analysis. The other two are:

Lintner, J. "The Valuation of Risk Assets and the Selection of Risky Investments in Stock Portfolios and Capital Budgets." *Review of Economics and Statistics,* February 1965.

Sharpe, W. F. "Capital Asset Prices: A Theory of Market Equilibrium under Conditions of Risk." *Journal of Finance,* September 1964.

20

THE INVESTMENT DECISION

I n the last two chapters we looked at profit maximization over time and under uncertainty. Given this background, we are now ready to look at the firm's investment decision, an application of profit maximization over time and under uncertainty.

Earlier in this text we looked at the questions the manager of the firm must answer in making production decisions:

How much output do I produce?

What price do I charge?

What level of input usage is optimal?

We now look at the final question the manager must answer, the investment decision:

What investment projects will I undertake?

We begin by looking at the net present value rule in the context of the investment decision. We then turn to a description and critique of some of the alternative investment criteria—payback, return to investment, and internal rate of return. Finally, we consider the case in which the manager's investment decision is affected by an expenditure constraint—the capital rationing problem.

20.1 THE NET PRESENT VALUE RULE FOR INVESTMENT

In Chapter 18, we provided the basics for the investment decision when we developed the net present value of a project or asset and the net present value rule: Accept projects that have a positive net present value and reject projects that have a negative net present value.

In Chapter 19, we incorporated uncertainty and considered the expected present value of a project. Extending this argument, we can define the expected net present value of investment project j as[1]

$$E(NPV_j) = E(PV_j) - (\text{Cost of investment project } j)$$

$$= \sum_{t=0}^{T} \frac{E(NCF_{j,t})}{(1 + r_{j,t})^t} - C_0.$$

Hence the decision rule for investment projects is to accept those for which the expected net present value is positive and reject those for which the expected net present value is negative,

$$E(NPV_j) > 0 \ . \ . \ . \ \text{Accept}$$
$$E(NPV_j) < 0 \ . \ . \ . \ \text{Reject}$$

Implementation of the rule is straightforward, involving the techniques we have described in this text:

1. Forecast demand to obtain estimates of expected revenues from the project, $E(R_{j,t})$.
2. Forecast (estimate) costs to provide estimates of the expected future costs associated with the project, $E(C_{j,t})$.
3. Combine the expected revenues and costs to obtain estimates of expected net cash flows for the project, $E(NCF_{j,t}) = E(R_{j,t}) - E(C_{j,t})$.
4. Determine the appropriate discount rate, $r_{j,t}$.
5. Discount the expected net cash flows to obtain the expected present value of the project.
6. Subtract the current cost of the project to obtain expected net present value.

To see how this might be accomplished, let's look at a simple example.

---

[1]We continue to consider a simple investment project for which the only outlay for the project occurs in the current period (C_0). However, it would not be difficult to generalize this expression to incorporate an investment project that requires outlays in future periods as well as the current period.

APPLICATION

An Investment Decision Using the Expected Net Present Value Rule

Nathan Matthew is the CEO of Travell Enterprises, a firm operating in an extremely competitive market. He is considering acquiring a new production facility for a purchase price of $5.3 million. The facility is essentially the same as Travell's existing plants. Matthew expects to use the production facility for five years and then resell it.

Matthew turned for advice to Cynthia Thomas, his chief of staff. She provided him with the following information and recommendation.

1. Expected Revenues from the Project

The economics staff of Travell had previously prepared forecasts for the price of Travell's product for the next five years. They summarized the probability distribution of future prices with three price forecasts: high, moderate, and low with probabilities 30 percent, 50 percent, and 20 percent, respectively. This price forecast is as follows:

| | Price Forecast | | |
Year	High	Moderate	Low
1	$20	$15	$ 7
2	20	15	10
3	24	20	10
4	24	20	15
5	24	20	15
Probabilities	30%	50%	20%

Using the estimated cost function for Travell's production facility (see #2 below), the economics staff was able to determine the optimal output for the new plant for each of the price forecasts. Then, multiplying price by quantity, they obtained a distribution of revenues for each year. Finally, using the probabilities for each of the prices, they were able to provide a measure of expected revenue for each year. These data are presented below.

Thomas also asked the economics staff for a forecast of the resale value of the plant at the end of the fifth year. The forecast provided was $3.5 million.

Year	Optimal Output (100,000 units)			Revenue ($ million per year)			Expected Revenue ($ million per year)
	High P	Mod. P	Low P	High P	Mod. P	Low P	
1	8	7.1	0	$16	$10.7	0	$10.2
2	8	7.1	0	16	10.7	0	10.2
3	8.6	8	0	20.6	16	0	14.2
4	8.6	8	7.1	20.6	16	$10.7	16.3
5	8.6	8	7.1	20.6	16	10.7	16.3

2. Expected Costs of the Project

Since the proposed acquisition is essentially identical to Travell's existing plants, the costs of operating the prospective facility could be obtained using data for Travell's existing facilities. The average variable cost function for one of Travell's plants has been estimated as

$$AVC = 20 - 3Q + 0.25Q^2,$$

where output Q is measured in 100,000 units per year. The annual fixed cost of operating the plant is $3.5 million. Using these estimates in conjunction with the output levels presented above, the economics staff provided a probability distribution for annual costs, for example, if the price in year 1 is $20, the optimal output is 800,000 units and the total variable cost per year is

$$\begin{aligned} TVC = AVC \times Q &= [20 - 3(8) + 0.25(8)^2] \times 800,000 \\ &= \$12.00 \times 800,000 \\ &= \$9,600,000. \end{aligned}$$

Rounding to the nearest $100,000, total variable cost is $9.6 million. Annual fixed cost for the next five years is expected to remain at $3.5 million. Hence, the total cost corresponding to a price of $20 in year 1 is $13.1 million. The cost estimates for the other output levels are provided below.

Year	Costs ($ million per year)			Expected Cost ($ million per year)
	High P	Mod. P	Low P	
1	$13.1	$11.5	$ 3.5	$10.4
2	13.1	11.5	3.5	10.4
3	14.4	13.1	3.5	11.6
4	14.4	13.1	11.5	13.2
5	14.4	13.1	11.5	13.2

Then, weighting the cost estimates by their respective probabilities, the expected cost for each year was determined. These expected cost data are provided in the right-hand column of the preceding table.

3. Expected Net Cash Flows

Combining expected revenues, the expected resale value of the plant, and the expected costs of operating the plant, Thomas obtained expected net cash flows from the project as follows:

Year	Expected Revenues*	Expected Resale Value*	Expected Cost*	Expected Net Cash Flows*
1	$10.2	—	$10.4	$ −0.2
2	10.2	—	10.4	−0.2
3	14.2	—	11.6	2.6
4	16.3	—	13.2	3.1
5	16.3	$3.5	13.2	6.6

*In million dollars per year.

4. The Appropriate Discount Rate

Thomas asked the finance director for the appropriate discount rate for each of the five net cash flows from the prospective plant. The finance director said that, since the investment project would look just like the existing firm, the appropriate risk premium for the new factory and therefore the appropriate discount rates, would be the same one as for Travell Enterprises itself.

Travell is currently using the capital asset pricing model (CAPM) to provide the discount rates it requires in making financing decisions. The estimate of the market model, using returns on shares of Travell stock, is

$$r_{TRAVELL} = 0.023 + 0.82\ r_{MARKET}.$$

So Travell's beta is 0.82.† The finance group is currrently using 9% as the market risk premium ($r_{m,t} - r_t$). Hence, the risk premium for Travell, and therefore the risk premium for this potential acquisition, is (0.82) (9%) = 7.38%. Therefore, the appropriate discount rates are obtained simply by adding this risk premium to the prevailing risk-free rate (i.e., the interest rate for U.S. government securities). These data are presented on the next page.

†As before, we will treat this equity beta as the beta for the firm's assets.

Year	Risk-Free Rate (percent)	Risk Premium (percent)	Discount Rate (percent)
1	5.75	7.38	13.13
2	6.00	7.38	13.38
3	6.25	7.38	13.63
4	6.50	7.38	13.88
5	6.75	7.38	14.13

5. Expected Present Value

Discounting each of the expected net cash flows by the appropriate discount rate and summing, Thomas obtained the expected present value of the new plant:

Year	Expected Net Cash Flow ($ million per year)	Discount Rate (percent)	Expected Present Value ($ million per year)
1	$-0.2	13.13	$-0.18
2	-0.2	13.38	-0.16
3	2.6	13.63	1.77
4	3.1	13.88	1.84
5	6.6	14.13	3.41
		Total	$ 6.68

6. Expected Net Present Value

Subtracting the cost of the project, $5.3 million, from the expected present value of the project, $6.68 million, the expected net present value of the plant is $1.38 million.

Recommendation

Since the expected net present value of the project is positive, the project should be undertaken.

As should be obvious, the discount rate plays a central role in the determination of the expected net present value and therefore in the investment decision. The expected present value equation indicates (and Problem 1 at end of chapter will reinforce) the inverse relation between the expected net present value and the discount rate: As the discount rate rises (falls), the expected net present value of the project will fall (rise).

For example, consider a one-year investment project which currently costs $100,000 and will generate an expected net cash flow of $108,000 at the end of one year. With a discount rate of 7 percent, the expected net present value of this project is $935. If the discount rate falls to 6 percent, the expected net present value of the project rises to $1,887. If the discount rate rises to 8 percent, the expected net present value of the project falls to zero. And, if the discount rate rises further to 9 percent, the net present value of the project becomes negative, -$917. This relation between the value of the project and the discount rate—sometimes referred to as the net present value profile—is illustrated in Figure 20.1. The firm should undertake an investment project as long as its expected net present value is positive. In the context of the example, the firm will undertake this project as long as the discount rate is less than 8 percent.

20.2 ALTERNATIVES TO THE NET PRESENT VALUE RULE

Although an economist would argue that the net present value rule is the "correct" investment criterion, it is not the only criterion available to managers. Three of those most widely cited are: payback, return on

Figure 20.1 **A Net Present Value Profile**

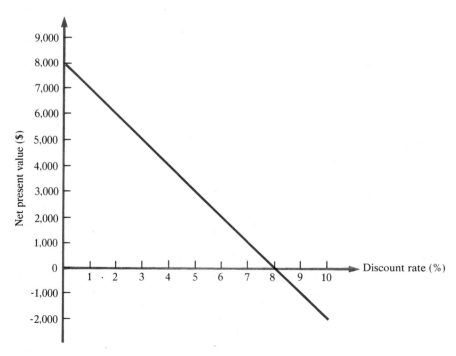

investment, and internal rate of return. Let's take a moment to look at these alternative criteria to see how they compare to the net present value rule.

Payback   The payback period for an investment project is the time required for the firm to recover its initial investment. For example, if a project costs $1 million and it is expected to return $250,000 per year, the payback period is four years; if expected returns are $500,000 per year, the payback period is two years.

Using the payback criterion, the payback period for the investment project is calculated and compared to some maximum payback period set by the firm. If the project's payback period is less than this maximum, the project is accepted.

APPLICATION

The Payback Rule

Matthew, the CEO of Travell Enterprises has set the maximum payback period for investment projects as three years. He asked Thomas for the payback period for the prospective production facility. She calculated the cumulative expected net cash flows from the project:

Year	Expected Net Cash Flow*	Cumulative Expected Net Cash Flow*
1	$ − 0.2	$ − 0.2
2	− 0.2	− 0.4
3	2.6	2.2
4	3.1	5.3
5	6.6	11.9

*In $ million.

The cumulative expected net cash flows equal (or exceed) the cost of the investment ($5.3 million) at the end of the fourth year. Hence, the payback period for this project is four years. And, since the payback period is longer than the maximum set by the firm, the project would be judged unacceptable using this criterion.

As the preceding example makes clear, the major problem with the payback criterion is that it can lead to the rejection of positive net present value projects—projects that will increase the value of the firm. Conversely, this rule could lead to accepting negative net present value projects. (This point will be reinforced by Technical Problem 3.)

As should be clear from our discussion to this point, the reason the payback rule can lead to this value reducing situation is that the cash flows are not discounted. Hence, the payback criterion gives too much weight to near returns and too little weight to distant returns: with the payback rule, net cash flows received after the maximum payback period have no value. This criterion ignores the time value of money and the time pattern of the cash flows generated by the investment project.

Interestingly Harold Bierman noted from his survey results that many users of the payback criterion think of the payback period as a measure of "risk." However, as Bierman correctly pointed out, gambling at the tables in Las Vegas may have a shorter payback period than purchasing a U.S. government security, but that doesn't mean the crap tables in Las Vegas are less risky than T-bills.

Return on Investment (ROI)   The average return on an investment project is defined as average returns from the investment divided by the average investment in the project. Then, using the ROI criterion, the decision whether or not to invest in the project is made by comparing the ROI for the project with the firm's target return.

APPLICATION

Investment Decisions Using the ROI Rule

Nathan Matthew has announced that Travell Enterprises requires a rate of return on investment of 60 percent. He asked his chief of staff, Cynthia Thomas, to look at the prospective investment again with this criterion in mind. From previous calculations, she knew that cumulative net cash flows from the project amounted to $11.9 million for the five years of the project's lifetime. Hence, the average net cash flow was $11.9/5 = $2.38 million. Dividing this average income by the average amount the firm has invested in the project over the five years, $5.3 million, the average return on the investment (ROI) is

$$2.38/5.3 = 45\%.$$

Since this ROI is less than the firm's target return of 60 percent, the project would be rejected using the rate of return on investment as the criterion.

As in the case of payback, the ROI criterion could result in positive net present value projects not being undertaken. And, also like the payback criterion, the problem with the return on investment criterion is that the cash flows are not discounted. However, unlike the payback criterion which gives *too little* weight to distant cash flows, the ROI criterion gives distant cash flows *too much* weight. With the ROI criterion, distant cash flows are treated as equivalent to current cash flows.

Internal Rate of Return   To understand the concept of the internal rate of return, let's consider again the single-period investment project we discussed earlier and illustrated in Figure 20.1:

Cost of investment	$100,000
Net cash flow at end of year 1	$108,000

The rate of return on this investment project is 8 percent,

$$\frac{108,000 - 100,000}{100,000} = 0.08 = 8\%.$$

Hence, for this single-period investment project, a criterion which is equivalent to the net present value rule is: accept the project if the discount rate for the project is less than 8 percent; reject the project if the discount rate is more than 8 percent.

Indeed, for any single-period investment project, we could implement the *NPV* rule by comparing the project's rate of return with its discount rate:

Rate of return > Discount rate→*NPV* > 0 → Accept project
Rate of return < Discount rate→*NPV* < 0 → Reject project.

From this, it follows that the rate of return on the project is the discount rate that makes the net present value of the project equal to zero:

NPV = 0 → Rate of return = Discount rate.

With investment projects having longer lifetimes (multiple-period projects), the rate of return becomes much more difficult to determine. Nonetheless, the definition of the internal rate of return (*IRR*) is simply a generalization of the preceding relation:

Definition.   The internal rate of return for an investment project is the discount rate that makes the net present value of.the project equal to zero.

Finding the IRR is not an easy arithmetic problem, since it involves solving for the discount rate at which the *NPV* of the project is zero. Operationally, that means that the equation

$$NPV = \sum_{t=1}^{T} \frac{NCF_t}{(1 + IRR)^t} - C_0 = 0$$

is solved for *IRR*. (Given (1) the complexity of this solution and (2) the wide acceptance of the *IRR* criterion, it is probably not surprising that most business calculators are pre-programmed to calculate this value.)

From the discussion of the single-period investment project, it should be clear that the investment criterion associated with the internal rate of return is to accept the project if the cost of capital to the firm is less than the *IRR* and reject the project if the cost of capital to the firm exceeds the *IRR*:

*Principle. **The internal rate of return (IRR) investment criterion is to accept projects if their** IRR **exceeds the firm's opportunity cost of capital.***

The *IRR* criterion can be illustrated graphically by looking again at the net present value profile for an investment project. A generalized profile is presented in Figure 20.2. As long as the internal rate of return exceeds the discount rate—the opportunity cost of capital—the NPV of the project

Figure 20.2 **A Generalized Net Present Value Profile**

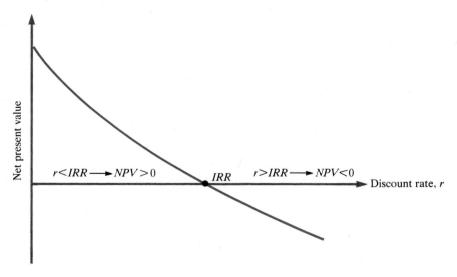

Part Six Time and Uncertainty

is positive and the project should be undertaken. However, if the *IRR* is less than the discount rate, the *NPV* of the project will be negative and the project should be rejected.

APPLICATION

Using the Internal Rate of Return as an Investment Criterion

After extensive consultations with the CFO, Matthew has determined that the cost to Travell of raising additional capital is 13.5 percent. That is, to raise money to finance investment projects, Travell will have to pay 13.5 percent annually. He asked Cynthia Thomas to reevaluate the proposed acquisition of the facility by looking at the project's rate of return relative to Travell's opportunity cost of capital.

To do so, Thomas calculated the internal rate of return for the project. That is, she found the single discount rate (the *IRR*) that would make the *NPV* of the project equal to zero by solving the following for the *IRR*:

$$NPV = \frac{-0.2}{(1 + IRR)} + \frac{-0.2}{(1 + IRR)^2} + \frac{2.6}{(1 + IRR)^3}$$
$$+ \frac{3.1}{(1 + IRR)^4} + \frac{6.6}{(1 + IRR)^5} - 6.5 = 0.$$

The resulting value for the *IRR* was 20.2 percent.

Hence, since the *IRR* for the project exceeded the firm's opportunity cost of capital, the project should be undertaken. On the basis of the IRR criterion, Thomas recommended going forward with the acquisition.

Note that, in contrast to the payback and return on investment criteria, the *IRR* criterion led to acceptance of our hypothetical investment project. In the context of our simple example it looks like the *IRR* criterion and the *NPV* criterion are equivalent rules. And they are: as long as the *NPV* of the project declines smoothly as the discount rate rises—as is illustrated in Figure 20.2—the two criteria are functionally equivalent (for evaluating single projects).

Thus, as long as the relation between *NPV* and the discount rate is smooth and negative, the *NPV* rule and the *IRR* rule will give the same results. However, there are times when the *IRR* rule does not work.

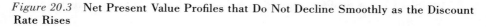

Figure 20.3 Net Present Value Profiles that Do Not Decline Smoothly as the Discount Rate Rises

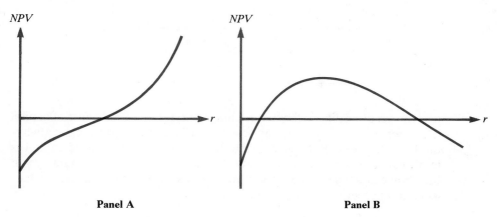

Panel A   Panel B

Clearly, if the net present value profile does not look like that in Figure 20.2, the *IRR* rule and *NPV* rule will no longer be equivalent. Most investment projects are like lending money: an original outflow is made in return for a stream of inflows thereby generating down-sloping net present value profiles like that in Figure 20.2. However, this need not always be the case; it is not always necessary that the largest expenditures on the project occur in the initial period. It could be that the inflows occur earlier than the outflows—the investment project could look more like borrowing than lending. In this case the net present value profile would look like that illustrated in Panel A of Figure 20.3. Or, it could be the case that the investment project will require net cash outflows both initially and in some subsequent period; for example, the project may require a retrofit at some date in the future. In this case, the net present value profile will look like that illustrated in Panel B of Figure 20.3. In either case, the IRR criterion is no longer equivalent to the *NPV* criterion.

Another case in which the *IRR* and *NPV* rules do not necessarily provide the same recommendation is when the decision concerns mutually exclusive projects. Consider a firm deciding whether to replace or refit a machine—decisions that are clearly mutually exclusive. Suppose the net cash flows from these two projects are as presented below:

	Refit	Replace
Current Cost	$100,000	$250,000
Net cash flow, year 1	75,000	125,000
Net cash flow, year 2	50,000	175,000

Which of these projects should be selected? Looking at the internal rates of return,

	Refit	Replace
IRR	17.5%	12.3%

it seems as if refitting is the better choice. And, if the firm's cost of capital is greater than 12.3 percent but less than 17.5 percent, refitting is always the best decision. But, what if the firm's opportunity cost of capital is less than 12.3 percent? Is the refit always the best choice? What about the choice at a 9 percent discount rate? Looking at the net present values using a 9 percent discount rate,

	Refit	Replace
NPV (r = 9%)	$10,900	$12,000

the choice is reversed; the better choice is now to replace the machine.

The reason for the inconsistency is provided in Figure 20.4. For discount rates in excess of 9.45 percent, the *IRR* criterion and the *NPV* criterion will be consistent. That is, with the discount rate in excess of 9.45 percent, the project with the higher *IRR* will have the higher *NPV*. However, for discount rates below 9.45 percent, the *IRR* is no longer a useful criterion. With a discount rate less than 9.45 percent, the project with the higher *IRR* has the lower *NPV*. And, with these lower discount rates, the *IRR* criterion would lead us to select the project with the lower, not higher, *NPV*.

Finally, you may have noted a methodological difference. When we worked with the net present value, we used different discount rates for different periods; payments received early were discounted at a different rate than those received late. The internal rate of return approach does not permit that differentiation. With the *IRR* approach, there is a single discount rate—payments received early are discounted using the same discount rate as those received late.

20.3 CAPITAL RATIONING

In the broadest perspective, capital rationing by the manager of a firm should not occur; there is no *external* constraint on the number of projects a firm can undertake. If the firm has available a project that will increase the value of the firm, the project should be undertaken. The capital con-

Figure 20.4 Net Present Value Profiles for Mutually Exclusive Projects

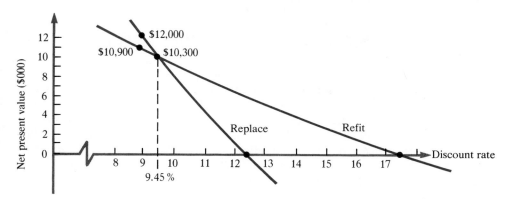

straint (the limit of available monies to finance the project) can always be eliminated by going to the credit market. If going to the credit market means that the firm will have to pay a higher and higher price for its capital (if the opportunity cost of capital is rising), the net present value of the project will decline. Indeed, if the opportunity cost of capital rises, some projects will no longer have a positive net present value. But in this case we are simply looking at the investment decision, not capital rationing.

From a more pragmatic perspective, most firms ration capital; most firms are subject to a constraint on the number of investment projects they can undertake. However, it is important to recognize that the constraint is, by and large, a *self-imposed constraint*. For some reason, the managers must believe that they will be unable to fund all of the investment projects available. And, if this is the case, they need some way to determine which projects to undertake.

When confronted by this constraint, many managers first think of the internal rate of return as a means of ranking the competing projects. We hope we have been able to convince you of the problems involved in using the *IRR* to choose among competing projects.

Then why not just rank projects according to their net present values? Suppose the firm had available the three projects ranked below by their net present values:

Project	NPV ($ million)	Rank
A	$10	1
B	7	2
C	5	3

Project A has the highest *NPV*. But, if the combination of Projects A and B costs less than A alone, it would be preferable to invest in the combination, since investing in both B and C would give a higher total *NPV* than would A alone. It is not sufficient to think simply about the project's net present value, rather we should think about the *NPV* per dollar spent on the project.

And this shouldn't be at all surprising. What we have here is a constrained optimization problem: the manager wants to maximize the value of the firm subject to the capital limitation. In Chapter 3, when we provided the basics of optimization, we noted that the rule for constrained optimization was to allocate such that the marginal benefit (the *NPV*) per dollar spent is equal among the competing activities. Hence, the most straightforward approach to the problem is to determine a *profitability index*—the ratio of the present value of the investment project to its cost. Presented below are data for the three projects introduced above.

Project	NPV ($ million)	Cost ($ million)	Present Value ($ million)	Profitability Index
A	$10	$5	$15	3.0
B	7	3	10	3.3
C	5	3	8	2.7

Given the values of the profitability index, the firm will allocate the first $3 million to Project B, since it has the largest ratio of marginal benefits to cost. The second project to be undertaken will be Project A. Project C will be undertaken only if the capital constraint is lifted.

The profitability index is, however, not without its own limitations. This approach fails if there is more than one constraint; for example, if the capital constraint is imposed in more than one period. It is also unreliable when the projects are mutually exclusive or when one project is dependent on another being undertaken. For such cases, more complicated techniques, including a linear programming approach, have been developed. (For these techniques the interested reader should see the references at the end of this chapter.)

20.4 SUMMARY

If the manager is maximizing the value of the firm, the investment criterion is simply the expected net present value rule.

The expected net present value rule for investment:
   If E(NPV) > 0, Accept the project.
   If E(NPV) < 0, Reject the project.

To implement the expected net present value rule, the manager will have to (1) forecast revenues, (2) forecast [estimate] operating costs for the project, and (3) determine the appropriate discount rate for the project. Particular emphasis was placed on the relation between expected net present value and the discount rate, a relation depicted graphically by the expected net present value profile.

While the expected net present value rule is the theoretically and analytically correct investment criterion, other rules continue to be used. Two rules of thumb were considered.

The Payback Rule.   The payback period is the time required for the firm to recover its initial investment. The investment criterion is to accept only those projects that have a payback period less than some arbitrary maximum set by the firm.

The Return on Investment (ROI) Rule.   The average return on investment is the ratio of average net cash flows to average investment. If the ROI *for the project is larger than the firm's arbitrary target return, the investment project will be undertaken.*

The primary shortcoming with these two ad hoc rules is that the net cash flows are not discounted; these rules ignore the time value of money. The payback rule gives too much weight to cash flows that will be received early; the *ROI* rule gives too much weight to distant cash flows. A more acceptable alternative investment criterion is the internal rate of return rule.

The Internal Rate of Return (IRR) Rule.   The IRR *is the discount rate that makes the* NPV *of the investment project equal to zero. The project should be accepted if the* IRR *is greater than the firm's opportunity cost of capital.*

As long as the expected net present value profile is a smooth, downward-sloping function, the *IRR* and expected *NPV* rules are functionally equivalent. However, the *IRR* rule can provide erroneous recommendations when mutually exclusive projects are considered. And, the *IRR* methodology requires that all net cash flows are discounted by the same rate—early and late cash flows are discounted using the same discount rate.

The constraint of limited funding for investment projects and the resulting capital rationing problem are, by and large, self-imposed by the management of the firm. Nonetheless, this is yet another constrained optimization problem: the solution must involve the ratio of marginal benefits to marginal costs (dollar expenditures). In this case,

The Profitability Index is the ratio of the present value of the investment project (the marginal benefit from undertaking the project) to its cost.

In order to maximize the value of the firm, managers will respond to the capital rationing problem by undertaking investment projects in the order of their profitability indexes.

TECHNICAL PROBLEMS

1. Nathan Matthew, the CEO of Travell Enterprises, wants some additional information to help him make his investment decision: "How sensitive is the expected net present value to changes in the risk-free rate? What will be the expected net present value if rates rise or fall?"

   To answer his question, reevaluate the investment decision using the two alternate schedules of risk-free interest rates provided below.

	Risk-Free Interest Rates	
Years to Maturity	Higher Rates	Lower Rates
1	7.00	4.50
2	7.25	4.75
3	7.50	5.00
4	7.75	5.25
5	8.00	5.50

2. Matthew wanted to see the expected net present value profile for the prospective facility discussed in this chapter. [Remember that this profile is drawn presuming a single discount rate for all of the net cash flows rather than a schedule (a term structure).]

   a. Calculate the expected net present value of the project for discount rates of 13.5 percent, 15.5 percent, 17.5 percent, and 19.5 percent.

   b. Sketch the expected net present value profile.

3. Your supervisor has asked you to evaluate two potential investment projects. Both of these projects cost $2 million. The net cash flows from the two projects are presented below. The firm's policy is that the maximum payback period for an investment project is two years. Evaluate the two projects using that criterion.

   Evaluate the two projects using the expected NPV criterion with a discount rate of 10 percent. Compare the two recommendations. What report would you make to your supervisor?

Year	Net Cash Flows ($ million)	
	Project A	Project B
1	2	1.0
2	0	0.8
3	0	0.6
4	0	0.4

4. Your firm has a target rate of return on investment of 35 percent. Using this criterion, you have been asked to evaluate two investment projects, both of which cost $20.5 million and have four-year lifetimes. The net cash flows from the two projects are provided below.

Year	Net Cash Flows ($ million)	
	Project A	Project B
1	$10	$ 4
2	8	6
3	6	9
4	4	11

Which, if either, of the two projects would be accepted using the ROI criterion?

Reevaluate the two projects using the expected *NPV* criterion and a discount rate of 15 percent. Compare the two recommendations. What report would you forward on these two projects?

5. Consider an investment project costing $162,500 that is expected to generate net cash flows of $100,000 in years 1 and 2.

  a. Calculate the expected *NPV* for this project using discount rates of 10 percent, 15 percent, and 20 percent.

  b. Sketch the expected *NPV* profile for this project.

  c. What is the *IRR* for this project?

6. Look again at the expected net present value profile you drew for Travell Enterprises' investment project (Problem 2). From this graph, what is the *IRR* for this project? How does this compare with the value calculated by Thomas?

For Problems 7 through 10, use the following data:

  Argonaut Enterprises had available four potential investment projects that would all begin in 1988. The characteristics of these projects are summarized in the table on the next page.

Project:	A	B	C	D
Cost:	$123,000	$89,200	$56,600	$55,800
Net cash flow*:				
1988	30,000	50,000	20,000	40,000
1989	30,000	50,000	20,000	20,000
1990	30,000	0	20,000	10,000
1991	30,000	0	20,000	0
Scrap or resale value at end of 1991:	50,000	0	10,000	0

*At year-end.

7. Evaluate these projects using the expected NPV criterion and a discount rate of 15 percent.

8. The expected NPV evaluation did not "sit very well" with the vice president for operations, for whom Project A was a particular favorite. He argued that the discount rate used in the calculation of the net present values was too high. In response, the board of directors asked to see the internal rates of return for each of the projects. Provide these values and an evaluation based on these values.

9. The vice president for operations came back to the board of directors with another argument: He believes that the resale value for Project A was underestimated and that the resale value should be $70,000 rather than $50,000. If this is true, should this project be undertaken, using 15 percent as the relevant discount rate? Use the net present value of the project to support your answer.

10. It turns out that Project B also has a supporter. The director of new-product development argues that the capital outlay necessary for Project B is $86,800 rather than $89,200. If this is true, what would be the internal rate of return for Project B? Would this project be undertaken, using 15 percent as the relevant opportunity cost of capital?

11. Your firm has to choose between repairing the existing plant or replacing it. If repaired at a cost of $2.5 million, the plant will be able to operate for two more years, generating expected net cash flows in each year of $1.5 million. If replaced at a cost of $9.5 million, the expected net cash flows for each of the next five years are $2.5 million.

    a. Calculate the expected net present values of each of these alternatives, using discount rates of 8 percent, 10 percent, 12 percent, and 14 percent.

    b. Sketch the expected net present value profiles.

    c. Determine the IRR for each of the alternatives.

    d. Over what range of discount rates would the expected *NPV* and the *IRR* provide consistent recommendations? Over what range of discount rates would the recommendations be inconsistent?

    e. At what discount rate would the firm be indifferent between the two alternatives?

12. Your firm has available four investment projects, the costs and expected net present values of which are presented below.

Project	Expected NPV	Cost
A	20	10
B	17	10
C	12	5
D	8	5

    a. Calculate the profitability index for each of the projects.

    b. Which projects will be undertaken if the firm has an expenditure (funding) constraint of 5? 10? 15? 20?

ANALYTICAL PROBLEMS

1. In general, when would the *IRR* and expected *NPV* investment criteria give conflicting recommendations?

2. Explain why "the payback rule gives too little weight to distant net cash flows and the ROI rule gives them too much weight."

3. If the payback period doesn't measure risk, what does?

4. "The capital rationing problem is, by and large, self-imposed." Explain why this is so. What could the management of a firm do to eliminate the constraint? Why do so many firms ration capital?

5. The tools we have developed for the investment decision can also be used in the firm's inventory decision. Why is this so? How would a firm go about deciding on the optimal inventory level?

6. The fact that you are attending a college or university indicates that you have made an investment decision. What kind of investment decision is this? What factors did you (at least implicitly) evaluate when making this decision? In what way would the decision to go to graduate school differ?

7. In this chapter we concentrated on investment projects, implicitly talking about investments in plant and equipment. However, the same techniques could be used to evaluate other investment projects, including new products.

Down-Home Eatin' is considering the introduction of Diet Grits. The proposal is to test market the new product for one year in two regions—Macon, Georgia, and northwest Bergen County, New Jersey. If the test markets are successful, the product will be introduced nationwide.

How would the investment decision be structured? What data are required to make the decision? How would the necessary data be obtained?

SUGGESTED ADDITIONAL REFERENCES

For a general discussion of the investment decision, see:

Bierman, Harold, Jr. *Implementation of Capital Budgeting Techniques,* Financial Management Survey and Synthesis Series. New York: Financial Management Association, 1986.

Brealey, Richard, and Stewart Myers. *Principles of Corporate Finance*. New York: McGraw-Hill, 1984.

The linear programming approach to the capital rationing problem was pioneered by H. M. Weingartner.

Weingartner, H. M. *Mathematical Programming and the Analysis of Capital Budgeting Problems*. Englewood Cliffs, N.J.: Prentice-Hall, 1963.

STATISTICAL TABLES

STUDENT'S t-DISTRIBUTION

Following is a table that provides the critical values of the t-distribution for three levels of confidence—90 percent, 95 percent, and 99 percent. It should be noted that these values are based on a two-tailed test for significance: tests to determine if an estimated coefficient is significantly *different* from zero (or one). For a discussion of one-tailed hypothesis tests, a topic not covered in this text, the reader is referred to R. J. Wonnacott and T. H. Wonnacott, *Econometrics,* 2d ed. (New York: John Wiley & Sons, 1979).

To illustrate the use of this table, return to an application presented in Chapter 4. In this example, 30 observations were used to estimate three coefficients, a, b, and c. Therefore, there are $30 - 3 = 27$ degrees of freedom. Then, the critical t-value for a 95 percent confidence level can be obtained from the table as 2.052. If a higher confidence level is required, the researcher can use the 99 percent confidence level column to obtain a critical value of 2.771. Conversely, if a lower confidence level is acceptable, the researcher can use the 90 percent confidence level column to obtain a critical value of 1.703.

THE F-DISTRIBUTION

Presented below is a table that provides the critical values of the F-distribution at both 95 percent and 99 percent confidence levels. To illustrate the manner in which this table is used, we return to an application

629

Critical T-Values

Degrees of Freedom	Confidence Level		
	90%	95%	99%
1	6.314	12.706	63.657
2	2.920	4.303	9.925
3	2.353	3.182	5.841
4	2.132	2.776	4.604
5	2.015	2.571	4.032
6	1.943	2.447	3.707
7	1.895	2.365	3.499
8	1.860	2.306	3.355
9	1.833	2.262	3.250
10	1.812	2.228	3.169
11	1.796	2.201	3.106
12	1.782	2.179	3.055
13	1.771	2.160	3.012
14	1.761	2.145	2.977
15	1.753	2.131	2.947
16	1.746	2.120	2.921
17	1.740	2.110	2.898
18	1.734	2.101	2.878
19	1.729	2.093	2.861
20	1.725	2.086	2.845
21	1.721	2.080	2.831
22	1.717	2.074	2.819
23	1.714	2.069	2.807
24	1.711	2.064	2.797
25	1.708	2.060	2.787
26	1.706	2.056	2.779
27	1.703	2.052	2.771
28	1.701	2.048	2.763
29	1.699	2.045	2.756
30	1.697	2.042	2.750
40	1.684	2.021	2.704
60	1.671	2.000	2.660
120	1.658	1.980	2.617
∞	1.645	1.960	2.576

Source: Adapted with permission from R. J. Wonnacott and T. H. Wonnacott, *Econometrics*, 2d. ed. (New York: John Wiley & Sons, 1979).

presented in Chapter 4. Again 30 observations were employed to estimate three coefficients—that is, $n = 30$ and $k = 3$. The appropriate F-statistic has $k - 1$ degrees of freedom for the numerator and $n - k$ degrees of freedom for the denominator. Thus, in the example, there are 2 and 27 degrees of freedom. From the table the critical F-value corresponding to a 95 percent confidence level is 3.35. If a 99 percent confidence level is desired, the critical value is 5.49.

Critical F-Values

Note: The values corresponding to a 95 percent confidence level are printed in roman type and the values corresponding to a 99 percent confidence level are printed in bold face type.

Degrees of freedom for denominator $(n - k)$

Degrees of freedom for the numerator $(k - 1)$

$(n-k)$	1	2	3	4	5	6	7	8	9	10	11	12	14	16	20	24	30	40	50	∞
1	161	200	216	225	230	234	237	239	241	242	243	244	245	246	248	249	250	251	252	254
	4052	**4999**	**5403**	**5625**	**5764**	**5859**	**5928**	**5981**	**6022**	**6056**	**6082**	**6106**	**6142**	**6169**	**6208**	**6234**	**6258**	**6286**	**6302**	**6366**
2	18.51	19.00	19.16	19.25	19.30	19.33	19.36	19.37	19.38	19.39	19.40	19.41	19.42	19.43	19.44	19.45	19.46	19.47	19.47	19.50
	98.49	**99.01**	**99.17**	**99.25**	**99.30**	**99.33**	**99.34**	**99.36**	**99.38**	**99.40**	**99.41**	**99.42**	**99.43**	**99.44**	**99.45**	**99.46**	**99.47**	**99.48**	**99.48**	**99.50**
3	10.13	9.55	9.28	9.12	9.01	8.94	8.88	8.84	8.81	8.78	8.76	8.74	8.71	8.69	8.66	8.64	8.62	8.60	8.58	8.53
	34.12	**30.81**	**29.46**	**28.71**	**28.24**	**27.91**	**27.67**	**27.49**	**27.34**	**27.23**	**27.13**	**27.05**	**26.92**	**26.83**	**26.69**	**26.60**	**26.50**	**26.41**	**26.30**	**26.12**
4	7.71	6.94	6.59	6.39	6.26	6.16	6.09	6.04	6.00	5.96	5.93	5.91	5.87	5.84	5.80	5.77	5.74	5.71	5.70	5.63
	21.20	**18.00**	**16.69**	**15.98**	**15.52**	**15.21**	**14.98**	**14.80**	**14.66**	**14.54**	**14.45**	**14.37**	**14.24**	**14.15**	**14.02**	**13.93**	**13.83**	**13.74**	**13.69**	**13.46**
5	6.61	5.79	5.41	5.19	5.05	4.95	4.88	4.82	4.78	4.74	4.70	4.68	4.64	4.60	4.56	4.53	4.50	4.46	4.44	4.36
	16.26	**13.27**	**12.06**	**11.39**	**10.97**	**10.67**	**10.45**	**10.27**	**10.15**	**10.05**	**9.96**	**9.89**	**9.77**	**9.68**	**9.55**	**9.47**	**9.38**	**9.29**	**9.24**	**9.02**
6	5.99	5.14	4.76	4.53	4.39	4.28	4.21	4.15	4.10	4.06	4.03	4.00	3.96	3.92	3.87	3.84	3.81	3.77	3.75	3.67
	13.74	**10.92**	**9.78**	**9.15**	**8.75**	**8.47**	**8.26**	**8.10**	**7.98**	**7.87**	**7.79**	**7.72**	**7.60**	**7.52**	**7.39**	**7.31**	**7.23**	**7.14**	**7.09**	**6.88**
7	5.59	4.74	4.35	4.12	3.97	3.87	3.79	3.73	3.68	3.63	3.60	3.57	3.52	3.49	3.44	3.41	3.38	3.34	3.32	3.23
	12.25	**9.55**	**8.45**	**7.85**	**7.46**	**7.19**	**7.00**	**6.84**	**6.71**	**6.62**	**6.54**	**6.47**	**6.35**	**6.27**	**6.15**	**6.07**	**5.98**	**5.90**	**5.85**	**5.65**
8	5.32	4.46	4.07	3.84	3.69	3.58	3.50	3.44	3.39	3.34	3.31	3.28	3.23	3.20	3.15	3.12	3.08	3.05	3.03	2.93
	11.26	**8.65**	**7.59**	**7.01**	**6.63**	**6.37**	**6.19**	**6.03**	**5.91**	**5.82**	**5.74**	**5.67**	**5.56**	**5.48**	**5.36**	**5.28**	**5.20**	**5.11**	**5.06**	**4.86**
9	5.12	4.26	3.86	3.63	3.48	3.37	3.29	3.23	3.18	3.13	3.10	3.07	3.02	2.98	2.93	2.90	2.86	2.82	2.80	2.71
	10.56	**8.02**	**6.99**	**6.42**	**6.06**	**5.80**	**5.62**	**5.47**	**5.35**	**5.26**	**5.18**	**5.11**	**5.00**	**4.92**	**4.80**	**4.73**	**4.64**	**4.56**	**4.51**	**4.31**
10	4.96	4.10	3.71	3.48	3.33	3.22	3.14	3.07	3.02	2.97	2.94	2.91	2.86	2.82	2.77	2.74	2.70	2.67	2.64	2.54
	10.04	**7.56**	**6.55**	**5.99**	**5.64**	**5.39**	**5.21**	**5.06**	**4.95**	**4.85**	**4.78**	**4.71**	**4.60**	**4.52**	**4.41**	**4.33**	**4.25**	**4.17**	**4.12**	**3.91**
11	4.84	3.98	3.59	3.36	3.20	3.09	3.01	2.95	2.90	2.86	2.82	2.79	2.74	2.70	2.65	2.61	2.57	2.53	2.50	2.40
	9.65	**7.20**	**6.22**	**5.67**	**5.32**	**5.07**	**4.88**	**4.74**	**4.63**	**4.54**	**4.46**	**4.40**	**4.29**	**4.21**	**4.10**	**4.02**	**3.94**	**3.86**	**3.80**	**3.60**
12	4.75	3.89	3.49	3.26	3.11	3.00	2.92	2.85	2.80	2.76	2.72	2.69	2.64	2.60	2.54	2.50	2.46	2.42	2.40	2.30
	9.33	**6.93**	**5.95**	**5.41**	**5.06**	**4.82**	**4.65**	**4.50**	**4.39**	**4.30**	**4.22**	**4.16**	**4.05**	**3.98**	**3.86**	**3.78**	**3.70**	**3.61**	**3.56**	**3.36**

Critical F-Values (continued)

Degrees of freedom for the numerator $(k-1)$

Degrees of freedom for denominator $(n-k)$	1	2	3	4	5	6	7	8	9	10	11	12	14	16	20	24	30	40	50	∞
13 …	4.67 **9.07**	3.80 **6.70**	3.41 **5.74**	3.18 **5.20**	3.02 **4.86**	2.92 **4.62**	2.84 **4.44**	2.77 **4.30**	2.72 **4.19**	2.67 **4.10**	2.63 **4.02**	2.60 **3.96**	2.55 **3.85**	2.51 **3.78**	2.46 **3.67**	2.42 **3.59**	2.38 **3.51**	2.34 **3.42**	2.32 **3.37**	2.21 **3.16**
14 …	4.60 **8.86**	3.74 **6.51**	3.34 **5.56**	3.11 **5.03**	2.96 **4.69**	2.85 **4.46**	2.77 **4.28**	2.70 **4.14**	2.65 **4.03**	2.60 **3.94**	2.56 **3.86**	2.53 **3.80**	2.48 **3.70**	2.44 **3.62**	2.39 **3.51**	2.35 **3.43**	2.31 **3.34**	2.27 **3.26**	2.24 **3.26**	2.13 **3.00**
15 …	4.54 **8.68**	3.68 **6.36**	3.29 **5.42**	3.06 **4.89**	2.90 **4.56**	2.79 **4.32**	2.70 **4.14**	2.64 **4.00**	2.59 **3.89**	2.55 **3.80**	2.51 **3.73**	2.48 **3.67**	2.43 **3.56**	2.39 **3.48**	2.33 **3.36**	2.29 **3.29**	2.25 **3.20**	2.21 **3.12**	2.18 **3.07**	2.07 **2.87**
16 …	4.49 **8.53**	3.63 **6.23**	3.24 **5.29**	3.01 **4.77**	2.85 **4.44**	2.74 **4.20**	2.66 **4.03**	2.59 **3.89**	2.54 **3.78**	2.49 **3.69**	2.45 **3.61**	2.42 **3.55**	2.37 **3.45**	2.33 **3.37**	2.28 **3.25**	2.24 **3.18**	2.20 **3.10**	2.16 **3.01**	2.13 **2.96**	2.01 **2.75**
17 …	4.45 **8.40**	3.59 **6.11**	3.20 **5.18**	2.96 **4.67**	2.81 **4.34**	2.70 **4.10**	2.62 **3.93**	2.55 **3.79**	2.50 **3.68**	2.45 **3.59**	2.41 **3.52**	2.38 **3.45**	2.33 **3.35**	2.29 **3.27**	2.23 **3.16**	2.19 **3.08**	2.15 **3.00**	2.11 **2.92**	2.08 **2.86**	1.96 **2.65**
18 …	4.41 **8.28**	3.55 **6.01**	3.16 **5.09**	2.93 **4.58**	2.77 **4.25**	2.66 **4.01**	2.58 **3.85**	2.51 **3.71**	2.46 **3.60**	2.41 **3.51**	2.37 **3.44**	2.34 **3.37**	2.29 **3.27**	2.25 **3.19**	2.19 **3.07**	2.15 **3.00**	2.11 **2.91**	2.07 **2.83**	2.04 **2.78**	1.92 **2.57**
19 …	4.38 **8.18**	3.52 **5.93**	3.13 **5.01**	2.90 **4.50**	2.74 **4.17**	2.63 **3.94**	2.55 **3.77**	2.48 **3.63**	2.43 **3.52**	2.38 **3.43**	2.34 **3.36**	2.31 **3.30**	2.26 **3.19**	2.21 **3.12**	2.15 **3.00**	2.11 **2.92**	2.07 **2.84**	2.02 **2.76**	2.00 **2.70**	1.88 **2.49**
20 …	4.35 **8.10**	3.49 **5.85**	3.10 **4.94**	2.87 **4.43**	2.71 **4.10**	2.60 **3.87**	2.52 **3.71**	2.45 **3.56**	2.40 **3.45**	2.35 **3.37**	2.31 **3.30**	2.28 **3.23**	2.23 **3.13**	2.18 **3.05**	2.12 **2.94**	2.08 **2.86**	2.04 **2.77**	1.99 **2.69**	1.96 **2.63**	1.84 **2.42**
21 …	4.32 **8.02**	3.47 **5.78**	3.07 **4.87**	2.84 **4.37**	2.68 **4.04**	2.57 **3.81**	2.49 **3.65**	2.42 **3.51**	2.37 **3.40**	2.32 **3.31**	2.28 **3.24**	2.25 **3.17**	2.20 **3.07**	2.15 **2.99**	2.09 **2.88**	2.05 **2.80**	2.00 **2.72**	1.96 **2.63**	1.93 **2.58**	1.81 **2.36**
22 …	4.30 **7.94**	3.44 **5.72**	3.05 **4.82**	2.82 **4.31**	2.66 **3.99**	2.55 **3.76**	2.47 **3.59**	2.40 **3.45**	2.35 **3.35**	2.30 **3.26**	2.26 **3.18**	2.23 **3.12**	2.18 **3.02**	2.13 **2.94**	2.07 **2.83**	2.03 **2.75**	1.98 **2.67**	1.93 **2.58**	1.91 **2.53**	1.78 **2.31**
23 …	4.28 **7.88**	3.42 **5.66**	3.03 **4.76**	2.80 **4.26**	2.64 **3.94**	2.53 **3.71**	2.45 **3.54**	2.38 **3.41**	2.32 **3.30**	2.28 **3.21**	2.24 **3.14**	2.20 **3.07**	2.14 **2.97**	2.10 **2.89**	2.04 **2.78**	2.00 **2.70**	1.96 **2.62**	1.91 **2.53**	1.88 **2.48**	1.76 **2.26**
24 …	4.26 **7.82**	3.40 **5.61**	3.01 **4.72**	2.78 **4.22**	2.62 **3.90**	2.51 **3.67**	2.43 **3.50**	2.36 **3.36**	2.30 **3.25**	2.26 **3.17**	2.22 **3.09**	2.18 **3.03**	2.13 **2.93**	2.09 **2.85**	2.02 **2.74**	1.98 **2.66**	1.94 **2.58**	1.89 **2.49**	1.86 **2.44**	1.73 **2.21**
25 …	4.24 **7.77**	3.38 **5.57**	2.99 **4.68**	2.76 **4.18**	2.60 **3.86**	2.49 **3.63**	2.41 **3.46**	2.34 **3.32**	2.28 **3.21**	2.24 **3.13**	2.20 **3.05**	2.16 **2.99**	2.11 **2.89**	2.06 **2.81**	2.00 **2.70**	1.96 **2.62**	1.92 **2.54**	1.87 **2.45**	1.84 **2.40**	1.71 **2.17**

26 ...	1.69	1.82	1.85	1.90	1.95	1.99	2.05	2.10	2.15	2.18	2.22	2.27	2.32	2.39	2.47	2.59	2.74	2.98	3.37	4.22
	2.13	2.36	2.41	2.50	2.58	2.66	2.77	2.86	2.96	3.02	3.09	3.17	3.29	3.42	3.59	3.82	4.14	4.64	5.53	7.72
27 ...	1.67	1.80	1.84	1.88	1.93	1.97	2.03	2.08	2.13	2.16	2.20	2.25	2.30	2.37	2.46	2.57	2.73	2.96	3.35	4.21
	2.10	2.33	2.38	2.47	2.55	2.63	2.74	2.83	2.93	2.98	3.06	3.14	3.26	3.39	3.56	3.79	4.11	4.60	5.49	7.68
28 ...	1.65	1.78	1.81	1.87	1.91	1.96	2.02	2.06	2.12	2.15	2.19	2.24	2.29	2.36	2.44	2.56	2.71	2.95	3.34	4.20
	2.06	2.30	2.35	2.44	2.52	2.60	2.71	2.80	2.90	2.95	3.03	3.11	3.23	3.36	3.53	3.76	4.07	4.57	5.45	7.64
29 ...	1.64	1.77	1.80	1.85	1.90	1.94	2.00	2.05	2.10	2.14	2.18	2.22	2.28	2.35	2.43	2.54	2.70	2.93	3.33	4.18
	2.03	2.27	2.32	2.41	2.49	2.57	2.68	2.77	2.87	2.92	3.00	3.08	3.20	3.33	3.50	3.73	4.04	4.54	5.42	7.60
30 ...	1.62	1.76	1.79	1.84	1.89	1.93	1.99	2.04	2.09	2.12	2.16	2.21	2.27	2.34	2.42	2.53	2.69	2.92	3.32	4.17
	2.01	2.24	2.29	2.38	2.47	2.55	2.66	2.74	2.84	2.90	2.98	3.06	3.17	3.30	3.47	3.70	4.02	4.51	5.39	7.56
32 ...	1.59	1.74	1.76	1.82	1.86	1.91	1.97	2.02	2.07	2.10	2.14	2.19	2.25	2.32	2.40	2.51	2.67	2.90	3.30	4.15
	1.96	2.20	2.25	2.34	2.42	2.51	2.62	2.70	2.80	2.86	2.94	3.01	3.12	3.25	3.42	3.66	3.97	4.46	5.34	7.50
34 ...	1.57	1.71	1.74	1.80	1.84	1.89	1.95	2.00	2.05	2.08	2.12	2.17	2.23	2.30	2.38	2.49	2.65	2.88	3.28	4.13
	1.91	2.15	2.21	2.30	2.38	2.47	2.58	2.66	2.76	2.82	2.89	2.97	3.08	3.21	3.38	3.61	3.93	4.42	5.29	7.44
36 ...	1.55	1.69	1.72	1.78	1.82	1.87	1.93	1.98	2.03	2.06	2.10	2.15	2.21	2.28	2.36	2.48	2.63	2.86	3.26	4.11
	1.87	2.12	2.17	2.26	2.35	2.43	2.54	2.62	2.72	2.78	2.86	2.94	3.04	3.18	3.35	3.58	3.89	4.38	5.25	7.39
38 ...	1.53	1.67	1.71	1.76	1.80	1.85	1.92	1.96	2.02	2.05	2.09	2.14	2.19	2.26	2.35	2.46	2.62	2.85	3.25	4.10
	1.84	2.08	2.14	2.22	2.32	2.40	2.51	2.59	2.69	2.75	2.82	2.91	3.02	3.15	3.32	3.54	3.86	4.34	5.21	7.35
40 ...	1.51	1.66	1.69	1.74	1.79	1.84	1.90	1.95	2.00	2.04	2.07	2.12	2.18	2.25	2.34	2.45	2.61	2.84	3.23	4.08
	1.81	2.05	2.11	2.20	2.29	2.37	2.49	2.56	2.66	2.73	2.80	2.88	2.99	3.12	3.29	3.51	3.83	4.31	5.18	7.31
42 ...	1.49	1.64	1.68	1.73	1.78	1.82	1.89	1.94	1.99	2.02	2.06	2.11	2.17	2.24	2.32	2.44	2.59	2.83	3.22	4.07
	1.78	2.02	2.08	2.17	2.26	2.35	2.46	2.54	2.64	2.70	2.77	2.86	2.96	3.10	3.26	3.49	3.80	4.29	5.15	7.27
44 ...	1.48	1.63	1.66	1.72	1.76	1.81	1.88	1.92	1.98	2.01	2.05	2.10	2.16	2.23	2.31	2.43	2.58	2.82	3.21	4.06
	1.75	2.00	2.06	2.15	2.24	2.32	2.44	2.52	2.62	2.68	2.75	2.84	2.94	3.07	3.24	3.46	3.78	4.26	5.12	7.24
46 ...	1.46	1.62	1.65	1.71	1.75	1.80	1.87	1.91	1.97	2.00	2.04	2.09	2.14	2.22	2.30	2.42	2.57	2.81	3.20	4.05
	1.72	1.98	2.04	2.13	2.22	2.30	2.42	2.50	2.60	2.66	2.73	2.82	2.92	3.05	3.22	3.44	3.76	4.24	5.10	7.21
48 ...	1.45	1.61	1.64	1.70	1.74	1.79	1.86	1.90	1.96	1.99	2.03	2.08	2.14	2.21	2.30	2.41	2.56	2.80	3.19	4.04
	1.70	1.96	2.02	2.11	2.20	2.28	2.40	2.48	2.58	2.64	2.71	2.80	2.90	3.04	3.20	3.42	3.74	4.22	5.08	7.19
50 ...	1.44	1.60	1.63	1.69	1.74	1.78	1.85	1.90	1.95	1.98	2.02	2.07	2.13	2.20	2.29	2.40	2.56	2.79	3.18	4.03
	1.68	1.94	2.00	2.10	2.18	2.26	2.39	2.46	2.56	2.62	2.70	2.78	2.88	3.02	3.18	3.41	3.72	4.20	5.06	7.17
55 ...	1.41	1.58	1.61	1.67	1.72	1.76	1.83	1.88	1.93	1.97	2.00	2.05	2.11	2.18	2.27	2.38	2.54	2.78	3.17	4.02
	1.64	1.90	1.96	2.06	2.15	2.23	2.35	2.43	2.53	2.59	2.66	2.75	2.85	2.98	3.15	3.37	3.68	4.16	5.01	7.12

Critical F-Values (concluded)

Degrees of freedom for the numerator $(k - 1)$

Degrees of freedom for denominator $(n - k)$	1	2	3	4	5	6	7	8	9	10	11	12	14	16	20	24	30	40	50	∞
60 …	4.00	3.15	2.76	2.52	2.37	2.25	2.17	2.10	2.04	1.99	1.95	1.92	1.86	1.81	1.75	1.70	1.65	1.59	1.56	1.39
	7.08	4.98	4.13	3.65	3.34	3.12	2.95	2.82	2.72	2.63	2.56	2.50	2.40	2.32	2.20	2.12	2.03	1.93	1.87	1.60
65 …	3.99	3.14	2.75	2.51	2.36	2.24	2.15	2.08	2.02	1.98	1.94	1.90	1.85	1.80	1.73	1.68	1.63	1.57	1.54	1.37
	7.04	4.95	4.10	3.62	3.31	3.09	2.93	2.79	2.70	2.61	2.54	2.47	2.37	2.30	2.18	2.09	2.00	1.90	1.84	1.56
70 …	3.98	3.13	2.74	2.50	2.35	2.32	2.14	2.07	2.01	1.97	1.93	1.80	1.84	1.79	1.72	1.67	1.62	1.56	1.53	1.35
	7.01	4.92	4.08	3.60	3.29	3.07	2.91	2.77	2.67	2.59	2.51	2.45	2.35	2.28	2.15	2.07	1.98	1.88	1.82	1.53
80 …	3.96	3.11	2.72	2.48	2.33	2.21	2.12	2.05	1.99	1.95	1.91	1.88	1.82	1.77	1.70	1.65	1.60	1.54	1.51	1.32
	6.95	4.88	4.04	3.56	3.25	3.04	2.87	2.74	2.64	2.55	2.48	2.41	2.32	2.24	2.11	2.03	1.94	1.84	1.78	1.49
100 …	3.94	3.09	2.70	2.46	2.30	2.19	2.10	2.03	1.97	1.92	1.88	1.85	1.79	1.75	1.68	1.63	1.57	1.51	1.48	1.28
	6.90	4.82	3.98	3.51	3.20	2.99	2.82	2.69	2.59	2.51	2.43	2.36	2.26	2.19	2.06	1.98	1.89	1.79	1.73	1.43
125 …	3.92	3.07	2.68	2.44	2.29	2.17	2.08	2.01	1.95	1.90	1.86	1.83	1.77	1.72	1.65	1.60	1.55	1.49	1.45	1.25
	6.84	4.78	3.94	3.47	3.17	2.95	2.79	2.65	2.56	2.47	2.40	2.33	2.23	2.15	2.03	1.94	1.85	1.75	1.68	1.37
150 …	3.91	3.06	2.67	2.43	2.27	2.16	2.07	2.00	1.94	1.89	1.85	1.82	1.76	1.71	1.64	1.59	1.54	1.47	1.44	1.22
	6.81	4.75	3.91	3.44	3.13	2.92	2.76	2.62	2.53	2.44	2.37	2.30	2.20	2.12	2.00	1.91	1.83	1.72	1.66	1.33
200 …	3.89	3.04	2.65	2.41	2.26	2.14	2.05	1.98	1.92	1.87	1.83	1.80	1.74	1.69	1.62	1.57	1.52	1.45	1.42	1.19
	6.76	4.71	3.88	3.41	3.11	2.90	2.73	2.60	2.50	2.41	2.34	2.28	1.17	2.09	1.97	1.88	1.79	1.69	1.62	1.28
400 …	3.86	3.02	2.62	2.39	2.23	2.12	2.03	1.96	1.90	1.85	1.81	1.78	1.72	1.67	1.60	1.54	1.49	1.42	1.38	1.13
	6.70	4.66	3.83	3.36	3.06	2.85	2.69	2.55	2.46	2.37	2.29	2.23	2.12	2.04	1.92	1.84	1.74	1.64	1.57	1.19
1000 …	3.85	3.00	2.61	2.38	2.22	2.10	2.02	1.95	1.89	1.84	1.80	1.76	1.70	1.65	1.58	1.53	1.47	1.41	1.36	1.08
	6.66	4.62	3.80	3.34	3.04	2.82	2.66	2.53	2.43	2.34	2.26	2.20	2.09	2.01	1.89	1.81	1.71	1.61	1.54	1.11
∞ …	3.84	2.99	2.60	2.37	2.21	2.09	2.01	1.94	1.88	1.83	1.79	1.75	1.69	1.64	1.57	1.52	1.46	1.40	1.35	1.00
	6.64	4.60	3.78	3.32	3.02	2.80	2.64	2.51	2.41	2.32	2.24	2.18	2.07	1.99	1.87	1.79	1.69	1.59	1.52	1.00

Source: Adapted with permission from R. J. Wonnacott and T. H. Wonnacott, *Econometrics*, 1st ed. (New York: John Wiley & Sons, Inc., 1970).

APPENDIX: LINEAR PROGRAMMING

L inear programming is a mathematical technique used to determine the optimal solutions to certain specific problems. This tool is frequently used to find the least cost combinations of inputs necessary to produce some desired level of output; that is, cost minimization problems. However, the same technique can be used to solve other types of optimization problems such as the optimal level of inventory, the least cost method of transporting commodities, and so on.

Basic Concepts

Let's begin with a practical problem: A firm produces two products, X_1 and X_2, which it can sell at fixed prices, P_1 and P_2. The production of X_1 and X_2 requires the use of three different types of machines which can be used for eight hours a day. The firm currently owns three type-1 machines, two type-2 machines, and five type-3 machines. Therefore, given the daily capacity of each machine, the firm has available 24 type-1 machine-hours, 16 type-2 machine-hours, and 40 type-3 machine-hours per period. In the short run, the firm cannot buy or sell any machines; but it can employ various amounts of labor or other inputs at prevailing market prices.[1]

---

[1]Outputs and inputs are assumed to be infinitely divisible, and the outputs are produced according to fixed proportions, constant-returns-to-scale processes.

Since labor and other inputs are obtainable in unlimited supplies, the firm first calculates the gross profit on each product net of labor and other input costs from the market prices for X_1 and X_2. These "net prices,"

$$p_1 = P_1 - \text{Labor cost per unit of } X_1 - \text{Other costs per unit of } X_1$$
$$p_2 = P_2 - \text{Labor cost per unit of } X_2 - \text{Other costs per unit of } X_2,$$

are the accountant's measure of gross profit. The problem for the firm is to choose the output combination that maximizes total (gross) profit.

To solve this problem, we must first know something about the actual productive capacity of each machine. Suppose that the number of type-1 machine-hours required per unit of X_1 is six, while only three type-1 machine-hours are required to produce a unit of X_2. Likewise, suppose each unit of X_1 requires two type-2 machine-hours and X_2 requires four hours per unit. Finally, suppose that eight type-3 machine-hours are required to produce a unit of either X_1 or X_2. Given the respective fixed quantities of machine-hours per period, these production relations may be written in the form of constraints,

$$6X_1 + 3X_2 \leq 24$$
$$2X_1 + 4X_2 \leq 16$$
$$8X_1 + 8X_2 \leq 40,$$

which show the possible combinations of X_1 and X_2, given machine availability. For example, the first constraint indicates that, if no X_2 is produced, the maximum daily production of X_1 is four units because each unit of X_1 requires six hours of type-1 machine and only 24 hours of type-1 are available. Similarly from the first constraint, if four units of X_2 are produced, only 12 hours of type-1 machine time are left to produce X_1; thus, only two units of X_1 can be produced. The other two constraints are interpreted similarly. Thus, all three constraints put a limit on the combinations of X_1 and X_2 that the firm can produce daily.

Suppose that the net prices of X_1 and X_2 are \$12 and \$8 per unit, respectively. The problem facing the firm is to choose the combination of X_1 and X_2 (X_1 and X_2 are the *choice variables*) that maximizes total gross income

$$\pi = 12X_1 + 8X_2$$

subject to the physical constraints imposed by the production processes and the limited availability of machines.

In general, we write this type of problem, a *linear program,* as

$$
\begin{aligned}
\max \pi = {} & p_1 X_1 + p_2 X_2 \\
\text{subject to} \quad & a_{11} X_1 + a_{12} X_2 \leq r_1 \\
& a_{21} X_1 + a_{22} X_2 \leq r_2 \\
& a_{31} X_1 + a_{32} X_2 \leq r_3 \\
& X_1, X_2 \geq 0,
\end{aligned}
$$

where a_{ij} ($i = 1, 2, 3; j = 1, 2$) is the required number of type-i machine-hours per unit of output j and r_i represent the "restrictions" on the program—in our example, the fixed quantities of machine-hours available. Of course, it should be noted that there could be any number of choice variables and constraints in any given linear program.

The first equation in the program, the total (gross) profit function, constitutes the objective function of the linear program; that is, it is the firm's *objective* to maximize total gross profits per production period. The three inequalities that follow are the *constraints* imposed on the linear program by the technological relations and the "restrictions." Finally, by the last two inequalities ($X_1, X_2 \geq 0$), referred to as the *nonnegativity restrictions,* we impose the restriction that negative outputs are impossible. Therefore, there are three essential ingredients to every linear program: an objective function, a set of constraints, and a set of nonnegativity restrictions.

Returning to our specific example, we may write our problem in this general form:

$$\max \pi = 12X_1 + 8X_2$$
$$\text{subject to} \quad 6X_1 + 3X_2 \leq 24$$
$$2X_1 + 4X_2 \leq 16$$
$$8X_1 + 8X_2 \leq 40$$
$$X_1, X_2 \geq 0.$$

Since our problem involves only two choice variables, X_1 and X_2, the linear program may be solved graphically. In Figure A.1 we plot X_1 along the horizontal axis and X_2 along the vertical axis. Because of the nonnegativity restrictions, we need only concern ourselves with the positive (nonnegative) quadrant.

To see what the constraints look like graphically, first treat them as equalities and plot them as straight lines as in Panel A. Since each constraint is of the "less-than-or-equal-to" type, only the points lying on the line or below it will satisfy the constraint. To satisfy all three constraints simultaneously, we can only accept those points that lie interior to all three constraint lines. The collection of all points that satisfy all three constraints simultaneously is called the *feasible region,* shown as the shaded region in Panel B. Each individual point in that region is known as *feasible solution.* It should be noted that the feasible region includes the points on the *boundary,* or the heavy line in Panel B. Note that in the present (two-dimensional) case, the corner points on the boundary are called *extreme points.* They occur either at the intersection of two constraints [(2,3) and (3,2)] or at the intersection of one constraint and one of the axes [(0,4) and (4,0)].

The feasible region contains all output combinations satisfying all three constraints and the nonnegativity restrictions. However, some of these points may entail a lower level of total profits than others. To maximize

Figure A.1 **Linear Constraints**

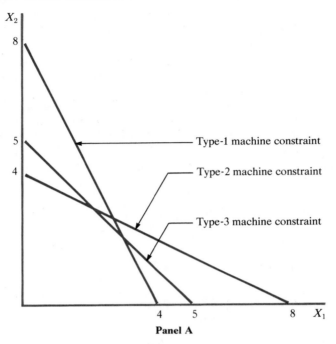

Panel A

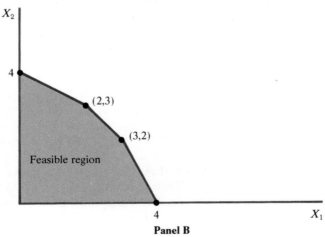

Panel B

profits, we must consider the objective function. To plot the profit function in (X_1, X_2) space we rewrite it as

$$X_2 = \frac{\pi}{8} - \frac{3}{2}X_1.$$

This equation represents a family of parallel straight lines corresponding to different levels of profits or values of π. Since each of these lines is

Figure A.2 An Optimal Solution

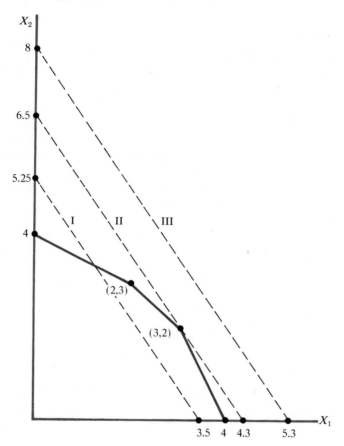

associated with a specific value of π, they are sometimes called *isoprofit curves*. Three isoprofit curves are shown in Figure A.2 as dashed lines, labeled I, II, and III.

The firm's objective is, of course, to attain the highest possible isoprofit curve while still remaining in the feasible region. In Figure A.2, isoprofit curve II satisfies this objective. While isoprofit curve III represents the highest level of profits, the combinations of X_1 and X_2 on this line are not in the feasible region, so this level of profit cannot be attained. Combinations on isoprofit line I clearly lie in the feasible region; however, a higher level of profit can be reached. Isoprofit line II represents the highest possible profit level that still incorporates a point in the feasible region. It coincides with the output combination of three units of X_1 and two units of X_2. Thus, the point (3,2) is the *optimal solution* to our linear program. Total profits for this optimal output combination can easily be obtained by using the values $X_1 = 3$ and $X_2 = 2$ in the objective function to yield the maximum profit, $\pi = \$52$ per production period.

Note that the optimal solution is an extreme point. In fact, the optimal solution to *any* linear program is always an extreme point. This fact will prove useful in developing a general solution methodology for linear programs.

General Solution Method

With two choice variables, the graphical method provided an optimal solution with little difficulty. This situation holds regardless of the number of constraints; additional constraints simply increase the number of extreme points, not the dimension of the diagram. When there are more than three choice variables, however, the graphical method becomes intractable, since we cannot draw a four-dimensional graph. Therefore, we need an analytical method to find the optimal solution to linear programs involving any number of choice variables.

As suggested above, the optimal solution of a linear program is one of the extreme points. Given a two-dimensional feasible region, it is relatively easy to find its extreme points, but finding them for the nongraphable *n*-variable case is more complex. Before considering the *n*-variable case, it will be instructive to return to our example. In Figure A.1, note that there are five extreme points—(0,4), (2,3), (3,2), (4,0), and (0,0)—all of which can be placed in one of three general categories.

The first category consists of those extreme points occurring at the intersection of two constraints. In our example, these points are (3,2) and (2,3). While such points exactly fulfill two of the three constraints, the remaining constraint is inexactly fulfilled. Consider the output combination (3,2). While the type-1 and type-3 machine constraints are exactly fulfilled, (3,2) lies inside the type-2 machine constraint and hence there is *slack* (or underutilization) in the use of type-2 machines.

Extreme points in the second category, illustrated by (0,4) and (4,0), occur at the intersection of a constraint and one of the axes. Because they are located on only one of the constraints, these points exactly fulfill only one constraint and, therefore, at such points there will be slack in the two remaining constraints. Lastly, the third category of extreme points consists of a single output combination, the origin (0,0), where there exists slack in all the constraints.

The point is that, whenever the number of constraints exceeds the number of choice variables, every extreme point will involve slack in at least one of the constraints. Furthermore, as is evident from Panel A of Figure A.1, the magnitude of the slack in any particular constraint can be calculated. Therefore, when we choose a particular extreme point as the optimal solution, we are not only choosing the optimal output combination (X_1, X_2) but also the optimal amount of slack in at least one constraint. Let us consider these slacks explicitly and denote the slack in the *i* constraint ($i = 1, 2, 3$ in our example) by S_i. We call these S_i's *slack variables*. Since we now explicitly consider the possible slack in each constraint, we can transform each inequality constraint into a strict equality by adding these S_i's to the left-hand side of the ith constraint.

Returning to our example and adding a slack variable to each constraint, we may rewrite our linear program as

$$\max \pi = 12X_1 + 8X_2$$

$$\text{subject to} \quad 6X_1 + 3X_2 + S_1 \quad = 24$$
$$2X_1 + 4X_2 + S_2 \quad = 16$$
$$8X_1 + 8X_2 + S_3 \quad = 40$$
$$X_1, X_2, S_1, S_2, S_3 \geq 0.$$

There are now five choice variables: X_1, X_2, S_1, S_2, and S_3. When $S_i > 0$ there is slack in the ith constraint (a *nonbinding* constraint); if $S_i = 0$, there is no slack and the ith constraint is exactly fulfilled (a *binding* constraint). Slack in a constraint for this particular problem could best be thought of as excess capacity or overcapitalization of a certain type of machine.

It is easy to determine the values of the slacks implied by each extreme point. If we start with the origin $(0,0)$, we substitute $X_1 = 0$ and $X_2 = 0$ into the transformed constraints and find that $S_1 = 24$, $S_2 = 16$, and $S_3 = 40$. Thus, the extreme point $(0,0)$ in output space can be mapped into *solution space* as the point

$$(X_1, X_2, S_1, S_2, S_3) = (0, 0, 24, 16, 40).$$

Similarly, we may map each extreme point in output space into solution space. The results are presented in Table A.1.

From Table A.1 the profit contribution at each extreme point can be calculated by inserting the values for X_1 and X_2 into the objective function. The point that yields the maximum profit is the constrained profit-maximizing output point—the solution to our linear-programming problem. The profit contributions of each point in solution space are shown in Table A.2. Again, we confirm that output combination $(3,2)$ is the profit-maximizing point. Note that $S_2 > 0$ at the optimum indicates that the constraint on the type-2 machine is nonbinding.

The procedure described above is used in solving more complex linear programming problems. Computer programs are available which find solution values for the variables at all extreme points, evaluate total profits at each potential extreme point, and then determine the extreme point at which the objective function is maximized.

The Dual in Linear Programming

For every maximization problem in linear programming there exists a symmetrical minimization problem and vice versa. The original programming problem is referred to as the *primal* program and its symmetrical counterpart is referred to as the *dual* program. The concept of this duality

Table A.1

	Output Space (X_1, X_2)	Solution Space $(X_1, X_2, S_1, S_2, S_3)$
	(0,0)	(0, 0, 24, 16, 40)
	(0,4)	(0, 4, 12, 0, 8)
	(4,0)	(4, 0, 0, 8, 8)
	(3,2)	(3, 2, 0, 2, 0)
	(2,3)	(2, 3, 3, 0, 0)

Table A.2

Solution at Extreme Point	Value of Variable					Total Profit Contribution
	X_1	X_2	S_1	S_2	S_3	
(0,0)	0	0	24	16	40	0
(0,4)	0	4	12	0	8	32
(4,0)	4	0	0	8	8	48
(3,2)	3	2	0	2	0	52
(2,3)	2	3	3	0	0	48

is quite significant because the optimal values of the objective functions in the primal and in the dual are always identical. Therefore, the analyst can pick the program, the primal or the dual, that is easiest to solve.

The linear program we have been using as an illustration—our *primal*—is a maximization problem: we wish to maximize total (gross) profit subject to the constraints imposed by the technology and machine time availability.

Primal

$$\max \pi = 12X_1 + 8X_2$$
$$\text{subject to} \quad 6X_1 + 3X_2 \le 24$$
$$2X_1 + 4X_2 \le 16$$
$$8X_1 + 8X_2 \le 40$$
$$X_1, X_2 \ge 0$$

Corresponding to this maximization problem there exists a *dual* minimization problem: Minimize the (opportunity) cost of using available machine-hours for the three machines subject to the constraints imposed by the production process and (gross) profitability of the two outputs.

Dual

$$\min \pi^\circ = 24y_1 + 16y_2 + 40y_3$$
$$\text{subject to} \quad 6y_1 + 2y_2 + 8y_3 \ge 12$$
$$3y_1 + 4y_2 + 8y_3 \ge 8$$
$$y_1, y_2, y_3 \ge 0$$

In the primal, the choice variables X_1 and X_2 are the output levels of the two products. In the dual, the choice variables y_1, y_2, and y_3 represent the "shadow prices" (or premiums) for the inputs. For example, the variable y_1 is the shadow price of using one hour of machine type-1, and, since we have 24 type-1 hours, the total cost of using machine type-1 is $24y_1$. A shadow price can be viewed as the implicit value to the firm of having one more unit of the input; that is, the marginal profit contribution of the input. We then attempt to determine minimum values, or "shadow prices," for each of the inputs, such that these shadow prices will be just sufficient to absorb the firm's total profit. In other words, we seek to assign "values" to each input so as to minimize the total inputed value of the firm's resources.

In the primal, the constraints reflected the fact that the total hours of each type of machine used in the production of X_1 and X_2 could not exceed the available number of hours of each type of machine. In the dual, the constraints state that the value assigned the inputs used in the production of one unit of X_1 or one unit of X_2 must not be less than the profit contribution provided by a unit of these products. Recall that $12 is the (gross) profit per unit of X_1 and $8 is the profit per unit of X_2. The constraints require that the shadow prices of the different types of machines times the hours of each type required to produce a unit of X_1 or X_2 must be greater than or equal to the gross (unit) profit of X_1 or X_2.

To solve the dual we again introduce slack variables, which allow us to write the constraint inequalities as strict equalities. Notice that in constrained minimization problems the constraints are of the "greater than or equal to" variety. Therefore, we introduce slack variables to the left-hand side of the constraints with a negative sign. (These negative S_i's used in the solution of minimization programs are often referred to as *surplus* variables). We can then write the dual program as:

$$\min \pi° = 24y_1 + 16y_2 + 40y_3$$
$$\text{subject to} \quad 6y_1 + 2y_2 + 8y_3 - S_1 = 12$$
$$3y_1 + 4y_2 + 8y_3 - S_2 = 8$$
$$y_1, y_2, y_3, S_1, S_2 \geq 0.$$

Since there are three choice variables (y_1, y_2, and y_3), a graphical solution would require a three-dimensional figure. Instead of such a complex diagram let's use the general techniques described above to find the solution space, evaluate the objective function for each feasible solution, and find that solution which minimizes the objective function.

A general rule illustrated in Table A.1 is that the maximum number of nonzero values in any solution is equal to the number of constraints. (In Table A.1, the number of constraints is three; so the maximum number of nonzero values in any solution is three.) Since there are two constraints in this dual problem, a maximum of two nonzero-valued variables define any solution point. Therefore, we can solve for the solutions by setting

Table A.3

Solution Number	Value of Variable					Feasible?
	y_1	y_2	y_3	S_1	S_2	
1	0	0	0	−12	−8	No
2	0	0	1	−4	0	No
3	0	0	1.5	0	4	Yes
4	0	2	0	−8	0	No
5	0	6	0	0	16	Yes
6	0	−2	2	0	0	No
7	2.66	0	0	4	0	Yes
8	2	0	0	0	−2	No
9	1.33	0	0.5	0	0	Yes
10	1.8	0.66	0	0	0	Yes

three of the variables—y_1, y_2, y_3, S_1, S_2—equal to zero and solving the constraint equations for the values of the remaining two.

For example, we can set y_1, y_2, and y_3 equal to zero and solve for S_1 and S_2. Using the first constraint,

$$6 \times 0 + 4 \times 0 + 8 \times 0 - S_1 = 12,$$

so $S_1 = -12$. Likewise, using the second constraint,

$$3 \times 0 + 4 \times 0 + 8 \times 0 - S_2 = 8$$

and $S_2 = -8$. However, since S_1 and S_2 cannot be negative, this solution is outside the feasible region. Alternatively, setting y_1, y_2, and S_1 equal to zero, $y_3 = 1.5$ and $S_2 = 4$. Since all of the values in this solution are positive, the solution lies in the feasible region. All of the potential solutions are presented in Table A.3.

It is apparent from the table that not all the solutions lie within the feasible region. Only solutions 3, 5, 7, 9, and 10 meet the nonnegativity restrictions; that is, these are the only feasible solutions.

Each of the feasible solutions is then used to calculate a corresponding value of the objective function. For example, using solution 3, the value of the objective function is

$$\pi^\circ = 24 \times 0 + 16 \times 0 + 40 \times 1.5 = 60.$$

All of these values are summarized in Table A.4.

With solution 9, the objective function—the total value inputed to the different types of machines—is minimized. As mentioned earlier, and confirmed in this example, the optimal value of the dual objective function is equal to the optimal value of the primal objective function (see Table A.2).

Note that at the optimum, the shadow price of type-2 machine-hours is zero. A zero shadow price implies that the input in question has a zero

Table A.4

Solution	(y_1, y_2, y_3)	Value of Objective Function	(S_1, S_2)
3	(0,0,1.5)	60	(0,4)
5	(0,6,0)	96	(0,16)
7	(2.66,0,0)	64	(4,0)
9	(1.33,0,0.5)	52	(0,0)
10	(1.8,0.66,0)	53.75	(0,0)

marginal value to the firm, adding another type-2 machine-hour adds nothing to the firm's maximum attainable profit. Thus, a zero shadow price for type-2 machines is consistent with our findings in the solution to the primal: the type-2 machine constraint is nonbinding. Excess capacity exists with respect to type-2 machines, so additional hours will not result in increased production of either X_1 or X_2. Analogously, we see that the shadow prices of type-1 and type-3 machines are positive. A positive shadow price indicates that the fixed number of these machines' hours imposes a binding constraint on the firm and that, if an additional hour of type-1 (type-3) machine work is added, the firm can increase its total profit by $1.33 ($0.50).

The dual solution has thus far not indicated the optimal output combination (X_1, X_2); however, it does provide all the information we need to determine these optimal values. Note first that the solution to the dual tells us that the type-2 machine constraint is nonbinding. Furthermore, it tells us that, at the optimal output combination, $\pi = \pi^\circ = \$52$. Now consider the three constraints in the primal, which we rewrite here for convenience.

$$6X_1 + 3X_2 + S_1 = 24 \quad \text{type-1}$$
$$2X_1 + 4X_2 + S_2 = 16 \quad \text{type-2}$$
$$8X_1 + 8X_2 + S_3 = 40 \quad \text{type-3}$$

From the solution to the dual we know that the type-1 and type-3 constraints are binding, because the dual found these inputs to have positive shadow prices. Accordingly, S_1 and S_3 equal zero in the primal program and the binding constraints can be rewritten as

$$6X_1 + 3X_2 = 24$$
$$8X_1 + 8X_2 = 40.$$

These two equations may be solved simultaneously to determine the optimal output combination. In this example, the solution is $X_1 = 3$ and $X_2 = 2$, the same output combination that was obtained in the primal problem.

Let us stress the two major points of this discussion and example. First, the choice between solving the primal or the dual of a linear programming problem is arbitrary, since both yield the same optimal value for the objective function. Second, the optimal solution obtained from the dual provides the information necessary to obtain the solution for the primal and vice versa. Thus, as we mentioned at the outset, one can elect to solve either the primal or the dual, depending on which one is easier to solve.

Activity Analysis: Linear Programming and Production Planning for a Single Output

As emphasized in Chapters 9 and 10, a decision problem faced by all firms is how to determine the least cost combination of inputs needed to produce a particular product. If the production process satisfies certain regularity conditions, linear programming may be applied to solve the cost minimization problem.

Suppose that a firm produces a single product, Q, using two inputs, capital (K) and labor (L). As long as the production processes are subject to fixed proportions and constant returns to scale, we can characterize the relation between input usage and output as linear functions and thereby use linear programming to obtain a solution.

To illustrate how this is accomplished, consider the four production processes depicted in Figure A.3. Since production is characterized by fixed proportions, the relations between input usage and output are shown by a straight line from the origin. These lines are referred to as *activity rays*—hence the title *activity analysis*.

In Figure A.3, production process A requires four units of K and four units of L to produce one unit of Q. This requirement is illustrated by point A_1. Process B uses four units of L and two units of K to produce one unit of output. Similarly, Process C uses one and a half units of K and five units of L, while Process D requires eight units of L and one unit of K to produce one unit of output. These input-output relations are illustrated by B_1, C_1, and D_1, respectively. If we recall the definition of an isoquant, that is, different input combinations for which the level of output is constant, we can connect points A_1 through D_1 and derive an isoquant corresponding to a level of output equal to one unit of Q. In Figure A.3 this piecewise linear isoquant is labeled Q_1. With constant returns to scale, doubling the amount of both inputs employed results in output also doubling. In our graph, this doubling of inputs is illustrated by points A_2, B_2, C_2, and D_2. Connecting these points, we derive an isoquant corresponding to two units of output; it is labeled Q_2. Similarly we may find isoquants Q_3 and Q_4 for three and four units of output, respectively.

Suppose that you are asked to determine the least cost combination of L and K, for an output level of four units when a unit of labor costs $4 (say the hourly wage rate is $4) and a unit of capital costs $8 (say it costs $8 to run a machine for one hour). This problem is simply a constrained

Figure A.3 Piecewise Linear Isoquants

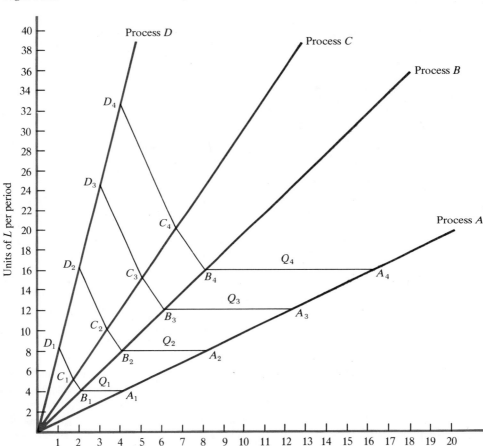

minimization problem, that is, we want to minimize the total cost of producing four units of output. Accordingly we may translate the problem into a linear programming problem. For illustrative purposes we will solve this program first graphically then solve it using our general algebraic method developed above.

The isoquant for four units of output is reproduced in Figure A.4. Since we know the price of a unit of K is \$8 and the price of a unit of labor is \$4 we can plot on this graph a family of *isocost* curves corresponding to different levels of total cost. These curves are derived by solving the total cost function $C = 8K + 4L$ to obtain

$$L = \frac{C}{4} - 2K.$$

Figure A.4 Solution to a Cost Minimization Problem

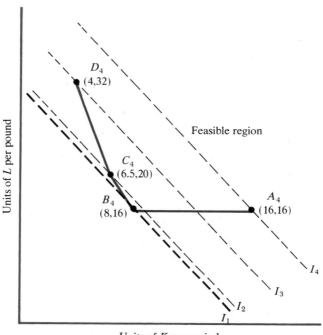

Units of K per period

Recall from Chapter 9 that we used a tangency rule to find the least cost combination of inputs: we find the isocost curve that is just tangent to the isoquant and, therefore, the closest to the origin. At that point of tangency, corresponding to a particular combination of inputs, total cost of production is minimized. In linear programming, the same process is used.

In Figure A.4 isocost curves (I_1, I_2, I_3, I_4) are draw through points B_4, C_4, D_4, and A_4. It is easy to see that isocost I_1 through point B_4 (8, 16) is closest to the origin and, therefore, represents the least cost possible of producing four units of output. If we use 8 units of K and 16 of L in our cost equation, we obtain a minimum total cost of production of $128.

We can use our algebraic method to solve the same problem. First note that there is only one constraint—the isoquant representing four units of output. Therefore, at the optimum there will be no slack or surplus in the constraint and we can determine the solution simply by substituting the values for the extreme points into the cost function (our objective function in this program). The results are shown in Table A.5.

Since our objective is to minimize total cost, we pick the input combination that does just that. Again we confirm our result from the graphical solution; the combination of 8 units of capital and 16 units of labor minimizes the total cost of producing 4 units of Q.

Table A.5

Extreme Point	Value of Variable		Total Cost
	K	L	
(4, 32)	4	32	$160
(6.5, 20)	6.5	20	132
(8, 16)	8	16	128
(16, 16)	16	16	192

TECHNICAL PROBLEMS

1. Solve the following linear programming problem graphically.

$$\text{maximize } \pi = 2X_1 + 3X_2$$
$$\text{subject to} \quad X_1 \le 8$$
$$X_2 \le 6$$
$$X_1 + 4X_2 \le 16$$
$$X_1, X_2 \ge 0$$

2. In Problem 1, how would the optimal solution change if the "restrictions" imposed (i.e., the r_i's) were all cut in half?

3. Solve the following linear programming problem using the general solution method.

$$\text{minimize } C = 3X_1 + 4X_2$$
$$\text{subject to} \quad X_1 + X_2 \ge 2$$
$$2X_1 + 4X_2 \ge 5$$
$$X_1, X_2 \ge 0$$

4. Form the dual to the linear programming problem presented in Problem 3, then solve it to obtain the optimal values of X_1 and X_2.

ANALYTICAL PROBLEMS

1. Provide an explanation of the nonnegativity constraints for the problem of minimizing cost subject to a desired level of output.

2. Give some examples of managerial decisions for which linear programming can provide useful information. For each of these, suggest the type of analysis that would be employed.

3. Suppose you were hired by a firm that produces several products. This firm needs to know the amounts of the different products it should produce to maximize total profit. What information would you require? How would you analyze this problem?

SUGGESTED ADDITIONAL REFERENCES

Archibald, G. C., and Lipsey, R. G. *An Introduction to Mathematical Economics: Methods and Applications*. New York: Harper & Row, 1976.

Baumol, W. J. *Economic Theory and Operations Analysis*. Englewood Cliffs, N.J.: Prentice-Hall, 1977.

Chiang, A. C. *Fundamental Methods of Mathematical Economics*. New York: McGraw-Hill, 1974.

Intriligator, M. D. *Econometric Models, Techniques, and Applications*. Englewood Cliffs, N.J.: Prentice-Hall, 1978.

INDEX

Key concepts are set in bold face type.